1800
75p

PSYCHOLOGICAL FOUNDATIONS OF EDUCATION

AN INTRODUCTION TO HUMAN MOTIVATION, DEVELOPMENT, AND LEARNING

THIRD EDITION

Morris L. Bigge and Maurice P. Hunt

HARPER & ROW, PUBLISHERS
New York   Hagerstown   Philadelphia   San Francisco   London

Sponsoring Editor: George A. Middendorf
Production Manager: Jeanie Berke
Compositor: Maryland Linotype Composition Co., Inc.
Printer and Binder: The Murray Printing Company
Art Studio: Vantage Art Inc.

PSYCHOLOGICAL FOUNDATIONS OF EDUCATION: AN INTRODUCTION
TO HUMAN MOTIVATION, DEVELOPMENT, AND LEARNING

Third edition

Library of Congress Cataloging in Publication Data

Bigge, Morris L
    Psychological foundations of education.
    Includes bibliographical references and index.
    1. Educational psychology. I. Hunt, Maurice P.,
joint author. II. Title. [DNLM: 1. Psychology,
Educational. LB1051 3592p]
LB1051.B45213   1979   370.15   79-52
ISBN 0-06-040681-X

CONTENTS

PREFACE

This book is designed as a basic text for courses in educational psychology, psychological foundations of education, or development and learning. Because of its rather extensive treatment of both learning and motivation theories, it might also have a place in introductory courses that focus on these aspects of psychology. Instructors of courses in introductory general psychology who wish to acquaint their students with a systematic development of cognitive-field psychology also will find the book useful.

The book centers upon the positions of major psychological outlooks in regard to four basic questions: What is the nature of human motivation; how do children and youths develop; how do they learn; and how can knowledge of motivation, development, and learning be related to the teaching-learning process? It emphasizes the cognitive-field position. But, it also develops the nature and implications of other leading prevailing and historical systematic and eclectic positions.

The approach is semihistorical and comparative but not eclectic. Features and implications of psychological systems are presented in such a way as to confront students with a need to make choices between conflicting points of view. The book contains much more historical analysis than is commonly found in books on psychological foundations. This appears to be the only means by which one can explain and clarify certain points of confusion in contemporary education.

During the twentieth century, the concepts of relativism have invaded virtually all of the natural and social sciences, as well as literature and the fine arts. So, in this book a strong attempt is made to describe what relativism means for psychology and to develop an educational psychology that consistently has a relativistic orientation. Through their development of positive relativistic cognitive-field psychology, the authors hope to dispel some of the confusion that exists concerning the general meaning of relativism.

Although this book is intended for use by college students who may have had only one or two courses in general psychology, the authors have deliberately tried to keep it challenging. They recognize that many text-books lately have resorted to a kind of "popular magazine treatment" of their subjects with a plethora of photographs or drawings and few words of more than two syllables. But, they think that a typical college student of today does not need to be talked down to. Serious treatment of issues in psychology should appeal not only to undergraduates but to graduate students and practicing teachers as well. The authors are even presumptuous enough to hope that some professors will find the book stimulating.

The primary goals in preparing this third edition of *Psychological Foundations of Education* have been to update factual materials and references and to make the book more readable and understandable for students. In keeping with these purposes, the writing has been refined throughout in the interest of greater readability, logical flow, and improved style.

The general plan of the book is as follows: Chapter 1, an introduction, presents the issue of eclectic versus systematic psychological outlooks. Then, Part I, Chapters 2 through 5, treats the leading mechanistic and nonmechanistic theories of motivation. Chapter 5, on achievement motivation, is rather technical but also rewarding in that it presents much recent thinking in the field. Chapter 6 presents some current biological research that contributes to an understanding of motivation.

Part II, Chapters 7 and 8, deals with physical, sociological, and psychological aspects of human development. Chapter 7 treats the nature and course of human development through the elementary school years. Chapter 8 deals with the physiological, sociological, and psychological meaning of adolescence.

Part III, Chapters 9 through 16, discusses the nature of learning, its transfer, and its application. Chapter 9 introduces the problem of learning and the various learning theories. Chapter 10 sets the historical stage by presenting the theories of *mental discipline*, *"natural unfoldment"* or *self-actualization*, and *apperception*. Chapter 11 broadly outlines what the authors see as the two major "families" of contemporary learning theory SR (stimulus-response) conditioning and Gestalt-field psychology. Chapter 12 gives in some detail a specific description of the learning process as offered by each of these two positions. Chapter 13 presents

B. F. Skinner's operant conditioning, a specific psychology of learning that represents the SR conditioning or behavioristic family. Chapters 14 and 15 present a relativistic cognitive-field psychology as a systematic representative of the Gestalt-field family. Chapter 16 treats Robert M. Gagné's and J. S. Bruner's eclectic psychologies and relates them to motivation and learning.

Part IV, Chapters 17 through 21, applies psychological theory to classroom practice. Chapter 17 applies the various meanings of intelligence to classroom relationships. Chapter 18 deals with the meaning and measurement of intelligence. Chapters 19 through 21 are essentially "how to do it" chapters, but at no time is practice divorced from theory. Chapter 19 relates learning theories to autonomous development, memory, explanatory understanding, and reflection levels of teaching and learning. Chapter 20 offers concrete directives for explanatory understanding level teaching and Chapter 21 for reflection level teaching. Finally, in the interest of pointing toward anticipated future directions of educational psychology, an epilogue has been appended.

The authors are indebted to so many persons that it would be futile to single out individuals for their influence and help. These persons include their former graduate and undergraduate professors, their many helpful students, and their colleagues at California State University, Fresno. But especially, the support and cooperation given us by our good wives, Ada June Bigge and F. A. Guerard, has been invaluable.

Morris L. Bigge
Maurice P. Hunt

IN MEMORIAM

Maurice P. Hunt
1915–1979

In 1955 there was little about Maurice Hunt that any of us—his advisees and students—could have identified with greatness. In that year I took my first course with him; it was also the year of publication of his and Lawrence Metcalf's *Teaching High School Social Studies.* At that time we saw him simply as a shy, unassertive man whose teaching consisted largely of asking questions. He began the class—a required methods course—by asking us our reaction to the problem of a well-to-do man who had installed a mistress in his townhouse but was still loyal to his own family. A fellow student, Ed, told me once or twice that this was the damndest methods course he had ever seen. Others were bewildered. But a number of us were intensely stimulated. Indeed, the words "stimulate" and "provocative" were, for Maury, words of high praise. I should, he urged, take a course from Bigge because he was "stimulating." And so I did. And Maury was right. Between Hunt and Bigge I was ruined; never thereafter could I tolerate the cant, clichés, and banalities that passed then—and now—for much scholarship in education.

Years later, after I had begun my own career, Maury's teaching and his published ideas began to fall into place. I saw that the emphasis on "provocativeness" was quite intelligible: One needed to be provoked into sensing a problem—for without this the rest of Dewey's complete act of thought would never take place. This simple notion has yet to find a place in education. Eventually, after I had consulted his works, not dozens but literally hundreds of times, I recognized that Hunt had attempted to capture the relationships among democracy, learning theory, problem-solving, social studies, and culture. It then became clear to me that, to use an uncongenial Aristotelian term, Maury had penetrated to the very essence of things.

In my last letter to Maury Hunt—unmailed and now lying on my desk, for I have just been told of his passing—I encouraged him to get well and to continue writing. The world, I thought, had much use for his unequalled scholarship, for his clarity of insight, and for his ability to express himself gracefully. Now, I can only take comfort in knowing that his writings will transcend his life and his death, and that in years to come those who are interested and can understand will be able to share his conviction that it is possible for education in our society to be the thoughtful, reconstructive act that Dewey originally described. There is enough substance in Maury's scholarship to keep the rest of us busy for many years to come.

S. Samuel Shermis
Purdue University

Chapter 1
INTRODUCTION: WHAT ARE SOME PRESSING ISSUES IN EDUCATIONAL PSYCHOLOGY TODAY?

Psychology is a biosocial science of human experience and behavior. Whereas sociology studies groups, psychology studies individuals alone and in relation to groups. *Educational psychology* is one area of applied psychology. Its primary concern is applying psychological knowledge to problems involving the teaching-learning process. Its principal functions are (1) to develop and evaluate theories of human motivation, development, learning, and instruction; (2) to examine, and propose modifications of, educational practices; (3) to evaluate teaching methodology in light of psychological theory; and (4) to provide scientific approaches to research in regard to psychological aspects of educational matters.

HOW DOES PHILOSOPHY RELATE TO SCIENCE?

Although many scientists do not mention philosophical issues in their books, they all assume—consciously or unconsciously—certain philosophical premises. We refer to the particular philosophical issues that underlie science as the *philosophy of science*. All science has had a beginning in philosophy. The highest university degree, even for scientists, is still called doctor of philosophy (Ph.D.). As late as the eighteenth century this degree required graduate students to study philosophy before working on their particular specialties.

What Is Philosophy?

There are, of course, many definitions of philosophy. One that might adequately serve the needs of scientists is: *a critical study of the basis for fundamental assumptions and beliefs and an analysis of the underlying concepts used in the expression of such concepts.* Another more understandable definition of philosophy might be: the statement and critical study of the premises that underlie and support the concrete study of a subject.

An example of the kind of philosophizing that scientists must do is to define scientific truth and then to decide the best methods for finding it. Defining what is true (and what is false) and what is the best means of seeking truth is a branch of general philosophy called *epistemology.* Scientists cannot even begin their work without deciding on an epistemology.

Philosophical ideas cannot be proved to be true or false in the same sense that we can prove a proposition like "Students develop and learn normally only if they have enough to eat." However, philosophical statements can be analyzed in terms of their history, their consistency, and the results of acting upon them.

What Is Science?

One meaning of science is *a body of knowledge whose truth is confirmed by the best methods available.* Examples are economics, sociology, anthropology, physics, chemistry, geology, and biology. When used in this sense, science is a thing: a body of presumably true statements that fit together in some logical fashion, and that can serve as a tool for analyzing new problems in the field.

Perhaps a more useful way of defining science is as a method. Defined in this sense, science and epistemology mean approximately the same. The purpose of the scientific method is to provide us with dependable knowledge rather than ignorance, misunderstanding, superstition, and confusion. The scientific method can be applied to almost any subject matter. It is usually described as a series of steps to be taken. However, since the steps need not be followed in any consecutive order, it is better to think of them as *aspects.*

What Are the Aspects of the Scientific Method?

These are the conventionally accepted aspects of the scientific method. In presenting them, we will look at issues.[1]
   • *Aspect One: Becoming Involved with a Problem.* The scientific method becomes relevant when people encounter something that puzzles

or frustrates them. People seem forever to be developing goals and usually making some effort to reach them, but their environment often poses obstacles. Trying to overcome the obstacles makes reaching the goal a problem.

If a problem grows out of more or less self-generated wants, persons, without pressure from parents, teachers, or peers, will typically show interest and try to solve it. However, if persons have foisted on them a problem that neither corresponds with their personal problems nor interests them, they will either not work on the problem at all, or do so only reluctantly.

• *Aspect Two: Gathering All Possible Data.* There are at least three tests for judging what are acceptable data: (1) internal consistency, (2) completeness, and (3) factual accuracy. Difficulties may arise in the gathering of data. The very concept of *data* confuses many people. Data are facts or logical constructions that are relevant to the problem, and relevance is often hard to determine.

Data also may be very hard to find. If only one or two facts are available, then in the absence of contrary facts, we must proceed on what data we have. Even worse, people keep developing problems for which there seem to be no data at all. In this case, they have the choice of abandoning the problem or proceeding by intuition, hunch, or guess.

• *Aspect Three: Making Hypotheses.* An hypothesis is an assertion that we tentatively assume to be true in order to proceed toward an answer to the problem. An hypothesis is a trial answer. Usually gathering facts about the problem will suggest at least one and sometimes many hypotheses that sound promising. We select the most attractive hypothesis and test it with factual data or logical constructs. If the data harmonize with one another and are relevant to the hypothesis, we have a good reason for regarding the hypothesis as true.

Making usable hypotheses can be a problem for students not well versed in the scientific method. First, ambiguity must be avoided. To be useful an hypothesis must be stated very clearly. Second, wishful thinking must be omitted.

• *Aspect Four: Testing Hypotheses.* This involves a review of available facts to see whether they support the hypotheses. It takes only one negative fact to challenge an hypothesis. If 72 facts support a proposition, but one is contrary, then the hypothesis is not absolutely true. In such cases the hypothesis can be either dropped or qualified in terms of probabilities. In the above case one could say that, "The hypothesis has 71 chances out of 72 of being right."

• *Aspect Five: Drawing a Conclusion.* This occurs automatically if all the data fall nicely into place around an hypothesis: the tested hypothesis is the conclusion. Conclusions, particularly in a field like psychology with all its uncertainties, should always be considered to some degree as tentative. Facts change with changing circumstances, and what is today's truth may well be tomorrow's falsehood.

What Is the Relation of Fact and Theory?

Students sometimes object to a course that is "all theory" or "has too much theory in relation to facts." Those who object to theory typically do not understand what theory is and are unaware of its role in problem solving.

A fact is relatively easy to define. It is a thing or process that actually exists. In scholarly literature the word *event* is often used to mean a fact. A *theory*, or *theoretical statement*, is a rule, principle, generalization, or law. The chief requirements of theoretical statements are that they must embrace all the facts or events they are supposed to and that they use present-tense verbs. If one is referring to the year 1776, one might say "Riding a horse was the fastest way to get from one place to another." This was a perfectly good generalization for that time in history, though it tells us nothing about the fastest way to travel now or in the foreseen future.

A theory or generalization with a present-tense verb implies past, present, and future applicability. Suppose we say that "People generally expect persons attending a wedding or a funeral to wear their best clothes." This is good social theory in 1766, at present, and insofar as we can tell within the foreseeable future. Commonly, but not necessarily, a theoretical statement takes the form of an "If . . . then" syntax. Two examples: "If water drops to 32 degrees Fahrenheit or 0 degrees Celsius then it will freeze"; "If a person has a large vocabulary, then that person can read better than one with a small vocabulary."

Thought without theory is impossible. When we dress in the morning, we must choose appropriate clothes to wear. We expect various events to occur. How do we choose? Suppose one expected event—if we are schoolteachers—will be a visit by the superintendent of schools. From experience we have learned a generalization—a theoretical statement— as follows: "School administrators like teachers to be neatly dressed." Since one of our goals is probably to stay in the good graces of the superintendent, we put on our best, most appropriate clothes. We spend some extra time grooming. Before the superintendent is due we recomb our hair. If teachers are going to get along, they need to have many hundreds of general statements—theories—about what administrators, students, and parents want teachers to be like.

If each day's decision had to be made as if it were a unique case and a problem to be solved upon each occurrence, we would simply not have adequate time to eat, work, or play. Most of our everyday behavior is governed by theory—those "if . . . then" statements discussed above. Our thinking involves the use of theory at many levels—from the student's deciding what to eat for breakfast, to a nuclear physicist's deciding what to work on next in a project. It is little wonder that writers have been so fond of quoting the statement of the late Kurt Lewin, "Nothing is so useful as a good theory."

Is There But One Scientific Method?

People usually tend to think of science as one method used for all subjects. They associate it with fact finding and drawing conclusions, and particularly with subjects in the physical sciences. This is unfortunate because each field of inquiry requires its own scientific procedures, with major differences between anthropology, geology, physics, biology, and psychology.

By the end of the nineteenth century many psychologists had begun to think that there was only one valid method of inquiry—that used by physicists. These people thought that to have science, one must simply deal with quantifiable data that could produce conclusions in the form of statistical tables or mathematical formulas. The reason psychologists began to emulate physical science was that they had come to believe that psychology of the past had not been a science. Psychology, they thought, relied entirely too much on introspection, intuition, and deduction from "made up" theories.

To emulate physical science, however, psychologists had to focus on those parts of people that could be studied in the manner of physics. Thus any aspect of psychology that could not be subjected to the methods of the physical scientists was considered irrelevant, pointless, and a waste of time.

From World War I to the 1960s, psychologists who espoused the physics model were greatly influential in the field of psychology. There is now, however, a new breed of psychologist, with new concepts of science, who insists that psychology should not exclude the study of any aspect of thought, feeling, or behavior. This important issue will be discussed more fully in other parts of the book.

WHAT IS THE PRESENT STATE OF PSYCHOLOGY—ECLECTIC OR SYSTEMATIC?

Psychology is a science that embraces a number of schools of thought. Some of these positions rest on such similar basic premises and assumptions that they are not seriously incompatible. Hence, they may be considered members of a psychological family. So, it is possible to group many different positions in psychology into a few "families."

Some positions in psychology, however, are not only incompatible with other positions, but their primary assumptions are so contradictory that the positions are mutually exclusive, that is, if one position is true, the other cannot be. In fact, there are enough positions in psychology that do not harmonize with one another to make the field quite fragmented. This state of affairs can make psychology a rather frustrating subject of study for many students; but the divisions also help make a challenging and, to most students, more interesting subject than it would be if all psychologists agreed.

Psychology, however, is no more fragmented than many other sciences. In fact, it is easier to group integrated positions in psychology in some orderly fashion than it is to group positions in economics, sociology, business management, medicine, and perhaps even physics. Psychology, including educational psychology, also has a number of positions that are intentionally or unknowingly *eclectic* rather than *systematic*. In the late 1970s, the issue of eclecticism vs. systematization is a key issue, the solution of which would solve a variety of other issues.

What Do We Mean by Eclectic and Eclecticism?

Eclectic and its noun form *eclecticism* refer to pulling sections or pieces from various positions, views, or schools of thought, and putting them together into a new position. At first thought, combining pieces of older positions seems like a good idea, particularly if one assumes that only the very best points go into the new school of thought. (A school of thought is a comprehensive treatment of a subject, put together in such a way that it is as complete as possible and free of internal contradictions.) We find different and competing schools of thought in almost every field of importance. Economics furnishes a good example. There are schools of thought referred to as Keynesian (after John Maynard Keynes), monitarism (Milton Friedman), democratic socialism (John Kenneth Galbraith), and several others. Some major schools of thought have been developed out of an eclectic assembly of fragments of knowledge.

Eclectics who are not extremely astute in identifying their deepest assumptions may very easily—and with good intentions—select from differing schools of thought ideas that on superficial examination seem very attractive. But suppose, when examined in the light of their *primary assumptions*, these ideas are contradictory? This is a risk that eclectics take, and they often fall into the trap of building a new point of view out of incompatible elements. What emerges is a position that may at first glance look logical, but on more careful scrutiny is a hodgepodge of contradictory and mutually exclusive components.

What Do We Mean by System and Systematic?

A definition of *system* is "an aggregation or assemblage of objects joined in regular interaction or interdependence: a set of units combined by nature or art to form an integral, organic, or organized whole: an orderly working totality."[2] Systematic means relating or pertaining to a system. Fairly satisfactory synonyms for system are *order, school of thought, frame of reference, position, view,* or *persuasion.*

A system may consist of physical or material objects such as the solar system. It also may combine living creatures and nonliving objects. For example, social institutions may be coherent patterns of human beings and nonliving objects—the latter including such items as buildings, offices, streets, automobiles, typewriters, and paper. Or a system may be composed primarily or even entirely of ideas, in which case we refer to it as a *cognitive system.*

Presumably, behind any system that includes man-made artifacts there is a cognitive system, although, as we will see, some psychologists would not use that terminology. Examples of cognitive systems are a system of mathematics (such as Euclidean geometry), an internally consistent body of theory about politics or economics, or a theory of the nature of the universe.

A cognitive system may include either a few or many verified facts, or it may consist only of assumptions, hypotheses, or postulates. As we will discover, within systems of psychology the nature of the assumptions greatly influences the kind of experimental evidence that will be sought. Some systems as now understood, such as our solar system, contain many verified facts. A system of geometry, in contrast, is entirely "made up"— a matter of creative imagination. As readers will discover throughout this book, within systems of psychology many facts have been verified; but more than in some sciences, psychological research begins with hunches or intuitions, some of which have been testable and the subject of much experimentation, while others have remained quite speculative.

How Do Static and Evolving Systems Differ?

By definition, a *static system* exhibits a given state of balance or equilibrium over an indefinite period of time. We may be justified in using the term static to refer to a system that, when disturbed by some outside force, tends to assimilate, modify, or divert the force so that it does not disrupt the system. A system that shows a strong tendency to maintain a steady state illustrates the principle of *homeostasis.* The human body's ability to maintain an average temperature of about 98.6 degrees F. is an example of a relatively dependable form of homeostasis.

However, there may not be any such thing as a truly static system. Physical systems, for example, always appear to be evolving in some direction: mountains erode, rivers change their courses, and the weather is relatively unpredictable. Cognitive systems sometimes show more stability than anything found in nature. Since some cognitive systems are highly subjective, they can be retained in comparatively static form over long periods of time, particularly if we are referring to systems of beliefs or ideologies. Even so, viewed historically, few examples of cognitive systems have not eventually eroded away and been supplanted by something new.

An *evolving system* is a body of interacting, interdependent elements that, although perhaps showing considerable balance or equilibrium, also exhibits more or less continuous change. An evolving system reflects *dynamic homeostasis*: although it keeps changing, it maintains a state of workable balance. The aging human body illustrates this concept very well.

How Do Nonpurposive and Situationally Purposive Systems Differ?

A nonpurposive system is mechanistic—it is incapable of developing its own goals or determining its own direction of movement. Presumably our solar system, a glacier, or pile of rocks are examples of nonpurposive systems. A nonpurposive system may change, but when this happens we assume it changes because of pressures exerted from outside the system (a comet of large mass might change our solar system significantly).

Situational purpose refers to a purpose that grows out of interactive human experience. The existing situation gives rise to the purposes to be agreed on and sought. Geologists are interested in nonpurposive systems whereas social scientists, particularly students of group behavior, are interested primarily in situational purpose as it emerges from human encounters. Situational purpose is sometimes referred to as immanent purpose.

To avoid confusion, we should point out that immanent purpose is quite different from transcendental purpose. Whereas immanent, situational purposes operate within a world of workaday life experiences, transcendental purposes extend beyond the world of experience to an assumed basic nature of the forces behind the entire universe. The concept *immanent purpose* simply means that any individual, in keeping with his (or her) state of development, does the best that he knows how for whatever he thinks he is.

WHAT HAS BEEN THE ROLE OF SYSTEMATIC THINKING IN THE HISTORY OF SCIENCE?

The history of science shows that periods of systematic and eclectic thinking have occurred both alternately and simultaneously. To illustrate what brings about these conditions during inquiry, we use examples mainly from physical science both because the first "scientific" psychology emerged from physics and biology as tempered by philosophy, and because physics probably provides more clear-cut examples than do other sciences. For us to understand the nature of systematic as opposed to eclectic thinking, it is essential that we consider another concept: *model.*

What Is a Model?

The kind of model used in scientific investigation is a simplified depiction of what an investigator thinks some aspect of reality may be like. (Models are also called exemplars or paradigms.) An investigator may have only a few hard facts to go on—perhaps scraps of experimental evidence— but these may suggest a relatively complete model. To complete the model *it is necessary to fill in imaginatively what is factually missing.* Sometimes existing facts enable the investigator to infer the missing facts with considerable certainty. In other cases there is so little ground for inference that the investigator must invent hypothetical facts that would at least complete the model enough for its use, even though there may be little experimental grounds to support their existence.

What Categories of Models Are There?

Even physical models (like an aircraft test body) have to be con- ceptualized by someone before being built. Hence, the models of methodological concern to us are *cognitive models, that is, systematic constructions of ideas.*

One way of categorizing models is by degree of formality. The least formal models are neither precise nor inflexible; they have a literary quality. The most formal are abstract to the point of lacking any ex- perimental content; put together with great precision they can usually be described only with mathematical or other abstract symbolism.[3]

Models that are used most successfully in the social sciences, educa- tion, and psychology tend to fall toward the informal end of the formal- informal continuum. They usually include at least some empirical or sense data, and they may make some use of statistics or mathematics of a more abstract nature. In some cases, however, they may be confined entirely to qualitative data.

How Have Models Successfully Used Unverifiable Themes as Substitutes for Sense Data?

Gerald Holton has traced the history of model building in the physical sciences (with some comments about social science and psychology). The themes he discusses are hypotheses that have been popular his- torically as substitutes for empirical knowledge in the building of models. They are no more than plausible assertions that can neither be proved nor disproved.

A remarkable and important feature of cognitive models is how useful many models have been, even when they were merely "dreamed up." In terms of eventual results some of the most potent models were selected over others because of characteristics unrelated to empirical verifiability—because they were more symmetrical, elegant, interesting, or literary. Copernicus defended his model of the solar system in part because it was "pleasing to the mind."[4] Einstein's papers, particularly the 1905 one on relativity, were largely intuitive; they contained only a few "empiricist and rationalistic elements . . . ." With respect to some of Einstein's key propositions, Holton tells us that Einstein could only have advanced them because of their attractions as "a statement of elegance, of arrogance, or ignorance of the detailed experiments [of others] . . . of lack of serious concern with the messy details of experimental physics, or even of mere lack of time . . . ."[5] Holton himself, as a careful student of Einstein, guesses that the most likely reason for much of Einstein's model building was a fondness for elegance. There is, it seems, more poetry in physics than laymen would dream of.

Why Are Models Reductionistic?

The construction of models necessarily involves *reductionism*, that is, omitting those parts of an idealized whole that seem peripheral or extraneous to what an investigator wants to study. Cognitive, as well as physical, models are by definition simplified depictions of a whole organization that is too complex to convert to "miniature form" without omitting some parts of the idealized whole. For instance, a miniature aircraft body designed for wind tunnel testing does not need to contain its own engines, passenger seats, and instrument panel. Similarly, a model of a human being can be very useful for study without its including all we know is a part of human form.

A model needs to contain only those empirical facts and postulates that seem pivotal. A very live issue in psychology is whether some basic positions employ a human model that is too simplified. Certainly, some outlooks in psychology are much more reductionist than others. This issue is of great importance and will be explored in several places later in the book.

What Is the Purpose of a Model?

Science could not proceed without model building. Those who tell us that science is essentially fact gathering—with the aim of drawing from collections of facts, rules, principles, or laws and of continuing this process until a body of law has accumulated which can then be called a "science"—are ignorant of the whole history of innovative science. Important scientific breakthroughs have nearly always been based on model building.

Whether models are mostly fact or mostly fiction, they are where one starts. Models are hypothetical (conjectural) structures from which one can deduce the kinds of facts that would have to be true if the hypotheses are to be verified. If the models "test out," then those parts that were originally imagined become verified facts.

In psychology, investigators proceed as they do in physics or any other science. They construct models of the human mind, the human neuroendocrine system, the whole human being, and the human person in relation to its environment.

What Is the Relationship Between Models and Systems?

As commonly used, there is no sharp distinction between the terms *model* and *system*. As we have seen, a model is a deliberately simplified depiction of someone's hypothesis of "reality." It should not overly offend semanticists to use the terms interchangeably. However, for our needs, we do make this distinction: we can regard a system as a model that has "tested out." That is, the empirical deductions made from the model stood the test of experimentation and, for a while at least, were regarded as factually grounded. Systems are the factual structures of their time, even though as opposing data accumulate they tend to become shaky and evolve sooner or later into new systems, inspired by new models.

Can Useful New Knowledge Be Achieved
Except Through Systematic Thinking?

There are innumerable examples of new facts about nature being found through accident. The discovery of penicillin is a classic example. However, when we examine these cases it appears that, taken by themselves, they have seldom been useful discoveries until it was seen how they would fit into some larger whole. It has been through attempts to build more plausible and encompassing systems that physicists moved from unworkable to workable concepts of gravitation, light, the structure of atoms, and the envisioning of energy and mass as different versions of the same entity.[6]

What Lessons of Physical Science Are Available to Psychology?

What can we learn from a "history" of the key system builders in physics and other sciences that will help us understand some of the dilemmas of psychology? We learn that their systems have generally proved faulty eventually as new and contrary findings emerged from further study. But at the same time, we learn that each new system was usually more useful than previous ones because it explained more; it offered a better basis for prediction and control. Some models have been highly reductionist, but this is not always a necessary characteristic. Other models have embraced not only virtually everything known but a relatively thorough filling in of unknowns with imaginative constructs. The long-range tendency is probably toward less reductionism, except perhaps in certain sciences where contemporary models vary greatly in amount of reductionism—as in psychology. We also find that model building does not occur in an emotional vacuum; models in science have always reflected the values of the scientist which in turn have tended to be influenced by the general intellectual state of some part of the scientific community.

How Useful Is Systematic Thinking?

Probably the most important lesson of an historical study of model and system building is that it has not been completed systems that have produced new knowledge. When an earlier explanation of things (system) had begun to fall apart and be of little use, systematic thinkers have tried to pick up any pieces still of apparent usefulness and invent a new system (an emergent) incorporating both what may have remained valid from the old and the new knowledge that may have been responsible for eroding the old system.[7] Of fundamental importance to innovators in education is the fact that major breakthroughs in science generally have occurred during attempts to build and validate new models or systems that explained research data that was inconsistent with the models or systems previously in use.

To answer the question posed earlier—Can useful knowledge be achieved except through systematic thinking?—it appears that even during times when satisfactory explanations of phenomena are not available, efforts that prove the most productive arise from attempts to arrange what is known into systematic models, even though the models may seem somewhat less than satisfactory.

In contrast, it is difficult to conceive how any intentional eclecticism can lead to further knowledge (or even valuable insights about current knowledge). Eclecticism may sometimes be impossible to avoid (as during the long period when the photon and wave theories of light existed side by side), but we know of no philosopher of science who would advocate that for purposes of inquiry investigators should create eclectic positions. Authentic scientists tolerate eclectic positions only when they must. By definition, eclecticism does not permit systematic model building or provide a basis for creative hypothesizing.

WHAT ARE SOME EXAMPLES OF OPPOSED SYSTEMATIC VIEWS IN PSYCHOLOGY?

To help readers understand more fully what we mean by a systematic position, we will briefly describe two very different frames of reference in psychology which we will temporarily call *mechanistic* and *humanistic*. In psychology the use of the term mechanistic in the sense in which we use it is anything but unusual. Its function to describe one component of human life, though not necessarily all of it, dates back at least to René Descartes (1569–1650) and continues into the 1970s. Deci, for instance, places all of the associationistic or behavioristic psychologies under the general rubric of mechanistic positions.[8]

In contrast the term *humanistic* as a generic label for a frame of reference in science and psychology is a comparatively new development not yet acceptable to many writers in psychology. Though *The Journal of Humanistic Psychology* was established in 1961, not until the present decade did the American Psychological Association add a Division of Humanistic Psychology. As of 1977, however, at least two distinctive "humanist" positions seem firmly established in American psychology.

What Are Some of the Key Assumptions of Mechanistic Psychology?

Mechanistic psychology was an outgrowth of the intellectual spirit of the seventeenth through the nineteenth centuries. The intellectual cast of these three centuries was profoundly influenced by the natural sciences, first astronomy and physics, later chemistry, and in the late nineteenth century by biology as exemplified in Darwinism. During these three centuries certain primary, cosmological assumptions were widely accepted in the Western world. Cosmology refers to a branch of philosophy that deals with the origin and structure of the universe. Mechanistic psychology cannot be understood apart from its dominating cosmological assumptions about nature and the relation of its parts. These assumptions, taken together, compose what are referred to as *classical mechanics*.[9]

What Were the Cosmological Assumptions of Classical Mechanics?

Within the pattern of classical mechanics it was held that the universe consists of a collection of isolated material bodies—ranging in size from atoms to the largest known body—that exert force on one another according to mechanical principles. These forces tend to be in the form of attractions or repulsions (pulls and pushes). Motion is "naturally" linear and continuous, unless disrupted by forces exerted by other bodies. Lowry suggests that under classical mechanics, "the whole of nature rather resemble a great game of billiards . . . ."[10]

Every event is explainable (given sufficient knowledge) as part of a lawful sequence of causes and effects. Also, provided enough is known about it, everything in nature can be described quantitatively, that is, mathematically.

It was further held that the laws of nature operate independently of human observers. This led to the assumption that the observer and the observed were always separate (often referred to as the separation of subject and object). The laws of nature were also held to be universal and eternal. These beliefs in the independence of nature from human beings, and the fixity, dependability, and universality of natural law gave cosmology a decidedly absolutistic flavor.

One aspect of the Newtonian system that was of great importance to the early development of psychology was that, in order to develop his laws of gravitation and motion and describe them mathematically, Newton found it necessary to treat bodies of matter (of whatever size) as *points*—hypothetical designations of place, without area or mass. Further, for purposes of science, the only reality was considered to be two kinds of relationships between points: spacial (synchronous) and temporal (successive).

What Has Classical Mechanics Assumed About Human Nature?

Classical mechanics led to three mechanistic positions in psychology, all united by common acceptance of some of the assumptions stated above, yet each distinctive. Here we state, with inescapable oversimplification, the basic outlines of mental, physiological, and behavioral mechanisms. Each is treated in considerable detail later in the book.

MENTAL MECHANISM

Mental mechanism was the first systematic "scientific" psychology. It began developing in the seventeenth century and became the predominant position in psychology in the eighteenth. Essentially, mental mechanists were trying to explain mental functioning, not that of the "whole person."

Many historians of psychology regard John Locke (1632–1704) as the initiator of mental mechanism and James Mill (1773–1836) as both the terminal figure and the one who gave mental mechanism its most complete and plausible form. Perhaps most important for educational psychologists was the noted mental mechanist and educator Johann Friedrich Herbart (1776–1841), whose theories are still influential. The contributions of both Locke and Herbart are described in detail in Chapter 10. The chief characteristics of mental mechanism can be stated briefly as follows.

Human beings are regarded as passive receivers of the contents of the environment. Environmental elements are perceived as unitary sensations. In the human mind, these sensations may link with previously gained ideas of varying degrees of complexity according to "laws of association." There are no innate or inborn ideas; whatever their degree of complexity, existing ideas are never more than products of sensations previously received. Ideas do not exist in space, nor do they have a solid form, rather they are the mentalistic equivalent of Newton's postulated "points."

Although mental mechanists did not all agree on the laws governing the association of ideas, they generally thought that ideas attracted one another if they had a *resemblance* or affinity with one another, or if they occurred either at the same time (*spacial contiguity*) or immediately following one another (*temporal or successive contiguity*). Mill dropped the principle of resemblance because it had no counterpart in classical mechanics. Spacial and temporal contiguity corresponded to two fundamental relationships in the Newtonian system. Also, ideas that do not attract one another may repel one another: thus mental mechanism includes the Newtonian concepts of attraction and repulsion.

Humans with normal sensory equipment cannot escape sensory stimulation, or the combining of sensations into ideas, according to the laws of association (a part of natural law). Therefore, mental mechanism—like the other mechanistic psychologies—implies *environmental determinism*.

PHYSIOLOGICAL MECHANISM

Physiological mechanism conceives of human beings as biological organisms—automatons, that are automatically, governed. René Descartes (1596–1650) came closer than any of his contemporaries to developing the concept of the human being as an automaton. Descartes reduced the functions of the soul to but one—thought. Later, Julien de la Mettrie (1709–1751) eliminated the soul (or mind) altogether to develop in its purest form the idea of the human being as an automaton. Physiological mechanism reached its zenith in the nineteenth century with the work of a succession of famous German psychologists, particularly Johannes Muller (1801–1858), Gustav Fechner (1801–1887), and Herman von Helmholtz (1821–1894). The concept of human beings as "mindless organisms" became increasingly plausible with new findings about the functioning of the nervous system, particularly the discovery that nervous impulses were electrical and one-directional. Organic chemistry was also making major strides in describing various bodily processes including metabolism.

Probably even more than did mental mechanism, physiological mechanism borrowed heavily from the concepts of classical mechanics. Some chief points of physiological mechanism are as follows.

All aspects of what we call life can be explained through the laws of physics and chemistry. The human machine consists only of particles in motion. The human machine contains nothing innate that would direct its actions; it is basically reflexively responsive to environmental pushes and pulls. Thus, physiological mechanism—like other mechanisms—assumed that life was governed by environmental pressures. Hence it too was an environmental determinism.

Nineteenth-century mechanists thought that the nervous system is basically an electrical conductor system. Afferent (in-leading) nerves transmit sensory impulses to a central switching or "projection area"; in turn, efferent (out-leading) nerves transmit command impulses to muscles and glands. Further, this version of the "reflex arc concept" was held to be the basic unit of behavior, capable of describing all behavior.

Sensory nerves react to small, discrete stimuli, and nerve impulses take the form of small, discrete (particulate) units. Or, to use nineteenth-century terminology, nervous excitation and corresponding sensations are *punctiform*. These unitary or punctiform neural impulses and corresponding sensations combine into mosaics in the central nervous system, thus accounting first for complex sensations and then for complex reactions. This combining of punctiform sensations into mosaic or complex forms is a matter of conscious or unconscious inference, but is fully automatic and irresistible.

Physiological mechanistic thought could—it was believed—at last be regarded as an "exact science," similar to physics, and susceptible to laboratory study with quantifiable results capable of statistical description. It followed that, once physiological psychologists knew enough, it should be possible to manufacture life in the laboratory.

BEHAVIORAL MECHANISM

If mental mechanism was the psychology of the eighteenth century and physiological mechanism that of the nineteenth, then behavioral mechanism—at least until the 1970s—has been the predominant psychology of the twentieth century. Behavioral mechanism represented a logical third step for mechanistic psychology. Mental mechanism (with its attempt to describe the mind in terms of sensation gathering and organizing) and physiological mechanism (with its attempt to depict humans as mindless bodies) had both reached dead ends. There was only one area left for mechanistic interpretation: to relegate both mind and body to the waste heap and focus on *behavior* alone.

Although behavioral mechanism has as its foundation essentially the same cosmological assumptions as earlier mechanisms, it does break the established pattern in one important way—its view of human beings incorporates the concept of *evolving*, rather than static homeostasis. As noted earlier, the concept *evolving* in this context need not mean more than *changing*; it is not to be confused with the concept *purposive*. The injection of change over time as a basic feature of life was made necessary by wide-spread acceptance of the evolutionary theory of Charles Darwin

(1809–1882). Early in life Darwin was a staunch mechanist committed to the idea of static homeostasis. His investigations led him to conclude that life could only be described in terms of adaptive change. This, too, was a form of environmental determinism; therefore it did not require psychologists to abandon mechanistic assumptions. It did require them to accept the idea of change, though still in terms of "blind, unthinking, 'mechanical' principles."[11]

Prominent early behavioral mechanists were Ivan Pavlov (1849–1936), the somewhat eclectic Edward L. Thorndike (1874–1949), and John B. Watson (1878–1958). In Richard Lowry's opinion behavioral mechanism found its most complete and sophisticated development in the system of Clark Hull (1884–1952). After Hull, probably the best known behavioral mechanist has been B. F. Skinner (1904–   ), whose views are described in some detail in Chapter 13.

Some of the principles of behavioral mechanism are:

1. The purpose of psychology is to learn how psychologists, teachers, advertisers, politicians, and so forth can modify the behavior of others. This point is of the greatest importance because, with a few notable exceptions, particularly Herbart, most mental and physiological mechanists had seemed somewhat unclear about the practical use of their theories.

2. The only things innately predetermined about human behavior are biological drives and a tendency toward reducing them. But the number of drives are assumed to be limited to what the organism requires for survival and health—for example, hunger, thirst, sex, freedom from pain, temperature extremes, and so on. A drive is a strong, persistent stimulus that demands an adjustive response.

3. Psychological processes are a product of evolutionary demands; they take whatever form will contribute most to the survival of a species, including *Homo sapiens. Hence, psychology deals with both racial and personal adaptation.*

4. Adaptive behavior can be explained in terms of relationships between stimuli (Ss) and responses (Rs). Stimuli consist of some physical excitement provided by the environment and impinging on the organism. Responses consist of organic reactions to the stimuli. Central to behavioral mechanism is some sort of S–R or R–S formula, the most popular at present being a form of temporal sequence of stimuli and responses that impresses either new or changed reactions on a pliable passive organism. In most cases an R is "fixed" or "stamped in" by what follows it, often called a "reward." A "reward," as used here, is simply a stimulus that follows a behavior and thereby increases the likelihood of that behavior's occurrence in the future. In no sense does it imply that the organism is trying to accomplish something.

5. All that needs to be known about adaptive human behavior can be

explained without reference to consciousness, mind, purposiveness, or any other mentalistic construct, or to neurological or other bodily phenomena.

Since behavior is adaptive (or adjustive), it is also passive in relation to environmental forces. Like other mechanisms, *behavioral mechanism assumes environmental determinism.*

What Are Some of the Key Assumptions of Humanistic Psychology?

There are at least three outlooks which have borne the label of humanism. In its most generic meaning humanism now usually means a philosophically oriented psychology that elevates human beings and human concerns to a central position—in contrast, say, to a philosophy that elevates above human concerns the world of nonhuman nature, or some supernatural or mystical realm.

We plan to elaborate in this chapter only one humanist position, namely scientific humanism. However, it may be helpful to describe two others briefly so readers may get some feel for the breadth of the general term *humanism.*

1. *Classical humanism* (also called classicism) refers to an interest in human culture as depicted in the classical literature of the ancient world. Classicism urges both individualism and a critical spirit. This interest was at high tide during the Renaissance, but has had its disciples ever since. It has a psychology implicit in it, including a theory of learning. We treat classicism in Chapter 10.

Beginning in the early 1970s, a movement developed in the United States to develop what were called "renaissance schools." This movement has not progressed very far, but those who promote it feel they are being innovative and progressive. It would appear, however, that they may be about five centuries behind in their thinking.

2. *Psychedelic humanism* is a position holding that human beings instinctively have within them a tendency toward goodness and the capability as individuals of finding their own road to personal development and fulfillment. The position strongly emphasizes self-growth. It had its origin in Rousseau's concept of "natural unfoldment" and an eighteenth and nineteenth century movement called *romantic naturalism.* Recent and contemporary exponents include Abraham Maslow, Paul Goodman, and John Holt. It implies a distinctive theory of development and learning, and is treated in Chapters 5 and 10.

3. *Scientific humanism* is the version of humanism we describe in this chapter to contrast with mechanism. Scientific humanism seems to rest on more carefully developed and internally consistent assumptions than does psychedelic humanism. Therefore, it better illustrates the issue between systematic and eclectic positions in psychology. The following definition of scientific humanism, though a simplification, may be useful.

Scientific humanism is an outlook that emphasizes the enhancement of human welfare through the application of scientific processes to the solution of problems of human beings. Its adherents assert "the essential dignity and worth of man and his capacity to achieve self-realization through the use of reason and scientific method."[12]

Scientific humanism has several other commonly used names. One of the authors has used the term *positive relativism* to label a philosophic position which seems to belong within the compass of scientific humanism. The psychology that harmonizes best with positive relativism is called *cognitive-field*.[13] These terms are used in later sections of the book.

What Are Some of the Key Assumptions of Scientific Humanism?

The assumptions of scientific humanism have only within the past 20 or 30 years been clearly stated. With the exception of those asserted in the thought and writing of John Dewey and his intellectual forebears, Charles Peirce and William James, much recent literature on humanism tends to mix together assumptions appropriate to both psychedelic and scientific humanism. Michael Littleford, for example, seems to do just this in his still useful 1970 article.[14] A number of the more than 20 assumptions stated by Littleford harmonize with both these branches of humanism. However, his tendency to depict reality as wholly subjective, rather than as a product of the interaction of a person and the person's perceived environment, would make most scientific humanists unhappy.

Scientific humanists have a great deal more to say about human beings than about "the nature of things in the universe." They are also more interested in process or method than in structure. Trying to state a large number of assumptions about the characteristics of human nature and the universe in which human nature has evolved would require assertions about fixed principles or unchanging essences ("objective natural law") which only classical humanists are willing to get involved with. Modern humanist positions tend to reflect a good deal of relativism, as exemplified in the term we will use most of the time in this book as a label for our version of scientific humanism—positive relativism.

SOME ASSUMPTIONS ABOUT THE UNIVERSE

The "new physics" of the twentieth century makes a few primary assumptions that harmonize well with humanist philosophy and psychology. For example, the new physics rejects the notion of a neat, finite universe describable by absolutistic natural law. It is now generally assumed by physicists that whatever the universe may be (if, indeed, anything exists which deserves such a name), it is open—open to change, open to an infinite amount of new conceptualization. The physicist Max Born has aptly referred to an "unbounded, restless," universe.[15]

Any description of the universe is now seen as being colored by the values of the scientist who is doing the describing. In the new physics, subject-object coupling is regarded as the common state of affairs, broken only by the most arbitrary of descriptions. As physicist Neils Bohr put it, "a 'phenomenon' is the description of that which is to be observed *and* of the apparatus [including the observer] used to obtain the observation."[16]

Since reality is no longer conceptualized as relationships between points but rather as the interaction of elements in a force field or system, the classical notions that spacial and temporal relationships provide a complete picture of reality is obviously now obsolete.

SOME ASSUMPTIONS ABOUT HUMAN NATURE

The radical shift in assumptions about the cosmos led to shifts in assumptions about human nature over a long period of time. The nature of the shifts required are spelled out in Lowry's work, which we cited on page 13. We will review a few of the assumptions about human nature implicit in scientific humanism—some of which are not necessarily directly related to the new physics.

The purpose of psychology is not to ascertain how people can manipulate one another, nor how as passive organisms they can adapt (adjust) to a determining environment. Rather, the primary goal of psychology is to devise ways of teaching—influencing—persons to think more productively.

Human beings are not to be regarded as machines in any of the usual senses of the word. They are neither passive receivers of stimuli, nor reflexive in relation to their surroundings. It is assumed that human beings are potentially purposive in a way that goes far beyond mere biological maintenance. Purposes arise from neither innate nor environmental factors alone, but from an interactive process between the two. Human behavior, like the new conception of the universe, is seen as basically restless or dynamic.

Except artificially, persons cannot be separated from their environments, whether the environment referred to is physical, social, or both. Interaction between self and environment, or subject and object, is continuous. In the process, both self and environment are changed (although in the case of physical environments, the change may be only in the meaning of the physical objects—which, psychologically speaking, is a real change). A fundamental aspect of life is psychological as well as physical change. Further, it is assumed that adults as well as children are capable of indefinite amounts of change. The new psychology stresses not mere homeostatic functioning, but a consciously purposive kind of seeking—a desire on the part of living creatures to seek competence and self-determination in relation to their environment.[17]

In view of the above ideas about human nature, it is obvious that humanist psychologists reject environmental determinism, as well as all its implications regarding absolutistic behavior and an absolutistic society. Like the new cosmology, the new psychology is fundamentally relativistic.

WHY IS ECLECTICISM PROFUSE
AMONG EDUCATIONAL PSYCHOLOGISTS?

A tendency in psychology during the past decade or two apparently has been toward more eclecticism and fewer attempts at systematization. This does not mean there are not a large number of psychologists who are attempting model and system building; but others select with varying degrees of care from existing systems and put together eclectic bodies of knowledge that exhibit more or less internal consistency. In Part III, we describe several well-known systematic and two eclectic positions.

One reason so many psychologists have turned away from system building is that they have linked philosophy to cosmology. Hence, they have had a desire to divorce philosophy from psychology. Whereas noted physical scientists and major creative mathematicians have known all along that physics, mathematics, and philosophy are inseparable, mechanistic psychologists particularly have insisted that to make a science out of psychology it must be kept uncontaminated by philosophical thought. Also, many educational psychologists, including some of those who write books in the field, seem rather unaware that there is an issue of substance here. Perhaps too many psychologists have come to reject large-scale theorizing (system building) and, instead, have resorted to building minimodels of a number of specific psychological or physiological processes.

How May the Nature of the Subject Matter
of Psychology Promote Eclecticism?

Psychologists, human biologists, and social scientists surely have chosen to work with the most complicated subject matter ever brought under investigation—Homo sapiens, perhaps better named Homo erraticus: "man" the unpredictable, "man" the capricious.

A human being lives in and interacts with an environment and cannot be well understood apart from this interactive process. We are probably well advised to think of the process of *interaction* as the fundamental datum of study. When we consider not only the complexity of the human organism but also the complexity of the total environment relevant to human behavior, it is clear that scientific humanist psychologists do not have an easy task.

If this interactive process is going to be the preferred focus of study by psychologists, no wonder the building of plausible systematic models of this whole process has given pause to even the most powerful intellects. Perhaps no model proposed so far seems adequately useful to many psychologists and teachers to be worth bothering with. If a subject matter is simply too complicated to make sense of, investigators may feel that they can only gather facts about small matters and hope that some picture will emerge. Or investigators can study the apparently unsatisfactory models and draw items from them selectively in the hope of putting together an admittedly eclectic body of knowledge about human-ity that will be more useful than no body of knowledge at all.

How May Erosion of an Established System Promote Eclecticism?

In the Western world, particularly the Anglo-Saxon world, the mechanistic model as described earlier has been the most popular one among psychologists. There is a good reason why this should be so. Psychology as a field of formal research began to develop in a major way while classical mechanics was still in favor. So the mechanistic approach eventually captured the imagination of thousands of psychologists. There was an optimism among these early mechanistic psychologists, marvel-ously expressed by the behaviorist John Watson when he wrote:

> Give me a dozen healthy infants, well-formed, and my own special world to bring them up in, and I'll guarantee to take any one at random and train him to become any kind of specialist I might select—doctor, lawyer, artist, merchant-chief, and yes beggarman and thief, regardless of his talents, penchants, tendencies, abilities, vocations, and the race of his ancestors.[18]

Mechanistic psychology clearly dominated education until the 1960s. The mechanists had an impressive leader in B. F. Skinner of Harvard, who vigorously presents his highly reductionistic psychological model of the human organism, but because of a chain of circumstances—including the impact in the United States of the humanistic German emigré Kurt Lewin, the cultural developments of the 1960s, and the success of human-ists in bolstering their position with empirical evidence—it appears that mechanistic psychologists may soon be on the defensive. As of now, mechanistic psychology is perhaps in about the same situation physics was in after classical mechanics was confronted with relativity.

What Are Two Opposing Views of Psychological Model Building?

The state of psychology today can be aptly illustrated by the opposing positions taken in two fairly recent books. Chaplin and Krawiec, after reviewing the rise and decline of the major systematic positions in psychology, including psychoanalysis and the humanistic model that emerged from Gestalt psychology, assert that the period when schools of thought in psychology were predominant is now over because psychology has outgrown schools. These authors place their stamp of approval on what they call "miniature systems," examples of which they give as "learning, motivation, or perception," and also "personality." Even these may be further broken down, the authors suggest, illustrating what would appear to be a plea for miniature systems within miniature systems. They suggest that learning can best be treated in its different aspects, such as "verbal learning," "conditioning," or "maze learning." What this amounts to is a call for eclecticism or at least psychologizing by bits and pieces.[19]

In a contrasting position, after suggesting that all the mechanistic models have proved inadequate, Schultz hypothesizes that the future of psychology may lie in the more systematic development of humanistic psychology, and argues that the times are finally ripe for the emergence of more sophisticated humanistic models. Schultz does agree that at present we are in a period where the focus is on miniature systems, and that perhaps for now this may be the best that can be accomplished.[20]

WHY HAS EDUCATION BEEN UNDER ATTACK?

Education in the sense of schooling has always been the subject of criticism by both educators and laypersons, but apparently criticism has been on the rise during the past 20 years. Such criticism has come from professional educators as well as from the lay public. In raising the following pertinent questions and suggesting possible answers we conclude our brief look at some of the current issues in educational psychology.

Is Education an Art or a Science?

Many scholars in the liberal arts and humanities have tended to argue that if teachers know the content of their subject specialties well, they don't need to take courses in education. These scholars argue that "teachers are born" and not made; if college graduates have stimulating personalities and know their specialties, they can go into the classroom and with a little practice become capable teachers.

In contrast, most professors of education have argued that, although there may be an artistic component in teaching, education also can and must be studied as a science. These professors point to the research-based content of such courses as educational psychology, counseling, teaching the handicapped and the gifted, modern curriculum design, and classroom teaching techniques. There is indeed an immense research literature in these and other education courses.

Our own opinion is that the argument concerning education as an art vs. a science is invalid. We feel that the highest quality of teaching inseparably combines both knowledge of scientific derivation *and* art. We also feel that though there is not much that programs in teacher education can do to impart the artistic component of teaching—except to demonstrate artistic procedures in their own teaching—such programs can give prospective teachers a good deal of scientifically based information.

Unfortunately we have serious reservations as to how well schools of education have been teaching prospective teachers what the relevant sciences (for example, psychology, sociology, and human biology) really have to offer education. What has gone wrong?

Have Education Courses Failed as Science?

This discussion should begin with a hasty caveat; obviously, not all education courses have failed to bring the best scientific knowledge available to students. Hundreds if not thousands of education professors have done a creditable job of trying to transmit the most recent and pertinent research to students. Unfortunately these professors have had to contend with a frustrating barrier; their students come to them saturated with misconceptions about what science is. Students' misconceptions run deep and are held with stubborn commitment because they are the very misconceptions that pervade American culture. Primary among them is the cultural belief that there is only one way of "doing science"—the way of classical, mechanistic physics. As we suggested earlier in the chapter, this belief is at least 70 years obsolete, but that does not seem to weaken its tenacity.

Practicing teachers have been influenced more or less by the type of courses that they took as college students. If much of what they encountered reflected a self-contradictory, psychological eclecticism, then we can hardly expect them to teach their students to think more productively, more systematically. For the above reasons, this book focuses on describing, comparing, and evaluating systematic views in educational psychology. The book does not purport to offer any final answers, but its authors do hope that it will give students some genuinely viable options to think about, and that it will clarify some of the confusion over systematic vs. eclectic thinking.

NOTES

[1] See John Dewey, *How We Think*, Lexington, Mass.: Heath, 1933.

[2] *Webster's New International Dictionary*, 3d ed., S. V. "system."

[3] Abraham Kaplan, *The Conduct of Inquiry: Methodology for Behavioral Science*, San Francisco: Chandler, 1964, pp. 259–262.

[4] Gerald Holton, *Thematic Origins of Scientific Thought*, Cambridge: Harvard University Press, 1975, p. 35.

[5] Holton, pp. 294–295.

[6] Stephen Toulmin and June Goodfield, *The Architecture of Matter*, New York: Harper & Row, 1962, pp. 296–297.

[7] See T. S. Kuhn, *The Structure of Scientific Revolutions*, 2d ed., University of Chicago Press, 1970, especially pp. 43–65.

[8] Edward L. Deci, *Intrinsic Motivation*, New York: Plenum Press, 1975.

[9] In developing the different cosmological assumptions underlying mechanistic psychologies, and the primary assumptions of the psychologies themselves, we have drawn freely from Holton; Toulmin and Goodfield; and Richard Lowry, *The Evolution of Psychological Theory: 1650 to the Present*, New York: Aldine-Atherton, 1975; Duane P. Schultz, *A History of Modern Psychology*, 2d ed., New York: Academic Press, 1975; and James P. Chaplin and T. S. Krawiec, *Systems and Theories of Psychology*, 3d ed., New York: Holt, Rinehart and Winston, 1974.

[10] Lowry, p. 16.
[11] Lowry, p. 113.
[12] *Webster's*, S. V. "humanism."
[13] Morris L. Bigge, *Positive Relativism: An Emergent Educational Philosophy*, New York: Harper & Row, 1971.
[14] Michael Littleford, "Some Philosophic Assumptions of Humanistic Philosophy," *Education Theory*, 20 (3), 1970: 229–244.
[15] Holton, p. 36.
[16] Holton, p. 118.
[17] Deci, pp. 55–63.
[18] John B. Watson, *Behaviorism*, rev. ed., New York: Norton, 1930, p. 104.
[19] Chaplin and Krawiec, pp. 67–68.
[20] Duane P. Schultz, *A History of Modern Psychology*, 2d ed., New York: Academic Press, 1975, pp. 362, 370–375.

BIBLIOGRAPHY

BERTALANFFY, LUDWIG VON. *General System Theory: Essays on Its Foundation and Development*. New York: Braziller, 1969. A provocative plea for systematic thinking in psychology and the social and natural sciences. The originator of what he calls "general systems theory," his contribution to scientific thought is considerable.

BORING, E. G. *A History of Experimental Psychology*. New York: Appleton-Century-Crofts, 1950. In spite of its copyright date, this remains one of the best histories of psychology written. Contains considerable material pertinent to Chapter 1.

BRIDGMAN, PERCY W. *The Way Things Are*. Cambridge, Mass.: Harvard University Press, 1959. One of Bridgman's later statements on relativistic thinking. Highly pertinent to Chapter 1.

CHAPLIN, JAMES P., and T. S. KRAWLEC. *Systems and Theories of Psychology*, 3d ed. New York: Holt, Rinehart and Winston, 1974. A rather simplified treatment of a number of branches of psychology, including motivation. The author argues that the period of major system-building in psychology is over and that psychologists should now focus on minisystems. See chapters 11 and 16 particularly.

DIAMOND, SOLOMON (ed.). *The Roots of Psychology: A Sourcebook in the History of Ideas*. New York: Basic Books, 1974. A book of readings on psychology that begins with the ancient world and brings us down to the twentieth century. Useful as a reference, especially for advanced students.

FEARING, F. *Reflex Action: A Study in the History of Physiological Psychology*. Baltimore: Williams & Wilkins, 1930.

HERRNSTEIN, R. J., and E. G. BORING (eds.). *A Source Book in the History of Psychology*. Cambridge, Mass.: Harvard University Press, 1966.

HOLTON, GERALD. *Thematic Origins of Scientific Thought*. Cambridge, Mass.: Harvard University Press, 1975. Holton demonstrates how science relies heavily on themes—that is, assertions of an intuitive or evaluative nature that cannot be proved or disproved with factual evidence. An excellent book for helping students understand the nature of science, including psychology.

KUHN, THOMAS S. *The Structure of Scientific Revolutions,* 2d ed., University of Chicago Press, 1970. An oft-cited short but profound book on how change occurs in scientific thinking. Kuhn argues that a given model dominates thought until a more useful model challenges it. It takes for granted that thought cannot claim to be scientific unless it is sweepingly systematic.

LOWRY, RICHARD. *The Evolution of Psychological Thought: 1650 to the Present.* New York: Aldine-Atherton, 1971. This is one of the best, if not the best, study in the history of philosophic assumptions behind schools of thought in psychology. Best treatment of how Newtonian-Galilean assumptions produced the three mechanistic psychologies—mental, physiological, and behavioral mechanism.

MILLER, GEORGE A. *Psychology: The Science of Mental Life.* New York: Harper & Row, 1962. This readable book more or less parallels the introductory course in psychology at Harvard during the 1960s. For an interesting two-page wrap-up, see Chapter 22, "In Conclusion."

MURPHY, GARDNER. *Historical Introduction to Modern Psychology.* New York: Harcourt Brace Jovanovich, 1949. Contains considerable material pertinent to Chapter 1. Murphy is regarded as being somewhat less scholarly than Boring, but also more readable for students.

MURPHY, GARDNER, and L. B. MURPHY (eds.). *Western Psychology: From the Greeks to William James.* New York: Basic Books, 1969.

SAHAKIAN, WILLIAM S. (ed.). *History of Psychology: A Sourcebook in Systematic Psychology.* Itasca, Ill.: F. E. Peacock, 1968. Probably the most comprehensive and best balanced book of readings on the history of psychology. Includes some areas not touched upon in other readers.

TOULMIN, S., and J. GOODFIELD. *The Architecture of Matter.* New York: Harper & Row, 1962. An interesting account of how conceptions of matter have evolved historically. Readable for most students, but one or more courses in physical science would be helpful background.

WARREN, H. C. *A History of Association Psychology.* New York: Scribner, 1921.

WATSON, JOHN. *Behaviorism.* New York: Norton, 1924. Watson's own description and explanation of his views about "scientific" psychology. Watson is the American originator of behaviorism (behavioral mechanism). Many students may find one of Watson's earlier books best to start with, for example, *Behavior: An Introduction to Comparative Psychology* (Holt, 1914).

WATSON, ROBERT I. *The Great Psychologists from Aristotle to Freud,* 2d ed. Philadelphia: Lippincott, 1968. A reference book describing positions in psychology from the ancient world to about 1945. Of chief interest to readers of the present book are his chapters on John Watson's behaviorism and Wertheimer and Gestalt psychology—the latter one of the antecedents of contemporary cognitive-field psychology.

WOLMAN, B. *Contemporary Theories and Systems in Psychology.* New York: Harper & Row, 1960.

WOLMAN, B. (ed.). *Historical Roots of Contemporary Psychology.* New York: Harper & Row, 1968.

Part I
WHY IS AN UNDERSTANDING OF MOTIVATION IMPORTANT TO CLASSROOM TEACHERS?

Part I deals with the subject of motivation. Some psychologists, notably certain mechanists, have not regarded motivation as an important issue in education. Some of these persons have insisted—and continue to insist—that learning and motivation are identical processes and that any treatment of learning theory is in itself an adequate treatment of motivation. On the other hand, there are psychologists, particularly those of humanistic persuasion, who distinguish sharply between motivation and learning, and argue that motivation must exist for learning to occur. Other views fall somewhere between these two extremes.

Chapter 2 provides readers with some needed historical background, including a treatment of some ideas about motivation that are prescientific in the sense that they are not based on experimental evidence and are incapable of furnishing us with hypotheses that could be tested scientifically. Despite this lack, these prescientific views of motivation are still held by numerous parents, teachers, and school administrators. Chapter 2 also briefly reviews some of the chief issues raised by twentieth-century scientific psychologists.

Chapter 3 treats motivational concepts as set forth by several prominent behavioral mechanists, with special attention to theories that stress innate biological drives as the force behind motivation. The views emphasized in Chapter 3 are commonly called behavioristic because of their special attention to overt behavior as the only valid source for the scientific study of motivation.

Chapter 4 treats motivational concepts as set forth by several prominent nonmechanistic twentieth-century psychologists. In general, these views assume the existence of some kind of basic need or needs, needs that are psychological rather than biological. Chapter 5 is devoted to achievement motivation and its special pertinence to problems of classroom education.

Chapter 6 treats some selected aspects of human biology that contribute to an understanding of psychology; it centers upon the nature and function of the nervous system and the biofeedback process. We placed it in this position because it contains important material about motivation from the view of a neurobiologist. We have not found much of this material in any other educational psychology book and feel that it will have a high level of interest for students.

Chapter 2
WHY DO TEACHERS NEED TO UNDERSTAND THEORIES OF MOTIVATION?

The purpose of this chapter is to establish the importance of motivation as a subject of study for teachers, and to introduce some competing theories about the fundamental sources of motives. Chapters 3 and 4 then delve into the subject as treated, first, by mechanistic psychologists and, second, by psychedelic and scientific humanists (particularly positive relativists).

Part III of this book deals with a number of theories of learning, some of which include a clearly stated theory of motivation. Motivation is so important a subject, however, that it deserves special treatment especially because of its value to readers as an introduction to Part II on human psychological development and Part III on learning.

Motivation has been a much neglected subject in educational psychology. Schultz tells us that

> Progress in the area has been deterred by the many opposing points of view, differing experimental approaches, and disagreements over proper terminology and problems of definition. A fundamental dichotomy exists between the behavioristic-comparative [mechanistic] theorists working with animal subjects, who are concerned with the physiological basis of motivation, and the often nonexperimental theorists of an analytic persuasion, concerned with the more psychological basis of motivation.[1]

Not all behavioral mechanists have ignored "inner processes," but most have agreed that conscious inner processes or feelings of purposiveness have no important bearing on the causes of behavior. B. F. Skinner, the most influential behavioral mechanist of the 1960s and still influential in the late 1970s, does not even include the concept of motivation in his description of behavior. Rather, he asserts that the concept of motivation should be eliminated from psychology because what has passed for motivation historically is no more than learned behavior.

Before pursuing the subject, we offer the following definitions: A *motive* is commonly defined as a "something" inside a laboratory animal or a human being that arouses the animal to act—to energize behavior, so to speak. Some motivational theorists include in motivated behavior also the direction and sustaining of behavior. *Motivation* refers to the act or process of motivating. If mechanistic (behavioristic) psychologists use the term at all, they are usually referring to *drives* (that push the organism) or *incentives* (that pull the organism)—all in mechanical fashion. Drives usually come from within—like the feeling of an empty stomach in which the object of the aroused behavior is food. Drives and incentives may, however, work together; an incentive refers to some characteristic of the goal object. Food may or may not be an incentive depending upon its nature. A lion that preys on live mammals would hardly be activated to move toward a dish of birdseed.

Nonmechanistic psychologies, such as are represented by the different varieties of humanism, commonly assume that motivation is a product of some inner need—that is felt as a psychological need. So, when they use the term motivation, as most of them do, they are referring to thoughts and feelings. However, cognitive-field psychologists (positive relativists or scientific humanists) tend to see the source of motivation as an interacting process—selves interacting with their perceived environments.

HOW HAS IGNORING MOTIVATION AFFECTED EDUCATION?

Historically, perhaps in part because educational psychology has tended either to play down or to ignore motivation, we have produced one generation after another of school teachers and administrators who have no clear theory of motivation. These persons may entertain theories of motivation based on folklore, or they may bypass the subject altogether. However, the absence or possession of a theory of motivation crucially affects both the selection of content to be taught and the methods used to teach it.

School personnel who lack a clear theory of motivation usually also lack a clear theory of learning. Learning theories that are at all comprehensive provide either explicitly or implicitly some explanation of what initiates behavior or thought. Teachers and administrators who have no clear-cut theory of learning and its motivation may possess a variety of beliefs about how learning is initiated and how it proceeds. So teachers quite often adhere to fragments of two or more theories of motivation that may be, and often are, contradictory.

It seems plausible to assume that this state of affairs is a result of teachers not having been able to reconcile the conflicting ideas they received from different education professors and from articles in the professional education journals. Further, teachers who have gained their theoretical grounding from these two sources are likely to be so confusedly eclectic that they uncritically combine whatever ideas they encounter. Hence, we can see in the work of large numbers of teachers the influence not only of portions of theories of motivation promoted by educational psychologists, but also scraps gleaned from folklore beliefs about what instigates learning.

How Is Inadequate Use of Motivational Theory Reflected in Contemporary School Situations?

As of this writing, public elementary and secondary education in the United States is receiving more caustic criticism than usual. One reason for the present wave of attacks is the wide-spread realization that high school seniors and entering college freshmen for several years have scored lower each year on the widely given Scholastic Aptitude Test (SAT). Since language and arithmetic skills play an important role in enabling students to do well on the SAT, the public schools are being charged with declining efficiency in teaching these skills. Whereas public blame for the results focuses on school administrators and teachers, these people in turn blame parental permissiveness, television, variations in students' cultural backgrounds, and each other's teaching methods.

Whether education in the 1970s has been less effective, about the same, or more effective than education 25, 50, or 100 years ago is likely to remain a matter of debate; but most educators seem to agree on two points. First, the schools could do a much better job. Second, educators blame television, parents, and peer group values for the poor results. They also point to what they see as an indisputable fact: according to the criteria of most teachers, elementary and secondary students are more apathetic toward learning, more disrespectful of authority, and more unruly than in "the good old days." This characterization of students fits some communities better than others, but most educators would agree that the complaint has merit. An unprecedentedly large number of students, from junior high through twelfth grade, act as if they did not want to be in school. Their rebellion against formal schooling takes the forms of tardiness, absence, disobedience, vandalism—and in some urban ghettoes, physical attacks on teachers.

How may this be explained? What we see is a lack of motivation among students to take school seriously. Although teachers tend to blame the various causes noted above, it may be that virtually all pupils could be motivated to achieve well in school if teachers themselves knew more about the nature and source of motivation. We have suggested that many teachers and administrators are apparently weak in their command of a learning theory that includes a theory of motivation. This is one variable in the total situation that teachers and administrators rarely seem to see as important. Possibly it was relatively unimportant 50 years ago. Perhaps students who finished high school then were motivated by factors other than those provided as a result of their teachers' understanding of what produces motivation. However, if these factors no longer exist, it would appear that today teachers need to understand motivation extremely well.

If hypotheses now being tested with apparently fruitful results by a goodly number of psychologists such as Edward L. Deci, whose findings are reported in Chapter 4, p. 92, do indeed prove verifiable, then many teaching strategies now used to produce or increase motivation are mistaken. The strategies are not only wrong in the sense of being ineffective, they may even demotivate pupils who might otherwise be motivated. New findings in the nature of motivation are explored in Chapter 4, and effective teaching for producing motivation strategies are considered in Chapter 21.

What Do Teachers Substitute for Effective Motivational Procedure?

If teachers lack a solid grounding in contemporary motivation theory, or in adequate theories of learning that include motivation theories, they have little choice but to engage in trial-and-error experimentation with all the devices they can think of to catch and hold the interest of pupils. *Devices* is an appropriate term to use, particularly if it means ruses, strategems, subterfuges, or tricks. A nontheoretical approach to teaching is often referred to as a "bag-of-tricks" approach. Many teachers accumulate a large repertoire of tricks, one or more for each class period—though some may be good enough for a teacher to use over and over—and select whichever trick or tricks they feel most appropriate for a given class period.

To a casual observer, many classroom tricks seem like first-rate teaching procedures. They may indeed capture students' attention. They may turn an otherwise chaotic situation into one of surface order. They may make the teacher popular with pupils. They may even make teachers popular with supervisors and administrators. If the tricks are unusual, the teacher is thought of as creative. But tricks they remain, not systematic approaches to motivation. A careful examination of prepackaged bag-of-tricks teaching materials suggests that many of them either are addressed to very superficial issues or no issues at all, or they contain built-in pro-status-quo biases unlikely to provoke thought. Some prepackaged teaching materials however do help teachers encourage students to critically examine serious, long-range cultural issues and problems. Some carefully designed teaching films and simulation games do provoke thought and produce understanding of issues related to the power structure, racial bigotry, distribution of wealth, sexism, foreign policy, ecological problems, and the like.

Nevertheless a bag-of-tricks recipe for teaching may prevent students' achieving both sustained motivation and the in-depth learning that results from sustained motivation. One reason for this is that most trick-kits separate means from long-range culturally significant ends. They are built to serve short-range objectives—objectives suited to either one or a few periods of classroom study. To be workable in this format the materials not only rely on prestated, short-range learnings, but promote a kind of fun-and-games procedure for reaching ends that are purportedly matters of very serious concern. Both teachers and pupils come to rely on the fun-and-games aspect of such strategies and in the process risk losing sight of long-range culturally important goals. Emphasis on short-range flashy means may submerge consideration of long-range serious ends.

The foregoing assertion is not intended to suggest that means and ends are separable, except artificially for purposes of analysis. Means and ends are integral, in that means tend to incorporate ends and vice versa. The ends we achieve are thus imbedded in the means. If the means are viewed by students as fun and games, then the ends actually achieved will be the enhanced ability to work with and to be entertained by fun and games.

How Does Thoughtless Eclecticism Contribute to Poor Understanding of Motivation?

It may be useful at this point to refer back to the central issue developed in Chapter 1—systematic vs. eclectic approaches to theory building. Teachers often combine motivational concepts appropriate to one or more of the mechanistic psychologies (mental mechanism, physiological mechanism, and behavioral mechanism) with motivational concepts appropriate to one or more of the humanistic psychologies (classical, psychedelic, and scientific humanism). Although what this kind of eclecticism really leads to will be discussed later, here we may note that many teachers mix incompatible assumptions about what motivates students, how motivation is sustained, and what the outcomes of study based on adequate motivation should be.

In the next section of this chapter we present a systematic overview of theories of motivation, including the theories that are still influential despite their ancient origins. In Chapters 3, 4, and 5 we pursue this task more specifically.

WHERE DO MOTIVES COME FROM?

According to which theory of motivation we adopt, motives will be seen as coming exclusively or mainly either from *within* the individual, from the individual's *outer* physical environment, or from the *interaction* between a person and that person's perceived environment. This classification is not always clear cut because to some extent these three categories of theories overlap and interpenetrate each other.

Furthermore, even if one category of theories (those harmonizing with cognitive-field psychology) seems to have more explanatory power than the others (as the authors tend to think), readers should note that humans often act as if one or more theories under the other two categories explain and predict their behavior better. This may be because of the highly developed ability of humans to role play and thus to veil the behavior toward which they are most inclined.

WHAT ARE SOME PRESCIENTIFIC THEORIES OF INNER MOTIVATION?

Under this head we describe what are commonly called *vitalistic* theories and *instinct* theories. These two classes of theories have in common the view that explanations of motivation should focus *within a person or biological organism,* not within either the environment or an interactive person-environment process.

How Do Vitalists View Motivation?

The central idea of vitalism is that the source of human motivation consists either entirely or partly of a vital or life force—*élan vital,* as it is often called. There are two major versions of vitalism. One version regards the total human as essentially a *life force* (or mind, spirit, or soul). The other regards a total human being as consisting of two parts— a life force and a more or less material and mechanical body. The first position is a *monism*—a term derived from the Greek *monismus,* meaning "oneness." (As we will see later, there are other views of the nature of human nature, quite unlike vitalism, that also promote a monistic interpretation of human beings.) The second position has traditionally been called a *dualism*—meaning "twoness," or consisting of two separate and different parts. The separate parts are a materialistic body on the one hand and a mind, spirit, or soul on the other.

Vitalists conceive the life force as an entity or substance that is nonmaterial, invisible, indestructible, and possessed of certain mental powers, most of which are related to thinking. (Mental powers include willing, purposing, reflecting, imagining, and remembering.) Alternative terms for life force are mind, spirit, or soul. Mind as a synonym for life force is defined in a special way. Though there are a variety of definitions of mind, here we treat only those that need concern students in an educational psychology course.[2]

MONISTIC VITALISM—IDEALISM

We commonly associate the origins of monistic vitalism with Plato (427–347 B.C.). Plato believed the essence of the universe consisted of pure ideas that are perfect in nature, but which are represented imperfectly and in a somewhat illusory form by what seems to be the reality around us. Because the fundamental structure of the universe was viewed as ideas, Platonic doctrine may be thought of as *idea-ism*. Although the term has merit because it describes what it refers to, it is awkward to pronounce. So, although misleading to students, the word *idealism* has been used historically to mean idea-ism.

Idealism has taken many forms throughout history and continues to attract many people today. Adherents of this position assume that in actuality the human body, and indeed all apparent material substance, is not a real substance at all, but a *projection* of either a finite human mind or the infinite mind of God. A leading exponent of the idea that perception of a thing is what gives it an apparent material existence was the Irish philosopher George Berkeley (1685–1753). Bishop Berkeley's position is known as *subjective idealism*.

In its extreme form, idealism holds that mind (soul, spirit, élan, or life force) is the only reality in the universe, and that material objects are not substantial realities. This view is associated with a philosophical school of thought known as *absolute idealism* which originated with the German philosopher G. W. F. Hegel (1770–1831).

As a philosophical position, idealism has usually pushed the assumption that the properties of the mind are fixed. However, the nineteenth-century interest in evolutionary change led to new forms of idealism that assumed that the properties of mind change or evolve over time. The views of two persons are important in this connection: the Italian Giovanni Gentile (1875–1944) and the French Jesuit paleontologist and religious philosopher Pierre Teilhard de Chardin (1881–1955).

Gentile did not refer to mind as an existent but rather as pure activity from which springs all that we know as existence. Since, according to Gentile, mind is activity or process in an everlasting state of change—and since all material substance is a product of mind-acts—it follows that all we call material is likewise in a state of constant flux. To Gentile, the universe consists basically of acts of thought, that is, acts of mind. Mind has no existence apart from its acts, and its actions have no limitations in space and time. Thus, Gentile went about as far as one can go in making mind or spirit the basis of everything that people are aware of, and at the same time eliminating any kind of eternal law or governing principle.

Chardin's "system" is a highly influential twentieth-century view that places psychic—or mind—force at the center of things. Chardin was a scientist. Hence he was more directly influenced by Darwinian concepts than was Gentile. Chardin postulated that energy is the basic substance of the universe. However, over the long course of the history of the universe, energy assumes increasingly complex forms, from atomic particles to human life. This evolutionary process is God expressing Himself. Chardin identified two modes in which energy is manifested—the energy familiar to physicists and psychic energy. As the organization of energy became more complex, the psychic mode of expression became more prominent and controlling. Psychic energy can be equated with consciousness, spirit, or soul; one of its properties is love.

Since the late 1950s idealism in the Western world has also received a renewed impetus through the wide-spread interest in Asiatic religions. Most of the various mystical religions of Asia which have been imported to the United States are apparently, in their basic nature, forms of idealism.

With respect to motivation, one of the chief influences of the various idealist positions is their common emphasis on individual will, purposiveness, and decision making. Will implies something like what is meant in the layperson's expression "will power." Another layperson's expression relating to the idealist view is "mind over matter." The meaning of mind, construed as an independent, willing, purposing entity or substance, provides a key to understanding motivation from an idealist's view. *An active mind decides on its own what to do and when and how.* What we call the body, and its physical environment, do not count for very much. People can, if they seriously try, free mind from bodily and environmental restraints. This is what the expression free will means.

DUALISTIC VITALISM

A position more widely accepted than pure idealism is mind-body dualism. According to this view, mind is defined very much as idealists define it. Mind is the *élan vital*, a nonmaterial substance, the equivalent of soul or spirit. But to dualists material entities are equally real. The notion that human beings were made up of two contrasting entities, spirit and body, was probably introduced to Europe from the Persian peninsula before the Christian era. A characteristic of early dualisms was the notion that the mind or spirit is perfectable but the physical body is intrinsically evil. St. Augustine (354–430 A.D.) preached this idea with great force, arguing that the body is inherently defiling—a prison of flesh against which the spirit wars until it is freed by the body's death.

René Descartes (1596–1650) gave dualism a more sophisticated form. As noted in Chapter 1, Descartes, drawing on the physiology of his time, described the body as a somewhat self-sufficient machine and reserved only one function for the mind or spirit—thought. According to

Descartes, the mind uses the body as its instrument. Hence, mind-body dualism in its more modern forms has portrayed mind as a force that makes the body go. To use some simple analogies, the body is like an automobile, the mind like the driver; or the body is like a piano, the mind like the player.

There are problems inherent in mind-body dualism as this position has been traditionally stated. Critics of the position argue that no dualist has ever provided an adequate explanation of how a nonmaterial substance, particularly of a mentalistic or spiritual nature, can act upon a material substance. Furthermore, it seems clear that mental and bodily functioning are tied together integrally. What we call mind seems profoundly affected by bodily states such as serious illness or damage to the brain; conversely, mental states seem to affect with equal potency the functioning of the body.

Despite these problems, until the middle of the twentieth century many eminent scientists have accepted some form of dualism as the best available explanation of the complexities of human life. The well-known physicist A. S. Eddington asserted what was essentially a dualist position (*The Philosophy of Physical Science*, 1939). C. S. Sherrington, a pioneer in neurophysiology, adopted a dualistic outlook (see his *Man on His Nature*, 1951). E. D. Adrian, earlier in the century one of the world's leading authorities on neural electrical phenomena, wrote in terms of a mind-brain dualism

> the addition of mental events . . . seems to rule out a purely physical description of all that happens . . . if it is found that physical mechanisms cannot even explain all that happens in the brain, we shall have to decide when and where *the mind* intervenes.[3]

Even a relatively pure Cartesian (term derived from the name Descartes) dualism was advocated as recently as the 1950s by the British neurophysiologist John C. Eccles, who proposed a theory of how a brain could interact with a life force not detectable by any instruments then available.[4]

Although today only a minority of psychologists, physiologists, or biologists are body-mind dualists, a kind of naive dualism seems acceptable to most laymen. Both Gallup and Harris public opinion polls, working with national samples of adults, found repeatedly that a large majority of Americans recurrently talk in terms of "mind and body" and of spirit or soul as a "something" which resides in or about the body and continues on after the body's demise.

Dualists who define mind in essentially the same manner as monistic vitalists generally would be likely to espouse the same concept of motivation. The life force, with its capacity for purposing, willing, and decision making, is capable of being self-starting; it not only can direct its own activities, but most dualists believe that it instigates and guides—motivates—activities of the body.

CURRENT EFFECTS OF VITALISM

When mind is defined as a nonmaterial substance different in kind from any entity in nature, then it is removed from the realm of scientific investigation. We have treated vitalism at such length not because it forms the basis of any current scientifically viable explanation of motivation, but because so many people, including school teachers and administrators, remain vitalists. As long as they are vitalists it is difficult for them to seriously entertain any nonvitalistic explanation of motivation without being trapped in a contradictary eclecticism. To be true to their own position, vitalists have to espouse some kind of doctrine of free will (see p. 37). A belief in free will does not mesh well with any current theory of motivation that can be experimented with in psychological laboratories or classrooms.

How Have Instinct Theories Developed?

An instinct is an unlearned or innate pattern of conduct. The notion that humans and other animals have implanted within them genetically based behavior patterns that will emerge more or less automatically at some time between birth and old age is longstanding. Dating back to the ancient world is the notion that behavior is rooted in a number of innate powers or "faculties," chief among which are free will and the capacity for reason. Humans and humans alone were thought to possess these faculties. It was also thought that human behavior is not entirely rational; much of it is governed by "lower" emotions that are animallike.

St. Thomas Aquinas (1225?–1274) was one of the earliest figures in the Christian era to talk about instincts, even though the word had not yet been coined. (Interestingly, apparently the first known use of the term instinct was in Shakespeare's play *Henry IV.*)

More recently, for example, about the time of René Descartes (1596–1650), religious beliefs came to play an important role in explaining what motivated humans. Human traits, including patterns of motivation, were widely believed in the seventeenth century to be God given. This God-given nature of the human mind was thought to contain within it the urges that impel humans to adapt to their environments and also to satisfy their necessary biological needs. But, in the thinking of Descartes and others, instincts were not mechanical (that is, not producing an imperative cause-and-effect relation, as mechanistic thinkers later would hold in their insistence that a given S [stimulus] is followed automatically by a given R [response]).

There was a competing line of thought about instincts derived from the materialistic thinking of the ancient Greek, Democritus. This was a mechanical view of which little was heard until Thomas Hobbes (1588–1679) proposed a strictly materialist view of instincts. Hobbes distinguished between two kinds of instinctive motion in humans. *Vital motion* was what many psychologists today would call autonomic—breathing, digesting food, the pumping of the heart, and so on. *Voluntary motion* was what humans did through conscious direction—such as moving an arm, smiling, or walking. Voluntary motions were so directed as to minimize pain and maximize pleasure. This pleasure-pain principle, we will find, has been held to be instinctively based by some psychologists well into the twentieth century.

How Do Instinct Theories Relate to Motivation?

We can identify two basic kinds of instinct theories: prescientific and scientific. Prescientific instinct theories are so labeled because they cannot be tested with evidence; they can only be taken on faith. Loosely defined, prescientific human instincts are inherent tendencies toward certain types of moral behavior. In this chapter we treat two prescientific theories because they are still widely espoused by laypersons and by a large number of professionals as well. The major scientific instinct theories are treated in Chapter 3.

THE BELIEF IN INNATELY EVIL HUMAN NATURE

Historically, many people who have assumed the existence of an instinctive human nature have described human nature in moralistic terms—as either bad or good. According to the notion that human beings are naturally bad, all humankind is thought to be afflicted with evil impulses. Thus, we should expect the fundamental motivation of people—that with which they are born—to be toward acts that are at best antisocial and at worst sinful in the eyes of God. We shall see just how compelling some people have thought humankind's motivation toward evil is.

The idea that human nature is instinctively evil is very old. Its origin is unknown and may lie farther back than recorded history. Noss reports the thinking of Hsun-tzu, a Chinese philosopher of the third century B.C., as follows: "The nature of man is evil . . . . Therefore to give rein to man's original nature, to follow man's feelings, inevitably results in strife and rapacity."[5] Hebraic thought during the pre-Christian era also seems to reflect this idea. In Genesis 8:21 we are told, "for the imagination of man's heart is evil from his youth" and in Psalm 51:5, "Behold, I was shapen in iniquity; and in sin did my mother conceive me."

The idea that humans have two selves, a higher and a lower, also developed at a relatively early period in human history. The ancient Egyptians, like the members of many nonliterate cultures before them, conceived of human beings as made up of two parts, body and spirit. A number of pre-Christian Greek philosophers made a very definite distinction between body and spirit. They believed that the body was an impure "prison of the soul," and that, in contrast, the soul was pure. This notion was shared by a number of religious sects of the Persian peninsula.

Early dualists, that is, those who assumed a twofold—body and spirit—nature of humankind, tended to think that, when bodily impulses got the upper hand, peoples' behavior was highly evil, but when the spirit or soul dominated, behavior was much better.

In the United States notions about the inherent evilness of human nature have come down to us most strongly through the Puritan tradition which put its stamp on much of American thought down to recent times. Of the Puritan outlook, Smith tells us

> The Puritan ideal was one of extreme personal righteousness, the Puritan consciousness of an everpresent sense of the all-pervading and innate character of sin. Emphasis on Augustine's theory of concupiscence and infant damnation . . . gave to all true Puritans a somber and gloomy character . . . [The emphasis of Puritanism] on original sin led it to distrust the child: infants are bound by their own innate fault; though they may not have given evidence of their iniquity, they have the seed shut up in them, their whole nature is a sort of seed of sin. . . .[6]

In the American colonies, Jonathan Edwards exemplified Puritan beliefs. Probably the colonies produced no more effective exponent of the notion that human nature is intrinsically vile. Referring to what he spoke of as "the total depravity and corruption of man's nature," Edwards argued that humans are "wholly under the power of sin, and . . . utterly unable, without the inter-position of sovereign grace . . . to do anything that is truly good," and that "the natural state of the mind of man . . . is corrupt and depraved with a moral depravity, that amounts to and implies their utter undoing." Edwards depicted humans as utterly repugnant to God because of their corrupt state. His most famous sermon on this theme, "Sinners in the Hands of an Angry God," was delivered July 8, 1741. Edwards that day told his Connecticut congregation:

> The God that holds you over the pit of hell, much as one holds a spider, or some loathsome insect over the fire, abhores you. . . . You are ten thousand times more abominable in his eyes, than the most hateful venemous serpent in ours.[7]

Although we are less extreme about it today than was Jonathan Edwards, there apparently remains a streak in American thought holding that the human race is a pretty despicable lot, with natural or instinctive "cussedness" taking a variety of forms. We still talk a great deal about such undesirable human traits as greed, violent aggressiveness, stealing, cheating, and laziness. "Most people on welfare are simply lazy and don't want to work" is a commonly expressed idea. Proponents of the idea that humans—of all ages—will do every evil thing they can get away with tend to urge the passage of increasingly comprehensive and severe laws to control other people's failings.

If one accepts the notion that human nature is intrinsically bad, and that this condition is common to the young as well as the old, then certain conclusions about motivation follow. The dominant motive of human beings is to behave immorally and illegally. Since this inner motivation is instinctive, all members of the human race will be impelled by it for life. However, it is usually assumed that the threat of punishment or, if necessary, punishment itself will keep most people within a relatively decent pattern of behavior. People will think evil thoughts—this no one can prevent—but if people can be made sufficiently afraid of translating these thoughts into action, they will be motivated to remain overtly good enough to make society work.

This may seem like a simplistic theory of motivation. Nevertheless, much of our criminal law assumes its correctness. "Rehabilitation" of criminals more often than not takes the form of punishment. The same principle operates in many schools. Students are assumed to have many evil characteristics such as being untrustworthy, thieving, and lazy—until they prove otherwise. The young are energetic enough to cause trouble, but seem too lethargic to do the constructive classroom work that teachers expect. Many people feel that it is only through moral or physical coercion that children do anything productive.

THE BELIEF IN INNATELY GOOD HUMAN NATURE

The idea that human nature is innately good, moral, compassionate, and so forth turns the conception of instinctive evil motivation upside down. Like notions of innate badness, the idea of innate goodness appears to have ancient origins. In the sense that in many primitive cultures people's natural impulses have been worshipped or idolized, the idea of innate goodness appears to date from the prehistoric era. Burtt comments that primitive man generally was not aware of any need to be "remade" or "reborn" in order to fulfill the demands of moral custom.

> Primitive religion . . . assumes that man's natural desires form the core of his true self; these desires press legitimately for satisfaction, and religion provides one important set of techniques by which their satisfaction can be assured.[8]

The chief role of the deities conceived by primitive men and women was to assist the natural impulses. Hence, sexual orgies, gluttonous banquets, and drunkenness were often a part of religious worship and ceremony. It would be easy, however, to oversimplify this picture. Primitive societies also entertained numerous taboos that had the effect of suppressing or denying an outlet to common impulses. Primitive man was not as uninhibited as some moderns have imagined.

When we analyze humankind's historical period, beginning with ancient Greece, we encounter two versions of the idea that human nature is intrinsically good. The first view holds that humans' natural (instinctive) impulses are good in themselves, and that if people live according to the dictates of their inborn motives they automatically will have a good life. This notion gained much force during the Renaissance; although sometimes associated with classical humanism, in retrospect it seems more like a forerunner of the psychedelic humanism of modern times. The second, related, view holds that even though humans are instinctively good, civilization—particularly in large cities—has a corrupting influence, so that many humans display very bad traits indeed. But if humans can be kept free from societal contamination, they should blossom like the loveliest flowers. This idea is usually associated with the thinking of Jean Jacques Rousseau (1712–1778), whose major idea we will examine.

Rousseau was a champion of the idea that a child at birth is naturally good; provided the child is not corrupted by society, this goodness will manifest itself in behavior. Rousseau's combined philosophy and psychology has been called *Romantic naturalism*.

There were at least two major themes in eighteenth-century thought. The use of reason and science in human affairs gained for the century the title "The Age of Enlightenment," but the other theme was essentially sentimental. It provided a foundation for the nineteenth-century movement known as *romanticism* with which we associate Rousseau. He exhibited a sentimental, worshipful attitude toward nature and all things close to nature. The first sentence of his famous book, *Emile*, states, "All things are good as they come out of the hands of their Creator, but every thing degenerates in the hands of man."[9] Thus, Rousseau found the inborn motivation for good primarily in unspoiled human nature—the nature of simple, uncorrupted persons such as "noble savages," peasants, preliterate tribal cultures, and children. Rousseau did not visualize this simple humankind as much given to reason or reflection. Humans, he thought, are like the lower animals in that they are almost purely creatures of impulse or spontaneous motivation.

As time passed, the concept of the innate goodness of human nature became increasingly influential. This influence has had a significant impact on American psychology. During the first half of the twentieth century, Arnold Gesell (1880–1961), a leader in child study, asserted that in describing a child it is best to use the analogy of a plant. One gets the impression from Gesell that children will show naturally good traits if their environment is sufficiently permissive. The influence of Rousseau was also conspicuous in the Progressive Education Movement, which was formalized in about 1920 and had some weight in public education until the late 1950s. Also of considerable importance in both England and the United States has been the work of Briton A. S. Neill (1883–1973) of Summerhill School fame who pushed the ideas of growth from within and permissive child rearing about as far as possible.

Even more notable has been the development in the United States of psychedelic humanism, a school of thought with clear roots in Rousseau. Psychedelic humanism also has been called "third force psychology" to set it apart from mechanistic and Freudian schools of thought. Among psychologists, the central figure in this movement was probably Abraham Maslow (1908–1970). This position is developed in more detail in Chapter 4.

Why Were Early Instinct Theories Unscientific?

Despite their continuing influence, theories of motivation which assume that humans have an instinctive penchant for either badness or goodness are prescientific because they are not stated in a way that permits empirical testing. To say that human nature is naturally (instinctively) either good or bad is to state a supposedly "self-evident" absolute—not a scientific hypothesis that can be tested through accuracy in interpretation or prediction. The only way something can be good or bad in a scientifically demonstrable way is for it to be dependably instrumental in the attainment of some generally agreed upon goal. For example, it can be shown in many cases that insulin injections are "good for" a person with diabetes; conversely, it can be shown that heavy indulgence in alcohol or cigarettes is "bad for" some persons. All that is meant by *good* and *bad*, as so used, is that something will or will not contribute toward attainment of a desired end.

Puritans took the view that human beings, instinctively, want to do the things that Western society historically has condemned—which in no way proves that these actions are "bad" in any universal or eternal sense (many such actions would be deemed good in numerous non-Western cultures). Likewise, Rousseau took the view that people, if uncorrupted by society, instinctively want to do what Western society historically has acclaimed as good. Neither outlook can be subjected to scientific test.

WHAT ARE SOME THEORIES OF OUTER MOTIVATION?

By outer motivation we are referring to motivation induced by environmental settings. This is environmental determinism, which mechanistic or behavioristic psychologists assume is the chief source and guide of human behavior. According to this general view, environmental pushes and pulls induce organisms to act, and guide action once it has been instigated.

What Is the Background of Mechanistic Theories of Motivation?

Mechanists (also sometimes called materialists) explain the whole of life in terms of the operation of the laws of physics and chemistry. They assume that living protoplasm is nothing more than a highly complex organization of chemical and electrical phenomena. They staunchly refuse to accept, as necessary in explaining life, any sort of nonmaterial mental or spiritual force. Behavior, they maintain, is best explained as responses to stimuli from either outside or inside an organism. H. G. Wells, J. S. Huxley, and G. P. Wells compare the mammalian body to a gasoline motor and go on to say,

> Now is this analysis sound? Is a living man fundamentally a machine? That is a question capable of experimental decision. We can measure the amount of food that a man or an animal consumes over a given period of time, and we can measure the energy yielded during the same period. If we burn an equal weight of similar food in a suitable apparatus and find out how much energy its combustion yields, and if this value is equal to the energy yielded by the experimental subject, then evidently the living organism, so far as its energy-output is concerned, is really and precisely a combustion engine.[10]

After citing experiments designed to test this proposition, these authors conclude that "man and the animals generally are fundamentally mechanisms, driven by the energy liberated in the oxidation of food."[11] They concede, however, that the machinelike properties of the body do not explain everything. For example, they do not explain growth, reproduction, and consciousness. But the latter phenomena are explainable, they reason, without resorting to a belief in soul, spirit, or mysterious "life force."[12] However, Huxley in his later writings, such as *Evolution in Action* and certain essays in *Man in the Modern World*, seems to move toward an outlook more like what we describe under our third—interactionist—category.

Mechanists have given much attention to the task of explaining mental phenomena in physical terms. The development of electronic computers ("electronic brains") has stimulated attempts to describe what we call mind as a product of a complex system of computation, making use of electrochemical processes. In a provocative paper delivered before the Hixon Symposium in 1948, the late John von Neumann, a brilliant mathematician associated with the Princeton Institute for Advanced Study, explored the question of whether it would be possible to build a computer having the essential attributes of a living organism. Von Neumann states,

> some regularities which we observe in the organization of . . . [natural organisms] may be quite instructive in our thinking and planning of . . . [automata, or computers]; and conversely, a good deal of our experience and difficulties with our artificial automata can be to some extent projected on our interpretations of natural organisms.[13]

Von Neumann compares an individual neuron with a vacuum tube or transistor of a computer. A vacuum tube in a digital computer is a yes-or-no organ; similarly, individual neurons discharge on a yes-or-no basis. Computing machines are capable, he says, of logical calculations and of memory. Von Neumann also elaborates on the idea that it is theoretically possible to build an artificial automaton that can reproduce itself.[14]

Early mechanists historically have favored some sort of reflex arc theory for explaining behavior. A reflex arc is defined as a circuit that consists of a sense organ (such as an eye), a nerve leading from the sense organ to a central "switching area" (the spinal cord or brain), and a nerve leading outward from the switching area to a muscle or gland. When the sense organ is stimulated, a "message" tours the circuit and produces a response of muscle or gland.

The reflex arc concept in biology has a long history. Descartes came to conceive of all the lower animals as simple machines. He noted that muscular reactions seemed to follow predictably from stimulation of sense organs and reasoned that there were incoming and outgoing pathways that provided fixed channels for an animal's whole repertory of acts. (As we have seen, Descartes placed man in a different category—man had a soul, or mind.) Pierre Cabanis (1757–1808), a French philosopher and physician, argued that human beings exhibit a level of behavior as mechanical as that of the lower animals. He asserted that stimulus-response connections in man that do not reach the brain but are channeled through the spinal cord show the same reflex quality that Descartes thought he had observed in the behavior of lower animals.[15] The term *reflected movement* (or reflex) was coined in 1736. Boring attributes the first detailed treatment of the subject to the German physiologist Müller who published his work on the subject between 1833 and 1840.[16]

It remained for psychologists of the late nineteenth and early twentieth centuries to extend the reflex arc concept to include all, or virtually all, of human behavior. Reflexes were thought to be either inborn—a part of a person's original biological equipment—or learned. In the latter case, they involved the fixing or *stamping in* of some new connection between specific afferent (incoming) and efferent (outgoing) nerves. The afferent *messages*, it was thought, might be channeled either through the spinal cord only, or through both cord and brain. Stimulation of the receptor (sense organ) was held to cause an automatic, predictable, and almost instantaneous response in the effector (reacting muscle or gland). Reflex arcs presumably are illustrated by such phenomena as knee jerk, blinking (when an eye is threatened), and withdrawal from a painful object. We associate such a development in biological and in psychological thought in Russia with I. P. Pavlov (1849–1936), a biologist, and Vladimir Bekhterev (1857–1927), a neuropathologist, and in this country with Edward L. Thorndike (1874–1949) and John B. Watson (1878–1958).

The reflex arc concept, particularly in the simple form in which it was held early in the twentieth century, has now fallen into disrepute. However, since the intent of this section of the chapter is to present early positions on motivation and to keep pros and cons to a minimum, we shall not describe here specific criticisms that have been leveled against it.

Most modern mechanists take for granted the inadequacy of the original reflex arc theory and describe behavior in different, but still essentially mechanistic, terms. For example, D. O. Hebb has constructed a rather elaborate theory that takes into account the criticisms of the reflex arc concept. Hebb is a mechanist who believes that we must be able to account for higher thought processes (such as purposing, valuing, and reflecting) as a product of the electrochemical activity of the body.[17] G. L. Freeman, also a mechanist, likewise develops a highly sophisticated conception of the life process in which he meets many of the traditional objections to a biology based on mechanistic premises. However, in so doing, Freeman's mechanistic view borrows from the interactionist view in that he defines a life form as a *system* that operates purposively.[18]

How Can Mechanists Use the Term Mind?

So far we have said nothing about how mechanists define mind. If they are pure mechanists, that is, if they have eliminated every trace of dualism, obviously they must reject the notion that mind is a nonmaterial vital force. If they are true to their materialistic principles, they must deny that any kind of nonmaterial force exists; or if they concede its existence, they must at least hold that such a force is inconsequential.

In what way, then, can mechanists use the term mind? They can use it only if they regard mind as a function—as a manner of behaving and not as a thing in itself. To mechanists, mind is learning, that is, the building and storing of neurological relationships. Most mechanists, however, avoid any use of the term *mind*, since from their point of view the term connotes a nonmaterial spiritual force. To them, an electronic computer is analogous to a mammalian brain; and a computer, even though it can solve many problems if the data are fed in correctly, cannot be said to have a mind.

Chapter 3 provides a rather detailed treatment of motivation as seen by mechanists. Our point here is that to a mechanist, mind can be nothing more than a physical function—a pattern of behavior resulting from the environmental forces acting upon a living organism. Adherents of the next position we describe also regard mind as a function. However, they define the nature and role of a functional mind—a psychological concept—in a fundamentally different manner.

WHAT IS AN INTERACTIVE VIEW OF MOTIVATION?

In this chapter, we treat three broad concepts of motivation in terms of their background. Since one's theory of motivation is an outgrowth of one's theory of human nature, to achieve a full understanding of motivational theory, we must link it to its corresponding theory of humanity. We have done this for theories of inner motivation and for theories of outer motivation—for motivation that arises within ourselves and motivation that is produced wholly by pushes and pulls exerted by our environment. We now turn to the theory of humanity that calls for an interactive concept of motivation. Motivation produced by an interaction of self and perceived environment links with the psychological position that we have called cognitive-field and its corresponding philosophical counterpart, positive relativism.

What Are Some Key Points
in the Background of the Interactive View?

Cognitive-field psychology is a relativistic psychology in contrast to the absolutistic *faculty* psychology attached to philosophical idealism and the absolutistic *stimulus-response* psychology attached to philosophical realism. The two latter are regarded as absolutistic because they are based on *fixed* premises about human nature. Human nature is portrayed by these two psychologies as essentially the same universally and eternally (if their adherents are consistent), even though they are completely separate positions and in relation to one another are mutually exclusive.

A central idea of relativism is that any object derives its qualities not merely from something inside itself but from the total situation—its surroundings as well as itself. Another way of putting it is that no object has meaning apart from its context. Applying this idea to humans, we can understand what people are like only by studying them as they operate in relation to their environments. Our object of study must be a *unit* that can be called "a discerning person interacting with his or her psychological-environment."

Since person-environment situations seem capable of endless variation, then human nature, too, is capable of endless variation. A San Franciscan is likely to have a different nature from a Bostonian. Both San Franciscan and Bostonian are likely to have different natures ten years from now than they have now. Human nature is not static.

At this point readers may feel inclined to ask how a relativistic definition of human nature differs from that of mechanists like Edward Thorndike, John Watson, Clark Hull, Kenneth Spence, and B. F. Skinner (see Chapter 3). The most significant difference lies in the relativistic conception of human beings as purposive, exploring persons. To environmental determinists (that is, mechanists) the habitual pose of humans is passivity or reactivity; people wait to act until they are stimulated either by internal stimuli (such as hunger) or external stimuli coming from the outer environment. On the other hand, cognitive-field theorists hold that persons are fundamentally purposive; they continuously generate wants and set out to satisfy them.

Despite their drastic differences, there are a few ideas that mechanists and cognitive-field theorists hold in common. One is that humans are born morally neutral. Unlike those instinct theorists who hold people to be born innately bad and those instinct theorists who hold people to be born innately good, relativists hold that people are born morally neutral. Mechanists think that people become bad or good or a combination of the two as a result of environmental forces alone, whereas cognitive-field psychologists think that people become bad, good, or some mixture of the two, through continuous interaction with their environments as they perceive them.

When human beings are considered neutral-interactive (the cognitive-field position), neutrality extends only to goodness-badness, not to activity-passivity. Cognitive-field psychologists assert that people are always dynamic in some way; they keep generating new wants or goals as fast as they satisfy the previous ones. Thus, their habitual relationship to their environments is purposive and exploratory. Their wants may or may not be related to fundamental biological drives, such as hunger or thirst, but they are not instinctual—inherited fixed patterns of behavior common to a species. Human wants are specific so far as individuals are concerned, but they vary greatly from one individual to another.

What Do Interactionists Mean by "Self"?

If we grant that human purpose is highly individualized, are there no common purposes, no common motivations apart from those directly related to fundamental biological drives? Are there no general principles governing human behavior? A human being has two kinds of "organization," physical and psychological. We do not mean to imply that they are unrelated, or, in fact, that they are anything other than different sides of a coin. But from the standpoint of an individual, it is possible to talk of one's physiology and one's purposive behavior in different terms. Therefore, it is fair to say that we have a physiological or bodily organization and a psychological organization. A prime goal in life is to maintain biological organization. Many persons, however, do not seek strongly to maintain their bodily organization; otherwise we would have no people eating or drinking themselves to death, or in other ways unnecessarily damaging their bodies. Some persons deliberately try to destroy their biological organization by committing suicide.

On the other hand, it is now fairly well established that people have certain relatively universal motivations toward maintenance and enhancement of their perceived selves. One's psychological organization is one's self or, as Combs and Snygg call it, one's *perceived self*[19] in relation with one's psychological environment. But how do people go about preserving their psychological or perceived selves? Various psychologists have postulated that human beings have an innate urge to feel competent and self-determining in relation to their environment.[20] Being competent means being capable of solving or partially solving the problems that grow out of the interaction of self and perceived environment. Being self-determining means that people try to exercise genuine choice in their decision making.

Once people have achieved reasonably adequate perceived selves, they may resist any change in thought pattern that would jeopardize their present organization. However, when they perceive their mental structures as inadequate, they may actively seek new ideas, and are therefore capable of change. They may even become revolutionaries. A relativistic psychologist's position is that human nature changes all the time and that the range of human capacities is doubtless tremendously wider than has been indicated in anything yet achieved or even envisioned.

What Is the Interactionist's Theory of Mind?

Interactionists view mind as a *function* of a living purposive person, and not a thing or substance. The difference between mechanist and interactionist theories of mind is major. To the mechanist, mind involves linking incoming nervous signals with outgoing signals and does not include purposiveness, ability to reflect, to be creative, and to be choice-making.

Interactionists go about defining mind as "cognitive events" that involve the entire person and his or her psychological field at once. The mind function probably does involve activity in the central nervous system, but it may also involve glands, hormones, and indeed any part of a living creature—the sensory organs being perhaps as important as the central nervous system. However, to interactionists, the physiological events accompanying thinking are secondary to the understanding of mind itself.

Mind is the capacity of a human being in an interactive situation to see and be guided by meanings. Meaning is the "sign quality" or "pointing quality" that objects come to have as a result of a person's experience with them. For example, the "sign quality" of a hot stove soon becomes apparent to a small child; a stove means "Touch me and you will get burned." To extend the illustration, growling dogs mean bite, thunderheads mean rain, paddles mean spank, the smell of cooking food means a meal. Human beings probably begin acquiring their first meanings in early infancy long before their thoughts can be verbalized.

Mind arises when the ongoing activity of an individual is, to some degree, blocked. In such situations, a person feels a state of perplexity—which translates into *tension*. It is in such doubtful or tensional situations that mind makes its appearance, serving the purpose of ministering to the demands or specific wants or goals of the person. Mind serves the purpose of resolving the ambiguity of such situations and enabling the person either to overcome the perceived barrier or decide that it cannot do so. This view, it should be noted, does not make thought instrumental to sheer activity but rather to satisfaction of specific wants or interests. Mind is a goal-oriented function in the sense that it is related to purposive behavior and is forever engaged in problem solving of a kind to help in the achievement of purposes.[21]

What View of Motivation Is Held by Interactionists?

Interactionists (cognitive-field psychologists) see motivation as a function arising from a situation that is unclear, puzzling, problematic, or frustrating. It is the desire to go ahead in the face of either barriers or conflicting goals of some sort, large or small. Thus, to an interactionist, motivation is an integral aspect of mind itself. Chapters 4 and 5 treat at length the motivational theory implied in the above concept of human nature.

NOTES

[1] Duane Schultz, *A History of Modern Psychology*, 2d ed., New York: Academic Press, 1975, p. 362.

[2] Although old, one of the best books on this subject remains Charles W. Morris, *Six Theories of Mind*, University of Chicago Press, 1932. Also highly pertinent in this connection is Boyd H. Bode, *How We Learn*, Boston: Heath, 1940.

[3] E. D. Adrian, *The Physical Background of Perception*, New York: Oxford University Press, 1947, p. 4 (our italics).

[4] John C. Eccles, *The Neurophysiological Basis of Mind*, New York: Oxford University Press (Clarendon Press), 1953, especially chapter 6.

[5] John B. Noss, *Man's Religions*, New York: Macmillan, 1949, p. 384.

[6] Homer W. Smith, *Man and His Gods*, Boston: Little, Brown, 1953, p. 379.

[7] Clarence H. Faust and Thomas H. Johnson, *Jonathan Edwards: Representative Selections with Introduction, Bibliography, and Notes*, New York: American Book Co., 1935, pp. 162–164, 321.

[8] Edwin A. Burtt, *Types of Religious Philosophy*, New York: Harper & Row, 1951, p. 439.

[9] Quoted in Robert Ulich, *Three Thousand Years of Educational Wisdom*, Cambridge: Harvard University Press, 1954, p. 383.

[10] H. G. Wells, Julian S. Huxley, and G. P. Wells, *The Science of Life*, Garden City New York: Literary Guild, 1934, pp. 29–30.

[11] Ibid., p. 30.

[12] Ibid., pp. 1270–1277.

[13] John von Neumann, "The General and Logical Theory of Automats," in Lloyd A. Jeffress (ed.), *Cerebral Mechanisms in Behavoir*, New York: Wiley, 1951, p. 2.

[14] Advanced students who wish to study further modern attempts to explain life in physicalist terms may find of interest Norbest Wiener's *Cybernetics*, New York: Wiley, 1948; or W. Ross Ashy's *An Introduction to Cybernetics*,

London: Chapman & Hall, 1956; also by the same author, *Design for a Brain*, New York: Wiley, 1952. John von Neumann's posthumously published *Computer and the Brain*, New Haven: Yale University Press, 1958, is also pertinent.

[15] Gardner Murphy, *Historical Introduction to Modern Psychology*, New York: Harcourt Brace Jovanovich, 1949, pp. 18, 38.

[16] Edwin G. Boring, *A History of Experimental Psychology*, New York: Appleton-Century-Crofts, 1929, p. 39.

[17] Donald O. Hebb, *A Textbook of Psychology*, Philadelphia: Saunders, 1958, chapters 2–5.

[18] G. L. Freeman, *The Energies of Human Behavior*, Ithaca, N.Y.: Cornell University Press, 1948.

[19] Arthur W. Combs and Donald Snygg, *Individual Behavior*, rev. ed., New York: Harper & Row, 1959, pp. 129–130.

[20] For one recent statement on this subject, see Edward L. Deci, *Intrinsic Motivation*, New York: Plenum Press, 1975, pp. 54–61.

[21] Charles W. Morris, *Six Theories of Mind*, University of Chicago Press, 1932, pp. 294–295.

BIBLIOGRAPHY

Because Chapters 2–5 should be studied as a unit, references for these chapters are found at the end of Chapter 5.

Chapter 3
WHAT ARE SOME MECHANISTIC THEORIES OF MOTIVATION?

In this chapter we treat three categories of mechanistic theories of motivation, namely, scientific instinct theories, drive theories, and reinforcement theories. This is roughly the order in which the categories appeared, although overlapping and backtracking make a neat historical chronology impossible.

Human instincts are inherent tendencies toward certain patterns of behavior. Scientific instinct theories are supported by some degree of empirical evidence. A *drive* is a strong, persistent internal stimulus that requires an adjustive response. *Reinforcement* is the process within which the reduction of an organic need or the satisfaction of a drive stimulus increases the probability of an organism's displaying a certain behavior in the future.

WHAT ARE SOME SCIENTIFIC INSTINCT THEORIES OF MOTIVATION?

Instinct theories present a special problem in the sense that the word has been defined very differently at different times by different psychologists. Instinct theory nearly became extinct after behaviorism's rise to dominance; but some conception of instincts is implicit in other schools of thought discussed in this chapter and under "needs" in Chapter 4. There seems to be some resurgency of the concept of instinct in one form or another in the 1970s.

Until the eighteenth century, people who talked about instincts had tended to assume that instinctive actions all had a purpose—either to fulfill God's plan or to satisfy a law of nature (see Chapter 2, pp. 38–43). Francis Hutcheson (1694–1746), a Scottish philosopher, was apparently the first to deny that instincts had to have a purpose. He defined instinct as a "propensity to act" and argued that such propensities were dependent neither on God's will nor on the seeking of pleasure and avoidance of pain. "Thus, in Hutcheson we find the first really modern view of instinct as a force that impels to action without the idea of the object of the action."[1]

What Was the Darwinian Concept of Instinct?

Instinct theory, by whatever name, had little profound impact until Charles Darwin (1809–1882) published his views on the origin and nature of the human species in his famous books, *On the Origin of Species* (1859) and *The Descent of Man* (1871). Darwin's views on instinct were the result of a long history of thinking on the subject. There is great similarity between Darwin's concept of instinct and that of Hutcheson, but Darwin expanded the concept giving it so special a force that instinct theory's great popularity would continue from late in the nineteenth century until about 1920.

One point Darwin established to his own satisfaction and that of his increasingly wide following was the biological continuity of humans and all other animal species. That is, all animal species differed in degree, not in kind. Humans happened, as a result of the process of natural selection, to be distinctive in many respects from the rest of the animal kingdom but also were an integral part of it. Darwin's view of instincts thus applied equally to humans and all other living creatures.

Darwin maintained that certain innate tendencies to act were biologically "built into" all living organisms. These innate tendencies to act were instincts. These behavioral tendencies responded automatically to certain inner and outer stimuli, such as hunger, thirst, and pain. The animal would then attempt to act in such a way as to reduce, if possible, these stimulated demands. In short, stimuli cause behaviors designed to eliminate the stimuli. Animals not programmed for such stimulus-reduction activity died out in the course of evolution while those that were suitably programmed lived to reproduce their own kind. Since stimulations might change—with changes in climate, for example—animals that were suitably programmed for survival during one historical epoch might cease to survive during another.[2]

After Darwin, the development of instinct theory took two directions. One group of theorists constructed lists of instincts that were considered responsible for a great variety of behavior, both simple and complex. These theorists included William James and William McDougall, of whom we will say more later. The second group attempted to use the concept of instincts to explain human motivation of a complicated, non-biological nature. Associated with this second direction of theorizing are both Sigmund Freud (1856–1939) and the American psychologist Clark Hull (1884–1952).

What Was the "Instinct-Naming" Approach?

William James (1842–1910) was the most noted American psychologist of the nineteenth century. In his most influential writing (1890), he denied the popular view that because humans have a monopoly on intelligence, they needed only a few instincts. James argued instead that humans have both more, and more complex, instincts than do lower animals. He claimed that the greater facility of humans for learning tended to obscure or modify their natural instinctive endowment. Contrary to Darwin, James also contended that instincts were not a blind force but were usually integrally linked to intelligence. That is, there were many complex relationships between instinct and learning. James defined an instinct as *"the faculty of acting in such a way as to produce certain ends, without foresight of the ends, and without previous education in the performance."*[3] An instinct would be blind only on its first expression; after that, it would be linked by foresight to its possible ends. If James had stuck with this definition his position would have been more defensible than it turned out to be. As it was, he went on an "instinct-naming" spree that included simple reflexes, such as sneezing, and very complex patterns of behavior, such as hunting. Altogether, James listed 32 human instincts.

Probably even more important than James as an instinct-naming theorist was William McDougall (1871–1938) who outlined his instinct theory most systematically in *An Introduction to Social Psychology* (1908). This volume passed through approximately 25 editions and impressions and was highly influential for many years. McDougall called his system "Hormic psychology." Hormic means striving, purposive, or nonmechanical; it derives from the Greek *horme*, an approximate synonym for which is "impulse," but which in McDougall's terminology could also mean instinct.

According to McDougall, instincts are much less specific in a child than in an adult. Since instincts are to some degree activated by learning, adults exhibit more of them than do children. In his 1908 volume, McDougall listed twelve instincts, seven considered primary (of greatest importance) and five secondary. Later he extended his list to 13, namely, flight, repulsion, curiosity, pugnacity, self-abasement, self-assertion, parental instinct, instinct of reproduction, sexual jealousy, female coyness, gregariousness, instinct for acquisition, and instinct for construction.[4]

Within McDougall's hormic psychology, each instinct expresses itself in three ways which have been called the perceptual, the emotional, and the conative. The perceptual aspect insures that its owner will see certain features of his environment in a certain way, for example, as menacing. The emotional aspect refers to the feeling deriving from perception, for example, fear. The conative aspect consists of appropriate action, for example, trying to run away, and might also be referred to as the *striving* aspect.

Whereas James had attributed motivation to more forces than pure instinct, McDougall contended that all behavior has an instinctive origin. McDougall asserted that without these inner prods to behave, humans would simply lie inert and presumably perish. To McDougall, instinctive behavior was both adaptable to changing situations and identified with goals rather than means. Means to a goal may be learned, but our goals (wants, desires, wishes) spring only from instincts. McDougall reminded us that human life can be characterized by its purposiveness and emotional characteristics.

What Was "The Great Instinct Controversy"?

Within 20 years after its publication, James's 1890 volume had been widely read. McDougall's first edition (1908) was also quickly popular. As dozens of psychologists, sociologists, and biologists jumped on the instinct bandwagon between about 1910 and 1920, "instinct naming" was much in vogue. A tendency developed to attribute almost every human or animal action to one or more instincts. By about 1920, however, the whole concept of human instincts was under attack. In part the attack was instigated by the newly developing group of behavioral mechanists, at this time led by John B. Watson. Watson insisted that virtually all human behavior is learned through a process of conditioning; this made the concept of instincts irrelevant.[5]

Even more potent, perhaps, than Watson's as yet unproved assertion was the rather obvious circularity of the argument for instincts. The then current argument for instincts was circular in the sense that a behavior was defined as a product of instinct. At the same time, when instinct theorists were asked to define an instinct, they cited the very behavior used to define instinct. Korman states this rather amusingly.

> Obviously one could not explain aggressive behavior by appealing to a basic instinct of aggressiveness and then cite as an example of this instinct the fact that the organism engaged in aggressive behavior. This is a circular definition, trivial in nature, and to quote an old saw, "you can't hardly lose that way."[6]

There are some obvious requirements if behavior is going to be attributed to instincts in a respectably scientific way. The instincts must be susceptible not only to definition but also either to experimental manipulation and/or empirical measurement independent of the behavior that they are used to predict. Preferably, such measurement should occur before the behavior being studied. Neither McDougall nor the numerous other instinct theorists of this period ever did develop such independent conceptualizations. Rather they kept expanding their lists of "basic instincts." By the middle teens, it was noted that almost 3000 instincts had been named as explanations of the causes of behavior.

By the 1920s few psychologists would use the word instinct because it had become so disreputable. It virtually disappeared from the vocabulary of psychology until the late 1930s when it reappeared as a purely descriptive term meaning *unlearned behavior*. By 1932 even McDougall quit using instinct and began using instead the terms propensity (meaning a disposition) and tendency (meaning the corresponding tendency to act).

How Has Ethology Reinstated a Theory of Instincts?

When we discuss *ethology* we are referring to a position in biology with important ramifications for psychology that attracted considerable attention between the 1930s and about 1970. Ethology systematically studies the formation of the character or nature of a species of animals and in so doing tries to make some sense of the largely discredited "nature-nurture" controversy. Ethology, in its modern sense, began with the German zoologist Konrad Lorenz's 1935 paper entitled "Companions in the Life of Birds." (Most of Lorenz's experimental work was done with geese.) Another prominent earlier book was that by Nikolaas Tinbergen (*The Study of Instincts*, 1951). Also contributing to ethology have been books by Robert Ardrey, Desmond Morris, Lionel Tiger, and Robin Fox.

Ethologists have tended to think of instincts as *releasing mechanisms* that perform the roles only of steering or guiding behavior according to an "imprinting" that occurs during an early formative period in the life of an animal. For example, Lorenz maintained that his geese had a "following instinct" and that as a newly hatched gosling a goose would follow whatever was most conspicuous and convenient for it to follow, including humans. Geese that had been imprinted with the urge to follow humans would follow only humans the rest of their lives. (Or dogs, chickens, cows—you name it.) Ethologists have tended to attribute the energizing of behavior to hormones or other internal stimuli, but such energizing performs no guiding role and is thus confined to the first phase of instinctive behavior.

Unlike experimental psychologists who have preferred studying animals in a laboratory situation, ethologists like to leave animals in their natural environment and do field studies there. Ethologists tend to think that any artificial situation, like a cage, causes animals to behave in unnatural ways, thus making it difficult for us to really find out much about their authentic natures. Some ethological study has had a great deal of intrinsic interest to humans, and several popular, but not so scholarly, books on ethology have had a large sale.[7]

One of the most pointed criticisms of ethology has been that most ethologists were not only "fixed on instinct theory" but they also insisted that, if instincts can be demonstrated in lower animals, they must likewise govern human behavior. There were other oversimplifications that space does not permit our treating here. Bolles asserts that in the 1970s ethologists have become more analytical and more inclined toward controlled experimentation. Further, D. S. Lehrmen emphasizes that

> We have come to realize that *no real distinction can be made between innate and learned behavior.* Even the most innate of behaviors is likely to be expressed only if certain developmental and other experiential conditions are met. And even the most learned of behaviors requires for its expression that there be an appropriate genetic background.[8]

Ethologists have become increasingly involved in the search for environmental controlling factors and less interested in trying to explain behavior by instinct.

How Has Sociobiology Treated Instincts?

Beginning in the 1960s, and attracting considerably more attention by the mid-1970s, a new field of inquiry is developing—*sociobiology.* Originally it was an attempt to synthesize several previously separate areas of study—such as ethology, neurophysiology, physiopsychology, and behavioral ecology.[9]

Most important for us here is the fact that sociobiology has a place for instinct theory defined in a new way. Wilson points out that the concept of instinct—which he says has never had more than an intuitive definition—has been broadly defined in two different ways. The least flexible definition Wilson states as follows:

> An instinct, or innate behavior pattern, is a behavior pattern that either is subject to relatively little modification in the lifetime of the organism or varies very little throughout the population, or (preferably) both.

The flexible definition, Wilson states as:

> An innate behavioral difference between two individuals or two species is one that is based at least in part on a genetic difference. We then speak of differences in the hereditary component of the behavior pattern, or of innate differences in behavior, or, most loosely, of differences in instinct.[10]

In accordance with the second, more flexible definition, it becomes meaningless to ask whether a trait is a product of instinct or environment because both are operating interactively to produce the final product. Wilson feels that this definition can be used appropriately with human beings and primates generally, but that it is not yet of great use because of the all-but-impossible (at least so far) task of distinguishing that which is instinctive from that which is learned. The more rigid of the two definitions, Wilson is convinced, is useful in studying the behavior of some species of animals, and he tries to demonstrate this with insects, a phylum on which he is one of the world's leading authorities.

Wilson described human instinctive behavior at three levels of probability: (1) highly probable if the behavior is shared by all social species of animals; (2) probable if it is shared with all or almost all other primates; and (3) possible and somewhat probable if it is shared with most or all other humans (but not necessarily other species).

In the first category (behavior shared among social animals), Wilson names two forms of behavior for which he feels instinctive direction is mandatory—otherwise, social species could never have developed in the first place, and, if developed, they could not have maintained themselves. These are

(1) a strong enough instinct toward altruistic behavior to overbalance intraspecies aggression that might decimate the species and (2) some instinctive social arrangement making possible the exchange of genes among different populations within the species.

In the second category (behaviors widely shared among primates) we find the following: (1) aggressive dominance systems, which produce social stratification; (2) male dominance over females; (3) a wide range of response capabilities, especially in aggressive interactions; (4) prolonged maternal care; (5) pronounced socialization of the young; and (6) matrilineal organization (that is, the social organization of the species is transmitted primarily by females).

Wilson's third category of possible instinctive behaviors (those shown by humans only) includes at least 15 items, the precise number hinging on whether one treats certain complex patterns of behavior as influenced by only one, or more than one, genetic trait. A brief sampling of these includes (1) reciprocal altruism through barter, (2) family ties extended across generations and over long distances, (3) relatively continuous sexual behavior with extended foreplay (sex not instinctively related to procreation), (4) extreme capacity for role playing, (5) ability to use highly complex language and other symbolic communication, (6) a persistent and universal tendency toward culture building, and (7) pluralism of moral values and tendency toward moral conflict.

Wilson thinks that there is neither a significant relationship between genetic inheritance and intelligence nor a genetic basis for religion as usually defined. He does, however, postulate that humans may need to see themselves in a broader setting than merely the social group (which leads people variously toward religion, philosophy, or cosmology).[11]

Reaction to Wilson's attempted synthesis has been varied. *Sociobiology* was widely reviewed, with most reviewers praising Wilson's efforts, but with reservations. His final chapter (27) on "Man: From Sociobiology to Sociology" has met with more criticism than the rest of his system. In what seems to be one of the more careful critiques of Wilson's attempted synthesis, C. H. Waddington argues that although much that Wilson says about animals, including humans, implies the existence of mentality and purposiveness, Wilson refuses to come openly to grips with the issue of whether mind exists and if so how it is to be defined.[12]

WHAT ARE SOME DRIVE THEORIES OF MOTIVATION?

When the early concept of instinct came under attack about 1920, an alternative theory was needed to explain what energizes, directs, and sustains a behavior. Thus, Weiner suggests, "as is so often true in science, a theory does not die—it is replaced. The instinct doctrine . . . was replaced with the concept of *drive*."[13]

The first person to use the word drive as a label for "what makes the organism go" was Robert S. Woodworth.[14] Woodworth was a transitional figure in the sense that although his innovative thinking helped lead the way to a purely mechanistic description of drives, Woodworth himself did not conceive of drives as mechanistic processes. He made a clear distinction between drives as *energizers* only—followed by mechanisms that gave behavior its specific directions—and other characteristics.

Woodworth asserted that as organisms develop physiological needs (now more often being called *tissue deficits*), these needs or tissue deficits produce motivation for fulfillment. Drives result from physiological imbalance (disequilibrium) or too much of one thing and too little of another. Disequilibrium produces uncomfortable and often dangerous physiological conditions. Therefore, when out of balance the organism tends to return to its previous state of balance or passivity. This tendency of disturbed organisms is known as the principle of *homeostasis*. *The function of a drive is to produce its own elimination so the organism can return to a passive or inert state.*

As a compromise term, drive—prior to its more precise and mechanistic definition by Clark Hull (see p. 60)—worked out very well. It gave almost everyone something. "Drives were manifest in behavior, had physiological correlates, and gave rise to man's desires. Thus they bridged all of the interdisciplinary gaps that instincts were supposed to bridge."[15]

For about 20 years after Woodworth's introduction of drives, numerous attempts were made to identify specific drives. Such obvious organic survival needs as oxygen, food, water, sexual reproduction, and freedom from pain were quickly identified as drives. But investigators were not willing to stop here. Through drive theory they sought to explain numerous other behaviors commonly observed in animals. Between about 1925 and the 1950s a drive to explore novel situations was generally accepted. Furthermore, it was asserted that in the absence of unchanging stimuli animals develop a boredom drive that incites them to explore. Between the 1940s and 1950s, drives for manipulation, mastery, visual exploration, use of sensory organs, and numerous other functions were proclaimed. This period has been called the "drive-naming era" and more than 2500 drives were proposed. Various psychologists pointed out that there was now very little difference between the concept *drive* and the earlier concept *instinct* that had become so thoroughly rejected by psychologists.

WHAT WAS HULL'S DRIVE THEORY OF MOTIVATION?

Psychologist Clark Hull (1884–1952) has frequently been proclaimed the world's greatest behaviorist psychologist. Because of the differences between his theorizing and that of other mechanists, Hull has often been called a *neobehaviorist.* However, his thinking was consistently mechanistic. He is remembered by many psychologists as the innovator of a highly experimental, rigorous, and mathematically oriented theory of motivation.

He rejected all mentalistic or subjective notions like purposiveness and will, and tried to develop an exclusively physicalistic psychology for which the basic premises of classical mechanics as introduced into biology by Darwin were the cornerstones (see Chapter 1, p. 16). Hull went through various stages, making rather drastic changes in his position.[16]

For Hull, the reason organisms behaved at all was the need to survive. When an organism was in a threatened situation, behavior was aroused that would have survival value. Though some behavior was innate (drive, or D) and some was learned (habit, or H), it was always the urge for survival that energized behavior. Hull recognized that many kinds of behavior seem unrelated to survival needs, but he felt that once psychologists knew enough they would be able to explain all behavior as originally stemming from demands for survival. Survival was threatened by unmet biological needs such as hunger, thirst, release from injury and pain, and absence of sex. The aroused behavior was of a sort to reduce or eliminate the threat, and would continue until the biological deficiency was abated. "Another way of saying this is that man (or better organisms in general) is motivated to achieve an inert condition, that is, a condition without stimulation."[17]

What Are Intervening Variables (O)?

Previously, behaviorists had tried to work primarily with only two variables, stimulus (S) and response (R). One of their primary assumptions was that incoming Ss connected with and originated outgoing Rs.

The central nervous system was seen as analogous to the switching center of a telephone system, where incoming messages are transferred mechanically into outgoing messages. Hull was largely instrumental in promoting the notion that something more happened between Ss and Rs than a simple switching operation. He pushed the idea that between Ss and Rs there were *intervening variables*. For this reason, he was known as an S–O–R theorist. The O denoted what happened within the organism after an S was received and before an R was emitted. The key concept that was associated with the intervening variables (O) was *effective reaction potential* (E). E is the potential that an organism has at any given time for making a particular response when the organism is confronted by an S (stimulus situation). The probability of an R occurring is directly related to the strength of E: when E is low there may be no response; when E is high, a response is virtually certain.

What Was Hull's Early Concept of Drive (D)?

Hull's concept of drive (D) was central to his whole position. An organism acts to reduce or eliminate the drive-state, whether primary or learned. The drive-state exists only when some need or combination of needs exist. Unsatisfied needs, whether biological or learned, produce discomfort. For these reasons, Hull's theoretical model is often called *drive-reduction theory.*

Hull envisioned D as coming from two fundamental kinds of stimuli, *internal* and *external*. He maintained that one category of drive-state emanated from internal stimuli that were not learned. These stimuli were simply there because of their function in preserving the biological needs of an animal. He referred to the drive-state that grew purely out of biological demands as *unlearned drive*. But through a process of *association*—being contiguous in time—drive stimuli bearing no evident relation to biological need could be learned. Hull referred to the general excitation caused by these learned drive stimuli as *secondary* or *acquired* drive. Thus he found a way in his master theory to explain why people may want to play cards, go for a car ride, watch television, or participate in any other activity not needed for biological survival.

In his later works, Hull redefined drive (D) and added the concept *incentive* (K).

How Did Hull Redefine Drive?

Hull had said that D was aroused by certain kinds of stimuli (stomach contractions, dry mouth, pain, and so forth). But increasingly it appeared that these stimuli were much more complex than Hull had first believed and could not be used in any clear-cut fashion in connection with D. Also damaging to the concept of D was the finding that in many situations D does not lead to behavior that reduces motivation; in the case of food and drink, drive plays a reasonably clear-cut role; but in other behaviors, D appears to have little or no capacity for reducing the stimuli related to it. One of many possible examples is that of rats in a copulation-without-ejaculation situation reinforcing their sex drive instead of reducing it. Behavior such as this violates Hull's basic contention that D leads to its own extinction rather than further stimulation. This finding raised questions about what Hull really meant by D.

Even more damaging to the drive concept was the finding that most drivelike behaviors have no basis in biological need. Dollard and Miller's experimentation showed that drive properties are found in any strong stimulus, including an infinite number of behaviors that have no bearing on the reduction of tissue needs. This influenced Hull to redefine drive as any strong stimulus. Prior to this shift in definition, Hull had been unable to account for attempts of an animal either to escape from or try to reduce obnoxious but biologically harmless stimuli such as strong lights, noises, numerous chemicals, or water only slightly warmer or cooler than body temperature. Furthermore, there was a rapidly growing tendency among psychologists to view incentive, rather than drive, as the main determinant of behavior.

Why Did Hull Add Incentive (K) to His Variables?

According to Hull's first concept of K, it refers to the amount of reward (usually food) that is given. In Hull's scheme of things, deprivation of a hungry animal increases incentive (K) and, since Hull defined incentive as a pull that varied positively or negatively in strength as it was increased or reduced, the concept could be quantified. D also increases with deprivation, so presumably a rat deprived of food for only three days will not hunt it as fast as a rat deprived for six days. This definition of K makes for easy quantification and supports Hull's physicalistic approach.

Why did Hull find it necessary to add K to his equation? Research demonstrating the existence of *latent learning* forced him to change his thinking. Satiated rats were found to explore and learn an unfamiliar maze in the absence of a reward, apparently for no reason at all (the Hullian hypothesis had held that satiated rats become passive until their biological urges goad them into trying to fulfill some need). But the rats that were apparently wandering, for reasons not understood, would, after becoming hungry again, proceed very quickly to the goal box—approximately as quickly as rats that had been trained and rewarded each time in this particular maze. The previously satiated, untrained rats when deprived of food required only one or two trails to learn the most efficient way to reach the goal box containing the food. It was evident that both groups of rats—the highly trained and consistently rewarded group and the untrained, unrewarded group—were both learning all along, but the unrewarded rats simply had no reason to show it until food was put in the box. The rats in the untrained, unrewarded group acted as if they had developed an expectancy of reward as well as the knowledge of how to get it.

What Was the Significance of Latent Learning?

The concepts of expectancy and knowledge are mentalistic concepts. They suggest a purposive mode of behavior, or foresight, as well as cognition—which does not harmonize with a mechanistic psychology. Findings about latent learning were difficult to reconcile with the "machine model" of animals that mechanists had always assumed. Do machines ever expect something? Does an automobile wait in a garage because it knows it is cold outside?

In addition to what appeared to be expectancy, it was found that rats that have been reinforced (rewarded) on all successful trials and had learned the maze well would quit seeking the goal box containing food within one or two trials after the food was removed. This suggested that as soon as expectancy changed, behavior of the animals changed. Who has ever heard of an automobile refusing to start because it expected to run out of gasoline even when there was still gasoline in the tank? Hull and Spence both attempted explanations of expectancy that would keep it within a mechanical, physicalistic framework, but did not succeed well enough to impress a large number of psychologists. Hull by now had little choice but to symbolize expectancy (incentive) with a K and include it with the other intervening variables, drive and habit. Hence the addition of K in Hull's 1952 volume.[18]

WHAT ARE THE IMPLICATIONS
OF DRIVE THEORY FOR EDUCATION?

It appears that drive theory has had much less impact on education than has B. F. Skinner's reinforcement theory (described in the following section). However, there are some important implications for education in drive theory. Drive theory stresses inner or intrinsic motivation as much as outer or extrinsic motivation, even though Hull himself was leery of innate drives when defined in a way similar to instincts.

Theoretically, teachers could utilize primary drives (food, drink, pain, and sex) as goads to learning. In practice, this general principle is seldom followed. However, children and youth could be driven to speed up some learning tasks because they were hungry or thirsty or uncomfortable in their seats, just as Hull's rats ran toward the food box faster the more days they had been deprived of food.

Two followers of Hull—Dollard and Miller[19]—have tried to spell out more fully what drive theory implies for teaching. Drive theory expresses itself in what students want for themselves—fundamentally, freedom from hunger, thirst, pain, or restrictions on sexual needs. Although one might argue that all learning is motivated by the desire to satiate innate drives, this general idea achieves much more significance if the drives referred to are acquired (learned) rather than innate ones.

According to drive theory, students have an almost unlimited number of acquired drives, even though their relation to the primary drives noted above is seldom very clear. It should be fairly obvious that many students want high grades, friends, social recognition, and the like—even though these achievements have little or nothing to do with biological survival.

Schools may try to give students acquired drives or to strengthen many that they already have. Most students have learned to be anxious, fearful, angry—or conversely, kindly, truthful, honest, and so on. If students feel strongly about these and dozens of other matters, they can be said to be exhibiting learned drives or motives. Schools, in essence, are places where it is hoped students will develop learned drives of a kind to keep school administrators, teachers, and parents happy.

HOW DO REINFORCEMENT THEORISTS VIEW MOTIVATION?

Among mechanistic psychologists, what is called *reinforcement* theory is, at the time of this writing, probably the most widely held position. Its best known proponent is B. F. Skinner (see chapter 13 for a description of Skinner's learning theory). Other well-known proponents are W. K. Estes and R. J. Herrnstein.

What Is Reinforcement Theory?

Reinforcement in psychology is the strengthening of a behavior by giving the right kind of stimuli to the organism after the correct performances of that behavior. By strengthening behavior we mean making it more likely to occur in the future, or to speed up or give more force to a behavior that is already occurring. Reinforcement theory is a body of knowledge about what will reinforce a desired behavior and thus make it habitual; or, conversely, what will decrease a behavior because it has either a neutral or a negative effect.

There is some debate as to whether the word theory should be used in connection with the position held by psychologists who experiment with, and approve of, reinforced (rewarded) behavior. Skinner, for example, disclaims that he is a theorist. According to his own view, he is only a researcher who describes what happens. Describing does not necessarily lead to theorizing. However, most of those who see the body of assumptions underlying Skinner's work, most of which must be re-garded as hypotheses still unproven, see in Skinner's position what may legitimately be called a theory.

Skinner has stated in considerable detail the assumptions that he sees as supporting his particular brand of behaviorism. According to his critics, he often fails to distinguish between his empirical (factual) findings (that is, his psychology) and his assumptions that cannot be tested (that is, his metapsychology). Some of Skinner's assumptions are held as absolutes (that is, fixed) and others as probabilities, thus leading Deci to say, in his summarization of Skinner's total position, "In practice, then, Skinnerian principles are stated in terms of probabilities, but in metatheory, they are stated as absolutes."[20]

REINFORCEMENT THEORY AND THE QUESTION
OF INTERVENING VARIABLES

Behavioristic psychologists between the time of John Watson and Clark Hull had worked with only two major variables, stimuli (Ss) and re-sponses (Rs). Their model of a living organism was based on the as-sumption that Ss and Rs become connected in the nervous system through some kind of switching mechanism, but that the organism itself played little role in determining its own behavior. Hence, early behaviorists talked about S-R models in psychology. But Hull asserted that there were so-called *intervening variables;* that is, something in the organism was involved between the time when it received an incoming signal through afferent nerves and discharged an outgoing signal through efferent nerves. So, Hull's S–O–R model indicated something other than a pure switching operation occurring between S and R. As noted earlier, the basic inter-vening variable was D, or drive.

Skinner's position marked a shift back to the simpler S–R model. He virtually ignored any possible inner controls over behavior, calling them unnecessarily complicated or irrelevant. According to Skinner, behavior at any given time is determined by the genetic pattern, the reinforcement history of the organism, and the contingencies (classes of occurrences) in the contemporary environment. Thus, to understand and control be-havior, it should be necessary only to take into account the nature of the organism, its history of conditioning, and the occurrences in the present situation that could have a further conditioning effect on the organism. Thus, once their genetic inheritances are set at the time of conception, organisms are seen as under the full control of their history and present environmental forces. This leaves no room for either free will or choice making on the organism's part. We should note that according to Skinner, a "reward" is not really a reward. The organism is never trying to do anything. A reinforcer is, therefore, any kind of stimulus that works effectively in making a behavior more precise and likely.

REINFORCEMENT AND THE CONTROL OF SUBJECTS

Reinforcement theorists maintain that one objective of reinforcement is the control it gives over the subjects whose behavior is being reinforced (whether rats or humans). Skinner has demonstrated this very well with laboratory animals. Reinforcers can be used to pull an animal along in virtually any direction the experimenter wants the animal to take, provided the direction of movement is within the capability of the organism. Using reinforcers to guide subjects into new patterns of response is referred to as *behavior modification.*

According to one view, the main purpose of reinforcement in either a psychological laboratory or a school is that of *control.* This position has been greeted with enthusiasm by some psychologists and many school administrators and teachers. It has also been greeted with hostility, particularly by those with strong democratic inclinations.

Although Skinner's explanation of the psychological nature of reinforcement or "behavior modification" is seriously challenged by cognitive-field and other psychologists, there is little doubt that the process works in the sense that it can be used to change overt behavior. When used with children, it appears that it may be more successful among those who are retarded than among the gifted. Also, the changes induced by behavior modification have a more lasting effect if children remain within the situation where the modification first occurred.

How Do Reinforcement Theorists
View the Concept of Motivation?

Any models of motivation set forth under reinforcement theory are likely to play down the concept of motivation and play up the concept of learning. Most reinforcement theorists go so far as to discard the concept of motivation and replace it with the assertion that all behavior that seems motivated is in fact learned. Skinner is the leading figure in promoting this view. Quite unlike the earlier instinct theorists, or drive or drive-incentive theorists like Hull and Spence, he denies the needfulness of postulating any kind of "inner force" in human behavior. Everything that an animal does during its periods of arousal can be explained as the reactivation of previously learned habits because of cues or signals in the present situation that were previously present when the habits were themselves learned by being reinforced. Bolles tells us that "This kind of explanatory model suggests that the phenomena that have been called motivation can be translated—without loss—into the phenomena of reinforcement."[21]

If reinforcement theorists are going to use any kind of motivational concept at all, in the interest of consistency they have to restrain themselves to saying that all motives are learned—that there is no pattern in an animal's seemingly motivated behavior that is innate. There is empirical evidence for this: Animals often seem more aroused—more motivated—after a series of training trials than at the start of training. This is quite the opposite of Hull's notion that the more learning that occurs, the less motivated an animal will be because the function of training or learning is to reduce the one or more drives that motivate the behavior.

Learned motivation (often called *incentive motivation*) is all we need to have any concern for, assert Skinnerians. Nearly all learning is induced by only one kind of event—the rewarding (reinforcement) of desired behavior or the nonreinforcement of undesired behavior. An example of learned motivation is the tendency of both humans and most laboratory animals to prefer sweetened to unsweetened liquids. The sweetened liquids—usually plain water laced with saccharin—do not need to have a positive physiological effect. Animals can be taught to react either positively or negatively to virtually every environmental object through reinforcement. Within motivational theory, these learnings—because they often seem to be motivated—are referred to merely as *reinforcement effects.*

To a large degree, the semantics (word usage) of reinforcement theorists parallel those of drive theorists such as Hull. To convert Hullian language to the language of reinforcement, we need only make lists of reinforcers to substitute for lists of drives. Learned drives, particularly, correspond to reinforcers. The two lists—of drives and reinforcers—should correspond in a one-to-one fashion. If a person can be said to have a learned drive for cherry pie, then he or she can also be said to have had ingestion of cherry pie reinforced.

Reinforcement theorists argue that by omitting the concept of motives and focusing on reinforcement we have a way of describing animal and human behavior that comes out the same but is simpler. As either a theoretical or descriptive statement, it takes fewer words to describe reinforced behavior than it takes to describe drive-induced behavior. Parsimony of statement (that is, using fewer words) is generally considered a mark of a good scientific theory, provided that nothing essential is lost in the process. Thus, it is contended that reinforcement theory is easier to explain to novices than is drive theory. Skinnerians feel that Skinner wins over Hull because he can be understood better by readers, especially student readers.

What Are Recent Criticisms of Reinforcement Theory?

Reinforcement theory makes little or no attempt to explain various phenomena that most motivational theorists have considered highly relevant to an understanding of behavior. There is rather general agreement among nonreinforcement theorists that among animals and humans there is a state properly called the energization of any activity. What makes animals and people want to do anything in the first place? The newly born among most animals and among humans behave as if activity were their preordained state. These animals are born moving in relation to what appear to be goals (newborn animals are capable of and seem to want to suck and engage in various other behaviors). This tendency to do something for the first time—prior to any possibility of reinforcement—can only be explained by drive theory or one of the various theories of needs, whether they are physiological or psychological.

Reinforcement theory has been under attack particularly since about 1970. Since then three important developments have occurred relating to the issue of active motivation vs. passive reinforcement. (1) Reinforcement theory has come to play a much smaller part than previously in explaining human behavior, particularly learning. The consequences of a subject's responses remain important but not because they strengthen mechanical habits.[22] (2) Reinforcement theorists themselves are becoming increasingly cagy about attributing a direct response-strengthening function to reinforcement. About all that matters now among reinforcement theorists is how to control behavior—behavior modification—as was mentioned above. (3) It has been established empirically that a reinforcer that is effective under one set of conditions may not be under another set of near-identical conditions. This permits a strong argument to the effect that some other factor or factors are at work in motivation—intervening mediators in the S–O–R model or the S–C–R model to be described in Chapter 4.

Bolles refers to the existence of a crisis within reinforcement theory, developing as of the middle to late 1970s. He treated reinforcement theory with sympathy if not affection in his 1967 book. However, his 1975 volume reviews reinforcement theory in detail and then rejects it.

Bolles describes one experiment among others that he feels is pivotal. Because of its interest, we briefly restate it here. In the 1960s two psychologists devised what they called "the bright, noisy water experiment" in which the subjects were laboratory rats. Half of a group of rats was trained to drink bright, noisy water. This was ordinary tap water so arranged that the moment a rat's tongue touched it a light would flash against the water's surface and a distinctive clicking sound would be heard. After learning to accept water under these unusual conditions the rats were divided into two subgroups. One of these subgroups was given a severe electric shock immediately after drinking the water. The other subgroup was made ill immediately after drinking by the administration of X-rays or lithium chloride. The next day, the rats were again presented with bright, noisy water. Those who had been shocked drank significantly less than before; those that were made ill, drank their usual amount of water.

The other half of the original group of rats was trained to like saccharin-sweetened water, which they tended to drink more of than ordinary-tasting water. Because saccharin was used, the sweetened water was no more nutritious than ordinary water; hence, it did not satisfy some physiological need and become preferred for that reason. Immediately after drinking sweetened water, half of this group was given a strong electric shock and the other half made ill in the manner described above. The following day, the animals that had been ill showed an aversion to sweetened water whereas the animals that had been shocked drank the normal amount.

In sum, electric shock had produced an aversion to bright noisy water but had no effect on drinking saccharin-sweetened water; at the same time, illness produced an aversion to sweetened water but not to bright, noisy water. The investigators concluded that among rats in situations that are comparable, sometimes learning occurs and sometimes it does not. The relation between the taste of the food and a following illness is particularly strong in rats and produces rapid learning—learning to avoid a food with a certain taste. But why wouldn't electric shock have the same effect? Apparently, it did in one case and not the other, but why?

Among reinforcement theorists it had always been assumed that so long as a stimulus is a stimulus it will sooner or later produce changed behavior (that is, learning); it had also been assumed that upon repetition of a response, if the stimulus situation is the same the response will be the same. The experiment described above raises serious questions about both of these assumptions. Before drawing conclusions, student readers should read and think seriously about the whole Skinnerian position as it is described in Chapter 13. Reinforcement theory is the dominant psychological theory underlying education at the present time. Are teachers simply being misled, or is reinforcement theory actually a valid basis for the education of children and youth?

HOW DOES THE ACCOUNTABILITY MOVEMENT RELATE TO REINFORCEMENT THEORY?

Beginning around 1970, the United States has been swept by a movement to make teachers accountable for what students learn. Although this movement has been interpreted by its critics as primarily a ploy of businessmen's groups, taxpayers' associations, politicians, schoolboards, and district school administrators to make public education cheaper and to produce a docile, procapitalist, technically trained labor force, there are many dedicated educators who are convinced that the accountability movement can improve education from the view of classroom teachers and students.[23]

It is not our purpose here to analyze the accountability movement in terms of its economic and political implications; our interest rather is in a psychological analysis. First, we will explain briefly what the accountability movement is.

What Is the Nature of the Accountability Movement?

One of the chief purposes claimed for the accountability movement is to reorganize the public school curriculum so that its results can be measured in a rather precise way and the effectiveness of teachers judged by the amount of training exhibited by their students. Teachers who can demonstrate a high level of efficiency in output are rewarded in some way; teachers who cannot may fail to get tenure or salary increments. Teachers are therefore subjected to extrinsic motivators of a rather compelling sort.

To install a program of accountability in a school, it is necessary that precise and detailed objectives be stated for every course. The objectives must be stated in terms of some outcome that can be quantified. In practice, this leads to what are called behavioral objectives, that is, objectives stated as overt behaviors to be demonstrated by pupils. An overt behavior might be something spoken or written on paper; a mark made on a test paper; the bodily skill required for an athletic task; or the completion of a shop or home economics project. Any behavior that cannot be measured with precision is excluded from the goals of the program. Such "behaviors" as meditating, reflecting, imagining, and reasoning are clearly not suited to an accountability program because they may never produce a measurable overt behavior, or if they do, it may be long after the pupil has completed the school year during which the teacher was accountable for visible training.

Once behavioral objectives are formulated, teachers deploy a content selected to be directly pertinent to the behaviors as stated. Both objectives and content are often accumulated around three categories of objectives: cognitive (intellectual), affective (emotional), and psychomotor (bodily skills). To measure behavioral outcomes, teachers either develop their own short-answer tests or use standardized achievement tests. Testing is frequent because the behavioral objectives to be achieved by students are typically both small and narrow in scope and can supposedly be achieved in a week or two of concentrated drill.

Although the above description of the accountability movement is in accord with the way the movement is typically implemented at the elementary and high school level, some defenders of the movement argue that there is nothing about the movement that mandates the use of purely behavioral objectives; objectives can be stated as understandings so long as they can be measured. It is also argued by the proponents of accountability that teachers are not restricted to short-answer tests to measure achievement of behavioral objectives. Another point they make is that units of work do not necessarily have to be short and narrow in focus;

they can be extended as long as necessary to take care of complex or long-range objectives.

Training under an accountability program has either of two names— performance based education (PBE) or competency based education (CBE). Curriculum and instructional procedure may be identical under these two labels; or there may be a significant difference in application of the two concepts. Performance implies the exclusive use of objectives that can be stated strictly in terms of overt performance. Competency can be defined broadly enough to include objectives that refer to thought processes, such as understandings, provided they can be measured objectively.

What Are Some Mechanist Assumptions Underlying Accountability?

Although usually not stated by proponents of accountability, the psychological assumptions of this movement are those of mechanistic psychology, particularly of reinforcement. They reflect the premises of behavioral mechanism, as described in Chapter 1. The assumptions of most concern are well stated by Martin et al., whose statements we will paraphrase:

1. Human behavior is determined by environmental forces. A related assumption is that learning can be defined exclusively as a change in overt behavior (in contrast to changing one's mind).

2. Overt behavior is both observable and testable, can be portrayed in operational definitions and quantified. Learning, defined as a change in overt behavior, is therefore observable and hence measurable; to measure it teachers only have to observe and measure overt changes in performance.

3. There is a stable, widely shared "observation language of behavior," and any behavior that cannot be translated into this special language should not be instilled in students. This leads to the notion that curriculums should and can have "clearly stated behavioral or competence- or performance-based objectives that entail both the content and method of instruction."

4. Society can be improved through the "science of behavior" and the development of technology. Linked to this assumption is the further assumption that curriculums and methods can be related to behavioral objectives as means are related to ends. By juggling and manipulating curriculums and methods we can produce whatever behaviors in pupils we see as desirable.[24]

According to the mandates of PBE or CBE, teachers have the primary responsibility for inducing in students the behaviors specified in the behavioral objectives. Objectives, presumably, will reflect strongly what adults want trained into pupils. Usually the only provision for individual differences among students is that some are allowed more time than others to acquire a given behavior. Presumably, in a given subject, all teachers will attempt to teach the same things about a subject, since they are all controlled by the same objectives.

Why Do PBE and CBE Rely Largely on Extrinsic Motivators (Reinforcements)?

There is nothing inherent in the accountability movement that provides students with much say over their own destinies. In fact, the overall nature of the movement denies any significant degree of autonomy to pupils. Adults decide for them what they should study, how they should study it, and how their achievement of objectives will be measured. If any of the subject matter chosen to implement PBE or CBE is of intrinsic interest to students, it is usually an accident. Since pupils sometimes become interested in a strange subject, when they are required to learn it to pass tests, accountabilitists argue that the potential for student interest is always present. However, when teachers are required to teach for literally hundreds of specific objectives and test frequently for their achievement, it is difficult to see how teachers can find the time to make a subject as colorful and lively as it conceivably could be. Accountability automatically produces in both teachers and pupils—a sense of urgency to get a necessary job done with the least input needed to achieve the required output.

Such a procedure necessarily requires the extensive use of rewards and sometimes punishments. Passing tests becomes one of the central reinforcers—for students who can be motivated this way. Since inter-school and interpupil competition is often emphasized in accountability programs, one's simply being a winner becomes crucial. In most school districts where accountability is policy, rewards are lavishly doled out to winners. Punishment for losers includes, but is not limited to, being held back because of failure to pass the tests.

Our intent is not to suggest that motivators other than those coming from pupils' environments can never be used under an accountability program. But the very nature of accountability programs tends to eliminate self-direction on the part of pupils and to place them under the control of teachers. Direction for study necessarily comes from outside the students. Accountability places virtually all pupils and many teachers in a situation in which environmental determiners rule.

Although some advocates of PBE and CBE argued that training can lead students into conceptualization and reflective problem solving, higher thought processes are rarely engaged, not only because of the difficulty of capturing them in behavioral objectives, but also because of the pace of instruction. The easiest way to cope with accountability is to train pupils to respond correctly with collections of discrete facts. Curriculums become atomistic because no one knows how to make them anything else and still meet the demands imposed by the rationale of accountability. Historians of education are aware that when curriculums have focused on fact memorization, students have rarely shown much inclination to be self-starting and self-sustaining in their study. To move over a specifically prescribed terrain, students require potent doses of outside motivators.

NOTES

[1] Robert C. Bolles, *Theory of Motivation*, 2d ed., New York: Harper & Row, 1975, p. 31.

[2] For a brief review of Darwinism and its role in the development of instinct theory see Korman, *The Psychology of Motivation*, Englewood Cliffs, N.J.: Prentice-Hall, 1974, pp. 15–16.

[3] William James, *Principles of Psychology*, vol. 2, New York: Henry Holt, 1890, p. 383.

[4] See William McDougall, *An Introduction To Social Psychology*, Boston: Luce, 1923, chapter 3.

[5] See John B. Watson, *Behaviorism*, rev. ed., New York: Norton, 1930.

[6] Korman, *The Psychology of Motivation*, p. 100.

[7] See particularly Robert Ardrey, *The Territorial Imperative*, New York: Atheneum, 1966; and Desmond Morris, *The Naked Ape*, New York: McGraw-Hill, 1967. Also interesting are the writings of Lionel Tiger and Robin Fox.

[8] Cited in Bolles, *Theory of Motivation*, p. 105. Italics added.

[9] See the widely discussed, controversial, Edward O. Wilson's *Sociobiology: The New Synthesis*, Cambridge, Mass.: Harvard University Press, 1975, p. 5.

[10] Wilson, *Sociobiology*, p. 26.

[11] Wilson, *Sociobiology*, chapter 27.

[12] C. H. Waddington, "Mindless Societies," *The New York Review of Books*, 7 August, 1975, pp. 30–32.

[13] Bernard Weiner, ed., *Theories of Motivation from Mechanism to Cognition*, Chicago: Markham, 1972, p. 13. Italics ours.

[14] Robert S. Woodworth, *Dynamic Psychology*. New York: Columbia University Press, 1918.

[15] Robert Bolles, *Theory of Motivation*, p. 101.

[16] Clark Hull, *Principles of Behavior*, New York: Appleton-Century-Crofts, 1943.

[17] Korman, *The Psychology of Motivation*, p. 27.

[18] See Clark Hull, *A Behavior System: An Introduction to Behavior Theory Covering the Individual Organism*. New Haven, Conn.: Yale University Press, 1952.

[19] John Dollard and Neal Miller, *Personality and Psychotherapy*. New York: McGraw-Hill, 1950; and Neal Miller, "Graphic Communication and the Crisis in Education," *Audio-visual Communication Review* 5, (1957): 3.

[20] Edward L. Deci, *Intrinsic Motivation*, New York: Plenum Press, 1975, p. 8.

[21] Bolles, *Theory of Motivation*, p. 304.

[22] W. K. Estes, "Reward in Human Learning: Theoretical Issues and Strategic Choice Points," in R. Glazer (ed.), *The Nature of Reinforcement*, New York: Academic Press, 1971.

[23] For an explanation and defense of the accountability movement, see Leon M. Lessinger, *Every Kid a Winner: Accountability in Education*, Palo Alto, Ca.: Science Research Associates, 1970; for a sharp critique of accountability, see Don T. Martin, George E. Overholt, and Wayne J. Urban, *Accountability in American Education: A Critique*, Princeton, N.J.: Princeton Book Company, 1976.

[24] M. Martin, R. Burkholder, R. L. Rosenthal, R. G. Tharp, and G. L. Thorne, "Programming Behavior Change and Reintegration into School Milieux of Extreme Adolescent Deviates," *Behavior Research and Therapy* 6, (1968): 371–396.

Chapter 4
WHAT ARE SOME IMPORTANT NONMECHANISTIC THEORIES OF MOTIVATION?

Though in the late 1970s a substantial number of academic, including educational, psychologists may prefer behavioristically oriented eclectic theories, a rapidly growing proportion of psychologists are apparently turning to various humanistic and cognitive psychologies. For example, Bernard Weiner of the University of California at Los Angeles says, "Mechanism no longer dominates psychology; the current trend is to conceptualize an active, information processing organism."[1] Whether this presages a major turning point in psychology with a new paradigm (system or model) dominating psychology for generations to come is, of course, unknown. But the feel of psychology in the late 1970s is quite different from that of 20 to 30 years ago when nonmechanists were often considered unscientific if not freakish.

Chapter 4 first treats the motivational theory attached to self-actualization psychology, a psychedelic version of humanistic psychology that has had only a minor impact on American classrooms. Then, the major part of the chapter is devoted to motivational theories classified as cognitive theory, field theory, and cognitive-field theory.

HOW DOES SELF-ACTUALIZATION THEORY VIEW MOTIVATION?

Psychologies that place strong emphasis on an evolving, individual self and its need to move through its own genetically decreed stages of development, or to fulfill its own distinctive inherent needs in relation to a potentially yielding environment, are properly called ego-development, self-development, or self-actualization psychologies. As indicated in Chapter 2, probably the most influential early popularizer of this view was Jean Jacques Rousseau.

In the twentieth century, led by the influential thinking of Abraham Maslow (1908–1970), a school of thought often referred to as *third force* psychology has arisen. The expression third force derives from the belief that Maslow's self-actualization psychology represents an alternative to the views dominant at mid-twentieth century—behaviorism (mechanism) and psychoanalytic theory (most often associated with Sigmund Freud). The idea of grouping all psychological theories into these three categories now seems outdated, since by the 1970s there are additional possibilities, particularly what the present writers call cognitive-field theory.

Another outdated idea is that of labeling self-actualization psychology as humanistic without qualifying the term. As this is only one type of humanism, we prefer to differentiate it as *psychedelic humanism*. This sets it apart from humanist *cognitive* psychology focusing on human thought, and from *interactive humanism* focusing on selves in interaction with their perceived environments.

Well known psychologists whose views are much like Maslow's include Carl Rogers, Eric Fromm, R. D. Laing, S. M. Jourard, Charlotte Buhler, and perhaps the motivational theorist, Richard de Charms. Among popular writers on education, John Holt seems clearly to belong to this group. Psychedelic humanists vary among themselves, of course, and individuals among them also change their positions over time.

In studying human nature Maslow accepted introspection as a valid method. To find out what people are really like, he believed the best approach is to get them to tell us. Often they cannot tell us directly and it then becomes necessary to use free association techniques or have them react to pictures or stories. Dream interpretation is also useful.

What Is Maslow's Theory of Human Nature?

Maslow was convinced that all psychologizing begins with a concept of the nature of human beings and this concept determines both what psychologists choose to study and the design of their research. To Maslow, everyone is guided by values—learned or otherwise—which emerge from their making free choices in situations where there is a choice among values. Maslow's conception of the nature of human beings breaks sharply from the Darwinian, or biological, conception of human nature. He apparently regarded humans as distinctively different from other members of the animal kingdom. Despite Maslow's rejection of the Darwinian biological model for humankind he did not consider humans divorced from nature's laws, but simply unique in certain important ways; "The laws of human psychology and of nonhuman nature are in some respects the same, but are in some respects utterly different."[2]

Maslow has also asserted that the "core" of human nature is a set of inborn, genetically determined needs and potentials, and that such a group of qualitative traits cannot be quantified in the sense of their existing in certain amounts. This view is very different from that of Hull and others who defined drives quantitatively in terms of the number of days of deprivation of food, water, or sex. Maslow believed, however, that the effects of society and culture on each individual shape these innate qualities, sometimes giving them what seemed like quantitative characteristics, such as so much need for physiological demands, and so much need for safety. However, society and culture cannot qualitatively change inborn possibilities.

Maslow referred to his view of human nature as *holisticdynamic*. The term holistic refers to unity of wholes. Maslow was convinced that a human being functions as one entity rather than a series of parts: for example, mind and body are both aspects of the same thing; all organs function in integral relationship to one another; and no single part of a human being can be understood without studying the whole mind-body entity.

By dynamic, Maslow meant that healthy persons generate their own purposes from within themselves and that they are fundamentally active, purposing, planning, anticipating organisms. Human beings are never passive—when one need is temporarily met, a person moves immediately to satisfy another. However, society and culture can exert forces that either reduce or eliminate the dynamic tendency in human nature.

Maslow thought that human beings are born essentially good in that their basic needs—if not frustrated by the environment—are not destructive of the interests of others. Second, they are born essentially active because their needs are genetically decreed (inborn) and will not be denied, except insofar as environmental barriers make gratification impossible.

What Are the Human Needs Hypothesized by Maslow?

It should be noted that Maslow used the terms *motive* and *desire* as apparently synonymous with need. He also used the word drive to refer to physiological needs, as noted above, but not in the sense in which Hull and Spence used it. Needs are "like instincts"; Maslow used the term "instinctoid." They thus come from within and are inner rather than outer in origin.

Needs exist in a hierarchy in the sense that when one category of needs is gratified, persons move to the next higher, but less immediately demanding, category. Psychological growth and psychophysical health require the gratification of needs at each level and the continued movement of the person to gratify needs at the next higher level, until the highest order need—self-actualization—becomes the focus of desire. Unsatisfied "lower" needs tend to dominate the need structure; until satisfied they overrule "higher needs." Maslow's categories of needs follow in a sequence from lower to higher, from most urgent to least urgent, in their demand for gratification:

1. *Physiological Needs.* These needs must be satisfied to some degree for a person to stay healthy. Maslow's list is similar to those of many other need theorists. Included are all the obvious bodily requirements for life to be maintained: food, water, sex, elimination of waste, and so forth. To some extent they are hierarchical—life and health can be maintained longer in the absence of some than of others. For example, Maslow considered the need for oxygen as most urgent, the need for food much less so. But the important point is that until the physiological needs are adequately met, people are hardly concerned with higher order needs.

2. *Safety Needs.* When physiological needs are sufficiently gratified, people begin feeling safety needs such as desire for security, stability, protection, structure, order, and law; and freedom from fear, anxiety, and chaos. Obviously the most urgent needs will not be the same for all people; urgency will depend on the total situation.

3. *Need For Belongingness and Love.* This need is called by many psychologists the need for affiliation. This category includes a number of needs concerned with relating sympathetically with others. It is manifested as a hunger for affectionate relationships with people one knows.

4. *Need For Self-Esteem.* The esteem needs consist of two subsidiary sets: (a) need for self-confidence, independence, and freedom in relationship to the environment which takes the form of desire for strength, achievement, adequacy, competence, and mastery; (b) need for being esteemed by other people, as manifested by their recognition, attention, and appreciation of one's importance, status, and prestige.

The four categories of needs mentioned above are regarded as deficiency needs. They are also regarded as basic, in that if the deficiencies are not corrected people tend to become ill. The general state of one's health is a function of how well they have been met.

5. *Need for Self-Actualization.* This is the "growth need" and is felt by normal humans only after the deficiency needs have been sufficiently gratified for health. Maslow's definition of self-actualization is the full development of one's potentials. Self-actualized persons tend to accept their own impulses, continue to grow and change even after the four basic need categories are gratified, think in terms of long-range rather than momentary goals, set individualistic goals, and accept others as they are. They also tend to be both largely self-determining in relation to the environment and to be species- or world-centered in their concerns (the idea of transcendent self).

Persons who have failed to gratify all their deficiency needs and consequently have not become self-actualizing have pretty much the opposite traits. They reject their own impulses, tend to become passive after meeting a given deficiency need, think in terms of both short-range and highly conforming goals, accept a state of environmental determinism, treat others as means to serve their own ends, and are egocentric. In Maslow's view these persons must be regarded as ill.

How Is Maslow's Psychology a Theory of Motivation?

Maslow's concept of instinctoid needs makes his theory of human nature largely a theory of motivation. It is a modern theory of how instinctive proclivities push a person along—of instincts energizing, guiding, and sustaining behavior. Further, since needs are biologically rooted (that is, carried in the genetic code), presumably all biologically normal human beings have essentially the same basic needs arranged in the same order of urgency. Becoming self-actualizing is a goal of all normal persons, although individual choices of expression vary widely. Potential fields to master as one's own are as divergent as vegetable gardening and brain surgery. Maslow allows for some interaction with environmental forces in shaping the behavior intended to satisfy one's innate needs, but within his frame of reference complete freedom of choice plays such a crucial role in relation to environmental pressures that his motivational theory cannot properly be called interactionist.

How Has Maslow Been Criticized?

Maslow urged that there should be an integral link between philosophy and psychology. In this connection, he thought that a philosophy of values should be a part of psychology. It is obvious that when he drew up specifications for a self-actualizing person he defined human nature and its potential in terms of his own preferred values. So, Maslow's theoretical structure has been criticized as being value laden rather than a factual description of "the way things are." However, Maslow was apparently aware of just what he was doing and felt it was justified.

The extent to which a psychological theory does or should rest on the values of the psychologist remains a matter of dispute. All psychological positions tend to represent both the philosophical premises and the values of the concerned psychologists. Maslow argued that one goal of self-actualization is one's reaching one's maximum potential in one's central area of interest. However, it has been pointed out that insane geniuses are then a problem for this definition. Van Gogh, for instance, had probably reached, or nearly so, the fullest possible development of the capability in which he was interested, but a Van Gogh could not qualify as a self-actualizing person because grave personal deficiencies in many areas contrasted with his genius in painting.

The most wide-spread criticism of Maslow concerns the difficulties involved in testing his theory empirically. Maslow's theory does not lend itself well to the making of testable hypotheses. The scant research to test Maslow's hypotheses has mostly produced negative or inconclusive findings.[3]

What Are Some Implications of Self-Actualization Theory for Teaching?

Self-actualization theory has probably been more popular among kindergarten and primary-level teachers than among others. Also, it has been more popular in some types of private schools than in public schools— particularly those based on the "free school" concept (such as Summerhill, the famous British school founded by the late A. S. Neill). To the extent that we find self-actualization theory visible at all in public secondary schools, its application usually appears as one element in a curriculum that is haphazardly eclectic (in the sense that an individual teacher works from one set of philosophical and psychological premises one day and often from opposite and mutually exclusive premises the next day). In common practice students are taught in relatively authoritarian fashion according to the precepts of a mechanistic psychology. To relieve the frequent oppressiveness of this approach, now and then a day is given over to letting students do as they please—presumably to strive toward meeting their instinctive needs.

In a school consistently devoted to self-actualization theory, teachers' chief work would be to remove insofar as possible environmental barriers that block need gratification. According to self-actualization theorists, if students are left to their own devices, much of what they do is simply to follow the dictates of innate needs or motives. This does not leave teachers much to do. Under self-actualization theory people are assumed to be self-motivating. Therefore, students do not need teachers goading them to keep busy and growing constructively. The chief role left for teachers is to prevent students being handicapped by any manipulable environmental obstacles such as classroom arrangements, enforced extrinsic motivators (such as grades), or the absence of study materials.

HOW HAVE COGNITIVE LEARNING THEORISTS VIEWED HUMAN MOTIVATION?

As its name implies, cognitive psychology is mainly concerned with cognition in the sense of conscious thought. It stands in sharp contrast to behaviorist and neobehaviorist psychologies, which have avoided the study of cognitive processes and focused on studying overt behavior. Cognitive theorists assert that overt behavior cannot be understood by studying overt behavior alone; first it is necessary to understand the thought processes behind overt behavior. Whereas the key concept in behaviorism has been *behavior*, the key concept in cognitive learning theory has been *awareness*.

David P. Ausubel and Floyd G. Robinson have been leaders in the development of cognitive theory in educational psychology.[4] Although cognitive theorists have strongly opposed many aspects of behaviorism, they do share some ideas with behaviorists. For instance, both positions hold that a person's future is the product of that person's past, and that this past can be analyzed in mechanistic ways. It remained for cognitive-field theory, discussed later in this chapter, to develop a clean break with behavioristic thinking.

How Do Cognitive Theorists View Learning?

Ausubel divides learning into two categories—rote and meaningful learning. Meaningful learning, a cognitive process, is given far greater emphasis than rote learning. Particular instances of learning are more or less meaningful and more or less rote.

Rote learning is

> the acquisition of arbitrary, verbatim associations in learning situations where either the learning task cannot be nonarbitrarily and substantively related to cognitive structure or where the learner exhibits a nonmeaningful learning set.[5]

Learning is relatively rote whenever, and to the degree that, (1) the material to be learned lacks logical meaningfulness, (2) the learner lacks relevant ideas in his or her own cognitive structure, or (3) the individual concerned lacks a meaningful learning set.

Rote learning is a conditioning process wherein learned materials tend to be relatively short-lived. Reinforcement occurs only in relation to rotely learned associations and instrumental responses; it does not characterize meaningful learning outcomes. Since the human mind is not designed for long-term verbatim storage of arbitrary associations, the retention span for rote learning is relatively brief.

Meaningful learning "is the human mechanism par excellence for acquiring and storing the vast quantity of ideas and information represented by any field of knowledge."[6] Such learning presupposes a meaningful learning set and a potentially meaningful learning task. So, meaningful learning refers to the differentiated cognitive content that may be evoked in a learner by a particular symbol or groups of symbols.

Meaning, for cognitive theorists, is a differentiated and sharply articulated *awareness* that either develops as a product of symbolic learning (concept formation) or that is evoked by a symbol or group of symbols after the latter have been related to one's cognitive structure (concept assimilation).

How Do Cognitive Psychologists View Human Motivation?

Cognitive theorists have tended to imply that people are basically neutral and active. However, they show overtones that imply that people are both neutral and passive and bad and active. For Ausubel and Robinson the concept *interaction* occurs between verbal stimuli—input and one's cognitive structure; it is a quite different concept from that of cognitive-field psychology where *interaction* is descriptive of the relationship of a person and his or her psychological environment.

> Typically, . . . motivational and attitudinal variables are not directly involved in the cognitive interactional process. . . . the effects of motivational variables on learning and retention respectively, unlike their cognitive counterparts, are not mediated through the same mechanisms.[7]

Although motivation is a highly significant factor in facilitation of learning, it is by no means an indispensable condition. "Much of the facilitating effect of motivation on learning is mediated by an increase in attention."[8] Available evidence "suggests that motivational factors influence *meaningful* retention selectively by inhibiting (raising) rather than facilitating (lowering) particular thresholds of recognition and recall".[9] Motivation, then, facilitates learning through increasing attention to the desired learning materials and directing attention away from the undesired ones.

Human motivation toward achievement consists of three basic components—cognitive drive, ego-enhancement, and affiliative motivation. Whereas cognitive drive is an intrinsic motive, the other two are extrinsic in nature. One may desire knowledge both as an end in itself and as a means of enhancing status and self-esteem.

COGNITIVE DRIVE MOTIVATION

Cognitive drive is the intrinsic need for acquiring knowledge and solving academic problems as ends in themselves; it is simply the need to know. This basic component underlies the need for academic achievement to the degree that such achievement represents to the learner the attainment of the knowledge that he or she seeks to acquire. It is completely task-oriented; the motive for becoming involved in the task in question is intrinsic to the task itself. The reward—attainment of knowledge—also inheres completely in the task itself, since it is capable of wholly satisfying the underlying motive.

"At the human level, cognitive drive . . . is more important in meaningful than in rote or instrumental learning, and is . . . the most important kind of motivation in classroom learning."[10] This desire to know and understand, to master knowledge, and to formulate and solve problems is derived from general human tendencies to be curious and to explore, manipulate, understand, and cope with the environment. Specific cognitive drives, however, are acquired from and dependent upon particular experiences. The awareness of successful learning reduces the state of the cognitive drive for a particular task, but increases cognitive drive generally. However, eventually in the life of a learner,

> the viability of the cognitive drive as an intrinsic, task oriented type of motivation is impaired as a consequence of the increasing, almost exclusive association of intellectual interests and activities with ego-enhancing and anxiety-reduction motives.[11]

EGO-ENHANCEMENT MOTIVATION

Ausubel states that

> The emphasis that has been placed on intrinsic motivation for learning should not be interpreted as a denigration of the importance of developing extrinsic motivations. . . . On the average, ego-enhancement [an extrinsic] motivation is undoubtedly the strongest motivation available during the active portion of an individual's academic and vocational career.[12]

Few people ever develop enough cognitive drive to master large bodies of subject matter as an end in itself. Hence, long-term ego-enhancement motivation becomes necessary.

Ego-enhancement motivation, for cognitive theorists, is non-task-oriented concern with achievement as a source of status. It is directed toward attainment of present scholastic achievement or prestige and future academic and career goals. A central ingredient in this type of motivation is anxiety. *Anxiety,* as used here, is a tendency to respond with fear to any current or anticipated situation that is perceived as a potential threat to self-esteem.

More than any other factor, ego-enhancement accounts for the persistence of high levels of aspiration. However, if carried to an extreme, this type of motivation may either generate sufficient anxiety to disrupt learning or lead to the formulation of unrealistic academic and vocational aspirations that point toward failure. Furthermore, exaggerated ego-enhancement motivation, because of its utilitarian orientation, often limits the pursuit of knowledge simply to vocational success. On the other hand, overemphasis on academic achievement may bring a premature extinction of motivation.

AFFILIATIVE MOTIVATION

Affiliative motivation is concern with academic achievement as a means of gaining and holding the approval of a superordinate person or group with whom individuals identify in a dependent way and from whose acceptance they obtain a derived status. Affiliative drive is most prominent during early childhood. Children first desire the approval of their parents, later that of their teachers. Then ego-enhancement becomes the dominant component of motivation in adolescence and adult life, especially among males and members of the middle class.

Do Reward and Punishment Motivate?

Ausubel states that "effective extrinsic motivation implies both reward and punishment."[13] The objective of punishment—aversive motivation— is facilitation of learning through anticipated threat of failure; its aim is to make students avoid punishment by their learning, rather than experience punishment by their failing to learn.

For sustaining the long-term academic achievement required for reaching professional goals, aversive motivation—the threat of penalties that are associated with failure—is as necessary as positive motivation that stems from anticipated rewards. Contrary to Skinner's findings, "punishment, conditioned fear, and anxiety have been remarkably effective in a wide variety of avoidance-training, instrumental conditioning, and discrimination learning experiments."[14]

In meaningful learning, reward and punishment have facilitating effects that are quite different from those in rote learning or conditioning. A person's awareness of successful learning—the satisfaction of cognitive, ego-enhancement, and affiliative drives for acquiring new knowledge— energizes subsequent learning efforts by enhancing self-confidence, encouraging perseverance, and increasing the subjective attractiveness of the learning task.

How Does Cognitive Motivational Theory Apply to Teaching?

We summarize cognitive motivational theory by listing nine practical implications for increasing classroom motivation as developed by Ausubel.

1. Since motivation is as much an effect as a cause of learning, do not wait for motivation to develop before engaging a student in learning activities.

> The causal relationship between motivation and learning is typically reciprocal rather than unidirectional. Both for this reason, and because motivation is not an indispensable condition of learning, it is unnecessary to postpone learning activities until appropriate interests and motivations have been developed.[15]

2. Always make the objective in a given learning task as explicit as possible. The relationship of specific learning tasks to other kinds of knowledge and intellectual capabilities should be pointed out.

3. Make full use of, but do not be limited by, existing interests and motivations.

> Although it is undoubtedly unrealistic and even undesirable in our culture to eschew entirely the utilitarian, ego-enhancement, and anxiety-

reduction motivations for learning, we must place increasingly greater emphasis upon the value of knowing and understanding as goals in their own right, quite apart from any practical benefits they may confer.[16]

4. Maximize cognitive drive by arousing intellectual curiosity, using attention-attracting materials, and arranging lessons so as to insure ultimate success in learning.

5. Set tasks that are appropriate to each learner's ability level. Nothing dampens motivation as much as a diet of failure and frustration.

6. Help students set realistic goals and evaluate their progress toward these goals by providing tasks that test the limits of their ability and by providing informative feedback.

7. Allow for developmental changes and individual differences in motivational patterns. Motivation becomes a progressively less important factor in learning as children advance in age. As children grow older material rewards and punishments become less salient factors in learning.

8. Make judicious use of extrinsic and aversive motivation, avoiding excessively high levels of each.

> Although educators theoretically decry the use of aversive motivation, they implicitly rely on it to keep students studying regularly for their credits, degrees, and diplomas. They do this because they know that cognitive drive and anticipated reward for hard work are not sufficient to overcome both inertia and the typical human proclivity toward procrastination and aversion to sustained, regular, and disciplined work. . . . The motivational force of an examination lies more in the fear of failure than in the hope of success.[17]

9. Since learning is an active process, place greater responsibility for its accomplishment in the hands of students.

> The teacher cannot learn for the pupil nor navigate intellectually for him. He can only present ideas as meaningfully as possible. The actual job of articulating new ideas into a personal frame of reference can only be performed by the learner.[18]

WHAT IS THE FIELD THEORY OF MOTIVATION?

Although field theory and cognitive psychology have become integrated under the rubric of cognitive-field psychology, field theory is still considered by most psychologists as a distinctive and original position and therefore warrants our attention here. The central figure in developing field theory was Kurt Lewin (1890–1947), a German emigrant to the United States in 1932. Though critical of Lewin in several respects, Korman says about his contribution that "it is vital for us to recognize that Lewin's importance as a figure in the psychology of motivation remains overwhelming."[19] This view is widely shared among psychologists. Lewin exerted a powerful influence on Tolman and such motivational theorists as Atkinson, McClelland, Rotter, and Vroom.

What Were Lewin's Major Contributions to Motivational Psychology?

Lewin is generally regarded as being primarily a motivational theorist. He asserted that an adequate theory of motivation must show how, given certain persons and certain environments at a particular point in time, certain behaviors are more likely to occur than others.

While Lewin felt that the experiential history of people was important, his theory of motivation assumed that one could build an adequate motivational theory by using only the elements in the contemporaneous situation. To understand the motivation of a particular individual, an investigator needed to know: the tensions (needs) of the individual, the individual's abilities, the characteristics of the environment, and a way to conceptualize these meaningfully. Lewin felt that, by understanding these factors and placing them within an adequate conceptual framework, the behavior of individual persons could in large measure be predicted.

Lewin spent most of his working career trying to devise procedures for conceptualizing the traits of people and the properties of perceived environments as interrelated components of an overall system or field of forces. He asserted that all behavior was a function of the field prevailing at the time. Thus Lewin's idea of *field* provided the conceptual framework within which the characteristics of both individuals and their perceived environments could be studied. This is why Lewinian psychology is generally called *field theory*.

What Is a Field?

To understand field psychology, is it necessary to understand the concept of "field" as it is now used in physics and the physical sciences generally. Lewin's formulation of "field" is derived from a statement by Albert Einstein. A simple definition of field is "a totality of coexisting facts which are conceived of as mutually interdependent . . . ."[20] A characteristic feature of a field is that, because of the interdependence of its elements, it tends to maintain some degree of balance or stability. If the equilibrium of a field of forces is disturbed, counterbalancing forces tend to arise which reinstate equilibrium. However, since the new equilibrium may—and usually does—incorporate factors not previously present, it will not necessarily consist of the same forces as existed prior to the disturbance. Most force fields are dynamic, not static.

Field theorists tend to regard all individual items as part of a field, small or large. An individual living cell is held to exhibit field characteristics. But this miniature field is a part of a larger field of forces, namely, a bodily organ. In turn, organs are seen as part of a still larger field, the entire organism. But even these are not self-sufficient; they are part of a larger field—the environment in which they live.

In studying persons and their environments, it is assumed that part of one's environment is other human beings. The behavior of any single human is incomprehensible apart from two influences—that exerted on it by other people and that which the single person is in turn able to exert on others. Accordingly, any position in psychology that emphasizes field theory is actually a social psychology.

What Are the Primary Features of Motivation in Field Psychology?

To explain motivation Lewin held it was necessary to assume that a person is motivated by psychological tensions produced by the interaction of a psychological self with a psychological environment; hence his statement that behavior is the function of a person and his environment.

Field psychologists do not deny the existence of organic or biological needs (drives) but assert that such needs are either translated into psychological needs by the person or are not felt at all. Most of us are aware that even small boys and girls often become so wrapped up in play that they do not want to take time to eat meals or go to the bathroom.

As is the case with most humanistic psychologies, field theory asserts that no amount of repetition of a particular S-R linkage will fix that response so that its automatic continuation will be assured. A particular response will occur only so long as it reduces a psychological tension of the person. As psychological needs shift, which may occur frequently and suddenly, action will shift in a way to keep it in the service of needs.

Another significant divergence from S-R mechanism to be found in the thinking of Lewin and other field psychologists is the idea that once an act has been completed the recurrence of the stimulus associated with the act will not produce a recurrence of the act unless the same tension persists. If an individual has a letter to mail, the sight of a mailbox may indeed guide the person's behavior and in that sense is a stimulus. But once the person has mailed that letter, the sight of further mailboxes does not elicit a "letter mailing response"—not, that is, until the person has another letter to mail. If Ss and Rs were linked blindly, as most mechanists assert, the sight of a mailbox should bring forth the same response every time.

What Is the Essence of Lewin's Concept of Motivation?

Psychological tensions are the energy source and the basis of motivation. Tensions lead to the formulation of aims or goals and psychological movement toward these goals. Tensions arise when there is an imbalance or discrepancy in the total force field affecting the person. A specific goal-related behavior ceases once its achievement is sufficient to allay feelings of tension. However, with the reduction of tension following successful pursuit of a goal, a person does not lapse into a state of passivity, as most behavioral mechanists have claimed. The force field in which a person functions is always in the process of becoming imbalanced so that tension at some level is ever present. Therefore, a person is forever formulating goals and acting on a psychological environment, which simultaneously acts on the individual. Mutual interaction is continuous and simultaneous.

Lewin did not suggest that there are certain psychological needs common to all normal humans, as did Maslow and some of the achievement-motivation theorists that are mentioned in the next chapter. Needs are situational in the sense that they take shape according to the situation at the time.

HOW DO COGNITIVE-FIELD PSYCHOLOGISTS VIEW MOTIVATION?

Cognitive-field psychology is a comparatively recent position. Basically, its adherents have constructed it through drawing from cognitive and field psychologies and forming an emergent synthesis that they hope is superior to either of these earlier psychologies alone or a combination of the two. As a position, it is a relatively complete theory and has inner consistency. Before discussing its implicit theory of motivation, we must briefly describe this position. (More details appear in Chapters 14 and 15.)

What Is Cognitive-Field Psychology?

Cognitive-field theory was developed primarily to help teachers understand people—especially students, but also themselves. Hence, it offers a psychological system that is fruitful in dealing with children and youth. With respect to motivation, cognitive-field theorists view psychological activity as dependent on psychological tension systems. In contrast to the practices of behavioral mechanists, cognitive-field psychologists stress, as crucial to a description of motivational processes, changes both in the values (valences) of a person's psychological environment and in the tension systems or needs of individuals in relation to their environment.

Cognitive-field psychology concerns itself with overt behavior only insofar as it may provide clues to what is transpiring psychologically. Psychological, as cognitive-field psychologists use the term, refers to purposive personal involvement. Cognitive-field–oriented teachers want to change overt behavior, but only if that behavior is an outcome of a change in outlook or thinking.

The purpose of cognitive-field psychology is to formulate tested relationships that will predict the purposive behavior of individual persons. To predict individual behavior, persons and their psychological environments must be studied as a pattern of interdependent factors and functions. Cognitive-field psychology is an interpersonal social psychology that constitutes an effective vehicle for understanding people.

What Is the Cognitive-Field View of Motivation?

The basic hypothesis of cognitive-field psychology in regard to human motivation is that any person—in keeping with an achieved level of development and understanding—does the best that he (or she) knows how for whatever he thinks he is. Vitalists do the best they know how for their substantive minds; biological mechanists do the best they know how for their passive bodies; and cognitive-field-oriented individuals do the best they know how for their psychological persons.

In a psychological field no distinction is made between inner and outer sources of motivation. Motivation results from the interplay among elements in the field. Its presence and intensity cannot be measured by studying changes in overt behavior. To determine what level of motivation exists, we must somehow "get inside" other persons and see the world through their eyes. This requires an understanding of individuals' needs—what they are, their relative intensity, and whether individuals can reasonably expect to achieve goals that would reduce the intensity of their needs.

Cognitive-field theorists think biological needs can be transcended—that is, overridden by psychological needs or motives. Otherwise how could we explain the deliberate ignoring of biological needs in order to serve psychological goals. Athletes often punish themselves severely in the interest of winning. Also, many persons commit suicide—the ultimate refusal to accommodate biological needs.

In dealing with motivation, cognitive-field psychologists decry the use of such concepts as drive and reinforcement. Instead, they prefer goal, expectancy, value, intention, interaction, and the like. They also prefer connecting success and failure to motivation (rather than pleasure and pain, which behavioral mechanists have considered to be central to motivation). People often choose pain and even bodily damage —that is, deny their biological needs—in the interest of achieving some transcending psychological goal. Long distance runners and politically motivated hunger strikers are but two of hundreds of possible examples.

For cognitive-field–oriented teachers, the essence of "reward" is a feeling of success. Such teachers recognize that students need to experience rewards for learning. But from a cognitive-field view, the best reward is psychological—any reward that makes students feel better about themselves—for example, by having satisfied felt needs for competence and self-determination. This requires that to some degree students feel they have some share in deciding what they are to do and considerable freedom in determining how they do it.

INTERACTIVE MOTIVATION

Motivation may be considered to be either extrinsic, intrinsic, or inter-active. *Extrinsic motivation* usually refers to needs or motives the source of which is largely "outer", that is, in the environments of humans. If extrinsic motivation prevails, there is little or no room for autonomous choice making. Among those tending to view motivation as extrinsic are the behavioral mechanists—not only those who are clearly reinforcement theorists, but even drive-incentive theorists. To the latter, in an im-portant sense even a hunger pain is "outer" in that it feeds highly de-manding stimuli into the central nervous system. Extrinsic motivation is usually linked to a belief in *environmental determinism*.

Intrinsic motivation commonly refers to needs or motives that are largely "inner," that is, coming from inside the persons' self structures. Psychologists who use this expression tend to assume that humans much of the time can choose their behavior according to personal choice. Some early instinct and drive theorists spoke of intrinsic motivation, but in the context of today's psychological thinking such usage would be incorrect. The psychologists who can now be most accurately identified as pro-moting inner motivation are the self-actualization theorists such as Maslow and Rogers.

There has been considerable confusion associated with the concept of intrinsic motivation. Even psychologists who promote intrinsic motiva-tion with the greatest dedication recognize that environmental barriers often make free choice difficult or impossible. In the view of these people, individuals try to adopt a position of "mind over matter" but are not always successful. In fighting the existence of environmental barriers, they may achieve their goals fully, partially, or not at all.

Although it has been widely held that not only the self-actualization position, but all the varieties of Gestalt and field psychologies prefer teaching that stresses intrinsic motivators, this would seem to be an oversimplification.

Though the expression has not yet been highly popularized, *inter-active motivation* would seem a better way of labeling the kind of motivation that harmonizes best with cognitive-field psychology. Cog-nitive-field psychology is an interactive position—the self and the person's perceived environment are always in the process of simultaneous mutual interaction (SMI). The self is using the environment, changing its meaning and often its objective qualities; at the same time the environ-ment is influencing the nature of the self. An interactionist theory of how people relate to their environments would seem to call for a theory of motivation in which no attempt is made to sort out inner cause of motiva-tion on the one hand and outer causes of motivation on the other. When Deci, who strongly advocates the intrinsic nature of motivation, says: "Children are born with a basic undifferentiated intrinsic motivation, the need for being competent and self-determining in relation to their en-vironment,"[21] and in other statements stresses intrinsic needs in relation to the environment, it appears that his theory is more an interactive than a purely intrinsic theory of motivation.

What Are Some Implications of Cognitive-Field Psychology for Classroom Teaching?

This subject is developed on a more "how-to-do-it" level later, particularly in Chapters 20 and 21. Here we only summarize and draw theoretical or quasitheoretical conclusions. However, readers should be able to infer much about classroom practice from this chapter—as was the case with Chapter 3.

PSYCHOLOGICAL NEEDS THE BASIS FOR MOTIVATION

Innate needs are purely physiological life needs, such as the need for oxygen. But psychological needs often transcend physiological ones; or at least they tend to color and transform biological demands in an infinite number of ways. Physiological needs are not innate; they develop through one's interaction with one's environment. Such needs usually exist in relation to goals, and they participate in determining behavior toward those goals.

The more teachers gear their selection of content and methodologies to the felt needs of students, the more motivating their teaching will be. Most young children are motivated to learn. Their curiosity seems boundless. Yet after a few years in school, children often lose most of their curiosity—at least about subjects taught in school.[22] Teachers can avoid the demotivation of students only by themselves understanding what produces motivation.

LEVELS OF MOTIVATION

Cognitive-field psychologists tend to believe that all people are always in some state of tension—ranging from the barely measurable to the extreme tension that produces psychosis. Jerome Bruner's research has led him to some interesting theorizing about what level of tension is best. Although eclectic in many of his views, Bruner appears to think like cognitive-field psychologists in certain areas including motivation. Bruner thinks there is a kind of "golden mean" in student motivation, somewhere between apathy and wild excitement, and that teachers should strive for this middle position. He says

> Frenzied activity fostered by the competitive project may leave no pause for reflection, for evaluation, for generalization, while excessive orderliness, with each student waiting passively for his turn, produces boredom and ultimate apathy.[23]

Cognitive-field theorists are perhaps a little more explicit about tension levels. They tend to believe that teachers should seek to involve students to a point just short of frustration. Teachers need to be able to recognize when students are approaching the frustration point. When students eagerly battle with conflicting or problematic ideas, we know that they are perplexed but not frustrated. However, when a student becomes unduly aggressive, perhaps impudent, in relations with others, this is displaying "fight." Or, if a student passively submits to a situation and appears to be doing nothing at all about it, this is psychological "flight." Both psychological *fight* and *flight* are symptoms of frustration.

THE THEORY OF COGNITIVE DISSONANCE

In 1957 Leon Festinger proposed a theory of cognitive dissonance that has generated an exceptional amount of interest among educational psychologists. Festinger maintained that if persons hold two or more cognitions that are discrepant (contradictory), and *if* they recognize the contradiction, they will feel uncomfortable and take steps to eliminate or reduce it. Festinger's theory may well have generated more follow-up research than any other assertion about motivation.[24]

Festinger proposed that people react negatively to conflicting perceptions or cognitions. That is, inconsistency in their psychological field makes them uncomfortable. People who perceive inconsistency become uncomfortable and seek to eliminate it. Further, they will seek to live so as to avoid the repetition of previous dissonance. Thus, incompatible cognitions energize behavior in the direction of reducing the dissonance; that is, people try to avoid uncertainty. Faced with cognitive dissonance, people usually either modify their attitudes and values or change their behavior.

In light of Festinger's studies it might appear that to motivate students all we need do is to put them in situations where they are made aware of their inconsistencies so they will engage in study and activities designed to eliminate the dissonance in perceptions. However, Festinger's early statements were shown to be oversimplified and have since been revised by him and many others. A large amount of empirical research has established that people do not prefer lives free of discrepancies. Normal people seek challenges, which may lead to inconsistent perceptions; these they will try to reconcile, and then proceed to the next challenge. Further, discrepancies in perception may not only fail to produce discomfort, but people may actively seek out challenges. Various investigators, including J. Mc V. Hunt and Edward Deci, prefer respectively the terms *incongruity* and *challenge* as broader terms than Festinger's dissonance. According to Deci:

> When a person sees that he is unable to behave so as to reduce the incongruity (i.e., to meet the challenge) he will begin to experience discomfort (i.e., dissonance). He then seeks to reduce this discomfort, most probably by changing one of his own internal states, such as an attitude, a motive, or an emotion. . . . all of these internal states have a cognitive component and can therefore be affected by the cognitive process of dissonance reduction.[25]

The approach to teaching implied in the foregoing line of thinking is one of arranging situations that are incongruous (puzzling) or challenging to students; sometimes no "arranging" is required in that students come to school with their minds well loaded with inconsistencies that they do not recognize. Then the teacher's job is to help expose these inconsistencies that already exist. Just how this may be done is illustrated in Chapter 21.

Specifically, what kinds of situations produce cognitive dissonance or uncertainty? They may evolve from incompatibility between cognitions, or between cognitions and behavior or experience, requiring persons to argue in favor of something with which they disagree, predicting future events that will have unpleasant consequencies, and perhaps other situations.

We have already noted, however, that few people want to eliminate all uncertainty from their lives. Most prefer an optimum level of dissonance but vary in their definitions of "optimum level." Some people are obviously more daring than others. The most daring are able to remain comfortable at a rather high level of dissonance in comparison to the least daring.

Using cognitive dissonance to motivate students is the preferred approach of most cognitive-field psychologists and most teachers in the cognitive-field framework. This means that doubt or uncertainty are deliberately injected into the classroom, either by exposing contradictions already existing in the students' thinking or by arranging a situation which will puzzle them. Problematic (puzzling) situations take certain distinctive forms which we may refer to as no-path situations and forked-path situations. They may be diagrammed as in Figure 4.1.

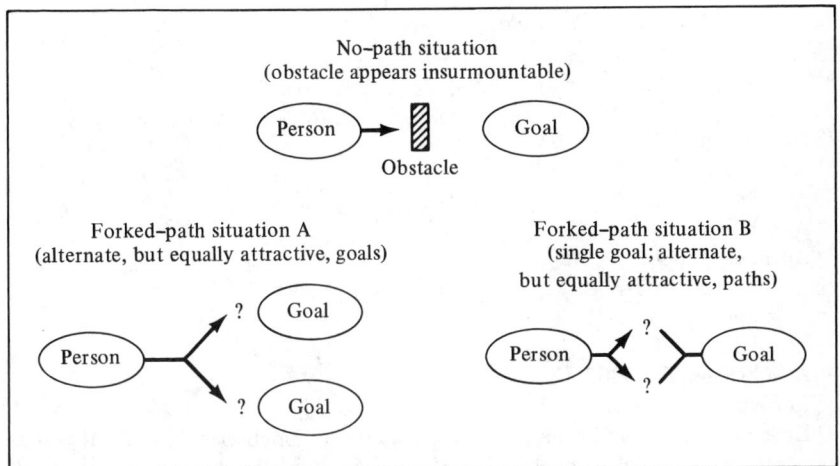

Figure 4.1   Problematic situations.

There is another dissonance-producing situation, not illustrated, that might best be called "making a choice between two evils." People often find themselves in situations in which they are unhappy with all possible choices—as in choosing between two candidates for public office when the voter really likes neither. This kind of situation requires a choice between negative goals, but the one that appears to represent the lesser of two or more evils takes on something of a positive nature. When people have to select one unpleasant choice, they tend to rationalize their behavior and exercise considerable ingenuity in defending their choice as "good."

Techniques through which teachers may clarify or induce dissonance are elaborated elsewhere in the book, particularly in Chapter 21.

NOTES

[1] Bernard Weiner et al., *Achievement Motivation and Attribution Theory*. Morristown, N.J.: General Learning Press, 1974, p. 4.
[2] Abraham Maslow, *Motivation and Personality*, 2d ed., New York: Harper & Row, 1970, p. 7.
[3] For a brief, clear discussion and critique of Maslow, see Edward L. Deci, *Intrinsic Motivation*, New York: Plenum Press, 1975, pp. 82–86. For a short, lucid account of the difficulties in testing Maslow's theory, see Abraham K. Korman, *The Psychology of Motivation*, Englewood Cliffs, N.J.: Prentice-Hall, 1974, pp. 247–248; and K. B. Madsen, *Modern Theories of Motivation*, New York: Wiley, 1974, chapter 15.
[4] David P. Ausubel, *Educational Psychology, A Cognitive View*, New York: Holt, Rinehart and Winston, 1968; Ausubel and Floyd G. Robinson, *School Learning, an Introduction to Educational Psychology*. New York: Holt, Rinehart and Winston, 1969.
[5] Ausubel and Robinson, *School Learning*, p. 608.
[6] Ausubel, *Educational Psychology*, p. 58.
[7] Ausubel, p. 369.
[8] Ausubel, p. 371.
[9] Ausubel, p. 373.
[10] Ausubel, p. 365.
[11] Ausubel, p. 368.
[12] Ausubel, p. 378.
[13] Ausubel, p. 381.
[14] Ausubel, p. 383.
[15] Ausubel, pp. 365–366.
[16] Ausubel, p. 368.
[17] Ausubel, p. 378.
[18] Ausubel, pp. 366–367.
[19] Korman, pp. 103–104.
[20] Kurt Lewin, "Behavior and Development as a Function of the Total Situation," in Leonard Carmichael (ed.), *Manual of Child Psychology*, 2d ed., New York: Wiley, 1954, p. 919.

[21] Deci, *Intrinsic Motivation*, especially chapter 4.
[22] Deci, p. 210.
[23] Jerome Bruner, *The Process of Education*, Cambridge: Harvard University Press, 1960, p. 72.
[24] Leon Festinger, *A Theory of Cognitive Dissonance*, Evanston, Ill.: Row, Petersen, 1957.
[25] Deci, p. 162.

Chapter 5
WHAT IS ACHIEVEMENT MOTIVATION?

Achievement motivation is the expectancy of finding satisfaction in mastering challenging and difficult performances. When discussed in relation to school achievement, achievement motivation is motivation to perform specific tasks for which there is a standard of excellence against which results can be judged. Typically, classroom teachers decide what learning tasks students are to perform and also evaluate the quality of achievement.

The conditions under which achievement motives best develop require that learners (1) can give reasons for developing a given motive, (2) understand that the motive is realistic, (3) can link the motive to deeds and daily events in life, (4) commit themselves to concrete goals, (5) keep a record of progress, (6) have honest and warm support, (7) engage in self-study, and (8) feel that they belong to a successful group.

Achievement motivational theory, as it has developed, accepts partly or wholly, some assumptions of the motivational theory implicit in field and cognitive-field psychology as portrayed in Chapter 4. Consequently, what achievement motivation theorists advocate as specific classroom practice may resemble or overlap the motivational practices advocated by field and cognitive-field psychologists. However, readers should keep in mind that motivational practices advocated by both field and cognitive-field psychologists rather sharply differ from, and may be more effective for classroom use than, the practice advocated by achievement theorists.

HOW SHOULD THIS CHAPTER BE STUDIED?

Achievement motivation can be divided into two periods: (1) an early period in which achievement motivation theorists incorporated into their models aspects of behavioristic and Freudian psychology and (2) a period marked by a more complete, balanced cognitive theory supported by "attribution theory." During the first period, achievement theory, while producing considerable useful knowledge about motivation, nevertheless exhibited considerable eclecticism. This period began to decline in the 1960s.

Although many psychologists are still trying to refine early achievement theory, major modifications began to emerge about 1970. Some modifications of the past decade are so new as to be revolutionary. The theory has developed new assumptions and new methods of investigation. Some of the new directions are more difficult to understand, more abstract, even more esoteric than the content of earlier theories. The new directions are so compelling and have so many implications other than achievement in school subjects that we may be seeing in it some kind of "wave of the future" in psychology.

How Should Students Study Early Achievement Theory?

Approximately the first half of the chapter is devoted to early achievement theory and the course it had taken into the 1960s. Although it is difficult enough to be challenging, the authors presume that most upper-division college students can understand it. All readers who expect to teach should read the first half of the chapter, if for no other reason than to comprehend the assumptions, research designs, and findings of psychologists within the framework of early achievement motivation theory. But more important, early achievement theory has produced findings that should be useful to any teacher under certain circumstances—especially in rather old-fashioned school situations.

How Should Students Study Achievement Theory of the 1970s?

What is now emerging in achievement theory is in large degree a new beginning along new lines. It has great practical potential, but has not gone very far in its development. In effect, it is a partial model that a number of relatively young and very innovative psychologists are developing step by step. The authors recognize that this is perhaps the most challenging section of the text, and will baffle some readers. We have written the book so that part of this chapter between pages 103–114 can be omitted without any loss of continuity. This material should therefore be considered optional. Although not necessary for following the major themes of the book, we do suggest that all students sample this material in order to get the feel of avant garde thinking about motivational theory, especially as it involves *cognitive attribution*.

WHAT ARE SOME KEY FEATURES OF EARLY ACHIEVEMENT MOTIVATION THEORY?

Early achievement motivation theory is based on the assumption that motives arise from changes in emotional states. This class of theories has been referred to as *affective arousal theories*.[1] Early achievement motivation theorists believed that achievement motives arise when learned cues reinstate emotional states or feelings. Motives for achievement usually refer to specific tasks. They can be identified on the basis of individuals' expectation of success, provided the persons are personally involved.

Attributing motivation to emotion only is not a widely accepted view. Other motivational theorists assert either that cognition (in the sense of information processing) determines motives or that some combination of cognition and emotion—thought of as two aspects of the same unitary process—produce motives. As we will see, one important aspect of the new generation of motivational theorists is their tendency to attribute motives to a cognition/emotion blend, with fear probably being the only "pure emotion" that generates motives.[2]

Achievement motivation theory prior to the late 1960s has sometimes been called a quasicognitive theory of motivation. As previously noted, it retains certain terms and concepts from behaviorism, adapts others from psychoanalysis, as well as inventing its own distinctive terminology and concepts. The focus of the early theory was not on cognitive processes as now understood.

How Did Achievement Motivation Theory Begin?

The first systematic work in achievement motivation theory in the United States was that of Henry H. Murray.[3] Murray's work can best be comprehended by realizing his strong interest in biology. His concept of innate needs is somewhat reminiscent of instinct theory, a popular concept among biologists and Freudian psychoanalysts. However, he recognized the importance of environmental factors in shaping needs, even though his theorizing never took the strongly interactionist position that can be seen in contemporary achievement motivation theory. Murray conceived of humans as active, growing organisms—a dynamic interpretation quite in opposition to the behavioristic view of organisms as passive receivers of stimuli.

Murray's central contribution was to personality theory. He felt it was possible to identify a variety of innate needs that give the human personality its enduring characteristics. They include a need for achievement. To determine the strength of various needs, including that for achievement, Murray invented a testing instrument that was to become quite popular among psychologists—the Thematic Apperception Test (TAT). The TAT consists of a series of ambiguous pictures; the testee is asked to tell or write what the picture means and through this activity is supposed to reveal both the force of various needs and the areas of conflict between them.

With the passage of time, Murray's work was seen as somewhat dated and narrow. However, his influence can be seen in the work of later psychologists, particularly McClelland, Atkinson, and their associates and followers.

What Are Some Central Features of the McClelland/Atkinson Model?

Following Murray, developments in achievement motivation theory are associated primarily with David C. McClelland and J. W. Atkinson.[4] Although these men did not take the same position on all issues, their theories can in large part be treated together. McClelland was a rather close student of Murray. His interest in the whole personality, particularly in the measurement of need systems, was directly in line with Murray's work. Like Murray, McClelland was also influenced by psychoanalytic theory. This helps explain his interest in the relationship between child-rearing practices and achievement motivation. He was also interested in sociology and anthropology. One of his more impressive accomplishments was his attempt to relate achievement motivation to societal economic growth (presented in *The Achieving Society*).

Atkinson, though largely in the same tradition as McClelland, was apparently more influenced by Hull, Lewin, and Tolman. Like these men, he tried to identify the causes of behavior and to develop a mathematical means of describing them. He is known for his mathematical model of motivational factors.

MOTIVES AS DEFINED
BY McCLELLAND AND ATKINSON

The McClelland/Atkinson concept of a motive is implicit in their acceptance of what has been labeled *optimal incongruity theory*. Incongruity refers to discrepancy, incompatibility, dissonance, or inconsistency. Although many mechanists have maintained that organisms prefer a situation of complete freedom from tension, by the early 1950s an impressive body of research data suggested that humans are comfortable within a range of current perceptions that contradict past perceptions of stimulus experience.

Often humans act as if they were passive because they are taking no apparent action toward a pleasant situation or away from an unpleasant one. If current perceived stimuli, whether positive or aversive, are only mildly different (ranked, say, at 1.5 on a continuum of 0 to 3) from past experience (set on the continuum at the point 0 and called the "adaptation level"), then the organism accepts the discrepancies between present and past experience. Such small deviations in stimulus input above (ranked as positive) or below (ranked as negative) the adaptation level are satisfying and generate positive emotions that motivate the organism either to stay with or approach the experience causing the good feelings. But large deviations cause negative emotions, which lead people to avoid highly discrepant experiences. Here we have the beginnings of a psychology of motivation based on perceived conflicts—similar to Festinger's theory of cognitive dissonance.

A discrepancy between current perception (information received) and the adaptation level (past experience) causes a primary emotional response when the discrepancy is first noticed. Such responses tend to be associated with mildly discrepant stimuli (cues) then present within either the individual or the environment. Encountering similar cues in the future renews the individual's original (primary) emotional response. McClelland defined this revised former emotional state as a *motive*.

Observe that in the McClelland/Atkinson conceptualization a feeling of disharmony or tension is not seen as necessary to induce motivation and ensuing action. All that is necessary are stimuli or cues that will restore the previous primary emotion originally developed by discrepant perceptions. McClelland and Atkinson saw all motives as learned—a position that contrasts with earlier instinct or biologically rooted theories of motivation. Motives were learned, as indicated above, by the pairing of cues with primary emotional responses. All behavior was viewed as motivated by the restoration of primary emotional states.

Revived primary emotional states produce "approach" or "avoidance" behaviors. Thus, if a student is assigned a task and the stimuli accompanying it restore a pleasant emotional state anticipating pleasant outcomes, the task will be pursued. If the task is associated with unpleasant outcomes, it will be avoided. If present cues, for example, suggest a hot stove and if prior hot-stove experience was emotionally negative (perhaps the student was burned), the student will avoid the stove. If prior experience was emotionally positive (perhaps the student had cooked a gourmet meal), the student will approach the stove.

MOTIVES AS PSYCHOLOGICAL

Although the McClelland/Atkinson model is not fully cognitive, neither is it traditionally mechanistic. These investigators did not recognize the existence of purely organic needs—analogous to Hull-Spence drive theory. They saw all human needs as psychological in that tissue deficits (like an empty stomach) do not in themselves translate directly into needs. All needs (motives) are construed as psychological. Thus, people learn to eat to satisfy hunger, but an empty stomach does not necessarily elicit an eating response. Most children's appetites seem voracious to adults;

but even though a child may not have eaten for a long time, the compelling cues in a situation may be revived positive emotions related not to food but to play. Both parents and teachers know how difficult it can be to persuade a playing child to take time out to eat.

ASSESSING NEEDS

The achievement motivation theory promoted by McClelland and Atkinson was directed at probing the content of thought. For this purpose, the TAT has been widely used. To serve as a research instrument, Murray's original TAT had to be "objectified" by devising interpretation formulas that would make the test equally reliable when used by numerous investigators. The formula developed made it possible to give a numerical score to the strength of a need.

The need to achieve (the success motive) was found to vary markedly from one individual to another. Though many persons would fall between the two extremes, a common research design began by categorizing subjects into two groups—those with a strong need to achieve and those with only a weak need. The discoveries about differences among people in their need to achieve lent ammunition to those psychologists who were promoting the concept of individual differences. Atkinson, particularly, is now regarded as having perhaps made his most important contribution in demonstrating the significance of individual differences in motivation.[5]

What Are Some of the Central Features of Atkinson's Model?

Perhaps the most interesting and useful treatment of achievement motivation until the late 1960s was that presented by Atkinson in 1964. By then he had developed a somewhat elaborate set of mathematical formulae for depicting the relationships between various determinants of behavior. Advanced students may want to dip into Atkinson's own writing for a more complete treatment, as space permits only a very brief outline here.

Atkinson asserted that people tend to approach and engage in achievement-related tasks if there is a probability of success and to avoid tasks if there is a probability of failure. Presumably everyone has a motive for success that is defined simply as the need to perform successfully according to some socially accepted standard. The strength of the motive for success varies greatly from one individual to another, but for any given person is thought to remain relatively stable. The strength of the motive for success, Atkinson felt, could be measured by the use of TAT tests.

The motive for success will be felt most strongly when one feels responsible for the outcome of one's acts, when there is quick feedback of results, and when there is some risk of failure. This view contrasts quite sharply with the Skinnerian view that people do not feel responsibility (at least not in the usual sense), and that tasks should always be kept easy enough so success on each trial is virtually assured.

The probability of success is based on one's expectations of reaching the goal and is a consequence of one's previous experiences in trying to cope with similar goals. Assessing the probability of success is a sub-jective process that can be undertaken only by the subject. Perhaps the most significant feature of Atkinson's model is that the probability of success needs to be less than certain—particularly in the case of high achieving students. Risk is thus a stimulator toward action rather than a deterrent in many cases.

Atkinson maintains that the value of success is related exclusively to goal difficulty. The harder the goal, the greater the pride its achieve-ment will bring. Conversely, the easier the goal, the greater the shame in not accomplishing it. Note that Atkinson makes no reference to the possible relevance or intrinsic interestingness of the goal, except insofar as goal difficulty itself makes for interest.

So far we have been considering students who tend to be normal or high achievers. But what about students who have been habitual failures and have been categorized as low achievers? Poor achievers may not have a motive for success. Instead, they may be motivated primarily to avoid failure. The motive to avoid failure is, of course, linked to the desire to avoid shame. The motive to avoid shame is felt to be a relatively stable part of the make-up of low achievers. This motive produces anxiety, which, it is believed, can be measured with the TAT. Again, the easier the goal, the greater the shame resulting from failure. Few people are ashamed at failing highly difficult tasks—they have lots of company.

Of What Value Has the Atkinson Model Been?

Atkinson's formulations can be criticized in various ways. An early criti-cism was that the model provides no genuine interaction between the perceived self and the perceived environment. It focuses on intrinsic (inner) factors—how persons feel about themselves in relation to achieve-ment. Extrinsic (outer or environmental) factors were ignored, par-ticularly the possibility that achievement may be related to rewards or punishments supplied by others, such as parents or teachers. However, Atkinson's final formulation did take cognizance of environmental factors in relation to both motive level and probability of success.[6] Deci sums up Atkinson's work by pointing out that "The extrinsic component of the model has received virtually no attention, yet it does set a precedent for the development of a model which is concerned with both intrinsic and extrinsic motivation."[7]

Atkinson's model might also be criticized for the narrowness of the definition of incentive. As seen by Atkinson, incentive is a function of the difficulty of the goal. The harder the goal, the more pride derives from its achievement, and thus the higher the incentive. This ignores the possibility that many easy goals may be sought because their achievement will be useful for reasons other than elevating pride. Some relatively easy achievement tasks are simply fun and worth doing for themselves.

(Optional Reading: The following section is included so students can get some feel for recent and current research. Its content may be too difficult for many students. Hence, we have written the chapter so the following section on cognitive attribution theory can be omitted without disturbing the general thought flow of the chapter.

HOW HAS THE COGNITIVE-ATTRIBUTION THEORY OF ACHIEVEMENT MOTIVATION DEVELOPED?

At least two important elements have been introduced to achievement motivation theory in the past decade: (1) a more complete and balanced cognitive theory and (2) the analysis of how both the causes that people attribute to their wanting to do things and the actual doing of them affect motivation and performance. This analysis is called by psychologists *cognitive-attribution theory.*

A large number of psychologists have applied recent versions of cognitive theory and its subfield, attribution theory, to the study of achievement motivation. A few of the more prominent ones are Julian Rotter, Fritz Heider, Richard Nisbett, Stuart Valins, Harold H. Kelley, Edward L. Deci, and Bernard Weiner. Perhaps the two most prolific researchers and writers of the 1970s are Deci and Weiner, who seem to be in essential agreement on many issues.

What Is Weiner's Basic Model?

Readers will note that although Weiner's overall conceptualization is fundamentally different from that of McClelland and Atkinson, much of the time he is indebted to them for some of his work. Weiner points out that until the late 1960s relatively little was known about the "experiential or phenomenological aspects of achievement" and that trying to explore these basically subjective components of human behavior has represented one of the major thrusts of work in achievement motivation in the 1970s.

Readers will recall from Chapter 3 that the Hull-Spence sequence of behavior was often portrayed as S–O–R, where S meant stimulus situation, O meant organism, and R meant overt response. S and R were defined as behaviorists have traditionally defined them, and O referred to a mediating process internal to the organism.

Cognitive-attribution theorists, including Weiner, use a model that can be stated in short form as S–C–R, where C stands for cognitions (the procees of knowing; also knowledge), and S and R are redefined in a fundamental way. Beginning with the assumption that people are purposive, and that behavior is a function of the interaction between the perceived self and perceived environment, they no longer can define S simply as any form of energy that arouses a response, but rather as consisting of information and concepts. Nor can R be defined as an automatic, thoughtless action resulting from S and O. Instead, it is an action intended to achieve a goal, but the goal may be thought itself or some combination of thought and overt behavior. Cognitive-attribution theorists commonly use the term behavior defined broadly to include any form of activity, mental or otherwise.

Weiner and others prefer to split S–C–R into two units. They see the S-C relationship as information and concepts that provide persons with their perceptions of their environment (or the "cognitive representation" of their environment). This *relationship* requires a model of thought. The second unit, C-R, or the *C-R connection* reflects the linkages between causal cognitions and behavioral response, and requires a model of action. The S-C and C-R units are not, of course, separate; they are discussed as two units or components only for clarity of explanation. Weiner suggests that just how thought influences action is not understood, but even so he assumes that all action is a product of thought.

Although a broader theory of motivation cannot ignore purposiveness, if a task is already set—as in achievement motivation—it is possible to view goal making as already determined by external forces (parents, teachers, textbook writers, counselors, custodians, and so on). The problem for the person with an assigned goal becomes the analysis of those causal factors that make achievement of the goal possible—or impossible. Note that these are causal factors as seen by achievers, and that only factors that achievers ascribe and the achievers' way of relating them to each other have relevance for achievement. It is the roles attributed by the achievers to these factors as they affect their own behavior that makes the prediction of individual behavior possible.

Although dozens of causal factors could be listed (both facilitators and barriers), for the sake of manageability and precision much recent experimentation in achievement motivation has been limited to the four causal factors—ability, effort, task difficulty, and luck. (One could add other causal factors—such as mood, fatigue, illness, teacher bias, fluctuations in skill—but additional factors would cause complications that present experimental designs cannot handle.)

Weiner and his associates, drawing from Heider, present the following classification of these four personally ascribed causes of behavior.[8] They note that these causal factors can be classified in two different ways (a "2 x 2 classification"). If they are classified on the basis of what persons see as the locus or source of control, then ability and effort will usually be viewed as coming from within oneself—as internal factors. But individuals usually see task difficulty and luck as coming from outside themselves—as external, environmentally determined factors.

Secondly, if the classification is based on the factors' relative stability, then experimentation seems to reveal that persons ascribe high stability to ability—as if it had innate or inheritable qualities. Likewise they tend to see task difficulty as stable—it has been determined by another person. But, they tend to see effort and luck as variable factors; they may change from moment to moment. This classification can be depicted as:

Locus or Source of Control		Factor's Relative Stability	
Internal:	ability	Stable:	ability
	effort		task difficulty
External:	task difficulty	Variable:	effort
	luck		luck

Achievement motivation theorists recognize that the above 2 x 2 classification is overly simple. Ability and effort are not always necessarily perceived by their holder as having exclusively internal sources; nor task difficulty and luck as having exclusively external sources ("If I owned a typewriter my ability might improve"; "By cheating, I can reduce task difficulty"). Likewise, ability and task difficulty are not always perceived as stable or effort and luck as unstable. ("My ability might be more dependable if I always ate breakfast"; "My effort fluctuates often depending on mood.") So, Weiner's model does not purport to be complete—only the most useful, to date.

What Are Some Ascribed Causes of Success and Failure?

We have noted that in the S–C–R sequence, for purposes of analysis the S-C component can be treated as a set of relationships that constitute a "model of thought"—although in real life, models of thought and models of action cannot be so neatly separated. The S of the S-C relationship consists of information (about causal factors), causal schema (theory of causal relationships), and individual predispositions (attitudes)—all of which Weiner places under the head of *antecedents* which means that which comes first and may influence what comes later.

The basic causal ascriptions—the information components of S— that have proved most usable to date are, as noted, ability, effort, task difficulty, and luck. Readers should remember at all times that these items are not "objective" in the sense of their having an independent existence of some kind—they are what individuals ascribe or attribute to themselves (self-perceptions).

1. Ability. People make inferences about their ability on the basis of their past history of success and failure, as judged by such items as making high grades or being a winning athlete. Social norms are commonly used as references by which to judge one's own ability.

2. *Effort.* Perceptions of effort are related to perceptions of ability in the sense that high previous performance is often ascribed to effort. Most high achievers see a decline or improvement in performance as a decline or gain in effort. Hence, effort is much more likely than ability to be seen as unstable—something that can be turned on or off at will.

3. *Task Difficulty.* People tend to judge the difficulty of tasks by social norms (How hard has the task seemed for others?), or by the obvious objective task difficulty (Is it harder to climb Mt. Everest than to walk around a city block?). But because people do vary in ability, and effort may increase or decrease, objective judgments of task difficulty are often not easy to make. There is, therefore, a strong tendency to fall back on social norms that give task difficulty a perceived stability.

4. *Luck.* People ascribe an event to luck if it seems completely beyond personal control and is also quite unpredictable. Luck is therefore considered highly variable. Even so, after a series of wins at a game of chance people may begin ascribing luck to skill or effort. Or they may begin perceiving themselves as "one of those rare lucky people" and include luck as an aspect of ability, thus giving luck a more stable role in causing success (or, conversely, failure).

HOW CAUSAL ASCRIPTIONS ARE MADE

There is considerable predictability in the way people use such cues as ability, effort, task difficulty, luck, and other possible variables to interpret their success or failure. Kelley has formulated some principles of processing behavior information that have helped predict how people tend to relate these factors.[9] Kelley maintains that three factors of behavior usually determine how people explain their successes and failures: (1) distinctiveness, (2) generality, and (3) social norms or consensus. How this works may be seen as follows.

In an experiment conducted by Weiner and Frieze,[10] an individual was described as either succeeding or failing at a task. Subjects were given information and were to answer questions that would lead to ascriptions of success or failure to one of the following factors having the following arbitrary meanings: (1) the *distinctiveness* of the performance (was the try a success or failure?); (2) the *generality* of the performance (was the try typical in success or failure for that individual?); and (3) social *consensus* (how did the individual perform in relation to other people?). The subjects were then asked to ascribe the individual's success or failure to some combination of ability, effort, task difficulty, or luck.

The results bore out Kelley's description of the role of the factors of distinctiveness, generality, and consensus. Virtually all subjects make the following ascriptions: (1) outcomes (success or failure) conforming to social consensus are attributed to the qualities of the task; (2) success tends to be attributed to internal factors (ability, effort) and failure to external factors (task difficulty and luck); (3) outcomes incompatible with previous outcomes are attributed to the unstable factors of effort and luck; and (4) the greater the degree of previous success or failure, the more likely is future success or failure to be ascribed to high or low ability.

What is the significance of all of this? It shows that subjects do use specific cues to make causal inferences and that the cues are related in a rational manner. But it also shows that the process of judgment relies on theoretical structures or models of what causes what. These theoretical structures—representing Kelley's main contribution—go beyond the "facts as given." They may properly be called *causal schema*, which Weiner defines as "a relatively permanent structure that refers to the beliefs that a person holds about the relationship between an observed event (and effect) and the perceived causes of that event."[11] Using less precise language, we may simply call these causal schema theories of causation.

It appears, therefore, that one's theory of causation is as important as specific information in making causal interpretations. In sum, one doesn't determine the causes of one's own or others' behavior (that is, their motivation) just by adding up facts, but rather by working back and forth thoughtfully between fact and theory, or data and frame of reference. This distinctively cognitivist and humanistic notion is quite in contrast with the most recent of popular behavioristic psychologies— Skinner's reinforcement theory which in fact denies any use for theory at all.

Readers might be left with the notion that there is something fixed or "absolute" about the theory imbedded in causal schema. This is not at all the case. New factual or reputedly factual data may contradict an established causal theory. For example, it seems a more-or-less standard bit of theory that success at a difficult task requires both high ability and high effort. But suppose we observe cases where success at a difficult task seems to have been achieved without high ability and effort, or, indeed, with neither high ability nor effort. The school's prime mathematical ignoramus doodles unintelligibly for half a minute on a scrap of paper and comes up with the right answer to a hard problem which it might have taken the teacher a week to do. When such oddities do sometimes happen, they produce a state of cognitive dissonance which may force observers to rethink the common notion that high performance requires both high ability and effort.

CAUSAL BIASES AND THEIR MAINTENANCE

Theories of causation tend to contain personal biases. For example, even when it can be demonstrated that they are equal in ability, students high in achievement needs tend to attribute all high achievement to ability and effort. Conversely, students low in achievement needs tend to attribute all low achievement to low ability and have little or no conception of the role that effort plays in achievement. Further, success and failure syndromes tend to be self-perpetuating. Kelley's concept of the role played by distinctiveness and social consensus helps explain the permanence of high and low self-images. When performance outcome is seen as low in distinctiveness and also low in social consensus, performers ascribe the results to their own inner qualities (performers normally perform well, and in comparison others perform poorly). Conversely, high distinctiveness coupled with high consensus causes the performers to place the blame on external factors (they have failed when they usually succeed, and others have also failed—so task difficulty, with perhaps some bad luck, become the culprits). This common tendency for people to rationalize, that is, to "make reasonable" both their successes and failures, is a useful insight for teachers and will be discussed in various contexts later in the book.[12]

What Are Some Consequences of Perceived Causes?

In this section, we turn our attention to the C–R component of the S–C–R paradigm assumed by Weiner and many others. We are here interested in performance as it is affected by how people interpret the causes of their behavior. Weiner and apparently most other cognitively oriented achievement theorists see behavior as partly or largely determined by the perceived expectancy of success or failure and the incentive value of the goal. Since goals involve values—something we want—this particular model of the immediate determinants of behavior is often called the expectancy value conception of behavior. The remainder of this section is devoted to how causal ascriptions influence expectancy and goal value.

STABLE VERSUS UNSTABLE CAUSAL FACTORS
Goals appear more attainable if persons either ascribe high ability to themselves or see the task as relatively easy. The easiest goals, of course, are those requiring a combination of perceived high ability and perceived task ease, although this combination is likely to bore most students. In any case, since ability and task difficulty are typically seen as unchanging (at least during a single task confrontation), then effort and luck are perceived as the crucial factors. Effort can be increased and luck may change. In fact, if the ability-task difficulty relationship—the "can" factor—is seen as potentially manageable, success or failure hinges on effort—the "try" factor—plus luck. Of these two, trying or expending effort is seen by most students as the more important, although in many situations students see luck as crucial. (A particular teacher, for example, may refuse to tell a class what to study for prior to an examination; in this

case, students may see success or failure on the exam as a matter of chance (luck), in which case they may try less hard.)

However, it must be stressed that the relative importance ascribed to ability, task difficulty, effort, and luck varies according to the situation. Students with a record of high achievement are likely to see effort as of major importance. Many teachers reward effort, even if it does not lead to successful performance. Students with a record of low achievement typically do not see the significance of effort—possibly because they are convinced that in relation to task difficulty their ability is so low that effort is inconsequential.

The expectancy of achieving a goal tends to change after experience in trying to attain a goal. In general, past success leads to the expectancy of future success with similar goals, and past failure leads to the expectancy of future failure. However, this is more likely to be the case if success or failure were attributed to ability to do the particular task, that is, to a stable factor. If success or failure are seen as attributable to bad luck, fatigue, mood, teacher bias, or other variable and often unpredictable factors, previous success or failure are less likely to change one's expectancy. At the same time, effort is seen as more important than luck and ranks second only to the stable factors—ability in relation to task difficulty.

EXPECTED SUCCESS AND EFFORT

The relationships depicted by Weiner and associates differ from those previously described by psychologists. The Atkinson model described earlier would lead us to think that only after expectancy of success is high-will performers be willing to exert effort. However, the research of Weiner and associates, and of others, suggests that anticipated effort is a highly important factor in determining expectancy of success (particularly in the case of relatively high achievers). Weiner feels he has established that among high achieving students effort often comes to be seen as a stable factor—students who have habitually tried in the past are certain that they will try equally hard again.

CAUSAL STABILITY AND "HOPE"

We have seen that people attribute stability to the causal factors of ability and task difficulty, and instability to effort, luck, mood, fatigue, and so on. They tend to believe it impossible to change either ability— which is often construed as innate—or task difficulty—which is imposed by others. Persons failing in situation in which they feel their behavior is fully under the control of unchangeable causes tend to develop a state of hopelessness. They no longer have positive anticipations. The term *learned helplessness* has been coined for this state of mind.

In achievement-oriented situations, it is aversive (painful) to ascribe the cause of failure to low ability. Such an ascription can only lead the person to believe that the future holds nothing but failure. The strict environmental determinism assumed by many mechanist psychologists may, therefore, have a potentially disastrous effect in that it produces learned helplessness. Of course, many mechanists have tended to assume that ability is a flexible quality determined by a combination of genetic and environmental factors. Ability is thus completely removed from the individual's control. This is the way most people now perceive ability. But they might learn to perceive it as continuously variable if determinism had not gained such a hold on large numbers of educational psychologists and professional educators.

An example of the kind of research that reveals learned helplessness is that of Dweck and Reppucci.[13] These investigators gave a group of subjects 30 trials at tasks rigged to make failure inevitable. These 30 failed tasks were followed by two at which success should have been relatively easy. In addition, all subjects were given the Intellectual Achievement Responsibility Scale (IAR) test, which permits subjects to attribute internal or external causes to their failures and successes.

Part of the sample failed the two soluble tasks assigned after they first failed 30. Another part of the sample solved these two additional tasks. Those who failed the two soluble tasks were labeled "helpless" and those who completed them successfully were labeled "persistent." By studying the IAR results, it was clear that the helpless subjects attributed their failure to external factors (environmental causes). But, the persistent subjects attributed their prior failures to low effort and their final successes to high effort. The persistent subjects attribute their performance to a factor they feel they can control, whereas the helpless attribute their performance to factors they feel they cannot control. Weiner thinks that results of experiments such as this have great therapeutic significance and that much more research along this line is probable.[14]

ASSIGNED CAUSES AND EMOTIONAL RESPONSE

So far we have paid relatively little attention to emotional (affective) states that appear to result from differing ascriptions of the causes of success and failure. In general, we are referring to feelings that contemporary achievement theorists label pride and shame. The research findings seem to show that the locus of control is of crucial importance in producing emotional states. If either success or failure is attributed to internal causes—thus making the individual responsible—pride or shame is experienced. Conversely, if success or failure is attributed to external causes such as task difficulty or luck, there is very little emotional reaction.

Emotional states aroused as a result of success or failure determine in large part the incentive value of a goal. Pride increases incentive and shame decreases it, although it should be noted that high achievers can suffer considerable shame and still come back trying (they have experienced pride often enough to want to continue seeking it).

Of all the ascriptions to causality, the belief that one has exerted a major effort and, as a result, has succeeded is more likely than any other to produce an "emotional high." The high will be especially marked if the individual does not see him or herself as high in ability or if the task achieved is one at which most others fail. Social norms are usually highly significant—if known by individuals in an achievement situation. "Performance consistent with social norms elicits external (task) ascriptions, while performance inconsistent with the norms results in personal attributions."[15]

Readers should note how different the above analysis of incentive is from that presented by Atkinson, who defined incentive as solely a function of task difficulty—the harder the task the higher the incentive value. A more balanced cognitive analysis ascribes goal-values as a function of externality vs. internality of control, among other possible factors.

Deci, in the tradition of Lewin, has proposed that a significant variable is the interestingness of the task itself. Although a given task may be interesting to one performer and dull to another, teachers have some objective grounds for judging: if most students show enthusiasm for a task and work hard at it in the absence of external rewards (such as pay), it may be assumed the task is interesting for its own sake. However, Deci reports research evidence to indicate that providing external rewards for doing a task which appears to have intrinsic interest tends to destroy the interest. When considered in the light of Deci's analysis, task difficulty takes on a new light: interesting tasks seem easier; boring tasks seem harder. Thus, subjectively, task difficulty may not have the stability ascribed to it in the experimental data reported by Weiner.[16]

Another example of how emotional factors may affect performance focuses on anxiety. We noted earlier that within the McClelland/Atkinson model of achievement performance, persons who fail habitually have a high anxiety level. Anxiety was assumed to be caused by failure. However, there is experimental evidence to show that, conversely, failure may be caused by anxiety.

Weiner and Sierad performed an experiment in which subjects of varying achievement needs were divided into experimental and control groups.[17] The experimental group was given a placebo but told that it was a drug that would interfere with hand-eye coordination—hence, failure at the task assigned in the experiment could be attributed to the effects of the drug.

It was hypothesized that among low achievers the expectancy of success would be low among members of both experimental and control groups but that the control group would react normally for them, that is, they would have a negative attitude toward the task and would perform at an unsatisfactory level; however, it was also hypothesized that the experimental group would not feel anxious about their expected failure and as a result might do comparatively well at the assigned task. In the case of high achievers, it was hypothesized that high achievers in the experimental group would have a low expectancy of success, would not feel anxious about the task ("Why worry—we're drugged and can't be expected to do it"), and would perform poorly.

After four trials, the results of the experiment confirmed the hypotheses. In fact, the low achievers in the "drugged" state achieved almost as well as the high achievers in the nondrugged control group. Both groups' performances improved on each trial, with the low achievers gaining sharply on the second.

Though teachers are not in a position to pretend to drug low achievers into not worrying, teachers should be aware of such experiments. These results confirm Weiner's earlier finding that high achievers are more realistic than low achievers in their causal ascriptions. More evidence is needed, but perhaps low achievers' misjudging of their own ability may be an important reason for their trying less hard.

How Do Rewards and Punishments Affect Motivation?

Since about 1970 there has been considerable empirical research on the effects of rewarding students for successful or wanted behavior. Such research virtually all leads to the conclusion that however much intrinsic motivation may exist, *it is either reduced or destroyed by rewards.* When children and youth are, first, allowed to do something intrinsically interesting, then separated into matched groups with one being paid to continue the activity and the other group not rewarded at all, and are finally allowed to pursue the activity on a "free will" basis—then virtually always the paid group soon loses interest and quits the activity, whereas the unpaid group continues with equal or greater enthusiasm. This basic type of study has been repeated enough times to have become accepted as the usual result of rewarding people for something they wanted to do anyway.

Such introduction of rewards apparently causes the subjects to shift the location of their original perceived reasons for performing the activity. Before the rewards, subjects see their reasons as inner—a matter of their own free choice. But later subjects see rewards as the cause of their activity; they then feel that someone else is controlling their activity. Thus, any classroom practice will decrease the intrinsic motivation related to a task if it causes students to see what they would do anyway because of intrinsic interest become something they do for others "for hire."[18]

The implication for teaching practice of these experiments is profound. First, it suggests that we eliminate rewards entirely if they are likely to be perceived by students as a means of "buying them off." Such practices as giving letter grades, rewarding students with special privileges, or maintaining a system whereby certain students are singled out for honors (for example, the valedictorian system) is likely to shift motivation from inner or interactive to extrinsic. When this happens students do not work because they want to learn something for their own purposes; they work in order to be paid in one form or another—and typically stop working when the payment ceases.

A second means by which intrinsic (internal) motivation can be changed is by changing students' feelings of competence and self-determination in relation to the environment. Any action taken by a teacher that boosts these feelings among students will encourage them to be intrinsically motivated; conversely, any action that reduces students' feelings of competence and self-determination reduces the amount of internal—intrinsic—motivation. Verbal rewards ("You are doing a very good piece of work, Johnny") do not seem to decrease the intrinsic motivation of boys but seem to destroy it for girls. Deci sees this as a result of the role playing we teach children from an early age: girls tend to take personally the feedback they get, linking it to their own likeability, whereas boys treat feedback as information ("The praise I got suggests that I am a competent person").[19] How might one explain the fact that some girls' intrinsic motivation decreased after receiving positive verbal feedback? Studies showed that the sex of the experimenter was not the cause. The answer seems to lie in a combination of the traditional socialization process and a tendency to reinforce its effects by emphasizing only one factor of verbal feedback. The control of girls by older persons is more pronounced than that of boys. That girls yield to the socialization process more readily has been verified by anthropologists, psychologists, sociologists, and other experts in human behavior, and, by them, this usually is considered to be a learned trait.

Verbal feedback has two factors—controlling and informing. It is the controlling factor of rewards that results in the persons' receiving the feedback shifting their perceived locus of causality from intrinsic to extrinsic. That is, they no longer see their behavior as being caused by their own inner wishes, but by the desires of some other controlling person. Studies have shown that this factor applies in teaching girls to be dependent on others and more subservient in a traditional society. Though the controlling factor is apparent in such rewards as money, avoidance of punishment for poor performance, and the receiving of awards for good behavior, girls see the controlling factor also in praise. Boys, on the other hand, tend to see rewards like praise to be information about their competence and their self-determination.

Deci believes that if the controlling aspect of feedback (verbal rewards) were avoided with girls, they would not shift their perceived locus of causality from inner to outer and so decrease their intrinsic motivation. One way of avoiding this decrease would be to avoid interpersonal feedback and allow the feedback to come from the girls' unrewarded success experiences. The girls could deduce the informational feedback from the experience and verbalize it to themselves. This would retain intrinsic motivation and tell the girls about their competence and self-determination.

Pertinent to the issue of intrinsic vs. extrinsic motivation, de Charms and his colleagues have been experimenting on the effects of encouraging students either to think they originate their own behavior (internal or intrinsic motivation) or to think they are the tools of someone else. The de Charms team found that students who had studied this issue and were taught to feel maximum personal autonomy (with some necessary practical restrictions) made significant gains over conventionally taught children in both realistic goal setting and academic achievement.[20]

WHAT ARE SOME IMPLICATIONS OF ACHIEVEMENT MOTIVATION THEORY FOR CLASSROOM TEACHING?

We have described some findings of McClelland, Atkinson, and their followers which may still be useful. Our interest here is to summarize what is now being said about achievement motivation from the view of an attribution theorist.[21]

Weiner and others are interested primarily in comparing how students attribute causes for success or failure with how teachers attribute causes for the students' success or failure. Attribution theory does not appear to conflict in its basic premise with cognitive dissonance theory; rather, the two approaches seem complementary. Weiner's focus is on how causal attributions affect the rewards and punishments administered by teachers and the accompanying pride and shame experienced by students. Obviously, events that make students proud are motivating—"nothing succeeds like success." Likewise, persistent failure seems to breed more failure.

How Do Teachers Apply Rewards and Punishments?

Weiner's conclusions are based on four studies which all led to the same conclusions. With respect to the tendency of teachers to reward or punish students, it seems well established that highly capable students who fail an easy task are punished more than anyone else. Teachers interpret this situation as a sign of laziness or simply not caring about school and perhaps not the teacher either. Inadequate "trying" bothers teachers more than anything else in their relations with students.

Students perceived as low in ability are punished less than any other category of students, but receive more punishment if they don't try than if they do. In fact, the students most highly thought of by teachers are students low in ability who try hard. These students are rewarded even more than students of high ability who try hard and achieve at a high level. Weiner suggests that American culture promotes what we find in school—little or no ability, coupled with some or perhaps a great deal of effort, is highly prized in the American value hierarchy. Americans generally are willing to reward incompetence so long as the incompetent person tries.

What Are the Bases for Students' and Pride and Shame?

Students appear to evaluate themselves much as teachers do. When incompetent students achieve success through effort, those students feel pride. Shame is suffered most when high-ability students fail because they did not try. In one experiment, students in the fourth and fifth grade were given an opportunity to take as many poker chips from a bowl as they thought they deserved for a successful performance. Conversely, they had to return as many chips as they thought they were obliged to after a failure.

The students had previously been given a test that revealed where they placed causation for their successes and failures. Those students predisposed to attribute success to effort but failure to factors other than effort ended with the most chips. Students predisposed to attribute failure to low effort but success to other factors ended with few chips. Thus we see divergent tendencies among the two student groups—a strong tendency to blame failure on lack of effort, but also: the most self-rewarding students tend not to attribute failure to lack of effort and the least self-rewarding students tend not to attribute success to effort. In sum, students who tend to be high achievers ascribe their success to effort and their failures to some other factor, whereas low achievers, while recognizing effort as a causal factor in failure, do not see effort as related to successful performance.

Pride results when students feel they have through effort conquered a task relatively difficult for them, whereas shame results when students fail to see a clear causal link between effort and success. It would appear that teachers need to take student ascriptions for success or failure much more seriously than they do. To develop pride and subsequently better performance among weak students, methods need to be devised to help them see the role of effort in achieving success.

NOTES

[1] Edward L. Deci, *Intrinsic Motivation*, New York: Plenum Press, 1975, pp. 14–15, 34, 104–106. See also Bernard Weiner, *Theories of Motivation from Mechanism to Cognition*, Chicago: Markham, 1972, pp. 173–174.

[2] Deci, pp. 14–15.

[3] Henry H. Murray, *Explorations in Personality,* New York: Oxford University Press, 1938.

[4] David D. McClelland, *Personality,* New York: Holt, Rinehart and Winston, 1951; McClelland, J. W. Atkinson, R. W. Clark, and E. L. Lowell, *The Achievement Motive,* New York: Appleton-Century-Crofts, 1953; McClelland, *The Achieving Society,* Princeton, N.J.: Van Nostrand, 1961; J. W. Atkinson, *An Introduction to Motivation,* Princeton, N.J.: Van Nostrand, 1964.

[5] Bernard Weiner, ed., *Achievement Motivation and Attribution Theory,* Morristown, N.J.: General Learning Press, 1974, Chapter 1, "Achievement Motivation as Conceptualized by an Attribution Theorist," by Bernard Weiner, p. 47.

[6] Ibid., Chapter 2, "The Emergence of a Cognitive Psychology of Motivation," by Heinz Heck Mausen and Bernard Weiner, p. 61.

[7] Deci, pp. 110–111.

[8] Weiner, ed., *Achievement Motivation,* chapter 1 by Warner, pp. 4, 5.

[9] H. H. Kelley, "The Process of Casual Attribution," *American Psychologist* 28, (1973):107–128.

[10] Weiner, ed., *Achievement Motivation,* chapter 3, "Cue Utilization and Attributional Judgments for Success and Failure," by I. Frieze and B. Weiner, pp. 69–74.

[11] Weiner, ed., *Achievement Motivation,* chapter 1 by Weiner, p. 13.

[12] Weiner, ed., *Achievement Motivation,* chapter 1 by Weiner, pp. 20–47.

[13] C. W. Dweck and N. D. Reppucci, "Learned Helplessness and Reinforcement Responsibility in Children," *Journal of Personality and Social Psychology* 25, (1973):109–116.

[14] Weiner, ed., *Achievement Motivation,* chapter 1 by Weiner, p. 31.

[15] Weiner, ed., *Achievement Motivation,* chapter 1 by Weiner, p. 33.

[16] Deci, pp. 265–268.

[17] Bernard Weiner and J. Sierad, "Misattribution for Failure and the Enhancement of Achievement Strivings: A Preliminary Report," unpublished manuscript, 1973, reported in Weiner, *Achievement Motivation,* pp. 40–43.

[18] Deci, chapter 5, especially pp. 137–139.

[19] Deci, pp. 142–146.

[20] Richard de Charms et al., *Enhancing Motivation: Change in the Classroom,* New York: Irvington Publishers, 1976, chapters 1 and 11.

[21] Weiner, ed., *Achievement Motivation,* chapter 12, Attribution Theory, Achievement Motivation, and the Educational Process, pp. 186–195.

BIBLIOGRAPHY

ALSCHULER, ALFRED S. *Developing Achievement Motivation in Adolescents: Education for Human Growth.* Englewood Cliffs, N.J.: Educational Technol-Publications, 1973. One of the best references on teaching achievement motivation to adolescent youth. Should be read by every prospective secondary school teacher.

ALSCHULER, ALFRED S., DIANE TABOR, and JAMES MCINTYRE. *Teaching Achievement Motivation: Theory and Practice in Psychological Education.* Middletown, Conn.: Education Ventures, 1971. This is essentially a how-to-do-it book in achievement motivation. Not a "cookbook" in the usual sense, this volume presents in readable form the major principles of teaching for achievement as they had been developed to 1970. Alschuler is involved in the Program in Humanistic Education at the State University of New York in Albany.

ATKINSON, J. W. *An Introduction to Motivation.* Princeton, N.J.: Van Nostrand 1964. Atkinson's interpretation of the contributions to motivational theory made by William James, Sigmund Freud, Kurt Lewin, Edward Tolman, and Clark Hull.

ATKINSON, JOHN W., and DAVID BIRCH. *The Dynamics of Action.* New York: Wiley, 1970. Atkinson's systematic approach to motivational theory. A mathematical model more sophisticated than anything we have suggested in Chapter 4. For graduate students and professors only.

ATKINSON, JOHN W., and NORMAN T. FEATHER (eds.). *A Theory of Achievement Motivation.* New York: Wiley, 1966. A book of readings containing essays by Atkinson, Feather, and others. More readable for students than the Atkinson volume cited above.

AUSUBEL, DAVID P., *Educational Psychology A Cognitive View.* New York: Holt, Rinehart and Winston, 1968. A systematic development of cognitive psychology.

AUSUBEL, DAVID P. and FLOYD G. ROBINSON, *School Learning an Introduction to Educational Psychology.* New York: Holt, Rinehart and Winston, 1969. Cognitive psychology developed with emphasis upon school application.

BOLLES, ROBERT C. *Theory of Motivation,* 2d ed. New York: Harper & Row, 1975. The most detailed up-to-date treatment of findings from animal research on motivation. In Bolles first edition (1967) he seemed a dedicated behaviorist; in the second edition, he raises some fundamental questions about the usefulness of behaviorism explaining human behavior.

BORING, EDWIN G. *A History of Experimental Psychology.* New York: Appleton-Century-Crofts, 1950. See annotation in Chapter 1.

BOULDING, KENNETH E. *The Image: Knowledge in Life and Society.* The University of Michigan Press, 1956. The "image" as analyzed by Boulding appears to be what the present volume refers to as the psychological or perceptual field—a person's interpretation of what comes to him or her through the senses. A profound little book, and a clearer treatment than offered in most psychology texts. Harmonizes with cognitive-field psychology.

DE CHARMS, RICHARD. *Personal Causation.* New York: Academic Press, 1968. De Charms is an advocate of personal-causation motivation, sometimes sounding like Maslow, but actually an interactionist. Assumes the need for competence and self-determination in relation to environment and in same general category of theorists as Edward Deci.

DE CHARMS, RICHARD, et al. *Enhancing Motivation: Change in the Classroom.* New York: Irvington Publishers, 1976. Reports an interesting study of motivation in children in which children and their teachers were taught a distinction between two personality types, labeled for the study Origins (people who set their own goals) and Pawns (people who let themselves be pushed around by others), and in which school settings were devised for producing attitudes favorable toward being Origins. The work of the two categories was studied, indicating that boys trained in this distinction have significantly higher achievement motivation than control groups.

DECI, EDWARD L. *Intrinsic Motivation.* New York: Plenum Press, 1975. Probably the best recent book available on intrinsic, as contrasted with extrinsic, motivation. Once readers have learned the technical vocabulary (all of which is in an unabridged dictionary), this is one of the easiest of the scholarly books on motivation suitable for student reading.

GLASSER, WILLIAM. *Schools without Failure.* New York: Harper & Row, 1969. Glasser offers us here a highly readable prescription for school reform. Many of his ideas are controversial, but he is always provocative. Glasser appears to fit somewhat within the cognitive-field framework.

GOBLE, FRANK. *The Third Force: The Psychology of Abraham Maslow, A Revolutionary New View of Man.* New York: Pocket Books, 1971. A highly readable explanation of Maslow's system. Maslow rejected both Freudian and behavioristic views of the nature of human nature and struck out in a "third" direction. The "fourth" direction would be cognitive-field psychology which Maslow either rejected or did not understand.

HALL, JOHN F. *Psychology of Motivation.* Chicago: Lippincott, 1961. This textbook, designed for upper division and graduate students, is interesting to sample in contrast to recent books on motivation. Hall is a behaviorist and his book gets us no farther than the experimental work surrounding the positions of Hull, Spence, and Skinner.

JONES, EDWARD, et al. *Attribution: Perceiving the Causes of Behavior.* Morristown, N.J.: General Learning Press, 1972. A collection of papers on the rationale and early research behind attribution theory. Perhaps the best introduction to the subject for student readers.

KELLEY, H. H. "Attribution Theory in Social Psychology." In D. Lewine (ed.), *Nebraska Symposium on Motivation.* University of Nebraska Press, 1967. On the nature and uses of attribution theory, by one of its leading theorists and practitioners.

KLAUSMEIER, HERBERT, et al. *Individually Guided Motivation,* 3d ed. Wisconsin Research and Development Center for Cognitive Learning, the University of Wisconsin, 1975. This is a simplified and down-to-earth manual for teachers and prospective teachers. Readers should check the "motivational principles" on p. 3 against other sources (such as the McClelland/Atkinson model) to note areas of disagreement.

KORMAN, ABRAHAM. *The Psychology of Motivation.* Englewood Cliffs, N.J.: Prentice-Hall, 1974. A comparatively short but very useful treatment of historical and comparative theories of motivation. Compare Korman's interpretations with those of Weiner (1972), cited below.

LESSINGER, LEON. *Every Kid a Winner.* Palo Alto, Ca.: Service Research Associates, 1970. One of the early and more impassioned pleas for installing accountability programs in every school.

LOGAN, FRANK A. *Fundamentals of Learning and Motivation,* 2d ed. Dubuque, Iowa: Brown, 1976. Logan is an example of a relatively pure behaviorist, and this short and comparatively readable book is a good entry into the behavioristic view for students of the late 1970s. Logan draws heavily from the experimentation of such well-known mechanistic psychologists as Hull, Miller, Pavlov, and Skinner.

MADSEN, K. B. *Modern Theories of Motivation: A Comparative Metascientific Study.* New York: Wiley, 1974. Madsen, of the Royal Danish School of Educational Studies, has written a book giving wide coverage to virtually every recognized theoretical position pertaining to motivation. If readers do not allow themselves to become confused by the space Madsen gives to semantics, this is one of the most readable and complete of the general treatments.

MARTIN, DON T., GEORGE E. OVERHOLD, and WAYNE J. URBAN. *Accountability in American Education: A Critique.* Princeton, N.J.: Princeton Book Company, 1976. Martin et al. criticize the accountability movement by exposing its underlying assumptions which are rarely stated by proponents of the idea.

MASLOW, ABRAHAM H. *Motivation and Personality,* 2d ed. New York: Harper & Row, 1970. Maslow's last treatment, prior to his death in 1970, of his concept of motivation.

MCCLELLAND, DAVID C., and R. S. STEELE. *Motivation Workshops: A Student Workbook for Experiential Learning in Human Motivation.* New York: General Learning Press, 1972. Designed for student use, this workbook is one of the easiest entries into McClelland's theory of motivation.

MONTAGU, ASHLEY. *The Nature of Human Aggression.* New York: Oxford University Press, 1976. Anthropologist Montagu here takes issue with Lorenz, Ardrey, and other ethologists on whether humans have an instinct for aggression. Montagu argues that they do not.

MURPHY, GARDNER. *Historical Introduction to Modern Psychology.* New York: Harcourt Brace Jovanovich, 1949. See annotation in Chapter 1.

NASH, R. J., and R. M. AGNE. "The Ethos of Accountability: A Critique." *Teachers College Record* 73, no. 3 (1972):357–370. A critique of the accountability movement written during the heyday of the movement.

SEAGOE, MAY V. *The Learning Process and School Practice.* Scranton, Pa.: Chandler, 1970. Chapters 2 through 6 offer a very simplified treatment of the theory and classroom use of motivation. Eclectic, but potentially useful. Easy to read.

WEINER, BERNARD (ed.). *Achievement Motivation and Attribution Theory.* Morristown, N.J.: General Learning Press, 1974. Although technical, this book is one of the best available on its subject. Reports on research completed and in progress on attribution theory as related to motivation theory and as viewed by several cognitive theorists.

WEINER, BERNARD (ed.). *Cognitive Views of Human Motivation.* New York: Academic Press, 1974. Papers presented during a symposium at the annual convention of the American Association for the Advancement of Science. Although these papers present views of motivation that are basically cognitivist, they vary considerably in basic assumptions. The first paper, by Robert C. Bolles, on the history of cognitive psychology departs from more conventional treatments by insisting that most psychological views called "mechanistic" contain a larger cognitive than mechanistic component. Bolles is particularly bothered by those who place Hull in the mechanistic camp.

WEINER, BERNARD. *Theories of Motivation from Mechanism to Cognition.*

Chicago: Markham, 1972. Probably the most useful book for students on the history of theories of motivation. Written from the viewpoint of a cognitive-field psychologist. Makes a sharp distinction between mechanistic psychology and what the present book refers to as humanistic psychologies.

WILSON, EDWARD O. *Sociobiology: The New Synthesis.* Cambridge: The Belknap Press of Harvard University Press, 1975. Wilson, the central figure in sociobiology, offers some provocative ideas about human nature. See especially chapter 27.

Chapter 6
HOW DOES HUMAN BIOLOGY CONTRIBUTE TO HUMAN PSYCHOLOGY?

Readers may wonder why we have included a chapter with a biological orientation in an educational psychology text. There are several reasons. Educational psychology has always drawn rather heavily from related subjects ranging from philosophy to medicine. The subject matters integrated into educational psychology at any given time hinge largely on what is happening in the numerous subject areas that have something to offer educational psychologists.

New developments have made human biology one of the most dynamic fields of inquiry in the 1970s. This dynamism is virtually certain to continue beyond the 1980s particularly in that branch of human biology that we refer to as *neurobiology,* also aptly named the "brain sciences." Its numerous contributions to educational psychology include applications to motivation, development, and learning.

We have placed this chapter at the end of Part I largely because it makes some fundamental contributions to motivation. It should also be seen as containing basic background material in neurobiology that will help students study the rest of the book, and of no less importance, themselves.

WHAT IS THE PRESENT STATE OF HUMAN BIOLOGY?

Human biology, particularly neurobiology, has undergone striking changes since 1950. Until the twentieth century, most psychologists had tried to learn about mind by studying the physiology of the body. As soon as a somewhat modern microscope was invented, study of the central nervous system became popular, but until the 1950s no significant breakthroughs were made—particularly in discovering the relation between nerve cell functioning and thoughts and feelings.

Trying to derive psychology from physiology had pretty much come to a dead end by the beginning of the twentieth century. So, most psychologists began seeking ways to pursue the study of psychology without reference to the physical body. Mechanistically inclined psychologists found their niche in the study of overt behavior—not so much human behavior but the behavior of those laboratory animals that were assumed to function much like humans—rats, cats, dogs, guinea pigs.

Humanistic psychologists sought to study mind directly by prying into how people thought and felt. From their strivings emerged various cognitive psychologies. But cognitivists, like behaviorists, shied away from bringing the affairs of the body into their research.

But now human biology is undergoing a revolution, and we are finding out undreamed-of things about the central nervous system. A time has again arrived when affairs of the body merit the attention of serious psychologists.

What Is the New Biology?

Although it is evident to biologists that biology has been in a revolutionary state since about 1950, most people are not biologists. We will therefore indicate a few of the most significant changes that we associate with the new biology.

THE TREND TOWARD HUMANISM

Since we define and discuss humanism in Chapter 1, we will treat briefly only some of its biological applications here. Historically, humans were not considered a desirable subject of biological inquiry. They were regarded as something more than animals, even though they did consist of living tissue. The study of the human body was largely confined to the field of physiology. Biology, unlike physiology, is much more interested in the *why* of things. Humanistic biology places human beings at the center of such study.

Just as mechanistic biology steered away from the issue of purposiveness in nature, humanistic biology assumes and welcomes the notion that most animal species, particularly humankind, act out of a purposiveness born of animals trying to satisfy their needs.

DEVELOPMENT OF ORGANISMIC BIOLOGY

Organismic biology is in part an offshoot of Gestalt psychology, which focuses on wholes rather than parts of life forms, and says in effect that "the whole is greater than the sum of its parts." Perhaps the most prominent advocate of organismic biology was the late Ludwig von Bertalanffy. His position can be summarized under three propositions:[1]

1. Life Is a "System" Rather Than a Collection of Cooperating Parts. To state the idea differently, life is characterized by organization—an interdependence of parts and some kind of coordinating agency. Further, a living organism is a "system of systems." That is, a single cell is a system in itself, although it may be controlled by the organ of which it is a part.

2. Life Is Dynamic Rather Than Static. Life is purposive in the sense that it tries to maintain and better itself and its environment. Its fundamental pose is "activity, exploration, movement." Life does not wait for environmental stimuli to impinge upon it and thus excite it to action.

3. Life Is Interactive Rather Than Reactive. Since the fundamental orientation of an organism is toward exploration and manipulation of its environment, it is unlike a slot machine, which is passive until someone pulls the lever. On the other hand, life forms are modified by environment; living is a two-way process in which a life form and its environment exert simultaneous influences upon each other.

Organismic biology has achieved a great deal of factual support within neurobiology and is no longer considered a mere hypothesis or tentative theory. Neurobiologists live by it. But biologists with other specialties are also increasingly adopting life-systems theory.

What Is Molecular Biology?

Historically, biology has proceeded through three main stages: (1) the focus was first on what could be seen with the unaided human eye; (2) new worlds of information were then opened to investigation by the invention of the ordinary microscope; and (3) even more fantastic worlds of information were opened to investigation by the invention of the electron microscope and other instrumentation designed to explore even the smallest molecules.

But molecular biology involves a great deal more than study of very small particles. Fundamentally, molecular biology has come to focus on the study of DNA, the nucleic acid of which the genes are composed, and RNA, a related nucleic acid that manufactures proteins under the directions of DNA molecules. Since the genes contain the code or set of abbreviated specifications that is at the center of the process of life, molecular biologists are searching for answers as fundamental as the nature of life itself. One of the chief technical problems confronting them is that of adequate seeing. We now describe some ways in which the problem of seeing has been met.

• *The Ordinary Light Microscope.* The first light microscopes came into use in the late seventeenth and early eighteenth centuries. Anton van Leeuwenhoek (1632–1723) invented a simple single-lens micro-scope. It is a fair guess that van Leeuwenhoek's microscope was fairly powerful since under the right conditions it permitted observation of average-sized bacteria. Magnified 1000 diameters, an average bacteria appears the size of a sharpened pencil point. The best of today's light microscopes can magnify either living or dead biological material about 2500 diameters. This limitation is imposed by the wave length of the visible light spectrum, and nothing can be done to make the light microscope a more powerful instrument.

 • *The X-Ray Photograph.* Based on the discovery of the x-ray in 1895 by Wilhelm Konrad Roentgen (1845–1923), the x-ray photograph is too familiar to require description. Readers may not be aware, however, that x-rays are only one five-thousandth of the length of visible light rays and therefore potentially capable of producing images with much greater detail than the light microscope. It is the shortness of the wave length that gives x-rays their "see-through" property.

 • *The X-Ray Scanner.* The x-ray scanner developed in the 1960s has become a powerful aid to medicine and tissue study generally. The scanner takes thousands of x-ray pictures very rapidly, each focused on tissue slightly farther from the machine. The pictures are then assembled by computer into a single picture that has three-dimensional qualities.

 • *The Transmission Electron Microscope.* First developed in the 1920s, the electron microscope "sees" with beams of electrons. Because of the extremely small diameter of an electron, the most advanced of these instruments can magnify an object about 20 million diameters. The electron microscope has made "seeable" for the first time objects never seen before—viruses, molecules, genes, and atoms only about four billionths of an inch in diameter. The disadvantages of the electron microscope are its size, cost, and the fact that it is used to examine only dead tissue.

 • *The Scanning Electron Microscope.* Invented about 1965, the elec-tron scanner has the advantage of providing three-dimensional images of living as well as dead organisms and tissues. The image of an object viewed with a scanner can be projected on a TV-like screen. As early as 1957, Nobel laureate Richard Feynman of the California Institute of Technology, referring to the electron microscope, said "It is a strange world in which new laws apply. Up to now man has been blind."[2]

How Can We See "Through the Mind's Eye"?

It is now possible to teach people to "read" what is going on inside them and to a greater or lesser degree voluntarily control it. This is done through biofeedback training (BFT). Although in some respects BFT has taken on cultish aspects and has drawn in unknowledgeable lay practitioners, there is an authentic biofeedback movement. One of the most impressive researchers in biofeedback is Barbara Brown. In his foreword to Brown's *New Mind, New Body,* Hugh Downs states her philosophical orientation and that of many of her co-workers:

> [authentic biofeedback research] cuts away the shackles of doctrinaire body-only behavioral attitudes, much as early twentieth-century physicists dismantled the rigid mechanical model of Newtonian reality, to replace it with the more versatile relativistic model of the universe.[3]

What Has the New Biology Accomplished?

Perhaps most biologists would agree that the first concrete biological discovery of revolutionary importance made by biologists in this century was the discovery of the structure and chemical make-up of DNA molecules. This milestone came in 1953.

Also fascinating is the new knowledge about how individuals can voluntarily control their own biological processes. In one passage of *New Mind, New Body,* Barbara Brown tells of being at the first meeting of the newly formed Biofeedback Research Society in 1969. After hearing several leaders in the field tell of mind-boggling accomplishments of human will, she tells us

> Then came the climax. The revelation, in all the true meaning of the word, that in some way the human mind, without even telling itself, could learn to control the electrical activity of a single [nerve] cell.
>
> I was, perhaps, more startled and more stunned than any layman ignorant of biological science. After a lifetime of studying the intricacies of man's body in both good functioning and bad, my memory banks of physiological, pathological, and biochemical information suddenly stalled. There was simply no scientifically explainable way in which man could learn to control a single cell of his body.[4]

HOW DO NEURONS FUNCTION?

Neurobiology centers upon the structure and function of nerve cells, the brain, and their ways of communication.

What Is the Basic Structure of a Nerve Cell or Neuron?

Although neurons are never exactly alike, each has three basic parts— cell body, axon, and dendrites. They are shown much oversimplified in Figure 6.1.

THE NEURON CELL BODY

The neuron cell body takes a variety of shapes and sizes. Like all living cells, it contains a nucleus that contains chromosomes, the genes of which contain coded instructions that allow them to play an "executive role." The chromosomes consist mainly of a complicated nucleic acid called DNA and another nucleic acid called RNA, which has the capacity to

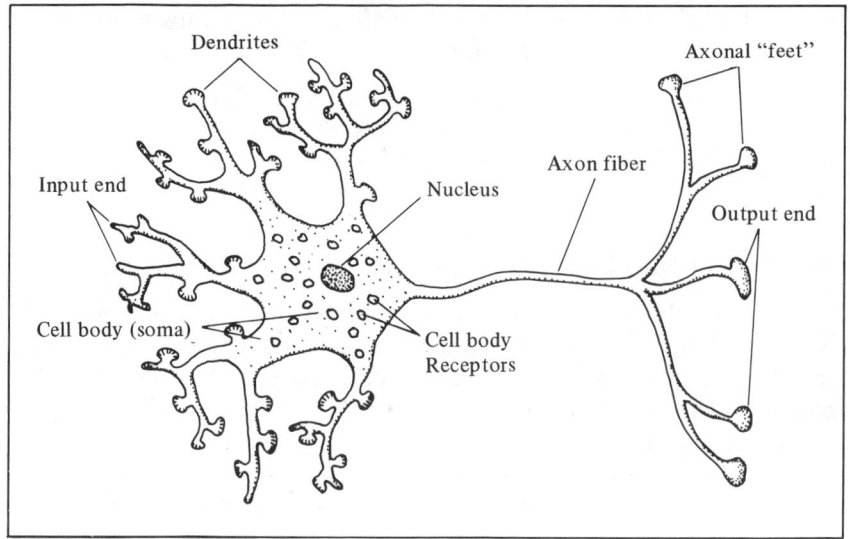

Figure 6.1   A simplified drawing of a neuron.

manufacture proteins on the command of the DNA. Each neuron has about 20 million molecules of RNA, each of which can manufacture any of 100,000 different proteins. The rest of the cell body contains a substance called soma. The surface of the cell body has as many as several thousand receptor—synapse—sites.

THE DENDRITES

The main receptors or receivers of messages are the dendrites—an extension of the cell body forming a kind of plume. Readers will note in Figure 6.1 the dendrites' innumerable branches. Each branch has tiny extensions. Under an electron microscope they appear like little blunt-ended stalks with a greater density of protoplasm at the end. These stalks (or twigs) are receptor sites for incoming messages. Their ends are potential synapse sites. A "close up" of an end section of a dendrite is shown in Figure 6.2. Note that the end of the dendrite fiber is also blunt and like the receptor stalks is a potential synapse site. Dendrites also have receptor sites that do not protrude except to form a low mound or knob. They are indicated in Figure 6.2 by small shaded and raised areas indicating the greater density of the tissue.

The dendrite fibers and cell body of a single neuron may have 80,000 synapse sites. Each neuron is capable of communicating with from 60,000 to 300,000 other neurons.

THE AXON

The axon is an elongated fiber that carries *outgoing* messages from the cell body to another neuron or group of neurons. Although small enough in diameter so that many millions can be carried in a bundle—as within the spinal cord—they may extend from the base of the brain to the feet. However, axons are usually about a millimeter to a few centimeters in length.

How Do Neurons Communicate?

Neurons do not quite touch one another. However they have a way of getting messages across the small gaps between them. The point at which one neuron can receive messages from adjacent neurons is called a *synapse*.

It is now clear that neurons perform many more functions than the simple sending of messages. A neuron is highly complex, both in structure and functioning. Individual neurons, or collections of communicating neurons, are decision-making entities and more.

An axon typically branches out into a number of fibers, the ends of which are little bulblike structures relatively flat on the terminal side. This little "foot" comes into proximity with the receptor sites on either the dendrites or cell bodies of the next neuron in the chain. Axons can carry messages only from the cell to which they belong toward another receptor. The axons of *motor neurons* link directly with a muscle, controlling the muscle's actions.

How Are Neurons Yes-No Organs?

Neural messages travel at speeds of up to about 900 miles per hour. When a neuron cell body sends a message to its axon, it is said to *fire*. A neuron ordinarily is constantly bombarded with messages from other neurons. Some messages say, in effect, "fire." Others say in effect, "don't fire." Each neuron is thus in a situation of conflict, but only when the number of fire and don't fire messages are about equal. If the messages to fire outnumber the inhibitory messages, the neuron fires. If the in-

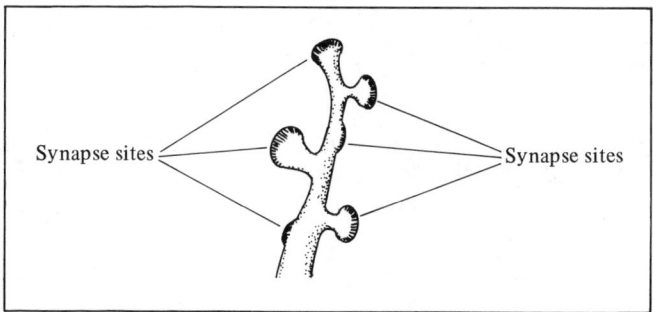

Figure 6.2   End section of a dendrite.

hibitory messages outnumber the encouraging messages, the neuron refuses to fire. It may also refuse to fire from apparent exhaustion, or may fire spontaneously without any urging from other neurons. It is speculated that each neuron in the body is to some degree an independent agent with "a mind of its own." In any case, a neuron either fires or it does not. We therefore refer to neurons as *yes-no organs*.

When a neuron fires, it is an ion (an atom with an electrical charge) that is fired. A fired ion is said to be a pulse (or impulse). The force of firing is always the same, and for a given neuron, every ion fired travels along the axon at the same speed. A number of ions fired in succession converts these fired ions into a coded message. Firing is analogous to the periodic firing of a machine gun. The number of ions in successive bursts is the message.

Figure 6.3 shows part of a neuron with its axonal input connections from other neurons. Although highly simplified, one gets some idea from the figure of the complexity of neural connections.

How Does Synaptic Transmission Work?

It is through synaptic transmission that neurons communicate with one another. A synapse is the narrow gap between the axonal foot and the dendritic or cell body receptor. This gap is usually called the *synaptic cleft*. It is about forty-billionths of an inch wide and can be seen clearly only under high magnification. Figure 6.4 shows the synaptic cleft between an axonal foot and a dendritic receptor stalk.

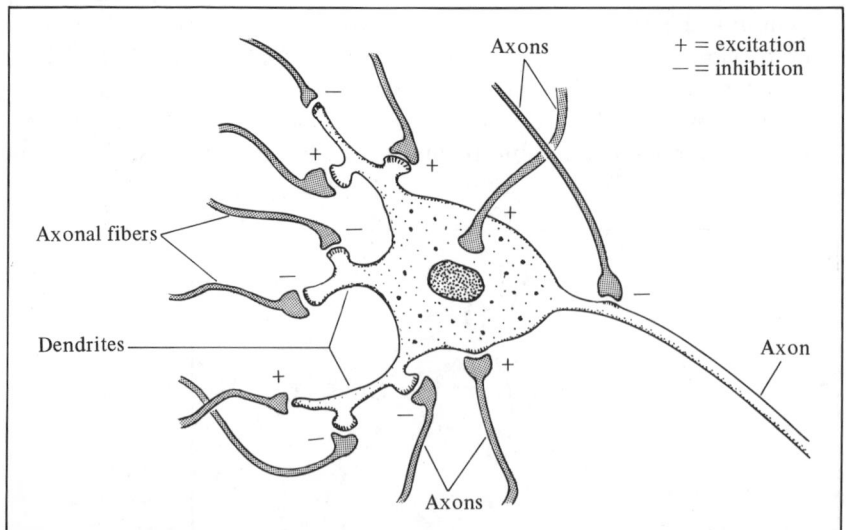

Figure 6.3   Neuron linked with excitatory and inhibitory axons.

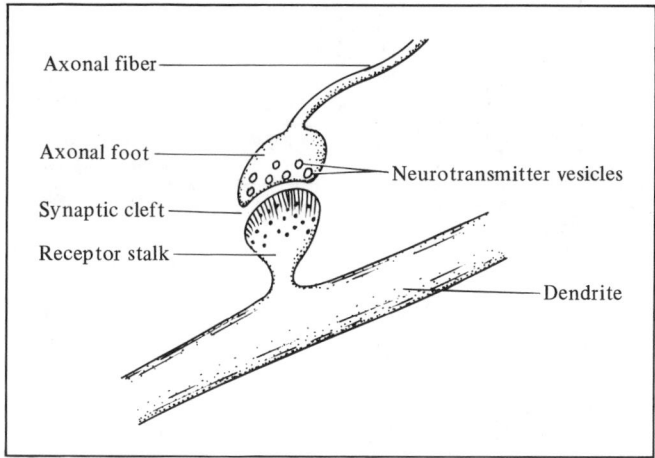

Figure 6.4   Synaptic site.

• *The Axonal Foot and Presynaptic Membrane.* The presynaptic membrane covers the outer end of the axonal foot. It can open and thus let chemicals inside the foot escape or it can refuse to. Vesicles within the foot look like little balloons. They contain one of several complex chemicals, all of which are potential carriers of messages across the cleft.

• *Receptors and Postsynaptic Membrane.* The dendritic or cell body receptor sites are also covered by a membrane with variable porosity. When excited, the postsynaptic membrane becomes porous and receptive to the admission of neurotransmitter fluids.

• *The Transmission Process.* When a sufficient number of ionic pulses reach the axonal foot to surpass its threshold level, the vesicles burst and the fluid droplets sprayed into the synapse becomes carriers in "piggyback" fashion of the ions that constitute the message. (See Figure 6.5.) These droplets have the quality of being able, in effect, to say to the postsynaptic membrane, "Let us in" or "Keep us out." If the postsynaptic membrane is not excited, no message gets through to the next neuron in the chain; if excitement occurs, the message gets through. Whether the next neuron in the chain fires depends on whether the total excitation messages being received by hundreds or thousands of synaptic receptors exceed the total inhibitory messages.

How Do Neurons "Think," Singly or in Groups?

Although very little is known about the biology of thinking, contrary to the simplistic "reflex arc" concept with its analogy to an automatic telephone system, it does seem highly probable, given our present knowledge of neurons, that they function as decision-making organs. Most of us now take for granted that it is the brain that "thinks" for us, and can override

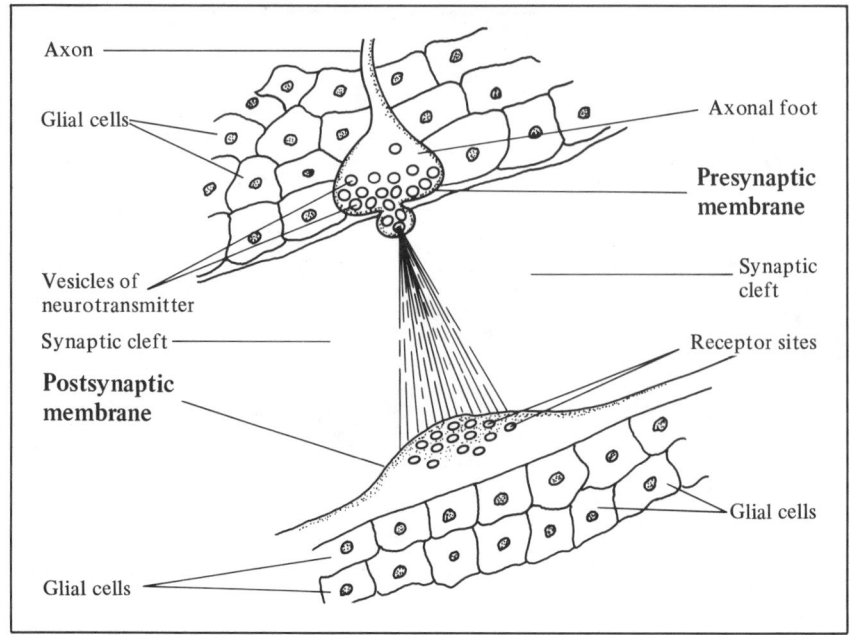

Figure 6.5   Synaptic transmission.

the "thoughts" of any spinal cord or peripheral nerve centers. We even think that the cerebral cortex is the executive of the brain. However, with the extraordinarily slender and sensitive censors that we now have to pick up minute voltages and that can be guided by x-ray to a single neuron inside the body, we can no longer take for granted the idea that the executive functions of neurons are only in the head. We know that individual neurons fire spontaneously, that neurons fire in groups of all sizes up into the millions or billions, and that in many instances most neurons in a group will fire "yes's" while others fire "no's" and vice versa. Hence, it is not an unreasonable hypothesis to suggest that we think "all over."

How Do Sensory Neurons Function?

There are many kinds of neurons in the human body, but two basic types—sensory and motor—are of primary interest to us here. Sensory neurons pick up and transmit to the cord or brain, or both, stimuli that arise from either outside or within the body. A pin prick to the skin tends to excite one or more sensory neurons which carry the information to the cord and usually to the brain. Information that can be processed and reacted to in the cord does not necessarily reach the brain, but all sensory impulses have the potential of reaching the brain via fibers in the cord. The more meaning a sensory message has to the total organism, the more likely it is to reach the cerebral cortex. In many situations, it appears that sensory neurons themselves choose, from all the available sensations, which ones to ignore and which ones to report to the brain.

A good example of this is the operation of sensory nerves in the retina of the eye. Some of the original research on the neural process of seeing has been done with frogs. Blakemore tells us, for example, that in the eye of the frog there are at least 100 million visual receptors. These visual neurons do not record everything in the visual field. They record selectively. They act as if in a cooperative way they were searching for meaning in the visual field. Meaning in this case involves relating three factors—the content of the present visual field, the past experience, and the present purposes of the animal. This same search for meaning by the retinal neurons has been proved to exist in frogs, cats, and monkeys, and it is assumed that even more sophisticated searches for meaning occur in the human eye.[5]

The selectivity of the visual neurons has been known for several years. In a special issue of *Saturday Review* we find this statement:

> Neurons are more than simple repeaters of the information they receive. . . . The process of passing on information about only certain select aspects of the stimulus and throwing out the rest is feature extraction, *presumably* saving those features of the stimulus that are important for the brain to receive.[6]

Blakemore sums up this phenomenon by saying "the eye has a language for its soliloquy to the brain. It speaks in symbols that define the important features of the visual scene."[7] According to presently available evidence, other sensory organs also search for meaning. If they cannot find it, they remain mute.

How Do Motor Neurons Function?

Motor neurons control the muscular activities of the body. It now seems apparent that they too react selectively to signals issued by the spinal cord or the brain. In the case of some signals to act, they simply stall. In other cases they issue orders to act. Classical examples of this have been derived from states of human hysteria: a leg may refuse to work no matter how insistent the cortex is in demanding it to. Just where the stalling occurs in the neural chain we do not know.

WHAT DO WE KNOW ABOUT THE STRUCTURE AND FUNCTIONS OF THE HUMAN BRAIN?

The human brain weighs, on the average, about three pounds or 1500 grams. The writers of one article tell us, however, that "they are a mighty three pounds—perhaps the most highly organized three pounds of matter in the known universe."[8]

What Are the Major Parts of the Brain?

Figure 6.6 is a simplified drawing of the left half of the brain as seen from the outside. The right half would appear virtually identical from the outside, except reversed. All that can be seen from the outside is the *cerebral cortex* (cortex means outer layer, in this case about one-tenth of an inch thick), a part of the *cerebellum,* and the lower *brain stem,* which is actually the upper end of the spinal cord. The cortex is extremely convoluted with many folds, ridges, and valleys.

Each half of the brain is called a hemisphere. They are connected by a thick bundle of nerve fibers. This bundle is called the *corpus callosum* and contains approximately 200 million axonal fibers, suggesting a very large amount of communication between the two hemispheres. Figure 6.7 depicts the brain from above. The two hemispheres are drawn unrealistically separated to show the location and relative size of the corpus callosum.

The human brain contains about 100 billion cells. About 10 billion of these are neurons. The remaining 90 billion are *glial cells* that support and hold the neurons in place, insulate the neurons from each other except at functional points of contact, and provide the surroundings for blood vessels that bring oxygen and glucose to the brain.

Since the brain has so large a number of parts, we describe only those of the greatest importance. Beginning at the bottom of the brain, we will work upward. The *brain stem* (old brain) is just above where the spinal cord attaches to the brain. Next up on the brain stem is the *midbrain.* The stem mediates "gut" reactions—those most essential for survival in any species of animal, such as eating and mating.

The *limbic brain* is almost in the center of the brain and is closely

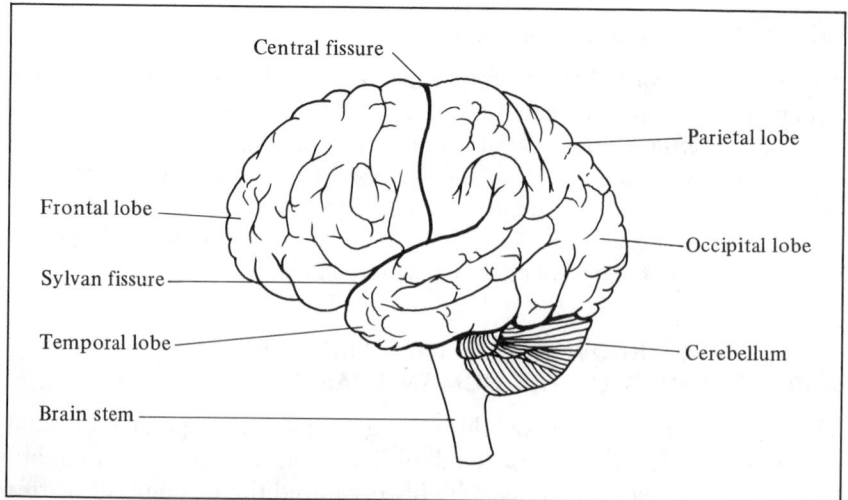

Figure 6.6   Side view of brain.

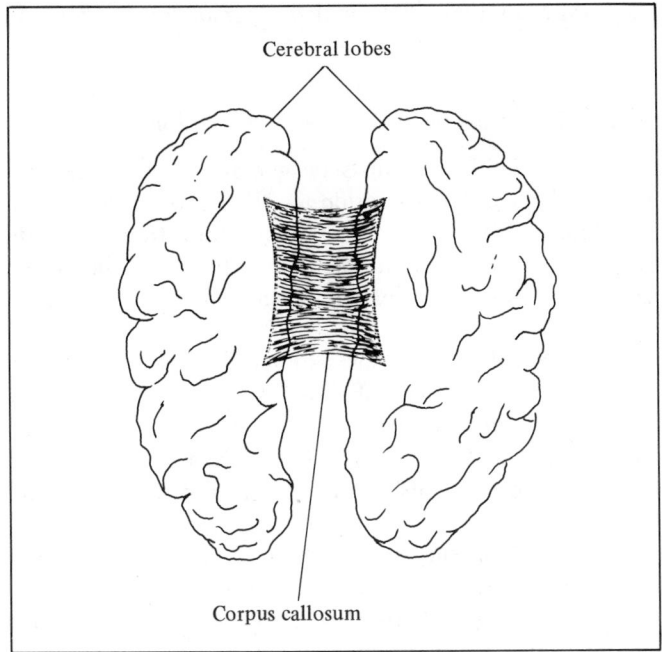

Figure 6.7   Hemispheres pulled apart to reveal corpus callosum.

associated with the sense of smell and taste. The limbic brain is involved in emotional behavior and regulates the *autonomic nervous system.*

The *cerebellum,* or *hindbrain,* is located under the rear of the cerebrum (see Figure 6.1). Like the cerebrum, it is divided into two apparently identical hemispheres. The cerebellum is a passageway that carries signals back and forth from the cerebrum to all parts of the body. It also performs the executive functions of keeping brain and body muscles working together. It also plays a crucial role in seeing, hearing, and general muscular control.

The *cerebrum* is the dominant part of the human brain. It provides us with the capacity to speak, learn, remember, reason abstractly, and carry on whatever other functions that might be labeled "higher thought processes." The critical part of the cerebrum is its outer layer, the *cortex,* which contains hundreds of millions of neurons. The cortex is a relatively large organ: if removed from the cerebrum and flattened out, it would more than cover a card table.

In the brain stem, neural fibers cross over so that the left brain controls the right side of the body, and the right brain controls the left side of the body. For reasons not understood, about 94 percent of people are so-called left-brain dominant and the remaining 6 percent are so-called right-brain dominant. Brain hemisphere dominance can usually be noted at a glance: left brain dominance makes a person right-handed and right-footed, while right brain dominance makes a person left-handed and left-footed.

Does the Brain Work Piecemeal or in Generalized Fashion?

Brain scientists tend to be either localists or generalists. Localists feel there is a great deal of local specialization in the parts of the brain, including the cerebrum and its cortex. Generalists think that the brain functions as a single unit. Those brain scientists who think that brain functions are somewhat but not entirely localized may be called *semilocalists*.

Many neurobiologists think the right and left halves of the brain play quite different roles in the control of thought, emotions, and bodily activity generally. One leading promoter of this idea is a well-known localist brain surgeon Roger W. Sperry of the California Institute of Technology.[9] Other major proponents are Robert E. Ornstein and Paul Baker.[10]

A most revealing kind of surgery, leading to knowledge of the specialization of each hemisphere, is that which severs completely the corpus callosum—the neural link of the two halves of the brain. This surgery has been done on a considerable number of persons who had severe epilepsy and were steadily getting worse. Severing the corpus callosum seems not only to reduce greatly the intensity of epileptic fits, but in some cases to eliminate them entirely. At the same time, although the subjects involved may be able to cope fairly well and even find work they can do skillfully, their personalities are quite changed.

Sperry says of people whose left and right brain had been disconnected:

> Everything we have seen so far indicated that the surgery has left these people with two separate minds, that is two separate spheres of consciousness. What is experienced in the right hemisphere seems to be entirely outside the realm of awareness of the left.[11]

This carries localism about as far as it can go; not only is each brain hemisphere divided into discrete areas of control, but the two hemispheres have little to do with one another—they are barely on "speaking terms."

LEFT BRAIN

The left brain, to quote Sperry, has a virtual monopoly in being "highly verbal, mathematical, performing with analytic, symbolic, sequential logic."[12] The left brain is analogous to a computer. It does most of the work in an advanced industrial society. It is called superior because its skills fit those needed in today's technological world.

RIGHT BRAIN

With respect to the right brain, Sperry tells us that it is "spatial and mute, performing with a synthetic-perceptual and mechanical kind of information processing that cannot be simulated by computers."[13] By being spatial, Sperry means that the right brain has a feel for shapes and forms. It innervates drawing, painting, making music, writing poetry, and sculpting. By muteness, Sperry means that the right brain cannot verbalize in linear, logical fashion.

Among reputable neurobiologists, there are a considerable number who feel that localists like Sperry are at best only half right. Such localization as can be demonstrated may be a result of learning. Dr. Gabriel Horn, a lecturer in anatomy at the University of Cambridge (England) says, "The experimental evidence demonstrates quite clearly . . . that persisting changes in the morphological and functional properties of neurones occur as a result of experience."[14] Other critics of the localist conception of brain functioning include Daniel Goleman, E. Roy John, Keith Killam, David Kleinman, Daniel Ruchkin, and Paul Eastman. Goleman, a generalist, tells us that the brain does not work like a printed circuit; it is like a symphony orchestra.[15]

John says, referring to localism,

> I think this view is only partly right. My research leads me to believe that vast regions of the brain are involved in every thought process, although some parts are more involved than others.[16]

What Do We Know About the Biology of Memory and Recall?

There has been a great deal of research on the neurobiological basis of remembering and forgetting. But this problem remains one of the more puzzling that neurobiologists have tackled. Earlier in the century it was thought that the memory of an event becomes encoded in a self-perpetuating electrical circuit in the brain called an *engram*. But the eminent Harvard neuropsychologist Karl Lashley (1890–1958) spent 30 years trying to discover engrams in the brains of trained rats without success. In a famous paper Lashley presented in 1950 he said "I sometimes feel in reviewing the evidence on localization of the memory trace, that the necessary conclusion is that learning just is not possible."[17]

What Lashley did was to teach rats a skill so well that they could remember it for weeks or months afterward. He then performed brain surgery on the rats, removing first one part of cortex and then another. He found he could remove any part of the cortex without destroying memory. He finally concluded that the cerebral hemispheres exhibit a sort of "mass action" in the recording of experiences. Starting as a localist in the matter of memory, Lashley ended up becoming a generalist.

All evidence points to the cortex generally as being the center of memory, but as yet no one knows how. Even if engrams exist, the research of Lashley and others suggests there must be some other way of retaining memory. This hypothesis led to the development of chemical theories of memory storage. If a memory can be encoded in a protein molecule manufactured especially for this memory, we have the beginning of a possibly viable theory of memory. The search began for a chemical that, taken internally, would affect memory.

It remained for a Dutch pharmacologist, David DeWeid of the University of Utrecht, to find a natural chemical, one manufactured by the experimental animals themselves that would enhance memory with no ill effects. He came up with a complicated hormone, ACTH, which tends to fix memories in animals for short to intermediate intervals. By now it seemed conclusive that chemicals were in some way related to the retention of experience.[18]

Since 1975 some new plausible theories about memory and recall have been formulated with some supporting evidence. One of the better reporters of what has happened is the previously cited University of Cambridge professor, Colin Blakemore. Blakemore tells us that

> Memory, its physical structure, is an unsolved challenge. It is perhaps, the *central* question, rather like the problem of the structure of DNA . . . for molecular biology and genetics. But theories about the nature of memory have still not really progressed beyond the stage of description through analogy.[19]

Finding the biological basis of memory and recall would indeed be one of the greatest scientific breakthroughs of all time. Neurobiologists are pursuing the problem with vigor, and in a decade or so may solve it.

What Is the Mind-Body Problem?

The mind-body problem, stated in its most basic terms, is whether the words "mind" and "body," or "mind" and "brain," mean the same thing or whether mind is a mysterious "something" that directs the brain to do what it does. If we assume that mind is an independent entity that tells the brain what to tell the rest of the body, then we are talking about *substantive mind theory,* often referred to as the *ghost in the machine* theory. Under this position the word mind is often used more-or-less interchangeably with soul or spirit. Adherents of this dualist position think that there is a fundamental difference between a free-flowing mind and a machinelike body.

Some neurobiologists of this century have used the words body (or brain) and mind interchangeably. This position is known as *monism.* When Blakemore entitles his book *Mechanics of the Mind* or Nigel Calder uses for his major book the title *The Mind of Man,* or when Steven Rose uses the title, *The Conscious Brain,* these men are all assuming that brain *is* mind.

But some twentieth century neurobiologists find the working of the human body inexplicable without assuming some sort of mysterious controlling force. Some of the most prominent among this century's neurobiologists who have switched from monism to dualism include C. S. Sherrington, E. D. Adrian, John S. Eccles, and Wilder Penfield.

Dualists cannot prove empirically that they are right, but then neither can monists. It is an issue of long standing, with its roots in the ancient world. Dualists of the 1970s find it pretty hard to explain away what seems like an integral relation between mind and brain. We can change our bodily states by how we think and feel, and our thoughts and feelings often appear to be inextricably related to bodily states.

We next present a list of some ways in which the mind-body problem has been "solved," so that readers will realize the effort that has gone into trying to explain what on the surface seems like a mind-brain dichotomy.

1. *Interactionism.* According to this view, mind and body are separate but engage in interactive relations with one another. That is, mind affects what the body does, but bodily states equally affect the way mind functions. The nature of the interactive mechanism—the way interaction happens—is not known. The word interaction in this context does not mean the same as the cognitive-field psychologists' concept of interaction between a self and its perceived environment.

2. *Parallelism.* This position also holds that humans are composed of two parts, mind and body; however, its exponents argue that body and mind do not interact—rather they go their own separate but parallel ways. This view eliminates the possibility of conflict between mind and body even as it leaves a host of other problems unanswered.

3. *Double Aspect Theory.* Slightly more complicated is the notion that body is mind when seen from one direction and that mind is body when viewed from another direction. So mind and body are both aspects of the same thing.

4. *Double Language Theory.* According to this position, mind and body are unitary but are differentiated by semantic problems. We use one kind of language to talk about bodily events and another kind of language to talk about mental events. If a new nondualistic language could be invented, then our talk about behavioral phenomena would not be couched in the dualistic terms of mind and body. Consequently some new words such as *psychophysical* and, still better, *psychosomatic* have been invented.

5. *Organismic Response Theory.* Persons who hold to this view think that mental processes are a distinctive kind of response made by individuals in the course of their interacting with their environment. That is to say, for example, that the language of behaviorism is appropriate and necessary if we assume that the environment is dominant and the person passive; and that the language of cognitive psychology is appropriate when the person exhibits purpose and at least partial free will and in so doing manipulates a passive environment somewhat to his or her own ends.

6. *Materialism.* This position, as we have indicated previously, holds that only that which is physical is real. Reality is limited to three-

dimensional solid or largely solid objects that can be seen, felt, tested, smelled, and so on, or to forces such as magnetism. Under this view, what is called mind does not exist, or if so, it is irrelevant clutter.

7. *Idealism.* This is the Platonic notion that the only genuine reality is mind, spirit, or soul. For the purposes of students the term would be more meaningul if spelled idea-ism.

8. *Mind as Functional Capacity of Organism.* This view parallels the position of cognitive-field psychologists. *Mind* is the functional capacity of an organism in a *psychologically interactive* situation to grasp and be guided by meanings.

Contemporary neurobiologists are very much interested in the mind-brain puzzle, and in a large sense, one of their fundamental purposes is to explain consciousness, thought, and feeling as centered in a function of the brain.

WHAT IS BIOFEEDBACK AND HOW DOES IT WORK?

This section is based primarily on the research of Barbara Brown who was mentioned earlier in the chapter. Her writing is lucid enough for an average student to read and she covers the field quite comprehensively.[20] Unlike many other biofeedback experimenters of the past decade, Brown is strikingly humanistic in her philosophical orientation. One of her foremost aims is to erase the distinction between mind and body. Hence, we commonly find the compound word mind-body in her writing. She tends to shy away from conditioning as a way of learning, although seeming to agree that under certain special circumstances conditioning, particularly B. F. Skinner's operant conditioning—reinforcement theory— may have a limited use. Both her major books have been widely read and in general highly praised.

Biofeedback as a means by which people can learn to "see" inside themselves is an aspect of the new biology. It does not require microscopy, but is nevertheless complementary to what we have treated previously in the chapter.

What Is Biofeedback?

Although the concept of feedback may be familiar enough to most readers, it is more complex than many people suppose. Its nature varies from one system to another, as noted below.

• *Feedback in a Strictly Mechanical System.* A simple example of this kind of feedback is a home furnace thermostat. The furnace heats the house to the desired temperature. At this point, feedback from the thermostat "tells" the furnace to stop burning. When the temperature drops below its setting, the thermostat "tells" the furnace to burn again.

This simple principle of feedback has many thousands of industrial applications.

   • *Feedback in a Hypothetical School Situation.* A teacher provides a task for students. If the students succeed, they are rewarded in some way, if only by a smile of approval. If the students fail they are not rewarded and may even be punished. In either case the teacher's response to the students' work provides feedback to the students. This system of feedback appears about as mechanical as the operation of the furnace thermostat.

   • *Experience as Feedback.* A purposive human being with a goal tries a hypothesized strategy to reach it. The person observes the results, which provide the feedback telling whether the judgment is good or bad. When people fail to reach a desired goal, they must choose whether to keep trying or turn their attention to something else; their choice will depend on the importance of the goal.

   • *Biofeedback.* Biofeedback refers to feedback within living systems. Living creatures of all kinds depend continuously on feedback from their external and internal environments to guide their behavior. To a large degree, this makes them self-regulating. In the case of a certain kind of experiment, T. George Harris, former editor of the magazine *Psychology Today,* referring to the work of Barbara Brown, has this to say.

> Body processes generate specific electrical waves. These can be measured by electronic sensors and reported by an indicator—often like the pointer on a speedometer. By watching the indicator we can follow what goes on inside us, anything from sphincter control to the firing of a single nerve in the brain.[21]

What Is Biofeedback Training (BFT)?

Biofeedback training is the method used to teach subjects how to exert maximum voluntary control over bodily functions formerly assumed to be always under the control of the autonomic nervous system. The aim of BFT is to help people learn to control their internal bodily phenomena on their own, without the use of any kind of electronic gadgetry.

   For most people, however, electrical gadgetry is essential in the beginning. The equipment consists basically of electrical sensors—small wires that can be pasted to any part of the body and carry the electrical current detected to an amplifier that steps up the voltage to a usable level. The current is filtered to eliminate the "noise" of unruly neurons firing erratically and to produce a clear electrical signal that can be attached to a variety of feedback indicators—lights or auditory signals.

   Just what other kinds of electronic equipment are connected with the system depends on what the experimenter and the subject want information about. If it is what kinds of brain waves are being emitted, an electroencephalogram (EEG) is used. If it is the voltage of electricity in the skin, investigators employ a device to measure the amount of current getting through the skin—the galvanic skin response (GSR). Muscle tension can be measured in much the same way.

How May Brain Waves Be Analyzed?

Brain scientists are now much more reserved about the measurement and interpretation of brain waves than they were even a few years ago. What is revealed on the EEG tape hinges on a number of variables including where on the head the electrodes are placed, the speed at which the EEG machine is operated, and the ever-changing thoughts and moods of the subject. Successive squiggles of the recording pen on the tape are rarely the same; what comes through is often pretty much of a jumble.

Brain waves are identified—according to their frequency measured by a unit named after its definer, H. R. Hertz, and abbreviated as Hz— in cycles per second as, 1 Hz = 1 cycle/second. Setting the boundaries of frequencies reflecting a particular wave has been fairly arbitrary. Four classes of brain waves that have been identified are: alpha (8 to 13 Hz), theta (3.5 to 6.5 Hz), beta (13 to 40 Hz), and delta (0.5 to 3 Hz).

• *Alpha Waves.* Alpha waves, the first to be identified, have medium frequencies and a relatively high voltage. They may vary from one person to another, however, and from one moment to the next in any person.

• *Theta Waves.* Theta waves are relatively low frequency rhythmic waves. They are relatively scarce, rarely being more than 5 percent of the total electrical pattern of the brain. They occur most frequently during drowsiness and dreaming. However, they also appear during wakefulness and are associated with recognition of something new in the environment (inner or outer) and with the sudden solution to problems—what is often called "Aha!" learning.

• *Beta Waves.* Nearly all waves with higher frequencies than alpha are called *beta waves.* Because of their low voltage, high frequency waves are difficult to identify; they often seem to be mixed with static from irregularly firing neurons. Beta waves are now considered significant because they are associated with alertness and concentrated mental activity, particularly abstract thought. The greater the frequency of beta waves (up to 40 Hz), the more likely they are to be associated with problem solving.

• *Delta Waves.* Delta waves appear on the tape as relatively long undulating smooth waves, usually single but sometimes in a series of four. They are almost exclusively associated with deep sleep and seem important mostly to verify living bodies.

How May Brain Wave Study Be Used?

As noted earlier, investigators can easily be fooled by what appears on the EEG tape. Problems in analyzing brain waves arise from their irregularity, deficiencies in recording equipment, and difficulty in documenting particular waves on tape. These problems, combined with lack of knowledge on composition, variation, and reactivity of components in typical EEG recording, have made brain wave researchers' analysis much more cautious than in the early 1970s.[22]

Despite these problems and others, Brown feels that brain wave research remains the most useful research instrument available in linking brain activity to specific mental and emotional states. Through biofeedback techniques, subjects can be taught to sustain a particular brain wave longer than otherwise so it can be studied better.

BFT is a diagnostic tool in medicine and education and a tool for psychological self-exploration, provided equipment and operator are sophisticated enough. Usually an EEG having alpha, but no beta, waves signals that the subject is awake and relaxed; this justifies its use in treating anxious and worried persons by increasing the output of alpha waves. Teaching people how to sustain alpha waves over a considerable period of time amounts to teaching them to "see inside themselves" or at least to have the tool to do so.

EXPERIMENTAL AND CLINICAL BIOFEEDBACK

Brown explains *experimental* biofeedback as employing rewards for "right performance" in relatively large numbers of matched subjects, and then calculating results statistically in terms of averages. In contrast with this, her approach to biofeedback is *clinical*. Of biofeedback work up to this time, Brown says

> The majority of psychologists working with alpha use the experimental designs of conditioned learning in which the alpha biofeedback is given as a reinforcement. . . . This "feedback signal" is often also supplemented by the reinforcement of verbal encouragement. The signals indicating satisfactory performance are post facto (almost posthumous).[23]

In Brown's context, clinical appears to mean that the subject receives minimal instructions (like "try to keep the light on") and is encouraged to take the time needed to ponder over what happened and why. No cues or instructions are given and there are no verbal rewards. The learner may not even regard success (keeping the light on) as an achievement, since the learner may not know that keeping the light on is an indication of alpha wave production. The learner will be told sometime later what the light signals.

Shortly after the learning session Brown asks a question such as: "How did you feel or what were you thinking about when the light came on?" and "How did you feel or what were you thinking when the light was not on?"

CHARACTERISTICS OF THE ALPHA STATE

When alpha waves predominate or at least show up frequently on the EEG tape, subjects typically report they were enjoying pleasant sensations—tranquility, lack of anxiety, general relaxation, and inward directedness. Also, all clinical reports to date indicate that this pleasant state of mind continues after training sessions.

If subjects are taught to produce more alpha through experimental conditioning techniques, they seem not to achieve the subjective satisfaction they do under the clinical approach; furthermore, such improvement as they may feel soon disappears. But when the clinical approach was used, subjects soon learned to turn on and off alpha states at will.

Brown tells us that

> The evidence that control, *voluntary* control, over brain wave activity can be developed is unequivocal. The intriguing aspect of learned control over alpha, or any physiologic activity, is that it cannot be proved to be a response to any specific situation or condition.[24]

She goes on to say:

> Except for my own publication, there has not been a single instance in which data has been provided that demonstrates subjects have learned to control alpha *without* the biofeedback signal, i.e., that they can consistently produce alpha upon demand, by intention. If biofeedback learning is indeed in the learning of voluntary control over physiologic functions, then it should be an absolute requirement that the control can be demonstrated in the absence of the feedback monitor.[25]

Why are so many neurobiologists interested in alpha waves, almost to the exclusion of other frequencies seen on the EEG tape? Alpha wave control seems to be the most practical means for persons to learn to study their inner selves.[26] Since alpha waves are relatively easy to detect because of their amplitude, persons who learn to turn on alpha at will have a ready means of assessing what is going on inside them.

It is an enticing hypothesis, with supporting evidence, that anyone who has achieved considerable voluntary control over bodily functions once thought to be governed exclusively by the autonomic nervous system, produces large amounts of alpha waves. For example, Zen meditation is almost always accompanied by a high component of alpha brain waves, and authentic yoga practitioners also show a high component of alpha.

WHAT ALPHA CONTROL CAN DO

Like Skinner with his ping pong playing pigeons, alpha waves can be used for stunts. If a subject who has learned to turn alpha wave production on and off at will is wired to an amplifier to step up the voltage from the brain—and if next in line is a filter to remove some overlapping brain waves and static and to emit only alpha—and if an integrator is attached to the whole hook-up to pull the bursts of alpha waves together, then the subject can at will produce a steady flow of alpha voltage.

To demonstrate that this voltage could be used to do something other than turn on a light of a given color, or produce a humming or clicking auditory signal, Brown brought into the lab a toy electric train.

Subjects who had had BFT and could produce alpha voltage at will, could start the train, control its speed, and stop it merely by getting into an "alpha state." Observers were impressed but

> What they didn't know, and I was too embarassed to reveal, was that I had a whole racing car set which I had arranged to operate from brain waves. Two people could be wired for brain wave recording and demonstrate their alpha wave control by racing their cars against each other, shooting the curves, plotting their track-crossing tactics, all in their heads and with their heads.[27]

LEFT-BRAIN RIGHT-BRAIN SYNCHRONY

It has been demonstrated that the right and left brains tend to produce different waves, but both include the alpha range. Brown speculates that people may be able to learn to produce the same alpha from each hemisphere. There is some empirical evidence for this hypothesis, but not enough to give it much support at this time. Brown's speculation includes the hypothesis that with sufficient education in alpha control, the left-brain right-brain dichotomy might be either reduced or eliminated. The tentative conclusion would seem to be that left-brain right-brain differences, as we have mentioned, are *learned* and through biofeedback training these differences might be unlearned. If this hypothesis can be confirmed it would force a revolutionary change in the thinking of the localists among neurobiologists.

HOW MAY BIOFEEDBACK BE USED THERAPEUTICALLY?

Learning to produce a high component of alpha and theta waves seems to have therapeutic value in the cases of various neuroses and psychoses. Alpha production has shown promise in helping drug addicts and people who suffer intractable pain, such as migraine headaches. Also, in many persons with colitis, alpha training has been helpful. Combining hypnosis and relaxation exercises with alpha biofeedback often produces better effects than biofeedback alone.

A common problem of people today is insomnia. Theta wave production, particularly, seems to reduce insomnia; if it does not put subjects fully to sleep, it promotes enough relaxation so that rest occurs.

Epileptics have their own distinctive brain wave patterns. If such persons can be taught to suppress these unwanted patterns—to better control alpha production and to control brain rhythms in the 12 to 16 Hz range—often their symptoms largely or completely disappear.

How May Biofeedback Reduce Stress and Muscular Tension?

Barbara Brown pushes the idea that stress (and resulting muscle tension) is behind many of the unwanted symptoms that both children and adults develop. In her latest book (*Stress and the Art of Biofeedback*) she places her heaviest emphasis on biofeedback directed toward relaxation of muscular tension.

Impulses carried by axonal fibers may terminate with a connection to a muscle. When impulses reach the muscle, the muscle contracts. But since most muscles of the body come in pairs, or two cooperating sets, the contraction of one muscle or a set requires the slackening of the opposing muscle or muscle set. This slackening occurs not because of messages sent to it by the central nervous system, but by an absence of messages. An absence of neuronal firing to a muscle reduces it to limpness. If the firing does not cease, we have two taut muscles "fighting each other." Under the ordinary circumstances of life, muscle tautness is never extreme or continuous; muscles contract only as much as is necessary to provide the desired movement.

Any situation—from a direct threat to a person's life to discomfort in a social situation—causes muscles to contract. This includes not only the large or small striated muscles (as in the arms or legs), but also the smaller smooth muscles that control internal organic functioning such as that of the glands and intestines. If a person is in a continuous state of stress, the continuous muscle tension associated with stress can have severely pathological effects. The degree of muscle tension is reported to the brain through neuronal chains, but such reports are often received at a subconscious level. Persons, then, are often not aware that their muscles are unnecessarily tense. Nor are they aware of the apparent fact that all muscular activity is ultimately controlled by the highest thought center—the cerebral cortex.

The problems caused by unruly muscles have been recognized for a long time, and programs for learning muscle relaxation have long been in existence. Two of the most popular of these are *autogenic training* and *progressive relaxation*. That they are both more-or-less effective seems to have been well confirmed, but as Brown tells us, "Both entail months, sometimes years, of relaxation practice."[28]

By pasting electrodes to the skin over key muscle sites, we can get a measure of how much tension is there and just where it is. The instrument used is the *electromyogram* (EMG); the program implemented is EMG biofeedback. Its advantage over the earliest programs for stress reduction is its speed. Even so, Brown recommends the use of all three methods of relaxation in conjunction where possible.

What Is EMG Biofeedback?

EMG biofeedback is the recorded pattern of muscle electrical activity. Electrical sensors are placed on the skin over "uptight" muscles, with a third electrode placed in a neutral spot for reference. After being amplified, the clear electrical signals are summarized and used to activate a visual or auditory signal for the subject. Brown asserts that EMG biofeedback is probably more useful in muscle control than any other biofeedback technique. The instrumentation is much simpler and learning to control muscle tension is easier than learning to control brain waves.

There is obviously an overlap here: brain wave biofeedback teaches a person body relaxation by bringing out the potential of the alpha state as a general relaxer. But if the same result can be achieved by EMG procedures more quickly and easily—and more cheaply—we should take it seriously. Theoretically, success with EMG training should help a person produce more alpha without need for the complicated electronic equipment necessary for brain-wave learning.

EMG biofeedback apparently is applicable not only in treating muscle tension but also in treating abnormal signals coming from the brain, such as those produced by emotional distress. Just how this works is not known, but one hypothesis is that a decrease in muscle tension alone shuts off tension-related signals going to the brain, so that the cortex will be less busy and can concentrate on resolving the emotional problems that produced the tension in the first place.

CONDITIONS FOR WHICH EEG AND EMG
BIOFEEDBACK MAY BE INDICATED

Among the disorders Brown lists as being helped by biofeedback are asthma, anxiety, depression, hyperactivity, learning disorders, muscle spasms, menstrual distress, and worry from social problems. She also makes a strong case for the curative effects of EMG relaxation training on headache, neuromuscular reeducation, and gastrointestinal problems.[29] Many of these and related problems require professional treatment. Only a tiny minority of schools are likely to have the sophisticated biofeedback equipment and personnel needed. However, teachers need to be aware that many conditions that interfere with motivation to learn in school may be helped by the new biology.

HOW MAY NEUROBIOLOGY AID IN MOTIVATING STUDENTS?

In this chapter, to a considerable extent we have been dealing with matters that are relatively new in that they are developments of this century, primarily of the 1960s and 1970s. The implications for human motivation are undoubtedly immense. This final section is probably more speculative than factual. However, we see no harm in speculation—up to a point—because it directs the thinking of readers forward and helps prepare them for fundamental changes very likely to arrive in the 1980s.

Where May the New Philosophical Orientation in Biology Lead Us?

Findings in neurobiology may force changes in both educational philosophy and educational psychology. Assuming that the already conspicuous findings in the brain sciences will continue apace with still more effective equipment and techniques, we are likely to get a far more humanistic psychology of education than we have had previously.

What Is the Promise of New Instrumentation?

It may be possible to find the biological source of many, or even most, kinds of defects that now make students slow learners. It is almost certain that neurobiology will enable us to treat or excise individual neurons or neuron clusters that are causing trouble. We may learn ways of "patching up" malfunctioning neurons caused by injury and disease. Neural transplants, although apparently impossible now, in less than ten years may turn out to be less difficult than it was to put men on the moon. Will it be more difficult to insert artificial organs that can perform the function of neurons now missing or damaged than to manufacture artificial hearts—a line of research that shows more promise each year? Any repair that makes people function better should prove motivating.

What More May We Learn About the Left-Brain–Right-Brain Dichotomy?

As we have seen, various writers may have gone overboard in stressing the differences in function between cerebral hemispheres. If they have exaggerated this difference, it may lead to major changes in school curriculums. Present critics of the left-brain–right-brain emphasis are now arguing that most present-day schools stress subjects controlled by the left brain and almost entirely neglect functions performed best by the right brain. A redress of the present imbalance—if it exists—would lead to much more emphasis on humanistically slanted courses and presumably fewer motivational problems.

Where May More Voluntary Control of Bodily Functions Take Us?

According to present theory, most of what goes on inside us occurs automatically. Barbara Brown and hundreds of other biofeedback practitioners are teaching people burdened with a variety of aches and pains that do not stem from serious disease or injury to eliminate them voluntarily. Students that do not feel well find it hard to become motivated. At any given time some proportion of any school population will have headaches, sprains, muscle spasms, and the like. As indicated earlier in the chapter, marked progress has already been made in techniques that teach people to reduce stressful pain.

How Does Purposiveness Relate to Motivation?

Humanistic neurobiologists such as Brown believe that most or all members of the animal kingdom are motivated by feelings of purposiveness.

This is so obvious as to be trite, but it still remains an issue among psychologists as to whether humans tend toward autonomy or passivity. Many neurobiologists have apparently made their case for purposiveness.

Bertalanffy, in his day, made a strong case for all biological systems being actively purposive. The ability of neurons to play an executive function—as decision-making organs—is coming to be increasingly accepted. It appears to be a fact that we can exercise a large amount of control over the "once uncontrollable" autonomic nervous system. The ability of brain neurons to "learn" how to take over the functions lost by the destruction of other neurons is often astounding.

But among these and other reasons that we could name for purposive motivation, the most impressive appears to be feature extraction—that is, the tendency of animals, presumably including humans, to be able to sense in their environments only that which has meaning in relation to the animal's purposes, and to remain unaware of objects that lack such meaning. Thus, the neurobiologists have provided critical scientific support for the notion that humans and lower animals are motivated by having felt needs and seeking to satisfy them.

NOTES

[1] Bertalanffy's books include *Problems of Life: An Evaluation of Modern Biological Thought*, New York: Wiley, 1952; and *Perspectives on General Systems Theory*, Edgar Taschdjian (ed.), New York: Braziller, 1975.

[2] Quoted in Kenneth F. Weaver, "Electronic Voyage through an Invisible World," *National Geographic Magazine*, February 1957, p. 279.

[3] From Hugh Downs' foreword to Barbara Brown, *New Mind, New Body: Biofeedback: New Directions for the Mind*, New York: Harper & Row, 1974, p. xii.

[4] Barbara Brown, *New Mind, New Body*, p. 156.

[5] Colin Blakemore, *Mechanics of the Mind*, Cambridge University Press, 1977, pp. 86–91. Blakemore is one of the world's most noted neurobiologists.

[6] "A Layman's Guide to the Brain," *Saturday Review*, 9 August, 1975, p. 15.

[7] Blakemore, p. 86.

[8] Albert Rosenfeld and Kenneth W. Klivington, "Inside the Brain: The Last Great Frontier," *Saturday Review*, 9 August, 1975, p. 13.

[9] R. W. Sperry, "Left-Brain, Right-Brain," *Saturday Review*, 9 August, 1975, p. 30 ff.

[10] Robert Ornstein, "Right and Left Thinking," *Psychology Today*, May 1973, pp. 87–92; Paul Baker, "The Right Brain Is the Dreamer," *Psychology Today*, November 1976, pp. 66–68.

[11] Quoted in Blakemore, p. 159.

[12] Sperry, pp. 30–32.

[13] Ibid.

[14] Gabriel Horn, "Experience and the Central Nervous System," *Intellectual Digest*, 1 September, 1971, p. 71. See also Gabriel Horn and Robert A. Hinde (eds.), *Short-term Changes in Neural Activity and Behavior*, Cambridge University Press, 1970.

[15] Daniel Goleman, "A New Computer Test of the Brain," *Psychology Today,* May 1976, pp. 44–48.
[16] E. Roy John, "How the Brain Works—a New Theory," *Psychology Today,* May 1976, pp. 48–52.
[17] Quoted in Blakemore, p. 103.
[18] Maya Pines, "Speak Memory: The Riddle of Recall and Forgetfulness," *Saturday Review,* 9 August, 1975, pp. 18–19.
[19] Blakemore, chapter 4, especially pp. 93–122.
[20] Barbara Brown, *New Mind, New Body;* "The Anatomy of a Phenomenon: Me and BFT," *Psychology Today,* August 1974—entire issue; "Biofeedback: An Exercise In 'Self Control,'" *Saturday Review,* 22 February, 1975, pp. 22–26; *Stress and the Art of Biofeedback,* with foreword by Hans Selye, New York: Harper & Row, 1977.
[21] T. George Harris, "Barbara Brown's Body: An Introduction," *Psychology Today,* August 1974, p. 45.
[22] Condensed from Brown's treatment in *Stress and the Art of Biofeedback,* pp. 149–152.
[23] Ibid., p. 230.
[24] Ibid., p. 231.
[25] Ibid., p. 233.
[26] Ibid., p. 236.
[27] Brown, "The Anatomy of a Phenomenon: Me and BFT," p. 51.
[28] Brown, *Stress,* p. 42.
[29] Ibid., pp. 54–55; also remainder of chapter 3, and chapters 4–6.

BIBLIOGRAPHY

BLAKEMORE, COLIN S. *Mechanics of the Mind.* New York: Cambridge University Press, 1977. One of the most fascinating and useful recent books on neurobiology. Historical and comparative. Very well illustrated. Mostly very readable, with but a few hard spots.

BROOKS, CHARLES V. W. *Sensory Awareness: The Rediscovery of Experiencing.* New York: Viking, 1975. Brooks, who sees people as wholes rather than as minds carried about by bodies, makes a strong argument in favor of a kind of naturalness of behavior that puts aside inhibitions (which he calls "holdings") and allows free growth. Reminiscent of Barbara Brown's special approach to biofeedback.

CALDER, NIGEL. *The Mind of Man.* New York: Viking, 1970. Although outdated in some matters, this remains one of the best comprehensive books on the brain-mind. Excellent illustrations and readable for college students.

CLARKE, EDWIN, and KENNETH DEWHURST. *An Illustrated History of Brain Function.* The University of California Press, 1972. A pictorial history of the believed localization of brain functions. Consists largely of brain drawings with their supposed functions labeled. Recommended as a historical record of what people have thought the brain does.

CRUICKSHANK, WILLIAM M. *The Brain-Injured Child in Home, School and Community.* Syracuse University Press, 1967. Although somewhat outdated, this is one of the better books on brain-injured children.

DOMAN, GLENN J. *What To Do about Your Brain Injured Child.* Garden City,

N.Y.: Doubleday, 1974. An easy-to-read handbook designed for both parents and teachers. Treats such defects as mental retardation, cerebral palsy, epilepsy, and autism.

ECCLES, JOHN C. *The Understanding of the Brain.* New York: McGraw-Hill, 1977. Eccles is considered by some as one of the major authorities on the brain. The paperback is short and readable and, as Eccles says, "is intended to be read right through." Eccles has been criticized by some of his colleagues for trying to use his brain research to support his religion.

ELLIOTT, H. CHANDLER. *The Shape of Intelligence: The Evolution of the Human Brain.* New York: Scribner's, 1969. An unusually readable treatment of the brain. Comprehensive, illustrated. A very useful reference for students interested in the central nervous system.

FELDENKRAIS, MOSHE. *The Case of Nora: Body Awareness as Healing Therapy.* New York: Harper & Row, 1977. Although this is about the healing of a woman in her sixties who had suffered stroke and lost the power to read or write, plus some motor functioning, Feldenkrais's recently developed technique for cure was highly successful. His "body awareness" therapy should apply equally to all age levels and apply to more than one kind of brain damage.

GAITO, JOHN. *Molecular Psychobiology: A Chemical Approach to Learning and Other Behavior.* Springfield, Ill.: Thomas, 1966. Probably the simplest and most readable book on cell biology, including neurons. A good book for starters to begin with. Well illustrated.

GARDENER, RICHARD A. *MBD: The Family Book about Minimal Brain Dysfunction.* New York: Jason Aronson, 1975. Gardener describes symptoms of MBD and how the mother's health contributes to its appearance. He points out the heresy that MBD children are necessarily of low intelligence; some are intellectually superior, but are still slow in learning and developing social relationships.

GARDNER, HOWARD. *The Shattered Mind.* New York: Knopf, 1975. A well-written and interesting book on what we can learn about normal brains by studying brains that have been severely damaged by stroke or accident. Gardner is influenced by Piaget in that he accepts Piaget's concept of saltatory mental development.

GREGORY, R. L. *The Intelligent Eye.* New York: McGraw-Hill, 1970. On how the eye distorts "what is there" so that it will be meaningful to the animal. Includes the research of Lettvin, Hubel, and Stent. Profusely illustrated and easy to read.

HAYWOOD, H. CARL (ed.). *Brain Damage in School Age Children.* Washington, D.C.: The Council for Exceptional Children, NEA, 1968. A book of readings on the nature and treatment of brain damaged children. By now, rather outdated, but contains some good background material on neural dysfunctions.

HYDEN, HOLGER (ed.). *The Neuron.* New York: Elsevier, 1967. Somewhat outdated and too technical for most students. Recommended here for its excellent electron microscope photographs and very good line drawings, and what they reveal about neuronal structure and functioning, but particularly the structure and role of RNA molecules.

JUNG, RICHARD (ed.). *Central Processing of Visual Information A: Integrative*

Functions and Comparative Data. New York: Springer-Verlag, 1973. In this book of readings, see material by David Hubel and Torsten Wiesel, who treat feature extraction (selective seeing) in cats and monkeys.

LASHLEY, KARL. *Brain Mechanisms and Learning.* New York: Dover, 1963. Lashley's famous book reporting his 30 years of brain research.

LAZARUS, RICHARD S. "A Cognitively Oriented Psychologist Looks at Biofeedback." *American Psychologist* 30 (1975):553–561. Offers both adverse criticism of the biofeedback movement and alternate means of coping with stress.

OATLEY, KEITH. *Brain Mechanisms and Mind.* New York: Dutton, 1972. A short, highly readable, book on the human brain. Eclectic with respect to the mind-body issue.

PENFIELD, WILDER. *The Mystery of the Mind: A Critical Study of Consciousness and the Human Brain.* Princeton University Press, 1975. Penfield, a British neurosurgeon and philosopher, presents one of the more recent arguments for mind-body dualism. He asserts that the brain is analagous to a computer and mind to the programmer. Short and readable.

PINES, MAYA. *The Brain Changers.* New York: Harcourt Brace Jovanovich, 1974. A fascinating account of our emerging ability to modify both brain and behavior. She wisely limits her coverage to a manageable number of subjects including biofeedback, drugs, and memory. Ms. Pine's writing is always highly readable without sacrificing scholarship.

ROSE, STEVEN. *The Conscious Brain.* New York: Knopf, 1974. This is one of the best "brain books" to appear during the 1970s. Rose is head of the Brain Research Group at the Open University in London. He treats with lucidity and a vast scholarship much that is known about the human brain. Highly recommended.

SAGAN, CARL. *The Dragons of Eden: Speculations on the Evolution of Human Intelligence.* New York: Random House, 1977. Sagan is a professor of astronomy and space sciences with a strong side interest in neurobiology. Flawed by often treating speculation as fact, this recent book is a wide-ranging and highly provocative treatment of many issues in neurobiology.

SCOTT, ALWYN C. *Neurophysics.* New York: Wiley, 1977. A physicist's view of neurology. Scott maintains that as neurobiology is much more complicated than physics, only some concepts and methodology of physics can be useful to neurobiologists. An excellent reference, best read by students with a physical science background.

SMITH, ADAM. *Powers of the Mind.* New York: Random House, 1976. A popular, somewhat breezily written, book on mental functioning. Smith is convinced that Western civilization has overvalued the role of the left-brain hemisphere to the neglect of the poetic, artistic, and creative powers of the right brain.

STENT, GUNTHER. *Molecular Biology of Bacterial Viruses.* San Francisco: Freeman, 1963. Stent, one of the country's best known molecular biologists, writes here of viruses (phages) that destroy bacteria. Recommended only for students with an organic chemistry background.

STENT, GUNTHER. *Molecular Genetics: An Introductive Narrative.* San Francisco: Freeman, 1971. A leading molecular biologist, who, drawing on the research of Hubel and Wiesel, supports the notion of psychological structures, that is, the interrelation of neurons as dominated by neural clusters of the rest of the body's nervous system. Highly recommended.

VALENSTEIN, ELLIOT S. *Brain Control: A Critical Examination of Brain Stimulation and Psychosurgery.* New York: Wiley, 1973. An assessment and critique of attempts to tamper with the human brain by using electrical stimulation, implantation of chemicals, and brain surgery. Good drawings.

WATSON, JAMES D. *The Double Helix: Being a Personal Account of the Discovery of DNA.* New York: Atheneum, 1968. One of the most fascinating science books of the century by one member of the team that discovered how heredity works. Highly readable.

Part II
HOW DO HUMAN
BEINGS DEVELOP?

Part II treats the development of children and youth from the time of conception to the late teens. The authors regard growth processes as essentially the same at all age levels. Psychological development is construed as a matter of persons' learning through their interaction with their psychological environments. Physical growth is thought to follow the same basic principles, irrespective of age. In both cases, the pattern fluctuates somewhat from one age level to another. In the case of physical growth, such variation stems from genetic endowment; in the case of psychological development, persons' interaction with their culture tends to produce a culture-related pattern. Adolescence, for example, has its genetically induced physical side, but psychological characteristics of adolescence appear to be largely the product of personal-cultural interactions.

The content of the two chapters that comprise Part II is as follows: Chapter 7 first explains the developmental concept of purposive persons interacting with their psychological environments; it then summarizes the physical, motivational, and cognitive development of children through the elementary school years. Chapter 8 focuses upon adolescence; it treats the physiological changes, sociological significance, and psychological meaning of this transitional period in the lives of persons.

Chapter 7
WHAT IS THE NATURE AND COURSE OF PSYCHOLOGICAL DEVELOPMENT THROUGH THE ELEMENTARY SCHOOL YEARS?

Psychological development is the process of persons' maturation and learning through their interaction with their environment. The psychological developmental process encompasses the expansion of individuals' abilities to learn through perception, to achieve judgments based on experience, and to think for themselves in imaginative, creative, and exploratory manners.

As in regard to motivation, discussed in Part I, there are several different viewpoints concerning both the nature and the course of psychological development. We may assume that the basic psychological nature of children is either good, bad, or neutral in innate moral nature or proclivity and either active, reactive, or interactive in relationship to their environments. Each outlook has definite implications for human psychological development. We may think that people develop through active unfolding of natural badness or goodness in a relatively passive environment, that they passively develop through reaction to their respective environments, or that their development is a matter neither of active unfolding nor passive nurture, but rather of person-environment interaction. The later position is the one that is developed in this chapter.

HOW MAY WE THINK OF A CHILD AS A PURPOSIVE PERSON WHO DEVELOPS THROUGH INTERACTION WITH HIS OR HER PSYCHOLOGICAL ENVIRONMENT?

The key concepts in the above heading are *person, interaction,* and *psychological environment.* In exploring this outlook in regard to human development we should be mindful that each concept has its special significance. Furthermore, each concept has arisen as an attempt to develop a more effectual expression to be used in place of less adequate concepts of the opposing outlooks toward development. Person and environment both are essential to any psychologically interactive process. However, to grasp their special meanings here, we must first understand the concept *simultaneous mutual interaction* (SMI).

What Is Person-Environment Simultaneous Mutual Interaction?

Simultaneous mutual interaction (SMI) is a cognitive experiential process within which a person, psychologically, simultaneously reaches out to the environment, encounters some aspects of it, brings those aspects into relationship with him or herself, makes something of those aspects, acts in relation to what he or she makes of them, and realizes the consequences of the entire process. The basic principle of interaction is that a thing cannot be perceived or experienced as a thing-in-itself, but only as it is related to other matters. Thus, the "reality"—psychological environment—with which a person interacts consists of what he (or she) *makes of* the things that he gains through his senses or any other sources available to him. Consequently, the meaning of any object arises from one's interpretation of the relationship between the object and oneself. When one interacts with an object or activity, one sizes it up. When a child sees a tiger as a kitty, psychologically it is a kitty; and a kitty that adults call a tiger is a part of the child's psychological environment.

When one attacks problems of development and learning within an interactionist frame of reference, one needs a systematic psychology that harmonizes with a *relativistic* outlook. This is cognitive-field psychology, described in detail in Chapters 14 and 15, only its developmental aspects are treated here. The task of cognitive-field psychology is to provide adequate ideological tools for describing person-environmental relationships. Accordingly, the aspects of a psychological field or life space are the central tools of cognitive-field psychology.

What Is the Meaning of Life Space?

Life space and the concepts associated with it are only introduced in this chapter on psychological development. They are explained in detail in Chapters 14 and 15 on the cognitive-field theory of learning. From a cognitive-field point of view, development is centered in the total psychological situation, which includes a person and his or her psychological environment considered simultaneously. A psychological situation is a functional interpretation and patterning of physical, social, and conceptual facts insofar as, and in the manner that, they involve the person under consideration.

Life space is a term that best describes a person's total psychological situation. It includes a psychological person and his or her psychological environment. So construed, this psychological concept represents all of the factors giving rise to an individual's behavior at a stated time. The times may vary in length, but strictly speaking, a life space has a duration of a moment. Thus, as a child develops, he or she lives through a more or less continuous and overlapping series of life spaces. Each life space of a moment or a longer juncture contains a person and his psychological environment of that moment or juncture of time.

A life space usually is represented by related geometric figures. However, it is important to keep in mind that the essence of a life space is its functional nature; it represents, not physical entities, but functional relationships. So it constitutes an instrument whereby one may be objective in studying child development by being, to some degree, subjective. Accordingly, a teacher may envision "What would I be thinking if I were a student and were acting that way?" or "If I were in his situation why would I be acting the way he is?" A life space is, uniquely, a psychological phenomenon. All psychological events—acting, thinking, learning, hoping, dreaming—are functions, not of isolated properties of an individual or his environment, but of mutual relations of a totality of coexisting facts that constitute a life space.

How Is One's Life Space Related to One's Development?

In terms of a psychological situation, development is a function of both a person and his or her psychological environment. Thus, actual behavior, in every case, depends upon a person's individual characteristics and the contemporary structure of his or her environment. This means that people with a cognitive-field emphasis in studying development do not center the process in either a child or the environment. Rather they think that development is defined most usefully as a situational process within which a person interacts with his environment.

Psychological development, relativistically defined, is the process whereby a psychological person emerges and grows. Thus, it is that procedure whereby a unique biological organism, lives in a human society and becomes a human—cultural—being. Whereas, from the viewpoint of biology, a human being is construed as a physical organism, psychologically he or she is a dynamic person who emerges in a social environment. Thus, psychological development has no necessary one-to-one relationship to physical or biological behavior. A child's becoming larger is biological growth and being moved from a theater to home while sleeping constitutes physical movement, but neither represents psychological development. Psychological development of a child cannot be ascertained merely through direct observation; it must be inferred through study of his total situation. And the total life situation is a *life space* or a *psychological field*. To summarize: the key concepts of a psychological situation or life space are psychological environment, person, and the interactive relationship between them—*simultaneous mutual interaction*.

What Is a Child's Psychological Environment?

A child's psychological environment is not an undifferentiated medium in which he or she is immersed. Rather, it is what the child "makes of" his physical-social environment, and it consists of everything around the child that has any meaning for him or her. Thus, it contains everything that a person purposively can do anything about. In the same sense that psychological development is distinctly different from physical or biological development, a psychological environment is distinctly different from a physical one.

Whereas the physical environments of a group of students in a classroom are relatively the same, each of their psychological environments is unique. Let us visit Miss Smith's classroom of sixth-grade students at Carbondale Elementary School. At 10:30 Tuesday morning, what is happening in the room? Miss Smith is holding reading class. What are Alice, Frank, Helen, and John doing? Alice is so absorbed with her teacher and school work that she is oblivious to everything else about her, including the other children. Frank is listening half-heartedly to the teacher but is concerned primarily with the other children in the room. Helen is a social butterfly; she wants the attention of most of the children in the classroom. She does give attention to the teacher from time to time, but right now she is concerned with other things. John's body is in the classroom but "psychologically" John is riding a shiny new tractor which is being operated in the field adjoining the school.

This classroom is illustrated in Figure 7.1. Each small circle represents a person and has his or her initial on it. Each person has his or her respective psychological environment, indicated by a larger figure that includes the person. Each person and his or her respective psychological environment constitute a life space. Practically everything within the four walls of the classroom, as well as much more, is included within either John's life space or his foreign hull. John's life space, drawn alone, would appear as in Figure 7.2.

Since a psychological environment, strictly speaking, is a momentary situation involving a specific person, such an environment and the person involved are constantly changing as the person actively lives in relation-

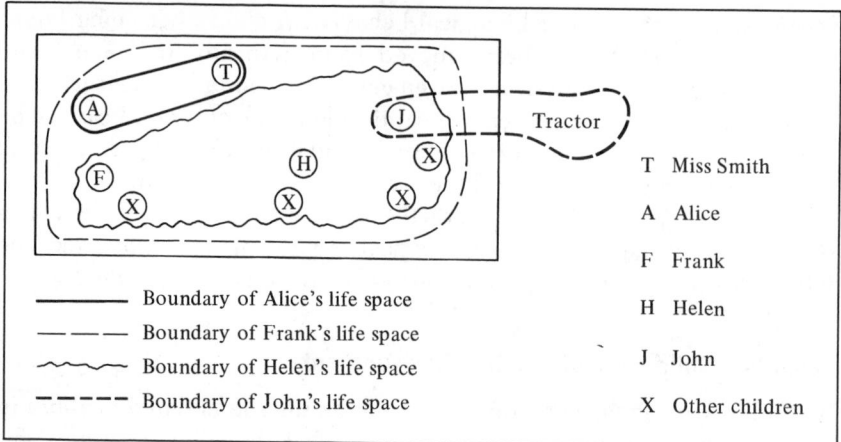

Figure 7.1   Life spaces involved in a classroom.

ship to that environment. What appears to an observer to constitute John's environment may include many elements not actually in John's psychological environment, and the observed environment may exclude some elements that, for John, psychologically are in it. For her to understand John, the teacher must study John in John's *psychological* environment, not his *physical* environment as such.

Thus, to be objective in dealing with the child, the teacher must be subjective. She must see the world as John sees it. In order to predict John's behavior accurately, the teacher must understand the interactive nature of John's life space—his person and his psychological environment—and she must be able to predict (anticipate) the boy's future life spaces. Then, for Miss Smith to be able to teach John in a significant way, it is imperative that there be some intersection of John's life space with hers and with the life spaces of other children in the room.

What Is a Psychological Person or Self?

A person or self is in no sense an abstract ego or self that can be experienced apart from any social context. It is within the social living of

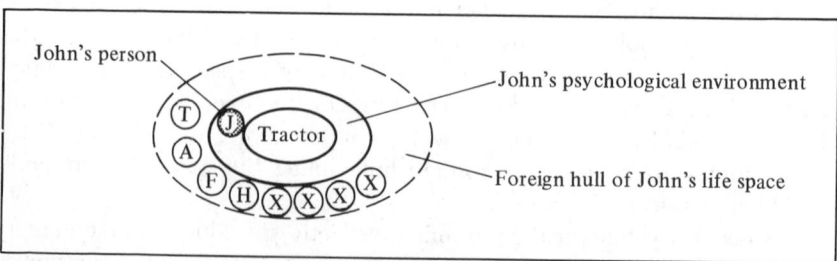

Figure 7.2   John's life space.

an individual that a person or self emerges and continues to change throughout life. Under normal conditions an individual's self is likely to involve his or her strongest motives. When a child uses the terms—*I, me, mine, you, yours, he* or *she, him* or *her*, or *his* or *hers*—a self is emerging. Such concepts arise only as a person interacts with other individuals and groups of people. Through this interactive process each person acquires such achievements as language, conceptual thinking, and moral, social, and religious predispositions and insights.

SELVES ARE ALWAYS IN THE PROCESS OF MAKING

Insofar as we know, a baby does not make sharp distinctions between his body, his environment, and the aspects of each; his life space is quite simple and undifferentiated. However, as a child lives and grows he extends his world of understanding in an attempt to have it encompass more and more of the world about him as he sees it—his world of effect or psychological environment. In turn, the resultant extension and differentiation of his life space leads to an enlargement of his psychological environment. It is in this dynamic process that essentially different facts acquire their psychological reality.

HOW A CHILD CONSTRUCTS A SELF

A young child, to a greater extent than an adult, is a dynamic unity. When the child cries, she cries all over; when she is hungry, all of her is hungry; and when she is frightened, she is startled completely. Later, the child comes to perceive her self only as she distinguishes it from her environment and various aspects of it from one another. The rather sharp distinction between one's person and one's psychological environment is something that grows in an individual's thinking, as the "I" or "self" is gradually formed. However, one's person grows so that soon the central feature of his or her social and personal motivation becomes the maintenance and furtherance of the welfare of that self. Hence, it may be said that the paramount human need is for preservation and enhancement of this emergent self or person. One even owns a "loyal" dog in order to enhance and give constancy to one's psychological person.

A child's awareness of his self or person is manifested in at least four different ways.

1. He (or she) reaches certain results by his own efforts and comes to feel responsible for his acts, priding himself on his achievements and blaming himself for his failures.
2. His self, being embodied in values and goals, is realized in his transactions with other people.
3. As he evaluates his conduct over and against an ideal, an ideal self emerges (people often identify this ideal self with "conscience").

4. His self grows to a prominent place in his memories of a past and his anticipations of a future.

The form that the development of selfhood takes depends upon the interaction of a person and his psychological environment. An organism, in a sense, is an aspect of each—person and environment. Whether a trait is primarily an aspect of the person or the environment depends, among other things, upon the person's present needs.

AN INDIVIDUAL HAS MANY SELVES

Selfhood, except as it has encased itself in a shell of routine, is always in the process of its making. Moreover, any self in process is capable of including a number of more or less inconsistent selves or unharmonized dispositions. So, in a sense, an individual has as many different selves as there are distinct groups for whose opinions he has concern. Thus, Margaret Jones at home is one self, in school another, on a date another, and on a basketball court still another. Every normal human being maintains a variety of interests or values in different situations, and so might be said to have a corresponding number of selves. However, although there is a different self in each successive life space of an individual, we can anticipate a continuity of selves of such nature that, in case of conflict, a deeper, continuous self pushes the others aside and becomes dominant. Consequently, each individual, if reasonably "normal," is a basic self or person made up of his or her major allegiances and commitments, among which there is some degree of harmony and continuity.

WHAT ARE THE ASPECTS OF "NORMAL" PSYCHOLOGICAL DEVELOPMENT THROUGH THE ELEMENTARY SCHOOL YEARS?

Although each child develops at his (or her) own rate and in his own unique way, children in a given culture all share some general aspects of development. Consequently, a description of psychological functions and changes at successive ages can be of great value to teachers in anticipating what their students are, and will be, doing and thinking. *Psychological* functions and changes are those involving a growing mind or intelligence.

Although it is somewhat fictitious to list the characteristics of any given age group, data descriptive of "normal" development of successive age groups do provide norms or averages which may be used effectually in understanding individual children and diagnosing problems in regard to their physical or psychological development and well-being. However, we constantly should be mindful of the fact that, although children all change with age, they show very great individual differences in the various aspects of their development. For instance, among a group of 4-year-olds in a nursery school, one may find children who still talk very much like babies along with others of the same age who sound much like adults in their speech.

Various aspects of a child's development are continuous with former and succeeding aspects and are closely interrelated with one another. Also, a child's manner and rate of development constantly vary from day to day. Nevertheless, in the interest of convenience and simplicity, we need some grouping of age periods as well as a system of classification of aspects of developmental changes. Consequently, in this text we separate the elementary school years into two groupings—early elementary (ages 5 through 8 or kindergarten through grade 3) and middle elementary (ages 9 through 11 or grades 4 through 6).[1] To provide teachers with some insight into the development of children prior to their formally entering regular elementary school, we preface our description of the elementary ages with a survey of the preschool or nursery school ages—3 through 4.

The more important aspects of psychological development of an age group include (1) physical growth pattern, (2) achievement of control and dexterity of motor skills, (3) changes in motivation, including the concept of self, (4) growth in personal-social relations, (5) cognitive or precept-concept development, (6) language development, and (7) modification of time and imaginative perspectives.

The various aspects are not discrete; some shade into, and others are subsumed under, one another. For instance, language development is a unique type of cognitive development. Nevertheless, to present more accurate word pictures, we describe the three levels of children—preschool, lower elementary, and middle elementary—according to the seven aspects in the order that they are listed.[2]

WHAT IS THE COURSE OF PSYCHOLOGICAL DEVELOPMENT DURING THE PRESCHOOL AGES 3 AND 4?

At ages 3 and 4 a child changes from a "toddler" to a "runabout." He (or she) loses most of his baby characteristics and becomes ready to move into formal school experiences. Many of the characteristics of 3s and 4s also extend to the 5s.

How Do 3s and 4s Grow?

At ages 3 and 4, a child's physical growth rate is slower than at any other time between infancy and pubescence. A child of this age usually eats regular meals plus midmorning and midafternoon snacks. However, his or her appetite is not particularly keen.

During this period muscle development accelerates to the point that about 75 percent of a 5-year-old's weight increase is due to muscular development. Whereas a 3- or 4-year-old's head growth is quite slow, his or her limb growth is rapid and the trunk growth is intermediate; the body grows taller and thinner and comes to have proportions and to appear more like that of an adult.

How Do 3s and 4s Achieve Control and Dexterity of Motor Skills?

Three's and 4s show a marked development of large muscle coordination, but small muscle and eye-hand coordination is not well developed. They run with more smoothness, speed up and slow down with greater ease, and negotiate sharp turns and sudden stops quite well. They can skip and jump, but not hop, smoothly, and, unaided, they can climb stairs by alternating their feet.

Because of their increased muscle coordination, they now are ready to replace their kiddy cars with tricycles. Three's and 4s make much use of swings, and they know how to "pump" and "go high in the sky." Many can hang by their feet and do some stunts on a trapeze or crossbar.

Even though small muscle coordination is not well developed in 3- and 4-year-olds, in drawing, their strokes become better defined, less diffuse, and less repetitive. Children's self-care motor skills generally are fairly well perfected during this period. These include feeding, dressing and undressing, toilet control, and self-care at the toilet.

What Changes in Motivation Occur in 3s and 4s?

Preschoolers are more open, direct, and spontaneous in their actions than are school-age children. They are almost constantly active, but they can remain quiet for short periods of time. They most like vigorous bodily activity and outdoor play. However, block building is a favorite indoor pastime and they construct simple towers or houses. They also combine blocks with other toys, dolls, animals, cars, trucks, and airplanes to construct farms and zoos. Finger painting is another popular activity. Four-year-olds chatter as they "work." They describe what they are doing, admire it, and expect others to do likewise.

Preschool-age children are alert, excited, exciting, and curious. They especially are curious about the nature of many objects and activities around them. These include cars, animals, the sky, sources of food, sources of babies, and anatomical differences of boys and girls. Their curiosity is evidenced by their constant queries in regard to "what is it?," "how does it work?," and "what makes it go?"

Three- or 4-year-olds definitely are aware of themselves as persons and they want and like to do things for themselves. This self-awareness consists largely of consciousness of what they can do, how they feel, and how they perceive the actions of others as they relate to them. They are conscious of their playmates and their actions toward them. They observe the activities of adults around them, especially their parents and grandparents, but also others such as the milkman and mailman. And they try fairly hard to imitate their behaviors.

As part of their self-realization, preschoolers are quite aggressive at times, as they assert themselves and attempt leadership over others. They engage in frequent and intense, but short-lived, quarrels in which they employ physical combat, loud noises, and some verbal argument. They also may display envy of other children who receive the attention of adults. At times they may even bite playmates of whom they are envious.

Many 3- and 4-year-olds discover or have discovered that touching and manipulating the genitals produce pleasant sensations. Thus, most of them practice some modified form of erotic self-stimulation. Each child also becomes interested in the genitals of others as well as his own. In our culture, he or she often becomes afraid of adult reactions to this curiosity about sexual matters.

What Growth Occurs in 3s' and 4s' Personal-Social Relations?

Preschool children widen their contacts with other people, especially children. Simultaneously, to some degree they wean themselves of dependence upon their mothers and other adults. Formerly solitary then parallel players, their parallel play now is giving way to group play in which they share materials and toys and hold conversations with others. A preschooler plays with both boys and girls, but usually his best friend is of the same sex as himself. He engages in a certain amount of verbal quarreling with his playmates and often resorts to hitting and fighting. For instance, he may say to a playmate, "go away you can't play here" or "this is mine you can't have it." He often runs to his mother with bitter complaints concerning the behavior of playmates. However, he also has developed some capacity for empathy. Thus, he may console a playmate who has been hurt.

Although 3- or 4-year-olds often venture beyond their homes into a world of playmates, they remain strongly attached to their mothers and become more or less attached to their fathers. Spontaneously, they turn to their mothers for comfort and care, and they like to tag after mother as she does her work. Their fathers now, are becoming increasingly important to them. They also are in the process of expanding this mother-father-self triangle to include other children in the family as well as adults with whom they are intimately associated—grandparents, uncles, and aunts.

Preschool children are highly imitative of each other and of adults. Furthermore, they generally want to please their parents. Thus, they are willing and eager to run simple errands, help with the dishes, and set the table. Their efforts usually are accompanied by questions as to whether "this is the right way." Though their interests in a project may fade quickly, their desire to help is genuine.

How Does Cognition Develop in 3s and 4s?

As teachers seek an understanding of the cognitive development of children of different ages, they can gain much from a study of Jean Piaget's *genetic epistemology*. For Piaget, the term "genetic" is synonymous with "developmental," and epistemology is the theory of knowledge acquisition. So, his genetic epistemology is devoted to a study of the developmental stages of children as they relate to the children's acquisition of knowledge.

For Piaget, the mental development of any child consists of a succession of three stages or periods, namely, sensorimotor, symbolic or pre-concrete-operational, and concrete-operational. Each stage extends the preceding stage, reconstructs cognition on a new level, and comes to surpass the earlier stage. Then, during preadolescence and adolescence, the stage of *formal operations* emerges. Youths become able to think about their thoughts, to construct ideals, and to reason realistically about the future.[3] They also become able to reason about contrary-to-fact propositions. For example, they can think of "white" coal.

The key processes in the stages of child development are *assimilation* and *accommodation*. Assimilation consists of the filtering or modification of the input from the environment. In this process, new knowledge meshes with the child's existing insights. Accommodation consists of the modification or change of the child's internal patterns of understanding to fit reality. In this process, existing internal insights are reconstructed so as to "accommodate" new data or information.

According to Piaget, during the sensorimotor stage (birth to 18 months or 2 years) a child lacks any symbolic function, so displays only direct action on reality. The 3s and 4s, however, are in the symbolic or pre-concrete-operational stage, which extends from 18 months to age 7 or 8. During this stage, children are developing their abilities to represent things with symbols and to use differentiated signifiers of objects. Evidences of the development of these abilities are children's acquisition of language, their indications of dreams, their development of symbolic play, and their attempts at drawing and graphic representations.

Three and 4-year-olds want to find out about most everything they touch, see, or hear. It is through their touching, seeing, and hearing objects and events that they form concepts or ideas. Through their asking countless questions, they manifest their great curiosity. Their psychological world is expanded to include a great variety of objects, animals, new experiences, and additional people. They sharpen and expand their perceptions of reality, and they develop more insightful perceptions of space, time, and people.

Mostly, 3s and 4s see objects as wholes and give only minor, if any, attention to component parts of things. In seeing objects as wholes, they learn to differentiate or classify them. Thus, they learn to distinguish a horse from a cow, a pig from a dog, or a truck from a car or trailer.

At this age there is some conception of forms and space. But, special concepts are limited to each individual's immediate environment. The children have some perception of down, up, around, beneath, inside, on top of, and beside as related to objects around them. They also are beginning to grasp some idea of the shorter units of space, that is, inch, foot, and so on.

Some conception of numbers also is achieved during this period. Children may be able to count to ten or higher. But, seldom do they understand quantity concepts beyond one, two, and three.

Children usually learn of the anatomical differences between sexes during the 3–4-year-old period. They also become aware of many sex-appropriate behaviors of the culture. Thus they learn to "be a lady" or that "little men don't cry."

How Does Language Develop During the Preschool Ages?

During the two preschool years, children are very talkative. Moreover, they move about and talk simultaneously. In their talk, they enthusiastically try new words. Four-year-olds often use all sorts of silly words and sounds in a joyous fashion. They also exercise some of the more famous "bathroom" and swear words of their culture. During this period, they are highly imitative in language as well as in other manners and habits.

Language develops rapidly during the preschool years, most children adding from 500 to 600 words per year to their speaking vocabulary between the ages two and five. Thus, a vocabulary of a few words is expanded into one of 2000 or more. Their understanding vocabulary is even larger.

The children sometimes want to say something but cannot find the right words or cannot get them to come forth properly. Consequently, they hesitate and repeat a good deal in their speech. This constitutes a simple type of stuttering which is of little consequence if parents and other adults do not make something big of it.

Three's and 4s not only acquire new words, they also develop endless strings of new four- to eight-word sentences. Furthermore, 4-year-olds organize subjects, predicates, and adjectives remarkably accurately. Of course, children in homes in which language use is encouraged and promoted develop more proficient language skills. It is interesting to note that, generally speaking, twins and triplets are slower in development of adult speech than are singletons; they probably develop their own means of communication and feel less need for formal cultural language.

Children of four are learning to express ideas and feelings with words. Their words come to be used in developing and settling disputes in place of earlier concrete methods of hitting, and snatching things from one another. They also are developing the language concepts or labels *good* and *bad* as an aspect of moral development.

How Are Time and Imaginative Perspectives of 3s' and 4s' Modified?

The preschool period is one of imaginative enterprise and creative, joyous play. The imaginative dramatic play takes up much of each day's time. In the early 3s imaginative play starts with playing house with a doll, being a horse or a train, and pretending to be animals who talk and play like children. Four's invent thrilling games of cowboy, spaceman, pirate, or doctor. This is the period of the "big lie," "imaginary playmate," and very real dreams. Since a child of 3 or 4 makes little or no distinction between imaginative and concrete reality, these figments really are not lies at all.

During the preschool period, a sense of a past and a future time begins to emerge. A child's past is very much in terms of herself. Thus, she always is curious to hear about herself as a baby. Furthermore, she never wearies of tales about herself and her playmates. The future which she begins to sense has a wobbly time framework and is not cut off from the present. However, conscience does begin to function as a check upon some behaviors. Also, children of this age may initiate defensive behaviors in reaction to anxiety-arousing situations. For example, a 3-year-old staying with her grandparents while her mother was in the hospital "getting a new brother" asked her grandfather to "burp" her soon after she was told of the new baby's arrival.

WHAT IS THE COURSE OF PSYCHOLOGICAL DEVELOPMENT DURING THE EARLY ELEMENTARY SCHOOL PERIOD (AGES 5 THROUGH 8)?

Early elementary childhood covers the years 5 through 8 and grades K (kindergarten) through 3. The elementary school span from age 5 through 11 is quite broad. Furthermore, there are some rather marked differences in development during the two halves of this period. Consequently, we discuss ages 5 through 8 and 9 through 11 separately. To repeat, we identify the two periods of development during the elementary school years as early elementary and middle elementary. The early elementary period sometimes is identified by the expression kindergarten-primary.

How Do Early Elementary Aged Children Grow?

By the time children have reached the age of 5, they have arrived at a state of physiological development that makes possible rather complex learnings, including those which can best be fostered in a school environment. After the extremely rapid physical growth of the first two or three years of life, a child settles down to a steady but decelerating rate of development until the preadolescent period.

The unspectacular but steady progress of physical growth from ages 5 through 8 (grades k through 3) is indicated in Table 7.1[4] During this

Table 7.1 AVERAGE HEIGHTS AND WEIGHTS (AGES 5–8)

	AVERAGE BOY		AVERAGE GIRL	
AGE	HEIGHT (IN INCHES)	WEIGHT (IN POUNDS)	HEIGHT (IN INCHES)	WEIGHT (IN POUNDS)
5	43.6	42.8	43.5	42.3
6	46.3	48.2	46.3	48.3
7	48.7	54.2	48.7	54.5
8	51.1	61.0	51.1	61.9

SOURCE: Derived from George H. Lowrey, *Growth and Development of Children*, 6th ed., Chicago: Year Book Medical Publishers, 1973, pp. 87–88. Data are based on American boys and girls.

period, ossification of cartilage proceeds at an even rate, making the skeleton more rigid and the joints less flexible. A child of 5 to 8, however, still has a much more flexible and less easily damaged skeleton than does an adult. By the end of the primary grades he or she has made a good start toward acquiring a permanent set of teeth; a typical child by this time has 12. His internal organs have kept pace generally with his bodily growth. His stomach soon will have a capacity almost two-thirds that of an adult—although it seems like much more. However, between the ages of 4 and 10, one's heart is smaller in relation to one's body size than at any other time in life, the lag being greatest at age 7. Lung capacity also remains smaller in relation to body size than it will be in adulthood.

By the early school years, a child's body proportions have come to be much better (judged by adult standards) than during infancy. His head by now is about one-sixth his body length. His face is larger in relation to the rest of his head. His legs are longer in relation to his arms and trunk. His muscles, which grew at about the same rate as the rest of him until age 4, now are developing more rapidly. From now on they will represent a steadily increasing proportion of total body weight. Kindergarten and primary children are highly susceptible to muscular fatigue. They tire much more rapidly than do adults; they also recover more rapidly.

The brain and nervous system of a first grader have already undergone their period of greatest growth. By the age of 2, sensorimotor equipment is relatively complete. By the age of 6, 90 percent of adult brain weight has been achieved. This does not mean, of course, that a 6-year-old is 90 percent as intelligent as an adult. It does mean that she has achieved an organic capacity for learning highly complex and closely coordinated motor activity.

What Control and Dexterity of Motor Skills Are Achieved During Early Elementary Childhood?

From 5 to 8, average youngsters are busy trying out a variety of new motor skills and improving their dexterity in them as well as bettering their techniques in skills acquired earlier. Although they are full of energy for trying various activities, they tire quite easily on each one.

They now become better coordinated and integrated. Thus, they are capable of learning more complex motor activities. In general, boys surpass girls of this age in speed of reaction and coordination of gross bodily movements. But, both boys and girls delight in putting their bodies through contortions, walking on high walls, and climbing trees. By 5, right- or left-handedness is fairly well established. Also, children are beginning to use their hands much more in small-muscle-dexterity movements.

By the age of 6, most children have developed a variety of physical skills. They climb with agility, often to the great but usually needless alarm of adults. They can hop, skip, jump, and gallop. They can bounce a ball and play catch. They can ride a child-size bicycle and roller-skate. Furthermore, by the end of the primary period the average child will have learned to do these things with a measure of grace, in contrast to the awkwardness with which he attempted them at age 4 or 5.

Kicking and throwing are favorite activities. Balls of various kinds are employed in play. A bat also becomes a comfortable instrument. Balls, rocks, and cans are kicked with glee. Bicycles and roller skates also are mastered. Running, jumping, swimming, diving, climbing, and hanging in apparently dangerous positions are other popular activities of this age group.

The picture we have drawn is of a fictitious average child. It must be remembered that in the various aspects of actual physiological development some children may be as much as two years ahead, and others two years behind, their age group. A child's growth pattern resembles that of other children, but his time table is strictly his own. Whereas one 6-year-old may be able to throw and catch a ball with considerable dexterity, another may be largely unable to do so. Differences in size and strength are marked. Boys of this age differ little from girls in size, weight, co-ordination, and physical strength. By the end of the primary period, however, an average girl is at least a year ahead of an average boy in bone development.

What Changes in Motivation Occur in the Early Elementary Years?

During the early elementary years, children work hard at becoming independent persons. They find their own way to school, make choices of friends, often choose what they are going to wear on most occasions, and seek responsibilities that give self-satisfaction.

Throughout their elementary-school life, children make three basic kinds of outgoing movements. They shift their center of interest from the home to their peer group. They become involved in games and other activities that require motor skills. Mentally and emotionally they assimilate a world of adult concepts, symbols, and instruments of communication.

Sixes and 7s often become ambivalent persons as contrasted with their earlier stable selves. This is evidenced by recurrent rebellion against parental authority and violent outbursts of temper. Such hostile episodes are interspersed with lovingness and cooperation.

Children at 5 to 8 strive hard to imitate the activities of children slightly older than themselves. This is particularly noticeable in siblings. Six-year-old George insists on his being able to perform the acts and receive the privileges that are accorded 7-year-old Roy. The children's attitudes and motives are strengthened or weakened, depending on how they harmonize or conflict with those of school mates or teachers. Thus, a child's acceptance or rejection by his peer group helps him develop his own ego structure or self concept.

During the early elementary years, children become highly sensitive to the difference between male personality characteristics, activities, and interests and female ones. Thus, the sex appropriateness of an activity exerts a major influence in direction of children's interests, goals, and vocational ambitions. Boys and girls still play together but sex differences in their play, as well as in their other activities, become evident.

Boys are expected to be strong, courageous, ambitious, assertive, aggressive, restless, daring, and tough. Girls, in contrast, supposedly are timid, amiable, docile, well-mannered, sociable, good looking, and tidy. They are expected to be afraid of many threatening situations and to withdraw from difficult problems. Peer-group acceptance and rejection promotes boys acting like "real boys" and girls being "little ladies." Boyish behavior in girls is branded tomboyish and girlish behavior in boys is the mark of a "sissy."

All this means that elementary-age boys and girls move farther apart in their attitudes, interests, and activities. However, this tendency is lessened by today's practices which extend much more freedom to girls than formerly. Thus, girls participate more in "boys'" games such as baseball, and those based on running and jumping activities. Yet, even today girls prefer games such as jacks, hopscotch, and jump rope more than boys do.

Children of this age appear to behave in extremes. They can assume more responsibility, but they often "forget." They both laugh and cry easily. They alternatingly are loving and aggressively hostile. They seek independence and feel insecure when they achieve it. Emotionally, they often vacillate between stability and ambivalence. Becoming more adult-like, they also develop their own conflicts and anxieties.

Important sources of their conflicts and anxieties are potential rejection by their parents, teachers, and peers; failure to fulfill their expected sex roles; lack of desired play skills and other competencies; and their aggression and rebellion against the authority of parents and teachers.

What Are the Personal-Social Relations of Early Elementary Years?

Five to 8-year-olds are exposed to an expanding social environment that requires new adjustments to school situations, neighborhood peers, and children's social class groups. At five, a child still primarily is a member of his family. By eight, he definitely also becomes a member of larger groups. These include his playmate peers, his classmates, his religious group, and organized groups such as scouts.

Early school-age children begin to idealize and glamorize prestigious individuals outside their immediate families. New heroes constantly emerge from television, movies, comic books, and printed sources. These heroes come to be much more colorful than one's own parents. Also, children tend to turn from parents to teachers and classmates for approval and praise.

For primary-age children, the school begins to function as a major socializing agency centered upon teacher and peer-group contacts. Although new experiences mean different things to different children, desire for acceptance, and anxiety in regard to rejection, are transferred to relationships with teachers and schoolmates. In school, group acceptance must be earned by achievements, as contrasted with that gained earlier through parental deference.

Although early elementary-age children want and need adult approval, they begin to resent adult control and to give it their own special names such as "bossy." They are somewhat able to evaluate their roles in relation to others. Their continuing growth from dependence to independence shows up in their concern for rightness and wrongness of events. They make much of fairness and demand their own turn and their own rights.

How Does Cognition Develop During the Early Elementary Period?

During early elementary childhood, one learns best through active participation in, and study of, concrete situations. A child's curiosity leads her to ask questions such as: What is that? What is that for? What makes it go? Thus, she discovers shapes, sights, sounds, feels, tastes, and smells in her world. She recognizes things all around her and feels a need to understand them and how they work.

Through their questioning, primary-school children learn that many things and events exist somewhat independently of them. They also learn that there are certain rules of games, as well as of life, that are not of their own making. They see that given behaviors have consequences by which they must abide, and they differentiate an outside world from themselves. They also begin to develop categories of objects and activities and to recognize likenesses and differences within a category.

During their early school years, children encounter a stress upon their intellectual achievement that is more or less new to them. Accordingly, they develop the intellectual skills that center on the three R's. Traditionally, reading, spelling, and speaking have been given precedence over arithmetic during this period. However, currently the trend is to emphasize arithmetic equally with the other disciplines even in the first grade. Along with their development of academic skills, our students acquire the ability to initiate and complete tasks that require some degree of persistence. They also learn to interact with their peers in an acceptable manner.

For Piaget, children of ages 5 through 8 are entering the stage of *concrete operations.* They are learning to "do in their heads" what previously they had accomplished only through physical actions. They are learning to think about things and thereby to deal with relations among classes of things.[5]

How Does Language Develop During the Early Elementary Years?

By age 6 or 7, perhaps earlier, most children's eyes have matured to the point that they can focus for rather extended periods on the relatively small print of children's books. Thus, they have developed from a far-seeing orientation into one in which they also can perform near-seeing operations.

By age 5, most children have acquired an oral vocabulary adequate for their exchange of thoughts and expression of meanings. At age 6, many children come to school with some small degree of reading ability. This ranges from ability to "read" titles of phonograph records and books to actual capacity to read children's simple stories.

As stated earlier, during the primary grades, most children learn to read, write, and do simple calculations. However, the big accomplishment in the primary grades is in the realm of language development. Since language development involves advancements in speaking, reading, and writing, we next list some of the more common achievements in each category which children in each of the first three probably will accomplish.

A large measure of a child's language development is acquired in school, and schools vary in regard to the ages at which specific matters are taught. Consequently, any listing of specific age or grade achievements of children can be only suggestive. However, it should provide a teacher with some broad guidelines in regard to the order in which language may be learned.[6]

FIRST GRADERS' USE OF LANGUAGE

SPEAKING—FIRST GRADERS

1. Articulate fairly well.
2. Speak in sentences, sometimes using complex structure.
3. Use verbs and pronouns in present and past tense.
4. Begin to hold to one topic when speaking.
5. Relate experiences through narration and description, and report incidents in limited detail.
6. Answer questions clearly.
7. Share ideas freely and contribute to discussions.
8. Associate words with pictures and locations.
9. Remember rhymes, songs, and short poems.
10. May produce one- or two-sentence oral compositions.

READING—FIRST GRADERS

1. Read first reader material fairly easily and with comprehension.
2. Read with vocalization, finger pointing, and head movement.
3. Read from left to right and top to bottom with few, if any, reversals.
4. Relate pictures to words and words to ideas.
5. Associate number words with numbers.
6. Note configurations of new words.
7. Read signs, labels, and page numbers.
8. Read directions, announcements, and other school bulletin board materials.
9. Interested in learning to read from books.
10. Recognize 20 to 50 or more words by sight.
11. Have ability to hear beginning sounds and detect words that begin with the same sound.
12. Refer to pictures for clues to recognize words.

WRITING—FIRST GRADERS

1. Copy labels and signs.
2. Draw pictures to tell a story.
3. Write simple declarative and interrogative sentences.
4. Capitalize first word in a sentence, I, dates, and name of mother and father.
5. Print or write own name.
6. Learn to spell new words.

SECOND GRADERS' USE OF LANGUAGE

SPEAKING—SECOND GRADERS

1. Use past as well as present tense of verbs.
2. Use pointing words such as *these* and *that*.
3. Use the pronoun *I* correctly.

4. Use words to express ideas.
5. Verbalize remembrances and simple requests or anticipations.
6. Begin to arrange events in sequence.
7. Take messages and respond over telephone.
8. Listen and participate to a limited degree in group discussion situations.
9. Progress in speaking complex sentences using adjectival and conditional clauses.

READING—SECOND GRADERS
1. Recognize and relate sounds and forms of most consonants.
2. Read silently from line to line.
3. In reading aloud make use of periods, quotation marks, and question marks.
4. Read preprimer, primer, first reader, and second reader with comprehension.
5. Read previously studied materials aloud with some ease and fluency.
6. Answer written questions and follow short written directions.
7. Read to find answers to questions.
8. Recognize a wide range of words, street signs, school signs, safety notices, and known parts of compound words and derived forms.
9. Readily grasp new words and recognize differences in word forms.
10. Learn the several meanings of some words.
11. Read simple informational and directional materials.
12. In oral reading, recognize thought units.
13. Use class or school library to find familiar books to enjoy.
14. Use tables of contents to find page numbers of stories.

WRITING—SECOND GRADERS
1. Accurately copy words, sentences, and short compositions.
2. Use question marks and periods correctly.
3. Write regular-sized, clearly formed, and on lines, most or all letters of the alphabet.
4. Capitalize proper names.
5. Learn six or seven new spelling words each week and ask for correct spellings of words as needed.

THIRD GRADERS' USE OF LANGUAGE

SPEAKING—THIRD GRADERS
1. Articulate sounds clearly.
2. Use near-adult sentence structure.
3. Participate well in discussions.
4. Can report on observed activities, interpret visual aids, construct definitions, and understand the differences between two ideas.
5. Use correctly *good* and *well* and words meaning *more* and *most*.

6. In speaking, classify objects and facts.
7. Frequent use of subordinate classes beginning with *when, if,* or *because*.

READING—THIRD GRADERS

1. Read silently with no observable lip movements or pointings.
2. Read aloud short stories, reports, and previously prepared materials 50 to 80 words per minute.
3. Can recognize sounds and forms of word variances when *s, ed,* and *ing* are added to sight words.
4. Can recognize, hear, and say consonant blends such as *ch* and *st*.
5. Build new words by adding *re, dis,* and *un* to known words.
6. Recognize word families such as the *at* words; fat, cat, etc.
7. Learn that different words may have the same meaning.
8. Interested in juvenile fiction and imaginative stories.
9. Read newspaper ads, timetables, menus, and words and numbers on admission tickets.
10. Can select words which have the same and opposite meanings.
11. Read to get factual information and answer specific questions.
12. Use telephone book and dictionary.

WRITING—THIRD GRADERS

1. Write and address post cards and short notes.
2. Can construct a beginning sentence and express thoughts in complete sentences.
3. Cooperatively, with other children, develop and write simple passages.
4. Capitalize titles of persons, teacher's name, days, month, holidays, salutation, and first word of closings of letters.
5. Use comma in a series of words, after the close and the salutation of a letter, in recording dates, and to separate the name of a city and state.
6. Use periods following abbreviations and initials.
7. Begin to use a pen.

How Do Early Elementary Children Modify Their Time and Imaginative Perspectives?

Whereas preschool children make little distinction between imaginative and concrete reality, children of school age begin to differentiate symbolic language and thought from concrete reality. Furthermore, they distinguish the characters of fairy tales and myths from "real" ones. Consequently, some symbolic objects cease to have the same potency as do aspects of the concrete physical world. However, primary children still enjoy fairy tales and myths as well as nature stories.

Children of early elementary age become greatly interested in causes and results. They think of physical causation in terms of historical precedence. Thus, they are curious and speculative about the origin and cause of natural phenomena such as wind, rain, thunder, and lightning.

Children of this age also begin to understand time and the use of money. They participate in much spontaneous and school-organized drama. Yet, they do not grasp the idea of sarcasm or irony, and they do little abstract thinking. They are increasing their capacity for self-evaluation and empathy for others. They also are developing a more differentiating conscience, which first emerged during the preschool years. Accordingly, they come to recognize rules that govern behavior. Also, they develop the counterpart of conscience—the tendency toward rationalization and self-justification of their mistakes.

WHAT IS THE COURSE OF PSYCHOLOGICAL DEVELOPMENT DURING THE MIDDLE ELEMENTARY YEARS (AGES 9 THROUGH 11)?

The middle elementary years cover ages 9 through 11 and grades 4 through 6. The most dominant characteristic of children of this age is their tendency to be together in gangs or clubs just for the sake of being with their pals. Gangs or clubs not only include certain boys or girls of the same sex, they also exclude others, often for reasons which to adults would seem inadequate and superficial.

How Do Middle Elementary Aged Children Grow?

Middle elementary children's lungs, digestive systems, and circulatory systems are almost mature. But, there is some evidence that this is a period of unusual strain upon children's hearts, which have grown less rapidly than other parts of their bodies.

During the middle elementary period, most children's slow, steady growth continues. However, some growth patterns actually level off into a plateau prior to the adolescent growth spurt. Furthermore, some girls in the sixth grade and a few in the fifth forge ahead into a growth spurt which may precede that of boys and some other girls by two or more years. Such rapid growth usually is accompanied by developing breasts and other adolescent growth characteristics. So some girls seemingly overnight may shoot up into near-adult size and find themselves actually head and shoulders taller than most of their classmates. Only occasionally does a boy in the sixth grade experience such a growth spurt. Even then, his growth, as such, is of little concern to him, whereas girls often are very sensitive about their height. Poor posture sometimes develops during the middle elementary period, and a prime cause of it is students' sensitivity to their atypical height and their stooping to conceal it. Girls may develop feelings of inferiority during this early rapid-growth period, which may persist even into adult life.

Table 7.2 AVERAGE HEIGHTS AND WEIGHTS (AGES 9 THROUGH 11)

AGE	AVERAGE BOY		AVERAGE GIRL	
	HEIGHT (IN INCHES)	WEIGHT (IN POUNDS)	HEIGHT (IN INCHES)	WEIGHT (IN POUNDS)
9	53.3	68.4	53.3	69.6
10	55.5	76.8	55.5	78.1
11	57.4	85.6	58.1	88.4

SOURCE: Derived from George H. Lowrey, *Growth and Development of Children*, 6th ed., Chicago: Year Book Medical Publishers, 1973, pp. 87–88. Data are based on American boys and girls.

Although growth is steady during the middle elementary period, it is proportionately less rapid than during the kindergarten and primary years. The middle elementary is a period of childhood when physiological change is not marked. Table 7.2 demonstrates the truth of this statement, so far as outward physical growth is concerned.

The growth trends established in the primary grades continue. That is, legs continue to grow at a rate exceeding that of trunk length, body continues to grow at a rate exceeding that of head, bones continue hardening, additional cartilage ossifies, new permanent teeth are acquired (an average 11-year-old has 20 of the 32 permanent teeth that he or she will eventually have), internal organs grow larger and more stable in their functioning. Faces mature somewhat during this period but remain relatively round in contour; noses remain small and foreheads convex. Gains are made in musculature, but physical stamina is still "childish" in the sense that muscular fatigue appears more rapidly than in healthy adults. Brain and nervous system reach virtual physiological maturity by the end of the elementary years.

What Control and Dexterity of Motor Skills Is Achieved During Middle Elementary Childhood?

During the middle elementary years, muscles become better coordinated and manipulative ability increases. Children's eyes come to function, with little strain, as well as those of adults on close and fine work. This is a period during which near-sightedness and other eye defects often are discovered.

During the middle elementary years, there is steady improvement in coordination and capacity to learn physical skills. Within this age period a child is likely to learn to ride a bike "no hands," to walk on top of a narrow fence, and to play ball with dexterity. Note that by the age of 11, girls have overtaken boys in both stature and weight. An average girl of this age has entered the phase of rapid growth which immediately precedes puberty. But, in general, children of this age have excellent control of fine as well as large muscles. They attain near-adult levels of power in coordinating their hands and eyes in manipulative skills and become quite adept in crafts and shop work.

This is the period during which many play skills also are acquired. Often, proficiency in these skills is a requisite for children's acceptance into groups with which they desire to be identified. Accordingly, in middle childhood, children grow to show appreciation of artistic skills in both work and play, and they develop accompanying standards of workmanship.

What Changes in Motivation Occur During Middle Elementary Years?

Middle elementary children display greater responsibility, dependability, and reasonableness than do those of a younger age. However, routine hygienic practices are of little interest to them. Earlier hand-washing, teeth-brushing, bathing, and neat-dressing practices now tend to be neglected. In fact, they may appear to be extending themselves to follow just the opposite of proper, neat procedures. Their clothes, pockets, and desks are likely to be sloppy. Because of their high-energy level, at times they may appear overactive, hurried, and careless.

Persons of this age develop a strong sense of right and wrong. Often, they are even perfectionists in their tasks. They so want to do well that they lose interest when they are either pressured or discouraged. They like to work on real jobs and are capable of prolonged interest and application. They can plan for an extended period of time, and, on occasion, go ahead with a project on their own.

They are less interested in fairy tales and fantasy than formerly. Their concern is centered more in stories of their and other countries and communities. They want their questions answered seriously. Furthermore, they want reasonable explanations of things and do not appreciate being talked down to. They also are more keenly conscious of their inadequacies and shortcomings and make definite efforts to compensate for them.

At this age, there is great interest in sexual matters, and information in regard to sex is avidly sought. The type of sex information that 9s to 11s seek includes biological facts surrounding reproduction and psychological understandings concerning the mating process. This is the age of some sexual experimentation. However, usually it is suggested or promoted by older playmates.

Nine to 11-year-old boys are beginning to show some interests that are different from those of girls of the same age. In their search for manhood, they acquire and transmit adult forbidden or tabooed information. This includes "dirty" stories, sex stories, ideas (mostly erroneous) in regard to sex, and the "proper" use of swear words.

Boys also make collections of articles such as pictures of baseball players and make a big thing of trading them with one another. Many collecting ambitions are only transitory. However, as boys grow older their special interests may bend their collecting fancies to articles in keeping with their occupational ambitions. A boy interested in music may collect records or one interested in biology may collect fossils or bugs.

Girls, too, have their unique interests. They are much more concerned with verbal imagery than are boys. An example of this is girls' mania to write and pass notes in school. Often, the notes are in secret language, and usually they transmit very little real information. But, they accomplish their mission, which is to give the girls satisfaction through the act of note passing, not through communication by means of the content of the notes. Many girls of this age daydream about romantic love affairs. They also devour romantic movies and stories in which the heroine ends up with a strong, virile man all her own.

What Are the Personal-Social Relations of Middle Elementary Years?

Between ages 9 and 11, children's social environments expand tremendously, and their world view is a rapidly changing one. In their world (life space) the gang is of paramount importance. Heroes and heroines constantly rise to challenge the place of earlier ones. However, those of the moment provide children with a set of goals, and foster skills which are relevant to the goals. A child in middle childhood who admires baseball players works hard at becoming one. One who admires biological scientists strives to learn about botany, zoology, and other aspects of nature.

Gangs appear in the lives of children even earlier than the middle childhood period. But, now they become more highly structured and more central in individuals' lives. Middle childhood gangs are characterized by special membership requirements and more or less elaborate rituals in conduct of meetings. Formal organizations such as Boy Scouts and Girl Scouts capitalize upon the gang-centeredness of children and make the "gangs" longer lived than those which spring up rather spontaneously.

Because of their identification with peer groups, 10- and 11-year-olds often come into real conflict with adult demands. The type of demands that gangs or peer groups make upon individuals seldom bring outright rebellion against adult authority, but they do lead to continuous conflict and aggression between children and adults. Parental admonitions are more likely to be ignored than challenged. Blowups occur only when children think they are being nagged or treated like babies. If there is some inconsistency between the values of a child's parents and teachers and those of his or her friends or gang, the child is likely to practice the behaviors that are encouraged by his or her peers. Acceptance by peer groups is so desperately needed that children may seek devious means to acquire it. If it cannot be gained through manifestation of skills in games, they may provide special treats and thereby attempt to buy their way into groups.

Girls' clubs seem to exist more for the girls to exercise verbal powers and imagery than for sociability. Accordingly, they have elaborate constitutions, membership rules, and by-laws. Girls' clubs also are likely to be more exclusive, autocratic, and rigidly organized than those of boys.

Boys of this age at least pose an anxiety in regard to their associating with girls, and they carefully guard against manifesting any interest in them. At the same time, they harbor a strong sexual interest and curiosity. As they grow out of this paradoxical condition near the close of the middle elementary period, they begin to recognize girls as quite interesting objects and express it by teasing, tripping, or poking them as they walk by.

As a child lives his (or her) life in the early preadolescent period, he comes to identify himself with a number of social groups and to reject membership in others. Thus, he may think of himself as a Christian, a Democrat, and a third-generation German and thereby prepare himself for future membership in adult organized groups.

How Does Cognition Develop During the Middle Elementary Years?

Middle-elementary-age children are persons with sufficient physical and mental strength to maintain themselves in a simple society. In a modern Western culture, it behooves them to recognize that they are dependent upon adults for food, clothing, shelter, and luxuries and, to some degree, their ideas. Although they are cognizant of cultural demands upon them, they do not always heed them. They are not enthusiastic about dressing for conventionality rather than comfort and using proper methods of communication when others will transmit ideas just as well. They want to know what they want to know, but they may take a dim view of matters that adults want to teach them. In areas that they consider important they collect many facts. These may pertain to ball players, movie stars, astronauts, mass media, biological knowledge, or humanity.

For Piaget, children in the ages 9 through 11 are well into the stage of concrete operations. They have become adept at doing thought problems and at combining and dividing classes of concepts. These children internalize actions as related to objects, but they do not yet use verbally stated hypotheses. Such hypotheses appear only in the ages 12 to 15, Piaget's fourth stage.[7]

By their middle years, children have accomplished sufficient skill in the three R's to use them as tools in acquiring more knowledge. So they apply their basic understandings to more complex problems and situations. They develop relationships between different areas of knowledge and they learn to deal with abstractions in a competent manner. Questions asked and information sought by children of the middle ages often involve biological phenomena (How do bees make honey?), celestial motions (If the earth is spinning, why can't we feel it?), human relationships (What is a Jew?), or causation (What makes turtle eggs hatch?).

How Does Language Develop During the Middle Elementary Years?

Most children in middle childhood can ably use words as tools for self-expression. They discuss current affairs with much understanding. They also describe experiences of groups or individuals, and express themselves in well-structured sentences. In discussions, they consider a number of factors and arrive at generalizations. They also are able to apply gained generalizations to new situations.

In reading, they recognize at sight a wide range of words, they divide words into syllables, and they can read ably in various subject matter areas. Also, they have developed ability to identify words that are spelled alike but are different in pronunciation and meaning. They also recognize many word variants which are formed by adding prefixes and suffixes.

They can write stories, diaries, and interesting letters on experiences in and outside school. In so doing, they can vary sentence structures and develop paragraphs properly. In most cases they capitalize and punctuate reasonably accurately. They spell most words correctly, and ably consult the dictionary for correct spellings of words as needed.

How Do Middle Elementary Children Modify Their Time and Imaginative Perspectives?

Children's mathematical and scientific knowledge varies with cultures, regions, and generations. However, fifth- and sixth-grade children are likely to comprehend concepts such as *zero, few, several,* and *hardly.* They also are coming to see the relationship between the spaces which they directly experience and those indicated on maps. But, their concepts of historical time still are somewhat inadequate. A relative perspective of periods of history is not yet achieved. However, during the latter part of middle childhood, as time and space perspective is achieved, children are fascinated by the study of distant places and remote future time.

Children of middle elementary age can distinguish between concrete reality and fantasy, and they have a fairly good idea when their thinking is centered in each. Nevertheless, they like to exercise their capacity for abstraction. Often this takes the form of "as if" gymnastics and games. For example, boys may say, "let's act as if the girls aren't here." Other times, the children present riddles which involve abstractions. Furthermore, they are intrigued by imaginative study of movements of celestial bodies and satellites.

Any attempt to describe the psychological development of children in one chapter is certain to be quite sketchy. Consequently, we urge readers, after they have studied this chapter, to extend their inquiry to books on child growth and development such as those listed in the bibliography of the chapter. The psychological development of adolescents is treated in Chapter 8.

NOTES

[1] The term "upper elementary," when used, refers to ages 12 through 13 and grades 7 and 8.
[2] Much of the information contained in this chapter has been gained from the basic books on child development that are listed in the bibliography. The books drawn upon most heavily are Paul H. Mussen, John J. Conger, and Jerome Kagan, *Child Development and Personality*, 3d ed., New York: Harper & Row, 1969; Ira J. Gordon, *Human Development: A Transactional Perspective*, New York: Harper & Row, 1975; David Elkind, *Children and Adolescents: Interpretive Essays on Jean Piaget*, 2d ed., New York: Oxford University Press, 1974; and George H. Lowrey, *Growth and Development of Children*, 6th ed., Chicago: Year Book Medical Publishers, 1973.
[3] See David Elkind, *Children and Adolescents: Interpretive Essays on Jean Piaget*, 2d ed., New York: Oxford University Press, 1974, p. 23.
[4] See George H. Lowrey, *Growth and Development of Children*, 6th ed., Chicago: Year Book Medical Publishers, 1973, pp. 77–88.
[5] Elkind, *Children and Adolescents*, pp. 23–24.
[6] See Walter Toban, *Language Development: Kindergarten Through Grade Twelve*, Urbana, Ill.: National Council of Teachers of English, 1976, for reports of recent research on childrens oral and written language development.
[7] Elkind, p. 24.

BIBLIOGRAPHY

BERNARD, HAROLD W. *Human Development in Western Culture*, 4th ed. Boston: Allyn & Bacon, 1975. Human development with a cultural emphasis.

BRECKENRIDGE, MARIAN E., and E. LEE VINCENT. *Child Development*, 4th ed. Philadelphia: Saunders, 1960. A popular text that surveys in considerable detail both physical growth and mental development from infancy through adolescence. The authors are highly eclectic in their approach.

DINKMEYER, DON C. *Child Development: The Emerging Self.* Englewood Cliffs, N.J.: Prentice-Hall, 1965. A survey of points of view concerning child development and learning. Stresses self theory.

ELKIND, DAVID. *Children and Adolescents: Interpretive Essays on Jean Piaget*, 2d ed. New York: Oxford University Press, 1974. Succinct presentation of Piaget's basic outlook and concepts treating child development.

FALKNER, FRANK (ed.). *Human Development.* Philadelphia: Saunders, 1966. Principles of human growth, genetics, and chemistry as related to physical and psychological development.

FORMANEK, RUTH, and ANITA GURIAN. *Charting Intellectual Development.*

Springfield, Ill.: Thomas, 1976. A practical guide to Piagetian teaching tasks on a how-to-do-it level.

GESELL, ARNOLD, and FRANCES L. ILG. *The First Five Years of Life; A Guide to the Study of the Preschool Child.* New York: Harper & Row, 1940. Detailed description of the physiological and behavioral characteristics of infants and small children, by the director of the Clinic of Child Development at the Yale University School of Medicine and a colleague. The assumption that a child unfolds both physically and mentally according to an innate growth plan runs through all of Gesell's writing.

GESELL, ARNOLD, and FRANCES L. ILG. *The Child from Five to Ten.* New York: Harper & Row, 1946. A rich fund of information about the physical and behavioral characteristics of 5- to 10-year-olds. Gesell's book treating the years from 10 to 16 is cited at the end of chapter 8.

GESELL, ARNOLD. *Studies in Child Development.* New York: Harper & Row, 1948. A description of general characteristics and conditions of child development, in a biological-psychological frame of reference.

GORDON, IRA J. *Human Development: A Transactional Perspective.* New York: Harper & Row, 1975. Survey of the development of selves as individuals from birth through adolescence. Attempts a "rapproachment" between phenomenology—neutral interactivity—and S-R associationistic behaviorism—neutral reactivity.

JENKINS, GLADYS, GARNER, and HELEN S. SHACLER. *These Are Your Children,* 4th ed. Glenview, Ill.: Scott, Foresman, 1975. A simply written and concise portrayal of physical and behavioral characteristics of children from infancy to age 14. Many pictures.

KAGAN, JEROME. *Understanding Children: Behavior, Motives and Thought.* New York: Harcourt Brace Jovanovich, 1971. Translates current psychological knowledge into practical suggestions for adults to use in dealing with children.

LANE, HOWARD A., and MARY L. BEAUCHAMP. *Understanding Human Development.* Englewood Cliffs, N.J.: Prentice-Hall, 1959. A lucid book, written in a personal and literary style. Discussions of physical and mental development are woven together. References are excellent.

LOWREY, GEORGE H. *Growth and Development of Children,* 6th ed. Year Book Medical Publishers, 1973. A compilation of developmental patterns and norms accompanied by constant emphasis upon the individuality of growth and development.

MARTIN, WILLIAM E., and CELIA BURNS STENDLER. *Child Behavior and Development.* New York: Harcourt Brace Jovanovich, 1959. Treatment of both physical and psychological development. Makes much use of the findings of cultural anthropologists.

MARTIN, WILLIAM E., and CELIA BURNS STENDLER. *Readings in Child Development.* New York: Harcourt Brace Jovanovich, 1954. An excellent selection of readings which cover numerous phases of development, both physical and psychological.

McCANDLESS, BOYD R. *Children and Adolescents Behavior and Development.* New York: Holt, Rinehart and Winston, 1961. A study of child development with a sociological emphasis. Intensive treatment of development of the social attitudes—prejudice, ethnocentrism, and authoritarianism.

MUSSEN, PAUL H. *The Psychological Development of the Child.* Englewood Cliffs, N.J.: Prentice-Hall, 1963. An excellent brief treatment of child development. Focuses upon basic ideas, problems, and issues which concern people interested in child study.

MUSSEN, PAUL H., JOHN J. CONGER, and JEROME KAGAN. *Child Development and Personality*, 3d ed. New York: Harper & Row, 1969. A general treatment of development from birth through adolescence. Follows development genetically from first year through adolescence.

PIAGET, JEAN. *The Child's Conception of the World.* New York: Harcourt Brace Jovanovich, 1929. A report of Piaget's observations and clinical study of children. More recent studies of this eminent Swiss psychologist concern the origin and development of intelligence and children's conceptions of morality, reality, space, physical causality, number, and geometry.

PULASKI, MARY A. S. *Understanding Piaget.* New York: Harper & Row, 1971. Introduction to children's cognitive development. Simplifies Piaget's difficult language.

ROWEN, BETTY. *The Children We See.* New York: Holt, Rinehart and Winston, 1973. An observational approach to child study. Prepares students to study child development through using their own observations. Emphasizes uniqueness of each child.

RUSSELL, DAVID H. *Children's Thinking.* Boston: Ginn, 1956. A psychological interpretation of backgrounds, materials, processes, and techniques for improvement of children's thinking based upon extensive research findings.

TRAVERS, JOHN F. *The Growing Child.* New York: Wiley, 1977. Aspects of, influences on, and problems of child development. Examines various theories of development.

Chapter 8
WHAT IS THE PSYCHOLOGICAL MEANING OF ADOLESCENCE?

Adolescence is the developmental period during which growing persons make a transition from childhood to adulthood. People in Western society generally recognize adolescence as a time of striking change. Adolescents often are considered problems to themselves as well as a source of perplexity and irritation to adults. Consequently, an understanding of this period is of great concern to high school teachers. However, teachers of all grade levels can benefit from a knowledge of this period of human development. When principles of development are interpreted broadly, those manifested by any age group will apply to all age levels. Furthermore, all elementary teachers help children develop understandings and appreciations that they carry with them into adolescence, and teachers in the upper elementary grades deal with some students actually entering this transitional period.

The early part of the chapter describes some common physiological and sociological characteristics of adolescence that provide a matrix or background for consideration of its psychological meaning. Then, later sections treat the psychological meanings of the period. However, there are at least two rather sharply conflicting outlooks in regard to the psychological interpretation of adolescence. We may identify these outlooks as *active-passive* and *interactive* positions. In the latter part of the chapter we describe each outlook in some detail with the hope that readers will evaluate them against one another. Here, we contrast them very briefly.

A human being, when considered both active and passive, is viewed as an actively maturing biological organism being passively conditioned by a physical-social environment. Thus, secondarily to being a biological organism, an individual is a socially nurtured being, and he (or she) is nurtured by the way his environment impinges upon him. In contrast, when considered interactive, a person is viewed as purposively reaching out and perceiving his environment in line with his goals at that particular time. Thus there is a critical difference between the conception of an active-passive adolescent organism in a physical and social environment and the idea of a purposive adolescent person interacting with his psychological environment.

In Western cultures adolescence, as a more or less unique interval in human development, has been institutionalized into a period of several years' extent during which individuals no longer are children but still are too immature to be treated as adults. It begins when young people enter pubescence and continues until they are sexually mature and have reached their maximum growth in height, and in mental ability as measured by intelligence tests. Chronologically, adolescence covers roughly the years from 12 to the early 20s. However, boys physiologically are about two years behind girls at the onset but catch up with them by age 17 or 18. During adolescence, youths are expected to attain physical, mental, and emotional maturity and to make some major effort in the direction of vocational and civic responsibility. The one word that best characterizes adolescence is *change*. The change is physiological, sociological, and psychological. The sociological changes of adolescence provide the matrix for the psychological ones. We treat each kind of change in order.

WHAT ARE THE PHYSIOLOGICAL CHANGES OF ADOLESCENCE?

One's body is the façade with which one faces one's world. Although physiological changes, in themselves, may not account adequately for the psychological changes of adolescence, they are of sufficient importance to merit careful consideration. Some physiological changes of adolescence, with some variations between boys and girls, happen through earlier childhood as well. These include decrease in pulse rate, rise in blood pressure, increase in total respiratory volume, and diminution of basal metabolism or heat production. But, there are other physiological changes that are unique to adolescence. These fall into three categories: (1) changes in both primary and secondary sex characteristics, (2) changes in skeletal dimensions, and (3) changes in body chemistry.[1]

What Are the Sexual Changes of Adolescence?

Maturation of sex organs and development of sex power are the most impressive physiological characteristics of adolescence. Pubescence and puberty describe respective aspects of the period and process within which sexual maturity is achieved. *Pubescence* is an approximately two-year period of physiological change that characterizes the biological onset of adolescence and culminates in a person's reaching puberty. Pubescence is marked by maturation of primary and secondary sex characteristics, related changes in glandular balances and body proportions, and a spurt in physical growth. *Puberty* is the point in biological development when sexual maturity appears. Puberty in girls usually develops within a few months after their first menstruation. In boys, the indicator is the presence of live sperm cells in their seminal discharges. However, since sperm cells cannot be detected by unaided eyes and boys' genitals are so obvious, the rapid growth of boys' genitals often is considered an indication of puberty. For American girls the average age of puberty ranges between 13 and 13½ and for boys it ranges from 14 to 14½. However, the range in ages of reaching puberty is at least from 9 to 17 for girls and from 11 to 18 for boys. In Western cultures, successive generations have been getting taller and attaining puberty at progressively earlier ages. For example, the average age of beginning of menstruation has declined from about 16 in 1860 to about 13 today.[2]

PRIMARY SEX CHARACTERISTICS

Features of an organism that are most immediately associated with procreation and reproduction are called primary sex characteristics. In boys they are penis and testes; in girls, ovaries, fallopian tubes, uterus, and vagina. As puberty is approached, genitals of both sexes make rapid growth. In boys this growth is quite apparent and is indicative of approaching manhood. Girls' sexual organs grow in parallel fashion but, since theirs are not so obvious, the advent of menstruation often is considered the indicator of puberty. However, anthropologists are acquiring more and more evidence that a period of some months usually elapses between a girl's first menstruation and her attainment of the capacity to become a mother. Nevertheless, tradition persists; people commonly connect the first menstrual period with the advent of female fertility.

SECONDARY SEX CHARACTERISTICS

Adolescent girls and boys manifest other distinctive sex characteristics that are not immediately related to reproduction and consequently are commonly labeled *secondary*. Girls' breasts develop and pelvises widen. They acquire fatty deposits in breasts and on hips. Also, clumps of hair appear in pubic regions and under arms. Boys, too, develop pubic and axillary hair but in addition to this they have their own secondary sexual characteristics. Hair develops rapidly on limbs and trunk, head hairlines develop a wedge shape, facial whiskers become pigmented, and voices drop in pitch. Boys also broaden through the shoulders and acquire larger chest cavities; whereas a normally proportioned adolescent girl takes on an hourglass shape, a normally built boy becomes the shape of a carrot. Sexual changes are accompanied by development of the sex drive in males and its partial development in girls. In the American culture, according to Kinsey, the sex drive of females in many cases does not appear to reach its fullest development until a decade or more later—perhaps not until the age of 30.[3] However, anthropological studies suggest that the later development of the sex urge among females is probably a culturally imposed trait; American parents typically make greater efforts to inhibit sexual expression in girls than in boys.

What Changes Occur in Skeletal Dimensions?

Sexual changes of adolescence are accompanied by noticeable modification of body height, weight, and proportions. Both boys and girls manifest a pubescent growth spurt about six months before the advent of puberty. However, the spurt in girls averages about one to two years ahead of that in boys.

The rate and span of changes in growth during adolescence are far from uniform. However, studies of the increments of growth of individuals show that each person has a period of sharp growth acceleration during pubescence. Some adolescents have been known to grow 6 or 7 inches in height and to gain 20 to 30 pounds in a single year. Since youths reach pubescent growth spurts at varying ages, growth changes tend to compensate for one another. Thus, when they are handled statistically, the astounding changes in individuals are concealed; growth curves plotted from averages of different ages of the two sexes tend to obliterate individual spurts and abatements of growth.

Not only does a person reach his (or her) pubescent growth spurt at his own particular time, but different organs and different parts of the body grow and develop at different speeds and their curves of growth take different forms. Thus, growth of organic systems and other physiological dimensions may either lag behind or overtake growth in stature. For instance, a very tall boy of 15 may appear to be a man and still have relatively undeveloped genitals.

THE JUNIOR HIGH SCHOOL YEARS (AGES 12 THROUGH 14)

Much more than in the few years preceding, the junior high school years are marked by rapid and conspicuous physiological changes. One of these is a resurgence of rapid growth, reminiscent of the infant growth rate. The preadolescent growth period is sometimes called the "pubescent spurt," because of its apparent close association with sexual maturation. The pubescent spurt typically occurs in girls between the ages of 10 and 13, with the greatest average annual weight gain, 12 pounds, occurring between 11 and 12. The growth spurt in boys is typically about two years later, between 12 and 15, with the greatest average weight gain, 13.4

Table 8.1 AVERAGE HEIGHTS AND WEIGHTS (AGES 12 THROUGH 14)

AGE	AVERAGE BOY		AVERAGE GIRL	
	HEIGHT (IN INCHES)	WEIGHT (IN POUNDS)	HEIGHT (IN INCHES)	WEIGHT (IN POUNDS)
12	59.6	95.2	60.7	100.4
13	62.0	105.7	62.8	110.5
14	64.9	119.1	64.1	120.1

SOURCE: Derived from George H. Lowrey, *Growth and Development of Children*, 6th ed., Chicago: Year Book Medical Publishers, 1973, pp. 79–88. Data are based on American boys and girls.

pounds, occurring at age 14 (see Table 8.1). It is only during the ages 10 to 13 that an average girl is taller and heavier than an average boy of the same age. Every junior high school teacher is aware of the fact that during these years boys seem small and childish in appearance—little changed from the late elementary years—but girls have moved far in the direction of physiological maturity.

Marked changes in relative configurational dimensions accompany the preadolescent growth spurt. Legs are the first part of the body to show conspicuous growth. This is followed by broadening of pelvis and change in hip contour in girls and broadening of shoulders and increase in chest cavity in boys. Faces assume the ovalness of adulthood, and noses and chins become more prominent. By the end of the pubescent growth spurt, hands and feet have reached adult size; this, combined with the natural awkwardness of the period, makes a youth seem all hand and feet.

Visceral growth is largely completed by the end of the pubescent spurt. However, the heart does not reach its full size until several years later. Muscle weight continues to gain in relation to total weight through the junior high school years, but the major gain in musculature does not occur until the senior high school period. Boys gain slightly in physical endurance; girls gain similarly until about the age of 13, when they reach a plateau.

Organs showing the most noticeable development during the junior high school age are the sex organs; however, quite a number of boys and an occasional girl do not mature sexually until after 14. For a majority of youth a most important feature of the junior high age level is sexual "coming of age." This is characterized by glandular development and hormone production, which are not externally visible, and by the appearance of the so-called primary and secondary sexual characteristics.

THE SENIOR HIGH SCHOOL YEARS (AGES 15 THROUGH 17)

The senior high period is characterized by virtual completion of physiological maturation. There is a reduced rate of growth in size during this period. A slight gain in stature may occur following the age of 18 and up to 20. Mature adults in the United States appear to be becoming relatively larger. Boys today are from 6 to 8 percent taller than were boys of similar age a half-century ago.

By age 18, youth have gained proportions characteristic of adulthood. The head is now about one-seventh of total body length; legs are one-half body length. Since infancy, the head has doubled in length, legs have increased by five times, and the trunk has tripled. One notable characteristic of this period is increased musculature of boys. By the age of 16, muscle weight has reached over 44 percent of total body weight—the adult proportion. Physical strength doubles between ages 11 and 16.

Stamina among males increases rapidly during the late teen years. However, capacity for sustained physical output appears to remain less than that of a well-conditioned male in his 20s and 30s. (Tenzing was 38 when, with Hillary, he conquered Mount Everest.) In the United States, girls typically have not progressed in this respect. After reaching a peak of endurance at about 13, females have declined in physical endurance; between the ages of 17 and 20, a typical female has had the physical endurance of a girl of 6 or 8. Cultural factors undoubtedly have accounted for this; girls become rather sedentary during the late teens. Because of a belief that boys do not prefer girls with muscles, feminine "softness" is cultivated in our society. This picture, however, is changing with the current changing roles of girls and women. In many countries, including those of western Europe and the Soviet Union, teen-age girls, with few exceptions, engage in fairly strenuous sports and calisthenics. In these countries differences in stamina and physical strength between the sexes are not great.

What Changes Occur in Body Chemistry?

In addition to glands like the liver and sweat glands, which have ducts to carry away their secretions, a human body also has ductless glands, or endocrines, which secrete hormones directly into the circulatory system. Normal physiological growth and development depend in part upon properly timed actions of the endocrines, which interact with one another. Thus, special changes in size and function of some endocrines are an important aspect of the physiology of adolescence. The endocrines most closely related to physiological changes of adolescence are the hypothalamus gland, the pituitary gland, and the gonads—the testes and ovaries.[4]

The hypothalamus is the part of the brain that lies beneath the thalamus on each side. Its secretions stimulate the anterior pituitary gland, which in turn stimulates the growth of the gonads. The pituitary gland, located at the base of the brain, controls general body growth. Its hormones bring about the various physical changes of pubescence.

The anterior branch of the pituitary gland also plays an important part in a change of glandular balance. It becomes more and more active in the period just preceding puberty, and its function is related to the rapid growth spurt of adolescence.

The pineal and thymus glands play a lesser part in sexual development. The pineal gland, attached to the underside of the brain, holds back sexual maturation during infancy and childhood. It seems to lose this function as adult sexual characteristics begin to appear.

The thymus gland, the "gland of childhood," is located in the upper breast. In the years just prior to adolescence it diminishes in size and activity. This is part of the shift of glandular balance, which begins at 9 or 10 in girls and 11 or 12 in boys. The shift takes several years to run its course.

Female gonads produce ova or egg cells and male gonads produce sperm cells, but in addition both produce the female sex hormones, estrogen and progesterone, and the male sex hormone, androgen or testosterone. There is a difference, but not utter dissimilarity, in gonadal glandular activity of an adolescent male and that of an adolescent female. Both estrogen and androgen are found in both sexes, but estrogen is more highly developed and more active in females and androgen more so in males.[5]

WHAT IS THE SOCIOLOGICAL SIGNIFICANCE OF ADOLESCENCE?

In discussions of adolescence, quite often the development of primary and secondary sex characteristics receives major attention. However, biological development of human beings is always paralleled by sociological development. The radical changes in adolescents' bodies are accompanied by equally significant changes in their relationships with groups with which they are associated and identified. Thus, changes in social attitudes parallel changes in physical structure. An adolescent, looking forward to and interesting him (or her) self in responsibilities of adult life, stands in sharp contrast to his earlier circumscribed, self-centered personality that existed when his mental horizons were relatively low and his bodily strength was more limited.

In the Western world, adolescence is more a cultural than a biological phenomenon. It is the period in a person's life when the society within which he (or she) functions ceases to regard him as a child but does not grant him full adult status, roles, and functions. Hence, the period is longest in a culture that is characterized by a high number of years of formal schooling, particularly among its high status families.

What Is the Sociological Nature of the Adolescent Transition?

The transition from childhood to adulthood can be very painful and difficult, but is not necessarily so. Adolescence is not by nature a period of storm and stress, as Margaret Mead's studies of Samoan youth so well demonstrate.[6] However, the value systems of adults in Western culture often lead it to be one. Western culture patterns (except those of Scandinavia and perhaps a few other European countries) are such that adolescents tend to find themselves in social environments full of continuing restrictions and frustrations for which they are inadequately prepared, and they commonly have no satisfactory solution. Although parents and other adults have definite ideas about how the transition from childhood to adulthood should proceed, usually these ideas seem rather nonsensical to adolescents, who must accomplish the change.

Adolescents must find their place in a society that is composed not only of their own peers but also of adults to whom they, as present citizens and members of society and as future job holders, parents, and voters must adjust. "Adjustment" means that they must learn to be socially acceptable and to accommodate themselves to the folkways, customs, and mores of their group. Furthermore, regardless of how much adult patterns of thinking and acting are out of tune with adolescent peer group ideals and values, adolescents are expected to adhere to those patterns.

ADOLESCENTS' PEER GROUP RELATIONSHIPS

In modern society informally organized groups, cliques, or gangs become especially widespread and important during adolescence. People of all ages, in large measure, draw upon their fellows for their thoughts, emotions, and modes of behavior. But as youths move into adolescence, peer groups become even more important to them. Whereas, during middle childhood, peer group influence supplements that of home and school, during adolescence it takes priority over, and may even supplant, the influence of these institutions. However, Remmers and Radler report that this generalization holds only in regard to matters involving present social participation. Adolescents turn to parents or other adults for advice on matters of more lasting importance such as political persuasions and personality problems.[7]

Informal groups of adolescent age mates often become the very center of a youth's experience with personal identity and stability. Adolescents will stake almost everything to win and hold the approval of their age mates, and frequently they are well aware of the great importance of age-mate groups in their lives. B. C. Rosen found that, for the group of youngsters he studied, peer groups tended to be more important than adults in influencing choices. He stated that, in cases where parent and peer groups had conflicting attitudes in regard to issues examined in the study, adolescents more often agreed with their peers than with their parents.[8]

Peer groups provide a variety of vital roles for adolescents that often are antithetical to the expectations of schools and society. Although peer groups are in continuous exchange with adult cultures, they also constitute separate subcultures.[9] Each group develops its respective code of conduct that sets limits to competition and cooperation, including acceptable upper and lower limits of academic achievement. Hence, peer groups support the activities of individuals by supplying them with social norms and giving them emotional support. For adolescents, then, peer groups are very important arbiters of social behavior. Through them dates are arranged, experiments with sex, smoking, and liquor consumption are discussed and provided, clothing styles are set, and moral reputations are both made and broken.

Groups with which adolescents identify themselves influence almost everything they do. Thus, peer groups influence an adolescent's speech, moral values, clothing habits, and modes of eating. Some by-products of group interaction are special catchwords, nicknames, jargon, and ambitions. Group approval, in fact, is so alluring to adolescents that they become virtual slaves to peer group customs and seem bound by certain peer group standards, ideals, and attitudes. This is true in a negative as well as a positive sense. If members of an adolescent's peer group frown upon his (or her) earlier ideals, he too is likely to belittle them. Thus, for the time being, peer groups become dominant reference groups that, to a considerable degree, regulate adolescents' attitudes, interests, activities, and aspirations. Consequently, within a peer-group–centered setting, parents and adults may become annoyances in many aspects of living that are vitally important to adolescents.

Identification with peer groups is not without problems. Since an American adolescent usually identifies with more than one group, he (or she) is subjected to conflicting loyalties. His roles are different in the various groups and not all are equally attractive. Yet, while he is with each group he must show unstinted loyalty and enthusiasm. Consequently, adolescent boys will manifest different languages and behaviors depending upon whether, at the moment, they are Future Farmers, Sunday school students, or pals on a Saturday night.

ADOLESCENTS' RELATIONS WITH ADULT SOCIETY

Adolescents not only must accept altered bodies and the necessity of adjusting to new motor and sensory patterns but they also must adapt themselves to a world of people and situations in which they must play new and different roles. Although, at least on a superficial level, they tend to feel competent to make these adjustments, their families are not so sure of his ability. Thus, there are many possibilities for conflict and misunderstanding.

Adolescents assert a desire for independence more aggressively than ever before, but economically and vocationally they are not yet able to escape from dependence on their families and homes. Consequently, many adolescents in present-day society regard themselves as rather useless and resent conditions which make them that way. Should society offer them adequate opportunities to participate in productive endeavors, it is rather doubtful that they would turn to extreme, escape types of activity for their basic satisfactions.

Adult-adolescent conflict is a common phenomenon in Western societies, where, to a large degree, expediency determines patterns of thought and behavior. The many inconsistencies and contradictions in adult society make it doubly difficult for adolescents to understand their society and adjust to it. When practices and values sanctioned by adults of a family and those sanctioned by an adolescent's peer groups point in opposite directions, conflict is certain to arise. In such situations, youths, in an attempt to maintain some degree of stability, gravitate back toward one another and their peer groups. Adult-adolescent conflict then becomes conflict between the family group and the adolescent peer group. The amount of difficulty adolescents encounter in relating themselves simultaneously to both their peer and their adult groups largely determines the degree to which the adolescent period is characterized by storm and stress.

In the lives of adolescents, both parents are important. If a father fails to convey warmth and acceptance to his son, his son stands a good chance of finding adolescence a difficult time. If a mother's family role is of minor importance with little respect for her husband, her daughter's acceptance of, and identification with, her female role is likely to be difficult.[10]

THE CONFUSED AMERICAN TEENAGER

Since there is no clear, consistent view in regard to the rights, duties, and obligations of adolescents, they are intermittently treated as children, as adults, or as marginal persons between the two. Although inconsistencies between the adult world and its expectations in regard to the lives of adolescents are most pronounced in the sexual sphere, they pervade the whole structure of society.[11] Hence, adolescents are uncertain about the expectations adults have for them and about their ability to meet societal expectations.

Obstacles to satisfactory socialization are likely to appear in their most conspicuous form during the teen years. By this time adults expect socialization to have been substantially accomplished. If it is not, glaring inadequacies appear. Various studies have been made of the state of American teenage minds. We already have mentioned the studies conducted at Purdue University under the direction of H. H. Remmers.[12] One conclusion to be drawn from the Purdue studies is that American youths do, after a fashion, become socialized but to a culture which in itself does not make as much sense as it should. Consequently, youth acquire the attitudes of the adult world in a way that would seem to an impartial observer to be senseless, irrational, and contradictory. For example, a sizeable minority—and on some issues a substantial majority— of the 7000 high school students sampled seemed to hold attitudes more appropriate to citizens of a police state than of a democracy.

On the positive side, adolescence is the period during which most individuals develop enough intellectual and social competence to become full-fledged adults through their gaining emotional maturity and ego identity along with their acquiring vocational education and establishing occupational goals. Despite adolescent flights, drug episodes, relaxed sexual mores, and extremes in grooming and clothing, most adolescents turn out to be reasonably stable as they proceed to their adult roles.

The Purdue studies also furnished empirical evidence to support the contention that there is much inconsistency, confusion, and irrationality in the "closed areas."[13] For instance, in the area of religion, students exhibited a confused combination of piety and doubt. However, high school seniors appeared to hold more orthodox views about religion than did freshmen; for example, a larger proportion of seniors rejected the theory of evolution. Also, in the area of sex, much ambivalence and confusion was shown. A considerable proportion of teenagers indicated that they were ashamed of their bodies and their natural functions. Most of those who dated said that they petted on occasion, but they confessed at the same time that they felt strong feelings of guilt about petting. When asked to list, in rank order, some of the "worst things which a person can do," a typical member of the Purdue sample rated "sexual misbehaving" as a more serious offense than stealing, cheating, lying, and being cruel to others.

GROWING INTO ADULTHOOD

Adolescents frequently continue to think of themselves as children beyond the time when it is most effective for them to do so or when it is justified by their biological development. Their resulting behavior leads adult associates to wonder why they do not "grow up and act their age." Only rarely is an adolescent in our society suddenly conscious that he (or she) is "grown up"; he lacks the evidence of some crowning event, like the rites which initiate boys and girls into adulthood in some primitive cultures. Even changes in the way others treat him as he grows up are so gradual that he is scarcely aware of them and would have great difficulty expressing them in words.

In societies where transition into adulthood is gradual and relatively easy, as in some primitive cultures, there is little need for youths to be conscious of their participation in developing new roles for themselves. Margaret Mead has described such developmental patterns of the mountain-dwelling Arapesh of New Guinea.[14] Both men and women are affectionate, trusting, and unaggressive. They consider bearing children and growing food the principal ends of life. The total community is the group to which all Arapesh feel they belong. Children refer to all adults by the same terms that they use in speaking of their fathers and mothers. After an initiation that involves much ceremony but little hardship, boys gradually take over adult economic and social responsibilities.

At the age of 7 or 8 years old a girl is betrothed to a boy several years her elder. She thereupon goes to live with his family. Some years later she too goes through initiation ceremonies, but her life goes on as before. Her future parents-in-law are as indulgent as her own parents. During their adolescent years, both she and her betrothed are members of the same family and community groups. Thus, there are no sudden shifts from one group to another, and the transition from childhood to married life is very gradual.

In societies such as the Arapesh, the passage from childhood to adulthood is so smooth that it goes unrecognized as a "special" period. So, adolescence, as experienced in Western societies, is not a world-wide phenomenon. *Adolescence, then, is a cultural invention.* However, in many primitive societies where the transition from childhood to adulthood is not so smooth, there is a ceremonial adolescence of relatively short duration. This usually takes the form of puberty rites or initiation ceremonies and is timed to occur near the onset of sexual maturity. Accordingly, the onset of puberty becomes the time to initiate boys and girls, often with bizarre and impressive ceremonies. Initiation rites include filing youths' teeth, isolating them for a period of time, or in various ways mutilating their genitals. In males this consists of circumcision or subincision; in females, clitoridectomy or laceration of the hymen or vaginal walls. At the conclusion of his puberty rites a young person enters into all adult activities of the group as a full-fledged member. These activities include marriage, preparation of puberty rites for other youth, and sharing in previously withheld secrets of the tribe.

In that initiation ceremonies dramatize achievement of full adult status, primitive groups may handle the problem of adolescence better than do our "civilized" societies. Today, in modern civilization some vestiges of primitive initiatory ceremonies remain. For example, initiations, some quite horrendous, are used to bring boys and girls into formal membership in various political, religious, and social organizations. However, such activities usually are not central to youths' really acquiring manhood or womanhood.

Some primitive societies, in contrast with ones we have mentioned, stretch adolescence over a considerable period of time. Up to the time of adolescence, both sexes of Tchambuli youth remain with groups of women and smaller children. The men spend most of their time by themselves planning ceremonials. When boys reach the age of nine or ten, they are eased out of the warm protective groups of women and children. However, they are not yet welcome to join men's groups. Men consider them mere boys who are not fit to be trusted with ceremonial property and secrets. Consequently, for three or four years, youths have the status neither of children nor of men.

In complex modern society, as in the Tchambuli society, transition from childhood to adulthood tends to be greatly prolonged. During this period, fulfillment of adult desires, in most instances, must be delayed. Youths no longer are considered children, yet they are not consistently accepted and treated as men and women. While adults who surround an adolescent still look upon him (or her) as a child to be petted and loved, or directed and commanded, the youth may have developed new powers, new interests, and a new sense of his personality. Consequently, at one moment he feels himself to be a man and tries to act like one; then at the next moment he may be forced again to act the part of a child.

Why Is Development of Heterosexuality a Problem?

Heterosexual literally means *other-sexual.* Heterosexuality involves various relationships between the two sexes. Prior to adolescence a child's dominant social interest is with children of his (or her) own sex. This interest continues into adolescence but is paralleled by rising heterosexual interests and activities. Ordinarily many of a person's childhood acquaintances and friendships extend over into the adolescent period. However, these must be restructured to harmonize with his new adolescent role. The socioeconomic status of his family and his friends becomes much more important to an adolescent than it was when he was a child. But, even more important, his motivations become heavily sex tinged. He becomes very much involved in learning all he can about members of the opposite sex. However, his answers usually come from inadequate, limited, and faulty sources. Consequently, typical adolescents in the United States avidly seek knowledge in regard to sex but are in the unfortunate position of not having adequate sources of such information.

SOCIAL MOTIVES AND SEXUALITY

Adolescent youths in modern society are preoccupied with social activities and experimentation, and high schools often serve as social laboratories. In the same sense that a group of people do not eat, sleep, and talk in just any way, adolescents do not choose just anybody as a steady boy or girl friend, and do not socialize with him or her in a completely random manner. As the social structure of a society becomes more highly developed, acquired tastes and motives become more numerous and complex and perhaps more inhibiting or coercing. This is particularly true for persons belonging to the middle and upper strata of a highly developed society. Many of an adolescent's ways of expressing his (or her) tastes and motives stem from social standards of his particular group. Thus, in his sexual relationships, as in others, he feels a need to keep pace with his group.

FROM HOMOSEXUALITY TO HETEROSEXUALITY

In itself, bodily and sexual maturation during adolescence has dramatic effects. Long before boys and girls reach adolescence, they have discovered their anatomical difference and have developed much curiosity with regard to sex and reproduction. However, generally speaking, it is only at the start of their pubescent period that youths begin really to feel the pressure of their organic sexual drives. Changes in their body and physical desires alter the way they see everything that is related to them, but naturally they bring the greatest modifications in their relationships with the opposite sex.

As adolescence is approached, there is a shift in composition of social groups from childhood gangs of one sex to adolescent groups composed of both sexes. Individual youths parallel this social change by shifting their center of interest from a chum of the same sex to a boy friend or girl friend of the opposite sex. Studies have shown that less than one-third of sixth graders voluntarily choose companions of the opposite sex. But by the twelfth grade almost two-thirds are doing so.

SEX-LINKED PROBLEMS OF ADOLESCENTS

Since adolescents' interests in the other sex are so new and so strong, and they have so little accurate understanding of their own sexual natures and that of the opposite sex, they are likely to blunder a good deal in their sexual lives. The wide individual variation in rates of sexual maturation often makes adolescents feel out of step and contributes further to their botching of heterosexual affairs.

Late-maturing boys or early-maturing girls especially are problems to themselves. To a high degree, an adolescent's physique represents his (or her) image of himself. Any atypical change, especially if it is relatively sudden, can be quite disconcerting. Although at the beginning of their teens, girls generally are taller than boys, some girls reach the adolescent growth spurt earlier than most others and are likely to be highly sensitive about their height and other bodily proportions which accompany this growth. It is rather common for tall junior high girls to develop hunched postures in an attempt to hide their atypical stature.

Adolescent girls not only disapprove of their own bodies' showing unusual growth or underdevelopment; they also spurn "mannish" physical characteristics in themselves or their female peers. Consequently, they often try to hide "male characteristics" such as unusual tallness, large hands, large feet, pigmented facial hair, hairiness of arms and legs, heaviness of the lower jaw, massiveness of body build, or underdeveloped breasts.

Whereas girls often are worried when they seem to mature too rapidly, boys typically become apprehensive that their manliness may not be appearing rapidly enough. Also, they frequently are concerned over the rate of growth of their genitals and body hair. At least 29 out of 93 adolescent boys, studied at the University of California, at some time during an eight-year period were disturbed over their physical characteristics. The greatest concern was about lack of body size, particularly height. It is significant, however, that only four of the seven boys concerned with their shortness were actually in the shortest 15 percent of the group of 93.[15]

Adolescent boys tend to stigmatize boys who exhibit feminine physical characteristics. Such traits include fat around the hips, scanty and colorless pubic hair, narrow shoulders, and fatty nipples. Some boys, at the onset of pubescence, still show these traits and are anxious for them to be replaced by adult characteristics as soon as possible.

Sex-linked problems during early adolescence are quite different from those of late adolescence. Problems of early adolescence involve matters such as physical build and proportions, bashfulness, being teased by elders, and accomplishment of a first "date." In late adolescence sex-linked interests center in regular dating, dating behavior, living together, selecting a mate, courtship, marriage, and participation in family life.

Since early-adolescent girls are more mature than boys of the same age, they tend to develop heterosexual interests one or two years sooner than boys. In the seventh and eighth grades, boys often find themselves almost literally being dragged toward heterosexual relationships which they do not welcome. During this period girls are prone to make overtures toward boys to the point that the so-called "dominant" males find their roles reversed. One of the authors vividly recalls sponsoring a party of 13-year-olds in a junior high school where he taught. Wistful females would wait in the ballroom or dance with another while the boys were either rough-housing or consuming soft drinks.

SEXUAL ACTIVITY OF ADOLESCENTS

By the time a primitive youth's sex drive ripens, his (or her) culture usually permits him to begin earning a living and to marry. In contrast, the economies, customs, and even laws of most industrialized societies make it virtually impossible for a 14- or 15-year-old boy and a 13-year-old girl to enter economic pursuits which would enable them to support a family. Even though organically there is little, if any, difference between pubescent youth of a primitive society and those of a civilized one, most adolescents of civilized society are still in school preparing themselves for the future. For them, economic independence is still only a dream. Furthermore, whereas many primitive societies sanction sexual mating of youth before or at least by the time of puberty, American society has in the past attempted to ban any sexual relations until after marriage. This is six or more years after sexual maturity has been reached.

The Kinsey and other studies indicate that a large percentage of boys and many girls are active sexually in some way even prior to adolescence, and that premarital sexual relations are not uncommon in the United States. This means that there is a wide discrepancy between sanctioned, professed, and discussed sexual relations of youth and their actual behavior. A possibly harmful result of this condition is development of guilt feelings which may hamper adult heterosexual adjustment.

Gordon thinks that the movement toward living together and early marriage may represent youths' search for solutions of conflicts.

> Youth wants independence but cannot fully achieve it in the home; youth wants a mature sex relationship and recognizes that clandestine or promiscuous relationships are unsatisfactory; youth wants to be adult in a society that requires that longer and longer years be devoted to education.[16]

In the early 1970s the conventional structure of organized clubs and planned activities in high schools has decayed markedly. Students are prone to say that this is because high schools, as presently operated, are "bad scenes"—they have little relevance to students' present and future needs. Hence, high schools tend to present to students a dual image of a formal adult-controlled and supervised program of instruction over against an informal peer group-controlled program of activities, each trying to dominate the other.

WHAT IS THE PSYCHOLOGICAL MEANING OF ADOLESCENCE?

Adolescence may be characterized psychologically in two quite different patterns of thinking. The key to the difference between the two alternative psychological approaches is the assumed nature of the relationship between a person and the objects that surround him (or her) and the groups of which he is a part. The pivotal question is: Are we to assume that an individual, and more specifically an adolescent, is a biological organism that recurrently is active and passive or that he is a psychological person who is always interactive with his physical-social environment?

The *active-passive* psychological approach to the study of adolescent development is an eclectic position that stems from two contrasting systematic outlooks. These are identified in Chapter 2 as active "saltatory development" and passive "conditioning." To review, "saltatory development" means that a child or adolescent is a natural enfoldment of innate abilities, characteristics, and talents, which unfold in such way that the person develops in a predetermined manner through rather sharply delineated successive stages. Thus, in the developmental process, the individual is considered inherently active; he (or she) carries within him the "blueprints" for his eventual unfoldment.

Passive "conditioning" signifies that an individual is an organism—a mass of protoplasm with a few basic drives—which has developed according to the way it has responded to stimuli, and that its future behavior will depend upon its prior conditioning—relations of stimuli and responses. Thus, in contrast with active unfoldment, conditioning is a mechanistic process of relating stimuli and responses.

An adolescent's being *interactive*, the key idea of the second approach, means that he (or she) is a dynamically purposive person who is at the center of the contemporaneous formulation of both himself and his environment. He is what he *makes of* his organism and all other features that he thinks of as his. Likewise, his environment is that which he *makes of* what to others seems to surround him. From this point of view, then, adolescence is that which adolescents psychologically make of themselves and their environments during that period when they, as developing youth, are growing into men and women.

Whereas the active-passive approach to adolescence centers in S-R conditioning behaviorism, the interactive position relates closely to cognitive-field psychology.[17] Psychologists or teachers working within a behavioristic frame of reference concentrates upon observing adolescents' sequential behavior. Thus, they emphasize organic developments and causal relationships that can be observed and measured. In their study, they look for such things as the correlation between different ages and speeds of growth, the relative positions in the sequence of appearance of respective secondary sex characteristics, and the rate at which a new behavior can be inculcated into the organism's repertoire of behaviors. Contrariwise, psychologists or teachers who operate within a cognitive-field pattern of thinking feel a necessity to think their way into the life spaces of adolescents—to see things as they see them. They concern themselves, primarily, with formulating hypotheses as to why adolescence often is a period of stress, and with testing these hypotheses in light of adolescents' apparently purposive actions. However, in formulating and testing their hypotheses, they take into consideration all of the available data that have been gained through behavioristic as well as cognitive studies.

Whereas behavioristic psychologies are biological-organism centered, cognitive-field psychologies are psychological-person centered. "Organism" suggests a mechanism and human passivity; "person," in contrast, suggests purposiveness and interactivity. The remaining sections of the chapter treat in turn the active-passive approach to adolescence within behaviorism and the interactive position within cognitive-field psychology.[18]

Within Behavioristic Psychology, How Are
Adolescents Considered both Active and Passive?

In the description of the active-passive approach to the study of adolescence we draw primarily from the works of G. Stanley Hall, Arnold Gesell and co-workers, and Karl C. Garrison (1900–   ). Hall was the father of adolescent psychology. Gesell is world renowned for his careful study of children and youth of various ages through the use of systematic observation and photography. Garrison is a leading contemporary adolescent psychologist.

Within the active-passive position in regard to development, adolescence fundamentally is the period and process within which a biological child changes into a biological adult. Social, mental, and psychological processes always are considered secondary to the biological ones. Essentially ". . . *the individual is a relational sum-total of behavior patterns developed in protoplasm in response to environment . . .*"[19] Such behavior patterns are the consequences of inherited physical constitutions being modified by environmental forces. An adolescent, then, grows and develops according to his (or her) genetic constitution and the various environmental forces that have affected that constitution from the time of its conception.

THE ACTIVE ASPECT OF ADOLESCENT DEVELOPMENT

Psychologists who base their theory of human development upon the assumption that human beings are active-passive must develop generalizations in regard to what active organisms are like. Their task is to ascertain the nature of the biological raw materials they have before them; then to describe what happens to biological organisms as they develop. An adolescent is what he (or she) is because of his unique naturally developed organic stage plus his learned responses to the environment which to date has impinged upon him.

In 1904, G. Stanley Hall wrote,

> Adolescence is a new birth, for the higher and more complete human traits are now born. The qualities of body and soul that now emerge are far newer. The child comes from and harks back to a remoter past; the adolescent is neo-atavistic and in him the latter acquisitions of the race slowly become prepotent. Development is less gradual and more saltatory, suggestive of some ancient period of storm and stress when old moorings were broken and a higher level attained.[20]

"Neo-atavistic" means that development of an individual reaches back to, and repeats, the history of the generations that have preceded him. Since adolescence is approaching adulthood, it is repetitive of a more recent, but still ancient, history of humanity.

Hall considered a child, adolescent, or adult to be the sum total of his or her movements or tendencies to move. These movements are based upon hereditary nature or instincts and are refined by the environmental accessory function of education. Furthermore, Hall thought that each stage in the life of an individual is marked by the rise of specific instinctive patterns, which determine his susceptibility to certain conditionings during that period. For example, he considered 8- to 12-year-olds, by their very instinctive nature, to be highly plastic and more susceptible to drill and discipline than they ever had been before or ever would be again.

Gesell, Ilg, and Ames exemplify more contemporary lines of thought within which adolescence is viewed as a step in the continued natural unfoldment of inherited patterns of development. These authors state that, "The cycles of development apply equally to the physical and mental aspects of an organism. The child comes by his mind as he comes by his body—through the organizing processes of growth."[21] They also further note that it took vast ages for human beings to bring their capacities for growth and learning up to their present form, and that in some condensed way infants, children, and youths must retraverse these immense ages of the past. Gesell and his associates recognized that an individual's growth career is not a literal recapitulation of his or her racial history, but they thought that it does reveal deeply seated stages and sequences. So, to develop adequately, an individual must activate a heritage of biological and social potentials as he responds to his surrounding culture.

Thus, according to Gesell, Ilg, and Ames, an innate ground plan is characteristic of the human species. However, each person develops uniquely as a variation of the basic plan. Culture influences and channels the development of human organisms, but it does not generate their developmental progressions and trends. Environmental factors support and modify, but in no sense create, the basic progressions of infant-child-adolescent-adult development.

In addition to the common, human developmental progressions, every person has a more-or-less unique metabolic pattern reflected in his or her body chemistry and endocrine functions. Thus, despite all of the cultural processes that make for standardization, an individual retains a measure of the individuality with which he is biologically endowed. Accordingly, the underlying innate individuality of a person gives form and foundation to his personality and life history. Six areas in which Gesell, Ilg, and Ames think that human organisms show inborn individuality are: sex differences, variations in physique and temperament, mental traits, intelligence, giftedness, and styles of growth.

In the life of an individual, the sequence of developmental stages always holds primary importance. The general tempo and specific timing of developmental stages vary from individual to individual. The general tempo may be accelerated or retarded. Progress may be reasonably constant or it may be irregular with spurts and plateaus. Nevertheless, as Gesell and his colleagues saw it, the sequence is always there.

Gesell's "developmental year" is a unit of developmental time which indicates the duration of inner stages of growth. Calendar time does not measure developmental time, but it does approximate it. Twelve-year-old behavior does not automatically begin on a twelfth birthday, but it does begin when one is approximately that age. A developmental year, unlike a chronological one, cannot be measured with mathematical accuracy. Yet by methods of systematic comparison, one may trace developmental trends over a series of years and ascertain trends which are characteristic of each successive year.

The single greatest source of an individual's responses is his innate organic needs and their corresponding drives. These are needs for food, rest, sleep, elimination, desirable temperature conditions, air, water, and sexual release. How one acts or responds in any situation is assumed to be dominated, but not fully determined, by the state of these organic needs and their related drives. Thus, they constitute the dynamics or movers of an organism.

The power of an individual's organic needs or drives is supplemented by the influence of her or his emotions. Emotion literally means "stirred up" behavior. "In the newborn period there is one universal response or unlearned emotional reaction. This is the so-called 'startle pattern' in response to sudden noise or sudden release of support."[22] This unlearned emotional reaction plus the innate needs and drives avowedly constitute the active psychological aspect of an individual and provide the "raw material" upon which the passive aspects of individuality develop.

THE PASSIVE ASPECT OF ADOLESCENT DEVELOPMENT

Adherents of the active-passive position emphasize two developmental processes—*maturation* and *enculturation*. Maturation means successive, *active* unfoldment of various innate bodily and mental functions and capacities. Enculturation is *passive* absorption of the ways of a culture or society. The two developmental processes interfuse. However, the mechanisms of maturation are so fundamental that they never are transcended; the basic aspects of individuality are assumed to be biochemical, metabolic, and physiological. Nevertheless, it is recognized that individuality also has its passive conditioned aspects. To these we now turn our attention.

Within an active-passive frame of reference, psychologists hold to an underlying conviction that an adolescent's mode of reaction to a situation arises from the nature of his (or her) original drives and emotions, the changes that have been wrought in his neuromuscular system up to that time, and the stimuli that impinge upon the organism just prior to its action. Also, they believe that attentive repetition of an act accompanied by proper stimuli makes it automatic. Furthermore, they think that, ". . . a habit once formed is never completely eradicated from man's neural structure, for all changes which are effected must be built upon the structural patterns existing at the time in the individual."[23]

Emotional reactions of infants are not highly specialized. The most common early emotional response is that of general agitation or excitement. From this, as a result of conditioning, a child learns to express or display responses of distress, fear, anger, delight, and love.[24] These later are differentiated further into diffused forms of behavior such as disgust, jealousy, elation, and affection. Thus, by the time a person reaches adolescence, most of his (or her) expressed fears, angers, and loves are *acquired* ways of responding to various stimuli and situations. "The adolescent is a product of his culture."[25]

To summarize the active-passive approach to development, we may say that basic organic drives and innate patterns of emotional responses furnish the foundation upon which is built a complex repertoire of adolescent behaviors. The nature of genes within one's germ plasm determines this foundation. A number of unconditioned—unlearned—reflexes are present at the birth of an organism. Others appear from time to time as an organism matures. An organism develops its learned habits as a system of conditioned or learned reflexes built upon its unconditioned or unlearned reflexes plus an equally important set of behaviors acquired through its emitted responses being reinforced through satisfaction of its biological needs or drives.

Perhaps an illustration will throw some light on this complicated, mechanistic process. The reader, however, should bear in mind that any verbalized description of mechanistic adolescent behavior tends to be an oversimplification. By the time people have lived 15 years or more in modern society, any of their traits represent the products of conditioning based upon other conditionings based upon other conditionings, and so on, to many levels.

Virginia, an adolescent girl, falls in love with Charles. Now "scientifically" how did this happen? "Falling in love" is a figurative expression which means that when Charles is near enough to Virginia to constitute a stimulus for her, she manifests a pattern of responses such as quickened heart beat, rise in blood pressure, and increased perspiration. Virginia has been conditioned to respond to Charles in this way. Although some responses cannot be easily observed, all can be measured, provided sufficiently sensitive instruments are available.

From birth, Virginia, like all human organisms, had manifested an unlearned tendency to be soothed when she was stroked gently in certain erogenous areas. Through learning, these have been generalized to include most of her body surfaces. She also has maintained an innate tendency to behave emotionally when she is held tightly. When these two emotional situations happen together, Virginia is restrained agitatingly and simultaneously stroked pleasantly, so is agitated pleasingly. Then, too, when previously Charles has impinged upon the sensory nerves of Virginia, accompanying objects and situations have satisfied some of her basic and learned drives. For example, the candy, which accompanied Charles, has satisfied her hunger drive. Through conditioning, Charles comes to evoke the same class of responses as did the pleasing accompanying objects such as candy.

ADULT-ADOLESCENT RELATIONSHIPS WITHIN
THE ACTIVE-PASSIVE OUTLOOK

Adults who hold the active-passive approach to adolescence make much of adolescents' interests, and interests are defined mechanistically. Each interest, so defined, is either an innate or a conditioned drive toward some special kind of activity. To a behaviorist, a drive is a strong, persistent, either innate or inculcated internal stimulus that spurs an organism to activity.

If an interest or drive is innately determined, there is not much that adults can do about changing it. However, when an interest is inculcated, it takes the form of a selective response or reaction that has been promoted through conditioning of the organism in such a way as to get the desired response. Consequently, almost of necessity, an active-passive outlook leads adults to impose their culture patterns upon adolescents. Adults strive to establish certain changes in neuromuscular systems of adolescent organisms that cause them to favor—tend to make—the desired reactions and exclude any others. Thus, certain parts of the environment are singled out as objects to which individuals respond, and they respond to them in the way they have been conditioned.

Garrison states, "Psychologically and sociologically adolescence ends when the individual attains a consistent and comparatively wide-spread level of maturity in his drives, interests, and behavior patterns."[26] Maturity, so used, can mean only conformity to the culture patterns or standards of an adult society. Consequently, within this frame of reference, the proper function of adults is to inculcate into adolescent organisms proper behaviors, worthy ideals, sound values, good character, and a sound verbalized philosophy relative to the nature, purpose, and destiny of man. In turn, achievement of these are some of the "developmental tasks" of adolescents.[27]

Within Cognitive-Field Psychology, How Are Adolescents Considered Interactive?

The most comprehensive concept within cognitive-field psychology is *life space*. In a life space—one's psychological world—everything of consequence is interrelated.[28] A life space is a cognitive map of an individual's personal and environmental factors in dynamic interaction. Such a map depicts one's environment as consisting primarily of a set of goals, the barriers to the goals, and the instrumentalities for achieving the goals. When we think of a person's being interactive, we see his (or her) psychological behavior as depending upon his perception of his current situation. Perception, so used, is given the broadest possible interpretation and coverage. It is the process of one's organizing and reorganizing one's life space—of one's organizing what is sensed and felt into a meaningful configuration related to the overall arrangement of one's world.

A teacher or psychologist construes a life space, as perceived by the person being studied, as consisting of two major regions—(1) the person or self and (2) the person's psychological environment. *Regions* of an individual's life space are those objects or activities or relationships between the two that are related to the individual in such a way as to have some degree of meaning or cognitive structure for him or her.

An adolescent's person or self is that which he or she means when saying "I" or "me"; it includes every idea, action, being, or relationship with which the individual identifies. One's self system is a construct; we cannot see it, but we infer it through observing the individual's patterned behavior. One's psychological environment consists of what one makes *of* one's physical-social environment.

Each of the two major regions—organized meanings—of a life space is differentiated into subregions, and subregions usually are separated further into lesser subregions. Each adolescent is a purposive, goal-oriented being who constructs his (or her) own world of meaning—the regional structure of his life space—through his (or her) experiencing his bodily actions and social milieu.

PSYCHOLOGICAL DIFFERS FROM EITHER
PHYSICAL OR BIOLOGICAL DEVELOPMENT

From a cognitive-field point of view, psychological development is neither physical development alone nor physical development plus other factors. Rather, it is the process whereby a person with a unique organism emerges and grows through interaction with his (or her) physical and social environment. In this process, an organism simultaneously is environmental as well as personal. In the sense that a person identifies himself with it, it is personal. In the sense that it is something with which a person must learn to live, it is environmental.[29] Thus, within the life space of a person, his (or her) organism is an aspect of his environment with which he deals and simultaneously is closely identified with his own self.

Cognitive-field psychologists make a sharp distinction between psychological adolescence and physical pubescence; a psychological person is a broader concept than a biological organism. Thus, to field theorists the social-psychological aspect of adolescence is its major feature. They recognize that changes in behavior that occur during the adolescent period seem at first sight to provide excellent support for a biological view, and that adolescence is related to sexual hormones and to certain periods of bodily growth. However, they note that, even though biological development as such is relatively the same in different societies, anthropological and sociological studies indicate that behavior typical of adolescent ages differs greatly from culture to culture. Consequently, there is little value in attempting to describe any universally generalized, biology-centered adolescent behavior patterns.

AN INTERPERSONAL, SOCIAL PSYCHOLOGY

A growing number of psychologists and educators are becoming convinced that interpersonal, social factors of adolescence are equally or even more important than physiological ones. Since the key factors of interpersonal, social situations are persons, cognitive-field psychologists place psychological persons at the center of the psychological scene. Thus, the pivotal question regarding adolescence becomes "What does adolescence mean to and for persons growing through it?"

Since the focal point of cognitive-field psychology is individuals in relationship with other individuals and with groups, it is an interpersonal, social psychology. When we refer to it as interpersonal, we mean that the interrelationships of persons are very important. However, neither the development of persons nor the development of groups receives exclusive emphasis. Rather, the two processes are considered complementary. Just as groups cannot develop without persons, persons cannot develop independently of groups. Furthermore, the nature of persons is influenced greatly by the nature of the groups with which they identify. Likewise, the nature of groups is influenced by the nature of interpersonal relationships within them.

Cognitive-field psychology, then, is an interpersonal, social psychology that constitutes an effective vehicle for characterization of both childhood and adolescence. It integrates biological and social factors and treats respective persons as interacting with them. In the interactive process a person and his (or her) environment are construed as interdependent variables. Thus, a person is neither dependent upon, nor independent of, his environment. Likewise, a person's environment is neither made by him nor independent of him.

The American social scene with its adolescent difficulties is a state of affairs within which children and adults constitute two clearly defined, distinguishable social groups. This contrasts with situations within which each society consists of one segmented but basically undifferentiated group with easy social locomotion or change from segment to segment. It is because of the sharp differences between child social groups and adult social groups in the American culture that the behaviors of the two groups are separated by an extended adolescence within which group memberships are somewhat unstable. Thus, whether, and to what degree, youngsters display adolescent vacillating behavior depends, in a large measure, upon the incidence of social-psychological conditions of conflict of group membership.

If special efforts were made early and gradually to provide increasingly mature experiences and constantly to introduce children to their larger environment, much of what is commonly considered adolescent behavior probably would not occur. Continuity of the life spaces of children, youth, and adults would persist to the point that any semblance of "stages" would be obliterated. Growth into adulthood would be marked by continuity; there would be no vestige of saltatory development. However, in our culture, spasmodic and rapid developmental changes tend to make adolescence a period of crises.

How Do Children and Youth, Through Psychological Interaction, Develop into Adulthood?

Children and youth accomplish their psychological development into adulthood through experiencing marked acceleration in at least five kinds of changes in the cognitive structures or meanings of their successive life spaces: (1) shifts in group belongingness or identification, (2) increasing conflicts in motivation, (3) intensification of self-awareness, (4) perplexity in regard to bodily appearance and functions, and (5) modifications of time and imaginative perspectives.[30] Note that all of these changes are modifications of the way youths perceive themselves and their environments, and that a perceived self and environment taken together constitute a life space.

SHIFTS IN GROUP BELONGINGNESS OR IDENTIFICATION

A social group is a dynamic whole based on the interdependence of its members. It is composed of two or more people who bear explicit psychological relationship to one another. Often people in a group are similar, but not always; it is their interdependence that makes them a group. Members of a family group—husband, wife, and children of, say, ages nine months, two years, and ten years—are less similar to each other than is a man to another man or a baby to another baby. High school boys of different racial and national background often weld themselves into a group on the basis of a feeling of similarity that constitutes their measuring stick for group belongingness. Note that it is *feeling* of similarity, not similarity in itself, that makes a group.

Any change in belongingness from one group to another is of great importance. A shift from a child group to an adult group makes possible certain activities that previously were forbidden but now are socially permitted. It also brings to the forefront certain taboos that exist for adults but do not apply to children in the same culture. A child usually does not smoke cigarettes or drink beer, whereas many adults do. In turn, a child, when he (or she) feels like crying, may do so; an adult, according to his or her group standards, may cry rarely, if ever.

An adolescent may wish not to belong to a children's group any longer and at the same time realize that he (or she) is not really accepted in an adult group. The inverse condition also may exist; an adolescent may want to continue his identification with a children's group and at the same time feel himself being "pushed" into adult status. In either case he has a position similar to that of what sociologists call a *marginal person*.

A marginal person is one who stands at the boundary between two groups. Thus, he (or she) is halfway between both and a full-fledged member of neither. Consequently, he is uncertain about belonging to either group and is ill at ease with both. Furthermore, he often is treated in an ambiguous manner by both groups. Similarly, an adolescent finds himself being treated ambiguously by his parents, teachers, and other adults as well as by children with whom he associates. An example of a marginal person is a second-generation immigrant who no longer is fully identified with the nationality of his parents but at the same time is not fully accepted as an "American." Characteristic symptoms of behavior of a marginal person are emotional instability and exaggerated sensitivity. To some extent, this symptomatic behavior can be found in most adolescents.

At the same time that a youth finds identity with a new group, he (or she) also experiences some degree of perplexity. His status with his peers in a group is contingent upon his degree of conformity, and often he is not sure of what constitutes conformity. Furthermore, the shift from a children's group to an adult group entails a movement to a more-or-less unknown position. The degree of its being unknown depends upon the habits of the particular culture involved. Thus, psychologically, a child's growing into adulthood is comparable to a person's moving to a new town. He does not know just what he is going to find there.

A child entering adolescence or an adolescent entering adulthood stands on shaky ground, never sure that he is doing the "right" thing. The adolescent no longer wishes to belong to a group that he now recognizes as less privileged than a group of adults, but at the same time he knows that he is not fully accepted by adults as one of them. Thus, he tends to be over-sensitive, he easily shifts from one extreme to another, and he is particularly cognizant of shortcomings of his younger companions who are still "children."

INCREASING CONFLICTS IN MOTIVATION

In modern Western society there is a more or less permanent conflict between children's attitudes, values, ideologies, and styles of living and those of adults. Adolescents often are caught midway in the conflict. Consequently, they experience great difficulty in defining their roles. In turn, the uncertainty in regard to their roles creates ambiguity in their motivation. Thus, they experience lack of social anchorage, except in their peer group. Consequently, they do not know when they should behave and be treated as adults and when they should continue as children. Then too, when they do desire to behave like adults, they lack understanding of the adult world which they are entering. Furthermore, they have little idea of the consequences of various kinds of adult behavior.

The broadening of adolescent life spaces to include both childhood and adult roles brings with it ambiguous situations that youth often are ill-equipped to handle. This results in increased emotional tensions. Then, the conflicts and inadequacies in adolescents' motivation lead adults to feel that adolescents manifest inadequate appreciation of values, emotional instabilities, tendencies to take extreme positions, and, at times, undue shyness and aggressiveness.

Adolescents' conflicts are magnified by the basic nature of the society within which they find themselves. What they learn from books, as well as from adult precepts about what they should accomplish, often is laden with contradictions. Also, in their day-by-day experiences they find a great variety of conflicting religious, political, economic, and occupational values being fostered within the groups with which they identify themselves. These conflicting principles often become personalized as individual conflicts in motivation.

Because of their unstable position in regard to values, adolescents are likely to be willing to follow anyone who will offer a definite pattern of values that fits all situations and thereby resolves their conflicts. This is one explanation of why adolescents are particularly susceptible to conversion to absolutistic systems of thinking that enable them to structure their fields, that is, make sense of their personal-environmental relationships in a rigid manner.

Within cognitive-field psychology, a person's motivation develops through his (or her) differentiating his life space into regions and subregions—functional objects and activities—and simultaneously his cognitively structuring the regions and subregions through grasping some of their meaningful relationships. As new regions and subregions emerge they, to some degree, also are structured cognitively; that is, they are made meaningful.

Although any child's development naturally leads to his experiencing some previously unknown functional subregions in his life space, a period of transition, such as adolescence, is characterized by a stronger than usual impact of the emergence of subregions. Moreover, the emergent subregions are cognitively structured but little, and what structurization does exist is not yet firm. This means that changes come relatively easily in life spaces of adolescents. Since an adolescent's life space tends to have comparatively little clear-cut structurization of subregions, what appears to an adult to be a major shift covering many steps of restructurization may, to an adolescent, involve only one step of change. Furthermore, the boundaries of the subregions of an adolescent's life space are less rigid than those of an adult's life space; in lay terms, he is less set in his ways. This flexibility makes further differentiation less difficult.

Meaningful objects and activities (regions) within a life space have valences (positive or negative drawing powers) of various strengths. The force that correlates with a positive valence of a region or subregion tends to move the person psychologically (not necessarily physically) in the direction of that region. Conversely, a force that correlates with a negative valence tends to move a person away from the region. Thus, objects and functions may have attractive positive valences or repulsive negative ones. Regions and subregions, then, actually are positive or negative *goal* regions. Any region that stands in the way of the person achieving a goal is a *barrier* region in relation to that goal.

In a weakly structured situation, such as that in which an adolescent often finds herself, the valences of an activity can be simultaneously both positive and negative. Thus, she may be inclined to advance toward a goal and to withdraw from it, both at the same time. For example, buying alcohol, having sexual relations, and getting married may be structured in an adolescent's life space with a very high positive valence. But, at the same time, religious scruples and parental authority may give these same activities equal or even higher negative valences.

Since adolescents' psychological directions are rather unclear, their behavior will likely be less effective than it had been in earlier childhood situations where directions were quite clear and habit had been reasonably reliable as a guide. This means that adolescents are in a state of psychosocial locomotion from a fairly well-structured field into a relatively unstructured one. This makes for environmental instability, and, since a person and his environment are closely interrelated, instability of a psychological environment makes for instability of the other major region of a life space—the person.

A person's space of free movement is limited by two types of barriers: (1) what is forbidden to him, and (2) what is beyond his or her ability. These barriers are unusually acute during the adolescent period, especially in American middle-class society. Thus, while self-awareness becomes intensified, self-realization may actually become impaired.

INTENSIFICATION OF SELF-AWARENESS

Self-awareness involves who and what a person seems to himself actually to be and what he is doing about it. From birth, a self is in constant process of emergence and development. However, one's awareness of oneself is sharpened as one becomes more cognizant of groups with which one associates. Personalization and socialization are complementary processes. A group, although different from the persons of which it is constituted, is dependent upon those persons for its very existence. In turn, a human organism without association with any social group probably would continue merely as a biological organism; no self or person would emerge.

An adolescent is very much aware of himself. At times he experiences agonies of self-consciousness as he attempts to come to terms with a new constellation of meanings. Some evidences of adolescents' intensification of self-awareness are their proneness to religious conversion, their some-time sense of the futility of it all, and their recurring idealism, rebellion, or cynicism. Adults might view a sloppily dressed adolescent and con-clude that the youth does not care about anything. However, should they gain the complete confidence of that same adolescent, they probably would find him deeply concerned with many things, but most of all with the enhancement of a self of which he is very much aware but does not understand.

PERPLEXITY IN REGARD TO BODILY APPEARANCE AND FUNCTIONS

Although physiological change in itself is not enough to account for the turmoil of an adolescent, his (or her) changing body with its new po-tential for feeling and behaving constitutes a region of his life space that is particularly close and important to him. Although people sometimes speak of their bodies and themselves as if they were identical, psycho-logically their bodies also are parts of their environments and are treated as such. A youth structures his body into a region of his life space in the same way that he perceives other parts of his environment. His psycho-logical body is that which he *makes of* his biological body.

Just prior to adolescence, a child generally knows his (or her) body quite well. He knows what he can expect from it and how it will act under given circumstances. Then come the glandular and primary sexual changes of pubescence with accompanying secondary sexual changes. The in-dividual becomes somewhat disturbed by the appearance and functioning of his own body. The strange new bodily experience causes this part of his life space that is so close and vital to him to become enigmatic and unknown. Such change tends to shake his faith in the stability of his psychological world and even himself. The kind of perplexity arising from a sharp change in an environment that formerly had been stabilized is quite different and more crucial than that experienced when one merely enters a new environment that never has been structured. It may be com-pared to the feeling of a midwesterner who, arriving in California, has the experience of standing on firm earth and suddenly having it move under him. Since an adolescent's body is a region of his life space that is very important and central for him, doubts in regard to its stability are crucial to his harmonious development.

MODIFICATIONS OF TIME AND REALITY PERSPECTIVES

Adolescence is a period of particularly deep changes in respect to time perspectives and of sharper distinctions of concrete from imaginative levels of reality. Man's "time-binding" ability is one of his most unique features. It grows from birth to adulthood, but at adolescence there is a definite expansion of its scope, paralleling that of physical growth. Whereas children consider days, weeks, or months in their goals, adolescents consider years. As one develops, more memories of a more distant past and anticipation of more projected future figure into one's motivation for present behavior. One's view of the future includes present expectations, fears, hopes, and dreams, projected in terms of a scope of time; they characterize the imaginative level of one's life space. However, one's expectations, hopes, fears, and dreams all are a part of a present life space and influence present concrete behavior.

Since a very young child cannot distinguish between the concreteness of things and figments of her (or his) imagination, in a sense she cannot tell a lie. However, by the time she reaches adulthood such a distinction is fairly well developed. Adults, too, operate on imaginative levels, but they are more likely than children to recognize that they are doing so.

An adolescent, being a marginal person in this regard too, fluctuates between making the sharper adult distinctions of reality levels and the quite fluid differentiation of late childhood. Even though she wanted to, she would encounter great difficulty in trying to make herself believe in the concreteness of Santa Claus. However, this does not mean that adolescents, or adults, completely cease attributing reality to figments of the imagination. Expansion of a person's time perspective and her discrimination of concrete objects from imaginative ones cannot adequately be described bimodally as either-or situations; rather they are a continuum of relationships.

For a child, ideal future goals and real ones are not sharply distinguished; thus, the future has a fluid, indefinite character. But, an adolescent makes a more definite differentiation in regard to time perspective. He (or she) usually feels the need to structure his time perspective in such a way that his ideal goals or values and the realities of life are both taken into account in developing realistic ambitions and expectations. Thus, he is likely to distinguish between what he dreams of or wishes for and what he really expects. The vague, imaginative ideas of childhood are replaced by more or less real decisions in regard to preparation for future occupations and positions.

NOTES

[1] See Nathan W. Shock, "Physiologic Growth," in Frank T. Falkner (ed.), *Human Development*, Philadelphia: Saunders, 1966, pp. 150–169.
[2] See Herant Katchadourian, *The Biology of Adolescence*, San Francisco: Freeman, 1977, pp. 84–85.
[3] Alfred C. Kinsey and others, *Sexual Behavior in the Human Female*, Philadelphia: Saunders, 1953, p. 549.
[4] See Karl C. Garrison, "Physiological Development," in James F. Adams, (ed.), *Understanding Adolescence*, Boston: Allyn & Bacon, 1976, pp. 118–120.

[5] Katchadourian, *The Biology of Adolescence*, pp. 90–114.

[6] Margaret Mead, *Coming of Age in Samoa*, New York: Morrow, 1928.

[7] See H. H. Remmers and D. H. Radler, *The American Teenager*, Indianapolis: Bobbs-Merrill, 1957, p. 222.

[8] B. C. Rosen, "Conflicting Group Membership: A Study of Parent-Peer Group Cross-Pressures," *American Sociological Review* 20, (1955):160.

[9] See Ira J. Gordon, *Human Development: A Transactional Perspective*, New York: Harper & Row, 1975, p. 314.

[10] Ibid., p. 305.

[11] Ibid., p. 312.

[12] Remmers and Radler, p. 222.

[13] See Maurice P. Hunt, *Foundations of Education, Social and Cultural Perspectives*, New York: Holt, Rinehart and Winston, 1975, for a discussion of "closed areas."

[14] See Margaret Mead, *Growing Up in New Guinea*. This book is the second in the triology *From the South Seas*, New York: Morrow, 1939.

[15] See Herbert R. Stolz and Lois M. Stolz, "Adolescent Problems Related to Somatic Variation," in Nelson B. Henry (ed.), *Adolescence*, Forty-third Yearbook of the National Society for the Study of Education, University of Chicago Press, 1944, pp. 85–87.

[16] Gordon, *Human Development*, p. 360.

[17] See Part III for an expansion of the difference between these systematic psychologies of learning.

[18] See Chapter 7, p. 154 for descriptions of various approaches to the study of development.

[19] Karl C. Garrison, *Psychology of Adolescence*, 6th ed., Englewood Cliffs, N.J.: Prentice-Hall, 1965, p. 37.

[20] G. Stanley Hall, *Adolescence*, vol. 1, New York: Appleton, 1904, p. xiii.

[21] Arnold Gesell, Frances L. Ilg, and Louise Bates Ames, *Youth: The Years from Ten to Sixteen*, New York: Harper & Row, 1956, p. 17.

[22] George H. Lowrey, *Growth and Development of Children*, 6th ed., Year Book Medical Publishers, 1973, p. 208.

[23] Garrison, p. 107.

[24] See Chapter 14, pp. 288–292, for an explanation of conditioning.

[25] Karl C. Garrison and Karl C. Garrison, Jr., *Psychology of Adolescence*, 7th ed., Englewood Cliffs, N.J.: Prentice-Hall, 1975, p. 64.

[26] Garrison, p. 433.

[27] Garrison and Garrison, pp. 10–14.

[28] See Chapter 7, pp. 155–156, for an introduction to the meaning of life space. The concept is developed in detail in Chapters 14 and 15.

[29] See Chapter 14, pp. 362–364.

[30] See Kurt Lewin, *Field Theory in Social Science*, New York: Harper & Row, 1951, pp. 137–141.

BIBLIOGRAPHY

ADAMS, JAMES F. (ed.). *Understanding Adolescence*. Boston: Allyn & Bacon, 1976. A timely symposium on many aspects of adolescence. Centers on understanding problems of today's youth.

BERNARD, HAROLD W. *Human Development in Western Culture*, 4th ed. Boston: Allyn & Bacon, 1975. Covers entire span of child and youth development. Chapters 10, 11, and 12 devoted to adolescence.

COLE, LUELLA, and IRMA NELSON HALL. *Psychology of Adolescence*, 7th ed. New York: Holt, Rinehart and Winston, 1970. A comprehensive treatment of all aspects of adolescent development. Contains many illustrative case studies and anecdotes. Applies adolescent psychology to teaching.

GALLATIN, JUDITH E. *Adolescence and Individuality*. New York: Harper & Row, 1975. Provides an integrated, coherent account of adolescent development. Emphasizes Erikson's theory of personality development.

GARRISON, KARL C. *Psychology of Adolescence*, 6th ed. Englewood Cliffs, N.J.: Prentice-Hall, 1965. A standard text for adolescent psychology. Adolescence is portrayed with a biological and social emphasis. Youth are pictured as personalities growing and developing according to their genetic constitutions and environmental factors.

GARRISON, KARL C., and KARL C. GARRISON, JR. *Psychology of Adolescence*, 7th ed. Englewood Chiffs, N.J.: Prentice-Hall, 1975. A complete reworking of *Psychology of Adolescence* within a sociological perspective. Excellent presentation of adolescent social psychology and sociology. Also has an active-passive orientation, but less sharply developed than in earlier editions.

GESELL, ARNOLD, FRANCES L. ILG, and LOUISE B. AMES. *Youth: The Years from Ten to Sixteen*, New York: Harper & Row, 1956. A report based upon study of a selected group of adolescents. This book traces development of behavior of each age group from 10 to 16 and interprets the patterns and trends of successive stages.

HENRY, NELSON B. (ed.). *Adolescence*. The Forty-Third Yearbook of the National Society for the Study of Education, University of Chicago Press, 1944. A balance of views on adolescents which covers their physical and psychological changes, development of physical and mental abilities, and socialization.

HURLOCK, ELIZABETH B. *Adolescent Development*. New York: McGraw-Hill, 1973. The adolescent transition—bodily, emotional, social status, interests, activities, morality, and sexual. Highlights important points in boxes.

KATCHADOURIAN, HERANT. *The Biology of Adolescence*. San Francisco: Freeman, 1977. The biological changes of adolescence including health hazards and ailments.

LEWIN, KURT. "Field Theory and Experiment in Social Psychology: Concepts and Method," *American Journal of Sociology* 44, (1939):868–896. (Also *Field Theory in Social Science*. New York: Harper & Row, 1951, chapter VI.) Discussion of the problem of adolescence and the social group concept provides examples of how it is necessary to represent the dynamics of a total situation to explain social behavior.

LOWREY, G. H. *Growth and Development of Children*, 6th ed. Chicago: Yearbook Publishers, 1973. Centers on children but contains excellent charts of adolescent development.

McCANDLESS, BOYD R. *Adolescents: Behavior and Development*. Hinsdale, Ill.: Dryden, 1970. Specific, unique, biological, personal, and social changes that characterize adolescents.

MEAD, MARGARET. *Coming of Age in Samoa.* New York: Morrow, 1928. A psychological study of the youth of Samoa. Comparison of Samoan youth with youth in "civilized" societies permits some deductions about "natural" behaviors.

MUUSS, ROLF E. *Theories of Adolescence.* New York: Random House, 1962. A chronological presentation of eight leading theories of the nature of adolescence. Followed by treatment of contemporary issues and some generalizations.

REMMERS, HERMANN H., and D. H. RADLER. *The American Teenager.* Indianapolis: Bobbs-Merrill, 1957. A research report on a cross section of American teenagers. Includes their conceptions of the world, their problems, their parental and school relations, and their outlook for the future.

A Study of Adolescent Boys, conducted by Survey Research Center, Institute for Social Research, University of Michigan, for the National Council, Boy Scouts of America, University of Michigan and Boy Scouts of America, 1956. A report of a national survey of 14- to 16-year-old boys. It analyzes dominant needs, problems, and concerns; kinds and amount of leisure-time activities; group membership and relationships; and sources of motivation of the boys.

SEIDMAN, JEROME M. (ed.). *The Adolescent—A Book of Reading,* rev. ed. New York: Holt, Rinehart and Winston, 1960. A broad selection of excellent outside readings by specialists in adolescent psychology. Includes adolescent transition, growth and development, peer group relations, multiple-group memberships, interests and attitudes, and problems.

Part III
HOW DO HUMAN
BEINGS LEARN?

Although both motivation and development are closely related to the learning process, we have not yet focused our discussion on learning per se. It is the purpose of Part III to treat learning explicitly and in some detail.

Chapter 9 introduces the problem of learning, the respective learning theories, and the concepts that characterize the learning theories. Chapter 10 presents the more prominent learning theories that emerged prior to the twentieth century and continue to influence today's schools. The chapter also shows the implications of these early developed theories for school practice.

Chapter 11 presents what the authors consider to be the two major competing "families" of learning theory of the twentieth century, namely, *stimulus-response conditioning* theory and *Gestalt-field* theory. The chapter also develops the theoretical backgrounds of the two families by explaining how they arose and how they relate to mechanistic and relativistic outlooks. Chapter 12 then focuses on the specific explanation of learning that each family offers. Chapter 13 presents the most prominent systematic version of stimulus-response conditioning theory or behaviorism—B. F. Skinner's mechanistic *operant conditioning* theory.

Chapters 14 and 15 are devoted to an explanation of *cognitive-field* learning theory. This learning theory is a prominent contemporary representative of the Gestalt-field family. Chapter 14 describes relativistic cognitive-field psychology and defines its key constructs. Then Chapter 15 applies this psychology to learning situations and processes. Chapter 16 presents Robert M. Gagné's and Jerome S. Bruner's cognitive-oriented eclectic psychologies.

Since each chapter, and its headings, is devoted to the presentation of a specific position on learning, all statements, even when they are not attributed to either the position or an adherent, should be construed to represent the respective position that is being presented.

Chapter 9
WHY IS CLASSROOM
LEARNING A PROBLEM?

Maturation or learning, or a combination of the two, is the means by which lasting changes in persons occur. Maturation is a developmental process within which a person from time to time manifests different traits, the "blueprints" for which have been carried in his (or her) cells from the time of his conception.

Learning, in contrast with maturation, is an enduring change in a living individual that is not heralded by his genetic inheritance. It may be considered a change in insights, behavior, perception, or motivation, or a combination of these.

> Learning is basic to the development of athletic prowess, of tastes in food and dress, and of the appreciation of art and music. It contributes to ethnic prejudice, to drug addiction, to fear, and to pathological maladjustment. It produces the miser and the philanthropist, the bigot and the patriot. In short, it influences our lives at every turn, accounting in part for the best and worst of human beings and for the best and worst in each of us.[1]

Since teachers can do little to influence the maturational patterns of students, except perhaps to accelerate or retard them to some degree, their most effectual area of endeavor always centers upon learning. Furthermore, because of people's unique traits and capacities, learning is far more crucial to them than it is to the lower animals.

Human beings have some distinguishing characteristics that give a unique quality to a study of them. First of all, they talk and they are time-binding individuals. Their being time-binding means that both a past and a future enter into their present perception of things. Secondly, they have a highly developed imaginative capacity. Also, they are cultural beings; they build on their past in a peculiarly selective fashion. Then, people have a unique capacity for social interaction with their fellows, which enables them to transcend concrete situations and live in a more or less imaginative realm. And most significantly of all, a human being, in his (or her) perceptual process, may view himself simultaneously as both the subject and the object, as a knower and as a known.

Whereas in the lower animals much behavior is instinctive, human children, benefiting from their high degree of plasticity, learn their many patterns of human behavior. The relatively long period of children's dependency upon adults, following their complete helplessness at birth, contributes to their acquisition of the culture of their group. Using their relatively high potential for intelligence and their capacity for communication through use of articulate speech and other symbols, members of each generation build upon the achievements—artifacts, ideas, customs, and traditions—of the generation before it. A culture—social heritage—of a society is the result of many generations of cumulative learning.

People share with other mammals some primary organic drives such as hunger, thirst, sex, cravings for oxygen, warmth, and rest, and possibly a few primary aversions such as fear and rage. The first expression of these drives and aversions is primarily a maturational process. But, in some way, human beings seem to transcend these hereditary drives and aversions. In large measure, this trancendence is centered in the human capacity to deal with a complex past, present, and future world so as to develop abstractions or generalizations that organize mazes of particulars into sensible patterns. Perhaps a desire to perceive, understand, imagine, and deal with ideas is just as much a part of people's basic nature as are the specific organic drives and aversions. Biologically, *Homo sapiens*— the human being—is a species of mammal characterized by superior knowing and discerning abilities.

There apparently is no group of human beings that has not, through learning, developed some devices for enriching its contacts with the world about it. In the development of these devices, people have attempted to derive satisfactions from understanding and manipulating their world as well as through merely touching, smelling, and tasting its various aspects. Moreover, contrasted with capacities of less advanced animals, people's potential for becoming human lies largely in their capacity for extension of experience to a world of symbolism—to operate on an imaginative level of reality.

Animals seem to derive satisfaction from using whatever abilities they have. Accordingly, human beings derive satisfaction from using both their innate and acquired abilities. Thus, the very process of learning, both concrete and abstract, can become satisfying to them. In their social, aesthetic, economic, religious, and political life they show a tendency to explore. Not all people develop sophisticated ideological outlooks. But, rarely if ever are there groups of people who subsist solely on a vegetative level with no imaginative or mentalistic endeavors. Even the most primitive cultures have developed some symbolistic folklore and ideology.

Not only have people wanted to learn, but often their curiosity has impelled them to try to learn how they learn. Since ancient times, at least some members of every civilized society have developed, and to some degree tested, ideas about the nature of the learning process. Thus, they have developed their respective learning theories.

WHAT IS A LEARNING THEORY?

A learning theory is a systematic integrated outlook in regard to the nature of the process whereby people relate to their environments in such a way as to enhance their ability to use both themselves and their environments more effectively. Everyone who teaches or professes to teach has a theory of learning. However, teachers may be able to describe their theories in explicit terms or they may not—in which case we usually can deduce from their actions the theories that they are not yet able to verbalize. So, the important question is not whether a teacher has a theory of learning, but rather how tenable it is.

Quite often in our scientific age we erroneously think of theory as indefinite or indefensible conjecture that existed prior to the use of scientific method and evidence. Consequently, although we might not object to using the term in a description of the historical development of modern concepts of learning, we would expect the word fact rather than theory to be used in describing the current scene. After all, are we not now on solid enough ground for the term theory to be discarded? This, however, is not the case; theory definitely should not be abolished.

Any sharp distinction between theoretical, imaginative knowledge and the action that stems from such knowledge is faulty. Action, whether a part of teaching or any other activity in life, either is linked with theory or it is blind and purposeless. Consequently, any purposeful action is governed by theory. Learning theory is a distinct area within theoretical psychology. In recent years, many psychologists have been dedicated to a study of learning theory. Thus, they have concentrated upon developing systematic theories supported by experimentation.

Since the seventeenth century, more or less systematic theories of learning have emerged periodically to challenge existing theories. Typically, a new theory of learning is not translated into school practice until 25 to 75 years have elapsed. Then, as a new theory eventually comes to affect school policy, it usually does not displace its predecessors; it merely competes with them. Thus, as new theories have been introduced they have been added to the old, and the educational scene has become more and more muddled. Probably most teachers, from time to time, have adopted conflicting features from a variety of learning theories without realizing that they were basically contradictory in nature and could not be brought into harmony with each other.

WHY ARE THERE THEORIES OF LEARNING?

In most life situations learning is not much of a problem. A (lay) person takes it for granted that we learn from experience and lets it go at that; he or she sees little that is problematic about learning. Throughout human history people have learned, in most cases without troubling themselves as to the nature of the process. Parents have taught children, and master workmen have taught apprentices. Both children and apprentices learned, and those who taught them felt little need for a grasp of learning theory. Teaching was done by "teachers" telling and showing students how, complimenting the learners when they did well and scolding or punishing them when they did poorly. Teachers simply taught the way that they had been taught as children or youth.

When schools were developed as special environments to facilitate learning, teaching ceased to be so simple a matter. The subjects taught in school were different from the matters learned as part of routine life in a tribe or society. Mastering school subjects, whether the three R's, foreign languages, geometry, history, or something else, appeared to children as an entirely different sort of learning task from those taken for granted in everyday life. Often their relevance to the problems of daily living seemed unclear. Such subjects, whose immediate usefulness is not obvious, strike a learner as quite different from the crafts and skills needed to carry on day-by-day social, economic, and political life.

Ever since education became formalized in schools, teachers have been aware that learning in school often is highly inefficient. For example, material to be learned may be presented to students innumerable times without noticeable results. Many students may appear uninterested. Many may become rebellious and make serious trouble for teachers. Consequently, classrooms often have seemed like battlegrounds in which teachers and students made war against each other. Such a state of affairs may come to be taken for granted by teachers, students, and parents. Consequently, they may consider it "natural" that youngsters dislike school and try to resist school learning. Thus, they may assume that it simply is one of the unpleasant facts of life that many children and youths will learn very little in school.

From the colonial period through the nineteenth century, most people in the United States probably made such placid assumptions concerning formal education. However, as soon as the professions of psychology and education developed, it was inevitable that professionals would begin asking questions. When teaching moved from the mother's knee to a formalized environment designed to promote learning, it was inescapable that a small group of persons would arise to begin speculating about whether schools were getting the best possible results. Then, professional psychologists and educators who critically analyzed school practices found that development of more or less systematic schools of thought in psychology offered a handy tool for crystallization of their thinking. Each of these schools of thought has contained, explicitly or implicitly, a theory of learning. In turn, a given theory of learning has implied a set of class-room practices. Thus, the way in which educators build curriculums, select materials, and choose instructional techniques depends, to a large degree, upon how they define "learning." Hence, a theory of learning may function as an analytical tool; its exponents can use it to judge the quality of a particular classroom situation.

Psychology is not a field of study characterized by a body of theory that is internally consistent and accepted by all psychologists. Rather, it is an area of knowledge characterized by the presence of several schools of thought. In some instances these may supplement one another, but at other times they are in open disagreement. Thus, we may find psychologist X, who is both scholarly and sincere, opposed to many of the crucial ideas of psychologist Y, who is equally scholarly and sincere. Such disagreement among psychologists may be disconcerting to students. But one of the challenges of psychological study lies in theoretical disagreement; only to the degree that students are willing to think for themselves can they emerge from their studies with something worthwhile. Some consolation may be had in the fact that similar disagreements also exist in the physical sciences. One's gaining an understanding and appreciation of the achievements of thinkers in any area is never easy. As stated by Taube, "After all, if the fox twists and turns, so must the hound."[2]

Everything teachers do is colored by the psychological theory they hold. Consequently, teachers who do not make use of a systematic body of theory in their day-by-day decisions are behaving blindly. Hence, little evidence of long-range rationale, purpose, or plan is observable in their teaching. So, teachers without a strong theoretical orientation inescapably make little more than busy work assignments. True, many teachers operate in this way and use only a hodgepodge of methods without theoretical orientation. However, this muddled kind of teaching undoubtedly is responsible for many of the current adverse criticisms of public education.

Yet, teachers need not base their thinking on tradition and folklore. Instead, they may be quite aware of the most important theories developed by professional educational psychologists, in which case their own psychological theory is likely to be quite sophisticated. The latter state of affairs is what professional psychologists interested in education of teachers are trying to induce. Teachers who are well grounded in scientific psychology—in contrast to "folklore psychology"—have a basis for making decisions that are much more likely to lead to effectual results in classrooms.

As a student, you may not have a large background of either practical experience or "book knowledge" to bring to bear on the question of how children and youth learn. Nevertheless, even before reading further in this book, you should realize that you do have some resources on which to draw. You have been learning all your life and are continuing to do so. And all your life you have been associating with others who were also learning, often from you. What seems to be the essential nature of the process called learning? What happens within, or to, you when you learn? Does the same thing happen to everyone? It probably would be helpful to you, now, to take paper and pen and write a one- or two-page essay on this subject. (You may not find this an easy assignment!) Repeat the assignment when you have mastered this book and see the difference in your two essays.

This book deliberately presents several competing theories of learning, providing different answers to many of the questions that might be raised, so that students will become increasingly sophisticated about the "schools of thought" that exist in psychology today and understand how differently each attacks respective problems. The "comparative" or "systematic" treatment herein employed requires, among other things, that students do considerable thinking for themselves.

HOW ARE LEARNING THEORIES EVALUATED?

It is one thing to talk about constructive thought and another actually to achieve it. Thinking for oneself is never easy. However, it may be easier for you to do a respectable job of critical thought if you are clearly aware of two competing kinds of criteria for judging the answers to questions, namely, *authoritarian* and *scientific*. Think about any statement that you consider to be true. Do you regard it as true merely because you read it somewhere or heard some teacher or other "authority" say it or because, when you examined all the available pertinent evidence, it seemed to have more factual support than any alternative statement? If you accept the statement "on faith" because someone told it to you, you have used an authoritarian criterion for judging truth. If you accept it because you either have pursued your own careful investigations of it or you have studied the investigations of others, you are operating within a more scientific framework.

Although we recognize the distinction between authoritarian and scientific approaches, the road to inquiry still may not be smooth. Often we are required to reach conclusions before we have had sufficient time either to conduct our own investigation or to study critically the investigations made by those who pose as authorities. In such cases we have no choice except to take someone else's word for it. Whose word do we take? In answering questions in psychology, we might turn to the writings of the most prominent psychologists. But, unfortunately, prominence does not guarantee reliability. Less well-known persons may be more nearly right. Furthermore, in the field of psychology it is common for top-ranking authorities, who have spent lifetimes in research, to disagree. Such disagreement is, in part, the result of differing basic assumptions.

So, there are no final answers to questions concerning learning, and no theory can be found to be absolutely superior to all others. Nevertheless, teachers can develop learning theories of their own that, because of their internal *harmony* and educational *adequacy*, they can support. Such theories may turn out to be somewhat replicas of ones introduced in this book, or readers may benefit by contributions of several theories and derive one of their own. In either event, the quality of their teaching will be enhanced by their having thought through the question of the nature of the learning process that teachers want to promote in students.

Through study of theories of learning and their historical development, teachers should gain insight into the harmonies and conflicts that prevail in present educational theory. Through this insight, they should move toward developing adequate theories of their own. Before attempting to formulate their own learning theory, they would do well to examine carefully and critically the prevalent theories that have been developed by professionals in the area.

WHAT LEARNING THEORIES ARE REFLECTED IN SCHOOL PRACTICE?

In the remaining section of this chapter, we present an abbreviated sketch of the major lines along which learning theory has developed and provide an example of teaching nonreaders to read using each. Then, in Chapters 10 to 17 we develop each line of thought in considerable detail. At least ten different theories in regard to the basic nature of the learning process either are prevalent in today's schools or are advocated by leading contemporary psychologists. Table 9.1 lists the ten major theories, groups some of them into families, and outlines the concepts involved. As students pursue the study of learning and teaching, they should find it helpful to refer to this table frequently.

What Are Some Leading Pre–Twentieth-Century Learning Theories?

Column I of Table 9.1 lists ten learning theories. The first four of these, namely, the two mental discipline theories of the mind substance family, *natural unfoldment* (or *self-actualization*) and *apperception*, were de-

Table 9.1 REPRESENTATIVE THEORIES OF LEARNING AND THEIR IMPLICATIONS FOR EDUCATION

	THEORY OF LEARNING I	PSYCHOLOGICAL SYSTEM OR OUTLOOK II	CONCEPTION OF MAN'S BASIC MORAL AND ACTIONAL NATURE III
Mental discipline theories of mind substance family	1. Theistic mental discipline	Faculty psychology	*Bad-active* mind substance continues active until curbed
	2. Humanistic mental discipline	Classical humanism	*Neutral-active* mind substance to be developed through exercise
	3. Natural unfoldment or self-actualization	Romantic naturalism or psychedelic humanism	*Good-active* natural personality to unfold
	4. Apperception or Herbartianism	Structuralism	*Neutral-passive* mind composed of active mental states or ideas
S-R (stimulus-response) conditioning theories of behavioristic family	5. S-R bond	Connectionism	*Neutral-passive* or *reactive* organism with many potential S-R connections
	6. Conditioning with no reinforcement	Behaviorism	*Neutral-passive* or *reactive* organism with innate reflexive drives and emotions
	7. Conditioning through reinforcement	Reinforcement	*Neutral-passive* or *reactive* organism with innate reflexes and needs with their drive stimuli
Cognitive theories of Gestalt-field family	8. Insight	Gestalt psychology	*Neutral-active* being whose activity follows psychological laws of organization
	9. Goal-insight	Configurationalism	*Neutral-interactive* purposive individual in sequential relationships with environment
	10. Cognitive-field	Field psychology or positive relativism	*Neutral-interactive* purposive person in simultaneous mutual interaction with psychological environment, including other persons

veloped prior to the twentieth century but continue to be highly influential in today's schools. (Chapter 10 is devoted to explanation and evaluation of these first four theories.)

Mental discipline, of both kinds, means that learning consists of

BASIS FOR TRANSFER OF LEARNING IV	EMPHASIS IN TEACHING V	KEY PERSONS VI	CONTEMPORARY EXPONENTS VII
Exercised faculties, automatic transfer	Exercise of faculties of the mind	St. Augustine J. Calvin C. Wolff J. Edwards	Many Hebraic-Christian fundamentalists
Cultivated mind or intellect	Training of intrinsic mental power	Plato Aristotle	M. J. Adler R. M. Hutchins
Recapitulation of racial history, no transfer needed	Negative or permissive education centered on feelings	J. J. Rousseau F. Froebel Progressivists	P. Goodman J. Holt A. H. Maslow
Growing apperceptive mass	Addition of new mental states or ideas to a store of old ones in subconscious mind	J. F. Herbart E. B. Titchener	Many teachers and administrators
Identical elements	Promotion of acquisition of desired S-R connections	E. L. Thorndike	A. I. Gates J. M. Stephens
Conditioned responses or reflexes	Promotion of adhesion of desired responses to appropriate stimuli	J. B. Watson	E. R. Guthrie
Reinforced or conditioned responses plus stimulus and response induction	Successive, systematic changes in organisms' environment to increase the probability of desired responses	C. L. Hull	B. F. Skinner K. W. Spence R. M. Gagné
Transposition of insights	Promotion of insightful learning	M. Wertheimer K. Koffka	W. Köhler
Tested insights	Aid students in developing high-quality insights	B. H. Bode R. H. Wheeler	E. E. Bayles
Continuity of life spaces, experience, or insights	Help students restructure their life spaces—gain new insights into their contemporaneous situations	K. Lewin E. C. Tolman J. Dewey G. W. Allport A. Ames, Jr. R. May	R. G. Barker M. L. Bigge J. S. Bruner D. Snygg M. Deutsch S. Koch

students' minds being disciplined or trained. In teaching nonreaders to read, teachers who are committed to mental discipline would instruct in a way that would exercise the "muscles" of students' minds. These teachers probably would first list words that they wanted students to be able to recognize, read, and spell. They would use flash cards in teaching them. They would drill their students extensively, test them daily, and have the low achievers return after school for further drill.

There would be "recitations" within which students would be drilled orally and would take turns reading passages of their daily lessons. Those who did poorly would be scolded when they made mistakes, and some of them would be sent to their seats to "study." Students would be driven to stay with their lessons, and thereby perseverance and willpower would be strengthened. Strict discipline would be maintained in order to strengthen the faculty of attention as well as those of memory, will, and perseverance. The teacher would have little hesitation in using various kinds of physical and mental punishment, as the situation required.

Natural unfoldment or *self-actualization*—the extreme opposite of mental discipline—is a procedure within which a child unfolds that which either nature or a creator has enfolded within him or her. Teachers who adhere to this position would first of all wait for students to express a desire to learn to read before they would make any attempt to teach them. Then, the teachers would be much more concerned with the children's development than with inculcation of any specific skills; they would make sure that each child's learning was a joyous experience.

Apperception is a process of new ideas associating themselves with old ones that already constitute a mind. Apperceptionists would teach students to read by starting with the alphabet and making sure that the students could recognize and say each letter. They then would tell them how letters are put together to make words, how letters make sounds, how sounds are telescoped together, and how vowels and consonants worked. In other words, the teachers would give them some rules. Next, they would talk to them about things that they already knew such as dogs, cats, boys, and girls. Then they would show them d o g and explain that it stands for dog. They would be concerned primarily with making reading interesting and being sure that their students got the right ideas from their reading.

What Are the Leading Twentieth-Century Learning Theories?

Twentieth-century systematic learning theories may be classified into two broad families, namely, *S-R* (*stimulus-response*) *conditioning* theories of the behavioristic family and *cognitive* theories of the Gestalt-field family. Thus, in Table 9.1 entries 5, 6, and 7—S-R bond, conditioning with no reinforcement, and conditioning through reinforcement—are encompassed by the generalized concepts *S-R conditioning theory* and *behaviorism*, which may be used interchangeably. Likewise, entries 8, 9, and 10— insight, goal-insight, and cognitive-field theory—are examples of the *Gestalt-field* family, which emphasizes cognition in learning.

Chapters 11 and 12 discuss the differences between the two families of twentieth-century scientific learning theories. Chapter 13 contains a description of a most popular contemporary psychology of learning that represents the behavioristic family—B. F. Skinner's operant conditioning theory. Chapters 14 and 15 present a leading contemporary representative of the Gestalt-field family—the cognitive-field theory of learning.

Since a large number of today's educators adhere to some sort of eclectic position in regard to learning, it behooves a teacher to have some idea of the forms that eclecticisms may take. In Chapter 16 we present Robert M. Gagné's behavioristic-oriented eclectic approach to learning and Jerome S. Bruner's cognitive-oriented eclectic psychology of learning and teaching. Gagné's psychology centers on behaviorism, loosely defined, and contains only marginal overtones gained from the Gestalt-field family. In contrast, Bruner's principal concern has been with describing the means whereby people cognitively select, retain, and transform information and with finding how they go beyond acquiring discrete information to gain the generalized insights or understandings that give them competence. Hence, his position has much in common with systematic Gestalt-field positions.

For behaviorists or S-R conditioning theorists, learning is a change in observable behavior. It occurs through stimuli and responses becoming related according to mechanistic principles. Thus, it involves the formation of relations of some sort between series of stimuli and responses. Stimuli—the causes of learning—are environmental agents that act upon an organism so as either to cause it to respond or to increase the probability of a response of a certain kind. Responses—effects—are physical reactions of an organism to either external or internal stimulation.

For Gestalt-field theorists, learning is a process of gaining or changing insights, outlooks, expectations, or thought patterns. In thinking about the learning processes of students, these theorists prefer the terms *person* to *organism, psychological environment* to *physical* or *biological environment,* and *interaction* to either *action* or *reaction.* Such preference is not merely a whim; there is a conviction that the concepts *person, psychological environment,* and *interaction* are highly advantageous for teachers in describing learning processes. They enable a teacher to see a person, his (or her) environment, and his interaction with his environment all occurring at once; this is the meaning of *field.*

To summarize the difference between the two families very briefly, S-R conditioning theorists interpret learning in terms of changes in strength of hypothetical variables called S-R connections, associations, habit strengths, or behavioral tendencies; Gestalt-field theorists define learning in terms of reorganization of perceptual or cognitive fields so as to gain understanding. Consequently, whereas a behavioristic teacher desires to change the observable behaviors of his or her students in a significant way, a Gestalt-field oriented teacher aspires to help students change their understandings of significant problems and situations.

Behavioristic teachers in teaching nonreaders to read, would first develop a list of words that they want to incorporate into the working vocabularies of their students. Prior to the introduction of specific letter sound relationships, they probably would teach students to read whole words and to express their meanings. Within the S-R conditioning process, students are taught using either one, or a combination, of two procedures, namely, the *stimulus substitution* method of classical conditioning or the *response modification* method of instrumental conditioning.

When using stimulus substitution, the teachers in any way possible, would get their students to say each specific word, then they would give them the appropriate stimulus in the form of the written word just prior to their saying that word. Consequently, in the future, upon being stimulated by that written word, students would be likely to say it.

Within response modification, or reinforcement, students would be given a "reward," that is, their behavior would be reinforced whenever they either completed a word properly or filled in the proper word in a blank space. There would be "feedback" from the reinforcing "reward," which would increase the probability that, on future occasions, students would accurately read or write the completed or filled-in words.

Gestalt-field–oriented teachers in teaching nonreaders to read, would set out to help them develop an intelligent "feel" for sound-symbol relationships.[3] Hence, they would help students get the ideas that surround the use of words. Accordingly, the teachers would spend a greater proportion of teaching time conversing with their students in regard to significant verbal relationships. Specifically, they would help students grasp the relation between individual letters and verbal sounds, blend verbal sounds that are represented by letter groupings, and learn that there are many phonetically regular words but also some irregular ones. Students' verbal skills would be in the form of learned insights in regard to such matters as rhyming, telescoping sounds together, and sounding out words that are encountered visually.

In deciding upon their outlook on learning, teachers have at least three kinds of choices:

1. They may adhere to one systematic position as much as possible.
2. They may eclectically, that is, selectively, borrow ideas from the various conflicting positions and arrange the borrowed ideas into a mosaic or patchwork that is available to be drawn upon as needed.
3. They may develop *emergent syntheses* from their study of the conflicting positions and their respective ideas.

An *emergent* outlook is something novel that appears in the course of the evolution of ideas. It is not an intermediate position but a genuinely new outlook or concept. When an emergent outlook reflects the results of the interplay of conflicting ideas in arriving at something new, it is a *synthesis*. Whereas one forms an *eclectic compromise* by selecting aspects of opposing theories and taking a position somewhere between them so as to form a mosaic pattern, one achieves an *emergent synthesis* by selecting and modifying knowledge from incompatible positions, adding new thinking as needed, and developing a new position that is internally consistent and still more adequate than its precursors. Hence, an emergent synthesis in learning theory is a somewhat new systematic outlook that benefits from the ideas that have been incorporated in prevailing psychologies of learning but does not form a compromise between those ideas.

Whereas mental discipline, apperception, natural unfoldment, behaviorism, and Gestalt-field theory may be considered traditional systematic positions, cognitive-field learning theory has been developed as an emergent synthesis that both benefits by, and develops from the conflicting outlooks of, these earlier positions.

WHAT CONCEPTS CHARACTERIZE
THE RESPECTIVE LEARNING THEORIES?

In addition to listing the ten learning theories, Table 9.1 catalogs the concepts that characterize each theory, together with some people who represent each one. It is difficult to make a sharp distinction between "key persons" (column VI) and "contemporary exponents" (column VII). However, the criterion for selection of key persons has been their making a major contribution to the theory under consideration and still not being a contemporary adherent of the theory as described.

Each learning theory represents a more or less comprehensive psychological system or basic outlook. Or, to say this in another way, each systematic psychological system or basic outlook has its unique approach to learning. Accordingly, column II of Table 9.1 describes systematic psychologies or basic outlooks that are reflected in each theory of learning. We allude to these psychologies or outlooks from place to place throughout the book as we treat learning, teaching, and related problems.[4] Column V of Table 9.1 contains the pivotal teaching concept of each learning theory. Below we briefly outline categories III and IV. They are expanded throughout the remainder of the book.

How May Teachers Picture the Innate Moral
and Actional Nature of Students?

A teacher's outlook in regard to the nature of the learning process is greatly influenced by his or her position in regard to the nature and source of human motivation. Such motivation arises from some kind of relationship of people and their respective environments. But what is the nature of this relationship? In other words, what is the basic moral and actional nature of human beings as it expresses itself through each individual's dealings with his (or her) environment? This question may be rephrased as, "What would children and youths be like if each should be left entirely on his (or her) own?" This is the raw material with which teachers must work. Although teachers may not have thought out their answers to this question, the way they teach inevitably implies some position in regard to its answer. In fact, each theory of learning, especially as it is applied in schools, is closely linked to a conception of the basic innate moral and actional nature of human beings as it expresses itself through each individual's dealings with his or her environment. Hence, when teachers seriously consider how they are going to teach children and youths, it is inevitable that they formulate some assumptions about the essential moral and actional nature of students as human beings. This is the topic of column III in Table 9.1 and also of Table 9.2 and Figure 9.1.

Teachers' conceptions of people's basic innate moral and actional nature involves the fundamental way in which they view their students, and this has a major influence upon the way that they operate in classrooms and the manner in which their students learn as well as upon the outcomes of the learning. There are at least five distinctly different ways in which teachers may view their students. Teachers may think that they are (1) innately bad individuals in need of discipline; (2) neutral-active rational animals; (3) active, innately planned personalities that develop through unfoldment of their native instincts, needs, abilities, and talents; (4) passive minds or organisms whose development depends upon their being conditioned by outside forces; or (5) purposive persons who develop through their interaction with their respective psychological environments. The following two pages are devoted to an explanation of the assumptions a teacher makes in deciding to which of these alternatives to adhere.

It is essential to make clear that we are using the word *people* in a generic sense. It applies collectively to all members of the human race, and thus to all students at all levels of education and ability. Furthermore, as used here, *innate* and *basic* are synonymous adjectives; both mean "original" or "unlearned." Consideration of the basic nature of people would be quite simple were there but one answer. But, interestingly, there are several distinctly different and mutually opposed answers to this

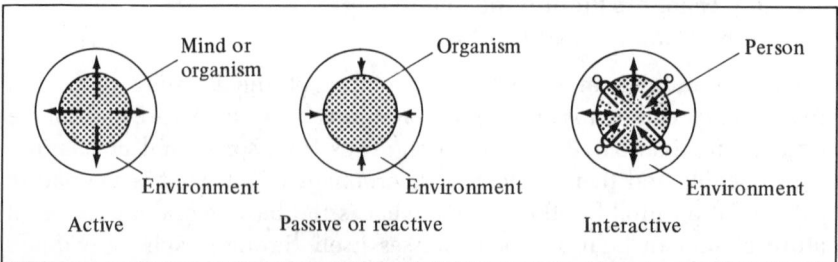

Figure 9.1 Models of mutually opposed assumptions in regard to the basic actional nature of people and their respective environmental relationships.

question, each enjoying a good deal of support. As students study this book, they should attempt to delineate their own positions in regard to this crucial problem.

Each of the two aspects of the problem of people's basic nature has at least three possible alternatives. They may be stated as follows: In *basic moral natures*, people are (1) innately *bad;* (2) innately *good;* or (3) their original moral nature is *neutral*, that is, originally neither good nor bad. Then, *actionally,* or in relationship to their environments, people are (1) innately *active;* (2) innately *passive* or *reactive;* or (3) basically *interactive*. We next review the nature of each set of alternatives and then describe their feasible combinations.

• *Three Alternate Assumptions Concerning People's Basic Moral Nature.* If we assume people's moral nature to be innately bad, then we can expect nothing good from them. If left to themselves, their badness will naturally unfold; persons will show no traits other than bad ones. Contrariwise, if we assume that people are innately good, then unless they are corrupted by some outside force, everything that comes from them will be good. Assumed neutrality in people's basic moral nature simply means that by nature they are neither bad nor good but merely "potential" in a way that has no connection with innate badness or goodness. Notice that people's neutrality, as used here, refers only to their innate goodness or badness; it in no sense means that students by nature are inactive.

• *Three Alternate Assumptions Concerning People's Actional Nature and Their Environmental Relationships.* If, in actional nature, children and youth are *active*, then their underlying characteristics are inborn. Hence, their psychological natures come from within them. Environments only serve as locations for their natural unfoldment. Notice that persons' merely moving physically does not mean that they necessarily are being psychologically active. For persons to be psychologically active, their personal motive power must be inner-directed and originate from within themselves. If persons are basically *passive* or *reactive* their characteristics are largely a product of environmental influences. Thus, their natures are determined by their environments. This does not mean that people do not move about. But it does mean that they are nonpurposive and that their behavior is caused by forces outside themselves.

If people are *interactive,* their psychological characteristics result from their making sense of their respective physical and social environments. So, their psychological natures arise from their personal-environmental relationships. Hence, one's psychological reality consists of that which one makes of what one gains through one's own unique experience. These three mutually opposed assumptions in regard to the nature of human beings and their environmental relationships may be illustrated by three models (Figure 9.1).

• *Five Alternate Combinations of Assumed Moral Natures with As-*

Table 9.2 ASSUMPTIONS ABOUT PEOPLE'S BASIC MORAL AND ACTIONAL NATURE AND THE LEARNING THEORIES THEY IMPLY

People's Basic Moral Nature	People's Basic Actional Nature
bad	active
good	passive
neutral	interactive

——————————— Possible, feasible conceptual patterns
— — — — — — — — — Possible, but unfeasible, conceptual patterns

Combination	Implied Learning Theory
Bad-active	Theistic mental discipline
Good-active	Natural unfoldment or self-actualization
Neutral-active	Humanistic mental discipline
Neutral-passive	Either apperception or S-R conditioning family
Neutral-interactive	Gestalt-field family

sumed Actional Natures and Their Implied Environmental Relationships. When we consider the possible, feasible combinations of assumptions concerning people's basic moral nature together with those concerning their actional relationship with their environment, we might reasonably assume the innate natures of students to be either bad-active, neutral-active, good-active, neutral-passive, or neutral-interactive (see Table 9.2).

Each of these assumptions in regard to the basic nature of students has definite implications for a theory of the learning process. If we assume students to be either bad-active or neutral-active, we will adhere to some form of mental discipline. This learning theory is described in the early part of Chapter 10 (pp. 240–252). If we assume students are good-active, we will think of learning as natural unfoldment or self-actualization (see pp. 252–254).

An assumption of neutral-passivity may take the form of either mentalistic apperception or physicalistic stimulus-response conditioning theory. Apperception theory occupies the last section of Chapter 10 (pp. 254–265). The different forms of S-R conditioning theory are discussed in Chapters 11 and 12. This theory is specifically represented by Skinner's operant conditioning theory, presented in Chapter 13.

The assumption that students are neutral-interactive is the pivotal thesis of Gestalt-field theories. These theories are described in Chapters 11 and 12 and specifically represented by cognitive-field theory, treated in detail in Chapters 14 and 15.

The following quotations from Gordon W. Allport and Rollo May summarize the importance of our assumptions concerning people's basic nature.

> Theories of learning (like much else in psychology) rest on the investigator's conception of the nature of man. In other words, every learning

theorist is a philosopher, though he may not know it. To put the matter more concretely, psychologists who investigate (and theorize about) learning start with some preconceived view of the nature of human motivation.[5]

The critical battles between approaches to psychology . . . in our culture in the next decades, I propose, will be on the battleground of the image of man—that is to say, on the conceptions of man which underlie the empirical research.[6]

What Is the Psychological Basis of Transfer of Learning to New Situations?

Transfer of learning, the subject of column IV of Table 9.1 is the relationship between the person's learning process and his (or her) using his learnings in future learning and life situations. Each learning theory has its correlative theory in regard to the nature of transfer and how it should be enhanced. A section of the explanation of each specific learning theory is devoted to the treatment of this subject. This, of course, is the key to the value of learning that occurs in schools. Schools should attempt to teach students in such a way that they not only accumulate many significant learnings applicable to life's situations, but they also develop a technique for acquiring new insights or understandings independently. These two goals of education constitute the realm of transfer.

Transfer of learning occurs when a person's learning in one situation influences his or her learning and performance in other situations. If there were no transfer at all, students would need to be taught specifically every act that they ever were to perform in any situation. Although, when we think of transfer, we usually consider how one learning experience strengthens another, we should remember that there also is a negative transfer process within which one learning experience interferes with, that is, weakens, another. However, generally speaking, what we learn in one situation tends to facilitate or help our learning in others. But the opposite effect, interference, can also occur. For example, a person's study of foreign language or philosophy can make him (or her) a slower reader of English literature, or his becoming committed to certain dogmas or absolutes can interfere with his future creative, reflective thought.

In its broadest sense, transfer of learning is basic to the whole notion of schooling. People who support, as well as those who conduct, our schools assume that matters being taught today will have some learning value in later times in different situations. Accordingly, the assumption that underlies our entire educational system is that knowledge gained in school not only will be available in the future but also will be applied in some degree to the solution of new problems as they arise in future school and life situations. For instance, we assume that today's lesson in arithmetic will help with tomorrow's problems in the same subject and that it also will help in dealing with algebra, geometry, and the physical sciences.

A predominant purpose of formal education in schools is to facilitate learning outside them. It would be difficult to justify any achievement of school learning that had no bearing upon students' future learning in life situations. Nevertheless, often what is learned in school contributes very little, if anything, to children's and youths' solving their future problems. Thus, there appears to be much room for improvement in our teaching procedures so that transfer of school learning to other situations will be enhanced to a much greater degree than at present.

The effectiveness of a school depends, in a large measure, upon the amount and quality of transfer potential of the materials that students learn. Thus, transfer of learning is the cornerstone upon which education should ultimately rest. Unless students learn in school those matters that help them in meeting situations more effectively further along the academic sequence and later in life as well as in the present, they are wasting much of their time.

We suggest that you reflect briefly upon the learning that you achieved while you were in high school. You studied, and apparently mastered, a number of different courses. These courses contained factual detail, generalizations, and techniques. Periodically, you showed on an examination that you had learned fairly well the content of each course. How much of your high school learning do you now retain in such a way as to be able to use it in contemporary situations? What dealings did the United States have with Napoleon? How does a participle differ from a gerund? If the school house is 1½ miles north and 2 miles east of a student's home, what is the shortest distance from home to school? What is the basic difference between the structure of San Francisco Bay and the Strait of Georgia? If you do not do very well with questions such as these, you need not be completely chagrined. Studies such as the Regents' Inquiry of the State of New York found such inability to be typical among students.

The basic problem of transfer is: In what way and to what extent will acquisition of skills, knowledge, understanding, behaviors, and attitudes in one subject or learning situation influence performance or learning in other subjects or situations? Knowing the answer to this and some subordinate problems will enable us to teach for maximum, effective transfer of learning.

Some subordinate transfer problems are:

1. How does a person's current learning assist him in meeting future learning situations?
2. How does what youngsters learn in school affect what they learn and what they do outside school?
3. Does school learning have as much effect as it should and how can it be made more effectual?

More specifically, in what manner and how much does the learning of a given material, say, memorizing the names of all the states and their capitals, aid, hinder, or have no effect upon subsequent learning, for example, learning the content of a textbook? To what extent and in what way does the study of Latin enhance English vocabulary and grammar, aid in learning French or German, or contribute to knowledge of ancient history? How does a study of theories of learning contribute to one's knowledge of how to teach fourth-grade reading or high school physics? Will an individual carry over the arithmetic ability he (or she) learned in a classroom to the problems he actually encounters in business or in tasks about the house? Does practice in memorizing, reasoning, per-severing, and willing improve the mental process in general? Can one improve his perception, retention, and imagination in all fields by practice in one?

The critical question in regard to transfer is not whether it takes place, but what conditions engender the greatest amount of it. Classroom teaching definitely can be conducted in such a way as to achieve transfer. Furthermore, it is highly probable that teaching can be brought to achieve a much higher degree of transfer than it now does. However, in order that we may teach for maximum transfer, we need to understand how transfer occurs. Having done this, we need to help students learn how to learn in such a way that transfer will reach a maximum level.

A book on learning theory, to be most meaningful to students, needs to treat, albeit in a theoretical manner, classroom application of psy-chological outlooks and principles. Such a treatment is the subject of Chapters 19, 20, and 21. Although teaching theory, as such, is emphasized only in these chapters, readers will do well to consider it to some degree along with the subject matter of the chapters on learning.

By reading across each entry in Table 9.1, we can get a picture of ten different ways of looking at the problem of how students learn. For example, a person who embraces number 4, apperception, is committed to psychological *structuralism;* assumes that students basically are of a *neutral-passive, mental* nature; sees the basis for transfer as the idea of *apperceptive mass;* and, in teaching, emphasizes addition of new mental states or ideas to a store of old ones "housed" in the subconscious mind. The key historical persons in development of this outlook are J. F. Herbart and E. B. Titchener, and many teachers and administrators are, perhaps unknowingly, its contemporary exponents.

NOTES

[1] Ernest R. Hilgard and Donald G. Marquis, *Conditioning and Learning*, 2d ed., New York: Appleton-Century-Crofts, 1961, p. 10.
[2] Mortimer Taube, *Computers and Common Sense*, New York: Columbia University Press, 1961, p. 2.
[3] See Siegfried Engelmann, *Preventing Failure in the Primary Grades*, Chicago: Science Research Associates, 1969, Chapter 4, "Reading for the Nonreader."
[4] The various systematic psychologies are described in Benjamin B. Wolman, *Contemporary Theories and Systems of Psychology*, New York: Harper & Row,

1960, and J. P. Chaplin and T. S. Krawiec, *Systems and Theories of Psychology,* 3d ed., New York: Holt, Rinehart and Winston, 1974.
[5] Gordon W. Allport, *Patterns and Growth in Personality,* New York: Holt, Rinehart and Winston, 1961, p. 84.
[6] Rollo May, *Psychology and the Human Dilemma,* New York: Van Nostrand Reinhold, 1967, p. 90.

BIBLIOGRAPHY

CANTOR, NATHANIEL F. *Dynamics of Learning.* New York: Lyle Stuart, 1956. One of the best books available on how to improve the effectiveness of teaching. The first few theoretical chapters require for their understanding a rich background in psychology and sociology. Read later chapters, which describe in detail how a teacher may conduct a class.

CANTRIL, HADLEY, and CHARLES H. BUMSTEAD. *Reflections on the Human Venture.* New York: New York University Press, 1960. Treatment of major issues in psychology from a relativistic view. Draws evidence largely from insights of novelists, poets, and playwrights. Excellent quotations. A profound book, likely to become a classic.

HALL, CALVIN S., and GARDNER LINDZEY. *Theories of Personality.* New York: Wiley, 1957. Description of twelve different "scientific" learning theories, including stimulus-response, Freudian and neo-Freudian, Lewin's, and other relativistic and nonrelativistic theories. Excellent as a reference source.

HILGARD, ERNEST R. (ed.). *Theories of Learning and Instruction.* The National Society for the Study of Education. Chicago: University of Chicago Press, 1964. A modern symposium on learning theory. Professional problems in developing psychological methodologies and educational technologies. Integrating psychologies of learning with technologies of instruction.

KRUTCH, JOSEPH WOOD. *Human Nature and the Human Condition.* New York: Random House, 1959. Krutch's attack on relativistic explanations in favor of a belief in an innate human nature. Contrasts with his attack, in his earlier book, on all mechanistic explanations of human nature.

KRUTCH, JOSEPH WOOD. *The Measure of Man.* Indianapolis: Bobbs-Merrill, 1953. An extraordinarily stimulating book on issues between mechanistic and nonmechanistic approaches in biology, psychology, and sociology, by a noted humanistic scholar and writer.

MONTAGU, M. F. ASHLEY. *The Direction of Human Development; Biological and Social Bases.* New York: Harper & Row, 1955. A book bearing on the question of what man's original nature is and how that nature is influenced to assume a socially functional form. Highly readable, considering the subject matter involved.

MURPHY, GARDNER. *Historical Introduction to Modern Psychology.* New York: Harcourt Brace Jovanovich, 1949. A history of psychological thought treating the positions of Locke and the modern scientific psychologists. Perhaps the most readable of the histories of psychology.

PIAGET, JEAN, and BÄRBEL INHELDER. *The Psychology of the Child.* New York: Basic Books, 1969. A definitive summary of Piaget's studies of child development. Traces the stages of cognitive development over the entire period from infancy to adolescence. Perhaps the best source for a teacher wanting to understand Piaget.

PIAGET, JEAN. *Psychology and Epistemology.* New York: Grossman, 1971. Presents the psychological and philosophical theory upon which Piaget's conclusions are based. Develops his meaning of genetic epistemology.

SPENCE, KENNETH W. "Theoretical Interpretations of Learning," in S. S. Stevens (ed.), *Handbook of Experimental Psychology,* pp. 690–729. New York: Wiley, 1951. A summarization of the task of learning theorists. Classifies kinds of learning theories into perceptual and S-R groups, and S-R groups into contiguity, reinforcement, and two-factor subgroups.

Chapter 10
WHAT EARLY THEORIES OF LEARNING ARE REFLECTED IN CURRENT SCHOOL PRACTICES?

This chapter is devoted to three conceptions of the learning process that emerged prior to the twentieth century but continue to have great influence in today's schools: (1) *mental discipline*, (2) *natural unfoldment* or self-actualization, and (3) *apperception.* These three theories have one characteristic in common: all were developed as nonexperimental psychologies of learning. That is, their basic orientation is philosophical or speculative. The method used to develop these three conceptions of learning has been introspective and subjective. The philosopher-psychologists who evolved these ideas tried to analyze their own thought processes and describe in general terms what they thought they found. Since, according to mental-discipline theory, mental training is imparted by the *form* of studies as distinguished from their content, mental discipline also is identified by the expression *formal discipline.* However, throughout this book we use *mental discipline* to denote this approach to learning.

WHAT IS MENTAL DISCIPLINE?

The central idea in mental discipline is that the mind, envisioned as a nonphysical substance, lies dormant until it is exercised. Faculties of the mind such as memory, will, reason, and perseverance are the "muscles of the mind"; like physiological muscles, they are strengthened only through exercise, and subsequent to their adequate exercise they operate automatically. Thus, learning is a matter of strengthening, or disciplining, the faculties of the mind, which combine to produce intelligent behavior.[1]

Adherents of mental discipline think that the primary value of history or any other disciplinary subject is the training effect it has on the minds of students. They are convinced that this effect will remain after the "learned" material has been forgotten. Furthermore, they consider the highest value of education to be its liberalizing effect. Education that is truly liberalizing prepares us not only to live in the world, but more important, to live with ourselves. In 1959 James D. Koerner, a contemporary exponent of mental discipline, wrote,

> the purpose of [liberalizing] education is the harmonious development of the mind, the will, and the conscience of each individual so that he may use to the full of his intrinsic powers and shoulder the responsibilities of citizenship.[2]

According to the doctrine of mental discipline, a person is either a bad-active or neutral-active "rational animal," and education is a process of disciplining or training minds, which are the most essential aspects of persons. Proponents of the doctrine believe that in this disciplining process mental faculties are strengthened through exercise. Just as exercising an arm develops the biceps, exercise of mental faculties makes them more powerful. Choice of learning materials is of some importance but always is secondary to the nature of minds, which undergo the disciplinary process. Within mental discipline, persons are thought to be composed of two kinds of basic substances or realities, namely, rational minds and biological organisms. Thus the concept "rational animal is used in characterizing a human being." That which is disciplined or trained through education is *mind substance*.

What Is Mind Substance?

Mind substance is a self-dependent, immaterial essence, which parallels the physical nature of human beings; it is just as real as matter, it has a nature of its own, and it operates in its own distinctive fashion. Furthermore, it usually is assigned the dominant position in a mind-body dualistic conception of humans. Physical substance—rocks, buildings, plants, and animals—is characterized by extension in time and space; it has length, breadth, thickness, and mass. Mind substance, in contrast, is not extended; it has no length, no breadth, no thickness, and no mass, yet it is as real as anything can be. In a sense, a human is considered a mental and physical whole. However, body and mind are of such a nature as to have no common characteristic.

How did primitive people acquire the idea that they had substantive minds? We do not know, but it is plausible to suppose that dreaming was partially responsible. Picture hunter A and hunter B lying down together after a hard day's hunting and a heavy feast. Hunter A has eaten too much and as a result is unable to sleep. Having been more moderate in his eating, hunter B sleeps all night but his sleep includes an adventurous dream. Upon awakening in the morning, hunter B relates the experience of finding and stalking game during the night. Hunter A expresses disbelief and insists that hunter B has been on the ground beside him all night. But hunter B is equally insistent that he spent the night hunting and describes his dream so convincingly that both men decide that there must be *two* hunter B's. One, the physical man, slept on the ground throughout the night; the other, the mental man, must have come from within the first and carried on his escapades unhampered by bodily form. Thus could have been born something like a modern concept of mind substance.

Now, the mind substance concept has been with us a long time. Furthermore, it has grown through the inventive genius of both primitive and civilized man, and it has become deeply imbedded in present-day cultures. Consequently, quite often its existence is considered a self-evident truth; the familiar has come to be accepted as the self-evident.

A defensible mind substance theory must take mind out of space completely. As long as one attributes to mind some characteristics of matter, even though they are very thin and elusive, one implies that mind is of essentially the same nature as matter. Thus, to gain an understanding of a mind substance theory of learning it is necessary for one to make a sharp distinction between mind and matter. One must remind oneself that, if a mind is nonspatial, it cannot be located in the brain or anywhere else, and that, to date, we have devised no way of determining experimentally the way in which spatial and nonspatial entities influence one another.

If one adheres to a mind substance theory, each student's substantive mind is assumed to be active in either an erroneous or an inadequate fashion until it is either curbed or trained. Hence, one sees all learning as basically a process of developing or training minds. Accordingly, learning becomes a process of inner development within which various powers such as imagination, memory, will, and thought are cultivated. Education becomes a process of mental discipline.

What Forms May Mental Discipline Take?

The theory of mental discipline has at least two versions—*classical humanism* and *faculty psychology*. Each is an outgrowth of different cultural traditions. Classical humanism stems from ancient Greece. It operates on the assumption that the mind of a human being is an active agent in relation to its environment and that it also is morally neutral at birth.

Humanism is an outlook and way of life that is centered upon human interests and values. Classical humanism is only one of its forms. Two other quite different forms of humanism are psychedelic humanism and scientific humanism. *Psychedelic humanism* emphasizes the autonomous, active nature of human beings within which each person "does his or her own thing." This type of humanism includes a self-actualization psychology of learning (see p. 253). *Scientific humanists* emphasize the enhancement of human welfare through the application of scientific processes to the solution of the problems of human beings (see pp. 18–20). This kind of humanism harmonizes with Gestalt-field psychologies of learning.

The psychology known as "faculty psychology" more often is associated with the *bad-active* principle of human nature than with the earlier Greek *neutral-active* principle. Because of differences in underlying assumptions concerning the basic nature of human beings, we find some difference between the kinds of education prescribed by classical humanists and that followed by faculty psychologists. However, all mental disciplinary approaches to learning have enough in common for them to be placed in a mind substance family (see Table 9.1).

How Did the Mental Discipline Theory of Learning Develop?

Mental discipline has roots extending into antiquity. Yet, its manifestations continue to be quite evident in present-day school practices. The theory was somewhat dormant during the first half of the twentieth century. However, the "post-Sputnik age" led to its revival and revitalization.

In the fourth century B.C., Plato believed that mental training or discipline in mathematics and philosophy was a person's best preparation for participation in the conduct of public affairs. Once trained, by having his (or her) faculties developed, a person was ready to solve problems of all kinds. Aristotle, who followed Plato, described at least five different faculties; the greatest, and the one unique to human beings, was reason. Faculties that humans had in common with lower animals were the vegetative, appetitive, sensory, and locomotive, but only human beings could reason.

At the close of the Middle Ages, during the Renaissance, *classical humanism* emerged as an endeavor of people to gain more understanding of the universe and themselves. These humanists believed that human beings, rather than the Scriptures, were to be the starting point in satisfying humanity's urge toward individual development. To gain understanding of the ideal nature of human beings, humanistic scholars turned to the classics of ancient Greece and Rome. The resulting classical humanism of the Renaissance was developed on the assumption that a person was a neutral-active rational animal whose direction of growth was to be provided from within, not by yielding to the behest of every chance impulse, but by following principles that an individual formulated for guidance of his or her conduct. Thus, learning was regarded as a process of firm self-discipline; it consisted of harmonious development of all of one's inherent powers so that no one faculty was overdeveloped at the expense of others.

Within classical humanism, the Socratic method was popular as a teaching procedure. A teacher's function was to help students recognize what already was in their minds; environmental influence was considered of little consequence:

> The Socratic method implies that the teacher has no knowledge, or at least professes to impart no information; instead, he seeks to draw the information from his students by means of skillfully directed questions. The method is predicated on the principle that knowledge is inborn but we cannot recall it without expert help.[3]

The nineteenth century could be characterized as the century of mental discipline. Rooted in European traditions of idealistic and rationalistic philosophy, the ideal of mental discipline had some currency in the early part of the century, and it gained great popularity in the middle and later decades. During this period education was regarded as necessarily laborious. Schoolroom atmospheres were at least austere and sometimes harsh. Teachers usually were dictators, sometimes benevolent, but sometimes even spiteful. Children were expected to be respectful and obedient and to accept at face value whatever teachers told them. Curriculums were relatively fixed with an almost exclusive emphasis in elementary schools on the fundamental skill subjects, and in secondary schools on such "disciplinary" subjects as Latin, history, and mathematics.

Traditionally, classical humanists have been more interested in perfecting the minds of a few superior individuals than in elevating the intelligence of mankind as a whole. Accordingly, some twentieth-century classical humanists are attempting to repudiate the intellectual leadership of natural and social scientists in the affairs of life and to revert to the precepts of traditional philosophers as represented by Plato, Aristotle, and the medieval scholastics. Whereas scientists make great use of other symbols, classical humanistic literary intellectuals center their activity in words. Some leading twentieth-century classical humanists are Robert M. Hutchins, Mortimer J. Adler, and Mark Van Doren.

The two most influential groups in the United States who continue to favor a mental-disciplinary approach to education are some leaders in parochial education and those liberal arts professors who are under the influence of faculty psychology and the classical tradition. In addition to these there are many thousands of other persons, including some public school teachers, who gravitate toward a theory of mental discipline. The current introduction of "renaissance schools" reflects this position, however in a somewhat confused manner.

MENTAL DISCIPLINE WITHIN THE CLASSICAL-HUMANISTIC TRADITION

Within the classical-humanistic tradition a human mind is assumed to be of such nature that, with adequate cultivation, it can know the world as it really is. A person, being a rational animal, is free within limits to act as he (she) chooses in the light of what he understands. Instead of our being creatures of instinct, we enjoy a complex and delicate faculty of apprehension, whose basic aspect is *reason*. This capacity resides in every normal human individual. It enables human beings to gain understanding of their needs and their environment, to direct their action in accordance with their understanding, and to communicate this understanding to other members of their group. Thus, it is assumed that the human mind is of such nature that, if it has been properly exercised and it has an opportunity, it will educe truth; it will develop outward manifestations of its innate potential.

Within the classical-humanistic frame of reference, knowledge assumes the character of a fixed body of true principles, handed down as a heritage of the race. These principles have been discovered by the great thinkers of human history and have been set down in the great books. Hence, classicists take the basic content of the school curriculum from philosophical and literary classics. To them, not only training the mind, but also studying the eternal truths contained in certain great books, is of primary importance.

FACULTY PSYCHOLOGY

Although faculty psychology had been implicit in the classical tradition and in virtually every early scheme of education proposed, it did not appear as an explicit, formalized psychological doctrine until the eighteenth century. Christian Wolff (1679–1754), a German philosopher, is credited with its development. His version was described in his *Rational Psychology*, published in 1734. Wolff's thesis was that the mind, although unitary, has different faculties that are distinct. The mind at times enters into particular activities in much the same way that the whole body at different times takes part in widely different acts. According to Wolff, the basic general faculties are knowing, feeling, and willing. The knowing faculty is divided into several others, which include perception, imagination, memory, and pure reason. The reasoning faculty is the ability to draw distinctions and form judgments.

The belief in a willing faculty is an outgrowth of the notion that human nature may be described in terms of the bad-active principle. If human nature is intrinsically evil, then a strongly developed will is necessary to harness inherent evilness. Without will, a person would be unable to function in human society. Will, in the sense in which it is employed here, refers to ability to implement, or put into effective practice, a decision that has been made. A strongly developed will enables a person to "see a decision through" even though such action violates natural, that is, evil, impulses. Hence, if one chooses to emancipate himself from his innate natural impulses, a well-developed will is necessary for success; he (or she) must make himself do that which he does not want to do. Faculty psychologists have held that if a person pursues any type of unpleasant work long enough his will will be strengthened.

Under faculty psychology, the task of a teacher is to find the kind of mental exercises that will train the various faculties most efficiently. Emphasis is not on acquiring knowledge, but rather on strengthening faculties. A consistent faculty psychologist would not be especially interested in teaching "great truths" or the "heritage of the past" or any other type of subject matter except insofar as it is a good medium for exercising the faculties.

The special attention given by faculty psychology to development of the will has led to the notion that school work is better for a child if it is somewhat distasteful. Consequently, when faculty psychology is a dominant influence in a school, teachers may deliberately keep their assignments both difficult and dull and use force if necessary to insure that students complete them. Also, use of severe punishment, including ridicule and whipping, may be found in frequent use in such a school.

THE WEDDING OF CLASSICISM AND FACULTY PSYCHOLOGY

Faculty psychology, as developed by Wolff and his followers, was at first a challenge to classical humanism. Logically, faculty psychologists should consider one subject as good as another for exercising a particular faculty; also, knowledge retained by a student was considered much less important than the disciplining effect of learning it. But these conclusions negate the classicist's insistence on the virtues of certain subjects and on learning and retaining the great truths that human experience has unveiled.

However, a rather easy compromise soon became apparent. If it could be established that the best subjects for training the faculties were the classics, then the classical curriculum could be defended. This argument gained strength, and by the late nineteenth century most secondary schools and colleges offered a curriculum limited mainly to the classical liberal arts. These subjects were regarded as valuable for a twofold reason: they were excellent tools for mind training and they incorporated the great truths of human experience.

AN HISTORICAL EXAMPLE OF MENTAL DISCIPLINE

A brief history of the teaching of Latin and Greek illustrates the development of mental discipline as a theory of learning. Throughout the Middle Ages, Latin served a practical purpose. It was the language of scholars throughout the Western world and the vehicle of instruction in schools. Thus, it was a living, growing, changing language that today we would call a "tool subject." During the Renaissance, Latin continued to be the language of scholarly communication, and both Latin and Greek were used in reading the classics, which contained those ideas considered the best that had been thought by humanity. To keep up with the thinking of his times, a scholar had to be able to read and use both Latin and Greek.

After the Renaissance, modern languages gradually came into more general use. English, German, and French rose to prominence and assumed the role previously played by Latin and Greek. By the end of the sixteenth century, the communicative value of the classical languages was beginning to wane. Supporters of these languages, however, made a determined fight to preserve them. No longer needed for basic communication, Latin and Greek came to be heralded as the best subject matter for mental discipline. Throughout most of the nineteenth century the doctrine of the disciplinary value of these languages was generally accepted in American educational circles. Since, according to the classical humanists, disciplinary values were intangible and not susceptible to statistical treatment, evaluation of them was limited to analysis of opinions of recognized authorities on educational matters.

During the early years of the twentieth century, when the mechanistic learning theories that were opposed to mental discipline—apperception, connectionism, and behaviorism—were on the upsurge in educational circles, Greek practically dropped out of the educational picture and Latin suffered a great decline. However, by the middle of the twentieth century a resurgence of the classical tradition was apparent. With it came its earlier associate, mental discipline, and the teaching of Latin began to be expanded again. Then, more recently, with the emphasis upon narrow vocationalism in schools, classical studies, including Latin, have dropped into the background once more.

How Do Mental Disciplinarians Treat Transfer of Learning?

To repeat, the basic problem of transfer is: In what way and to what extent will acquisition of skills, knowledge, understanding, behaviors, and attitudes in one subject or learning situation influence performance or learning in other subjects or situations? (See Chapter 9, p. 235.) For mental disciplinarians, the basis for transfer of learning consists of trained mental faculties and cultivated intellectual powers. According to mental discipline, germs of the various mental faculties are in each individual from birth, and learning is a process of developing these germinal, undeveloped faculties into powers or capacities. When teachers are asked about the value of studying a particular subject and they reply, "It sharpens the mind and improves the memory," or "It cultivates the reasoning faculty," they are thinking of learning as mental discipline and of that which is transferred as being generally exercised germinal capacity. Thus, the teachers think they are building in their students a great power reservoir that will automatically go into operation in any kind of subsequent mental activity.

The various inherited faculties can be developed through training and become capable of effective performance in all areas in which they are involved. Thus, the training of the faculty of memory through memorizing nonsense syllables presumably improves one's memory for names, for meaningful material, and in fact for anything that calls for memory. Likewise, after receiving training in reasoning through a study of geometry, a person can reason effectively in realms of philosophy, mathematics, social issues, and housekeeping. Accordingly, education largely is a matter of training or disciplining minds with vigorous mental exercise in the classics, grammar, logic, mathematics, and pure science on the assumption that such training makes a person equally effective in all areas where a given faculty is employed. Since, within mental discipline theory, transfer is assumed to be automatic, once a faculty has developed it goes into operation whenever its use is appropriate.

How Do Mental Disciplinarians Promote Transfer?

Educational practice based on the theory of mental discipline stresses the necessity for developing the "muscles of the mind" by rigorous exercise. Mental disciplinarians have little desire to make schoolwork pleasant or interesting. In fact, more discipline is engendered if the tasks are unpleasant and burdensome; the harder the exercise, the more the faculties are disciplined. Thus, the more difficult the schoolwork, the more effective it is thought to be. Since subjects such as Latin, mathematics, and science taught arbitrarily seem particularly arduous, these subjects have been enthusiastically taught in the schools for their disciplinary value.

To a mental disciplinarian the direct utility of a subject is of little consequence; exercise of the mental faculties is what is important. The material or content upon which the exercise is expended makes little difference, except that it must be of such nature as to require strenuous exertion. Certain mental powers or faculties such as tenacity and logicality, exercised and developed in the study of, say, botany, carry over automatically to all aspects of life wherein the same mental powers are required.

Since mental disciplinarians are not interested in anything like life-adjustment education, they work to stretch, not relax, the minds of their students. They are convinced that a teacher should be not an amateur psychiatrist, social worker, and baby-sitter, but a scholarly educator. Since faculties are strengthened through mental practice much as muscles are strengthened through physical exercise, the most difficult subjects are the most desirable for stretching the mind. Furthermore, long, difficult assignments develop the faculties of willpower and attention.

How Has Mental Discipline Been Evaluated?

Mental discipline proponents generally have held that learning theory, curriculum construction, teaching methods, and educational practices cannot be evaluated scientifically; they are derived philosophically, hence they can only be evaluated philosophically. However, by the early twentieth century, an imposing array of psychologists and educators had become captivated by the potentiality of scientific processes, particularly objective and statistical procedures as exemplified in such fields as physics and chemistry.

Whereas on the one hand mental disciplinarians insisted that science could not be applied in such a human enterprise as education, on the other hand scientifically oriented educators and psychologists insisted that science could and must be used in education.

When the classical-humanistic curriculum first took form, it represented the point of view of liberals of the time and reflected a desire for progress. Its adherents were sufficiently open-minded to permit changes. However, by the beginning of the twentieth century the classical curriculum had come under such sharp attack that its proponents were placed on the defensive. They pleaded for a return to a rigid Renaissance ideal, forgetting that the Renaissance ideal itself was an example of change and growth.

Almost to the end of the 1890s public high schools in the United States were loyal to the classical liberal tradition with its psychology of mental discipline. The famous Committee of Ten on Secondary School Studies upheld a doctrine of mental discipline throughout its 1893 report.

In the early 1900s Edward L. Thorndike (1874–1949) and Robert S. Woodworth (1869–1962), in a newer tradition of scientific psychology, performed experiments at Columbia University to test the validity of mental discipline as a psychology of learning. Their basic conclusion was that the idea of mental discipline is scientifically untenable. Their experiments showed that drill or training in performing certain tasks did not strengthen people's so-called faculties for performing such tasks. For example, students' development of neatness in one area of activity showed no or very little improvement of their neatness in other areas; students' arithmetic papers may be noticeably improved in neatness with no parallel improvement in neatness appearing in language and spelling papers.[4]

Thorndike also noted that the results of his experimentation, if corroborated by similar experiments, would prove that the amount of general improvement, or mental discipline, that students achieve due to the study of any school subject is small and that the differences in improvement as a result of their studying different subjects also are small. Thus, he concluded that the value of each subject must be decided largely by the special learnings that it provides; the languages, or any other liberal arts subjects, have no claims to preeminence as an educational medium. The order of influence, if any, of specific subjects upon the growth of intellect ranged from, first, arithmetic and bookkeeping to, last, biological sciences. The so-called disciplinary subjects appeared at all levels interwoven with nondisciplinary subjects. Thorndike reported in the *Journal of Educational Psychology:*

> If our inquiry had been carried out by a psychologist from Mars, who knew nothing of theories of mental discipline, and simply tried to answer the question, "What are the amounts of influence of sex, race, age, amounts of ability, and studies taken, upon the gain made during the year in power to think, or intellect, or whatever our stock intelligence tests measure?" he might even dismiss "studies taken" with the comment, "The differences are so small and the unreliabilities are relatively so large that this factor seems unimportant." The one causal factor which he would be sure was at work would be the intellect already existent. Those who have the most to begin with gain the most during the year. Whatever studies they take will seem to produce large gains in intellect.[5]

Thorndike was convinced that the principal reason that good thinkers seemed to have been made good thinkers by certain subjects that they had pursued is that good students tend to take the subjects that people generally identify with good thinking. Good students gain more than do poor students from the study of any subject. When good thinkers study Latin and Greek, these subjects seem to cultivate good thinking. However, "If the abler pupils should all study Physical Education and Dramatic Arts, these subjects would seem to make good thinkers."[6]

In 1914 Thorndike disposed of inborn faculties with two sentences:

> [There is] the opinion that attention, memory, reasoning, choice and the like are mystical powers given to man as his birth-right which weigh the dice in favor of thinking or doing one thing rather than another. . . . This opinion is vanishing from the world of expert thought and no more need to be said about it than that it is false and would be useless to human welfare if true.[7]

In 1944 Alexander Wesman made a study following up Thorndike's earlier mental discipline studies. High school students were tested at the start and end of an academic year with a series of general intelligence and achievement tests. Gains on the tests during the year were observed for students taking differing course patterns to see whether some patterns of courses contributed more to gained intelligence than did others. Wesman's study revealed no superiority of any one school subject over any of the others studied; there was no superior addition to intelligence for any one of the achievement areas measured.[8]

A curriculum based on a classical-humanistic philosophy and the liberal arts may not seem very practical to most persons today. However, mental disciplinarians deliberately make a distinction between knowledge of immediate usefulness and practicality and essential matters grounded in eternal standards of truth, goodness, and beauty. Mental disciplinarians are convinced that knowledge of immediate practical value is of little importance. They hold that only the abstract principles of pure theory can free the human mind and promote people's distinctively human capacity for reason.

This emphasis is understandable. Most adherents of mental discipline are mind-body dualists who feel that mind is much the more important member of the partnership. Identification of education with development of minds tends to disparage other aspects of human activity. Thus, we are told that "Education, as a whole, can never be a 'science' in the strict sense of the term. It is part of the 'humanities.' "[9] Even in the face of James's, Thorndike's, and Woodworth's research in this area, many scholars continue to endow certain subjects, particularly the more abstract ones, with immensely superior transfer power.

Students who have mastered difficult subjects usually do have above-average proficiency in whatever areas of study and thinking they happen to pursue. Although it doesn't necessarily follow, it is easy to assign credit for this proficiency to the nature of the specific subjects that have been studied; it often is overlooked that people who elect or survive difficult subjects perhaps had more ability when they started them. This is an example of the *post hoc ergo propter hoc*—"after this, therefore on account of it"—fallacy; instructors and others may fallaciously reason that after taking certain courses youth are good students therefore, the courses made them into good students. We should recognize, however, that, even though mental disciplinarians' reasoning may be fallacious in this regard, their procedure becomes a screening device, whether or not it is an educating one. A school may "maintain high standards" through teaching for mental discipline and grading so rigorously that a high percentage of students fail and drop out. By so doing, it can raise the quality of its students; but the increased quality of students, so gained, is no indication of improved quality of instruction.

Today the concept *mental discipline* is unpopular with most psychologists and professional educators. Experimental evidence indicates that memory as a general function is not improved by strenuous memorization of poetry. Likewise, reasoning in fields other than mathematics is not automatically improved by studying algebra and geometry. However, there still are scholars, parents, and other school patrons who are convinced that Latin, science, and mathematics should be included in the school curriculum because they are "good for the students' minds."

In light of current psychological knowledge, it is difficult to justify school subjects purely in terms of improving students' minds through exercise. Evidently there is transfer of learning, but not the general transfer implied in mental discipline. Methods of solving arithmetic problems can be transferred to the solution of problems in algebra. The learning of Latin may, and often does, facilitate the learning of English grammar. However, if experimental research is to be trusted, transfer is not automatic, and it is not a matter of disciplining minds.

WHAT IS LEARNING THROUGH UNFOLDMENT OR SELF-ACTUALIZATION?

We come now to the second major position to be treated in this chapter, often called "learning through unfoldment." This outlook on the nature of learning stems logically from the theory that people are naturally *good* and at the same time *active* in relation to their environments. All people are assumed to be free, autonomous, and forwardly active persons who are reaching out from themselves to make their worlds. Unless and until they are corrupted by some influences from outside themselves, every act that comes from them will be good. Each student is subjectively free, and his (or her) own personal choice and responsibility account for his life. He and he alone, is the architect and builder of that life.

Early development of this point of view usually is associated with Jean J. Rousseau (1712–1778). Later, the Swiss educational reformer Heinrich Pestalozzi (1746–1827) and the German philosopher, educator, and founder of the kindergarten movement Friedrich Froebel (1782–1852), to a large degree, used this outlook as a basis for their pedagogical thinking. The over-all philosophical framework of the natural unfoldment position often has been labeled *romantic naturalism.*

A contemporary position that implies that human beings are good and active is psychedelic humanism, which harmonizes with a radical existentialist philosophy. Psychedelic humanism contrasts with both classical humanism within which people are considered neutral and active and scientific humanism within which they are considered neutral and interactive.

Rousseau's position was that everything in nature is basically good. Since human hereditary nature is good, it need only be permitted to develop in a natural environment free from corruption. Rousseau qualified his interpretation of human nature as an active, self-directing agent by conceding that a bad social environment could make bad human beings; to him social institutions are not natural. Thus, his rejection of environmentalism was not complete. However, his emphasis was on natural, active self-determination.

Rousseau urged teachers to permit students to live close to nature so that they might indulge freely in their natural impulses, instincts, and feelings. He emphasized that in rural areas children need practically no schooling or tutoring. An example which he gave related to the learning of speech. A country boy, he said, ordinarily did not need instruction in speech. He called to his parents and playmates from considerable distances and thus practiced making himself heard; consequently, without tutoring, he developed an adequate power of speech. It was only the city boy, growing up in close quarters with no opportunity to exercise his voice in a natural way, who had need for speech instruction. Thus, Rousseau recommended that in teaching city boys teachers should, insofar as possible, adopt the method through which country boys learn.

Within current psychedelic humanism the essence of a human being lies within his conscious self; each person, completely, on his (or her) own, is deemed sufficient for every situation. His free-flowing emotional feelings, not his intellectual thoughts, are taken to be the final authority for truth. Hence, he arrives at decisions on all issues in accordance with the way he feels, and he is completely confident that he is right.

Since, according to the good-active definition of human nature, children grow up unfolding that which nature has enfolded within them, devotees of this position tend to place great emphasis on the study of child growth and development and to minimize the study of learning. When they allude to learning, they seem to assume or imply that it, too, is little more than a process of growth and development in accordance with the genetic patterns of individuals.

Learning, in the traditional sense, generally is conceived to be some form of imposition of ideas or standards upon a person or organism. However, within psychedelic humanism there is little need for this kind of learning. Instead, a student is expected to learn through the promptings of his (or her) own interests. Hence, there should be no coercion or prescription. A mind, in its growth process, may be considered analogous to an egg in the process of hatching. Its growth is a natural operation, which, without imposition from any outside source, carries its own momentum.

As a psychedelic humanist views matters, his (or her) learning process runs counter to conventional orthodoxies and dogmas. Accordingly, his approach to learning contradicts most of the elements of conventional schools. Since he wants his learning to center on his feelings, he expresses his feelings freely and thereby lives his way into learning.

Since psychedelic humanists depreciate the value of learning as such, they give a prominent place to the concept *needs*. Needs are considered person-centered, as contrasted with their being either environment- or situation-centered. As an organism or mind naturally unfolds through a series of stages, each stage is assumed to have its unique needs. Such child-centered needs have much in common with instincts; they are innate determining tendencies or permanent trends of human nature that underlie behavior from birth to death under all circumstances in all kinds of societies.

By its very nature, *natural unfoldment* has few, if any, positive implications for transfer of learning. Hence, we deal with it here only briefly. Exponents of natural unfoldment regard intellectual development as something that "just naturally happens." To be consistent with their over-all outlook, they would reject any kind of formal teaching for the purpose of stimulating development of intelligence. Instead, they stress student-planned activities including highly permissive types of projects as the means for releasing or developing latent intellectual performance. In this way, contemporary psychedelic humanists promote the development of autonomous, self-actualizing persons who exercise almost unlimited freedom.

WHAT IS APPERCEPTION?

The third major outlook toward learning that we describe—apperception—is far more complicated than either mental discipline or learning as unfoldment. Apperception is idea-centered learning. An idea is apperceived when it appears in consciousness and is assimilated to other conscious ideas. Thus, apperception is a process of new ideas associating themselves with old ones.

Adherents of both mental discipline and natural unfoldment either assume or imply the existence of an inborn human nature, some aspects of which are common to all people. Although, in their treatment of learning, supporters of both theories sharply differ from one another, they agree that the "furniture of minds" is innate. Whereas romantic naturalists in their emphasis upon natural unfoldment have expounded instinctive natural development of persons, mental disciplinarians often agree that knowledge is inborn but insist that students need expert help to enable them to recall it.

Apperception, in contrast to both mental discipline and natural unfoldment, is a dynamic mental *associationism* based upon the fundamental premise that there are no innate ideas; everything a person knows comes to him (or her) from outside himself. This means that mind is wholly a matter of content—it is a compound of elemental impressions bound together by association, and it is formed when subject matter is presented from without and makes certain associations or connections with prior content of the mind.

An *associationism* is any general psychological theory within which it is assumed that the process of learning is one of combining irreducible elements. In recall, we connect ideas or actions simply because they were connected in our earlier experiences with them. There are two broad types of associationisms: (1) early mentalistic associationisms such as apperception, which focus upon the association of ideas in a mind, and (2) more modern physicalistic stimulus-response associationisms, which concern themselves with formation of connections either between cells in a brain and peripheral nervous system or between organic responses and environmental stimuli.

The method of studying human beings within a framework of associationism is analytic or reductionistic; learnings are reduced to their component structural parts. The basic elements that are associated may be mental, physical, or a combination of both. But, within apperception, the associated elements are completely mental and constitute the *structures* of minds. Hence, whereas mental discipline implies that a mind is a *substance,* apperception implies that it is a *structure.*

How Did Apperception Develop?

The thinking that underlies modern associationism goes back to Aristotle. Aristotle, in the fourth century B.C., observed that recollection of an item of knowledge was facilitated by a person's associating that item or idea with another when he (or she) learned it. He maintained that four kinds of connections or associations would aid or strengthen memory: contiguity of one idea with another, succession of ideas in a series, similarity of ideas, and contrast of ideas.[10] Contiguity means "being together." If children told about Eskimos and igloos at the same time, future mention of *Eskimo* will help them recall *igloo.* "A tiger is a big kitty" uses the principle of similarity. If children learn that pleasure is the opposite of pain (contrast), mention of *pain* will aid them in thinking of *pleasure.*

In the seventeenth century John Locke (1632–1704) challenged the whole notion of innate faculties or ideas and with it the conception of learning as a development of innate potentialities or faculties. He replaced this notion with the idea that learning consists of persons gaining ideas in originally empty minds. Locke observed that he could find no common human nature at all. Realizing that he could find no ideas common to all people in any one society or to people in different societies, he developed his *tabula rasa* theory of the human mind. *Tabula rasa*— blank tablet—means that there are no innate ideas. Locke was convinced that not only was a mind empty at birth, but also any ideas that one holds must have come to one originally through one's senses.

Locke's theory that all of a person's ideas must come to him (or her) through his senses is called *empiricism.* Locke's empiricism was directly opposed to the earlier *rationalism* of Plato. Whereas Plato considered *reason* the source of knowledge, Locke insisted that knowledge was derived from *sense experience.*

For Locke, ideas were the units of a mind, and *associations* consisted of combinations of ideas. Ideas were either simple or complex. One of the operations of a mind was thought to be a compounding of complex ideas from simple ones. This notion of mental combination and analysis was a beginning of the "mental chemistry" which later characterized apperception.

Locke's writings spearheaded a shift in the conception of education from mental discipline to habit formation. His *tabula rasa* theory implied that the original nature of human beings is neither morally good nor bad, nor actionally active. Instead, it is deemed morally neutral and actionally passive. So, a mind is the product of life experiences. Locke's thinking opened the way for psychologists to place their emphasis upon environmental nurture rather than hereditary nature. In school, this meant that teachers were to be the architects and builders of minds of children and youths. They were to develop a systematic instructional program centered in procedures designed to form proper habits in students. Teaching, then, became a matter of stimulating the senses as opposed to training the mental faculties.

Locke's work constituted a turning point in professional thinking about learning. Up to the seventeenth century, most psychological thinking consisted of restatements and reinterpretations of the psychology of antiquity—mental discipline. This trend continued into the seventeenth and eighteenth centuries, but alongside it, Locke spearheaded modern associationism—a new line of thought in regard to learning.

What Is Herbart's Apperception Theory of Learning?

Johann Friedrich Herbart (1776–1841) developed the first modern systematic psychology of learning to emerge from a *tabula rasa* theory of mind. Herbart was an eminent German philosopher-psychologist and a skilled teacher. In 1809 he succeeded Immanuel Kant in the world's most distinguished chair of philosophy at Königsberg, Germany, and held it until 1833. His speculative thinking developed from his dealing with problems of education. To him, morality was the supreme objective of education; he wanted to make children good. Thus, he developed a psychology to achieve this goal.

Herbart's influence on twentieth-century American education has been great. Although his theory was developed early in the nineteenth century, it did not reach the United States until the 1880s, when four young Americans—Charles DeGarmo, Frank McMurry, Charles A. McMurry, and Charles C. Van Liew—studied at the University of Jena and returned to the United States to spread Herbartian doctrine with religious fervor. "Like a tidal wave, interest in this elaborate system swept over American teachers and students of education during the nineties."[11]

From the early years of the twentieth century to the time its tenets were seriously challenged by behaviorism, Herbartianism dominated teacher education institutions in the United States. Thus, if one is to comprehend the psychological atmosphere of today's schools, it is essential that one understand the development, principles, and implications of the theory of apperception. Today, one seldom meets an avowed Herbartian; however, much of what takes place in our public schools carries with it the implicit assumption that the neutral and passive minds of children are being filled. Although apperceptive teaching seldom is advocated systematically in teacher education institutions, much actual teaching continues to follow a pattern in harmony with the theory of apperception.

Herbart perpetuated a mind-body dualism that was prevalent in his time. This was a psychophysical parallelism within which the psychic aspect—mind—played the major role, particularly in the learning process. *Psychophysical parallelism* is a theory of mind and body according to which, for every variation in conscious or mental process, there is a concomitant, parallel neurological or body process. Yet there is no causal relation between body and mind; a person's mind does not affect his (or her) body, nor his body his mind.

Through the use of the concepts *presentations, mental states apperception,* and *apperceptive mass,* Herbart expanded the notion of a mind's neutral passivity into a systematic theory of learning and teaching. He thought that a mind had no innate natural faculties or talents whatsoever either for receiving or for producing ideas. In it lay not even remote dispositions toward perception, thought, willing, or action. He regarded a mind as nothing more than a battleground and storehouse of ideas. Ideas, he thought, had an active quality. They could lead a life of their own in a mind, which was completely passive. A mind was an aggregate, not of faculties, but of ideas or mental states. John Dewey (1859–1952) described the apperceptionists' view of mind in this way: "The 'furniture' of the mind *is* the mind. Mind is wholly a matter of 'contents.' "[12]

In his metaphysics, Herbart posited for each person a unitary mind or soul that is part of ultimate reality and consequently exists prior to experience. Such a soul or mind (*Wesen*) really has no spatial or temporal nature. However, as with a mathematical point, in thinking about it we give it space and time dimensions.

> The soul has no innate natural talents nor faculties whatever, either for the purpose of receiving or for the purpose of producing. It is, therefore no *tabula rasa* in the sense that impressions foreign to itself may be made upon it; moreover . . . it is not a [mind] substance which includes in itself original activity. It has originally neither concepts, nor feeling, nor desires.[13]

The mind's being no *tabula rasa* means that it has its own unique receptivity.

Herbart's ambition was to build a science of human minds that would parallel the physical and biological sciences. He thought that the actual character of a mind consists of an arrangement of ideas, which are very much like the electrons of modern physics—they make up the object that contains them. Accordingly, a mind is an aggregate of contents resulting from a person's being presented certain ideas. Since he thought of psychology as "mental chemistry," he felt that the chief role of psychology was to study the various blendings and amalgamations of ideas or mental states in minds. Discovery of the principles by which ideas combine and recombine like chemical elements was Herbart's object in psychological investigation.

Although Herbart felt that his psychology was scientific, probably most experimental psychologists today would not agree; he rejected experimentation and the use of physiological data, both of which have been cornerstones of twentieth-century behavioristic psychology. To him, observation and thought were the proper methods for psychological inquiry. Furthermore, the observation he had in mind was self-observation, or introspection. By looking into his own mind, Herbart thought that its "chemistry" could be observed and described. He felt it proper that a science like physics was experimental, but equally appropriate that the "science" of psychology should be metaphysical and introspective.

How Does Apperception Work?

Herbart used the German term *Vorstellungen* to name the mental elements, which he deemed the constituent parts of a mind. *Vorstellungen* may be translated to mean presentations, mental states, or ideas. According to Herbartian psychologists, mental states constitute a nonspatial, mental reality that is experienced firsthand and stored in the subconscious mind. They have three forms: sense impressions, images or copies of previous sense impressions, and affective elements such as pleasure and pain. Such mental states furnish the total source of mental activity. The derived states, feeling and willing, are secondary factors that accompany mental states but are not a source or cause of mental activity. So, volitional willing has its roots in thought; right thinking produces right actions.

Mind is an aggregate of mental states and a person's stock of mental states at any given time is his or her "apperceptive mass." Until a first presentation occurs, there is nothing whatever present in a mind; except for its inherent receptivity, it is completely passive. Mental states, the active structure of a mind, become associated to produce experience. Thus, new ideas are learned only as they are related to what is already in an apperceptive mass. Hence, it is the addition of new mental states to the old ones that produces the various types of mental processes. Furthermore, the particular combination of ideas that is predominant at any given time determines what will hold a person's attention at that time.

Within Herbart's system of "mental chemistry" every mental state has an inherent quality, giving it an affinity for certain other mental states and an aversion for some others; respective ideas either attract or repel one another. Whereas the ideas of "book" and "school" would have an affinity and attract each other, the ideas of "book" and "fishing rod" probably would have a repugnancy and repel one another.

A Herbartian regards a mind as a battleground of contending ideas. Each idea in the mind of a person has once been in the center of his consciousness and it strives to return; it seeks self-preservation. Furthermore, it tries to enter into relations with other ideas. Having once held the center of consciousness and subsequently lost it, each idea, like a deposed king, keeps trying to occupy the throne once again. Compatible ideas may operate as teams, helping each other to remain in a conscious mind. But, when two ideas are incompatible, one is likely to be submerged.

To Herbartians, all perception is apperception; it is a process of new ideas relating themselves to the store of old mental states. A mind is like an iceberg in that most of it is submerged below the level of consciousness. Memories stored in the subconscious enable one to interpret experience of the moment. Without a background of experience, any new sensation would mean almost nothing at all. In picturing a mind, Herbart introduced the idea of threshold of consciousness. Objects occupying consciousness are constantly changing. At any moment, several ideas may occupy the consciousness. However, one will be at the focus of attention, some will be sinking below the threshold, and others will be striving to rise into consciousness.

The subconscious aspect of mind contains the store of perceptions and images that have been accumulated during all past experiences of an individual. These constitute one's apperceptive mass. Any of these ideas are ready to spring back into consciousness whenever a propitious opportunity occurs. The content of consciousness at any moment is the result of an interplay of many ideas. Apperception is a process not only of a person's becoming consciously aware of an idea but also of the idea's assimilation into a totality of conscious ideas.

Within the apperceptive process Herbart saw the principles of frequency and association in operation. The principle of frequency means that the more often an idea or concept has risen into consciousness, the easier becomes its return. The principle of association holds that, when a number of presentations or ideas associate, or form a mass, the combined powers of the mass determine the ideas that will enter consciousness.

Herbart recognized three levels or stages of learning. First is the stage of predominately sense activity. This is followed by the stage of memory; this second stage is characterized by exact reproductions of previously formed ideas. The third and highest level is that of conceptual thinking or understanding. Understanding occurs when the common, or shared, attributes of a series of ideas make themselves seen. It involves generalization—deriving rules, principles, or laws from a group of specifics.

What Does Apperception Mean for Teaching?

According to apperception, right thinking will produce right action; volition or willing has its roots in thought. If a teacher builds up the right sequence of ideas, the right conduct follows. Hence, the real work of instruction is implantation not only of knowledge but also of inner discipline or will by means of presented ideas. Psychologically, students' mentalities are determined by the kind of ideas that are presented to them from without.

Since, in apperception, there is no substantive mind to be trained, it can no longer be said that learning is a matter of disciplining or training a mind; rather learning has to do with the formation of the apperceptive mass that constitutes a mind. Thus, the task of education is to cause present appropriate experiences to combine with a background. The problem of education, then, is to select the right materials for forming the backgrounds or apperceptive masses of students. Teachers must start with the experiences that pupils already have had and enlarge and enrich these experiences.

To Herbartians, the art of teaching consists of bringing to the attention of students those ideas that a teacher would like to have dominate their lives. Through controlling the experiences of students, an instructor builds up masses of ideas, which develop by assimilation of new ideas to them. Thus, by manipulating ideas the teacher constructs a student's "circle of thought." The goal is a comprehensive circle of thought closely connected or integrated in all its parts. A teacher is the architect and builder of the minds, and hence the characters, of students.

According to Herbart, at no time should a teacher enter into debate with his or her students on any matter. "Cases may arise when the impetuosity of the pupil challenges the teacher to a kind of combat. Rather than accept such a challenge, he will usually find it sufficient at first to reprove calmly, to look on quietly, to wait until fatigue sets in."[14]

What Are the Herbartian Five Steps in Learning?

Herbart and his followers were convinced that the learning process proceeds through an ordered series of steps that a teacher should understand and follow. Accordingly, effective teaching requires that, regardless of obstacles, the proper succession of steps be pursued. Herbart's four steps, clearness, association, system, and method, were expanded to five by American Herbartians. Clearness became (1) preparation and (2) presentation; association became (3) comparison and abstraction; system became (4) generalization; and method became (5) application. Use of these steps came to be regarded as the general method to be followed in all teaching. The steps may be demonstrated by the following example, which involves a teacher's teaching students the generalization that any object will float in liquid or in air if it weighs less than an equal volume of the liquid or air in which it is suspended.

1. Preparation. To bring into consciousness relevant ideas, the teacher reminds students of certain experiences they have had with floating objects. The students will recall the floating of boats, balloons, bubbles, and the like.

2. Presentation. The teacher presents new facts about floating, perhaps through means of demonstrations. For example, he (she) might demonstrate how oil floats on water or how a steel ball will float on mercury.

3. Comparison and Abstraction. If the teacher has performed the first two steps properly, students will see that the new facts have similarities with those already known. Hence, in the students' consciousness, the new and old ideas associate; they are welded together because of their natural affinity for each other. At this point students also should see the nature of the common elements that give the two sets of facts their mutual attractiveness. Sorting out this common element is what is meant by abstraction.

4. Generalization. In this step, students attempt to name the common elements of the two sets of facts as a principle of generalization. They arrive at the principle of flotation—the stated objective of instruction.

5. Application. The newly learned principle then is used to explain further facts or solve problems relating to flotation. This is done through assigned tasks or problems. The teacher might ask students to explain why boats can be made successfully from steel. Or he or she might give them a problem that requires them to determine whether a certain object would float in a certain medium. For example, the teacher might ask, "Given a freight barge of specified weight and displacement, how much weight could be placed in it without causing it to sink?"

What Is the Herbartian Doctrine of Interest?

The importance of student interest held a prominent place in the theory of apperception. Present-day policy of "making subject matter interesting" probably has strong roots in apperception. Whereas followers of faculty psychology saw little or no point in student interest (some even saw it as a deterrent to developing willpower), Herbartians gave it a central place in their system. But, since the Herbartian doctrine of interest implied that students were neutral and passive, students' being interested did not mean that they necessarily were either involved or perplexed; it merely meant that they were receptive to certain ideas.

Interest means "the natural bent or inclination of the mind to find satisfaction in a subject when it is properly presented."[15] Thus, it is an active power residing in the *contents* of the mind. It depends upon the nature of the apperceptive mass and determines what ideas are to receive attention. A person thinks, feels, and wills in accordance with his or her dominant mental states. To develop a variety of interests one must acquire a large apperceptive mass. Herbart listed six classes of interests under two major categories—those awakened by the phenomena of nature apart from people and those involving the direct study of human affairs. He then assumed a sort of affinity between the historical development of the race and the stages of mental development of children. He was convinced that the history and great literature of the world, when properly selected and arranged, would make a strong appeal to the interests and understanding of children at their successive periods of growth.

How Do Apperceptionists Define Transfer of Learning?

To summarize, apperception is a process of relating new ideas or mental states to a store of old ones. One's store of ideas constitutes one's apperceptive mass. Memories stored in the subconscious and brought into the conscious enable one to interpret experiences of the moment. New ideas are learned through their being related to what already is in an apperceptive mass. Thus, apperception consists of an idea assimilating itself with other, already acquired ideas. A student's mentality is made up of the apperceptive mass of ideas that have come to him or her from without.

Learning, then, is not a matter of developing or training a mind, but rather one of formation of an apperceptive mass. Education is a process of a teacher's causing present, specified experiences of students to combine with appropriate backgrounds. Consequently, apperceptionists emphasize implantation in the minds of students of a great mass of facts and ideas that have been organized by someone other than the learner—usually the author of a text or a teacher. The stored ideas lead to feelings and willings, and these lead to acts.

According to apperception theory, a student's "subconscious mind" contains a quantity of mental states that have been accumulated during his or her experiences. Any one of these elements of the apperceptive mass stands ready to spring back into consciousness when the appropriate occasion occurs; it is ready to join other mental elements with which it has an affinity.

By use of textbooks and lectures, apperceptionists "cover" their subject. Students learn the material, retain much of it in their apperceptive masses, and carry it over to meet future situations in and out of school. This information will be used whenever a situation arises in which it is needed. Appropriateness, however, is determined by the nature of the mental states or ideas, not by the person.

Apperception, as a theory of transfer of learning, has been a vital force in attacking its predecessor—mental discipline. However, the jump from the assumption that people innately are either bad and active or neutral and active to the assumption that they are inertly passive was not all to the good. John Locke's *tabula rasa* theory of mind upon which apperception is based is perhaps as vulnerable as is mental discipline. Within apperception, transfer becomes completely a matter of mechanistic storage of ideas in a mind, which is composed only of those ideas. As such it implies that teaching is an indoctrination procedure. Thus, it throws schools out of harmony with the democratic structure of American society.

How Do Apperceptionists Promote Transfer of Learning?

Fundamentally, apperceptionists promote transfer by building up the apperceptive masses of their students. The Herbartian principles of *association* and *frequency* are the heart of apperception. To repeat, the association principle is that, when a number of ideas form a mass, the combined powers of the mass determine the new ideas that will enter consciousness; this is the basis of interest. The coordinate principle of frequency is that the more often an idea has been brought into consciousness, the easier it is for it to return. Application of these two laws leads teachers to emphasize frequent presentation of the proper ideas to students. Teachers are convinced that transfer is best when a goodly supply of facts and principles are stored for later use. If people know facts and principles pertinent to a given area of learning or living, they automatically will use them as appropriate occasions occur.

How Does Apperception Influence Today's Schools?

Since it was the approach to teaching that was stressed most in a great many of our teacher education institutions from about 1900 to 1920, and then much later was used alongside conflicting theories of learning and teaching, apperception remains influential even today. Large numbers of persons now teaching or holding administrative posts in schools continue to adhere more closely to apperception than to any other systematics learning theory.

One area in which Herbartian influence frequently is still seen is that of lesson plans. In the Herbartian system, actual teaching was always preceded by the teacher's construction of a formal lesson plan, built around the "five steps." Teachers followed these plans, more or less rigidly, on the assumption that the thinking of students could be made to conform to the formal steps. Today, many professors of education continue to insist that there is a fixed order of steps for teaching and learning. They require their students to write lesson plans in which the material to be taught is arranged according to definite steps, and in supervising student teachers they insist that the prepared lesson plans be followed.

Herbartianism has its weaknesses; nevertheless it has made some important contributions to the development of education. Its attack upon the doctrine of mental discipline and faculty psychology has been of great significance. In a more positive vein, it has emphasized a psychological approach to teaching and learning that implies a need for sound methods of teaching based upon knowledge of people and their mental functions. Thus, it has directed attention to a need for adequate teachers and enriched curriculums. Hence, preparation of teachers has been made an important business. Also, it has made student "interest" a significant idea, and it has emphasized the importance of a background of experience in the process of perception.

Furthermore, Herbart, in developing a scientific though not experimental psychology, pointed the way for the later experimental scientific movement in psychology named *structuralism.* Structuralism was developed in the nineteenth century by Wundt in Germany and Titchener in the United States. Its subject matter is the content of consciousness, which is studied only by introspection. Nevertheless, structuralism was highly important in that it helped pave the way for modern psychologies that have focused on mental processes and at the same time have been experimental in the best scientific sense.

Although apperceptionist psychology was built on fundamentally different premises from the natural unfoldment theory of followers of Rousseau, it was equally incompatible with mental discipline. Hence, apperception, like Roussellian permissiveness, can be considered a counterinfluence to mental discipline. However, the formal, rigid approach of apperceptionists, coupled with what seemed to be emphasis upon rote learning, made their teaching appear on the surface to be much like the kind of education practiced by the mental disciplinarians. The teacher remained central and dominant in the educational process. Herbartianism seems to commit teachers to a program of indoctrination. Its approach to teaching requires teachers to determine precisely what their pupils are to be taught. Each lesson plan includes the answers as well as the questions. Students arrive at these answers through a largely mechanical process completely dominated by the teacher. Apperceptive education is conceived as a process similar to filling a storage container. Since students depend completely upon the teacher, who provides all of the leadership in learning, critical thinking is discouraged and students tend to be docile. Facts are acquired for test purposes, then rapidly forgotten; their transfer value tends to be very low. Furthermore, problem-centered teaching is largely disregarded. If learning is the mechanical process that Herbart and Herbartians describe, then how does reflective, creative thinking enter the educational scene?

Within Herbartianism, a teacher might teach for explanatory understanding, but not for reflection or exploratory understanding.[16] In commenting upon Herbartianism, John Dewey felt constrained to say, "It takes . . . everything educational into account save its essence—vital energy seeking opportunity for effective exercise."[17] Since Herbartian theory at no time suggests that a person is psychologically interactive with his (or her) environment, it inescapably gives students little or no chance for active participation and constructive thinking.

Another criticism of Herbartianism is theoretical, but nevertheless vitally important. Explanations of the apperceptive process seem to contain no adequate treatment of how the first ideas enter a mind so that apperception—perception upon perception—can take effect. How does the first idea tie up with an old one?

We should recognize, however, that, regardless of their shortcomings, apperceptionists have told us much about experience that otherwise might escape our attention. They have realized that when a person has a new experience there is a "reception committee" of background ideas that helps him interpret it. Furthermore, they have noted that experiences, in some way, abide after they have been undergone, and that they have considerable influence in determining the nature of subsequent experiences.

Apperception was a connecting link that led the way for development of both mechanistic and purposive contemporary psychologies. Although apperception preceded the physicalistic stimulus-response conditioning psychologies or behaviorisms on the psychological and educational scenes, a case may be made for its equality to, or even superiority over, these later psychologies as a foundation for teaching procedures.

NOTES

[1] See Walter B. Kolesnik, *Mental Discipline in Modern Education*, University of Wisconsin Press, 1958.

[2] James D. Koerner (ed.). *The Case for Basic Education*, Boston: Little, Brown, 1959, p. v.

[3] George F. Kneller, *Existentialism and Education*, New York: Philosophical Library, 1958, p. 134.

[4] See Edward L. Thorndike and R. S. Woodworth, "The Influence of Improvement in One Mental Function upon the Efficiency of Other Functions," *Psychological Review* 8 (May 1901):247–261; (July 1901):384–395; (November 1901):553–564.

[5] Edward L. Thorndike, "Mental Discipline in High School Studies," *Journal of Educational Psychology*, 15, no. 2 (February 1924):95.

[6] Ibid., pp. 96–98.

[7] Edward L. Thorndike, *Educational Psychology*, New York: Teachers College Press, 1914, p. 73.

[8] Alexander Wesman, "A Study of Transfer of Training from High School Subjects to Intelligence," *Teachers College Record*, (October 1944):391–393.

[9] Robert Ulich, *Professional Education as a Humane Study*, New York: Macmillan, 1956, pp. 112–113.

[10] John S. Brubacher, *A History of the Problems of Education*, 2d ed., New York: McGraw-Hill, 1966, p. 145.

[11] Frederick Eby and C. F. Arrowood, *The Development of Modern Education*, Englewood Cliffs, N.J.: Prentice-Hall, 1934, p. 786.

[12] John Dewey, *Democracy and Education*, New York: Macmillan, 1916, p. 84.

[13] Johann Friedrich Herbart, *A Text-Book in Psychology*, trans. Margaret K. Smith, New York: Appleton-Century-Crofts, 1891, p. 120.

[14] Johann Friedrich Herbart, *Outlines of Educational Doctrine*, New York: Macmillan, 1904, p. 165.

[15] Charles A. McMurry, *The Elements of General Method,* New York: Macmillan, 1903, p. 85.
[16] See Chapter 19 for development of the difference between these processes.
[17] Dewey, *Democracy and Education,* p. 84.

BIBLIOGRAPHY

ADLER, MORTIMER J., and MILTON MAYER. *The Revolution in Education.* Chicago: University of Chicago Press, 1958. Sympathetic criticism of present-day teaching and an attempt to ask the right questions, that is, those questions that might help teachers resolve issues confronting them. The frame of reference is that of a classical scholar but the analysis is impartial. Bibliography covers span from ancient world to 1950s.

BODE, BOYD H. *How We Learn.* Boston: Heath, 1940. A discussion of four distinct theories of mind—mind substance, mental states, behaviorism, and pragmatism. Excellent for historical background as well as for description of the outlooks.

BRUBACHER, JOHN S. *A History of the Problems of Education,* 2d ed. New York: McGraw-Hill, 1966. One of the best overviews of outlooks on learning. Chapter 5, "Philosophy of Education," provides theoretical background for learning theory. Chapter 6, "Educational Psychology," summarizes mental discipline, apperception, behaviorism, and Gestalt psychology.

DEWEY, JOHN. *Democracy and Education.* New York: Macmillan, 1916 (also in paperback, 1961 edition). Incisive, enlightening statements concerning natural unfoldment, apperception, and mental (formal) discipline. Pages 130–138 are devoted to Roussellian natural development; 65–68 to Froebelian unfoldment; 70–79 to mental discipline; and 81–84 to Herbartian apperception.

EBY, FREDERICK. *The Development of Modern Education.* Englewood Cliffs, N.J.: Prentice-Hall, 1952. An excellent account of Herbart and Herbartian education (chapter 18). Chapter 19 is equally good on Froebel and his system of education through self-activity.

HERBART, JOHANN FRIEDRICH. *Outlines of Educational Doctrine.* New York: Macmillan, 1904. The best source in English for Herbart's views on education. It gives Herbart's psychological orientation, then follows with practical advice for instruction.

KOLESNIK, WALTER B. *Mental Discipline in Modern Education.* University of Wisconsin Press, 1958. Review of the historical background and recent evidence on mental discipline. The author traces the changes in the meaning of mental discipline and attempts to give a dispassionate overview of the subject. He sees the viewpoints of the Harvard Committee on General Education, of Robert M. Hutchins, and of John Dewey as three approaches to mental discipline.

McMURRY, CHARLES A. *The Elements of General Method, Based on the Principles of Herbart.* New York: Macmillan, 1903. A textbook for teachers presenting Herbartian apperception, with its American modifications, by an early twentieth-century leader in American education.

Rousseau, Jean Jacques. *Émile*, trans. Barbara Foxley. New York: Dutton, 1911, in the Everyman's Library. A complete translation of Rousseau's *Émile*. It is Rousseau's account of his rearing and educating a fictitious boy born to eighteenth-century city dwellers.

Ulich, Robert. *History of Educational Thought*, rev. ed. New York: American Book, 1968. Educational thought followed through lives and thoughts of great thinkers. Separate chapters are devoted to Rousseau, Froebel, Herbart, and so on.

Chapter 11
WHAT ARE THE TWO MAJOR FAMILIES OF CONTEMPORARY LEARNING THEORY?

The two most prominent families of contemporary learning theory are the *behavioristic* family of *stimulus-response conditioning theories* and the *Gestalt-field* family of *cognitive theories*. These have been in the process of development throughout the twentieth century and have roots that extend back into even earlier periods. In a sense, both families have been protests against the inadequacies and inconsistencies of earlier psychological systems. Their immediate forerunners are mental discipline and apperception. To repeat, items 5, 6, and 7 of Table 9.1 refer to the behavioristic or S-R conditioning theories, and items 8, 9, and 10 refer to the cognitive or Gestalt-field theories.

Although the two psychological approaches contrast in most respects, they also have an area of commonality; they both are scientific approaches to the study of human beings and they both assume people's basic moral proclivity to be neutral—neither innately bad nor innately good. Their great difference centers upon the behavioristic assumption that human beings are *passive* or *reactive* and the Gestalt-field assumption that they are *interactive* in relationship with their environments. In this and the succeeding chapter, we explain in some detail the basic differences between the two families of learning theories by showing the respective presuppositions, assumptions, or commitments of adherents of each approach in regard to some specific issues.

Students should realize that within each of the two families of psychological theory there is considerable diversity. For example, in the behavioristic family, followers of K. W. Spence and B. F. Skinner are in disagreement on many points. Likewise, in the Gestalt-field family, followers of Kurt Lewin differ considerably in outlook from followers of Kurt Koffka, and proponents of cognitive-field theory differ significantly with both. For example, whereas contemporary representatives of this family consider persons to be neutral-interactive, early Gestaltists, because of their roots in German idealism, often implied that persons were neutral-active. Thus, the situation in psychology is somewhat like that in politics; many persons gravitate toward one or the other of our two political parties, but in spite of some common interests both the Democrats and the Republicans exhibit wide ranges of views. In the final analysis, however, behaviorists have certain key ideas in common, just as do Gestalt-field psychologists. Hence, it is proper to consider each family as a definite grouping that can be discussed in terms of the ideas common to its members.

If students are aware that despite variance within each family the two families do differ sharply, they will better understand the ensuing chapters on learning. The two families provide answers to fundamental issues in psychology that are often quite incompatible. Thus, in dealing with the following questions, a person oriented toward behaviorism is likely to give a significantly different answer from that given by a Gestalt-field theorist: What is intelligence? What happens when we remember and when we forget? What is perception? What is motivation? What is thinking? What is the role of practice in learning? How does learning transfer to other situations?

Before students adopt the orientation of one family of psychology or the other, they should recognize that objections may be made to any position one takes in psychology and to any currently available theory of learning. However, although the evidence is not clear enough to warrant dogmatic assertions about learning, one may emerge from a careful study with the knowledge that the ideas central to one family of psychological theory may be more tenable and have fewer disadvantages than the ideas central to the other.

Although all modern psychologists, irrespective of their orientation, generally accept the methods and results of experimentation, there is wide divergence in interpretation of experimental results and equally wide divergence on how a given interpretation should be applied to the solution of a concrete learning problem. These differences appear to stem from disagreement over the fundamental nature of human beings and their relationship to their environment, and the nature of motivation and perception. In spite of disclaimers by some psychologists, it also appears advisable to attach a number of issues in psychology to related issues in philosophy. A psychologist's philosophical leaning may not only determine the kinds of experiments he (or she) conducts but also influence the conclusions he or she draws from the evidence that is secured through experimentation.

This chapter develops the background thinking that underpins the position of each family in regard to the nature of learning. In so doing, it traces each family's historical roots, philosophical thinking, and assumptions concerning the role of psychology. Chapter 12 focuses on the more technical aspects of each family of learning theory. These aspects include the meaning of motivation and thinking.

WHAT ARE THE HISTORICAL AND IDEOLOGICAL ROOTS OF CURRENT BEHAVIORISMS?

During the 1920s and 1930s teachers' colleges moved away from the promotion of Herbartianism as such. But this does not mean that Herbartian ideas were completely abandoned in schools. They were then, and are today, accepted and practiced by many teachers. However, before the twentieth century had been under way very long, a new form of associationism had become popular. This was a nonmentalistic, physiological associationism. Its chief exponents during the first third of the century were John B. Watson (1878–1958) and Edward L. Thorndike. Watson's psychology was known as behaviorism. Thorndike's was called connectionism, but it too, in the broadest sense of the term, was "behavioristic."

Although the psychological systems of Thorndike and Watson no longer are advocated in their original forms, many contemporary psychologists have orientations sufficiently similar to theirs to be termed *neobehaviorists*.[1] Some leading contemporary neobehaviorists or S-R conditioning theorists are Robert M. Gagné, Robert Glasser, Donald O. Hebb, Neal E. Miller, O. Hobart Mowrer, Burrhus F. Skinner, and J. M. Stephens. In its broadest sense the term *behaviorism* encompasses all S-R conditioning theories; these include S-R bond or connectionism, behaviorism, and neobehaviorism. So, we may use the expressions *behaviorism* and *S-R conditioning theory* interchangeably.

Nineteenth-century forerunners of modern experimental psychology tended to be philosophical dualists; they considered people to consist of minds and bodies, each genuinely real. There was a good deal of speculation in regard to the nature of the relationship of minds and bodies but seldom a denial of the reality of either. In the transition period between apperception and behaviorism, much vacillation took place between emphasis upon the workings of biological organisms and the functions of either substantive or structural minds.

During the first half of the nineteenth century, experimental psychology got its start within experimental physiology. Ivan Petrovich Pavlov (1849–1936) was a physiologist and pharmacologist who wrote about "psychical processes" during his study of the digestive juices. Wilhelm Wundt (1832–1920) was trained in medicine. He turned from medicine to physiology and from physiology to psychology. In 1879 he established the first psychological laboratory of modern history. His method was introspection; he and his students observed the workings of their respective minds. Students from various parts of the world went to Wundt's laboratory at Leipzig to study introspection. But many became psychological heretics; they turned to study of observable behavior of other persons and animals.

Late in the nineteenth century interest in bodily functioning became apparent among many psychologists. This group of "physiological psychologists" thought that psychology could become a true science only if it switched its focus to bodily processes. In a century that placed ever-increasing emphasis upon experimental science, introspection came more and more to appear a highly unreliable procedure. One could reflect upon the workings of one's own mind, but what did this prove? Scientists were ceasing to be concerned with any kind of evidence that was not "publicly verifiable," that is, subject to public observation and tests. Thus, they began to focus their attention on objects or events that could be observed with the "five senses," could be studied in the same manner by any number of trained investigators, and would lead to uniform conclusions.

To a growing number of psychologists, the only logical alternative to the method of introspection was to focus on observable forms of behavior. Such behavior included not only bodily movement as seen by an observer watching a subject but also the internal physical processes that were related to overt bodily behavior. Why epinephrine is secreted and how long it takes one to react to a pinprick are equally challenging questions to a physiological psychologist. Both can be measured objectively described in terms of definite mechanical sequences or quantities, and reported statistically. Before the twentieth century was very far along, a large number of psychologists had come to feel that psychology, in time, could be made as "scientific" as physics.

Early in the nineteenth century, psychologists such as Pierre Florens (1794–1867) proposed that conclusions drawn from animal experimentation should be equally applicable to man. This notion gained wide acceptance and greatly simplified the work of experimental psychologists: after all, it is much cheaper and more convenient to experiment with rats than with human beings.

Some of the most notable animal learning experiments of the late nineteenth and early twentieth centuries were conducted by the Russian physiologist Pavlov and the American psychologist Thorndike. Pavlov put food before a hungry dog and sounded a bell or tuning fork. He found that if this procedure was repeated enough times, the sound alone would cause the dog to salivate. As we shall see, Pavlov's work was extremely influential, and nowhere more so than among the growing group of behaviorists in the United States.

Thorndike's animal experiments, making use of chicks, dogs, and cats, were possibly even more comprehensive than Pavlov's and, over the long run, more influential in the United States. Thorndike's famous "laws of learning" were derived mainly from his interpretation of how hungry cats behave when placed in a cage from which they cannot escape—until they learn how to so so. Since Thorndike was a dominant figure in the psychology of learning for almost half a century, we describe some of his ideas in detail.

What Was Thorndike's Connectionism?

Edward L. Thorndike, whose behavioristic psychology was called *connectionism*, was an "eclectic" in the sense that he retained in his thinking certain elements of Herbartian "idea associationism," and, at the same time, was strongly influenced by the new physiological psychology (see p. 6 for an explanation of eclecticism). Consequently, he assumed that there were both physical and mental events or units, and that learning was a process of linking the two in various combinations. A mental unit was something sensed or perceived; a physical unit was a stimulus or a response. Specifically, he saw learning as a process of connecting a mental with a physical unit, a physical with a mental unit, a mental with a mental unit, or a physical with a physical unit.

Thorndike's theory of learning, connectionism, also is called S-R *bond* theory. It implies that, through conditioning, specific responses come to be linked with specific stimuli. These links, bonds, or connections are products of biological, that is, synaptic, changes in a nervous system. Thorndike thought that the principal way in which S-R connections are formed is through random trial and error (or selecting and connecting). It is probably because of Thorndike's influence that the term *trial-and-error* became popularized and found its way into the vocabularies of many American educators.

In a typical trial-and-error experiment, Thorndike would place a "hungry" cat in a cage that could be opened from inside only by striking a latch or button. He also would place some food that the cat relished outside the cage. The cat would claw, bite, and scurry wildly about until it accidentally touched the release and was freed. The experiment would be repeated and the animal would behave the same except that over the course of a number of successive "trials" the total time required by the cat to get out of the cage and to the food would decrease. Eventually the cat would learn to escape immediately without random activity. Thorndike inferred from the timed behavior of his cats that learning was a process of "stamping in" connections in the nervous system and had nothing to do with insight or "catching on."

Thorndike formulated a number of "laws" of learning and classified them as either primary or secondary. He expressed his primary laws by the terms *readiness, exercise,* and *effect.* His secondary or subordinate laws were identified by the expressions *multiple response, set* or *attitude, prepotency of elements, response by analogy,* and *associative shifting.*[2] We describe here only his three primary laws:

1. The Law of Readiness. Thorndike termed the neuron (or neurons) and the synapse (or synapses) involved in establishment of a specific bond or connection a *conduction unit.* He assumed that, because of the structure of a nervous system, in a given situation certain conduction units are more predisposed to conduct than others. He also thought that *"for a conduction unit ready to conduct to do so is satisfying,* and *for it not to do so is annoying."*[3]

2. The Law of Exercise or Repetition. According to this law, the more times a stimulus-induced response is repeated, the longer it will be retained. As Thorndike put it, "Other things being equal, *exercise strengthens the bond between situation and response."*[4]

3. The Law of Effect. The law of effect stated the famous pleasure-pain principle so frequently associated with Thorndike's name. A response is strengthened if it is followed by pleasure and weakened if followed by displeasure. In Thorndike's words, "[to] a modifiable connection being made . . . between an S and an R and being accompanied or followed by a satisfying state of affairs man responds, other things being equal, by an increase in the strength of that connection. To a connection similar, save that an *annoying* state of affairs goes with or follows it, man responds, other things being equal, by a decrease in the strength of the connection."[5] "By a satisfying state of affairs [positive reinforcer] is meant one that the animal does nothing to avoid, often doing such things as attain and preserve it. By a discomforting or annoying state of affairs is meant one which the animal commonly avoids and abandons."[6]

In his later writings Thorndike disavowed his law of exercise or repetition and one-half—the annoyance aspect—of his law of effect. But he seemed not to have had the courage of his convictions. Through implication, he continued to emphasize repetition in learning. His law of effect shifted its emphasis to pleasure, but the pain aspect was not completely discarded.

Students will readily see that Thorndike's laws of learning are closely related and may operate together. For example, if an organism is ready to respond, then response is pleasurable and this fact in itself will tend to fix the response. Also, the laws appear to be exceedingly mechanical. Furthermore, they seem to leave no room for any sort of thought or insight, and they do not appear to require the assumption of any kind of purposiveness of man or lower animals.

The psychological concept *purposiveness* has no direct relationship to the problem of cosmic or teleological purpose. Within a purposive psychology, as contrasted with a mechanistic one, we assume that each animal or person, whatever its developmental level, is seeking some end or purpose and that we can predict its behavior most accurately when we anticipate what it is trying to accomplish.

What Was Watson's Behaviorism?

John B. Watson, much more strongly than Thorndike, felt the need to base psychology exclusively on the concepts of physics and chemistry. To his way of thinking, mind and all kinds of mentalistic concepts were not only unsusceptible to scientific inquiry but also irrelevant to the real task of psychology. Watson drew heavily upon Pavlov's work and became convinced that learning was as Pavlov described it, namely, a process of building conditioned reflexes through the substitution of one stimulus for another.

Watson and other "pure behaviorists" came to reject certain of Thorndike's ideas because it seemed impossible to exclude mind and mind-related concepts from them. The pure behaviorists were also bothered by Thorndike's concepts of satisfaction and annoyance. To behaviorists these seemed to be mentalistic concepts, which should be repudiated in a truly scientific psychology. So, Watson confined his study to only those aspects of animal life that are sufficiently overt to make possible highly objective observation and measurement of them.

Although Watson rejected some of Thorndike's ideas, he saw great promise in one of his secondary laws *associative shifting.* The principle enunciated by this law became the keystone for the behavioristic movement of the 1920s. According to this law, we may *"get any response of which a learner is capable associated with any situation to which he is sensitive."*[7] In other words, any response that is possible can be linked with any stimulus. An animal's "purposes or thoughts" have nothing to do with such learnings. We may illustrate this law by using an example involving the training of an animal. Suppose we wish to train a dog to sit up at the verbal command "Up." It is only necessary to induce the dog to sit up repeatedly by dangling a piece of meat or other food above him immediately after the verbal command "Up" is issued. Once this procedure has been repeated enough times, the dog should respond properly —without error—whenever the command is given. In this example, as long as the same "adequate stimulus" is used throughout the experiment, it would not matter if the command were replaced by any other accompanying stimulus to which a dog is sensitive—a light, a bell, snapping the fingers, whistling. Furthermore, by using the same basic procedure, it should be possible to teach a dog to perform any other act of which it is capable—standing on its rear legs, rolling over, playing dead, etc. This principle of learning, fundamental to behaviorism, is the principle of *stimulus substitution.*

Behaviorists have defined a living organism as a self-maintaining mechanism. They have assumed that the essence of a human machine is a system of receptors (sense organs), conductors (neurons), switching organs (brain and spinal cord), and effectors (muscles) attached to levers (bones)—plus, of course, fueling and controlling organs such as the stomach and glands. When an organism is defined in such mechanistic terms, mentalistic concepts can be entirely eliminated. Not only can they be dropped out of the picture but they actually begin to seem rather fanciful. Can one imagine a machine "having tender sentiments" or "soaring on the imagination"? Thus, among behaviorists, there developed an attitude toward the earlier mentalistic psychologists similar to that of a modern physician toward a primitive witch doctor.

The position of a Watsonian behaviorist can be illustrated amusingly in a morning conversation. Ordinarily, a conventional greeting would go as follows: "Good morning, how are you?" "I'm fine, and yourself?" "Just fine." But such a greeting implies introspection. Each person is "looking into himself" in order to decide what kind of shape he (or she) is in. Presumably (according to a behaviorist) this is scientifically impossible; instead the two persons would need to inspect each other. The proper salutation of a behaviorist would be, "Good morning, you appear to be fine; how am I?"

Who Are the Neobehaviorists?

There is a large group of American psychologists today who assume that life can be explained in essentially mechanistic terms but who have adopted positions somewhat different from that of the Watsonian behaviorists. Probably the best term to apply to contemporary S-R conditioning theorists is *neobehaviorists.*

Contemporary S-R conditioning theorists continue to assume that life can be explained in essentially mechanistic terms, but they do not place nearly as much emphasis upon the operation of the brain and nervous system as did their predecessors. Watson himself had felt that the precise nature of neural mechanisms was largely irrelevant to an understanding of learning; but Watson's followers, like Thorndike, exhibited a strong interest in neural physiology and the physical mechanics of S-R linkages.

Neobehaviorists differ from the original behaviorists in another respect. In their experimentation, they have tended to focus attention more upon response modification than stimulus substitution. Response modification refers to the fate of responses that are made—whether they will be strengthened, weakened, or changed by subsequent events. Since Thorndike's concept of learning as a process of "stamping in" a response that was originally accidental is a form of response modification, one might say that many neobehaviorists have returned to Thorndike's conception of learning. However, most neobehaviorists are better systematizers than Thorndike. Furthermore, they are more consistent, largely by virtue of their building systems that do not at any point require a study of human consciousness.

Another interesting feature of neobehaviorism is its attempt to explain behavior that appears to be purposive. The apparent purposiveness of organisms has always bothered psychologists who are behavioristically oriented because they have felt that it is difficult to recognize purposiveness without slipping into a mind-body dualism and its accompanying mysticism. However, since what seems purposive must be explained in some way, neobehaviorists have tended to develop mechanical explanations for apparent purposiveness. So, apparent purposiveness either is regarded as a product of a pattern of stimulation in which certain stimuli are more potent than the rest and thus lead an organism in one way rather than another, or it is interpreted as "drive reduction," that is, as a relieving reaction to the stimulation induced by organic drives such as hunger or sex. Thus, neobehaviorists continue to be careful to explain apparent purposiveness in a way that does not require the assumption of conscious behavior or intelligent experience.

WHAT ARE THE ORIGINS OF GESTALT-FIELD PSYCHOLOGY?

The second major family of contemporary learning theories, Gestalt-field psychology, originated in Germany during the early part of the twentieth century. The four leaders in its development were Max Wertheimer (1880–1943), Wolfgang Köhler (1887–1967), Kurt Koffka (1886–1941), and Kurt Lewin (1890–1947). All four of these men migrated to the United States where they devoted their professional lives to the development and refinement of their psychological position.

Gestalt-field psychologists consider learning phenomena to be closely related to perception. Consequently, they define learning in terms of reorganization of the learner's perceptual or psychological world—his or her *field*. Some contemporary leaders whom we may identify with this family are Roger G. Barker, Ernest E. Bayles, Jerome S. Bruner, Morton Deutsch, Donald Snygg, and Herbert F. Wright.

Gestalt is a German noun for which there is no equivalent English word, so the term was carried over into English psychological literature. The nearest English translation of *Gestalt* is an organized "configuration" or "pattern," including all that the pattern is composed of. Thus, we refer to related theories that either represented or grew out of Gestalt psychology as Gestalt-field or configurational psychology. As configurational psychology has evolved, other names such as *organismic, field phenomenological,* and *cognitive-field psychology* have become associated with it. Gestalt-field psychology was introduced into the United States in the middle 1920s. It has gathered a large number of exponents and now can be considered the leading rival of the behaviorisms. However, a great many psychologists are eclectic in the sense that they borrow elements from both schools of thought and identify themselves with neither. The position of Gestalt psychology was formally stated first by the German philosopher-psychologist Max Wertheimer in 1912. The central idea of Wertheimer's point of view is that an organized whole is greater than the sum of its parts. For example, a triangle is greater than the sum of the three line segments that form it. This is because of its Gestalt.

Wertheimer and his followers formulated a series of "laws" of perception. These laws were identified by the concepts *Prägnanz, similarity, proximity, closure, good continuation,* and *membership character.* According to the *basic law* of *Prägnanz,* if a perceptual field is disorganized when a person first experiences it, he or she imposes order on that field in a predictable way. The "predictable way" follows the other five laws. *Similarity* means that similar items (dots, for instance) tend to form groups in perception. *Proximity* means that perceptual groups are favored according to the nearness of their respective parts.

Closure means that closed areas are more stable than unclosed ones. Draw a 340° arc and ask a viewer what you have drawn. He (or she) very likely will say "a circle." This is an example of closure. Since to achieve closure is satisfying to one, closure might be considered a dynamic alternative to Thorndike's mechanistic law of effect. *Good continuation* is closely related to closure. It means that, in perception, one tends to continue straight lines as straight lines and curves as curves.

According to the law of *membership character,* a single part of a whole does not have fixed characteristics; it gets its characteristics from the context in which it appears. As Gardner Murphy puts it, "The Gestaltist insists that the attributes or aspects of the component parts, insofar as they can be defined, are defined by their relations to the system as a whole in which they are functioning."[8] For example, a patch of color in a painting derives its quality from its context—the surrounding picture pattern—rather than from anything inherent in itself.

The Gestalt "laws" imply that in perception, one's organization of a field tends to be as simple and clear as the existing conditions allow. Hence, a person, in experiencing his (or her) world, imposes an organization that is characterized by stability, simplicity, regularity, and symmetry. A viewer groups individual items in a field so they will have a pattern. He relates similar items as are required for completeness, and if present patterns are meaningful he tries to maintain them into the future. Imposing a "good" Gestalt, as happens when the foregoing events occur, is a psychological task. It does not necessarily involve any change in the physical environment. Rather, it represents a change in how a viewer "sees" or perceives his physical environment.

Two of Wertheimer's German colleagues, Wolfgang Köhler and Kurt Koffka, were primarily responsible for publicizing Gestalt psychology and establishing it in the United States. Köhler is famous, among other things, for his celebrated study of the learning process in chimpanzees (*The Mentality of Apes*, 1925). He set out to test Thorndike's hypothesis that learning is a matter of random trial and error in which correct responses are gradually stamped in. Köhler observed that, in addition to their exhibiting learning that might appear accidental, his apes also displayed a type of learning that appeared insightful. Hence, Köhler concluded that Thorndike's laws of learning were inadequate. Koffka's book *Growth of the Mind* (1924) contained a detailed criticism of trial-and-error learning as conceived by Thorndike. Koffka not only criticized Thorndike, his book also was a critique of the major ideas of behaviorism.

Kurt Lewin took the spirit of Gestalt theory, added to it some new concepts, and coined a new terminology. He developed a *field* psychology also called *topological and vector psychology*. Lewin spent his later years in the United States, where he acquired a considerable following. Lewin's psychological theory has contributed much to current cognitive-field theory, which is developed in Chapters 14 and 15.

During the development of the Gestalt-field family, its adherents have made two significant changes in their position concerning the presumed moral and actional nature of human beings. The original German Gestaltists—Köhler, Koffka, and Wertheimer—thought that people were neutral-active beings whose activities conformed to a set of psychological laws of organization. But, the American Gestaltists such as Raymond H. Wheeler and Ernest E. Bayles considered people to be neutral-interactive, purposive individuals whose interaction consisted of *sequential* relationships with their environments. Then, cognitive-field theorists adopted the Lewinian position, and built their thinking around neutral-interactive persons in *simultaneous mutual interaction* with their psychological environments.

It is in the process of developing an *emergent synthesis* from the two horns of the active-passive or subjective-objective dilemma that cognitive-field learning theory emerges (see pp. 230–231 for an explanation of the meaning of an emergent synthesis). Within this psychology, learning is not equated with unfoldment and sheer expression of inner urges. Nor is it a conditioning process, which comes from the environment's impinging upon a biological organism from without. Instead, cognitive-field psychologists find the clue to the meaning of learning in the aspects of a situation within which a person and his (or her) psychological environment come together in a psychological field or life space.

As a result of experimentation conducted by the Gestalt-field psychologists, behaviorists generally are coming to recognize that the earlier atomistic stimulus-response idea, based as it was on the principle of simple reflex arcs, does not explain human behavior or learning adequately. Thus, there is a tendency among contemporary S-R conditioning theorists to speak of "molar behavior" or behavior of the whole organism in contrast to piecemeal or "molecular" behavior. Accordingly, such psychologists characteristically refer to "total responses to patterns of stimulation." However, since these psychologists continue to think in terms of mechanically relating stimuli and responses, they still are within the basic pattern of S-R conditioning theory. Despite their adoption of the concept of molar behavior, their point of view tends to be fundamentally different from that of Gestalt-field psychologists.

WHAT IS THE PHILOSOPHICAL THINKING BEHIND THE TWO PSYCHOLOGICAL FAMILIES?

It is the purpose of this part of the chapter to explore some of the philosophical implications of the two families of psychology. When a contrast is drawn between their underlying philosophical premises, differences between the two families are made much clearer. Although many psychologists have tried during the past century to divorce psychology from philosophy, it is doubtful that this is possible. There is no science so "pure" that it lacks philosophical implications. Even physicists find it helpful to make assumptions about the basic nature of their materials and processes; hence they too become involved in philosophical formulations.

Since any psychological system rests upon some particular conception of basic human nature, psychology is deeply involved with philosophy from the very start. The issues among contemporary psychologists is whether a human being is an active creature of instincts and needs (as exemplified in the self-actualization of psychedelic humanism), an essentially *passive* or *reactive* organism that is the product of a unique stimulus-response history in a determining environment (as implied in S-R conditioning theory), or a *purposive person* who is interacting with his or her psychological environment (as currently implied in contemporary cognitive-field psychology). Each of the two latter positions harmonizes with an allied philosophical outlook: S-R conditioning theory with earlier *scientific realism* or contemporary *logical empiricism* and cognitive-field theory with earlier *pragmatism* or contemporary *positive relativism*.

Both logical empiricism and positive relativism are empiricistic in the sense that they center on knowledge gained through experience. But, in contrast with *logical* empiricism, positive relativism is a *psychological* empiricism within which one's experience grows out of one's pursuing one's purposes.

How Does Scientific Realism Relate to S-R Conditioning?

Scientific realists have been convinced that the physical world that is experienced by human beings is real and essentially what it appears to be when observed through the senses. Furthermore, even if there were no human beings around to observe it, it would exist in the same state. Reality, like existence, is independent of a thing's being known. Scientific realists have assumed that the physical world is governed by natural laws, which operate inexorably and without change. They further have assumed that a basic principle of the universe is sequential cause and effect; every event is determined by events that have gone before it. Thus, the universe is a vast mechanism governed by natural laws, which are essentially mechanical in nature.

Contemporary logical empiricists—the current representatives of scientific realism—think that we should abandon dogmatic, other worldly, supernaturalistic, and tender-minded ways of thinking and replace them with critical, worldly, naturalistic, and empirical fact-minded outlooks and procedures. Logical empiricists are likely to assume that there is a kind of hierarchy of the sciences, some being much more objective and reliable than others. They place at the top of the hierarchy physics and chemistry, aided by mathematics. These sciences are regarded as models that other sciences should emulate. For logical empiricists, just as the art of agriculture is based upon biological and chemical scientific knowledge, so education should be based upon the pure sciences of biology and psychology. To a consistent logical empiricist, nothing should be asserted to be real or meaningful unless, through observation, it can be subjected to objective study, using only publicly verifiable data. If anything exists, it exists in some amount; if it exists in some amount, it can be measured.

Let us trace how this overall point of view has been transplanted to psychology. Early in human history, people commonly believed in animism, that is, that all objects, including even rocks, have minds or spirits. Since primitive people had no other way of explaining most types of natural events, animism provided at least some basis for understanding their surroundings. However, as people learned more about natural causation, animism declined in popularity. In other words, when human beings came to understand something about gravity, a person no longer needed to attribute a mind and will to a rock to know why it fell on his (or her) head.

As time went on, mechanical explanations began to be applied to all sorts of physical events involving nonliving objects. Increasingly the nonliving parts of the universe were believed to consist of atoms in motion, each inert by itself, but subject to the push and pull of lawful forces external to itself.

Since living objects, especially human beings, seemed, on the surface at least, to be willful and unpredictable, they did not appear to conform to the mechanical concepts that applied to the world of nature. Thus, some kind of vitalistic mind-force was attributed to them. The belief in a nonmaterial mind-force as applied to human beings led to a distinctive conception of learning as a process of disciplining or training minds. This gave us the classical humanistic tradition in education. Although actual teaching under the classical mind-training approach may appear to be highly mechanical, the conception of human nature that underlies it definitely is nonmechanistic in that it assumes the existence of a mind substance, which is capable both of free will and of spontaneous "uncaused" behavior.

Apperception, the first modern associationism, was a mechanistic, albeit mental, psychology. Although in developing his learning theory Herbart perpetuated the idea of the human being's having a mystical aspect, his mechanistic psychology opened the way for rejection of vitalism and accompanying mentalistic concepts, which are inconsistent with a "realistic" interpretation of the universe. Consequently, as the associationistic psychologies developed, psychologists found themselves in increasing sympathy with the tenets of scientific realistic philosophy.

Realistic, mechanistic psychology, then, has been an outgrowth of the attempt of S-R conditioning theorists to make psychology as "scientific" as physics. Thus, S-R theorists have equated stimulus and response in psychology with cause and effect in physics.

The issue between mechanistic and nonmechanistic psychology is nowhere stated more clearly than by the contemporary neobehaviorist Donald O. Hebb. Hebb says flatly that psychology's only hope of remaining scientific is to assume that a person is basically a mechanism. Thus, as far as the basic outlook of a psychologist is concerned, there are for Hebb only two alternatives—mechanism and vitalism (see Chapter 2, pp. 34–46). With respect to the type of study that psychologists can undertake, Hebb says, "All one can know about another's feeling and awareness is an inference from what he *does*—from his muscular contractions and glandular secretions."[9] To a psychologist such as Hebb, Gestalt-field psychology would appear to be little more than "confusionism." The philosophical orientation of a behavioristic psychologist usually is so thoroughly mechanistic that any other outlook seems untenable.

Logical empiricists and their behavioristic psychological counterparts continue to think in terms of stimuli being causes and responses being effects and of there being a time lapse between physical stimuli and organic responses. To quote Hebb further, "Temporarily integrated behavior, extended over a period of time, is treated as a series of reactions to a series of stimulations. . . . Stimulus followed directly by response is the archetype of behavior."[10] Accordingly, logical empiricists, in harmony with behaviorists, treat human beings as basically extremely well-designed, clever machines, who learn through accumulating memories in an additive process. Human responses are a chance affair and a human being is a biological organism with a history of conditioned behavior. For logical empiricists, words such as *foresight, purpose,* and *desire* are literary terms, but not scientific ones.

In their approach to education logical empiricists, and likewise behaviorists, are very much environmentalists and determinists in the sense that they assume that the surrounding environment should, and inescapably will, largely control the behavior and learning of students. Thus, teaching practices advocated by behavioristic psychologists are closely in tune with the logical empiricistic-realistic outlook. Such psychologists tend to recommend that subject matter be selected by qualified adults prior to the teaching act, that it reflect facts and skills useful in contemporary society, and that it be inculcated into students. There is an implicit assumption that, if a given item of subject matter impinges upon a student, there will be a definite and predictable effect. Only secondary, if any, mention is made of such concepts as student goals or problem solving.

How Does Positive Relativism Relate to Cognitive-Field Psychology?

Positive relativism has emerged during the past 70 or 80 years and is, in a sense, a reaction against the absolutistic ways that have characterized many facets of human thinking throughout history; thus, it contrasts sharply with logical empiricism. Logical empiricists assume the existence of an ultimate reality, which consists of fixed natural laws, and they define truth as that which corresponds to natural law and consequently is unchanging. In contrast with logical empiricists, positive relativists neither assert nor deny an absolute existent reality. Rather, they define psychological reality as that which we "make of" what we gain from our environment. They then deal with reality, so defined, in achieving truth and designing behavior. Thus, whereas for a logical empiricist reality is the same as an objective existence, for a positive relativist reality is psychological and thereby different from any objective existence; it is what people gain through their five-plus senses.

The *positive* aspect of positive relativism denotes that such a relativism, to quote Webster's is "logically affirmative" and "capable of being constructively applied" as in "positive proposals for the betterment of society."[11] Accordingly, the philosophy's being affirmative implies that its proponents assert the availability of truth and reality and thereby affirm the feasibility of a body of constructive knowledge. Furthermore, its capability of being constructively applied signifies that it is structured in such a way as to direct its adherents toward promotion of further development, improvement, and advancement of themselves and society. Hence, a person is being positively relativistic in his (or her) thinking and action when he harbors no absolutes and simultaneously attempts to strengthen or improve matters or to develop something better to take their place.

The positive-relativistic position often is designated by the one word *relativism*. A central idea of relativism is that a thing derives its qualities from its relationship to other things. A person may look at a patch of grass that is in shadow. Compared with grass in the full rays of the sun, the patch appears dark; but compared with grass at night, it appears light. A tall girl, seen in the company of girls even taller may appear short. Thus, the way we perceive any object or event is colored by the total situation. This principle is actually one with which everyone is familiar. Relativistic philosophy does little more than explore and develop the numerous ramifications and implications of this basic idea.

It might appear that if relativism were a valid concept a person could never make a definitive statement about anything, except to say that it "is closer than something else," "is to the left of something else," "is darker than something else," or "is smaller than something else." However, this is not an insurmountable problem. In order to view a thing relativistically, one simply determines a convenient vantage point for reference. One can say that one's automobile has 200 horsepower, and in such an assertion be quite confident. The unit of measure, one horsepower, is an arbitrary standard humanly contrived and susceptible to future change, yet it has definite usefulness as a point of reference. Such relatively fixed points of reference are *relatively absolute*. The word *absolute,* so used, is an adjective; it means no more than that the point of reference is one of relative fixity or stability.[12]

If one assumes that objects have to be dealt with relationally, rather than as things-in-themselves, then a distinctive method of defining truth, or knowledge, and an equally distinctive method of arriving at truth are required. Relativists questions the notion that human beings are able to find and use final or absolute truth. Consequently, they have little interest in "eternal verities." Nevertheless, they are deeply concerned with truths, relativistically defined. Relativists regard knowledge as insights developed and held by human beings using human methods.

The development of the notion that knowledge is a matter of human interpretation, and not a literal description of what exists external to people, reflects a shift from an absolutistic to a relative view of science. A scientific law (including a principle of psychology) is a statement that seems true to all or most of those who are competent to study the matter. The relativistic test of truth is *anticipatory accuracy*, not correspondence to ultimate reality. Thus, in a sense, a scientific law is a generalization about which there is considerable agreement among those scientifically competent in its area; it is in a way a matter of consensus. Its test, however, is not the consensus, but its predictive accuracy. Relativists assume that no scientific law is "sacred"; any law may change, and indeed, over the course of time most will. A significant aspect of the thinking of relativists is their expectancy of change. They are much more likely than are logical empiricists to think of both nature and culture as undergoing continuous modification.

Positive relativists do not mean that truth has no objective standard and that it always varies from person to person, group to group, and time to time. In fact, they recognize that, fortunately, many truths have been so adequately tested that we may safely treat them as if they were certainties. However, their definition of certainty "is something in which I have tremendous faith."[13]

But what grounds does a relativist have for judging anything true? To quote Bayles, an insight is considered true "if, and only if, the deduced behavior pattern, when tested experientially or experimentally, produces the results which were anticipated."[14] Thus, an insight is true if it proves to be reasonably accurate—if what one supposes will follow from its application actually does follow. So, for a relativist, truth is not based upon eternal and universal principles. Rather, it is of human origin and humanity will change it as need be. But, this does not mean that truth is unimportant or ephemeral. It does mean that truth tends to evolve as human experience evolves.

Both logical empiricists and positive relativists assume that the most valid method of inquiry is scientific in nature; it is based on testable evidence. But they define "scientific method" in quite different ways and, as the foregoing discussion has indicated, they seek different ends from it. To a relativist, scientific method is not merely a sequence of steps such as a physicist supposedly uses. Scientific thinking is any form of intellectual pursuit that is based on testable evidence and is productive in relation to the goals of the thinker. To be sure, there are some measuring sticks or criteria of scientific truth; these criteria may be encompassed under the headings of *pertinency; adequacy,* and *harmony* in light of obtainable data. A conclusion, to be properly scientific, must be based on adequate pertinent data, and it must harmonize all the data, that is, it must make the data add up. If a single pertinent fact seems to be contradictory, if it remains unexplained, then the conclusion is not to be trusted. According to the principle of *adequacy,* all known pertinent facts must be taken into consideration. None may be ignored, no matter how unpalatable it might seem.

Positive relativists construe science much more broadly than do logical empiricists. They assume that the scientific approach can be applied in a wide range of situations. They do not think in terms of a hierarchy of sciences, with physics, chemistry, and mathematics at the top. They are also more flexible with respect to the kinds of data that will be considered. In psychological research, logical empiricists are likely to admit only data of observable physical objects or substances. Conversely, positive relativists in psychology will consider all the data of human experience, including that which may seem introspective. So, in the formation of hypotheses to be tested, they may go beyond the information that is at hand.

Current positive-relativistic cognitive-field psychology essentially is an emergent synthesis, but not a compromise, that has developed from an ideological conflict between the psychological tenets of psychedelic humanistic self-actualization and those of logical empiricist behaviorism (see pp. 230–231 for an explanation of the concept *emergent synthesis*).

To psychedelic humanists, learning is largely equated with unfoldment and is a product of inner urges. Logical empiricist psychologists, at the other extreme, have considered all development to be a product of biological maturation and learning, and have assumed that learning is a conditioning process that occurs through the environment's impinging upon an individual from without.

In bridging the two positions, positive relativists assume that a child or youth is what he (or she) is because of the psychological interaction between himself and his culture. With the emphasis upon interaction, the responsibility for development rests neither with the person alone nor with the environment alone. Instead, it is in a person and his environment coming together in a psychological field that cognitive-field psychologists find their clue to psychological development and learning. Since the number of possible culture patterns is infinite, the possibilities for variety in human development likewise become infinite. Thus, within its biological limits, human nature might become anything.

NOTES

[1] *Neo* is a word element meaning "new," "recent," or "modified." When used as a prefix, it refers to a school of thought that is derived from an earlier school of thought but refined in various ways. See T. W. Wann (ed.), *Behaviorism and Phenomenology*, Chicago: University of Chicago Press, 1965, pp. 7–21.

[2] See Ernest R. Hilgard and Gordon H. Bower, *Theories of Learning*, 4th ed., Englewood Cliffs, N.J.: Prentice-Hall, 1975, pp. 34–36 for descriptions of the subordinate laws.

[3] Edward L. Thorndike, *Educational Psychology*, vol. 1, New York: Teachers College Press, 1913, p. 127 (italics in original).

[4] Edward L. Thorndike, *Education*, New York: Macmillan, 1912, p. 95 (italics in original).

[5] Thorndike, *Educational Psychology*, p. 172.

[6] Edward L. Thorndike, *Animal Intelligence*, New York: Macmillan, 1911, p. 245.

[7] Thorndike, *Educational Psychology*, p. 15 (italics in original).

[8] Gardner Murphy, *Historical Introduction to Modern Psychology*, New York: Harcourt Brace Jovanovich, 1949, p. 288.

[9] Donald O. Hebb, *The Organization of Behavior; A Neuro-Psychological Theory*, New York: Wiley, 1949, p. xiii.

[10] Donald O. Hebb, *A Textbook of Psychology*, Philadelphia: Saunders, 1958, p. 46.

[11] From *Webster's Third New International Dictionary*, copyright 1961 by

G. & C. Merriam Company, publishers of the Merriam-Webster dictionaries, p. 1770, definition 4a (1) of *positive*. By permission.

[12] The present discussion of relativism follows closely that in Ernest E. Bayles, *Democratic Educational Theory*, New York: Harper & Row, 1960; see particularly chaps. 4 and 7.

[13] Hugh Skilling, "An Operational View," *American Scientist* 52, no. 4, December 1964:390A.

[14] Bayles, p. 113.

BIBLIOGRAPHY

References for Chapter 11 will be found at the end of Chapter 12. These two chapters should be studied as a unit.

Chapter 12
HOW DO THE TWO FAMILIES OF CONTEMPORARY LEARNING THEORY DESCRIBE THE LEARNING PROCESS?

In Chapter 11 we open discussion of the two major contemporary versions of the nature of learning. We now treat them in some detail. As already noted, whereas contemporary S-R conditioning theorists—the neobehaviorists—conceive of learning as *conditioning* or *reinforcement* of behaviors, Gestalt-field psychologists think of it as *development of insights,* which provide a potential guide for behavior.

IS LEARNING STIMULUS-RESPONSE CONDITIONING?

Neobehavioristic psychologists construe behavior to be observable actions that result from forces or stimuli being exerted upon an organism. Explanation for what organisms, including people, do is sought in their genetic endowment, the environmental circumstances that surround them, the stimuli that impinge upon them, and the actions, including verbalizations, that they emit. These actions or behaviors are either respondents or operants. A respondent is behavior that is elicited by a stimulus. An operant is behavior that is controlled by its consequences, that is, the stimulus that follows it.

A child or youth is something to be molded in the proper fashion. Learning primarily is a process within which both verbal and nonverbal behaviors are changed. Such behaviors are inculcated by adults telling, showing, directing, guiding, arranging, manipulating, rewarding, punishing, and, at times, coercing the activities of children and youth. Accordingly, teaching is a matter of adults setting behavioristic environmental conditions—stimuli—to make sure that the students accomplish those goals.

So, in the eyes of neobehaviorists, learning is a more or less permanent change of behavior that occurs as a result of conditioning. Accordingly, the learning process consists of impressions of new reaction patterns on pliable, passive organisms. Since learning arises, in some way, from the impingement of environment upon organisms, the key concepts of neobehaviorists are *stimuli,* which consist of excitement provided by an environment and *responses,* which consist of reactions made by an organism. Consequently, the problem of the nature of the learning process is centered in a study of the relationships of processions of stimuli and responses and what occurs between them. Since the focus always is upon behavior, in practical application, neobehavioristically oriented teachers strive to change behaviors of their students in the desired direction by providing the right stimuli at the proper time.

What Are the Two Forms of Stimulus-Response Conditioning?

Conditioning is the formation of some sort of stimulus-response sequential relation that results in an enduring change in either the pattern of behavior or the likelihood of a response of an organism. It takes either one or a combination of two forms called classical and instrumental conditioning. *Classical conditioning* is conditioning that occurs without reinforcement. It is a process of *stimulus substitution,* which is based on the *adhesive principle.* The adhesive principle means that a response is attached to a stimulus through the stimulus's occurring just prior to the response so that the recurrence of the stimulus will evoke or cause the response.

Instrumental conditioning is also called reinforcement or operant conditioning. It is a process of response change or modification that is based on the feedback principle. The *feedback principle* means that the reduction or satisfaction of an organic need or drive stimulus increases the probability of occurrence of future responses of the kind that the organism emitted immediately prior to its being fed, watered, satisfied sexually, or otherwise satiated; there is feedback from the satisfaction of some deprivation to reinforcement of the type of behavior that preceded it.

A *need* as used here is an objective, biological requirement of an organism, which must be met if the organism is to survive and grow. Examples of needs are an organism's requirement for food or escape from pain. A *drive stimulus* is an aroused state of an organism. It is closely related to the need that sets the organism into action and may be defined as a strong, persistent stimulus that demands an adjustive response.

Table 12.1 TWO BASIC FORMS OF STIMULUS-RESPONSE CONDITIONING

	CLASSICAL CONDITIONING	INSTRUMENTAL CONDITIONING
Order of stimulus and response	S-R conditioning	R-S conditioning
Nature of the process	Stimulus substitution	Response modification
Psychological principle involved	Contiguity (no reinforcement)	Reinforcement
	Adhesive principle	Feedback principle
The basic paradigm	$\begin{array}{c} S_1 \searrow \\ \quad\quad \to R \\ S_2 \nearrow \end{array}$	R ← S

Whenever an organism is deprived of satisfaction of a need, drive stimuli occur. In Table 12.1 under classical conditioning, S_1 is the originally adequate, unconditioned stimulus, S_2 is the conditioned stimulus, and R is the conditioned response; under instrumental conditioning, S is the reinforcing stimulus and R is the reinforced response.

CLASSICAL CONDITIONING

Classical conditioning usually is associated with such incidents as Pavlov's teaching a dog to salivate at the ringing of a bell, thus it is *stimulus substitution*. In Pavlov's conditioning experiment, the sound of a bell occurred prior to, or simultaneously with, the dog's salivation, which was caused by the presence of food. Then in the future the dog salivated at the ringing of the bell, even when the food was not present.

In classical conditioning a new stimulus is presented along with an already adequate stimulus—such as the smell of food—and just prior to the response that is evoked by that stimulus. Thus, an organism learns to respond to a new stimulus in the same, or similar, way it responds to the old, unconditioned stimulus—one already adequate to evoke the response. The new stimulus becomes the conditioned one, and the response that follows both stimuli becomes the conditioned response. A *conditioned response*, then, is one that is associated with, or evoked by, a new—conditioned—stimulus. In Pavlov's experiment, the sound of the bell became the new, conditioned stimulus that evoked the old, unconditioned response—salivation. Then, salivation became a conditioned response.

Classical conditioned learning is revealed in the behavior of an organism by the increasing capacity of a previously neutral stimulus, with successive training trials, to evoke a response that originally was evoked by some other stimulus. A *neutral stimulus* is one whose first occurrence does nothing toward either evoking or reinforcing the response that is under study.

INSTRUMENTAL CONDITIONING

Just as classical conditioning theory derives from the early work of Pavlov, instrumental conditioning theory has emerged from the foundation built by Thorndike. Instrumental conditioning or reinforcement is *response modification* or *change*. An animal first makes a response, then receives a "reward"; the response is instrumental in bringing about its reinforcement. There is a *feedback* from the reinforcing stimulus that follows the response that the organism is learning; a dog is fed after he "speaks" and, thereby, the likelihood of his "speaking" in the future is increased.

How Does Reinforcement Occur?

Neobehaviorists who emphasize the importance of reinforcement in learning assume that some psychological conclusions are fairly well established: (1) patterns of action develop through an organism's responses to repeated stimuli accompanied by "fumble and success" type of trial-and-error learning under conditions of positive or negative reinforcement; (2) reinforcement occurs through satisfaction of either basic biological needs like hunger or sex, or secondary needs such as a need for security, recognition, or aesthetic gratification; and (3) educational encouragement must take the form of positive and negative reinforcers. A positive reinforcer is a stimulus whose presence strengthens a behavior; a negative one is a stimulus whose *withdrawal* strengthens a behavior. Note that negative reinforcement psychologically is different from punishment.[1] Reinforcement may be either *primary* or *secondary*.

PRIMARY REINFORCEMENT

Primary reinforcement strengthens a certain behavior through the satisfaction of a basic biological need or drive. Secondary reinforcement sometimes is called high-order reinforcement. The reinforcers in secondary or high-order reinforcement have acquired their power of reinforcement indirectly through learning; poker chips for which a chimpanzee will work and money for which a person will do almost anything are secondary reinforcers.

The drive-reduction sequence of primary reinforcement proceeds as follows:

1. Deprivation of satisfaction of a basic requirement, such as that for food, produces a state of need in an organism.
2. The need expresses itself as a tension state or drive stimulus, which energizes the organism into action (a food-deprived animal shows the restless activity whose manifestation is called the hunger drive).
3. The activity achieves satisfaction of the need and relieves the tension state.
4. The form of the activity that immediately preceded the satisfaction of the need or reduction of the drive is reinforced.

SECONDARY REINFORCEMENT

Secondary reinforcement is reinforcement that is brought about by occurrence of an originally neutral stimulus along with a reinforcing stimulus. When a neutral stimulus such as a sound or light is repeatedly paired with food in the presence of a food-deprived (hungry) animal, the formerly neutral stimulus becomes a secondary, conditioned reinforcer. Thus, secondary reinforcement results when originally neutral stimuli become associated with primary reinforcing stimuli and thereby become effective in reducing needs. In this way, neutral stimuli acquire the power of acting as reinforcing agents; a chimpanzee learns to accept the poker chips that accompany food as a "reward" just as readily as he accepts food. Consequently, future actions of the chimpanzee are reinforced by his receiving poker chips immediately after he performs them; this is secondary reinforcement.

EXTINCTION

In addition to the two kinds of positive conditioning—*classical* and *instrumental*—there also is a negative conditioning process—*extinction*. Through classical and instrumental conditioning, an organism *gains* responses or habits; through extinction it *loses* them. Extinction is the process whereby an organism gradually loses a response or habit through its repeating the response a number of times while no reinforcing stimulus accompanies it. Any habits gained through either classical or instrumental conditioning may be lost through extinction.[2]

How May We Group S-R Conditioning Theories?

On the basis of their respective positions in regard to the specific nature of learning, we may divide behaviorists into three groups. One group makes conditioning the heart of the learning process but holds that reinforcement is not necessary for conditioning to occur. A second group is committed to reinforcement or law-of-effect theories. The third group consists of two-factor theorists, who contend that there are two basically different learning processes—conditioning independent of reinforcement and conditioning governed by principles of reinforcement.[3]

Edwin R. Guthrie's (1886–1959) *contiguous conditioning* is most representative of the first—conditioning, nonreinforcement—group. The names of Clark L. Hull (1884–1952) and B. F. Skinner are most often associated with the *reinforcement* group. However, Hull and Skinner have differed sharply in regard to the nature of the reinforcement process. Three prominent *two-factor psychologies* are those of Kenneth W. Spence, Edward C. Tolman (1886–1959), and O. H. Mower (1904–   ). Hence, four representative neobehaviorisms are Guthrie's *contiguous conditioning*, Hull's *deductive behaviorism* or *reinforcement theory*, Skinner's *operant conditioning*, and Spence's *quantitative S-R theory*. All four are alike in their emphasis upon a mechanical treatment of stimuli and responses. Hence, they agree that at no time is purposiveness to be attributed to human behavior. But, they differ rather sharply in their interpretations of stimulus-response relationships that occur in learning procedures. Guthrie was convinced that learning occurs when a stimulus and a response happen simultaneously; Hull centered the essence of learning in what occurs between the stimulus and the response; and Skinner places his emphasis upon the stimulus that follows a response. When we express these serial relationships symbolically, using S for stimulus, R for response, and O for organism, Guthrie has held to an S-R, Hull to an S-O-R, and Skinner to an R-S learning theory. Since Spence incorporated both contiguity and reinforcement into his theory, it cannot be categorized in this way.

IS LEARNING DEVELOPMENT OF INSIGHT?

The key word of Gestalt-field psychologists in describing learning is *insight*. They regard learning as a process of developing new insights or changing old ones. Insights occur when an individual, in pursuing his (or her) purposes, sees new ways of utilizing elements of his environment, including his own bodily structure. The noun *learning* denotes the new insights or meanings that are acquired.

Gestalt-field theorists attack three weaknesses in the theory that learning is conditioning: (1) the attempt of behaviorists to explain complex interrelated organizations in terms of simpler elements, that is, to insist that learning consists of an accumulation of individual conditioned responses or operants, each relatively simple in itself, but eventuating in a complicated pattern of habits; (2) their tendency to attribute learning to reduction of basic organic drives; and (3) the behaviorists' tendency to ignore the apparent purposiveness of much behavior. So, "The chief trouble with behaviorism . . . is that it leaves out so much behavior."[4]

Gestalt-field psychologists view learning as a purposive, explorative, imaginative, and creative enterprise. This conception breaks completely with the idea that learning consists of either linking one thing to another according to certain principles of association or building behaviors in a deterministic, mechanistic fashion. Instead, the learning process is identified with nonmechanical development or change of insight.

Behaviorists also sometimes use the term insight, but when they do they mean something quite different from what Gestalt-field theorists mean. When used by behaviorists, the term describes a special and rare kind of learning. To use Woodworth's definition, insight is "some penetration into the [absolutely] true nature of things."[5] But to Woodworth and other behaviorists, the ordinary form that learning takes is S-R conditioning. In fact, the most systematic of the behaviorists deny that there can be two entirely different kinds of learning; therefore they prefer to describe *all* learning as conditioning. Since insight obviously implies something very different from conditioning, many behaviorists do not use the term at all. To them it connotes something intuitive and mystical that cannot be described operationally. In contrast, Gestalt-field psychologists do not like to use the term *conditioning;* they regard *development of insight* as the most descriptive phrase available to describe the manner in which learning actually takes place.

The Gestalt-field definition of insight is a sense of, or feeling for, pattern or relationships. To state it differently, insight is the "sensed way through" or "solution" of a problematic situation. Insights often first appear as vague "hunches." We might say that an insight is a kind of intelligent "feel" we get about a situation that permits us to continue to strive actively to serve our purposes. When are insights verbalized? Perhaps at once; perhaps never. We probably know many things that we never manage to put into words. This is a problem on which animal experimentation sheds some light. Animals below human beings cannot talk; they can communicate but not by placing sounds together in coherent subject-predicate sentences. Yet the evidence indicates that, when they are confronted with what to them are problems, they insightfully learn.[6]

Gestalt-field psychologists do not use the term insights in a way to imply that they are necessarily true. Granted, the term sometimes is used this way by others. But the relativistic orientation of Gestalt-field theorists necessarily leads them to think of insights as trial answers or hypotheses, that either may or may not help a person toward his or her goal. Hence, they may or they may not be true. Truth, relativistically defined, is that quality of a tested insight that enables its possessor to design behavior that is successful in achievement of whatever it is designed to achieve.

Insights, then, are to be considered not literal descriptions of objective physical-social situations, but rather as interpretations of one's self and one's perceived environment on the basis of which pertinent action may be designed. Although insights are not physicalistic descriptions of objects or processes in the environment, they necessarily do take account of the physical environment. Their usability depends in part on how well this is done. Insights may misinterpret a physical environment so badly that they are useless as rules of action, in which case they are to be regarded as false.

It is important to understand that insights are always a learner's own. It is true, of course, that they may become his (or her) own through adoption. An insight is usable to a learner only if he can "fit it in," that is, understand its significance—for him. A teacher cannot give an insight to a student as we serve a person meat on a platter. He (or she) may acquaint students with his insights, but they do not become insights for students until students see their meaning for themselves and adopt them as their own.

One objection frequently raised against the Gestalt-field tendency to construe all learning as insightful is that some learning tasks are performed successfully without apparent development of insight—as, for example, when a child memorizes the multiplication tables. Gestalt-field psychologists concede that some learning appears highly mechanical, but they are convinced that it is not necessarily as mechanical as it appears. Accordingly, they contend that even though children may repeat the multiplication tables until they appear to have memorized them by rote, what they actually have done is to get the feel of some pattern that is present in the tables. The pattern may lie in the relationship of the numbers or perhaps merely in the order in which the student placed the numbers to "memorize" them.

One's use of the term insight does not imply that for a person to learn something he (or she) must understand all aspects of its use. Any degree of "feel for a pattern" is sufficient to constitute insightful learning. For example, in learning to extract the square root of a number, one might develop insight as to why the method works. Or the insight gained might be much more superficial; it might be merely a "feel" for the method—the pattern of steps—with no real understanding of the basic algebraic formula $(x + y)^2 = x^2 + 2xy + y^2$.

What Are Some Examples of Insightful Learning?

Before a military rifleman can become a sharpshooter, he must get a "feel" for his rifle. Often a Tennessee squirrel hunter was slow in learning to be an army rifleman. He had an excellent feel for his squirrel gun, but a squirrel gun was not an army rifle. In his army training he had to change old insights as well as develop new ones. On his squirrel gun his sights were fixed immovably to the barrel. To hit a squirrel he had to take wind and distance into consideration and move the rifle away from a line on the target (windward and upward) to give "Tennessee windage" and "Kentucky elevation." He had developed truthful insights to the point that he could behave intelligently without thinking; he could aim his gun and pull the trigger while giving very little attention to what he was doing.

Since his army rifle had movable sights, which prior to the rifle's being aimed were to be adjusted to allow for windage and elevation, he was supposed to set his sights and then line them directly on his target. But under pressure of target practice he used his new insights to adjust his sights correctly, then when he began to fire he gave his rifle Tennessee windage and Kentucky elevation and missed the target completely. He had used two sets of incompatible insights. He could learn to shoot his army rifle accurately only by getting a complete feel for his army rifle and leaving most of his squirrel-gun-aiming insights out of the picture.

What is the answer to $\sqrt{(\text{dog})^2} = ?$ How did you know it was "dog"? Had you ever before worked with square root and "dog" at the same time? If you knew the answer was "dog," you had an insight into the problem. Perhaps you had never put the insight into words, but you knew[7] that $\sqrt{x^2} = x$ and $\sqrt{4^2} = 4$. Your insight, when verbalized, would run something like, "The square root of anything squared is that thing." Conversely, you may have "learned"—memorized—"The square root of a quantity squared is that quantity" and still not know the answer to $\sqrt{(\text{dog})^2} = ?$.

Teaching for development of insight has definite implication for methods of teaching and learning spelling. Groups or families of words might be studied in such a way that students develop a feeling for a certain spelling pattern. Once a pattern is discovered, other words can be sought that conform to it. *Cat, fat,* and *bat* are "at" words. Now what about *hat, mat, pat, rat,* and *sat?* As students, working cooperatively with their teacher, find other word families, they soon will encounter words that apparently should, but do not, fit a given family—they find some limitations to an insight. They then seek other words with the same divergence from the "rule" and make a family of them. Or, in case there is only one divergent word, they think of it as an exception. As the insights into patterns of spelling are put into words, a class can formulate rules. But now rules will be generalized verbalizations of student's insight as contrasted with meaningless statements memorized at the beginning of study.[8]

How Is Insight Related to Understanding and Generalization?

Often when an insight is first "caught" it applies to a single case. Even so, a person is likely to assume that the insight may work in similar situations. Suppose, for example, that, after studying a particular situation, we hypothesize, "Mary became a shoplifter because she felt unwanted by her parents." The natural next step is to think, "Boys and girls who feel unwanted at home tend to become thieves." Of course, this generalization is only suggested. It is not warranted by evidence from a single case. Before generalizations become reliable, that is, before they become understandings, it is usually necessary that they rest on a number of specific insights, all suggesting the same conclusion. In short, dependable generalizations, that is, understandings, usually are products of considerable experience. Furthermore, they are prone to change in the course of experience, evolving continuously in the direction of greater usefulness as tools of thought.

An *understanding* of a thing or process is its generalized meaning, that is, it is a tested generalized insight. Thus, it entails one's ability to use an object, fact, process, or idea in several or even many somewhat different situations. It is one's understandings that enable one to behave intelligently, that is, with foresight of consequences. A tested generalization or understanding is assumed to be valid in any future situation similar to the situations in which it was tested. Tested generalizations have the character of rules, principles, or laws. Such generalizations are frequently if-then statements: If we take a given action, then the probability is high that a given consequence will follow.

We emphasize that tested generalizations should be regarded as probabilities, not absolute answers. Although, to behave with foresight, we must assume that our generalizations have predictive value, the predictions are always, to some degree, based on probability. Yet many insights have been so adequately tested that we may safely treat them as if they were certainties. Certainties, so construed, are insights in which we have tremendous faith but still not absolute commitment.

WHAT DOES MOTIVATION MEAN FOR EACH FAMILY?

Motivation refers to the "mainsprings" or instigative forces of behavior. But S-R conditioning theorists and Gestalt-field psychologists hold contrasting and seemingly incompatible ideas about the nature of human motivation. These differences arise from the contrasting conceptions of the basic human nature held by the two schools of thought. If one views human beings mechanistically, as do most behaviorists, one will prefer a theory of motivation compatible with this outlook. Contrariwise, if one views human beings as purposeful, reflective, and creative individuals, as do most Gestalt-field theorists, one will have a quite different theory of motivation. Since Part I of the book treats human motivation in detail, we here only summarize the two views on motivation as they relate to theories of learning.

What Is Motivation to Adherents of S-R Conditioning?

As we have seen, adherents of S-R conditioning tend to regard a human being as an intricate machine. Machines operate with induced regularity, according to fixed principles. Even a machine as complicated as an electronic brain does not operate purposefully as we usually use the term. An electronic brain does not know what to do until it has been set by a human being. Even electronic brains that can correct their own errors and do other seemingly fantastic tasks still behave as they do because some person has designed and regulated them. In a sense, a machine has no more purpose than a falling rock; it acts, but it has no thought-out goal. S-R conditioning theorists generally attribute this same quality to the nature of human beings.

To a behaviorist, all motivation arises either directly from one's organic drives or basic emotions or from a tendency to respond that has been established by prior conditioning of the drives and emotions. Motivation means that an organism either is deprived of something toward which there is an appetitional need or is confronted with a discomforting stimulus. Organic drives, such as hunger, thirst, and sexual need, and the emotions—fear, anger, and "love"—produce behaviors that are both predictable and irresistible. The drives and emotions are "built into" the organism, and it can do nothing to resist them. Conditioning produces a series of learned behaviors that spring into action whenever relevant stimuli appear. These conditioned responses and operants operate more or less automatically; a person makes them because he (she) must. Thus, through conditioning, the machinelike body has been regulated to behave in a predictable manner. All behavior is either stimulus-directed or stimulus-determined, whether the stimulus comes from within the organism or without. Motivation is defined as the urge to act that results from prior stimulation.

There are certain obvious aspects of the behavior of people or lower animals that do not appear to be adequately explained by the mechanical concepts of S-R conditioning theory. One of these is attention. At any given time, a person pays attention to one thing rather than another. At this moment, the reader of this book is "attending" to this page rather than to a television program or a poker game. So the fact of attention may seem to demonstrate that human behavior is governed by purpose. However, though S-R conditioning theorists concede that a person may often respond selectively to one or a small group of stimuli at a time, they believe that what appear to be selective responses can be explained according to S-R conditioning principles and that the existence of purpose need not be assumed. According to an adherent of S-R conditioning, an organism selects one response rather than another because of the particular combination of its genetic inheritance, its prior conditioning, and the present physiological drives and stimuli that are operating at the moment of perception. To a behaviorist, for one to introduce purpose as an explanation of motivation is to risk introducing some kind of metaphysical guiding force and to make impossible a truly scientific approach to the study of behavior.

A behavioristic theory of motivation has important implications for education. According to this viewpoint, children do not have to "want" to learn history in order to learn it. They do have to be persuaded to study it, to repeat the verbal responses that we associate with a knowledge of history. Anyone can learn anything of which he (or she) is capable if he will only allow himself to be put through the pattern of activity necessary for conditioning to take place. Thus, behaviorists do not talk much about such things as "psychological involvement" or "helping students see the point of learning." Instead, they engage students in behavior and assume that behavior with appropriate conditioning automatically produces learning. Teachers carefully plan which learnings (responses) they want students to develop. They then induce these responses and condition them with stimuli.

What Is Motivation to Gestalt-Field Theorists?

Present-day Gestalt-field theorists tend to avoid the use of concepts such as *drive, effect,* and *reinforcement* on the one hand and concepts such as *vitalism* and *consciousness* on the other. For them, some key concepts in dealing with motivation are *goal, expectancy, intention,* and *purpose.* Within the Gestalt-field frame of reference, behavior is a function of a total situation—a person interacting within a field of psychological forces. A psychological field includes purposes and goals, interpretation of relevant physical objects and events, and memories and anticipations. Motivation cannot be described as merely an impulse to act triggered by a stimulus. Rather, it emerges from a dynamic psychological situation, characterized by a person's desire to do something.

A Gestalt-field psychologist regards motivation as a product of disequilibrium within a life space. A life space includes goals and often barriers to the achievement of these goals. A goal may be either positive or negative—something one wants to achieve or something one wants to avoid. When a barrier, that is, any obstacle to the direct and immediate achievement of a goal, appears, a person feels tension. He (or she) tries to relieve tension either by surmounting or circumventing the barrier. The tendency to release tension by proceeding toward a goal, including the overcoming of whatever barriers are in the way, is motivation.

The particular form that motivation takes, and its intensity, are functions of a field of psychological forces in which no distinction can be made between "inner" and "outer." That is, one cannot identify a category of forces that stems exclusively from physiological drives and another category that stems from the outside environment. Hence, Gestalt-field psychologists object to the manner in which behaviorists attribute motivation to independently acting organic drives and stimuli.

Whereas S-R theorists in the Thorndikean tradition make much of pleasure and pain, or satisfaction and annoyance, as instigators of behavior, Gestalt-field psychologists are more likely to talk about *success* and *failure* as motivators. Success and failure are not merely achievements as such but represent the relationship between a person's ambitions and his (or her) achievements. If one has a certain level of aspiration and is able to achieve this level, one feels good about it. If one attains success at one level of aspiration, one is likely to raise the level and to continue doing so as long as one is able to perform successfully.

Another feature of the Gestalt-field theory of motivation that sets it apart from S-R conditioning theory is the emphasis placed on the present situation. Motivation, to a Gestalt-field theorist, grows out of one's contemporary life space—the psychological forces that are operating right then. In contrast, a behaviorist tends to think of motivation as emerging from a combination of genetically determined biological conditions and prior environmental influences. Consequently, an S-R conditioning theorist looks backward into a person's life to determine why he (or she) behaves as he does now. Gestalt-field psychologists do not ignore the impact of previous experience on a person's contemporary life space, but in explaining the causes of behavior they focus on the present scene as the person experiences it. For these reasons, it is common to think of behavioristic psychology as embodying a *historical* approach and Gestalt-field psychology as embodying a *situational* approach to the study of motivation and behavior.

Teachers who accept the Gestalt-field concept of motivation are likely to approach teaching in fundamentally different ways from teachers who operate within a behavioristic framework. Such teachers are deeply concerned with the problem of personal involvement, that is, in helping students see a need to learn. Hence, the personal goals of students always are observed. This does not mean that the teachers cater to students' every whim. Often they try to help them rethink their goals and discard those that are trivial and whimsical. Much of the time the teachers attempt to arrange the teaching-learning situation so that students will adopt goals quite new to them. They are convinced that, unless a child or youth realizes a need to learn something, the child or youth either will not learn it at all or will learn it only in a transitory and functionally useless way.

HOW IS OBSERVABLE BEHAVIOR CHANGE RELATED TO LEARNING?

Gestalt-field theories contrast sharply with S-R conditioning theories in regard to the manner in which adherents of the two respective positions use observable behavior of persons as psychological data. Behaviorists use observable behavior and only observable behavior as data. Consequently, they restrict learning objectives to those expressible in terms of observable behaviors. In contrast, Gestalt-field psychologists also study observable behaviors, but they infer from them the changing personalities, environments, and insights of the persons being studied. So, whereas for behaviorists one's physical behavior also is one's psychological behavior, for Gestalt-field theorists psychological behavior is something quite different from mere physical movement.

For behaviorists, *"behavior,* as a technical psychological term, may be defined as the publicly observable activity of muscles or glands of external secretion as manifested for example in movements of parts of the body or the appearance of tears, sweat, saliva and so forth."[9] But, when

Gestalt-field psychologists use the term behavior, they give it a quite different meaning. For them, it is any change in a person, the person's perceived environment, or the relation between the two that is subject to psychological principles or laws. Psychological, as used here, means their involving purpose and intelligence. Hence, psychological behavior is not the same as physical movement. Such behavior is not directly observable but must be inferred from the observable actions and demeanors of persons.

Learning and change in observable behavior often occur side by side and seem to be interrelated. So, behaviorists contend that any change of behavior is learning and, conversely, that any learning is a change of behavior. Thus, the current practice among many educators of defining learning as "change in behavior" usually reflects a behavioristic psychology. But, Gestalt-field psychologists maintain that not only may a change in behavior occur without learning, but also learning may occur without any *observable,* related changes in behavior. This is true in innumerable situations. There may be an insight but no opportunity or occasion for a change in behavior, as when one decides it would be nice to give more to charity but does not have the money to do so. Also, when new insights compete with older ones that have a strong hold on a person, the new insights may fail to change the person's behavior. For example, one may decide that racial discrimination is bad but continue to practice it.

The emphasis of behaviorists upon changed behavior often has led to school practices designed to produce a desired kind of behavior and to methods of evaluation that measure overt behavior—and little else. Teachers, or other school authorities, decide which specific behaviors they want students to display. They then stimulate the students in such a way as to evoke the desired behaviors. The success of the process is judged by how dependably the behavior can be invoked in the future (usually on tests). Gestalt-field psychologists protest this approach to education. They emphasize changes in experience rather than behavior, with experience defined as an interactive event within which a person, through acting and seeing what happens, comes to see and feel the consequences of a given course of action. They grant that when a person learns something, his or her behavior usually changes; but they further note that it does not follow that, for learning to take place, a change in observable behavior must occur at the same time, or that from a change in overt behavior we always can accurately infer the full nature of the insight related to it.

For Gestalt-field psychologists, learning is a persistent change in knowledge, skills, attitudes, values, or commitments. It may, or it may not, be reflected in changes in overt behavior. One does not "learn by doing" except insofar as one's doing contributes to a change in one's insights. For learning to result, the doing must be accompanied by the doer's realization of the consequences of the act. Thus learning occurs through, and results from, experience, and "Mere activity does not constitute experience."[10] For an activity to be included in experience, it must be interrelated with a realization of the consequences that accompany it.

DO HUMAN BEINGS AND LOWER ANIMALS LEARN ALIKE?

During the latter part of the nineteenth century the idea that there is a continuity among animal species, and that behavioral tendencies, including learning, are broadly similar throughout the animal world, rapidly gained in popularity among biologists and psychologists. The use of results of animal experimentation in the study of learning is governed by the assumptions that the learning process is essentially the same throughout the animal kingdom and that what we discover about learning in lower animals is transferable to human situations. These assumptions would have been thought ridiculous, if not heretical, a few centuries back. Until modern times, philosophers took for granted that there was an unbridgeable gulf between human beings and lower animals. It was thought that human beings possessed a unique quality: they could reason, whereas animals could not. This quality was believed to arise from the existence of a substantive mind—a mind-force, relatively independent of a body, which only man, among the earth's creatures, possessed.

In addition to the advantage of cheapness and convenience in using lower animals rather than humans in a psychological laboratory, obviously experiments that our mores would prevent being tried on people can be performed on animals. Furthermore, many persons have thought that it is easier to isolate simple units of behavior in lower animals than in human beings; although in humans the units may be substantially the same, they are often combined in a manner too complex for ready study.

Whereas behaviorists have assumed that people learn like lower animals, and more specifically like their own experimental animals in their own types of experiments, Gestalt-field psychologists have given this issue a reverse twist. For them lower animals learn like people do. Of course, if there is a continuity between humans and the lower animals, both ideas should make equal sense. But Gestalt-field psychologists had something else in mind. While not denying the likelihood of a fundamental similarity in the behavior of people and lower animals, Gestalt-field theorists have been interested in raising questions about the whole approach of the behaviorists.

One of the sharpest criticisms that a Gestalt-field theorist can make of the behavioristic conception of learning is directed against the tendency of the latter to deny purpose a central role in learning. Accordingly, Gestalt-field psychologists note that behaviorists usually placed their animals in situations entirely foreign to them and often allowed them only a bare minimum of freedom. Consequently, there was no place for their animals to begin a solution and little opportunity for them really to try various alternatives. Since the locks, levers, and mechanical devices that were used were above the animals' level of comprehension, for them to achieve the correct procedure it was necessary that they stumble upon the key by chance. Because lower animals are less discerning of the kind of relationships that seem important to people than are human beings, animals appear, in a humanly contrived "problem," to make completely random movements. Thus, on the surface, the nature of the discovery of the relationship between the release mechanism and an animal's escaping from a puzzle box appeared to be completely mechanical. Having set the stage against animals displaying genuinely purposive, problem-solving activity, even if they are capable of such, behaviorists have concluded that learning is a product of a mechanical trial-and-error process.

To Gestalt-field psychologists the tension that motivates an animal to learn is tension toward a goal. Thus, to some degree learning always involves purpose. Furthermore, purposiveness in learning is not restricted to humanity. Abundant experimental evidence indicates that learning is purposive, even among animals quite low on the phylogenetic scale.

An animal behaving purposively does not make random motions—even though on the surface it may appear to do so. Instead, it tries everything at its command, but if the problem is too difficult its trial moves will appear to an observer as random. If one eye of a slug or a honeybee is blinded, the animal at first glance appears to go through meaningless motions. However, more careful observation reveals that it is demonstrating something other than mere random responses. It assumes a posture which orients its body toward the light source; thus it flexes its legs on one side and extends them on the other as if it wanted to move in relationship to the light.

Gestalt-field psychologists further have criticized behaviorists' experimentation on the ground that it has been so arranged that, even if animal learning were insightful, the development of insight would not be noticed. The real nature of any psychological process can be concealed by the experimenter's designing his or her experiments in line with adverse predetermined conclusions, and this is precisely what the Gestaltists have insisted that behaviorists have been inclined to do. In an attempt to refute the contention of behaviorists that learning is mechanical—a mere matter of forming series of behaviors through either design or chance—the Gestaltists designed entirely different types of animal experiments. Their experiments involved creation of problematic situations that animals might conceivably resolve through development of insight. Such situations were geared in difficulty to the presumed potential intelligence of the animals being studied.

Köhler's experiments with chimpanzees and chickens illustrate the Gestalt-field approach to animal experimentation. Köhler spent four years on the island of Tenerife working with chimpanzees. A typical experiment involved suspending food (usually bananas) from the ceiling of a cage and then providing a chimpanzee with a tool or tools with which to knock down or reach for the fruit. The tool might be a pole of adequate length, a pole in sections that could be joined, or boxes that could be stacked and climbed. Köhler's chimpanzees, rather than gradually acquiring right responses and eliminating wrong ones, seemed at some point in a problem to develop insight into it—to grasp, often rather suddenly, the relationship involved. The chimpanzees seemed to get the idea of "tool use" and to apply it in new situations calling for tool use.[11]

Köhler experimented with chickens and found considerable evidence that even they can sense relationships and that it is relationships to which they respond rather than specific stimuli. He taught chickens to expect food only from the darker of two papers placed side by side. For the lighter paper he then substituted one even darker than the original dark one. In 70 percent of the trials the chickens switched their preference from the originally preferred dark paper to the paper that was still darker, suggesting that they had achieved an insight: "If I go to the darker of two surfaces, I will get food." The chickens had "generalized," that is, sensed the relationship of darker to lighter as a general principle in "food getting."[12]

Two American Gestalt psychologists, Raymond H. Wheeler and Francis T. Perkins, performed a great deal of animal experimentation in the 1920s and 1930s. Among their most frequently cited experiments was one with goldfish in which the fish received food after responding properly to a configuration of lighting. The fish learned to pick the light of brightest, medium, or dimmest intensity, even though the experimenters kept varying the absolute intensity and the serial arrangement of lights. Wheeler and Perkins also have reported numerous other studies made by themselves and others in which animals ordinarily regarded as not very intelligent learned to respond to relationships in an apparently intelligent way.[13]

The question arises, How far down the phylogenetic scale can an investigator go and still observe animals behaving as if they could perceive a relationship? To perceive a relationship one must get the feel of how a thing works. At first thought, it would seem that to do this an animal must have a certain minimum of sensory and neural equipment— perhaps a brain, even if it is only rudimentary. However, one well-known American biologist, H. S. Jennings (1868–1947), concluded differently. Jennings spent much time observing the behavior of protozoa, such as euglenae, paramecia, and amoebae. He found that the actions of protozoa are not only highly variable but also readily modified, and he decided that their behavior could not be explained merely in terms of simple physiochemical reactions. Jennings thought that, insofar as their observable behavior was revealing, it was as reasonable to infer the presence of purposive behavior among protozoa as among men and women.[14]

Adolf Portmann, a contemporary biologist, supports Jenning's earlier thinking in this regard. He states, "Biological research today must concentrate, therefore, on how things appear to animals, not what they actually are—which is a great change from the days a few decades back when biologists were supposed to reduce everything to physio-chemical laws."[15]

What are we to conclude from all this? One possible conclusion is that animal experiments, depending upon their orientation, are likely to arrange their experiments so that animal behavior appears to be either chancelike and mechanical or insightful. A famous philosopher, Bertrand Russell, noted before the end of the 1920s that psychologists could demonstrate two fundamentally different types of response in their animal experiments, depending entirely on how they arranged the experimental situation. Russell commented humorously: "Animals studied by Americans rush about frantically, with an incredible display of hustle and pep, and at last achieve the desired result by chance. Animals observed by Germans sit still and think, and at last evolve the solution out of their inner consciousness."[16] However, the state of affairs with regard to experimentation with lower animals is probably not as indecisive as Russell's comment would lead one to think. Once a student sets his or her orientation in either a behavioristic or a Gestalt-field direction, he benefits by the broadest possible knowledge of all available experimental, as well as other, evidence.

Behaviorists have clearly shown that animals can be put in experimental situations where they demonstrate overt behavior that seems trial-and-error, chancelike, blind, and mechanical. Furthermore, there seems to be little question but that human experimental subjects can be put in situations causing them to appear to demonstrate the same kind of behavior. The only requirement for such an experiment seems to be that the problem presented the learner be one with which his (or her) previous experience has in no way equipped him to cope.

On the other hand, Gestalt-field psychologists have demonstrated that whether one is dealing with the lower animals or human beings, situations can be arranged in which learning shows an "Aha!" quality. That is, experimental subject, in learning something, seems to "catch the point" or get the feel of a confronting situation. If people and the lower animals do seem to learn insightfully in situations that permit it, then serious doubt is cast upon the validity of the behaviorist notion that learning is purposeless, mechanical, and chancelike.

Gestalt-field psychologists insist that, to describe learning throughout the animal kingdom, we do well to begin with human examples. As we examine the purposive behavior of ourselves or others, learning often, perhaps always, appears to be a matter of seeing through things, of gaining understanding. If we start with the assumption that lower animals learn in the same way, we devise experiments that enable them to reveal such learning.

This does not mean that if we are studying, say, a dog, we dare anthropomorphize it—attribute to it human characteristics; it does mean that we must guard against mechanizing it—making a machine of it. The way to study a dog is to "dogize" it, just as in studying a child we should "childize" it. In short, we must consider each lower animal as well as each human being on its own level. If we always keep this in mind, we can probably make some generalized statements about learning that will hold true with respect to most or even all forms of animal life.

HOW DO ADHERENTS OF THE TWO LEARNING FAMILIES DESCRIBE THE THINKING PROCESS?

In its broadest meaning, the term *thinking* may embrace simple association or recall, reverie, fantasy, dreams, autism, and animism as well as creative ideational activity. However, in the more restricted sense in which we use the term herein, it is a directed, goal-oriented activity of an individual; in other words, it is a creative, problem-solving process.

Thinking, then, is goal-related problem solving. It is an attempt to work through a situation in order to find the means to achieve an end. For the purpose of analysis, we may distinguish two levels of problem solving, but any line drawn between them is necessarily arbitrary. One level may be termed *simple problem solving*. Simple problem solving does not involve weighty decisions. Examples of problems on this level are expressed in the following questions: Shall I wear a red or green tie today? Shall I drive or walk to work? Shall I spend the evening reading a book or watching a motion picture? During the solution of problems of this kind, our tension level remains relatively low, and we usually solve these problems without lengthy deliberation. Once we have made a decision, we are unlikely to worry about it later.

The other level of thinking may be termed *complex problem solving*. This level of problem solving usually requires much effort and time and is accompanied by relatively high tension. The distinguishing characteristic of this level is that each problem presents the person involved with something new. Although many elements of the problem may be familiar, some are unfamiliar. Consequently, each act of complex problem solving requires some degree of originality or creativity. Examples of problems on this level are suggested by questions such as: Shall I encourage my son to go to college? Shall I seek a divorce? Shall I change my registration from Democrat to Republican? Of course, not all complex problem solving involves questions as weighty as these. Deciding which insecticide to use or which service station to patronize might also require complex problem-solving procedures.

How Is Thinking Associated with Learning?

Since our principal tools of thought—concepts—are learned, people generally associate learning and thinking quite closely. Furthermore, one objective of education upon which persons of various shades of opinion seem to agree is that "Students should be taught to think." However, when people attempt to define thinking and to specify the proper procedure for its promotion, the apparent agreement soon fades away. Let us now take the question, "Should students be taught to think as part of their activity in school?"

Readers will recall that, prior to the advent of scientific approaches to psychological study in the eighteenth century, the main thrust of psychology, back into antiquity, was mental discipline with its accompanying mind-substance theory. Mental disciplinarians have thought that thinking was the operation of a trained faculty of a substantive mind. This trained faculty has been called *rational power* or *reason*. Hence, students' learning to think consists of their exercising this faculty of their mind. Accordingly, there are two kinds of subject matter—one, like geometry, that trains minds and one that merely gives students information.

Both behaviorists and Gestalt-field theorists construe thinking within a scientific frame of reference, albeit in their respective manners. Hence, both take strong exceptions to a mental-disciplinary conception of thinking, but they differ sharply in their scientific conceptions and explanations of the thinking process. In the next sections we outline in some detail the psychological meaning of thinking within the two scientific approaches.

Within Behaviorism, What Is Thinking?

For most behaviorists, an "idea" or "thought" consists of a symbolic movement that constitutes an intermediate step between overt stimuli and responses. *Symbols* are events that represent something beyond themselves. They may be either substitute stimuli or substitute responses. Whenever an organism is responding in a certain way and the stimulus that originally was adequate to evoke the response is absent, it is responding to a symbolic stimulus. A symbolic response is an incipient or partial movement that takes the place of a completely expressed pattern of behavior. It may take the form of a shrug of the shoulders, a facial expression, a nod of the head, or a change in posture. In thinking, symbolic movements may be so slight that the individual may be aware of only a "thought" divorced from any movement. Nevertheless, when one thinks some slight muscular or neural action occurs.

A person's thinking, then, is his or her behaving or responding symbolically in response to symbolic stimuli. Thought is not some mysterious mentalistic process that is the cause of behavior, but the behavior itself. Thus, thinking is symbolic or incipient trial-and-error behavior that culminates in learning. Like all other instances of an organism's behavior, it is a function or result of a set of antecedent or preceding conditions.

In thinking, an organism makes symbolic, miniature responses that sample the feedbacks that would occur if the action represented symbolically or incipiently were really carried out. Thus, to S-R conditioning theorists, thought consists of very small preparatory responses. These can be observed in the incipient or miniature trial-and-error movements of a rat at a "choice point" in a maze. Here, small movements, this way and that, often precede the rat's actually moving down a pathway. In human beings, this process is more subtle and elaborated but no different in kind from that of rats and other lower animals.

In its broadest sense, thinking behavior is both verbal and non-verbal and both overt and covert. However, any nonverbal or covert aspects are considered to function much like the observable ones; they too are segments of stimulus-response sequences. Accordingly, behaviorists assume that, once natural laws governing the relationship of observable stimuli and responses are identified and established, internal processes likewise can be described in terms of stimulus-response sequences that conform to the same laws. Thus, ideational thought, a variable that intervenes between observable stimuli and responses, likewise consist of stimuli and responses, albeit covert ones.

Although B. F. Skinner and some other contemporary neobehaviorists consider the study of any private, internal events irrelevant to a functional analysis of behavior, many others follow John B. Watson's earlier leadership in considering thinking basically to be implicit speech—talking to oneself. Thus, they associate thought very closely with language, which is a rich collection of symbols. So considered, thought basically is laryngeal activity supported by oral and nasal functions. However, it is closely aligned with gestures, frowns, shrugs, and grimaces, which stand for more overt actions or behaviors.

In the thinking process, words, other symbols, and incipient movements become *cues* for behavior. Cues are stimuli of faint intensity that evoke or guide an organism's movements. Any uniqueness people may have involves their "better" use of cues. Thus, three principal factors make human thinking processes "higher" than those of other animals:

1. People have greater capacity to respond selectively to more subtle aspects of the environment as cues.

2. They are also able to make a greater variety of distinctive responses that constitute cues for their actions; they are more able to stimulate themselves.

3. They can emit a greater number of cue-responses simultaneously. Thus, they can elicit many more of their own future responses based on patterns of cues, which represent, or result from, several different earlier patterns of stimulation.[17]

How Does Gestalt-Field Psychology Treat Reflective Thinking?

Gestalt-field psychologists interpret thinking to be a reflective process within which persons develop either new, or changed, tested generalized insights or understanding. So construed, reflective thinking combines both inductive—fact gathering—and deductive processes in such a way as to find, elaborate, and test hypotheses. Thus, there is no essential difference between reflective thinking and scientific processes, broadly defined. However, the term *reflective* does carry a connotation that is somewhat better suited to a description of student thinking than does the term *scientific*.

In the thinking of many persons science implies white-gowned technicians, microscopes and telescopes, chemical tables, and cyclotrons. Furthermore, it suggests precise measurement, use of mathematics, a large amount of rather esoteric wizardry, and neglect of moral values. However, scientific in its broadest sense covers not only a special kind of gadgetry and techniques but also a unique outlook, attitude, and method of inquiry.

Reflective thinking refers to the essential but nongadgetlike features of scientific method with which we may approach all problems, whether they are physical, social, or psychological. John Dewey gave us a classic definition of reflective thinking when he characterized it as the "active, persistent, and careful consideration of any belief or supposed form of knowledge in the light of the grounds that support it and the further conclusions to which it tends."[18]

Five rather definite aspects are present in each complete act of reflection. However, no one should suppose that a person goes through them in the consecutive, orderly fashion in which they may be listed on paper. Any or even all of the aspects may develop concurrently. Moreover, reflection normally is characterized by confusion, hesitation, backtracking, and "going around in circles." In many cases it appears to a thinker that he or she will never reach a solution at all. And once reached, a conclusion often must be abandoned and the process started all over again. Reflection is seldom easy; at best it is exhilarating and exciting, and at worst it is painfully hard work beset with many frustrating moments.

The principal aspects of reflective thinking are as follows:

1. *Recognition and definition of a problem.* This occurs when we become aware either of conflicting goals or of a goal and an intervening obstacle to its achievement. Often a problem consists of a newly sensed discrepancy in known data.

2. *Formulation of hypotheses.* Hypotheses are possible answers in the form of invented generalizations that, to be used most successfully, must be verified by human experience. In a relativistic sense, all scientific generalizations are hypotheses in which greater or lesser degrees of assurance can be placed. They range from hunches based on minimum data to laws, which reflect a very high degree of factual verification.

3. *Elaboration of logical implications of hypotheses.* This process includes our deducing the implications or consequences of the hypotheses whose observations already have been made so that the hypotheses may

be checked against present knowledge, and our deducing implications or consequences of the hypotheses whose observations have not yet been made so that the hypotheses may be tested through experiments yet to be designed.

4. *Testing of hypotheses.* This involves attempts to verify the implications or consequences that were deduced under the third aspect, in terms of both the data of previous experience—*scrutiny-explanation*—and data procured in experimental tests—*prediction-verification.*

5. *Drawing conclusions.* This consists of our either accepting, modifying, or rejecting the hypotheses, or our concluding that as of now the available pertinent evidence does not warrant taking any stand at all. (See Chapter 21 for the development of reflective teaching based on reflective thinking.)

NOTES

[1] See Chapter 13, pp. 325–326, for further treatment of positive and negative reinforcement and the differences between negative reinforcement and punishment.

[2] See Chapter 13, pp. 328–329, for a more extensive description of extinction.

[3] See Table 9.1, items 5, 6, and 7 for a classification of S-R conditioning learning theories.

[4] Rollo May, *Psychology and the Human Dilemma*, New York: Van Nostrand Reinhold, 1967, p. 190.

[5] R. S. Woodworth, *Psychology*, New York: Holt, Rinehart and Winston, 1940, pp. 299–300.

[6] See Wolfgang Köhler, *The Mentality of Apes*, New York: Vintage Books, 1959.

[7] This holds true when x is equal to or greater than zero.

[8] Chapters 15 and 16 continue the discussion of the nature of insightful learning and teaching.

[9] Donald O. Hebb, *A Textbook of Psychology*, 3d ed., Philadelphia: Saunders, 1972, p. 15.

[10] John Dewey, *Democracy and Education*, New York: Macmillan, 1916, p. 163.

[11] Köhler, *The Mentality of Apes.*

[12] See Henry E. Garrett, *Great Experiments in Psychology*, New York: Appleton-Century-Crofts, 1941, pp. 216–219.

[13] Raymond H. Wheeler and Francis T. Perkins, *Principles of Mental Development*, New York: Crowell, 1932.

[14] H. S. Jennings, *Behavior of the Lower Organisms*, New York: Columbia University Press, 1923, p. 335.

[15] Adolf Portmann, *New Paths in Biology*, New York: Harper & Row, 1964, pp. 91–92.

[16] Bertrand Russell, *Philosophy*, New York: Norton, 1927. The Germans referred to obviously are the Gestaltists.

[17] See Sigmund Koch (ed.), *Psychology: A Study of a Science*, vol. 2, *General Systematic Formulations, Learning, and Special Processes*, New York: McGraw-Hill, 1959, p. 247.

[18] John Dewey, *How We Think*, Lexington, Mass.: Raytheon/Heath, 1933, p. 9.

BIBLIOGRAPHY

BRUNER, J. S. et al. *Contemporary Approaches to Cognition.* A symposium held at the University of Colorado. Cambridge, Mass.: Harvard University Press, 1957. For the advanced student. Includes a range of positions, all of which focus on psychological, rather than behavioral, facts.

CHAPLIN, JAMES P., and T. S. KRAWIEC. *Systems and Theories of Psychology,* 3d ed. New York: Holt, Rinehart and Winston, 1974. A treatment of the evolution of psychological thought, which is traced from classical scholars to the major contemporary theories. Shows the continuity of thought from philosophy and physiology to psychology. Contains a good list of biographical sketches of contributors to psychological thought. Chapters 6–10 are especially pertinent to learning.

CONANT, JAMES B. *Modern Science and Modern Man.* Garden City, N.Y.: Doubleday, 1953. An explanation of how every phase of our lives is becoming involved with scientific procedures, and how this revolution in living has carried with it a revolution in scientific outlook. Human beings, as scientists, are no longer seeking absolute, but rather, workable, truth; they are becoming relativistic.

FRANK, PHILIPP. *Relativity—A Richer Truth.* Boston: Beacon Press, 1950. An examination and evaluation of the relativistic outlook, with a foreword by Albert Einstein. A key chapter, Chapter 22, is "How Can an Anti-Metaphysical View of Science Help Democracy?"

GALL, MEREDITH D., and BEATRICE A. WARD. *Critical Issues in Educational Psychology.* Boston: Little, Brown, 1974. An excellent book of readings to supplement this volume. Chapters represent the various psychological issues as represented by leading figures in learning theory.

GEIGER, GEORGE RAYMOND. *John Dewey in Perspective.* New York: Oxford University Press, 1958. By an astute student of Dewey and the "relativistic" position that Dewey helped develop. This book is somewhat easier reading than most of Dewey's works, yet it gives an accurate picture of Dewey's thoughts.

HEBB, DONALD O. *A Textbook of Psychology,* 3d ed. Philadelphia: Saunders, 1972. A textbook in general psychology that treats psychology as a biological, not a social, science. Mechanisms of behavior in learning, perception, and emotion are discussed in a thoroughly behavioristic manner. Learning is considered a neural change that continues to exist after the learning act.

HENRY, NELSON B., ed. *The Psychology of Learning,* part 2, *The Forty-first Yearbook of the National Society for the Study of Education.* Chicago: University of Chicago Press, 1942. In section 1: contemporary theories of learning; in section 2: the implications of learning theories for education. Chapter 7, by T. R. McConnell, is an attempt to reconcile conditioning, connectionism, and field theory to form a synthesis of learning theories.

HILGARD, ERNEST R., and GORDON H. BOWER. *Theories of Learning,* 4th ed.

Englewood Cliffs, N.J.: Prentice-Hall, 1975. A systematic, critical presentation of the most prominent learning theories current among contemporary psychologists.

HOOK, SIDNEY (ed.). *Dimensions of Mind.* New York University Press, 1960. A symposium of 29 papers on the mind-body, mind-brain problem. Papers are grouped under "The Mind-Body Problem," "The Brain and the Machine," and "Concept Formation." Three major kinds of considerations undergird the papers—nature of experience or "raw feel," traditional dualistic language habits, and results of modern psychology and brain physiology.

HULSE, STEWART, H. et al., *The Psychology of Learning,* 4th ed. New York: McGraw-Hill, 1975. A scholarly but difficult presentation of neobehavioristic theory of learning. Includes an extensive list of references on learning.

IRWIN, FRANCIS W. *Intentional Behavior and Motivation.* Philadelphia: Lippincott, 1971. A cognitive-behavioral approach to human motivation within a logical-empiricistic frame of reference. Key concepts—situation, act, and outcome—are defined behavioristically and as occurring serially. Emphasizes expectancies and intentions at the expense of effect, drive, and reinforcement on one hand and vitalism, mentalism, and consciousness on the other.

KOCH, SIGMUND. *Psychology: A Study of a Science, 2, General Systematic Formulations, Learning, and Special Processes.* New York: McGraw-Hill, 1959. A technical but highly informative volume, concerned with the general conceptual formulations of current psychologies. Each approach or theory is represented by a distinguished psychologist.

KOFFKA, KURT. *The Growth of the Mind,* trans. R. M. Ogden. London: Routledge & Kegan Paul, 1924. A Gestaltist child psychology text.

KÖHLER, WOLFGANG. *The Mentality of Apes.* New York: Vintage Books, 1959. Especially Chapter 7. An extensive report of Köhler's experiments with animal learning during the period of World War I, at Tenerife.

LINDZEY, GARDNER, and ELLIOT ARONSON (eds.). *The Handbook of Social Psychology,* 2d ed., vol. 1, *Historical Introduction and Systematic Positions.* Reading, Mass.: Addison-Wesley, 1968. Contains excellent presentations of seven systematic psychological approaches that have definite implications for learning as well as for social psychology. Stimulus-response, mathematical, cognitive, psychoanalytic, field, role, and organization positions are presented.

LOGAN, FRANK A. *Fundamentals of Learning and Motivation.* Boston: Little, Brown, 1970. Presents various constructs of behavioristic psychology. Includes a glossary of terms.

MAY, ROLLO. *Psychology and the Human Dilemma.* New York: Van Nostrand Reinhold, 1967. A psychiatrist's presentation of views that harmonize with Gestalt-field learning theory.

PITTENGER, OWEN E., and C. THOMAS GOODING. *Learning Theories in Educational Practice.* New York: Wiley, 1971. Integrates traditional, technological, and transactional educational philosophies with S-R associationist, Gestalt, and phenomenological learning theories in an attempt to bring educational philosophy, psychological theory, and classroom practice into closer harmony.

SAHAKIAN, WILLIAM S. *Psychology of Learning: Systems, Models, and Theories.* Chicago: Markham, 1970. A contemporary summary of scientific learning systems. Somewhat encyclopaedic, but a good reference source.

SCHULTZ, DUANE P. *A History of Modern Psychology.* New York: Academic Press, 1969. Traces 100 years of psychological thought, including the rise and outcome of each system or school.

SNELBECKER, GLENN E. *Learning Theory, Instructional Theory, and Psychoeducational Design.* New York: McGraw-Hill, 1974. Develops historical and contemporary psychological learning theories along with related instructional theories and "psychoeducational" innovations. Good background reading.

THORNDIKE, EDWARD L. *Selected Writings from a Connectionist's Psychology.* New York: Appleton-Century-Crofts, 1949. A collection of Thorndike's papers to give students a firsthand knowledge of connectionist psychology. His autobiography gives the reader a picture of how educational psychology has developed.

WATSON, JOHN B. *Psychology from the Standpoint of a Behaviorist,* 2d ed. Philadelphia: Lippincott, 1924. An introductory psychology textbook written strictly from a mechanistic, behavioristic point of view.

WATSON, JOHN B. *The Ways of Behaviorism.* New York: Harper & Row, 1928. An explanation of the what and why of behaviorism (which had been growing some 15 years) and why it opposes mentalistic concepts like instinct and unconscious.

WATSON, JOHN B., and WILLIAM McDOUGALL. *The Battle of Behaviorism.* New York: Norton, 1929. A debate between McDougall, the eminent psychologist of instinct theory, and Watson, the upsurging behaviorist. The sharp conflict between mentalistic and physicalistic psychology becomes clear.

WERTHEIMER, MAX. *Productive Thinking,* enlarged ed., Michael Wertheimer (ed.). New York: Harper & Row, 1959. An analysis of the thinking process by one of the three leading Gestalt psychologists. He developed the differences between associationistic and field study of thinking and showed how Gestalt psychology and reflective thinking are closely related.

WOLMAN, BENJAMIN B. *Contemporary Theories and Systems in Psychology.* New York: Harper & Row, 1960. A comprehensive picture of contemporary psychological theory. It emphasizes concept formation, relationship of psychology to other sciences, and methods of research. Chapters 1–4 present S-R conditioning theories, and chapters 10–13 Gestalt-field theories.

Chapter 13
HOW DOES SKINNER'S OPERANT CONDITIONING WORK?

Let the reader picture him or herself as a fourth grader, Betty Cooper, in a rather special type of classroom. At the first bell students enter the room; at the second bell they become silent. When opening exercises have been completed, the teacher says, "Arithmetic." Betty has been conditioned at this signal to place her arithmetic cylinder on her teaching machine, find where she left off yesterday, and proceed with conditioning herself to solve arithmetic problems. After 20 minutes the teacher says, "Reading," and in another 20 minutes, "Spelling." Each word is the appropriate stimulus for Betty to change cylinders on her machine. Then comes recess. At the sound of a bell with a different tone from that of the one that brought students into the room, they go out to the playground. Here, playground equipment has been adequately mechanized and sequenced so that there is little need for a teacher or any other supervisory personnel. The teacher uses the recess period to check, repair, and lubricate the machines.

The psychology that would support the emphasis on teaching machines for Betty's education has been developed by B. F. Skinner. Skinner has found *operant conditioning* highly effective in training lower animals, and he is confident that it promises equal success when used with children and youth. In operant conditioning, teachers are considered architects and builders of students' behavior. Learning objectives are divided into a large number of very small tasks and reinforced one by one. Operants—sets of acts—are reinforced or strengthened so as to increase the probability of their recurrence in the future. In this process it is of prime importance that teachers employ properly timed and spaced schedules of reinforcement.

Professor Skinner considers it the purpose of psychology to predict and control the behavior of individual organisms. He insists upon limiting scientific psychological study to the observable behavior of the organism; his only data are those acquired by sensory observation. Since such terms as *will power, sensation, image, drive,* or *instinct* imply nonphysical events, he opposes their use by psychologists or teachers in any connection with their thinking scientifically about people. For Skinner, a member of the human species "begins as an organism and becomes a person or self as he acquires a repertoire of behavior. . . . There is no place in the scientific position for a self as a true originator or initiator of action."[1] Behavior is "the movement of an organism or of its parts in a frame of reference provided by the organism itself or by various external objects or fields of force."[2]

Skinner's psychology is a strictly engineering type of science that is devoid of theory in any usual sense. He insists that psychology is a science of overt behavior and only overt behavior. Accordingly, he defines learning as a change in either the form or the probability of responses. In most cases this change is brought about by operant conditioning.

Operant conditioning is the learning process whereby a response is made more probable or more frequent; an *operant* is strengthened— reinforced. (Reinforcement is explained in Chapter 12, p. 290.) An operant is a set of acts that constitutes an organism's doing something—raising its head, pushing a lever, saying "horse." It is so called because behavior operates upon the environment and generates consequences. In the process of operant conditioning, operant responses are modified or changed. Reinforcement means that the probability of the repetition of certain classes of responses is increased.

Skinner thinks that nearly all human behavior is a product of operant reinforcement. He notes that in everyday life, in various fields including education, people constantly change the probabilities of responses of others by arranging reinforcing consequences. Furthermore, through their being operantly reinforced, people learn to keep their balance, walk, talk, play games, and handle tools and instruments; they perform a set of motions, reinforcement occurs, and the likelihood of their repeating the motions is increased. Thus, operant reinforcement improves the efficiency of behavior.

Whenever something reinforces a particular form of behavior, the chances are better that that behavior will be repeated. The task of psychologists is to gain more understanding of conditions under which reinforcement works best, and thereby open the way for cultural control through social engineering. To the many "natural" reinforcers of behavior, a host of artificial reinforcers may be added.

Any list of values is a list of reinforcers—conditioned or otherwise. We are so constituted that under certain circumstances food, water, sexual contact, and so on, will make any behavior which produces them more likely to occur again. Other things may acquire this power. . . . An organism can be reinforced by—can be made to "choose"—almost any given state of affairs.[3]

A list of values, then, actually is a list of reinforcers. "People behave in ways which, as we say, conform to ethical, governmental, or religious patterns because they are reinforced for doing so."[4] An organism can be reinforced by (that is, it can be made to "choose") almost any given state of affairs. Literature, art, and entertainment are contrived reinforcers. Whether a person buys a book, a ticket to a performance, or a work of art depends upon whether it is reinforcing to him (or her), and usually it is reinforcing to him if he had been reinforced when he previously purchased such an article.

HOW HAS SKINNER USED ANIMALS TO STUDY OPERANT REINFORCEMENT?

In general, experimental psychologists have tended not to relate their laws and theories to instances of learning in real life.[5] However, Professor Skinner and his associates have experienced remarkable success in training animals. It is probable that even professional animal trainers, through study of the procedures used in operant conditioning, could improve their techniques. In one college class period, by presenting food to a hungry pigeon at the right time, Skinner has implanted in the bird three or four well-defined responses such as turning around, pacing the floor in a figure-eight pattern, stretching the neck, and stamping the foot.

Skinner's basic thesis is that, since an organism tends in the future to do what it was doing at the time of reinforcement, one can, by baiting each step of the way, lead it to do very much what the experimenter wishes it to do. Using this thesis as a basis for his procedure, he has taught rats to use a marble to obtain food from a vending machine, pigeons to play a modified game of tennis, and dogs to operate the pedal of a refuse can so as to retrieve a bone.

Skinner focused his early study on lower animals because their behavior is simpler, conditions surrounding them may be controlled better, basic processes are revealed more readily and can be recorded over longer periods of time, and observations are not complicated by social relations between subjects and the psychologist.[6] However, more recently he has conducted research on learning using human beings of various ages and abilities.

The "Skinner box" is a simple box that contains a rat, a lever, and a device for delivering a pellet of food each time the rat presses the lever. Recording devices are set outside the box so that the experimenter can go home at night and see in the morning what the rat has been doing. There also are Skinner boxes for the study of pigeons and other animals. A rat or pigeon learns rapidly in a Skinner box because in the box there is little else for it to do. Skinner says, "The barest possible statement of the process is this: we make a given consequence contingent [dependent] upon certain physical properties of behavior (the upward movement of the head), and the behavior is then observed to increase in frequency."[7]

A pigeon's behavior can be reinforced in such a way that neck stretching will become habitual. The pigeon is placed in a cage so that the experimenter can sight across its head at a scale pinned on the far wall of the cage. The height at which the head is normally held is established on the scale; then some line, which is reached only infrequently, is selected. The experimenter, keeping his eye on the scale, quickly opens the food tray whenever the bird's head rises above the established line. As a result, learning occurs:

> We observe an immediate change in the frequency with which the head crosses the line. We also observe, and this is of some importance theoretically, that higher lines are now being crossed. We may advance almost immediately to a higher line in determining when food is to be presented. In a minute or two, the bird's posture has changed so that the top of the head seldom falls below the line which we first chose.[8]

By training two pigeons separately to do their parts in a total performance, Skinner has constructed a social scene within which competition is exemplified by two pigeons playing a modified game of ping-pong. He accomplished the training through operant reinforcement. First, the pigeons were reinforced when they merely pushed the ball. Then, when the ball got by one pigeon, the other was reinforced. He also has trained pigeons to coordinate their behavior in dancing in a cooperative manner that rivals the skills of human dancers.

Reinforcement procedures may vary according to intervals of time and the number of responses between reinforcements. A schedule of reinforcement is a pattern of "rewarding" behavior based upon a fixed time interval and a fixed number of responses between "rewards." In a laboratory, Skinner and Ferster have obtained performances appropriate to each of nine different ratio-interval schedules.[9] Skinner thinks that this achievement makes more plausible the extension of laboratory results to daily human life. To him learning, in the everyday life of people, is more complicated but nevertheless of the same basic nature as a lower animal's learning through operant conditioning.

In operant conditioning experiments, the species of organism studied has made surprisingly little difference. "Comparable results have been obtained with pigeons, rats, dogs, monkeys, human children, and psychotic subjects. In spite of great phylogenetic differences, all these organisms show amazingly similar properties of the learning process."[10]

WHAT PSYCHOLOGICAL THEORY UNDERLIES SKINNER'S TEACHING PROCEDURES?

Throughout his study and writings, Professor Skinner has adhered rigorously to a basic conviction that psychologists should restrict their study to the correlations between stimuli and responses and not meddle with any "make-believe" psychology that constructs intervening physiological or mental links between stimuli and responses. He considers only past events to be relevant to prediction of behavior. Accordingly he states, "Even if we could discover a spider's felt intention or sense of purpose, we could not offer it as a cause of the behavior."[11] So, any mentalistic description of behavior offers no real explanation of it. Instead, it only impedes its more effective analysis. Skinner, like both Thorndike and Watson before him, assumes that human beings are neutral and passive and that all behavior can be described in sequential mechanistic terms. In his study of human beings and animals, he constantly is mechanistic and elementistic; to him, psychology is the science of behavior.

What Is the Meaning of the "Science of Behavior"?

Skinner sees a great and crucial future for a science of behavior. In his view, since a science of behavior is concerned with demonstrating the consequences of cultural practices, the presence of such a science will be an essential mark of the culture or cultures that will survive in the future. The culture most likely to survive is the one in which the methods of science are most effectively applied to the problems of human behavior.[12] Consequently, throughout his work he has striven constantly to be scientific to the nth degree. He sees science as "more than a set of attitudes. It is a search for order, for uniformities, for lawful relations among the events in nature. It begins, as we all begin, by observing single episodes, but it quickly passes on to the general rule, to scientific law."[13]

A SCIENTIFIC-REALISTIC DEFINITION OF SCIENCE

Skinner works on the basic assumption that there is order in nature, including human behavior, and that it is the function of science to discover the order; this is the commitment of a scientific-realistic, as opposed to a positive-relativistic, scientist. Within Skinner's scientific-realistic outlook, science is concerned with the discovery of preexistent laws, which govern the world about us. Knowledge of these laws enhances predictability, and thereby control, of the variables that cause events to occur. This is as true in psychology as in physics or chemistry. Thus, human beings, through discovery of laws and organization of them into systems, enable themselves to deal effectively with aspects of the naturalistic world. "Science is in large part a direct analysis of reinforcing systems found in nature; it is concerned with facilitating the behavior which is reinforced by them."[14]

HUMAN BEHAVIOR, A SUBJECT OF SCIENCE

According to Skinner, it is not to be assumed that human behavior has any peculiar properties that require a unique method or special kind of knowledge. "The experimental analysis of behavior is a rigorous, extensive, and rapidly advancing branch of biology."[15] So, the variables of psychology, like the variables of any other science, must be described in physical terms. In Skinner's psychology, the *dependent variable* in a situation is the behavior of an individual organism. The *independent variable* consists of external conditions of which the behavior is a function. This means that behavior operates upon the environment to generate consequences. Notice that in this process neither the person nor the environment but it—behavior—behaves; behavior is a phenomenon of nature. Just as wind blows, behavior behaves.

The laws of the science of psychology are as definite as those of any other science. Skinner says, "It is decidedly not true that a horse may be led to water but cannot be made to drink."[16] Through applying the laws of psychology and arranging a history of severe deprivation, it can be made absolutely sure that drinking will occur; likewise, a desired behavior can be caused in a human being.

Skinner's goal in psychology is to achieve the degree of prediction and control in regard to human behavior that has been achieved by the physical sciences. The scientist of behavior evaluates probability of behavior and explores conditions that determine it. Through gathering data in regard to the frequencies of responses that have already occurred, he or she is able to make accurate statements about the likelihood of occurrence of a single future response of the same kind; frequency of response indicates probability of response.

> We are concerned, then, with the causes of human behavior. We want to know why men behave as they do. Any condition or event which can be shown to have an effect upon behavior must be taken into account. By discovering and analyzing these causes, we can predict behavior; to the extent that we can manipulate them, we can control behavior.[17]

In keeping with his physicalistic commitment (a physicalist is one who holds human thoughts and actions to be determined by physical laws), Professor Skinner states, "I do not see any distinction between predicting what an individual is going to do and predicting what, let us say, a sailboat is going to do."[18] "Operant conditioning shapes behavior as the sculptor shapes a lump of clay."[19]

How Is the Science of Behavior Related to Determinism?

Skinner's psychology implies a strictly naturalistic determinism. He notes that a scientific conception of human behavior dictates one practice and a philosophy of personal freedom another, and that a scientific conception of human behavior entails the acceptance of an assumption of determinism. Determinism means that behavior is caused, and that the behavior that appears is the only kind that could have appeared. Skinner emphasizes that the same type of determinism that is commonly accepted as applying to machines applies equally to human beings. Accordingly he states, "Man is a machine, but he is a very complex one. At present he is far beyond the powers of men to construct—except, of course, in the usual biological way."[20]

As machines have become more lifelike, living organisms have been found to be more like machines. Today, many machines are deliberately designed to operate in ways that resemble "human behavior." "Man has, in short, created the machine in his own image."[21] Since mechanical calculators now solve equations either too difficult or too time-consuming even for mathematicians to conquer, human beings have lost much of their uniqueness.

Determinism carries with it the implication that environment determines an individual even when he (or she) alters his own environment.

> It does not matter that the individual may take it upon himself to control the variables of which his own behavior is a function or, in a broad sense, to engage in the design of his own culture. He does this only because he is the product of a culture which generates self-control or cultural design as a mode of behavior.[22]

> All human behavior, including the behavior of machines which man builds to behave in his place, is ultimately to be accounted for in terms of the phylogenic contingencies of survival which have produced man as a species and the ontogenic contingencies of reinforcement which have produced him as an individual.[23]

"As accidental traits, arising from mutations, are selected by their contribution to survival, so accidental variations in behavior are selected by their reinforcing consequences."[24] "The scientist, like any organism, is the product of a unique history."[25] Science is of major importance in human affairs but even scientists and science are not free. Science, too, is a part of a naturally determined course of events, and it cannot interfere with that course.[26]

HOW IS OPERANT CONDITIONING NONPHYSIOLOGICAL AND NONPHENOMENOLOGICAL?

Skinner's system of operant conditioning has no place for study of either physiological or phenomenological psychology. *Physiological psychology* is devoted to study of physiological, neurological, and biological functions within an organism. *Phenomenological psychology* centers upon what events mean to the persons involved. In a sense it is similar to physiological psychology in that it, too, is centered upon what takes place within a person. However, it differs sharply from physiological psychology in that major emphasis is placed upon the process of conscious experiencing. Because Skinner rejects the use of the intervening variables of both physiological and phenomenological psychology, his friends sometimes speak of his dealing with the "empty organism." (Intervening variables intervene between stimuli and responses; they constitute the "O" of S-O-R psychology.)

How Is Operant Conditioning a Nonphysiological Psychology?

Skinner is convinced that the practice of looking inside an organism for an explanation of behavior has tended to obscure the variables that lie outside the organism and are immediately available for scientific analysis. These variables outside the organism are in its environmental history and its immediate environment. Psychologists' study of them permits behavior to be explained scientifically just as behavior of nonliving objects is explained scientifically by physicists. These independent variables are of many sorts and their relation to behavior often is subtle and complex; nevertheless, according to Skinner, it is only through analyzing them that we may hope to reach an adequate account of behavior.

Since statements about operations of the nervous system are not expressed in the same terms and cannot be confirmed by the same method of observation as the facts for which they are supposed to account, they are theories. Thus, Skinner feels that they can make little contribution to a scientific psychology. In the present stage of science an adequate neurological explanation of behavior is impossible. However, this fact in no way implies that a scientific psychology of learning cannot be established separate from any neurological theory.

How Is Operant Conditioning a Nonphenomenological Psychology?

Statements about mental events, like neurological statements, also are theoretical. Thus, Skinner belittles attempts of psychologists to infer what a physical situation means to an organism or to distinguish between the physical world and the psychological world of experience. He constantly emphasizes that events affecting an organism must be capable of being described in the language of physical science. Accordingly, he states, "I regard myself as an organism responding to its environment."[27] To him, the "free inner man," who is held responsible for the behavior of the external biological organism, is only a prescientific substitute for the external causes of behavior, which are susceptible to scientific analysis. Hence, there is no place in scientific psychology for study of the intrapersonal experiences of people as such. Accordingly, he writes, "What we have learned from the experimental analysis of behavior suggests that the environment performs the functions previously assigned to feelings and introspectively observed inner states of the organism."[28]

Skinner regards the practice of some scientists who indicate that they are describing only half the universe and that there is another half —a world of self, mind, or consciousness—as a part of the cultural heritage from which science has emerged but which now stands in the way of a unified scientific account of nature. Even in discussing the higher human function, thinking, Skinner sees little need for the concept *self*. He recognizes that behavior is a function of the environment, that environment presumably means any event in the universe capable of affecting the organism, and that a very small part of this universe is private, that is, enclosed within the organism's own skin. Thus, some independent variables, for example, an aching tooth, may be related to behavior in a unique way. However, he sees no reason to suppose that the stimulating effect of an inflamed tooth is essentially different from that of a hot stove.[29] "The alternative to the use of the concept [self] is simply to deal with demonstrated covariations in the strength of responses."[30]

PRIVATE EVENTS

Skinner thinks that students of a science of behavior should face the problem of privacy, but that they should do so without abandoning the basic position of "radical behaviorism." Radical behaviorists, including Professor Skinner, think that "An adequate science of behavior must consider events taking place within the skin of the organism, not as physiological mediators of behavior, but as part of behavior itself."[31] Both private and public events have the same kind of physical dimensions. Thus, contingencies that involve private stimuli also follow from simple mechanical relations between stimuli, responses, and reinforcing consequences.

Private stimuli are either interoceptive or proprioceptive ones. Interoceptive stimuli are those received by nerve endings in the internal organs, for example, the stimuli provided by hunger pangs or a full bladder. Proprioceptive stimuli are received through afferent nerve endings in the muscles of the body, for example, the stimuli provided by lame or sore muscles. All of the ways of changing a person's mind consist of either verbal or nonverbal manipulation of his or her environment.

CONSCIOUS EXPERIENCE AND FEELINGS

Persons learn to see that they are seeing, that is, to behave consciously only because verbal community arranges for them to do so. Even when the thing being seen is not present, as in a dream, contingencies produced by the verbal environment may set up self-descriptive responses that describe the behavior of seeing.

Any personal feelings, at their best, are accompaniments, not causes, of behavior. Furthermore, covert responses are not the causes of related overt ones; both are the products of common independent variables. Consequently, the conditions that one feels, not one's feelings as such, are the important factors in a study of behavior. "A radical behaviorism denies the existence of a mental world, not because it is contentious or jealous of a rival, but because those who claim to be studying the other world necessarily talk about the world of behavior in ways which conflict with an experimental analysis."[32] Radical behaviorism "does not *reduce* feelings to bodily states; it simply argues that bodily states are and always have been what are felt. It does not *reduce* thought processes to behavior; it simply analyzes the behavior previously explained by the invention of thought processes."[33] "No matter how defective a behavioral account may be, we must remember that mentalistic explanations explain nothing."[34]

In Skinner's system there is no place for the statement that behavior is under the control of an incentive or goal. A scientific psychology, as Skinner defines it, replaces statements that might use such words as *incentive, goal,* or *purpose* with statements about conditioning. A person may feel a purpose, but such a feel has no casual effect. "A person is not an originating agent; he is a locus, a point at which many genetic and environmental conditions come together in a joint effect."[35]

Instead of saying that a person behaves because of the consequences that are to follow his (or her) behavior, we simply state that he behaves thus and so because of the consequences that have followed similar behavior in the past. When one is "looking for something" one is emitting responses that in the past produced something as a consequence. When one says, "I am looking for my glasses," what one really means is " 'I have lost my glasses,' 'I shall stop what I am doing when I find my glasses,' or 'When I have done this in the past, I have found my glasses.' "[36]

Professor Skinner uses the analogy that astronomers may speak figuratively of the sun rising and setting, but they do not do so when they are performing the role of scientists. Likewise, psychologists and teachers properly may use such literary descriptions of human activity as the person *expected, hoped, observed, felt, knew, remembered, feared, was hungry,* or *was anxious.* But as behavioral scientists they should report only observed facts such as the *organism was reinforced when it pushed the lever,* the *intake of food was so much,* or *aversive stimuli or pre-aversive stimuli were present.*[37]

Since the terms *pleasant* and *satisfying* do not refer to any physical property of reinforcing events, and physical sciences use neither of these terms nor their equivalents, they, too, should be deleted from the language of a science of psychology. Furthermore, since behavior is always the behavior of an individual, a science of behavior that concerns only the behavior of groups is not likely to be of help in understanding particular cases. Thus, "A 'social force' is no more useful in manipulating behavior than an inner state of hunger, anxiety, or skepticism."[38]

WHAT IS THE NATURE OF OPERANT CONDITIONING OR REINFORCEMENT?

Operant conditioning is a learning process whereby a given response is made either more probable or more frequent by the occurrence of a reinforcing stimulus immediately following the response. In the pigeon experiment, reported on page 316, the process of operant conditioning is the change in frequency with which the head is lifted to a given height, the *reinforcer* is food, and the *reinforcement* is food presentation after the response is emitted. The *operant* is the behavior upon which the reinforcement is contingent—the height to which the head must be raised.

In operant conditioning, the important stimulus is the one immediately following the response, not the one preceding it. Any emitted response that leads to reinforcement is thereby strengthened. However, it is not the specific response that is strengthened, but rather the general tendency to make the response. Hence, carefully stated, an operant is a class of responses of which a specific response is an instance or member. A rat presses a lever and gets food. Because of this, the rat will be more likely to press the lever again. "What is changed is the future probability of response in the same class."[39] The operant as a class of behavior, rather than the response as a particular instance, is reinforced. It is not correct to say that an operant reinforcement strengthened the response that preceded it; the response has already occurred and cannot be changed. What has been changed is that the probability that that class of responses will occur in the future has been increased. Since each reinforcement builds up a reserve of responses, a pigeon may continue to raise its head or a rat to press the lever several, or even many, times after food has ceased to appear.

The *law of operant conditioning* is that, if the occurrence of an operant is followed by presentation of a reinforcing stimulus, the strength —probability—is increased. What is strengthened is not a stimulus-response connection; the operant requires no specific eliciting stimulus. Insofar as the organism is concerned, the only important property of the operant contingency is time; the reinforcer follows the response. How this is brought about does not matter. The process of operant conditioning may be described adequately without any mention of a stimulus that acts before the response is made. In reinforcing a pigeon's neck stretching, it is necessary only for one to wait for neck stretching to occur. It is not necessary for the experimenter to elicit it. "The statement that the bird 'learns that it will get food by stretching its neck' is an inaccurate report of what has happened."[40] A Gestalt-field explanation of how the bird learns, of course, would be just this.

What Is a Contingency of Reinforcement?

Skinner's units of learning are "contingencies of reinforcement." A *contingency of reinforcement* is a sequence within which a response is followed by a reinforcing stimulus. The ordered interrelations between three terms or variables compose such a contingency. These variables are (1) a discriminative stimulus (S^D); (2) the behavior or response itself (R); and (3) the reinforcing stimulus (S^{rein}). So, Skinner's paradigm of reinforcement is (S^D—R—S^{rein}). A discriminative stimulus (S^D) occurs prior to the response (R) being reinforced. It is any stimulus or pattern of stimuli that arises from the nature of the space within which the organism is placed, the apparatus used to sense occurrences of the response, or any special stimulating devices that may be used. Thus, it sets, or discriminates, the conditions under which a behavior occurs. The reinforcing stimulus (S^{rein}) follows the discriminative stimulus and the response and renders consequences to the organism.[41]

A hen that plays a piano at a fair, when a person places a dime in the appropriate slot, is an example of applied operant conditioning. The cage, the piano, the feed trough, and the lighted bulb in the corner of the cage constitute the S^D—discriminative stimulus—playing the piano is the operant that is being reinforced, and pellets being eaten constitute the S^{rein}—reinforcing stimulus. Pellets have been given her only after she had played the piano when the light was on. At no other time has she received a pellet. So, when the dime drops the light is turned on, the hen strikes the keys the required number of times, then a pellet is dropped and the hen eats the pellet.

Operant reinforcement, then, not only strengthens a given response; it also may bring the response under the control of a discriminative stimulus. But the discriminative or controlling stimulus does not elicit the response; it merely sets the occasion upon which the response is more likely to occur.[42] So, when a response occurs and is reinforced the probability that it will occur again in the presence of similar stimuli is increased.

In a contingency the occurrence of an operant—response—is *followed* by presentation of a reinforcing stimulus, and the strength—probability—of recurrence of the operant is increased. The three-term contingency of operant reinforcement occurs when a child is taught to read; a given response is reinforced with "right" or "wrong" according to how the student responds to the appropriate visual stimulus—word or sentence.

The key to successful teaching or training is to analyze the effect of reinforcement and design techniques that manipulate the process with considerable precision—to set up specific reinforcing contingencies. In this way the behavior of an individual organism may be brought under precise control. Implicit in operant behaviorism is the conviction that

"When all relevant variables have been arranged, an organism will or will not respond. If it does not, it cannot. If it can, it will."[43]

How Does Operant Differ from Respondent or Reflexive Conditioning?

Skinner acknowledges two kinds of learning—operant and respondent or reflexive. But, he places far greater emphasis upon operant learning. *Respondent* or reflexive behavior is behavior that is elicited by a stimulus; *operant* behavior is behavior that is controlled by its consequences, that is, what follows it.

Reflexive learning involves such situations as are described in the Pavlovian dog studies. Essentially it is a process of stimulus substitution. An organism already responds reflexively to a natural or unconditioned stimulus. Then, a new stimulus is presented along with the original stimulus and the organism comes to respond to the new stimulus in the same way it formerly did to the original one. In reflexive or respondent conditioning the key stimulus is the one that precedes the response. Whereas reflexive learning is an S-R process, operant learning is an R-S one. In operant learning, the most significant stimulus is that which immediately follows the response. Any modification of the environment constitutes a stimulus. (See Table 12.1, p. 289.)

WHAT ARE THE PROCESSES OF OPERANT REINFORCEMENT AND EXTINCTION?

In operant conditioning, an operant is strengthened through its *reinforcement* or weakened through its *extinction*. The psychologist's task is simply to account for probability of responses in terms of a history of reinforcement and extinction. The effect of reinforcement always is to increase the probability of response. Extinction is the reverse of reinforcement. When a reinforcing stimulus no longer occurs following a response, the response becomes less and less frequent; this is operant extinction. "Conditioning builds up a predisposition to respond—a 'reserve'—which extinction exhausts."[44] We discuss extinction on pages 328–329, but first we describe the kinds of reinforcers and types of reinforcement.

What Are the Two Kinds of Reinforcers?

Any stimulus whose presentation or removal increases the probability of a response is a reinforcer. Consequently, there are two kinds of reinforcers or reinforcing events—positive and negative. A positive reinforcer is any stimulus whose *presentation* strengthens the behavior upon which it is made contingent; a negative reinforcer is any stimulus whose *withdrawal* strengthens that behavior. Since in both cases responses are strengthened, reinforcement is taking place. A positive reinforcement consists of presenting a stimulus, of adding something—food, water, or a teacher's smile—to an organism's environment. A negative reinforcement consists of removing something—a loud noise, an electric shock, or a teacher's frown—from the situation. In both of these cases the probability that the response will recur is increased.

Although in lay usage both positive and negative reinforcers are "rewards," Skinner warns against defining a positive reinforcer as pleasant or satisfying and a negative reinforcer as annoying. "It would be as difficult to show that the reinforcing power of an aversion stimulus is due to its unpleasantness as to show that the reinforcing power of a positive reinforcer is due to its pleasantness."[45] When a person reports that an event is pleasant, this simply means that the event is of such kind that it reinforces him. Physical science uses no such terms as "pleasant" and "unpleasant" or their equivalents. The terms in no way refer to physical properties of reinforcing agents.

Is Punishment Reinforcement?

Punishment is a basically different process from reinforcement. Whereas reinforcement involves presentation of a positive stimulus or removal of a negative one, punishment consists of presentation of a negative stimulus or removal of a positive one. Again, whereas reinforcement is defined in terms of strengthening of a response, punishment is a process that weakens a response. Putting it succinctly, when a stimulus is involved in *strengthening* a response there is reinforcement; when a stimulus is either presented or withdrawn in an attempt to *weaken* a response, there is punishment.

Results of experiments indicate that punishment does not permanently reduce a tendency to respond. Thorndike's experiments with human subjects indicated that a reward strengthened the behavior that preceded it but that punishment did not weaken it. Through reward, behavior may be stamped in; but the converse, though punishment behavior can be stamped out, does not hold. Whereas reinforcement can be used to good advantage in controlling other organisms, in the long run punishment works to the disadvantage of both the punished organism and the punishing agency. Its results are neither predictable nor dependable. Extinction—permitting a behavior to die out by not reinforcing it—and not punishment is the appropriate process for breaking habits.

What Are the Types of Operant Reinforcement?

There are two rather distinct types of operant reinforcement—stimulus discrimination and response differentiation. Nearly all human learning can be classified under these two. However, the process of respondent or reflexive conditioning should not be completely ignored. Through operant reinforcement a relatively complete new unit of behavior may be learned or an existing unit of behavior may be refined. In general, reinforcement that leads to behavior acquirement is a process of discrimination of stimuli, whereas behavior refinement or skill development is a process of differentiation of responses.

DISCRIMINATION OF STIMULI

Operant discrimination is the establishment of a certain type of behavior that occurs as the result of a given stimulus either preceding or accompanying that behavior and the behavior's then being reinforced. If an operant behavior is reinforced by S^{rein} when a discriminative stimulus S^D is present but is not reinforced when that S^D is not present, the tendency for the organism to respond with that operant behavior when the S^D is present gradually becomes strengthened, and the tendency for it to respond in like manner when not that S^D but some other stimuli are present is gradually extinguished. As stated before, S^{rein} symbolizes the reinforcing stimulus, which follows the operant response (R), and S^D indicates the discriminative stimulus, which is the stimulus that either precedes or accompanies the operant response or behavior (R).

Through the use of a discriminative stimulus followed by reinforcement, that is, giving a pigeon pellets when it stretches its neck while a light is on, it can be made to be more likely to respond by stretching its neck at times when the light is on. Imitative behavior is an example of the result of discriminative operant reinforcement. Such behavior does not arise because of any inherent reflexive or mentalistic mechanism but develops in the history of an individual as a result of discriminative reinforcements. The visual stimulation of someone's waving a hand is the occasion upon which waving a hand probably received reinforcement. The reinforcement, not the stimulation from the other person's waving his or her hand, is the cause of future hand waving in similar situations. Because objects in shop windows into which other people are looking are likely to reinforce looking into such windows, when a person sees other people looking into a shop window she too is likely to look. So, "Attention is a controlling *relation*—the relation between a response and a discriminative stimulus. When someone is paying attention he is under special control of a stimulus."[46]

Operant discrimination of a stimulus causes an organism readily to respond in a given manner when the occasion is appropriate for it to do so. In an elementary school room a teacher says "yellow"; a girl points to yellow on a color chart; she then is reinforced for doing so, but only on those occasions when the teacher first has said "yellow." In this way the girl is conditioned to point to yellow only after the teacher, or someone similar to the teacher, has said "yellow."

Rules, laws, and maxims constitute a special category of discriminative stimuli; as well as specifying the occasions upon which a behavior will occur, they also often describe the behavior itself, and its reinforcing consequences. Thus, each rule, law, or maxim is effective as the first part of a set of contingencies of reinforcement.[47] Whereas behavior that is reinforced is under the control of succeeding stimuli, rules, laws, and maxims are under the control of prior ones.

DIFFERENTIATION OF RESPONSES

Skills are improved through differentiating reinforcements of varying responses. Many differentiating reinforcements may be supplied automatically by mechanical exigencies of the environment of an organism. To throw a ball skillfully, a person must release it at the proper moment; instances in which release comes before or after the proper moment are not reinforced. However, in more complex skill learning, reinforcement must be supplied by a teacher. In this process, any reinforcement that develops skill must be immediate. "By reinforcing a series of successive approximations, we bring a rare response to a very high probability in a short time.[48]

Through the procedure of operant conditioning, within which differentiation of responses is reinforced, a hungry pigeon that is well adapted to the experimental situation and the food tray can usually be brought to respond by pecking a specific spot in two or three minutes. To get the pigeon to peck a specific spot as quickly as possible, the bird first is given food when it turns slightly in the direction of the spot. This increases the frequency of turning toward the spot. Reinforcement is then withheld until the bird makes a slight movement toward the spot. Then positions that are successively closer to the spot are reinforced. Then reinforcement is given only when the head is moved slightly forward, and finally only when the beak actually makes contact with the spot.

What Is Extinction?

Extinction is a process whereby a learned behavior or response either becomes less and less frequent or completely disappears as the result of its repetition while receiving no further reinforcement. Whereas the mere passage of time after reinforcement has surprisingly little effect upon loss of an act or habit, extinction is an effective way of removing an operant from the habit repertoire of an organism. When unaccompanied by extinction, forgetting takes place very slowly if at all. Note the key difference here: whereas mere forgetting is the losing of a habit through the passage of time, extinction requires that the response be emitted without reinforcement.

Operant extinction takes place much more slowly than does operant reinforcement. However, as an organism responds less and less, a gradual process of extinction may be detected. Since behavior during extinction is a result of the conditioning that preceded it, extinction occurs quickly when only a few incidents of a given response have been reinforced and is greatly protracted when there has been a long history of reinforcement.

The extinction process includes the interesting phenomenon of spontaneous recovery. Even after prolonged extinction, an organism, at the beginning of another session of an activity in which it had been trained but now is no longer being reinforced, often will respond at a higher rate for at least a few moments.

Sometimes an extinction curve is disturbed by an emotional effect. Failure of a response to be reinforced not only leads to operant extinction but also may be accompanied by a reaction commonly called frustration or rage. A pigeon that has failed to receive reinforcement flaps its wings and engages in other emotional behavior. An auto mechanic, who is in the habit of having bolts unscrew when he turns his wrench, vents his spleen when one breaks off instead. However, after exercising his vocabulary, he turns back to the next bolt. Likewise a pigeon or rat will turn again to the operating key of the box when the emotional response has subsided. Extinction curves often show cyclic oscillation as the emotional response builds up, disappears, and builds up again.

The resistance to extinction generated by intermittent reinforcement of a response is much greater than that achieved by the same number of reinforcements being given for consecutive responses. If we only occasionally reinforce a child's good behavior, the behavior survives after reinforcement is discontinued much longer than if we had reinforced every instance up to the same total number of reinforcements. Since intermittent reinforcement generates longer extinction curves than does continuous reinforcement, there is no simple relation between the number of reinforcements and the number of unreinforced responses necessary for extinction.

WHAT DOES SKINNER'S OPERANT CONDITIONING IMPLY ABOUT THE NATURE OF TRANSFER OF LEARNING?

Skinner's operant conditioning theory of learning carries with it definite implications in regard to the nature of transfer and its role in teaching and learning. Since Skinner questions the reality of the inner qualities and faculties to which human achievements in the past often have been attributed, in his study of learning and transfer he turns from ill-defined and remote explanations of behavior to the study of observable and manipulatable behavior. For Skinner, the basic object of psychological study is the probability of observable behavior, which "is accounted for by appeal to the genetic endowment of the organism and its past and present environment, described wholly in the language of physics and biology."[49]

Since within operant conditioning learning simply is a change in the form and probability of a response, transfer likewise is an increased probability of responses of a certain class occurring in the future. Remember that a reinforcer is any stimulus whose presentation or removal increases the probability of a response; there are both positive and negative reinforcers. Because a single instance of a response or operant may be strengthened by being followed by a reinforcing event and the effect survive for a long time even though the same consequence never recurs, operant reinforcement provides a strong theoretical basis for transfer.

Skinner thinks that nearly all human behavior is the product of operant reinforcement and that most reinforcement improves the efficiency of behavior through continuously reshaping it. Thus, to his way of thinking, one's repertoire of conditioned operants is the basis for transfer of one's learning.

The three key concepts in understanding the meaning of transfer within operant conditioning are *conditioned reinforcement, stimulus* and *response induction,* and *conditioned generalized reinforcement.*

What Is Conditioned Reinforcement?

In conditioned reinforcement, a new stimulus becomes a conditioned reinforcer, that is, a new reinforcer (stimulus B) is conditioned through its occurrence along with an originally adequate reinforcing stimulus (stimulus A). Thus, stimulus B comes to reinforce an act operantly in the same way as would the originally adequate reinforcing stimulus (stimulus A). So, stimulus B becomes a conditioned reinforcer.

An example of conditioned reinforcement is that, if each time we give food to a "hungry" pigeon to reinforce an act that we are teaching it we turn on a light, the light eventually will become a conditioned reinforcer; it may be used to reinforce the act or some other operant just as food formerly was used.[50] "If we have frequently presented a dish of food to a hungry organism, the empty dish will elicit the animal's salivation. To some extent the empty dish will also reinforce an operant."[51] Thus, through conditioned reinforcement, other things may acquire the reinforcing power that food, water, and sexual contact originally had.

A characteristic of human behavior is that primary—originally adequate—reinforcers may be effective even after long delays. This presumably is only because in intervening events other objects such as symbols become conditioned reinforcers. In education, techniques are deliberately designed to create appropriate conditioned reinforcers and thereby transfer is promoted. When a student performs properly, the teacher gives him a smile and an A. An A thereby comes to be a conditioned reinforcer; it will "reward" the student for many kinds of activity—operants.

What Is Stimulus and Response Induction?

Skinner prefers the term *induction* for what more commonly is called stimulus or response *generalization*. Thus, induction occurs in regard to both stimuli and responses; that is, there is both stimulus induction and response induction.[52]

Stimulus induction is a process through which a stimulus either acquires or loses its capacity to elicit a response, control a discriminative response, or set up an emotional "state," because of its similarity to a stimulus that has acquired or lost such a capacity through direct conditioning. If a red light is established as a discriminative stimulus, an orange (or even yellow) light may be found to share the same function, perhaps in a lesser degree.

Response induction is a process through which a response changes its probability or rate because it shares properties with another response that has changed its probability or rate through reinforcement. When a dog has been trained to roll over by being rewarded and it is "told" to "roll over," it may make a twisting motion while remaining on its feet.

For us to understand Skinner's induction theory, we must remember that reinforcement does not strengthen the response that preceded it; it increases the probability of a class of responses, and the class is represented by certain specific responses that occur in the future. Furthermore, we must keep in mind that a class of responses consists of those responses that contain the same elements. Thus, Skinner's basic measure of behavior is a response element rather than a response itself. A *response element* "is a sort of behavioral atom, which may never appear by itself upon any single occasion but is the essential ingredient or component of all observed instances. The reinforcement of a response increases the probability [of occurrence] of all responses containing the same elements."[53]

A large complex of words—an idiom, a phrase, or a memorized passage—may be under the control of a single variable and thus constitute a functional unit.[54] Functional units of behavior, however, consist of a number of basic *behavioral atoms* or elements. Behavioral atoms, as contrasted with functional units, are at least as small as separate speech sounds. We must recognize these small behavioral atoms in order to account for distorted verbal responses such as spoonerisms and other verbal slips (a spoonerism is an accidental transposition of sounds—saying "blushing crow" for "crushing blow"). These "atoms" also are evident in the stylistic devices of alliteration, rhyme, and rhythm. When we identify elements rather than responses as units of behavior, we then say "the *elements* [atoms] *are* strengthened wherever they occur."[55]

In the life of each organism, through the process of stimulus and response induction, there is constant movement from primary to generalized reinforcement. Usually, in this process, a conditioned reinforcer is being generalized.

What Is Conditioned Generalized Reinforcement?

Conditioned reinforcement and induction or generalization combine to give conditioned generalized reinforcement. A stimulus that is a conditioned reinforcer is generalized when, in the process of its becoming a conditioned reinforcer, it is paired with more than one primary reinforcer; "if a conditioned reinforcer has been paired with reinforcers appropriate to many conditions, at least one appropriate state of deprivation is more likely to prevail upon a later occasion."[56] Thus, a response is more likely to occur. For example, when we reinforce behavior with money, our subsequent control of the behavior of an individual is relatively independent of any momentary deprivation. Money becomes a conditioned, generalized reinforcer because, from time to time, money occurs along with many primary reinformers. Thus, it acquires the capacity to reinforce many behaviors.

Skinner observes that a token such as money is a conditioned generalized reinforcer distinguished by its physical specifications. He further notes that money is not the only token that is a conditioned generalized reinforcer. In education an individual behaves as he (or she) does, in part, because of the marks, grades, and diplomas that he previously has received. These are not as readily exchanged for primary reinforcement as money, but the possibility of exchange is there. Educational tokens form a series in which one token may be exchanged for the next, and the commercial or prestige value of the final token, the diploma, is usually quite clear.

The maintenance of behavior in strength after it has been acquired is as much a function of reinforcement as is the original learning. After an organism has learned how to do something, that is, after it has acquired a behavior, further reinforcements are necessary to maintain the behavior in strength. In this process, various schedules of reinforcement are of special importance. So, transfer of learning is promoted by repeated reinforcement of desired behaviors and by following the most effective schedules of reinforcement.

HOW MAY OPERANT CONDITIONING BE APPLIED TO SCHOOLROOM PRACTICES?

For Professor Skinner, "Teaching is the arrangement of contingencies of reinforcement which expedite learning."[57] He is convinced that operant conditioning, so effectual when applied to animal training, promises equal success when used in schools. Furthermore, he thinks that the most effective control of human learning requires instrumental aid. He is appalled at the present inefficient practices in schools and recommends a procedure whereby they can be corrected. He thinks that, when teachers have taught successfully, regardless of whether they have thought in mental disciplinary, apperceptive, or behavioristic terms, they actually have arranged effective contingencies of reinforcement. But, he also thinks that teachers are more likely to do this well if they understand what it is that they are doing.

He recognizes that the first task of teachers is to shape proper responses, to get children to pronounce and write responses properly. But he sees their principal task as bringing proper behavior under many sorts of stimulus control. "Teaching spelling is mainly a process of shaping complex forms of behavior. In other subjects—for example, arithmetic—the same machine can be used to bring responses under the control of appropriate stimuli."[58] To achieve this task, Skinner recommends the use of programmed instruction.

Programmed instruction is a system of teaching and learning within which preestablished subject matter is broken down into small, discrete steps and carefully organized into a logical sequence in which it can be learned readily by the students. Each step builds deliberately upon the preceding one. A learner can progress through the sequence of steps at his own rate, he or she is nearly always right, and he is reinforced immediately after each step. Reinforcement consists of the learner's either being given the correct response immediately after his registering it or his being permitted to proceed to the next step only after he has registered that response. Programmed instruction may be accomplished either with or without the use of teaching machines. (A teaching machine is described on p. 337.)

Skinner's linear programming[59] presents a series of frames to a student. A *frame* constitutes a contingency of reinforcement. It consists of a discriminative stimulus in the form of a question. The student's answer is the response, and the student's making the "right" response in the form of the "right" answer is the reinforcing stimulus. The following is an example of a frame: "A warm-blooded animal that suckles its young is called a _____."

Succeeding frames develop new learning in such small increments that students get the "right" answer on more than 90 percent of the frames. It is assumed that a student's making a right response and immediately learning that it is right is in itself a reinforcer. Consequently, the student is more likely to repeat that response or answer in a future similar situation. Also, he (or she) will move on to the next frame. So, a pellet is to a rat what an M&M is to a small child, and what making the "right" response is to an older student.

What Are the Shortcomings of Current Educational Practice?

Skinner believes that it is in bringing correct responses under stimulus control that the greatest inefficiency of current teaching procedures occurs. "In education we design and redesign our curricula in a desperate attempt to provide a liberal education while steadfastly refusing to employ available engineering techniques which would efficiently build the interests and instill the knowledge which are the goals of education."[60] Consequently, he notes the following current weaknesses in educational practices:

1. Behavior is dominated by aversion (escape) stimulation.
2. Too great a lapse of time exists between behavior and its reinforcement.
3. A skillful program of reinforcement that moves forward through a series of progressive approximations to the final complex desired behavior is lacking.
4. Reinforcement of desired behavior occurs much too infrequently.

• *Behavior Dominated by Aversion Stimulation.* Although the type of threatened displeasure or pain has been changed in the past 50 years, behavior in the lower grades is still dominated by aversive stimulation—children are trying to escape or keep away from something. Fifty years ago children read numbers, copied numbers, and memorized tables to escape the birch rod or cane, that is, as far as they were concerned, they did these things to avoid or escape punishment. Today, students behave the way they do primarily to escape the threat of a series of minor distasteful events—the teacher's displeasure, criticism or ridicule by their classmates, a poor showing in competition, low marks, or a trip to the principal's office. When children are dominated by this atmosphere, getting the right answer is in itself a rather insignificant event. Thus, the emphasis in teaching and learning is not centered where it should be—in operant conditioning.

• *Excessive Time Lapse between Behavior and Reinforcement.* Unless explicit mediating behavior has been set up, the lapse of only a few seconds between a response and its reinforcement destroys most of the effect. A grade on a test taken near the end of the week is too far away from the behaviors the students emitted—sent out—in studying the subject matter earlier in the week. Reinforcing stimuli should follow the desired responses immediately.

Through use of the generalized reinforcer—approval—schools and society reinforce acquisition of the type of behavior learned in school. This is done by awarding grades, promotions, keys, diplomas, degrees, and medals. Skinner notes that these reinforcers do reinforce students' going to school and gaining a diploma or degree; their shortcoming is that they seldom if ever reinforce the subject matter elements themselves.

• *Absence of a Program of Serial Reinforcement.* A carefully planned program of teaching should move forward step by step by reinforcing a series of progressive approximations to the final behavior that is desired. To bring a human organism into possession of mathematical, or any other systematic, behavior most efficiently, a long series of reinforcement contingencies is necessary. Since teachers have only so much time, they cannot deal with students' responses one at a time; it is usually necessary for them to reinforce the desired behavior only in blocks of responses.

• *Infrequency of Reinforcement.* Perhaps the most serious criticism of current classroom procedures is the relative infrequency of reinforcement of the desired acts of students. It is just not humanly possible for one teacher to provide an adequate number of reinforcement contingencies for a class of 30 or 40 children. Skinner estimates that, although adequate efficient mathematical behavior at the level of the first four grades requires somewhere between 25,000 and 50,000 reinforcement contingencies, a teacher at best could provide only a few thousand. Thus, even our best schools may be criticized for their inefficiency in teaching drill subjects such as arithmetic. Skinner believes that advances recently made in techniques for control of the learning process suggest that classroom practices should be thoroughly revised.

What Are the Relevant Considerations in Conditioning (Teaching) a Child?

In order to plan a procedure for inculcating certain desired behavior in a child some specific questions need to be answered:

1. What behavior is to be established?
2. What reinforcers are available?
3. What responses are available?
4. How can reinforcements be most efficiently scheduled?[61]

• *Behavior to be Established.* To teach efficiently, the first job of a teacher who is an adherent of operant conditioning is to determine carefully just what it is he plans to teach at a specific time; the teacher is the architect and builder of behaviors. He (or she) must decide what he wants to teach, then teach it. His objectives are specific, and they are defined in terms of desired behaviors. Thus, operant behaviorism requires a teacher-centered classroom.

• *Reinforcers Available.* What does a school have in its possession that will reinforce a child? Since the sheer control of nature in itself is reinforcing, the material to be learned may provide considerable automatic reinforcement. Children play for hours with mechanical toys, paints, and puzzles. These feed back significant changes in the environment and are reasonably free of aversive stimulation. Automatic reinforcement from manipulation of the environment is probably rather mild. However, in teaching, the net amount of reinforcement in each contingency is of little significance. When properly and carefully used, a series of very slight reinforcements may be tremendously effective in controlling behavior.

In addition to automatic reinforcement arising from manipulation of the environment, some other reinforcers are available and often used. A child behaves in a certain way and the behavior is reinforced by its immediate consequences. Reinforcement may follow from a child's excelling others. However, when children are competitively "rewarded," the reinforcement of one child is, of necessity, aversive—"punishing"— to others. The good will and affection of the teacher also may be reinforcing. A positive "reward" or "consequence" (stimulus) strengthens the behavior that is part of the contingency including that stimulus; it has nothing to do with satisfying organismic purpose.

• *Responses Available.* In planning a program of progressive approximations that will lead to the desired final form of behavior a teacher must have at hand an inventory of the responses that are available throughout the conditioning process.

• *Most Efficient Scheduling of Reinforcements.* To schedule reinforcements efficiently means to make them contingent upon the desired behavior. Here two considerations are involved: (1) gradual elaboration of extremely complex patterns of behavior into small units or stages; and (2) maintenance of the behavior in strength at each stage.

> The whole process of becoming competent in any field must be divided into a very large number of very small steps, and reinforcement must be contingent upon the accomplishment of each step. . . . By making each successive step as small as possible, the frequency of reinforcement can be raised to a maximum, while the possibly aversive consequences of being wrong are reduced to a minimum.[62]

This is the purpose of programmed instruction.

According to operant conditioning,

> learning a subject like fundamentals of electricity is largely a matter of learning (or giving) a large number of correct responses to logically related sequences of questions that constitute the subject. . . . Once a subject has been carefully divided ("programmed") into a series of many small bits of information ("steps") a student has only to learn by repetition and reward ("rapid and frequent reinforcement") the correct answer to a series of questions about the small bits of information.[63]

Skinner contends that the necessary requirements for adequate reinforcement are not excessive, but they probably are incompatible with current realities of present-day classrooms. Experimental studies of learning have indicated that, in order to arrange the contingencies of reinforcement that are most efficient in controlling learning in an organism, mechanical and electrical devices must be used. As mere reinforcing mechanisms, teachers are out-of-date—and would be so even if each teacher devoted all his or her time to a single child. Only through mechanical devices can the necessarily large number of contingencies be provided. "We have every reason to expect, therefore, that the most effective control of human learning will require instrumental aid."[64]

How Do Teaching Machines Work?

In Skinner's view, education must become more efficient to a degree that cannot be accomplished merely by our building more schools and preparing more teachers; adequate systems of labor-saving capital equipment, that is, teaching machines, must be developed. He is critical, too, of traditional education, which makes students more and more the passive receivers of instruction. Teaching machines, he feels, encourage students to take an "active" role in the instructional process—they must develop the answers before they are reinforced.

• *Requirements of an Appropriate Teaching Machine.* Skinner thinks that, in light of modern psychological knowledge, an appropriate teaching machine has two basic requirements: First, a student must compose his or her response rather than select it from a set of alternatives. Second, in acquiring complex behavior, a student must pass through a carefully designed sequence of steps; each step must be so small that it always can be taken, yet in taking it the student must move somewhat closer to fully competent behavior, and the machine must operate so as to make sure that steps are taken in a carefully prescribed order.[65]

• *Operation of a Teaching Machine.* Let's see how Skinner describes a teaching device.

> The device consists of a box about the size of a small record player. On the top surface is a glazed window through which a question or problem printed on a paper tape may be seen. The child answers the question by moving one or more sliders upon which the digits 0 through 9 are printed. The answer appears in square holes punched in the paper upon which the question is printed. When the answer has been set, the child turns a knob. The operation is as simple as adjusting a television set. If the answer is right, the knob turns freely and can be made to ring a bell or provide some other conditioned reinforcement. If the answer is wrong, the knob will not turn. A counter may be added to tally wrong answers. The knob must then be reversed slightly and a second attempt at a right answer made. (Unlike the flash card, the device reports a wrong answer without giving the right answer.) When the answer is right, a further turn of the knob engages a clutch which moves the next problem into place in the window. This movement cannot be completed, however, until the sliders have been returned to zero.[66]

What Are the Advantages of the Use of Mechanical Teaching Devices?

Skinner claims a long list of advantages available through use of mechanical teaching devices in present-day classrooms.[67]

1. Reinforcement for the right answer is immediate.
2. Provided traces of earlier aversive control can be erased, mere manipulation of the device probably will be reinforcing enough to keep an average student at work for a suitable period each day.
3. All at one time, a teacher may supervise an entire class at work on such devices; yet each student may complete as many problems as possible in the class period and progress at his or her own rate.
4. Any person who is forced to leave school for a period may return at any time and continue from where he left off.
5. Each person may advance at his own rate and when he gets too far ahead of the class may be assigned to other tasks.
6. Through carefully designing materials, teachers may arrange problems in a serial order in the direction of an immensely complex repertoire.
7. Since the machines record the number of mistakes, tapes can be modified to enhance their effectiveness.
8. Knowing just what each student has done, a teacher can apply necessary supplementary reinforcement at the greatest vantage point.

In building a case for teaching machines, Skinner states, "the effect upon each student is surprisingly like that of a private tutor."[68] He then elaborates the nature of this similarity with the following points:

1. There is a constant interchange between programs and students; thus, the machine induces sustained activity.
2. The machine insists that a given point be thoroughly understood before the student moves on.
3. It presents that material for which the student is ready.
4. Partly through its constructed program and partly through its techniques of prompting or hinting, the machine helps the student to come up with the right answer.
5. Like a private tutor, it reinforces the student for every correct response.

Can Machines Teach a Child to Think?

Professor Skinner recognizes that "It is quite possible that the behavior of a man thinking is the most subtle and complex phenomenon ever submitted to scientific analysis."[69] But, he also emphasizes that thinking or originality is not absence of lawfulness and it should never be considered a spontaneous process. He points out that as long as thinking is identified with spontaneity or lawlessness it is a hopeless task to attempt systematically to influence a child's thinking in any way. Thinking, like the rest of the behavior of an organism, is a lawful process. Thus, verbal behavior, in terms of which human thinking eventually must be defined, should be treated in its own right as a substantial goal of education. In inculcating this behavior, learning devices can teach verbal thinking—establish the large and important repertoire of verbal relationships encountered in science and logic.

Skinner thinks it is of critical importance for us to realize that, in radical behaviorism, thought is not some mysterious process that is the cause of behavior, but the behavior itself. A human being thinking is a human being behaving, and human thought is operant, not reflexive, behavior. "Shakespeare's thought was his behavior *with respect to his extremely complex environment.*"[70] "In the broadest possible sense, the thought of Julius Caesar was simply the sum total of his responses to the complex world in which he lived."[71]

Skinner observes that study of what traditionally has been called the human mind is more appropriately a study of concepts and methods that have emerged from an analysis of behavior. Thinking behavior is verbal or nonverbal, overt or covert. It is primarily the verbal behavior of humanity that has survived in recorded form, but from this and other records we can know something about human nonverbal behavior. When we say that Caesar thought Brutus could be trusted we do not necessarily mean that he ever said as much. Rather he behaved verbally and otherwise as if Brutus could be trusted. The rest of Caesar's behavior, his nonverbal plans and achievements, were also part of his thoughts.

Although in earlier behavioristic analyses thinking was identified with subaudible talking, Skinner feels that nothing is gained by so doing. There are difficulties in assuming that covert behavior is always executed by the muscular apparatus responsible for the overt form. Furthermore, the data that give rise to the notion of covert speech can be treated, as such, with a high degree of rigor. Rather than identifying thinking with talking, a better case can be made for identifying it with a special kind of behaving, that which automatically affects behavior and is reinforcing because it does.

"It is important that the student should learn without being taught, solve problems by himself, explore the unknown, make decisions, and behave in original ways, and these activities should, if possible, be taught."[72] But we should not attempt to teach thinking while teaching subject matter. "If thinking can be analyzed and taught separately, the already-known can be transmitted with maximal efficiency."[73] "It is as important to define the terminal behavior in teaching thinking as in teaching knowledge."[74]

Thinking is more productive when verbal responses lead to specific consequences and are reinforced because they do so. Just as an artist paints what reinforces him visually, a speaker or writer says that which is reinforced by hearing it, or writes that which is reinforced by reading it. However, in any case the solution to a problem is simply a response that alters the situation so that another strong response can be emitted. "Reinforcing contingencies shape the behavior of the individual, and novel contingencies generate novel forms of behavior."[75]

The key to effective teaching of thinking, as well as any other behavior, is immediate feedback. To teach thinking, we should "analyze the behavior called 'thinking' and produce it according to specifications. A program specifically concerned with such behavior could be composed of material already available in logic, mathematics, scientific method, and psychology."[76]

NOTES

[1] B. F. Skinner, *About Behaviorism*, New York: Knopf, 1974, p. 225.

[2] B. F. Skinner, *The Behavior of Organisms*, New York: Appleton-Century-Crofts, 1938, p. 6.

[3] B. F. Skinner, *Cumulative Record*, 3d ed., New York: Appleton-Century-Crofts, 1972, p. 35. (This and other excerpts from *Cumulative Record* are reprinted by permission of Appleton-Century-Crofts.)

[4] Skinner, *Cumulative Record*, p. 34.

[5] See Donald K. Adams et al., *Learning Theory, Personality Theory, and Clinical Research*, New York: Wiley, 1954, p. 2.

[6] B. F. Skinner, *Science and Human Behavior*, New York: Macmillan, 1953, p. 38.

[7] Ibid., p. 64. (This and other excerpts from *Science and Human Behavior* are reprinted by permission of The Macmillan Company.)

[8] Ibid., pp. 63–64.

[9] See C. B. Ferster and B. F. Skinner, *Schedules of Reinforcement*, New York: Appleton-Century-Crofts, 1957.

[10] See B. F. Skinner, *The Technology of Teaching*, New York: Appleton-Century-Crofts, 1968, p. 14.

[11] B. F. Skinner, *Contingencies of Reinforcement*, New York: Appleton-Century-Crofts, 1969, p. 194.

[12] Skinner, *Science and Human Behavior*, p. 446.

[13] Ibid., p. 13.

[14] Skinner, *Contingencies of Reinforcement*, p. 143.

[15] Skinner, *About Behaviorism*, p. 231.

[16] Skinner, *Science and Human Behavior*, p. 32.

[17] Ibid., p. 23.

[18] B. F. Skinner, *Cumulative Record*, New York: Appleton-Century-Crofts, 1961, p. 201.

[19] B. F. Skinner, *Science and Human Behavior*, New York: Macmillan, 1953, p. 91.

[20] Skinner, *Contingencies of Reinforcement*, p. 294.

[21] Skinner, *Science and Human Behavior*, p. 46.

[22] Ibid., p. 448.

[23] Skinner, *Contingencies of Reinforcement*, p. 297.

[24] Skinner, *About Behaviorism*, p. 114.

[25] Skinner, *Cumulative Record*, p. 123.

[26] Skinner, *Science and Human Behavior*, p. 446.

[27] Richard I. Evans, *B. F. Skinner: The Man and His Ideas*, New York: Dutton, 1968, p. 65.

[28] Skinner, *About Behaviorism*, p. 248.

[29] Skinner, *Science and Human Behavior*, p. 258.

[30] Ibid., p. 286.

[31] Skinner, *Contingencies of Reinforcement*, p. 228.

[32] Ibid., p. 267.

[33] Skinner, *About Behaviorism*, p. 241.

[34] Ibid., p. 224.

[35] Ibid., p. 168.

[36] Skinner, *Science and Human Behavior*, p. 90.

[37] Skinner, *Contingencies of Reinforcement*, pp. 236–240.

[38] Skinner, *Science and Human Behavior*, p. 36.

[39] Ibid., p. 87.

[40] Ibid., p. 64.

[41] Skinner, *Contingencies of Reinforcement*, p. 23.

[42] Ibid., p. 175.

[43] Skinner, *Science and Human Behavior*, p. 112.

[44] Skinner, *Cumulative Record*, p. 82.

[45] Skinner, *Science and Human Behavior*, p. 173.

[46] Ibid., p. 123.

[47] Skinner, *Contingencies of Reinforcement*, pp. 160–170.

[48] Skinner, *Science and Human Behavior*, p. 92.

[49] B. F. Skinner, "The Design of Cultures," in Roger Ulrich, Thomas Stachnik, and John Mabry (eds.), *Control of Human Behavior*, Glenview, Ill.: Scott, Foresman, 1966, p. 333.

[50] See "How To Teach Animals," in Skinner, *Cumulative Record*, pp. 412–419.

[51] Skinner, *Science and Human Behavior*, p. 76.

[52] See B. F. Skinner, *Schedules of Reinforcement*, New York: Appleton-Century-Crofts, 1957, p. 728.

[53] Skinner, *Science and Human Behavior*, p. 94.

[54] Ibid., pp. 94–95.

[55] Ibid., p. 94.

[56] Ibid., p. 77.

[57] Skinner, *Contingencies of Reinforcement*, p. 15.

[58] Skinner, *The Technology of Teaching*, p. 41.

[59] See James G. Holland and B. F. Skinner, *The Analysis of Behavior*, New York: McGraw-Hill, 1961.

[60] Skinner, *Cumulative Record*, p. 300.

[61] Skinner, *The Technology of Teaching*, pp. 19–20.

[62] Ibid., p. 21.

[63] H. T. Fitzgerald, "Teaching Machines: A Demurrer," *The School Review* 70(Autumn 1962):248–249.

[64] Skinner, *The Technology of Teaching*, p. 22.

[65] Ibid., pp. 33–34.

[66] B. F. Skinner, *Cumulative Record*, p. 154.

[67] Skinner, *The Technology of Teaching*, p. 24.

[68] B. F. Skinner, "Teaching Machines," *Science* 128(October 24, 1958):971.

[69] Skinner, *The Technology of Teaching*, p. 140.

[70] B. F. Skinner, *Verbal Behavior*, New York: Appleton-Century-Crofts, 1957, p. 450.

[71] Ibid., pp. 451–452.

[72] Skinner, *The Technology of Teaching*, p. 116.

[73] Ibid., p. 116.

[74] Ibid., p. 117.

[75] Skinner, *Verbal Behavior*, p. 255.

[76] Skinner, *The Technology of Teaching*, p. 52.

BIBLIOGRAPHY

EVANS, RICHARD I. *B. F. Skinner: The Man and His Ideas.* New York: Dutton, 1968. A transcription of a taped interview with Professor Skinner wherein his position is set forth sharply and highly understandably. Recommended order of reading is chapters 3, 2, 1, 4, and 5.

FERSTER, C. B., and B. F. SKINNER. *Schedules of Reinforcement.* New York: Appleton-Century-Crofts, 1957. A report of scientific study of various reinforcement schedules.

FITZGERALD, H. T. "Teaching Machines: A Demurrer." *The School Review* 70(Autumn 1962):247–256. A well-written, sobering critique of machine teaching written by a director of education and training for an automotive parts plant. He considers mechanical reinforcement theory "an intrinsically undemocratic—worse, an antiintellectual—theory of learning" and concludes with the statement, "Teaching machines only teach (condition) machines."

GALANTER, EUGENE. *Automatic Teaching: The State of the Art.* New York: Wiley, 1959. A collection of papers, including one by B. F. Skinner, that treat the experimentation, analysis, and programming related to machine teaching. Chapter 15, "Teaching Machines and Psychological Theory," by Howard H. Kindler, is an excellent critique on the teaching machine movement.

HILGARD, ERNEST R., and GORDON H. BOWER. *Theories of Learning*, 4th ed. Englewood Cliffs, N.J.: Prentice-Hall, 1975. Chapter 7, "Skinner's Operant Conditioning," is a descriptive interpretation of Skinner's operant conditioning theory of learning.

HOLLAND, JAMES G., and B. F. SKINNER. *The Analysis of Behavior.* New York: McGraw-Hill, 1961. A programmed textbook for an introductory course in psychology to be used as a substitute for a teaching machine. A student is to learn the basic terms and principles of behavioristic conditioning; he writes the correct answer to a question, then is reinforced by finding it on the next page.

LUMSDAINE, A. A. "Educational Technology, Programmed Learning, and Instructional Science," in Ernest R. Hilgard, *Theories of Learning and Instruction*, National Society for the Study of Education. Chicago: University of Chicago Press, 1964. A comprehensive treatment of applications of programming to instructional procedures.

PRYOR, KAREN. "Behavior Modification: The Porpoise Caper." *Psychology Today* 3, no. 7 (December 1969):46–49, 64. Porpoises, in having their behaviors modified, seem to get the idea in regard to the "pay-off" and behave beyond the expectations of their trainers, that is, to show creative behavior. "Some of Malia's spontaneous stunts were so unusual that the trainers couldn't imagine achieving them with the shaping system."

SKINNER, B. F. *About Behaviorism.* New York: Knopf, 1974. Skinner's statement of the philosophy of the science of human behavior. His controversion of psychological positions that conflict with behaviorism. Lists and criticizes 20 statements commonly made about behaviorism. Behavioristically describes knowing and thinking processes.

SKINNER, B. F. *The Behavior of Organisms.* New York: Appleton-Century-Crofts, 1938. Skinner's early systematic statement of operant behavior and conditioning.

SKINNER, B. F. *Beyond Freedom and Dignity.* New York: Knopf, 1971. A presentation of Skinner's psychology for general consumption. Denies existence of either autonomous or cognitive man. An attack on the concepts human freedom and dignity.

SKINNER, B. F. "A Case History in Scientific Method," in Sigmund Koch, *Psychology: A Study of Science,* 2, *General Systematic Formulations, Learning, and Special Processes.* New York: McGraw-Hill, 1959. Skinner's own personal history illustrating his philosophy of science and psychology of behavior. He relates how he was operant-conditioned to perform in certain ways as he studied the conditioning of animals. The chapter is interesting reading. See pages 359–379.

SKINNER, B. F. *Contingencies of Reinforcement.* New York: Appleton-Century-Crofts, 1969. Professor Skinner's theoretical analysis of his psychological system and its comparison with other systems.

SKINNER, B. F. *Cumulative Record,* 3d ed. New York: Appleton-Century-Crofts, 1972. A series of Skinner's papers that reflect the implications of his position. Chapters on "The Science of Learning and the Art of Teaching" and "Teaching Machines" are particularly pertinent to our discussion in chapter 5.

SKINNER, B. F. "The Machine That Is Man." *Psychology Today* 2 (April 1969): 22–25, 60–64. Disposes of "inner man" by replacing him with genetic and environmental variables. "In pigeon and Indian alike, adventitious reinforcements generate ritualistic behavior."

SKINNER, B. F. *Science and Human Behavior.* New York: Macmillan, 1953. An application of "realistic" scientific method to a study of human behavior centered around operant conditioning. Scientific analysis is extended to the behavior of people in groups and the operation of controlling agencies such as government and religion. Its final section analyzes education as a process of control of human behavior.

SKINNER, B. F. "Teaching Machines." *Science* 128 (October 24, 1958): 969–977. Professor Skinner's strongest presentation of the use for teaching machines.

SKINNER, B. F. *The Technology of Teaching.* New York: Appleton-Century-Crofts, 1968. An expansion of the concept that teaching consists of arranging contingencies of reinforcement. Provides psychological rationale for making teaching a process of changing the behaviors of organisms.

SKINNER, B. F. *Verbal Behavior.* New York: Appleton-Century-Crofts, 1957. An explanation of how verbal behavior, including thinking, takes its place in the larger field of human behavior; it too is learned through operant conditioning. Ways of manipulating verbal behavior of individuals are tested.

SKINNER, B. F. *Walden Two.* New York: Macmillan, 1948. A novel proposing and describing a community within which maximum use is made of conditioning to control human welfare. It deals with the educational and social implications of behaviorism.

Chapter 14
WHAT IS THE COGNITIVE-FIELD THEORY OF LEARNING?

The basic thesis of cognitive-field psychology is that each person, in keeping with his (or her) attained level of development and understanding, does the best that he knows how for whatever he thinks he is. One's person, as used here, includes everything that one is involved in taking care of; it consists of every thing, idea, or principle with which one identifies one's self and to which one gives one's allegiance. The cognitive-field theory of learning is closely related to, and derived from, *cognitive* and *field* psychological theories.[1] The term *cognitive* is derived from the Latin verb *cognoscere*, which means "to know." The *cognitive* aspect of cognitive-field theory deals with the problem of how people gain an understanding of themselves and their environments and how, using their cognitions, they act in relation to their environments. A psychological *field* consists of the simultaneous concurrent interrelationships of a person and his (or her) psychological environment in any one situation. Hence, field theory in psychology centers on the idea that all psychological activity of a person, at a given juncture of time, is a function of a totality of coexisting factors that are mutually interdependent.

An astronomer uses field to describe the universe and predict the orbits of stars. A biologist relates the function of cells to their location in a growth "field." A physicist uses field in his study of the structure of an atom. Similarly, a cognitive-field oriented psychologist uses field to mean the total psychological world in which a person lives at a given time. It includes a *psychological* past, present, and future, also a certain concrete or imaginative level of psychological reality—all interpreted as simultaneous aspects of a current situation.

Cognitive-field learning theory draws heavily from the pioneer field psychology of Kurt Lewin (1890–1947). The German-American psychologist Lewin was interested primarily in a study of human motivation. Consequently, his field theory was developed not as a theory of learning, but as a theory of motivation and perception. However, he was concerned with the application of his theory to learning situations, and he did some writing in this vein.[2] Lewin's basic, comprehensive concept was *life space*. Consequently, life space has become a model for relativistic psychological thinking. It includes everything that one needs to know about a person in order to understand his (or her) concrete behavior in a specific psychological environment at a given time. Accordingly, it encompasses the *person* under consideration and his (or her) *psychological environment*.

Lewin's field psychology more precisely is called *topological and vector* psychology. In developing his psychology he borrowed ideas and concepts from other disciplines, especially geometry and physics. The key concepts that he borrowed were *topology* from geometry and *vector* from physics. However, in using these and related concepts, he did not adhere rigidly to the definitions of their mother sciences, but construed them in a manner most useful to his system of psychology. (The meanings of these concepts are developed in pp. 363–366.)

Some others who have made worthy contributions to cognitive-field theory are Gordon W. Allport, Adelbert Ames, Jr., Roger G. Barker, Ernest E. Bayles, Boyd H. Bode, Jerome S. Bruner, Hadley Cantril, Arthur W. Combs, Morton Deutsch, John Dewey, Sigmund Koch, Rollo May, Donald Snygg, Edward C. Tolman, and Herbert F. Wright.

WHAT IS THE PURPOSE OF COGNITIVE-FIELD LEARNING THEORY?

The purpose of cognitive-field psychology is to formulate tested relationships that are predictive of the behavior of individual persons in their specific life spaces or psychological situations. In order to understand and predict such behavior one must consider a person and his (or her) psychological environment as a pattern of interdependent facts and functions. Cognitive-field psychology is an interpersonal, social psychology that constitutes an effective vehicle for understanding people as interacting persons. In the interactive process a person and his psychological environment are construed as *interdependent* variables. Thus, a person is neither dependent upon, nor independent of, his environment. Likewise, a person's environment is neither made by him nor independent of him.

The cognitive-field theory of learning has been developed primarily for the purpose of helping teachers understand other people, especially students. But it also may help teachers understand themselves better.

Within cognitive-field theory, learning, briefly defined, is an interactional process within which a person attains new insights or cognitive structures or changes old ones. To promote learning effectively, teachers must concern themselves with other people. So, the ideas of cognitive-field psychology have been developed with the hope and expectation that they will help teachers do a better job of understanding other persons. Because of its unique purpose, cognitive-field psychology makes no attempt to describe some absolute reality that is just there independently of our experiencing it. Instead, it develops a psychological system that is fruitful in dealing with children and youth in learning situations.

This theory of learning has been formulated in an attempt to construct scientific principles that are highly applicable to classroom situations. Its advocates are convinced that, in light of the present stage of scientific development, this theory of learning is more likely than any other of which they are cognizant to lead to the most productive results in classroom procedures.

A cognitive-field theory of learning describes how a person gains understanding of himself and his universe in a situation so construed that his self and his psychological environment compose a totality of mutually interdependent, coexisting factors. It involves the kind of generalizations about learning that may be applied to actual persons in school situations, and it is associated with the knowing and understanding functions that give meaning to situations. It is built around the purposes that underlie behavior, the goals that are involved in behavior, and persons' means and processes of understanding themselves and their environments as they function in relation to their goals. Any understandings that persons gain in regard to themselves and their worlds are generalized *insights*.

WHAT IS AN INSIGHT?

An insight, concisely defined, is a basic sense of, or feeling for, relationships. Thus, it is a meaning or discernment. A tested generalized insight is an understanding, that is, it is a meaning or discernment that one may apply to several or even many similar, but not necessarily identical, situations or processes. In other words, it is an expectation or recognized rule. Although there is nothing about an insight that requires it to be right in any absolutistic sense, it is a grasp of a situation that often does go deeper than words. Thus, it is a realizing sense of a matter. So, insight into a situation is its meaning. *Meaning*, so used, denotes that to which an object or idea points or what it signifies. The insights of a person, however, are not equated with either his (or her) consciousness or awareness or his ability to describe them verbally; instead, their essence is a sense of, or feeling for, pattern in a life situation. (See Chapter 15, p. 379, for further explanation of insight.) A person may gain an insight through experiencing only one case. However, the most valuable insights are those confirmed by enough similar cases to be generalized into an understanding.

A person's insights collectively constitute the cognitive structure of her (or his) life space. However, the term insight sometimes also is used in a generic sense to mean cognitive structure. *Cognitive structure* means the person's perception of the psychological aspects of the personal, physical, and social world. Such a world includes a person and all of his or her facts, concepts, beliefs, memory traces, and expectations. Consequently, changes in the cognitive structure of life spaces prevail in the learning of language, emotions, attitudes, actions, and social interrelations. Now, let us review an episode of insightful learning as observed by one of the authors.

During World War II, the author watched a group of noncommissioned officers teaching recruits in basic training to fire army rifles (the author was one of these recruits). Army rifles have a powerful recoil or kick. A soldier is supposed to squeeze the trigger gradually and smoothly until the rifle fires. Recruits usually anticipate the recoil and jump before the shell explodes; thus, their aim is completely spoiled. The problem for a noncom was to teach his "student" not to make the anticipatory jump. Recruits were convinced that they really did not jump until after the explosion, thus hours of pointed verbal comment had little, if any, effect. Corporal Jones helped his "student" gain an insight: He "scolded" him several times for jumping, with no avail. Then while his student's attention was diverted to a fellow sufferer, the corporal slipped a fired cartridge into the firing chamber. The recruit aimed, started to squeeze, and again jumped, thereby gaining an insight. He was jumping before his rifle fired and thus ruining his aim. His jumping before the rifle had fired soon ceased.

HOW MIGHT WE TEACH INSIGHTFULLY?

Next, let us examine how we might teach a school subject insightfully. Our illustration is taken from the subject of arithmetic, specifically the teaching of the multiplication combinations involving the 9s. We use the 9s because these combinations generally are considered the most difficult. Furthermore, we use arithmetic because many teachers feel that, however one might teach other subjects, arithmetic must be taught by rote.

In what specific ways does this lesson in arithmetic differ from traditional procedures used in teaching the multiplication tables? The answer to this question will express the significance of cognitive-field psychology for learning and teaching.

This arithmetic lesson, as it develops, reflects the teacher's conviction that learning is an insightful process. The teacher is attempting to aid students in improving their understandings or insights in regard to multiplying by 9 and is doing it in such a way as to heighten their abilities to achieve new insights independently; he or she is not merely giving students a gimmick.

Let us assume that we are in a fourth-grade class and are ready to attack the 9s. We already have learned the 2s, 3s, 5s, 10s, and 11s, and we have learned them in such a way as to have developed insight into the relationships involved in these tables. We can anticipate a dialogue between students and teacher that might go somewhat as follows:

The teacher reminds the students of the combinations they already know and has them review these until it is clear that they know them well. The review process might appear on the surface as drill in the old-fashioned sense, but there is a fundamental difference. The teacher makes certain that students understand the relationships involved, that is, relationships of the same general type as those they are about to learn in connection with the 9s. After the review, the teacher suggests that the class advance to the 9s. (Some students are likely to protest that the 9s are more difficult than any of the others.)

The teacher begins writing the 9s table on the chalkboard, at the same time asking members of the class to supply answers that they already will have learned from their earlier study of the other tables. A "side trip" may be necessary to help students grasp, or perhaps only review, the insight that the product of 9×2 is the same as that of 2×9 (the commutative property). What appears on the chalkboard is something like this.

$$9 \times 1 = 09 \qquad 9 \times 7 =$$
$$9 \times 2 = 18 \qquad 9 \times 8 =$$
$$9 \times 3 = 27 \qquad 9 \times 9 =$$
$$9 \times 4 = \qquad 9 \times 10 = 90$$
$$9 \times 5 = 45 \qquad 9 \times 11 = 99$$
$$9 \times 6 = \qquad 9 \times 12 =$$

To this point, the answers supplied are based on students' prior learning of the 2s, 3s, 5s, 10s, and 11s. Let us now envisage the following dialogue:

TEACHER: How do we know the answers to 9×1, 9×2, and 9×3?

CLASS: Because we know the 1s, 2s, and 3s.

TEACHER: And what about 9×5, 9×10, and 9×11?

CLASS: We know these because we know the 5s, 10s, and 11s.

TEACHER: The ones that are left are the hard ones, aren't they? What is the answer to 9×7, Jimmie? Tell me without looking at the tables in your book. (Within this type of instruction procedure, when addressing Jimmie or any other pupil, the teacher anticipates that at least most members of the class are thinking along with the obvious student participant.)

Jimmie probably will say nothing but will stare at the teacher, baffled. The teacher may then ask various other members of the class the answer to 9×6, 9×8, and 9×4. After the class begins to demonstrate a certain amount of bafflement (perhaps approaching the point of mild frustration), the teacher may entice them in this manner: "Would you like to gain enough understanding of the rest of the 9s so that after today you will know the answers to all of them?" The class is likely to respond in the affirmative with considerable enthusiasm.

TEACHER: All right, let's work at this thing together. June, go to the board and write the 10s up to 10×5 right beside the 9s. (The class now will have before it the following combinations.)

$10 \times 1 = 10$	$9 \times 1 = 09$
$10 \times 2 = 20$	$9 \times 2 = 18$
$10 \times 3 = 30$	$9 \times 3 = 27$
$10 \times 4 = 40$	$9 \times 4 =$
$10 \times 5 = 50$	$9 \times 5 = 45$

TEACHER: When we compare the 9s that we have answered to the 10s, what difference do we see in the answers? What happens in the case of the 9s which did not happen in the 10s?

CLASS: Each step we move up in the 9s, one is lost.

TEACHER: How do you mean?

CLASS: 9×1 is one fewer than 10×1, 9×2 is two fewer than 10×2, and 9×3 is three fewer than 10×3. That is why we get the answers 09, 18, and 27.

Of course, finding this principle may not come as easily as the foregoing dialogue might suggest. The teacher might need to do quite a lot more "fishing" by rephrasing the question and perhaps even offering some hints. The speed with which a class comes to see for itself principles that are new to it depends much upon what atmosphere has been established and, of course, on the brightness of the students.

The teacher next helps students see that as in the 10s, the first digit goes up one each time, 09, 18, 27. By this time, the stage should be set for supplying the missing answers.

TEACHER: Now think carefully about what we have learned. Since $9 \times 2 = 18$ and $9 \times 3 = 27$, Gary, what is the answer to 9×4?

GARY: 36.

TEACHER: Why?

GARY: Well, if the first number increases by one for each larger table, and if we lose one in the last number of each table upward, it would have to be 36.

TEACHER: You already know the answer to 9×5. Judy, does it check with the idea that we have learned?

JUDY: Sure the first number will be one larger, and we will have lost five numbers from the second number. That makes 45.

The reader should not be misled by the foregoing hypothetical dialogue. In order to economize on space, students have been pictured as saying the right thing the first time. In an actual classroom situation there would be more hesitancy, more fumbling, more tries on the part of students and teacher. But the process would remain essentially the same.

The class now is ready to deepen its insights in relation to the multiplication process.

TEACHER: Look again at the first digit of each answer. (Teacher points to the 9s through 9×5.) Look at each of these digits in relation to the multipliers, 1, 2, 3, 4, and 5. Do you see anything interesting?

GARY: Why, the first digit of the answer is always just one number smaller than the multiplier.

TEACHER: Why do you think this is so?

GARY: Would this be caused by losing a number each time—I mean, losing a number as compared with the 10s?

The teacher has succeeded in evoking the insight (at least in Gary) that when one multiplies by 9 rather than 10, there is a loss of one at each step, including the first. The answers "never catch up," so to speak. They keep falling behind, but according to a definite and predictable pattern.

Still another relationship may be taught the class:

TEACHER: Look carefully at the answers that we have so far. (The teacher points to 09, 18, 27, 36, and 45.) Add the two digits of each answer and see what happens.

CLASS: The sum of the digits is the same in each answer. The sum is always 9.

TEACHER: Yes. $0 + 9 = 9$; $1 + 8 = 9$; $2 + 7 = 9$. Why is this so?

CLASS: $9 \times 1 = 9$, then the first digit always increases by one, and the second digit decreases by one. They kind of balance each other, so the sum remains the same.

By this time the stage has been set for teaching the remaining combinations involving the 9s. When asked the answer to 9×7, students should reason that the first digit of the answer will be 6 $(7 - 1)$ and that the second digit should be 3 $(9 - 6)$. The class now should be able to complete the combinations through 9×10 easily. At 9×11, the first digit of the answer becomes two less than the multiplier. (Why?) Furthermore, the sum of the two digits of the answer does not equal 9, as it did in each preceding step. (Again, why?) Students will know the answer is 99. The problem is, why? Answer: $9 \times 10 = 90$; at 9×11 "we start around again"; $90 + 9 = 99$. At 9×11 the first digit of the answer has lost two from the multiplier: $11 - 2 = 9$, so in 9×12 the first part of the answer is $12 - 2$ or 10. For the sum of the digits to add to 9, the last digit is 8. Thus, $12 \times 9 = 108$. This can be extended into a game.

$13 \times 9 = 117$
$14 \times 9 = 126$
$15 \times 9 = 135$

The class members now are ready to test their new insights to see whether they will work. The teacher may suggest to his or her better students that they put into words the insights they have learned. However, it should be borne in mind that it is not always necessary for one to put an insight into words in order to use it.

HOW DOES COGNITIVE-FIELD LEARNING THEORY DIFFER FROM THE STIMULUS-RESPONSE CONDITIONING THEORIES?

Some features of cognitive-field learning theory make it distinctly different from the mechanistic S-R conditioning theories. The most important of these features are (1) cognitive-field theory's emphasis upon psychological functions rather than objects, (2) its focus upon contemporaneous situations, (3) its relativistic-interactional approach to an understanding of perception, and (4) its interpretation of intelligent behavior as being purposive. We expand each of these features in the following sections.

Why Emphasis upon Psychological Functions?

A fallacy of behaviorists, noted by relativistic cognitive-field theorists, has been their tendency to describe the character of an activity by its physical aspects only and to neglect the great effect of the psychological setting. Psychological, as used here, means in accordance with the logic of a growing mind or intelligence. So, to be psychological in his or her pursuits, a cognitive-field psychologist looks at the world through the eyes of the learner. To describe a situation psychologically, he (or she), to the best of his ability, describes the situation that confronts the individual under study. So, cognitive-field psychology emphasizes psychological functions, relationships, and events as contrasted with physical objects and their movement.

Advocates of cognitive-field psychology do not deny the importance of the workings of the nervous system. Furthermore, they are interested in the results of recent research in neurophysiological functions. But, they do challenge the need to understand biological neurology in order to develop an adequate picture of the learning process. In 1975, Hilgard and Bower wrote, "both the nervous system and its behavior are complicated and neither will be understood with any completeness for a long time."[3]

But, for cognitive-field theorists, this does not mean that it is impossible to develop an adequate and harmonious conception of learning.

A "psychological" interpretation of life opens the way for extensive use of systematic constructs. Whereas a behaviorist restricts his or her generalizations to those based on the use of "objective" data, a cognitive-field psychologist knowingly uses constructs that go beyond the observable data. A *construct* is an invented idea. It is a named generalized concept that is not directly observable but formed from data that are observed. Its purpose is to correlate a broad range of data having some basic functional similarity, despite their marked superficial differences. A *need*, psychologically defined, is an example of a construct. Since it has no length, breadth, thickness, or mass, it cannot be observed. Yet it is a crucial, functional concept in studying human activity.

Why the Focus upon Contemporaneous Situations?

Whereas mental discipline, apperception, and behaviorism are historical approaches to the study of human behavior and motivation, cognitive-field psychology is a situational or ahistorical approach. That is, whereas the first three psychologies study the pasts of individuals in order to predict their futures, cognitive-field psychology studies the presents of persons in order to apprehend their presents and thereby predict their futures.

SITUATIONAL EMPHASIS

A definitive characteristic of cognitive-field learning theory is that a study always begins with a description of a current situation as a whole—the psychological field or life space—and proceeds to specific detailed analyses of various aspects of the situation. At no time are aspects of a field viewed as isolated elements. In the study of a life space with its various constructs, the idea constantly is kept to the forefront that no two constructs or concepts are mutually exclusive, but that everything to some degree and in some sense is dependent upon everything else. Readers are cautioned that, should they slip into giving the constructs independent physical or biological existence, they will be attempting to understand a relativistic psychology in a mechanistic fashion. A person's living in a world entails his or her living in a series of situations. The person is in the situation and the situation is in the person.

PRINCIPLE OF CONTEMPORANEITY

The principle of contemporaneity is the essential feature of cognitive-field psychology that is most often misunderstood. *Contemporaneity* literally means "all at one time." A psychological field or life space is a construct of such nature that it contains everything psychological that is taking place in relation to a specific person at a given time. The unit of time, microscopically viewed, is a moment; however, macroscopically considered, it may cover hours or even weeks. Whatever the expanse of time, everything is going on at once—that is the meaning of field. Readers are urged neither to reject the concept of contemporaneity summarily nor to give it an oversimplified interpretation.

The principle of contemporaneity means that *psychological* events are activated by conditions that prevail at the time behavior occurs. One cannot derive behavior from either the future or the past as such. Both behaviorists and cognitive-field psychologists see little basis for supposing a future cause of present events. However, cognitive-field psychologists differ sharply from behaviorists in their insistence that any attempts at derivation of the cause of human behavior from the past is equally metaphysical, that is, beyond the realm of science. Since past events do not now exist, they cannot as such have any effect on the present. Thus, influence of a future can only be anticipatory, and effects of a past can only be indirect. Nevertheless, through the continuity of life spaces, past psychological fields do have their "trace" or residue in a present field, which influences a person's behavior. *Trace* is a region or condition of a present life space that has similarity to a characteristic of earlier life spaces. In other words, trace means that there is some similarity between respective regions of succeeding life spaces. This is the psychological basis of memory. When, in solving a current problem, a person uses an insight acquired earlier, the insight is an example of trace.

An individual's views about the past, as about the rest of the physical and social world, are often incorrect; nevertheless, they constitute a significant psychological past in his (or her) own life space. Furthermore, the goals of an individual as a psychological fact lie in the present, and they too constitute an essential part of his current life space. The contents of the goals may lie in the future, and they may never occur; but the nature of an expectation is not dependent upon the event's coming to pass. If a high school student is studying chemistry so that in the future she is more likely to gain admittance to a medical school, whether or not she eventually is actually admitted to a medical school has no bearing upon her studying chemistry in high school. Her studying chemistry is a part—a goal region—of her contemporaneous life space; it takes the form of a current expectation.

Cognitive-field psychologists grant that in order for them to understand a person's present personality structure, it is often convenient and perhaps necessary to inquire into the individual's personal history. But, such inquiry is merely a means of knowing the present structure of his (or her) life space. A person's psychological field that exists at a given time contains, as well as the environment of the present, the views of that individual about his future and his past. So, any psychological past or psychological future is a simultaneous part of a psychological field or life space that exists at a given time. It is the contemporary meaning of events that influences our behavior in relation to them. Present situations are influenced by past or future ones if, and only if, the past or future ones, as viewed in the present, make the present appear differently than it otherwise would. So, psychologically, there is no past or future except as it enters into the present (see Figure 15.2, p. 377).

Why a Relativistic-Interactional Approach to an Understanding of Perception?

When a person perceives his (or her) world, he does not develop a photographic image of exactly what is "out there." Instead, he views, selects, simplifies, compares, completes, combines, separates, and places into context the objects of his experience. Furthermore, it is only through his viewing his patterns of experience as a whole that he comes to understand, and thereby is able to explain, what he experiences.

Psychologically speaking, a human life may be considered to consist of a series of distinguishable person-environment interactions within which neither objective physical nor objective social factors have a one-to-one psychological relation to a person. Thus, there is no known way that a person can experience the absolute nature of things-in-themselves. What a person does experience is *that which he (or she) makes of* what he gains from his environment as he pursues his various goals. Accordingly, cognitive-field theory represents a relativistic, as opposed to an absolutistic mechanistic, way of viewing human beings and their learning process. Readers are warned that should they attempt to understand its concepts mechanistically, they will not grasp this theory. (See pages 43–50 for a contrast of mechanistic and purposive outlooks.)

Mechanists attempt to explain all the fullness and variety of a universe in terms of machinelike objects and movements. Thus, mechanists in psychology consider a person an organism that is a product of its unique history of stimulus-response patterns. Consequently, they reduce all human activities to movements, usually in terms of stimuli and responses. Just as an automobile is built by workers who assemble its respective parts, a person is educated by teachers who feed into his (or her) physiological make-up the various aspects of environment that make him what mechanistic teachers want him to be.

The basic principle of *relativism* or *interactionism* is that nothing is perceivable or conceivable as a thing-in-itself. Rather, everything is perceived or conceived in relation to other things. That is, a thing is perceived as a figure against a background, experienced from a given angle or direction of envisionment. Furthermore, how a person perceives his (or her) environment depends upon the degree of his maturity, his knowledge, and his goals. Consequently, relativism means that psychological reality is defined, not in "objective," physical terms, but in psychological, perceptual ones.[4]

The term interaction is commonly used by both behavioristic and cognitive-field theorists in describing the person-environment process through which reality is perceived. But, the families of psychology define the term in sharply different ways. Whereas S-R conditioning theorists mean the *serial alternating reaction* first of organism, then of environment, cognitive-field psychologists imply that the interaction of a person and his or her environment is *simultaneous* and *mutual*—both participate at the same time.

BEHAVIORISTIC ALTERNATING REACTION

Alternating reaction, that is, passive interaction, begins with a reaction of a person or organism to a stimulus. The person is regarded as a passively waiting receiver of stimuli. When one receives a stimulus one responds in whatever way one must, that is, in accordance with both the conditioned and the innate behaviors that are called into play. Then, in turn, when one reacts, one is likely to change one's physical or social environment in some way. Thus, there is passive interaction. (The environment also is passive, in the sense that it "waits" for the organism to do something to it.) To a behaviorist, the temporal sequence of the interactive process is stimulus-reaction-stimulus-reaction, and so on. The chain of S-Rs may continue indefinitely. Consider an example. A dog bites a person; the person kicks the dog. Let us suppose the kick conditions the dog not to bite. The dog is friendly toward the next person he encounters, and the person reacts by patting him on the head. The dog may then react by licking the person's hand. The person may then give the dog a bite of hamburger. And so on, ad infinitum.

Behaviorists tend to think of interaction as involving only physical processes, that is, material objects reacting to other material objects. So interaction between human beings is analogous to interaction of molecules in a chemical compound. One molecule strikes another, which is deflected against another, which hits another, and so on. Thus, the interactive process is regarded as a chain of causes and effects; stimuli are causes and responses are effects.

COGNITIVE-FIELD SIMULTANEOUS MUTUAL INTERACTION

Interaction, when used by cognitive-field psychologists, refers to a relationship between a person and his (or her) psychological environment in which the person in purposeful fashion tries to give meaning to his environment and use objects in his environment in advantageous ways. The field or life space that influences an individual is described not in "objective," physical terms, but in the way it exists for that person at that time. Thus, there is no attempt to explain psychological behavior in terms of the relationship of a biological organism and its physical or geographical environment. In field psychology, the psychological concept *person* is much broader than is the biological concept *organism*. Gone from the cognitive-field concept of interaction is the idea of the reaction of a passive organism to a stimulus and an ensuing chain of S-Rs running back and forth from organism to environment. Rather, we now have a simultaneous mutual relation of a person and his or her psychological environment, during which the two are not mutually exclusive, so we do not make a sharp distinction between them. In symbolic terms, this concept is *simultaneous mutual interaction*—the *SMI* concept. So, *perception, relativistically and interactionally defined, is a cognitive experiential process within which a person, psychologically, simultaneously reaches out to his (or her) environment, encounters some aspects of it, brings those aspects into relationship with himself, makes something of those aspects, acts in relation to what he makes of them, and realizes the consequences of the entire process.*

Perception, here, is interpreted in its broadest possible sense. It does not mean mere consciousness. There is evidence from observation of both human and lower animal behavior that one cannot use consciousness as the sole criterion of what is a part of a life space. A child playing in the yard behaves differently when his mother is home than when she is out, yet he probably at no time verbalizes—is specifically aware of—her being either home or away. Children in a schoolroom with teacher A conduct themselves quite differently from when they are with teacher B. Yet they may at no time consciously formulate the two patterns of behavior.

To a cognitive-field psychologist, it is what occurs psychologically in a person's life space at that moment, or a longer juncture of time, that is most important to that person. A person interacts by relating himself, as he (or she) understands himself, to his interpretation of what is around him. Of course, while interacting, one may move one's body and manipulate objects in one's physical environment in ways conspicuous to observers. But psychological interaction and physical reaction are two different processes. A person can interact within a psychological field while sitting in an armchair in front of a fireplace. Human experience is synonymous with an interactive event. It does not necessarily require any kind of motion that an observer can detect.

Any idea can be ridden too hard, and the reader has probably already thought of cases in which the concept *SMI* does not seem to fit. For example, a person who is not aware of danger may be shot in the back. It seems fairly clear that in such a case the person has been a passive victim of a feature of the environment that was active in relation to him or her. However, all this example suggests is that there are situations in which a person has little control over what happens to him. Adherents of cognitive-field psychology do not deny this; instead, they operate on the assumption that, whenever a person can, he (or she) seeks to manipulate purposefully all those aspects of the environment that at the time mean anything to him. He may or may not be successful, but whether or not he is, his life space will be different as a result of the attempt.

EXAMPLES OF PERCEPTUAL INTERACTION

In apparently the same situation, a person at different times may perceive quite different aspects of a situation and behave accordingly. Furthermore, provision of opportunity for one to perceive certain aspects of a physical or social environment in a certain way by no means guarantees that that particular perception will occur or that the perception that does occur will have anything like a one-to-one relationship to the objective environment as it appears to someone else. Adelbert Ames, E. Engel, and Hadley Cantril have performed experiments at the Institute for Associated Research, Hanover, New Hampshire, that show that in perception nothing is absolutely fixed. Rather, one interprets everything in terms of the situation as a whole. What one perceives, that is, one's psychological reality, consists of what one *makes of* what seems to be oneself and one's environment. Depending on the insights or understandings that a person brings to a particular occasion, he (or she) seems to give meaning and order to things in terms of his own needs, abilities, and purposes.[5] A description of an experiment performed at the Hanover Institute will give some idea of the nature and significance of these studies.

Cantril experimented with a pair of stereograms. Each stereogram was a photograph of a statue in the Louvre; one a madonna with child, the other a lovely young female nude. A typical simultaneous viewing of the pair of stereograms proceeded as follows: The subject first saw only a madonna with child, then a few seconds later exclaimed, "But now she is undressing!" She had somehow lost the baby she was holding and her robe had slipped from her shoulders. Then in a few more seconds she lost her robe completely and became the young nude. Sometimes the process is reversed. Other people never see the nude and other never see the madonna. Apparently, what a person "sees" in a situation depends upon his needs, abilities, purposes, and insights, as well as upon what is "out there."

Now, one more example of perceptual interaction. Parents and siblings usually constitute important aspects of a child's psychological environment. When a second child arrives in a family, the first child sizes up—perceives—the situation. Whether the first child feels rejected depends, not upon the physical stimuli as such that he (or she) receives from his parents and the sibling, but upon what he makes of the relationship of the parents and the second child. The important question is not, Do the parents actually favor child number two? but rather, Does child number one "see" child number two as favored over child number one—himself? In this situation, the parents and the other child are key aspects of each child's and parent's psychological environment. The way child number one perceives the situation has important bearing upon the environments of child number two and the parents. Each person in a situation interacts with the others.

EXPERIENCE: AN INSIGHTFUL PROCESS

Cognitive-field psychologists, in general, give their conception of *experience* a major place in their learning theories. But, they define experience in terms of persons' purposively interacting with their respective psychological environments. Many behaviorists, led by B. F. Skinner, espouse *radical behaviorism*, which means that they have little or no place in their learning theory for such concepts as experience, awareness, or consciousness. They may concede that thought appears to occur, but they are likely to insist that, if human beings are to be studied with true scientific objectivity, most kinds of mentalistic concepts must be ruled out of bounds. Professor Skinner has expressed this notion clearly:

> the private event [that is, thought or consciousness] is at best no more than a link in a causal chain, and it is usually not even that. We may think before we act in the sense that we may behave covertly before we behave overtly, but our action is not an "expression" of the covert reponse [that is, thought] or the consequence of it. The two are attributable to the same variables.[6]

Some other behaviorists do use the term *experience*, but they interpret it mechanistically. Accordingly, to them, it means the conditioning process by which a human organism either learns new responses or changes old ones as the result of stimuli impinging on its sensory organs. If a child touches a hot stove and a link is formed between the sight of a stove and a withdrawal response, then it might be said that the child has had an experience. No thought needs to have occurred and no insights need to have been developed.

Cognitive-field psychologists use the term experience extensively, but define it in a way consistent with their positive-relativistic outlook. Accordingly, they regard experience as being rooted in insightful behavior. From this point of view, experience is a psychological event that involves a person's acting purposefully with anticipation of the probable or possible consequences of such action. So, experience is interaction of a person and his or her perceived environment. This is what Dewey meant when he said, "An experience is always what it is because of a transaction taking place between an individual and what, *at the time*, constitutes his environment."[7]

Why the Emphasis upon Purposiveness of Intelligent Behavior?

To repeat, the basic thesis of cognitive-field psychology is that any person, at his (or her) level of development and understanding, does the best that he knows how for whatever he thinks he is. In other words, any boy or girl in any situation, at the time that he is doing whatever he is doing, is doing that because, in keeping with the understandings that he holds at that particular time, it is the best way that he knows how to take care of himself.

A human being is born a very complex biological organism in a social environment. Throughout his (or her) waking hours, as a baby, later as a child, and then as a youth, he learns by trying various acts and seeing what happens. Thus, through his purposive living in a human environment, an individual develops as a person or self. (Within cognitive-field psychology person and self are synonymous concepts and so are used here interchangeably.)

Only by his living in a human world and having a biological organism of a unique type does a biological human being emerge as a psychological person or self. The form that the development of selfhood takes depends upon the learning that results from the purposive interaction of the person and his psychological environment. This contrasts sharply with S-R conditioning theories, which either ignore goal or purpose completely or make it only peripheral and incidental. Behaviorists have tended to consider any concept of goal direction or purposiveness to be teleological. To them, teleological means deriving present behavior from the future. Consequently it sounds mystical and superstitious. Thus, they have placed emphasis upon past events as the cause of present behavior. They have seemed to overlook the possibility of the "presentness" of causes of behavior. It is because cognitive-field psychology is goal centered that its theorists inveigh against the use of such mechanistic terms as reflex arc, connectionism, conditioning, associationism, and reinforcement in dealing with learning.

Within cognitive-field psychology, *purposive* is virtually a synonym for *intelligent;* it signifies an intentionality that need not be conscious. A unique characteristic of human beings is their capacity to pursue long-sighted, as well as short-sighted, self-interests. Cognitive-field psychologists recognize the significance of this fact. When a child or youth is behaving purposively, he (or she) is pursuing his goals in light of the insights he has available; he is behaving intelligently. The goal or goals toward which the individual strives psychologically exist in his present life space. The phenomenon of goal is such that expectation—not actual realization—is its essence. Although the content of a goal may be in the future or may not occur at all, the goal as a psychological fact necessarily lies in the present life space. For example, a student's goal to become a teacher is a goal toward teaching as the student now sees it. However, this goal may be a far cry from teaching as it eventually is experienced.

The *purposiveness* of cognitive-field psychology is *immanent in*—operating within, *not transcendental to*—not extending beyond—the world of experience; it prevails in workaday life situations. That is, careful study of children and youth (as well as of other animate beings) in life situations indicates that if they are acting at all they are trying to do something, and that it is only through our anticipating what they are trying to do that we can predict most accurately what they are going to do. Whether there is transcendental, supernatural purpose in the universe is another problem, which is related only indirectly to the concept *purposive* as developed in cognitive-field psychology. Relativistic purposiveness is immanent. Purposiveness, so construed, simply means that individuals act in such a way as to achieve their goal or goals—satisfy their wants or desires—in the quickest and easiest way that they comprehend or sense as possible under existing conditions. When one is motivated toward doing something, one's description of the matter is that one wants or desires to do it. So, one's purposive activity is carried forward toward a goal by a process of one's constantly searching out the conditions for the next step all along the way.

Whereas mental disciplinarians generally have held that people are endowed with *free will,* and logical empiricistic behaviorists have adhered to *determinism*—the opposite of free will—positive relativistic cognitive-field theorists emphasize *situational choice.* This means that, at any juncture of a person's continuous, overlapping life spaces, he (or she), to some extent, may choose which way he is going to turn next. So, cognitive-field theorists postulate that people exercise choice, but they neither assert nor imply identification with either side of the metaphysical free will-determinism antimony. Instead, they simply mean, to quote Dewey, that "Every intelligent act involves selection of certain things as means to other things as their consequences."[8]

WHAT ARE THE KEY CONSTRUCTS OF COGNITIVE-FIELD THEORY?

We may divide the key constructs or invented ideas of cognitive-field psychology into five pivotal concepts and a number of auxiliary ones. The pivotal concepts are *life space, topology, vector, person,* and *psychological environment.* Life space, the principal construct, is an individual's psychological world or contemporaneous situation, which includes the person and his (or her) psychological environment. We describe each of the pivotal concepts in some detail, after which we provide definitions of the auxiliary concepts.

For one to grasp fully the ideas of a cognitive-field psychology, it is essential that its key concepts be defined precisely as they are used in this frame of reference. In studying these concepts, readers should keep in mind the essential idea of field psychology, that is, the meanings of all its constructs are mutually interdependent. Each depends for its meaning upon the meanings of all the others. Thus, there are no independent, intervening, and dependent variables as in S-R conditioning theories;

instead, all of the variables or constructs of cognitive-field psychology are interdependent.

What Is a Life Space?

The concept *life space* constitutes an instrument whereby one may be objective in studying human activity by being, to some degree, subjective. A teacher may conjecture, "What would I be thinking if I were a student and were acting that way?" or "If I were in his situation, why would I be acting the way he is?" Life space, then, is a model of psychological reality or functional relationships developed for the purpose of describing what is possible and what is impossible for the person being studied, and of anticipating or predicting what he (she) is likely to be thinking and doing now as well as what his subsequent thoughts and actions will be.

A life space represents not physical objects as such, but functional and symbolic relationships. Hence, it includes not only presently perceived objects but also memories, language, myths, art, anticipation, and religion. A continuous series of overlapping life spaces represents the total psychological world in which a person lives. This psychological world may include the person's precepts, knowledge, and beliefs; his (or her) forward and backward time perspective; and abstract ideas as well as concrete objects.

We should remember that a diagram of a life space is figurative. It is difficult, perhaps impossible, to show everything at once. A complete and accurate image of a life space would show all of the psychological facts and constructs in a total situation represented by a differentiated person and a differentiated psychological environment. A differentiated person or environment is one functionally divided into various aspects as perceived by the one being studied (see Figure 14.1). Some differentiated aspects of a person are friends, ambitions, self-aggrandizement, and needs

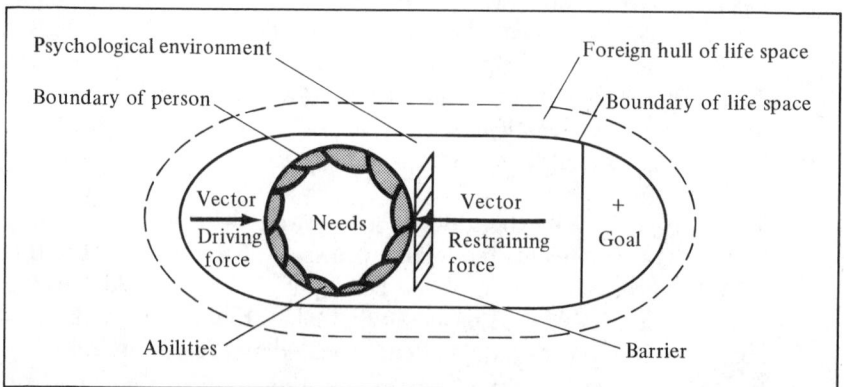

Figure 14.1 Life space of an individual.

and abilities to know about various matters and to carry out activities of different kinds. A differentiated psychological environment contains everything perceived by the person at the time under study.

Also, we should guard against making physical things of the psychological constructs whose purpose is to symbolize relationships, primarily functional in nature. For example, we should at no time think of a psychological person as being synonymous with a biological organism or of a psychological and a physical environment as being the same concept.

The two principal aspects of a life space are a person and his or her psychological environment. The two are not completely separate from each other. However, they do function as subwholes of a person's psychological field or life space. Both are surrounded by a *nonpsychological foreign hull*. The foreign hull of a life space is the nonpsychological environment. It is composed of those aspects of a person's physical-social environment that are observable by the one who is studying the particular person but which, at the juncture under consideration, have no significance for the person being studied.

A person, his psychological environment, and the foreign hull of his life space are represented by concentric figures. A person is within his psychological environment and both are surrounded by a foreign hull. The boundaries of the respective regions of a life space are characterized by permeability. Nonpsychological factors observed only by an outsider can at the next moment become psychological ones for the person being studied. There can be movement both ways through the boundary of a person or a life space or through any of their regions. For an aspect of the physical-social world to influence the intelligent behavior of a person, it must be moved from a foreign hull into his life space through his interaction with it.

As succeeding nonpsychological physical and social environments or foreign hulls are outside their respective psychological environments, they can have no immediate effect upon a person's intelligent behavior. However, through a person's interaction with the environment, parts of a present foreign hull can be transformed into goals, barriers, and other psychological factors of succeeding life spaces. They then are no longer a part of the foreign hull. Factors so transformed become parts of either psychological persons or environments. Thus, what a moment before constituted only a part of the foreign hull may at a succeeding moment be a central part of either the person or his psychological environment.

What Is the Topology of a Life Space?

The topology of a life space is its psychological structure. In mathematics, topology is a nonmetrical geometry, which encompasses concepts such as *inside, outside,* and *boundary* but has no dealings with length, breadth, or thickness. No distances are defined. Rather, topology is concerned with the relative position of the geometric figures being considered. "Topologically there is no difference between a circle, an ellipse, a regular or irregular polygon with any number of sides. . . . A drop of water and the earth are, from a topological point of view, fully equivalent."[9] It is helpful to think of a topological plane figure as being made of a highly elastic sheet of rubber; we may stretch, twist, pull, and bend it at pleasure, but the relationships it represents remain the same.

Two basic concepts that topological space denotes are connectedness and part-whole relationships. Topologically, things may be next to, inside, or outside one another. Size or shape has no significance in a topological figure. "Two figures are *topologically equivalent if* [and only if] one figure can be made to coincide with the other by an elastic motion."[10] The life spaces in Figure 14.2 are topologically equal. Each is a completely bounded area within a larger bounded area.

Topological concepts are used to represent the structure of a life space in such a way as to define the range of possible perceptions and actions. This is accomplished by showing the arrangement of the functional parts of a life space. The parts are shown as various regions and their boundaries. When an individual structures, that is, makes sense of, his (or her) life space, he divides it into regions. Boundaries of the major parts of a life space and their respective regions are either quite firm or more or less porous and permeable. So, topological ideas or terms, when applied to psychology, represent the position of a person in reference to his functional goals and the barriers to their achievement. Thus, topology shows the various possibilities for psychological behavior or locomotion.

In addition to aspects of the person whose life space is being studied, regions represent operative activities such as eating, going to the movies, and making decisions; more passive incidents such as being fired or being rewarded; and social entities such as family, church, school, and gang. If the region "going to the movies" is located in a person's life space, the

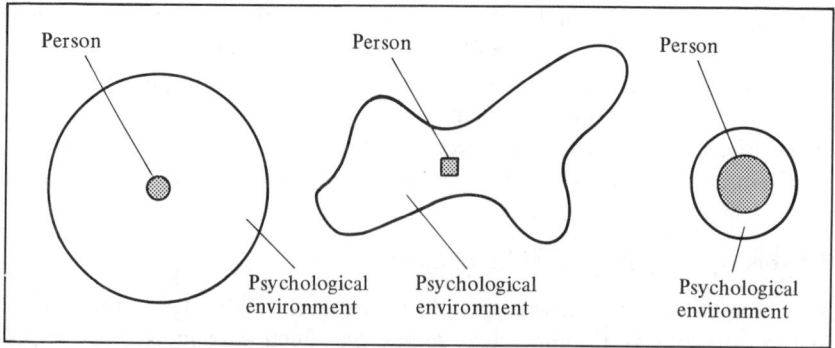

Figure 14.2   Topology of life space—three equal figures.

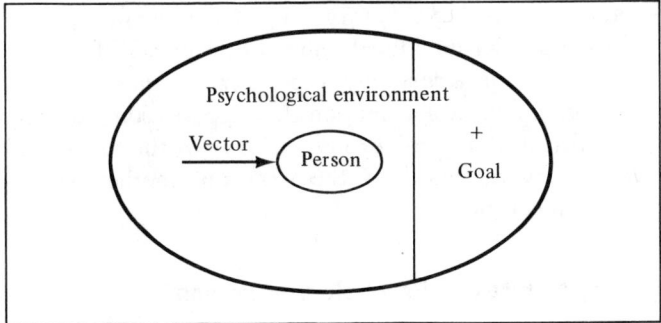

Figure 14.3   A vector.

person is either engaging in or thinking about engaging in that activity. If "being fired" is in his life space, the person is perceiving that incident and its consequences. "Church" in a life space involves what one makes of what "church" means to one.[11]

How Are Vectors Used in Describing a Life Space?

Whereas topological concepts are used to illustrate structurally what is possible, vectorial concepts describe the dynamics of a situation—what is happening or is likely to happen. The concept *vector* is borrowed from a system used in mechanics to represent direction and strength; these are two properties of a force. The third property is its point of application. In psychology a *vector* represents a force that is influencing psychological movement toward or away from a goal (see Figure 14.3). A *force* is a tendency to act in a certain way or direction. A vector is a concept equivalent to, and descriptive of, a psychological force. If there is only one vector—force—there is locomotion in the direction that the vector points. However, if two or more vectors are pointing in several different ways, movement is in the direction of the resultant force.

Vectors indicate the moving forces within a topological structure; they picture what is happening or likely to happen. Hence, vectors indicate the *valences* of respective environmental regions or functional parts of a life space. Valences are the attracting or repelling powers of regions; they may be either positive or negative. A *positive valence* means that the environmental object or event under consideration is attractive to the person; it supports the fulfillment of a psychological need. A *negative valence* means that the object or event is repulsive to the person; it either prevents or obstructs fulfillment of a psychological need or threatens injury to the person. Goal regions have either positive or negative valences; barrier regions have only negative ones.

Each vector is drawn as an arrow that shows the respective force's direction, strength, and point of application. A vector may represent either a driving or a restraining force. A *driving force* is a tendency of a person to move either toward or away from a goal region of his or her life space; it represents either a *drawing* or a *repelling* force. A *restraining force* is a barrier or obstacle to psychological locomotion that opposes some driving force. Both driving and restraining forces may arise from the needs and abilities of the person being studied, from the actions of another person, or from the impersonal aspects of a situation.

What Is the Origin and Nature of a Psychological Person?

Cognitive-field psychologists place one's person at the center of his (or her) psychological field. A person is that body or configuration of matters with which an individual becomes identified, of which he takes care, and to which he gives his allegiance. So defined, it is not a fixed quantity or static thing. It is achieved, as contrasted with being inherently possessed. So, briefly stated, a self or person consists of everything an individual takes care of.

Under no circumstances is a psychological person considered identical with a biological organism. Nor is it limited either to a substantive mind alone or to a combination of a substantive mind and a physical body. Rather, a person is a purposive behaving self. It is the center of abilities and needs, and it is what a child or adolescent, and later an adult, means when he says "I" or "me." The concept person may be considered synonymous with self. Whereas teachers more often think of Billy Smith and Sally Anderson as persons, Billy and Sally, when thinking of themselves, are more likely to use the term self.

Self, person, and interests, then, are names for the same psychological phenomenon. Depending upon the way individuals view matters, their persons take varying forms. There are individuals who are primarily concerned with keeping their bodies well fed, their temperatures well controlled, and the right amount of physical release, and those are their goals in life. Other people may think that their whole person is their mind. Still others may think of themselves as beings that are neither bodies alone, minds alone, nor combinations of physical bodies and nonphysical minds. But, whatever an individual is concerned with taking care of constitutes that person. Let us consider one example. A person's speech, whatever it might be, usually is a part of his (or her) self. So, any time we negatively criticize a student's speech, we are criticizing him. The individual's speech is part of his person, not merely an organic operation or behavior. Hence, in its widest possible sense, a child's self is the total configuration of all that he (or she) calls or thinks of as his. This can include his body, speech, thoughts, clothes, home, parents, grandparents, brothers and sisters as well as his reputation in various groups, his personal property, and his attitudes toward all these and the institutions for their realization.

A person may be represented as a differentiated region of a life space. The field of a newborn baby is something like "one big blooming buzzing confusion." Then, as one lives one's life, although one may not think of it in these specific terms, one's total situation is structured as one's self or person and one's psychological environment. Some aspects of experience involve the central core of a person; they are very near and dear to him. Others are of a less vital, peripheral sort.

Psychologically, a person is composed of (1) a motor-perceptual stratum or region and (2) an inner-personal stratum or region. The inner-personal region is the innermost part of a psychological person; it represents the person's needs. The motor-perceptual stratum has the position of a boundary zone between the inner-personal region and the psychological environment. It represents the cognitive or knowing and the manipulative abilities of a person. The practice of cognitive abilities entails the person's using his senses to know about things. Manipulative abilities involve the use of muscles and glands to do things.

In a sense, the motor-perceptual system is the tool of the inner-personal system. Like regions of the psychological environment, it provides opportunity and limits opportunity. However, it is more closely identified with the person than with the environment. While abilities are identified with the motor-perceptual system, needs are centered in the inner-personal system. A need is a state of a person that has a part in determining behavior toward any goal that may exist in relation to that state; it corresponds to a personal tension. Since the motor-perceptual region is *functionally* located between the inner-personal region and the environment, it performs functions of both person and environment. This means that a person acts in relation to his psychological environment and simultaneously realizes the consequences of so doing.

How Is Psychological Environment a Part of a Life Space?

Cognitive-field theorists treat the meaning of environment much differently than do S-R conditioning theorists. S-R conditioning theorists maintain that a person's psychological and physical environments are identical; his (or her) environment consists of all his physical and social surroundings. Because environment is defined in objective, physicalistic terms, presumably anyone can see, hear, smell, feel, or taste the environment of anyone else.

In contrast, cognitive-field psychologists think of a person's environment as being psychological. A person's psychological environment consists of every thing, function, and relationship that, at a given time, surrounds the person and means anything to him as well as the meaning that it has for him. It is that part of one's physical and social environment with which one is psychologically engaged at a specific juncture of a moment's, or longer period's duration, because it is relevant to one's purposes at that juncture. Such an environment consists of objects and events, not a sum total of optical, acoustical, and tactile sensations. A psychological environment, then, is what a person makes *of* his physical-social environment.

The meaning of *makes of* deserves our special attention. It means that some physical objects and events surround a person, and that the person reaches out and makes some kind of sense of some of them as he (or her) brings them into relationship with himself and his goals. Whatever a person makes of that which seems to be surrounding him is his psychological environment. Thus, one's psychological environment is not merely what is "out there" in a purely physical sense. Anything that appears to be in a student's physical environment, but of which he is completely oblivious, is in the foreign hull of his life space. However, if the person interacts with that thing in any way, either positively or negatively, it no longer is in his foreign hull but in his life space proper.

Now, let us see what all this means. When one of the writers was teaching in a Kansas high school some years ago, he had a student (let's call him Louis Brock) who was not mad at the teacher, neither did he love him, he was just oblivious to him. Louis was usually there physically, but he seldom if ever was there psychologically. Now, what the teacher attempted to do was to get Louis to pay attention to him, so he moved Louis right up to the center of the front row under his nose. But, Louis still was neither mad at nor attracted by the teacher; as far as Louis was concerned, the teacher just didn't exist. So, where was the teacher? He was part of the foreign hull of Louis' life space. Consequently, the only way that the teacher would ever teach Louis anything was to so maneuver that Louis would pull the teacher into his life space. Until he accomplished this, all the gyrations he performed would not teach Louis anything. This illustrates why it is so crucial that we recognize that every student's life space has a foreign hull as well as a psychological environment proper.

HOW DOES PSYCHOLOGICAL ENVIRONMENT DIFFER
FROM PHYSICAL-SOCIAL ENVIRONMENT?

A person's psychological environment includes impressions of parts of the physical environment but not necessarily all of it. It also extends beyond its physical environment. Sometimes a person's psychological environment includes largely memories or anticipations; in this case he (or she) is scarcely aware of the physical world currently around him. Hence, he is operating on a highly imaginative level.

Since each person's psychological environment is unique, obviously two persons may appear to be in the same location in space and time (or as nearly so as possible) and yet have very different psychological environments. Furthermore, the behaviors of two equally intelligent persons who are confronted with the same "objective facts" may differ drastically because each is different in his purposes and experiential background. Whenever a person has a new experience, he changes his environment and will never again be able to recapture the old environment in its identical form. The cognitive-field conception of environment helps explain why in a particular family one son may become a minister and another turn to crime; their interpretations of their world differ radically, even though to an outsider their social and physical environments appear quite similar.

IS AN ORGANISM CONSIDERED PERSON OR ENVIRONMENT?

In a relativistic sense, an individual's biological organism is an aspect of both his (or her) person and his psychological environment. A person usually closely identifies his biological organism with himself; he is concerned with taking care of it. But the person also sees his organism in another light as an important aspect of his environment; it is part of that with which that person must learn to live. A child's or youth's being crippled or abnormal in physical size or proportions may color everything he or she says or does. A 12-year-old girl who reaches the adolescent growth spurt early and becomes head and shoulders taller than any other student in her class may consider her physical stature a critical aspect of her psychological environment; she must live with what she "makes of" her physical stature.

We may illustrate the relation of a biological organism to a person in two different ways. The organism may be considered a boundary region of a person, which mediates between the person and his environment by providing cognitive and manipulative abilities (Figure 14.4A), or the functions of the organism may be pictured as a factor common to both a psychological person and his psychological environment (Figure 14.4B).

The basic formula of cognitive-field psychology is that psychological, as contrasted with physical, behavior is a function of a person and his or her psychological environment—B = f (P, E). The pivotal concepts—life space, topology, vector, person, and psychological environment—and the

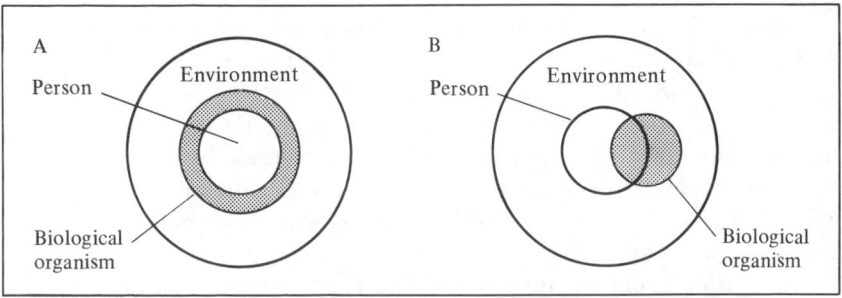

Figure 14.4 Relationship of a biological organism to a psychological person.

constructs that are auxiliary to the basic formula are illustrated in Figure 14.1, page 362. The auxiliary concepts are defined in the following glossary.

Glossary of Key Auxiliary Concepts of Field Psychology

Foreign hull of life space. Complex of all nonpsychological facts that surround a life space. That part of a person's physical and social environment that, at a particular juncture, is not included in his or her psychological environment. Physical and social raw materials. Foreign hull both provides and limits behavioral possibilities.

Regions. Psychologically significant conditions, places, things, and activities defined functionally as parts of a life space. They have positive or negative valences.

Valences (environment-centered). Positive or negative imperative environmental facts. Properties that regions of a life space have when an individual is either drawn toward them or repelled away from them. A region that possesses a positive valence is one of such nature that forces correlated with the valence of that region tend psychologically to move the person in the direction of that region. A negative valence means that forces tend to move the person away from that region.

Needs (person-centered). States of a person which, if they exist in relation to a goal, have a part in determining behavior toward that goal. Correspond to a tension system of the inner-personal region of a person. Needs develop through one's interaction with one's environment.

Abilities (person-centered). Cognitive abilities constitute a person's capacity to know his (or her) environment. Manipulative abilities constitute a person's capacity to affect his environment.

Tension. Very closely related to, and descriptive of, psychological needs. The state of one system relative to the state of surrounding systems. Release of tension may be achieved either through reaching a goal or through restructuring the life space. The release of tension corresponds to the satisfaction of a need.

Goal. A region of a life space toward, or away from, which a person is psychologically drawn.

Barrier. Dynamic part of an environment that resists motion through it. That which stands in the way of a person's reaching his or her goal.

Force. Immediate determinant of the locomotions of a person. The tendency to act in a certain direction. Its properties are strength, direction, and point of application. It is represented by a vector. The strength of a force is related to, but not identical with, the strength of a valence. The combination of forces acting at the same point at a given time is a resultant force.

Cognitive structure. An environment and a person, as known by the person. Synonyms are generalized insight or understanding.

NOTES

[1] See Gardner Lindzey and Elliott Aronson, *Handbook of Social Psychology*, 2d ed., 1, Reading, Mass.: Addison-Wesley, 1968, chapters 5, 6.

[2] See Kurt Lewin, "Field Theory and Learning," in Nelson B. Henry (ed.), *The Psychology of Learning*, part 2, *The Forty-First Yearbook of the National Society for the Study of Education*, Chicago: University of Chicago Press, 1942, pp. 215–242.

[3] See Ernest R. Hilgard and Gordon H. Bower, *Theories of Learning*, 4th ed., Englewood Cliffs, N.J.: Prentice-Hall, 1975, chapter 14; also see D. O. Hebb, *Textbook of Psychology*, 3d ed., Philadelphia: Saunders, 1972, pp. 275–280.

[4] See Hadley Cantril, "Perception and Interpersonal Relations," *American Journal of Psychiatry* 114 (August 1957): 126.

[5] These experiments are summarized in Alfred Kuenzli, *The Phenomenological Problem*, New York: Harper & Row, 1959, chapter 8.

[6] B. F. Skinner, *Science and Human Behavior*, New York: Macmillan, 1953, p. 279.

[7] John Dewey, *Experience and Education*, New York: Macmillan, 1938, p. 41.

[8] John Dewey, *Logic: The Theory of Inquiry*, New York: Holt, Rinehart and Winston, 1938, p. 460.

[9] Kurt Lewin, *Principles of Topological Psychology*, New York: McGraw-Hill, 1936, p. 88.

[10] Bradford H. Arnold, *Intuitive Concepts in Elementary Topology*, Englewood Cliffs, N.J.: Prentice-Hall, 1962, p. 24.

[11] See Dorwin Cartwright, "Lewinian Theory as a Contemporary Systematic Framework," in Sigmund Koch (ed.), *Psychology: A Study of a Science*, vol. 2, New York: McGraw-Hill, 1959, p. 25.

BIBLIOGRAPHY

References pertaining to Chapters 14 and 15 are at the end of Chapter 15. These two chapters should be studied as a unit.

Chapter 15
HOW DO COGNITIVE-FIELD THEORISTS USE THE CONCEPT OF LIFE SPACE?

Cognitive-field–oriented teachers use the concept *life space* to describe various situations that people find themselves in and their tendencies to behave in certain ways because of how they size matters up. Within cognitive-field psychology, a person's motivation develops through his (or her) differentiating his life space into regions and subregions—functional objects and activities—and through his simultaneously cognitively structuring the regions and subregions by grasping some of their meaningful relationships. As new regions and subregions emerge, they also are to some degree structured cognitively, that is, they are made meaningful in line with the person's purposes. A person's motivation occurs, not because of his past experience of conditioning as such, but as an aspect of his current psychological situation.

WHAT PSYCHOLOGICAL PROCESSES CHARACTERIZE ONE'S LIFE SPACES?

Because of the nature of human motivation and experience, cognitive-field theorists think of four concurrent psychological processes transpiring in the life of a person. It is within the course of a combination of these processes that learning occurs. The processes are (1) interaction, within each life space, of a person and his (or her) psychological environment; (2) continuity of succeeding life spaces; (3) differentiation in the person's time perspective; and (4) changes in the concrete-imaginative levels of reality. Since these four processes are occurring simultaneously, any adequate understanding of people becomes somewhat complicated. But people are complicated, and it is doubtful that we will ever get an adequate understanding of them unless we do have a rather complicated paradigm.

What Does Interaction Within Each Life Space Mean?

Interaction is the psychological process within which one makes something of one's person and one's psychological environment. To repeat, perceptual interaction, for cognitive-field psychologists, is a cognitive experiential process within which a person, psychologically, simultaneously reaches out to his (or her) psychological environment, encounters some aspects of it, brings those aspects into relationship with himself, makes something of those aspects, acts in relation to what he makes of them, and realizes the consequences of the entire process. This process is discussed in some detail on pages 356–359, we only summarize it at this point.

In a life space, a person and his (or her) psychological environment are in simultaneous mutual interaction (SMI) and are mutually interdependent. Each depends upon the other for its nature and functions; it is impossible to treat one adequately without also treating the other. Accordingly, one's person is definitive of one's environment and likewise one's environment is definitive of oneself. A person's perceived reality consists of that which he gains through the use of his five-plus senses in the manner of his sizing things up. Hence, one's person consists of what one *makes* of oneself, and one's psychological environment consists of what one *makes* of that which seems to surround one.

What Does Continuity of Succeeding Life Spaces Mean?

Since each life space covers only a limited expanse of time, an individual lives through a continuous series of overlapping life spaces that have much in common but seldom if ever are identical. Thus, an individual's life spaces are characterized by continuity of both his (or her) successive persons and their psychological environments. Each life space, to some degree, is different from the one that preceded it and the one that follows. This is illustrated in Figure 15.1. Since we can anticipate some degree of similarity and continuity of life spaces as the experiences of one moment shade into those of the next, for practical schoolroom procedures (depending upon the purposes being pursued), we may assume a fixity of life spaces for longer periods than a moment—perhaps a class period, a week, or a month.

Within a series of overlapping life spaces, a person's life is a continuity of psychological tensions, locomotions, and new equilibriums.

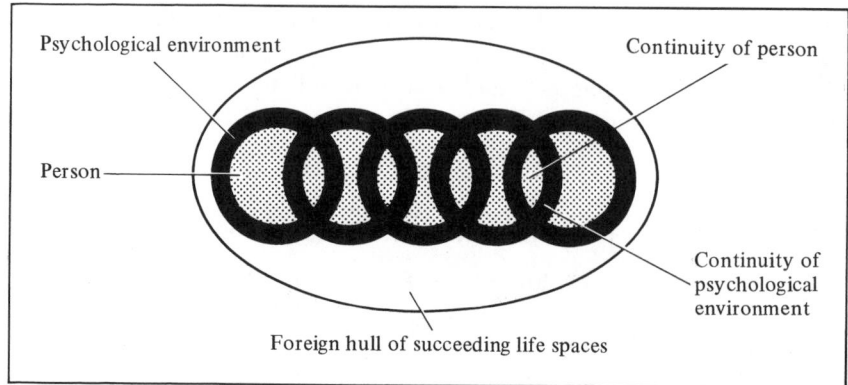

Figure 15.1   Continuity of a person's life spaces.

When there is an increase of tension in one part of a life space relative to the rest of the system, disequilibrium occurs. When a person finds himself in a state of disequilibrium and attempts to return to equilibrium, psychic energy is expended; he (or she) engages in psychological behavior. Should tension throughout the system become completely equalized, output of energy would cease; the total system would come to rest.

Of course, throughout a life span this absolute balance is never achieved. Since a person is intelligent and purposive, he constantly expands and restructures his life space to some degree. Consequently, new disequilibriums continuously emerge. This process gives a dynamic nature to human living that makes it immensely interesting and challenging.

Nonpsychological factors observed only by an outsider can at the next moment become psychological ones for the person being studied. A prime characteristic of the boundaries of a life space and its regions is their permeability. There can be movement both ways through the boundary of a person or a psychological environment or through the boundaries of any of their regions. Aspects of one's person may move into future environmental regions of the one's life space or even into its foreign hull, and vice versa. Only the inner stratum of self—needs—remains relatively stable, although it too may change drastically over periods of time, as when a person changes his religious faith.

What Is Differentiation in a Person's Time Perspective?

The basic idea of cognitive-field psychology is that everyone lives in the present; a person can't really live in either the physical past or future. In other words, each person lives when he or she lives, which is right now. So, psychologically speaking, the past is past-present, the future is future-present, and the present is present-present. The past-present consists of what we ordinarily call memories, and the future-present consists of what we ordinarily call anticipations or expectations.

During a person's development, an enlargement of his time perspective occurs; a psychological past and future become more significant. A small child lives very much in the present. His time perspective includes only an immediate past and an immediate future. However, as one's age increases, one's time perspective tends to expand. Thus, anticipations of more and more remote future events and growing memories of past events come to influence one's present behavior. These time-bending events occupy such a central part of many adult life spaces that it is often assumed that a past and a future actually exist in their own right. Careful thought, however, will bring the realization that the only past which a person can deal is what he thinks happened in the past. Likewise, the only future that can influence a person now is his anticipation of a future that he thinks may, or is going to, eventuate.

A person's present life situation contains "traces," or memories, of past incidents, but all of these are in his present situation or life space. When a second child has appeared in a family at some time in the past, the important factor now, as far as the first child is concerned, is not whether his mother rejected him when the second child was born, but whether the child interpreted the past situation as one of rejection and carried the rejection into his present life space. The past can be of present significance only through the operation of factors in the present that are identified as "past." That which persists from prior experience so that it is a "past" in the present is *trace*.

Anticipation of a future also occurs in the present; it is how one envisions the future, not what will actually happen then, that counts in the present. If a child is good in school on Monday so that he (or she) will get a star on Friday, whether or not he actually receives a star on Friday has nothing to do with his being good on the previous Monday. His anticipation of the star is his motivation for his goodness on Monday. Recognition of the "presentness" of any psychological past and future in no way depreciates them; it merely places them in a contemporaneous frame of reference within which growth of a person's time perspective is conceived in terms of memory traces and anticipations, which are functional parts of a present life space.

What Are Changes in Concrete-Imaginative Levels of Reality?

Normal human development carries with it not only an enlargement of time perspective but also an increased differentiation of the concrete-imaginative dimensions of one's life space. As used in cognitive-field psychology, *imaginative processes* are wishing, dreaming, imagining, symbolic thinking, and kindred practices. To young children, their products are concretely real; then gradually they are distinguished more and more from actual physical reality.

A young child does not clearly distinguish imaginary objects from concrete facts, wishes from goals, or hopes from expectations. Thus, to him, Santa Claus and Satan may be as real as any concrete object. However, when a child realizes that there "really" is no Santa Claus but still continues to talk about him, the child is differentiating an imaginative realm from that of concrete reality. Then, as the child grows older, he tends to make an even sharper distinction between concrete and imaginative reality. True, fantasy in the form of wishful thinking is also common in adults. However, adults generally are better able to distinguish imaginative processes from concrete experience. Furthermore, mature adults should recognize the degree to which they are engaging in each.

How Are Concrete-Imaginative Levels Related to Time Dimensions of a Life Space?

Two salient characteristics of a life space at any given time are (1) the level of concrete-imaginative reality at which the person is operating, and (2) the degree to which the individual's life space encompasses a psychological past and future. There is a direct relationship between the respective concrete-imaginative levels of reality and the degree of time-binding that pervades the life space of a person at a given time. At the level of concrete facts, immediate goals, and practical expectations, a life space contains only an incipient past and future; they are just beginning to be. But, as a person's life space assumes more imaginative dimensions, his time-binding functions become increasingly extended and significant until, at an extremely imaginative level, his (or her) entire life space may be centered on either a psychological past or future. But, even then, the time and imaginative dimensions of a life space continue to be both contemporaneous and present.

We should not confuse the adjectives *imaginative* and *imaginary;* the two words have significantly different meanings. Whereas imaginary means purely fictitious or fanciful and existing only in the imagination, imaginative applies to that which arises through one's cognitively creating concepts or plans for action. Thus, imaginative is a much more constructive term than is imaginary. In fact, a person's being imaginative is much the same as his being creative.

Imaginative levels of realty range from mere expectations and their means of fulfillment to hallucinations that give rise to extreme guilts and fears. Some levels between the two extremes, ranging from concrete reality to extremely imaginative reality, involve aspirations, wishes, imagination, symbolic thought, creativity, fancy, fantasy, dreams, and nightmares. In the psychological past, these take the form of memory, pride, innocence, error, fault, sin, and guilt. In the psychological future, they embrace goals, hopes, anticipations, conjectures, fabrications, visions, fears, and despair.

Figure 15.2 symbolically depicts the interrelationship of the concrete-imaginative dimension of a life space of a person and his (or her) time perspective. The figure should be interpreted to signify not merely two but numerous levels of reality, which may range from life on a purely biological level to one of complete autism—absorption in fantasy. The figure illustrates both the concrete-imaginative and the time-binding dimensions of a life space. Think of the figure's being three-dimensional. Its lower and upper bases represent extreme levels of concrete and imaginative reality. The part of the figure to the left of the vertical left-hand dotted line represents the person's psychological past, the part to the right of the vertical right-hand dotted line represents his psychological future. Notice that, when the person is operating on an extreme level of concrete reality, there is very little psychological past or future in his life. The person is little concerned with either yesterday or tomorrow; he simply lives each day—day by day. This type of individual, of course, is difficult to teach for the future.

As a person functions on more imaginative levels, his psychological past and future also become more salient aspects of his life space. Thus, whereas on the level of concrete reality a psychological past and future

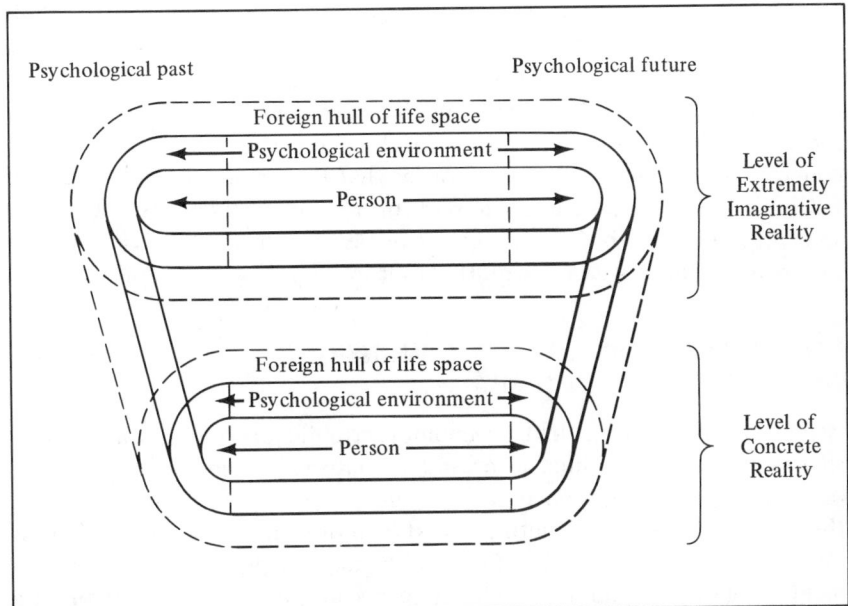

Figure 15.2 Concrete-imaginative levels of a life space as related to its psychological past and future.

hold only a relatively minor significance, as a person operates on more imaginative levels the time dimension of his life space becomes more and more important.

Now, how may an adult's understanding of the concrete-imaginative levels of life spaces contribute to his being a more effective teacher, especially when he (or she) is teaching boys and girls of a social class other than his own? For one to teach a child or youth successfully, one must meet him on the level of reality where his life space is focused at the time. Recognition of this key principle is highly essential, if a typical "middle-class" teacher is to reach and teach a child or youth from unskilled laboring class homes.

In working for marginal wages and barely earning a living, the parents of those boys and girls are likely to maintain their life spaces on a low, subsistence level of concrete reality; their primary goals involve the acquisition of food, clothing, and shelter. Because of their home conditions, children of unskilled laborers are also likely to center their realities on a concrete level. However, from time to time, both parents and children leave this concrete level, and, when they do, they are most likely to jump to an extremely imaginative level of reality. This imaginative level, reflected in persons' daydreams and fantasy, is focused largely on a psychological future; it is a flight from routine drudgery and boredom. An example of their swinging to a highly imaginative level of reality is their watching movies in which people dress formally, drink champagne, and drive Cadillacs.

Reserved and dignified "middle-class" people generally do not pitch their psychological realities on either of the extremes that are characteristic of unskilled laborers. Consequently, teachers, in their earlier contacts with boys and girls from the laboring class, should deliberately focus their interest, thoughts, and teaching on extreme levels of either concrete or imaginative reality in order that their students will make the teacher's attitudes and ideas a part or region of their respective life spaces. Then, students' life spaces may be constructively reviewed and progressively improved through the joint inquiry of teacher and students.

HOW IS LEARNING A CHANGE IN INSIGHT OR COGNITIVE STRUCTURE?

According to cognitive-field psychology, a child or youth in a learning situation is not unfolding according to nature; neither is he (or she) being passively conditioned always to respond in a desired manner. Rather, at his level of maturity and comprehension, an individual is differentiating and restructuring himself and his psychological environment; he (she) is gaining or changing his insights. Learning, then, is a dynamic process whereby, through interactive experience, insights or cognitive structures of life spaces are changed so as to become more serviceable for future guidance. Insights or cognitive structure are answers to questions concerning such matters as how something is made up, what is related to what, how one does something, of what good a thing or action is, and what one should be doing. They may be preverbal, verbal, or nonverbal; one may gain an insight before one has words to express it, one may achieve an insight and its verbalization simultaneously, or one may accomplish an insight that he does not verbalize at all.

There is evidence that even nonverbal animals solve mazes by formulating a series of cognitive structures and testing them, and that they solve their problems through gaining insight into their situations.[1] What occurs psychologically when by being given food, a dachshund is taught to sit up on its rear end at the command, "up," and later, when it wants a toy that it sees on a table, it goes to the table, assumes its "up" position, and barks?

Insights derive from an individual's best interpretations of what comes to him or her; they may be deeply discerning or they may be shallow. They may serve as dependable guides for action or they may prove ruinous. Chica, one of Köhler's apes, attempted to reach a banana by placing a box beneath it and jumping as high as possible from the box. After several failures, she suddenly held the box as high as possible, pressed it against the wall, and attempted to climb up on it. Chica had an insight, but not a true one.[2]

It is an insightful process when a ball player gets a feel for the correct swing of his bat, when a little girl discovers how to dress herself, when a youth learns to drive an automobile, when a child gets the idea of multiplication, perhaps through addition, or when a college student learns how to "read" Shakespeare.

A person's behavior, to a very large degree, depends upon the cognitive structure of his (or her) life space. Learning results in building psychological traces, which contribute to the structure and dynamics of both present and future life spaces and thus affect both present and future performance. Memory processes refer to cognitively structured similarities between an individual's life spaces that exist at different times. It is because of the continuity of life spaces and their cognitive structures that learning is of value to a person.

Good insight into a present life space or situation tends to provide excellent foresight into the cognitive structure of future life spaces. Suppose a college student wishes to understand and appreciate principles of human development and learning and to prepare himself to apply them in future teaching situations. An excellent procedure would be for him (or her) to acquire a deep understanding of himself, his psychological environment, and their relationships in his current series of life spaces.

One's learning consists of (1) one's changes in cognitive structure, (2) one's changes in motivation, (3) one's changes in group belongingness and ideology, and (4) one's gains in muscular control and dexterity. We may distinguish between the first two types of changes rather sharply. A change in cognitive structure means development of perceptual knowledge. It is centered in the topological or structural aspects of a situation. A change in motivation, in contrast, is centered in the vectorial or dynamic aspects of a situation; it means learning either to like or dislike certain regions or aspects of a life space. However, even changes in motivation arise from changes in cognitive structure; for a person to change the valence of an activity he (or she) must change the cognitive structure of his life space in regard to it.

Growing into a culture through one's change in group belongingness and ideology and one's development of muscular skills also involves primarily perceptions of oneself and the people and objects around one and one's getting the feel of performing various actions. Thus, these two types of change also are principally a process that involves changes in the cognitive structure of one's life space. Consequently, in treating learning, the pivotal concept is *change in cognitive structure*. "A change in action ideology, a real acceptance of a changed set of facts and values, a change in the perceived social world—all three are but different expressions of the same process."[3]

HOW MAY THE COGNITIVE STRUCTURES OF LIFE SPACES CHANGE?

A person changes the cognitive structure of his (or her) life space through *differentiation, generalization,* and *restructurization* of its respective regions or aspects. A region is a distinguishable, functional part of a life space. Hence, it is the psychological meaning of an object or activity. The object or activity may be either a remembered, a contemplated, or a presently existing one. Regions of a life space may include conceptions of aspects of one's self, specific activities such as working and eating, states of being such as being frightened or feeling secure, and membership in groups and classes as well as the personalities, objects, and events that one perceives. The cognitive structure of one's life space includes not only the arrangement and conditions of existing regions but also an understanding of what movements may occur and what may be the consequences of such movements. The relation of the region in which a person's activity is centered in reference to the other regions of his life space delineates the qualities of his immediate surroundings, the kind of regions adjacent to other regions (that is, the possibilities for his next steps), and what steps mean actions toward and what ones mean actions away from goals.

What Is Cognitive or Perceptual Differentiation?

Cognitive differentiation is the process within which regions are sub-divided into smaller regions. In differentiation, relatively vague and un-structured regions of a life space become cognitively structured and more specific. Thus, the person comes to see as different some things that he (or she) had previously thought to be parts of the same thing. Differentiation, then, means discerning more and more specific aspects of one's environment and oneself. What once were "kitties" come to be "leopards," "tigers," "lions," and "cats." What once was "toast" comes to be "crackers," "doughnuts," and "bread." What once was "baby" comes to be "me," "my arms," or "my legs," and, later, "student," "members of club," and "ball player."

Differentiation proceeds at different rates at different times, and during crisis periods such as adolescence its speed rapidly fluctuates. As a child grows he differentiates (1) himself or his person from his environment, (2) different aspects of his person and environment from each other, (3) a psychological past and future from the present, and (4) imaginative reality levels from the concrete reality level of his life space. (The latter two kinds of differentiation are explained on pp. 374–378 as two of the most important features of cognitive-field psychology.)

What Is Cognitive Generalization?

Cognitive generalization is a process whereby one formulates a general-ized idea or concept through discerning some common characteristics of a number of individual cases and identifies the cases as a class of ideas or objects. Thus, a person identifies similarities among aspects of himself or his environment that had previously seemed quite different. When a child learns that vegetables, flowers, bushes, and trees are plants, or a student learns that his hopes, dreams, beliefs, and anticipations are all subregions of a "future" region in his contemporaneous life space, he (she) is generalizing. A student of professional education, through differentiation of various instances of learning, may develop a generalized concept, learning, to cover any learning in any situation.

Although in common usage generalization is the opposite of differen-tiation, psychologically they are mutually complementary. Generalization is the process whereby one groups a number of particular objects or functions under a single heading or in a single category. Thus, one generalizes when one forms a concept that includes previously differen-tiated aspects of oneself or one's environment. When a child learns that cats, dogs, horses, and birds are animals he is generalizing. Then, through a combination of differentiation and generalization, he may divide the physical world into vegetable, animal, and mineral classes.

What Is Cognitive Restructurization?

Cognitive restructurization of one's life space means one's making more or different sense of oneself and one's world. A person not only differentiates and generalizes his (or her) life space into new regions but simultaneously restructures his life space; he changes the meanings of respective regions in relationship to himself and to one another. Thus, a person discovers some significant new relationships between some aspects of his life space and some nonrelationships between others that he had previously considered related. Within the process of restructurization, one defines or redefines directions in one's life space; one learns what actions will lead to what results. One does this through perception of significant relationships of different functional regions of his life space. Restructurization, then, consists of separating certain regions that have been connected and connecting certain regions that have been separated. (Remember that regions are defined as functionally distinguishable parts of a life space.)

When we were quite young, most of us differentiated people from their environments. Later we differentiated people into various races, classes, and groups. Perhaps about the same time we generalized them into Republicans and Democrats, or Christians and non-Christians. As persons learn, they continue to differentiate and generalize themselves and their environments, but they also restructure the differentiated and generalized regions of their life spaces so as to give them new meanings. In this way, persons become, or at least should become, increasingly better thinkers.

Restructurization includes not only extensions of time perspectives and increased differentiation of imaginative from concrete levels of reality, but also changes in motivation and group identification and changes in bodily coordination. A person's change in motivation arises through his seeing regions or factors of his life space in a new light. To a 14-year-old boy, a girl, once something to be teased, comes to be a thing to be quite gently cuddled. A change in motivation is also closely related to changes in group identification. To a large degree it is the groups to which one belongs that are the source of one's ideology and consequently one's motivation. One's person changes as one changes one's group allegiances. An adolescent's conformity to his peer group standards is a striking example of this developmental process.

HOW DOES COGNITIVE-FIELD PSYCHOLOGY TREAT TRANSFER OF LEARNING?

For cognitive-field theorists, continuity of life spaces is the pivotal concept in their theory of transfer of learning. Along with the perceptual interaction, which occurs in each life space of a person, there is a continuity of cognitive structures of succeeding life spaces. Although in the most technical sense a life space is of a moment's duration, for actual schoolroom purposes it is generally taken to extend over a juncture of some time. Furthermore, succeeding life spaces are not completely different from each other; rather, there is a continuity of a person's life spaces, and it is within this continuity that transfer of learning occurs. The cognitive structure of each life space overlaps, and shades into, that of the life space that succeeds it.

Learning that is transferred consists of the cognitive structure of a present life space that is extended to future life spaces of an individual. Cognitive-field psychologists note that when transfer of learning occurs, it is in the form of generalizations, concepts, or insights that are developed in one learning situation being employed in others; this process is called *transposition*. Transposition of insights may also be described in terms of habits, but under cognitive-field psychology, *habit* has a special definition. A habit is a skillfully executed application of a principle in a situation wherein application of that principle will apparently help a person achieve a goal. Nevertheless, even habits are not blind, automatic behaviors. Rather, they are products of tested insights being used in new situations. They are, therefore, precise adjustments to situations that call for them. One may operate on habit, and transfer may occur with little or no reflection. Or transfer may occur in a highly reflective situation. In either case, transfer is not automatic.

Cognitive-field psychologists think that transfer of learning occurs because of perceptual similarities between situations, and that it is in the form of meanings, expectations, generalizations, concepts, or insights that are developed in one learning situation and are usable in others. However, to cognitive-field psychologists, it seems as futile to expect a generalization to spring into action whenever the environment sets the stage for it as to expect such of a faculty or of an identical element. For teachers to promote transfer in a dependable way, something more than commonness of elements or appropriateness of generalizations is necessary.

Experience shows that in actual practice transfer of a generalization will not always occur even when a person understands a principle thoroughly and has applied it often. For instance, a natural scientist repeatedly can be scientific in dealing with problems of natural science and simultaneously resort to folklore and superstition in dealing with problems of the social sciences and humanities. He (or she) either may not recognize that scientific method is applicable to problems in the social sciences and humanities, or he may recognize such applicability but have no desire to use it in the other areas of endeavor.

A person is in the best frame of mind for transfer to occur when he (or she) is aware of acquiring meanings and abilities that are widely applicable in learning and living. However, important as this is for cognitive-field psychologists, it is not enough. A person must also want to solve new problems, or approach new situations, in the light of the insights gained through previous experience. For transfer to occur, individuals must generalize, that is, perceive common factors in different situations; they must comprehend the factors as applicable and appropriate to both and thereby understand how a generalization can be used; and they must desire to benefit by the sensed commonality. Ernest E. Bayles tells us that any insight susceptible of generalized application *"will transfer if and when—and only if and when—(1) opportunity offers, (2) a trained individual sees or senses it as an opportunity, and (3) he is disposed to take advantage of the opportunity."*[4]

Cognitive-field theorists are committed to the proposition that transfer of learning to new tasks will be better if, in learning, the learner can discover relationships for himself, and if he has opportunities to apply his learning to a variety of tasks. Consequently, they think that, for transfer to occur at its highest level, we must help students understand many widely useful relationships, principles, or generalizations; we must foster sensitivity to the presence of opportunities for transfer so that likelihood of recognition is high; and we must encourage students to embrace goals, attitudes, and ideals that support the conviction that progressive refinement of outlooks on life is possible and commendable.

The crucial points of cognitive-field psychology in regard to transfer of learning and its promotion may be summarized in seven points:

1. Opportunity for transfer may occur in many situations. It is not inherent in any subject but is possible from any field of knowledge.
2. Transfer is not dependent upon mental exercise with disciplinary school subjects.
3. Transfer is dependent upon methods of teaching and learning that use lifelike situations. It is facilitated by teaching for large generalizations that have transfer value.
4. Transfer is not automatic; opportunities for transfer must be recognized, and the person concerned must want to use them.
5. Transfer varies according to difficulty of generalization of subject matter and the intellectual ability of individuals.
6. Insights need not be put into words for their transfer to occur.
7. The amount of intraproblem insightful learning, not the number of trials as such, determines the amount of interproblem transfer.[5]

WHAT IS THE MEANING OF COGNITIVE-FIELD PSYCHOLOGY FOR TEACHING SITUATIONS?

To summarize a cognitive-field theory of learning, we may say that a person learns through differentiating, generalizing, and restructuring his (or her) person and his psychological environment in such a way as to acquire new or changed insights, understandings, or meanings concerning them, and thereby achieves changes in motivation, group belongingness, muscular skills, time perspective, and ideology. In this way, he gains greater control of himself and the world. So learning, concisely defined, is a process of one's either gaining or changing his insights, outlook, expectations, or thought patterns. Now, how is this learning theory applicable to teaching theory and practice?

Within the learning process, a constantly expanding world of understanding reaches out to encompass a constantly expanding psychological world. At birth, a child's psychological world is very small. But on his (or her) level each child is trying to understand that small world. He is trying to understand how to get food. Soon he will be seeking warmth. Later the child will seek means of getting attention. As he grows, in order more adequately to influence his own destiny, he will seek insights into his world as it affects him (see Figure 17.1, p. 424).

A completely new situation would be cognitively unstructured; a person would have no knowledge of what would lead or point to what. Thus, at that moment his behavior would be completely random. (This is the position of a lower animal when it is first placed in a "problem box.") However, rarely, if ever, does a person function in a completely unstructured situation. More often we find people in situations that are inadequately or inharmoniously structured. This means that they have problems and need to extend their learning, that is, to change the cognitive structures of their life spaces.

Within a cognitive-field approach to a school situation, each teacher and each student is considered a discerning person in interaction with his psychological environment. A teacher's unique function is to implement and promote the development of serviceable insights of students so as to help students become more adequate and harmonious personalities—that is, more intelligent. To accomplish this, a teacher needs a basic understanding of the structure and dynamics of life spaces. The structure of a life space is its topology; its dynamics are its forces as represented by vectors.

The *topology*, or *structure*, of a life space shows the various possibilities for psychological movement or action; *vectors*, or *dynamics*, show the moving forces within the topological structure. To understand the behavior of a student, a teacher must determine the psychological position of the student's person in reference to the goal regions of his (or her) life space, that is, the topology of his life space. This entails knowing the student's social position within and outside various groups, his position in relation to various ideas and activities, and the role of physical objects in his life space. The relationship of a student's person to the environmental regions of his life space determines the qualities of his immediate surroundings, and it sets the possibilities for the student's next step in his psychological life. The dynamics of a life space are indicated by vectors.

They show what step or event means action toward and what step means action away from a person's goals. Thus, they represent psychological moving forces engendered by goals or barriers; they picture what is happening or likely to happen. The forces represented by vectors are equal to the valences—the attracting and repelling powers—of respective regions of the student's psychological environment.

A student's life space on a given evening, topologically, may contain a television set, a book, and a movie. Vectorially, each object and activity has some degree of valence—alluring or repelling power. Should the student go to the movie, this means that the movie valence is greatest of all. When one behaves intelligently, one does what one wants to do; if one does not want to do it more than one wants not to do it, one does not do it.

To analyze a psychological situation, a teacher should comprehend the structure of a person and his (or her) psychological environment and ascertain their dynamic properties—what they have to do with the student's behavior. That is, the teacher must see the relationships between the regions or parts of the student's life space, and he must establish the nature of the respective factors residing within, at, and outside its boundary. Furthermore, he must assess the degree of permeability of the boundaries of the various regions of the student's life space. Such permeability means how susceptible the student is to change.

Factors outside the boundary of a life space, the foreign hull, are those that may be perceived by others but at the moment have no place in the perceptual world of the person being studied. Knowing these facts helps a teacher determine what is possible and what is not, and what might happen and what might not. Then, to understand and accurately predict a student's behavior, a teacher, in addition to understanding the structure of the student's field—the interpositional relationships between the parts in his life space—must also ascertain the dynamic properties of the person's life space in terms of the valences of his goals and the barriers between himself and his goals.

Now what does all this mean in a school situation? Let us review the situation described on pages 157–159. "Alice is so absorbed with her teacher and schoolwork that she is oblivious to everything else about her, including the other children." The teacher is central in Alice's life space. Alice's schoolwork also is far within the border of her life space. The other children and everything else in the room that is not part of Alice's schoolwork are in the foreign hull of her life space. "Helen is a social butterfly; she wants the attention of most of the children in the classroom. She does give attention to the teacher from time to time, but right now she is concerned with other things." The other children are in Helen's life space; the teacher is at the margin, sometimes in and sometimes out. "John's body is in the classroom, but 'psychologically' John is riding a shiny new tractor which is being operated in the field adjoining the school." John's school environment and his psychological environment have little in common. Whereas little within the room is in his life space, the tractor is as central as it can be and its valence is very high.

For a teacher to teach a student in a significant way, it is imperative that there be an intersection of the student's life space with the teacher's and with the other life spaces in the room. Life spaces intersect when they have some regions in common. To insure an adequate intersection of life spaces, a teacher must probe the various regions of the life spaces of his or her students.

Peripheral regions of a person are quite accessible in ordinary conversation. But, it is more difficult to reach more central regions, that is, those that are near and dear to him. However, a teacher who is thinking in dynamic field terms is probably more likely to see larger intrapersonal and interpersonal issues. To gain an understanding of each student and his cognitive world, a teacher has to develop a sort of disciplined naiveté. In order adequately to see John through he must see through John. He (or she) must see John's person and environment as John sees them. When a teacher gains rapport with a student and thereby gains his confidence, the teacher's influence can extend to the student's central regions. The teacher now is in a position to speak of the student's needs. What a person needs depends primarily upon how he sizes up himself and his physical and social environment.

Teachers should bear in mind that a self or person is in the making constantly as one develops new insights, or changes old ones, and forms new habits. Furthermore, a far-reaching change in the structure of a self or person can occur through one's developing a significant educational insight. And, finally, a student's acquiring a new educational insight can be as significant and far-reaching as his falling in love, becoming converted, or realizing a great change in his physical and social environment.

Teachers who are committed to the application of cognitive-field psychology in their teaching may encourage students to memorize certain items that seem to be worth knowing verbatim, but they will strive to teach as much as possible on the *exploratory-understanding* or *reflection* level. At times, due to human limitations, they may drop back to an *explanatory-understanding* level. But, they will guard against regressing to a memory level of teaching and learning. The levels of teaching and learning are developed in Chapters 19–21.

NOTES

[1] See Edward C. Tolman, "Cognitive Maps in Rats and Men," *Psychological Review* 55 (July 1948): 189–208.
[2] See Wolfgang Köhler, *The Mentality of Apes*, New York: Vintage Books, 1959, p. 139.
[3] Kurt Lewin, *Resolving Social Conflicts*, New York: Harper & Row, 1948, p. 64.

[4] Ernest E. Bayles, *Democratic Educational Theory*, New York: Harper & Row, 1960, p. 58.
[5] See Harry F. Harlow, "Learning Sets and Error Factor Theory," in Sigmund Koch (ed.), *Psychology: A Study of a Science*, 2, New York: McGraw-Hill, 1959, p. 502.

BIBLIOGRAPHY

ADAMS, DONALD K. *The Anatomy of Personality*. New York: Random House, 1954. A short treatise that applies field theory to personality development.

ARNOLD, BRADFORD H. *Intuitive Concepts in Elementary Topology*. Englewood Cliffs, N.J.: Prentice-Hall, 1962. A readable explanation of topology—the "rubber sheet geometry"—from an intuitive viewpoint. Chapter 1 is especially helpful.

BAKER, BRUCE F. "Buber: Pointing Beyond the Funnel and the Pump." Paideia (1973): 34–37. Employs Buber's symbols of the funnel and the pump to represent autocratic and anarchic education. Then develops interaction as a desirable emergent synthesis.

BAYLES, ERNEST E. *Democratic Educational Theory*. New York: Harper & Row, 1960. Chapter 3, "Learning and Transfer," pages 45–62, develops a goal-insight theory of learning that is closely related to cognitive-field theory, then states four conditions necessary to transfer of learning.

BAYLES, ERNEST E. *The Theory and Practice of Teaching*. New York: Harper & Row, 1950. Chapter 6, "The Transfer of Training," pages 85–98, is a historical summary of outlooks on transfer. Probably the best brief treatment of transfer available.

BIGGE, MORRIS L. "A Relativistic Approach to the Learning Aspect of Educational Psychology." *Educational Theory* IV, no. 3 (July 1954): 213–220. A proposed harmonization of the topological and vector psychology of Lewin with the pragmatic educational philosophy of John Dewey and Boyd H. Bode. It suggests that a relativistic approach to learning is highly predictive of individual behavior.

BIGGE, MORRIS L. "A Relativistic Definition of Stimulus-Response." *Journal of Educational Psychology* 46, no. 8 (December 1955): 457–464. Implications of situational psychology for relativism. Stimulus and response gained their currency within mechanistic approaches to learning. If they are to be retained within relativism, they should be redefined. Stimulus does not occur first, followed by response; nor vice versa. Rather, the two operate simultaneously. Stimulus is environment-centered and response is person-centered.

BODE, BOYD H. *How We Learn*. Lexington, Mass.: Raytheon/Heath, 1940. A classic in learning theory. Bode's views in Chapters 14–17 provide a precursor of present-day cognitive-field learning theory.

BROWN, BOB BURTON. *The Experimental Mind in Education*. New York: Harper & Row, 1968. A book on general methods that applies Dewey's educational philosophy. Opens the way for using cognitive-field psychology.

BUGENTAL, JAMES F. T. (ed.). *Challenges of Humanistic Psychology*. New York: McGraw-Hill, 1967. Chapters 1, 2, 3, 8, 9, 18, 30, and 34 contribute to an understanding of cognitive-field psychology.

CANTRIL, HADLEY. (ed.), *The Morning Notes of Adelbert Ames, Jr.* New Brunswick, N.J.: Rutgers University Press, 1960. Ruminations of Ames in regard to his activities and thoughts. Notes that, whereas the assumptive world is a common one, a perceptual world is an individual one. Develops interdependencies of perceptions, purposes, and actions.

COMBS, ARTHUR W. *The Professional Education of Teachers.* Boston: Allyn & Bacon, 1965. Application of a perceptual view of students and teacher to effective teaching. Perceptual as used here is analogous to interactive. Shifts emphasis from a mechanistic to a personal view of teacher-student relations.

COMBS, ARTHUR W., and DONALD SNYGG. *Individual Behavior,* rev. ed. New York: Harper & Row, 1959. A perceptual approach to psychology which supports the SMI position. Study centers upon perceived selves and their needs, goals, and purposes.

DEWEY, JOHN. *Human Nature and Conduct.* New York: Holt, Rinehart and Winston, 1922. Dewey's "psychology." It describes human nature in relativistic terms. Difficult but extremely rewarding for superior students.

GAGE, N. L. (ed.). *Handbook of Research on Teaching.* Chicago: Rand McNally, 1963. Pages 1014–1021 review research on consequences of teaching secondary school mathematics by tell-and-do methods as compared with heuristic—discovery—methods.

GIBSON, JAMES J. "The Concept of the Stimulus in Psychology." *American Psychologist* 15 (1960): 694–703. Thesis: When psychologists pick the variables of physics as they appear in physics textbooks, they choose the wrong variables. Whether a potential stimulus becomes effective depends upon the individual's perception of it.

GROSE, ROBERT F., and ROBERT C. BIRNEY. *Transfer of Learning.* New York: Van Nostrand Reinhold, 1963. A book of well-selected original writings on transfer of learning. Traces historical growth of the concept up to the present time.

HARLOW, HARRY F. "The Formation of Learning Sets." *Psychological Review* 56 (January 1949): 51–65. Based on research with animals, Harlow emphasizes the importance of learning how to learn—learning sets. Emphasizes problems as contrasted with trials in learning.

HASLERUD, GEORGE M., and SHIRLEY MEYERS. "The Transfer Value of Given and Individually Derived Principles." *Journal of Educational Psychology* 49 (December 1958): 293–298. Compares retention and transfer value of direct teaching and independent discovery and finds independent discovery method more effective.

HILGARD, ERNEST R., ROBERT P. IRVINE, and JAMES E. WHIPPLE. "Rote Memorization, Understanding, and Transfer: An Extension of Katona's Card-Trick Experiments." *Journal of Experimental Psychology* 46 (October 1953): 288–292. A review of Katona's card-trick experiments and findings and a report of further research to check the findings. Supports teaching for understanding as compared with rote learning, especially when transfer of learning to new problem-solving situations is involved.

KEMP, C. GRATTON. *Foundations of Group Counseling.* New York: McGraw-Hill, 1970. Develops group counseling as a means for people gaining understanding of themselves and their situations through development of interpersonal relations.

KNELLER, GEORGE F. "Automation and Learning Theory." *The School Review* 70 (Summer 1962): 220–232. Analyzes the nature of automation and its relation to learning. Points up that Skinner's teaching machines are effective only if the teacher accepts Skinner's special interpretation of behaviorism within which learning is considered to be always additive.

KUENZLI, ALFRED E. *The Phenomenological Problem.* New York: Harper & Row, 1959. A collection of technical papers clarifying the phenomenological—perceptual—approach in modern psychology which harmonizes with the SMI outlook.

LEWIN, KURT. *A Dynamic Theory of Personality,* trans. D. K. Adams and Karl Zener. New York: McGraw-Hill, 1935. A collection of articles that Lewin wrote prior to 1935 and a new survey chapter. This book shows Lewin's earlier thinking as his topological and vector psychology was emerging.

LEWIN, KURT. "Field Theory and Learning," in Nelson B. Henry (ed.). *The Psychology of Learning,* part 2, *The Forty-First Yearbook of the National Society for the Study of Education,* pp. 215–242. Chicago: University of Chicago Press, 1942. Probably Lewin's best brief presentation of the learning theory that is implicit in his field psychology.

LEWIN, KURT. *Field Theory in Social Science.* New York: Harper & Row, 1951. A collection of Kurt Lewin's papers. The first three chapters and the last chapter develop guiding principles and constructs of field psychology. The remaining six chapters demonstrate application of field psychology principles to study of learning, development and regression, ecology, group dynamics, and social psychology.

LEWIN, KURT. *Principles of Topological Psychology,* trans. Fritz and Grace M. Heider. New York: McGraw-Hill, 1936. One of the two basic books written by Lewin in German and translated into English. It contains practically all of the structure of his field psychology but is more difficult to read than are his later works. The later pages contain a valuable glossary of field concepts.

LINDZEY, GARDNER, and ELLIOT ARONSON (ed.). *The Handbook of Social Psychology,* 2d ed., 1, *Historical Introduction and Systematic Positions.* Reading, Mass.: Addison-Wesley, 1968. In Chapter 6 is an excellent description by Morton Deutsch of field theory as it has been developed by Lewin and his students. Chapter 5 on cognitive theory and Chapter 7 on role theory contribute to understanding of the cognitive-field position.

MARROW, ALFRED J. *The Practical Theorist: The Life and Work of Kurt Lewin.* New York: Basic Books, 1969. Develops the three areas of action that shaped Lewin's career: (1) his independent style of life, his constant involvement in cooperative enterprises, and his continued collaboration with former students; (2) his persistent integration of theory and practical action, his exposure of theory to ingenious experimentation, and his close coordination of seemingly abstruse hypotheses with affairs of everyday life; and (3) his successful combination of scientific concerns with personal and civic ones.

MAY, ROLLO. *Psychology and the Human Dilemma.* New York: Van Nostrand Reinhold, 1967. The human dilemma results from man's capacity to experience himself as both subject and object simultaneously. Man's being purely free or purely determined is not the way out.

ROGERS, CARL R. *Freedom to Learn*. Columbus, Ohio: Merrill, 1969. Chapter 7 regarding the facilitation of learning contributes much to an understanding of cognitive-field theory. However, Rogers considers people active more often than he considers them interactive.

SALTZ, ELI. *The Cognitive Bases of Human Learning*. Homewood, Ill.: Dorsey Press, 1971. An examination of the cognitive processes basic to learning. Centers on the nature and function of concepts.

SNYGG, DONALD. "Another Look at Learning Theory." *Educational Psychologist* 1, no. 1 (October, 1963). Pages 9–11 present the case for cognitive-field learning theory.

STEPHENS, JOHN M. "Transfer of Learning," *Encyclopedia of Educational Research*. New York: Macmillan, 1960. Pages 1535–1543 are an excellent summary of research pertinent to transfer of learning. Treats definition, characteristics, and conditions affecting the amount of transfer.

SYMONDS, PERCIVAL M. "What Education Has To Learn from Psychology, Transfer and Formal Discipline." *Teachers College Record* 61 (October 1959): 30–45. A good historical summary of the transfer problem and pertinent research. Emphasizes transfer through application of general principles.

TOLMAN, EDWARD C. *Collected Papers in Psychology*. Berkeley: University of California Press, 1951. Also published in 1958 under the title *Behavior and Psychological Man*. Papers reflecting Tolman's unit of psychological study as molar behavior purposively organized. Tolman's ideas bridged S-R associationism and Lewin's field theory. He accepted many field concepts, such as purpose and insight, but remained a behaviorist. He was critical of S-R connectionistic theories.

TOLMAN, EDWARD C. "Kurt Lewin: 1890–1947." *The Psychological Review* 55 (January 1948): 1–4. A tribute to Lewin shortly after his death. A good, very brief professional appraisal of his work.

WALLACE, JOHN. *Psychology: A Social Science*. Philadelphia: Saunders, 1971. Emphasizes the study of persons in many social contexts. Develops alternative conceptions of the person, including several cognitive theories.

WOLMAN, BENJAMIN B. *Contemporary Theories and Systems in Psychology*. New York: Harper & Row, 1960. Chapter 13, "Field Theory," is an excellent overview of Lewin's field theory as an approach to general psychology. Develops historical background as well as basic concepts of the theory.

Chapter 16
HOW DO ECLECTIC THEORISTS DEAL WITH LEARNING?

Some learning theorists are eclectic in their treatment of learning. An eclectic theorist is one who deliberately borrows ideas and concepts selectively from several systematic outlooks and arranges them into his or her own mosaic or patchwork (see Chapter 1, pp. 21–22 for a discussion of eclecticism). In their borrowing from several systems, some eclectics center their position on behaviorism and others center theirs on cognitive learning. In this chapter we develop some of the key ideas of Robert M. Gagné's behavioristic eclecticism and Jerome S. Bruner's cognitive oriented eclectic psychology.

HOW DOES GAGNÉ'S BEHAVIORISTIC-ECLECTIC PSYCHOLOGY DESCRIBE THE LEARNING PROCESS?

Robert M. Gagné (1916–   ) is a prominent educational psychologist whose *conditions of learning*[1] often are employed by methodologists and curriculum specialists to implement the achievement of the stated performance objectives of their behavioristic, eclectic methodologies. Hence, Gagné's psychology often is used to underpin the mechanistic instructional technology that is associated with behavior modification and *performance-* or *competency-based education*. Gagné's conceptional model is an *information-processing procedure* within which human learning processes are taken to be similar to the operations of a computer.

Because of his low esteem for the concept *insight,* Gagné depreciates the use of such verbs as know, understand, and appreciate in statements of educational objectives. In their place he promotes the use of overt action verbs such as state, derive, and identify. He then characterizes the use of the first group of verbs in statements of objectives as "ambiguous" and the use of the second group as involving "true" definitions of objectives.[2]

What Is Gagné's Definition of Learning?

For Gagné, "*Learning is a change in human disposition or capability, which can be retained, and which is not simply ascribable to the process of growth.*"[3] It exhibits itself as a change in observable behavior that happens under certain observable conditions. But the "Learning is something that takes place inside an individual's head—in his brain. Learning is called a *process* because it is formally comparable to other organic processes such as digestion and respiration."[4] "People do not learn in a general sense, but always in the sense of a change in behavior that can be described in terms of an observable type of human performance."[5]

Gagné distinguishes external conditions from internal conditions of learning. External conditions involve the arrangement and timing of stimulus events. Internal conditions include states such as attention, motivation, and the recall of the previously learned capabilities that are relevant to the person's present learning events.

The most important aspects of a learner, according to Gagné, "are his senses, his central nervous system, and his muscles."[6] For him, the learner's glands, motives, goals, intentions, and expectations, and his (or her) insights in regard to them, are only of secondary importance. Any learning capabilities that can be transferred must be stored in the learner's nervous system. Hence, all initial capabilities possessed by a learner must be conditions internal to him. Then, just as factors that influence growth are to a very large extent genetically determined, factors that influence learning are chiefly determined by events in an individual's environment. The input stimulus situation and the output response of the organism are directly observable variables. In contrast, "the nature of the connection between an S and an R cannot be directly observed."[7]

Gagné emphasizes the role of instrumental conditioning in learning and gives classical conditioning only minimal importance. For him, instrumental conditioning, as it occurs in school, is largely a matter of *information processing*, which is a complex of processes that take place in a learner's central nervous system. Within these processes, "Learning as a total process begins with a phase of apprehending the stimulus situation, proceeds to the stage of acquisition, then to storage, and finally to retrieval."[8]

Whereas radical behaviorists such as Professor Skinner emphasize the shaping of behavior through development of desired responses, Gagné stresses the organism's selection of stimuli. His basic paradigm is Ss → R. The symbol S represents the external stimulus, s represents the accompanying internal proprioceptive stimulation, and R represents the external response. Gagné thinks that stimuli are processed in quite a number of different ways by the human central nervous system and that our understanding learning is a matter of our figuring out how these various processes operate. The ways in which these processes operate are the conditions of learning.

What Are Gagné's Eight Conditions of Learning?

Gagné's eight conditions of learning or *learning types* are (1) signal learning, (2) stimulus-response learning, (3) chaining, (4) verbal association, (5) discrimination learning, (6) concept learning, (7) rule learning, and (8) problem solving. He states that his describing eight varieties of learning implies "that there are eight corresponding kinds of changes in the nervous system which need to be identified and ultimately accounted for."[9]

Each variety of learning begins with a different state of the organism and ends with a different capability for performance. "The most important class of conditions that distinguishes one form of learning from another is the initial state of the learning—in other words, its prerequisites."[10] In general, learning types 3 and 4 require type 2 as a prerequisite; type 5 requires types 2, 3, and 4; type 6 requires type 5; type 7 requires type 6; and type 8 requires type 7. Type 1 is reasonably important in its own right, but it is not considered a prerequisite to any of the other seven types of learning. Gagné's concept *learning hierarchies* implies that all eight kinds of learning are reducible to mechanistic S-R conditioning processes, and that the learning of any new capability requires the prior learning of subordinate capabilities.

Signal learning (type 1) is the classical conditioned response of Pavlov and Watson. It is stimulus substitution of such a nature that the organism learns to make a generalized response to a signal or stimulus. (See Chapter 12, p. 289 for a description of classical conditioning.)

Stimulus-response learning (type 2) is the instrumental conditioning of Thorndike. It is a process of response modification or change within which the learner acquires a precise response to a discriminated stimulus. "Thus the learning is really a matter of discrimination of correct and incorrect stimulation; of [discrimination of] that set of stimuli which produces reward (reinforcement) and that set of stimuli which does not. It is equally true to say that the response . . . becomes progressively differentiated."[11]

Behavioristic *chaining* may be either *motor* (type 3) or *verbal association* (type 4). "By chaining is meant the connection of a set of individual Ss → R's in a sequence."[12] Verbal association is the learning of verbal chains. Its conditions resemble those of learning motor chains. However, internal links may be selected from any part of the individual's previously learned repertoire of language. Gagné emphasizes that "the chain as a chain *cannot be learned unless the individual is capable of performing the individual* [Ss → R] *links*."[13] He also observes that the occurrence of some terminal satisfaction appears to be essential to the establishment of chains. But, he does little to develop the psychological significance of this observation.

Discrimination learning (type 5) is the process within which the individual that is involved learns to make a number of different identifying responses to as many different stimuli that, to some degree, may resemble one another in physical appearance. Discrimination learning is often concerned with distinctive features of objects. For example, a child learns to make distinctive responses to each of the printed letters of the alphabet.

Gagné observes that "most instruction in school subjects is concerned with the learning and use of concepts [type 6] and rules [type 7] and with problem solving [type 8]."[14] For him, *concept learning* is one's making a common response to a class of stimuli that may differ from each other widely in physical appearance. Within this process, the learner becomes able to respond in a single way to a collection of objects as a class; this response then becomes extended to include the learner's responding to other than the particular objects that were originally present. So, concept learning depends upon discrimination learning, which in turn depends upon verbal chaining, which is based on the S-R conditioning processes.

For Gagné, *rule learning* (type 7) is the formation of a chain of two or more concepts in the form of a built-in type of behavior that occurs in response to a class of stimulus situations. A rule "must be an internal state of the individual, which governs his behavior."[15] It is "*an inferred capability that enables the individual to respond to a class of stimulus situations with a class of performances*."[16] So, a rule is a superconcept. An example of a rule is "a pint doubled is a quart." The three concepts that are involved are "pint," "quart," and "doubled."

A rule may be stated verbally, but the rule itself is an inferred capability. To have a student learn the rule that "round things roll," "he must be asked to exhibit terminal responses that are possible only if he can, in fact, put together the concepts *round* and *roll*. Knowing the rule means [one's] being able to demonstrate that round things roll, not simply to say the words."[17] Whereas various kinds of verbal information such as facts, propositions, and generalizations do play an important role in the learning of new intellectual skills, for Gagné, they do not represent a stable basis for describing what the individual takes away with him from his education. Intellectual skills, on the contrary, do tend to remain with the individual over long periods of time.

Here we see an example of the psychological underpinning of the curricular dichotomy that is emphasized by many adherents of performance-based education. They set teaching for behaviors over against teaching for knowledge in such a way as to imply that knowledge consists of mere verbalizations. In contrast, Gestalt-field theorists emphasize that knowledge may better be defined in terms of expectancies or understandings that may be expressed in words, but need not be.

Gagné's *problem solving* (type 8) is "a natural extension of rule learning, in which the most important part of the process takes place *within the learner*."[18] It consists of the use of the "discovery method." Problem solving occurs when the instructions that are provided the learner do not include a verbally stated solution, but require him to construct such a solution on his (or her) own. In problem solving, the learner discovers a combination of previously learned rules that he can apply to achieve a solution for a novel problem situation. In this process, the learner combines two or more previously acquired rules to produce a new capability in the form of a higher-order rule. Extremely higher-order rules are *learning strategies*. So, "Rules are the stuff of thinking."[19]

What Are the Categories of Learning Outcomes?

For Gagné, the five major categories of human capabilities that are the outcomes of learning are (1) verbal information, (2) intellectual skills, (3) cognitive strategies, (4) attitudes, and (5) motor skills.[20] Whereas *verbal information* consists of a student's merely stating the desired information, *intellectual skills* involve the student's knowing how to perform an act as contrasted with knowing that certain conditions exist.[21] For example, an intellectual skill is one's distinguishing between a *b* and a *d*.

Gagné emphasizes that intellectual skills are not units of verbalized knowledge. So he states that in deriving them "one must carefully record statements of 'what the individual can do' and just as carefully avoid statements about 'what the individual knows.' . . . What learning hierarchies describe is, in computer language, subroutines of a program; what they do not describe [are] the facts or propositions retrievable from memory as verbalized statements."[22] Gagné does not completely discard verbalized knowledge. But, he does think that "the most important things learned in school are intellectual skills, and not verbalized knowledge."[23]

Cognitive strategies are a special kind of intellectual skills that pertain to the behavior of a learner, regardless of what he (or she) is studying. Specifically, they are internally organized capabilities that a learner employs in guiding his processes of attending, learning, remembering, and thinking.

For Gagné, What Is Teaching?

A teacher, according to Gagné, is a designer and manager of instruction and an evaluator of student learning. A total act of learning consists of the series of eight phases. Listed in the order of their occurrence, they are (1) motivation, (2) apprehension, (3) acquisition, (4) retention, (5) recall, (6) generalization, (7) performance, and (8) feedback.[24] For each phase of learning, one or more internal processes that correlate with the conditions of learning occur in the learner's central nervous system. Here, information is transformed from form to form until the individual responds with an outward performance.

Gagné thinks that after learning outcomes have been established they should be arranged in appropriate sequences of performance objectives for instruction. Then effective conditions of learning, should be brought into play. Finally, step by step, student achievement should be evaluated to make sure that the listed objectives are achieved.

The four most general components of instruction that a teacher has available for influencing the learning process in students are (1) the stimulation of recall of previously learned capabilities, (2) the direct presentation of appropriate stimuli, (3) the activation of desired mental sets, and (4) the provision of feedback.

A proper mental set for a given learning often is induced by verbal instructions. For example, the teacher tells the students to observe the shapes of a given group of figures, not their color.

Feedback is anything transpiring as the last phase of a learning event that is of such nature that it influences the learning that occurred during that event. To achieve feedback, in most instances teachers must communicate to students the outcomes of their learned performances as accurately as possible. For example, the teacher tells the students the degree of accuracy in their reporting an historical event.

In a typical instance of reinforcing feedback, the learner makes a response that reflects his (or her) newly acquired capability and then is told whether his response is right or wrong. More subtle cues also may be used for reinforcement of student behaviors. For instance, a teacher may either nod, smile, glance at the student, or proceed to the next point in the lesson. A student also may check his learning internally and provide self-reinforcement in terms of his knowing he (or she) has the right answer.

In Gagnéan problem solving, a student typically is *given a problem* by the teacher. The solution of the problem consists of the student's supplying the rules and the steps in applying them that will achieve the expected answer. For example, a problem for a class in social studies might involve the students' predicting the growth of stores in a local shopping center based on the projected pattern of housing that existed in the surrounding area. That which Gagné means by problem solving and discovery is quite different from what cognitive-field–oriented teachers mean by the concepts. Cognitive-field–oriented teachers help students *develop* and *solve* problems; they do not *give* problems to students.

HOW DOES BRUNER'S COGNITIVE-ORIENTED ECLECTIC PSYCHOLOGY TREAT LEARNING AND TEACHING?

Jerome S. Bruner (1915–   ) is a cognitive learning and developmental psychologist. His approach to psychology is eclectic, but in a highly sophisticated sense. In his study of human beings, he thinks of them as being information processors, thinkers, and creators. Bruner's eclecticism extends beyond benefiting from the contributions of various systematic psychologies to integrate with psychology knowledge from biology, anthropology, linguistics, philosophy, and sociology.

Although Bruner has not developed a systematic learning theory as such, a generalized theory about, and outlook concerning, learning is implicit in his various works. His principal concern has been with the means whereby people actively select, structure, retain, and transform information, and this is the essence of learning. Accordingly, he has centered his interests on the problem of what people do with information that they receive and how they go beyond discrete information to achieve generalized insights or understandings that give them competence. Bruner's approach has enough in common with cognitive-field psychology that a teacher may quite consistently use many of his ideas in implementing the application of cognitive-field theory to teaching-learning situations.

Two central unifying themes characterize Bruner's writing. The first is that the acquisition of knowledge, whatever its form, is a dynamic interactive process. The second is that a person constructs his (or her) knowledge through his relating incoming information to a previously acquired psychological frame of reference. This frame of reference is a "system of representation" or "internal model" that gives meaning and organization to the regularities in experience and permits an individual to go beyond the information given him. So, each person is regarded as a purposive participant in the knowledge-getting process who selects and transforms information, constructs hypotheses, and alters his hypotheses in light of inconsistent or discrepant evidence.

How Does Bruner View Human Motivation?

For Bruner, an individual is best viewed as neither a mystical active self nor a passive recipient of information. Accordingly, he has steered a middle course between mystical vitalism and behavioristic environmental determinism. He rejects any kind of transcendental vitalistic "purposivism" by saying that it has nothing to offer but "cheap solutions."[25] His psychology, however, is immanently purposive in the sense that he sees learning's being goal-directed. Accordingly, he makes such statements as "It is this future-oriented aspect of categorizing behavior in all organisms that impresses us most."[26]

Bruner suggests that people have a primary need, other than the "animal drives," that might be called "curiosity" and that keeps an organism active even in the absence of organic tensional states. So, our cognitive activity is not dominated at all times by concerns for only such things as food and sex.

How Is Learning a Cognitive Process?

Bruner sees learning as a cognitive process that involves three "almost simultaneous processes," namely, (1) acquisition of new information, (2) transformation of knowledge, and (3) checking the pertinence and adequacy of knowledge. A person's new information may either refine or contradict his (or her) previous knowledge. For example, a person may learn the details of the circulatory system after his already knowing vaguely that blood circulates. In transformation of knowledge one manipulates it to make it fit new tasks. Transformation, then, entails the way we deal with information so as to go beyond it either through extrapolation, interpolation, or converting it into another form. (To extrapolate is to extend experienced knowledge into an area not yet experienced; to interpolate is to alter knowledge by insertion of ideas.) We check the pertinence and adequacy of knowledge or information by evaluating whether the way we manipulate it is adequate to the task at hand; such an evaluation often involves judgments of knowledge's plausibility.

Bruner labels his view of learning "instrumental conceptualism."[27] This view is centered on two tenets concerning the nature of the knowing process: (1) a person's knowledge of the world is based on his or her constructed models of reality, and (2) such models are first adopted from one's culture, then they are adapted to one's individual use. So, Bruner makes much of the structured models of the world with which a culture equips its members. He states that

> Our knowledge of the world is not merely a mirroring or reflection of order and structure "out there" but consists rather of a construct or model that can, so to speak, be spun a bit ahead to things to predict how the world will be or might be.[28]

Models, in essence, are expectancies. Through his construction of models, a person does not simply deal with the information before him, but goes far beyond it. So, "Almost by definition, the exercise of intellect, involving as it must the use of short cuts and of leaps from partial evidence, always courts the possibility of error."[29]

A person's perception of an event is essentially a constructive process within which the person infers a hypothesis by relating his (or her) sense data to his model of the world and then checks his hypothesis against additional properties of the event. So, a perceiver is viewed not as a passive, reactive organism but rather as a person who actively selects information, forms perceptual hypotheses, and on occasion distorts the environmental input in the interest of reducing surprise and attaining valued goals. The act of perception, then, is one of categorization that is based upon a person's making an *inferential leap* from observed cues to his identifying a class of objects.

For Bruner,

> mental growth is not a gradual accretion, either of associations or of stimulus-response connections or of means-end readiness or of anything else. It appears to be much more like a staircase with rather sharp risers, more a matter of spurts and rests. The spurts ahead in growth seem to be touched off when certain capacities begin to develop.[30]

What Are Bruner's Three Modes of Representation?

Most mature persons, in their development, have proceeded through the elaboration of three systems of skills that correspond to the three major tool systems to which they must link themselves to fully express their capacities. These three systems of skills are Bruner's three *modes of representation* of reality. Bruner identifies these models of representation as *enactive, iconic,* and *symbolic* modes. *Representations* consist of systems of rules or generalizations by means of which an individual, in a manageable way, conserves the recurrent features of his (or her) environment. A person's representations collectively constitute his model of reality. They usually appear in the life of a child in the above order, and each depends upon the previous one for its development. Yet, all three of them extend more or less intact throughout an individual's life, and they are partially translatable into one another.

The *enactive* mode of representation is highly manipulative in character. It is one's knowing some aspect of reality without the use of imagery or words. Hence, it consists of one's representing past events through one's making appropriate motor responses. This mode is marked by an individual's single-track attention. Within it, one's knowing consists primarily in one's knowing how to do something; it consists of a set of actions that are appropriate for achieving a certain result. For example, a child enactively knows how to ride a bike or tie a knot.

Iconic representation is based upon internal imagery. Knowledge is represented by a set of images or graphics that stand for a concept but do not fully define it. For example, a diagrammatic triangle stands for the concept of triangularity. Iconic representation depends upon visual or other sensory organization along with the use of summarizing images that represent greater "chunks" of the environment. Iconic representation, then, is mainly governed by principles of perceptual organization and by techniques for making economical transformations in perceptual organization.

As a person approaches adolescence, language becomes increasingly important as a medium of thought. Then, the individual achieves a transition from the use of iconic representations based upon sensory imagery to the use of symbolic representation based upon an abstract, arbitrary, and more flexible system of thought. Language is the archetype of symbolic representation. It enables individuals to deal with what might or what might not exist, as well as with what does exist in experience. Hence, it is the principal tool of reflective thinking. The symbolic mode of representation is evidenced by a person's ability to consider propositions rather than objects, to give concepts a hierarchical structure, and to consider alternative possibilities in a "combinatorial fashion."[31]

Bruner uses the study of a balance beam to illustrate the distinction between the three modes of representation:

> A quite young child can plainly act on the basis of the "principles" of a balance beam, and indicates that he can do so by being able to handle himself on a see-saw. He knows that to get his side to go down farther he has to move out farther from the center. A somewhat older child can represent the balance beam to himself either by a model on which rings can be hung and balanced or by a drawing. The "image" of the balance beam can be varyingly refined, with fewer and fewer irrelevant details present, as in the typical diagrams in an introductory textbook in physics. Finally, a balance beam can be [symbolically] described in ordinary English, without diagrammatic aids, or it can be even better described mathematically by reference to Newton's Law of Moments in inertial physics.[32]

How Does Bruner Center Learning upon Conceptualization or Categorization?

For Bruner, learning is one's connecting things that are akin and connecting them into structures that give them significance. Remembering is not merely one's recitation of fixed, lifeless traces, but more a matter of one's achieving imaginative reconstructions. Bruner opposes the notion that people are passive receptors in perception, concept attainment, and reasoning. He thinks that in each case the acquisition of knowledge depends upon an imaginative process of construction. Learning at its best is thinking, and thinking is the process whereby one makes sense of a hodgepodge of perceived facts through a process called either *conceptualization* or *categorization*. Hence, the goal of Bruner's research is "to describe and in a small measure to explain what happens when an intelligent human being seeks to sort the environment into significant classes of events so that he may end by treating discriminably different things as equivalents."[33] Individuals categorize all discriminable colors into one concept, color, or into a few concepts, such as the "primary colors" or "the colors most fashionable in clothing this season." Similarly, they categorize people by social class, common personality traits, religious affiliation, nationality, size, or age.

Bruner's two basic types of categories are those of *identity* and *equivalence.* An identity category is formed by putting into one intellectual barrel or class a number of different variations of the same object. The moon goes through a series of phases ranging from a barely visible crescent to a full orb, yet we classify each phase of the moon as "moon." An equivalence category is one in which different kinds of objects are considered quite similar to one another and so are placed in the same barrel. Equivalence categories take three forms: affective, functional, and formal. However, the forms are not completely separated from each other.

What Is Bruner's Theory of Instruction?

Bruner has emphasized "the training of our students in the use of mind . . . with confidence, energy, honesty, and technique. It is in these processes that we place our confidence, not in any particular outcome."[34] "What is learned is competence, not particular performances."[35] To accomplish this goal, a teacher should be a day-to-day working model with whom students interact, not merely one to imitate.

A learned discipline may be conceived as a way of thinking about certain phenomena, and there is nothing more central to a discipline than its way of thinking. Hence, a school should provide students early opportunities to learn the ways of thinking, that is, to solve problems, to conjecture, and to dispute much as these processes are carried on at the heart of a discipline.

Professor Bruner states that a theory of instruction should take into account (1) the nature of persons as knowers, (2) the nature of knowledge, and (3) the nature of the knowledge-getting process. He thinks that

> Man is not a naked ape but a culture-clothed human being, hopelessly ineffective without the prosthesis provided by culture. The very nature of his characteristics as a species provides a guide to appropriate pedagogy, and the nature of his nervous system and its constraints provides a basis for devising reasonable if not inevitable principles for designing a testable pedagogy.[36]

In regard to the nature of knowledge, Bruner emphasizes that knowledge as it appears in our schooling should be put into the context of action and commitment. Hence, we should provide students with opportunities to learn skills in problem solving by giving them a chance to develop these skills on problems that, for them, have an inherent passion, for example, racism, crimes in the street, pollution, war and aggression, or marriage and the family. So, education should concentrate more on the unknown and the speculative, using what is known as a basis for extrapolation. It particularly should concentrate on subjects that have a visible growing edge but whose problems have no clearly known solutions, for example, the life sciences and the human sciences. However, adequate study in these areas entails study in the arts, literature, philosophy, science, mathematics, and logic.

In regard to the knowledge-getting process, the critical question is as follows: "How do you teach something to a child, arrange a child's environment, if you will, in such a way that he can learn something with some assurance that he will use the material that he has learned appropriately in a variety of situations?"[37] This includes a student's development of an approach to learning that enables him (or her) not only to learn it in such a way that he (she) will use the information in the solution of problems.

For Bruner, a theory of instruction should cover five major aspects:

1. The Optimum Experiences to Predispose Learners to Learn. These should highlight the role of students' intention and goal directedness in learning. Learning and problem solving entail the exploration of alternatives. Students should be in on where they are trying to go, what they are trying to get hold of, and how much pertinent progress they are making.

2. Structuring Knowledge for Optimum Comprehension. The ultimate aim in teaching is, "general understanding of the structure of a subject matter."[38] Students should be helped to discern knowledge that is significant from information that is less so. Knowledgeable experience should be coded in such a way that it is usable by students in both present and future learning and living situations.

Bruner defines a *coding system* as "a set of contingently related, non-specific categories"[39] that makes up one's pattern of enactive, iconic, and symbolic representations. So, one's coding system constitutes the means whereby one's concepts come to be combined into the structure of one's knowledge. It is a person's manner of grouping and relating information concerning the world. One's coding system is a hypothetical construct that is not directly observed, but is inferred from the nature of observable antecedent and consequent events and is subject to constant change and reorganization.

It is one's coding system that enables one to go beyond the information given, that is, to develop inventive behavior or to be creative. Bruner proposes that when a person goes beyond the information given he (or she) does so by virtue of his being able to place available empirical facts into a more generic coding system. Then, based upon either learned probabilities or learned principles of relating materials, he deduces additional information from his coding system.

As code is built upon code, or generalization is built upon generalization, a learner achieves increasingly "large" grasps of a subject. That is, he (or she) sees an ever increasing number of concepts and generalizations as related. The more generalized a coding system is, the more useful it is to a learner in that it relieves him of any need to learn and try to remember a great mass of isolated facts.

3. Specification of Optimal Sequences of Presentation of Materials to be Learned. For Bruner, an important task of an instructor is to convert knowledge into forms that fit growing minds. Materials to be taught should be properly tailored, sequenced, and put in forms appropriate to respective learners' existing modes of representation. Bruner states repeatedly that "Any idea or problem or body of knowledge can be presented in a form simple enough so that any particular learner can understand it in a recognizable form."[40] "Any subject, in short, can be taught to anybody at any age in some form that is honest and useful."[41] The task of schools, then, is to convert knowledge into structures that are within the grasp of learners of respective ages and to arrange the structures in an optimum sequence of materials to be learned.

The road, then, to a teacher's successful structuring of a subject matter is the development of a *spiral curriculum.* Such a curriculum begins with rudiments that children already have learned and builds upon them by adding more complex and subtle categories and codes; teaching, as it moves upward, constantly circles back to build upon previous understandings.

4. The Role of Success and Failure and the Nature of Reward and Punishment. Bruner distinguishes between two terminal alternative states that follow one's attempt either to know something or to master some task— success and failure and reward and punishment. Success and failure are inherent to the task at hand; thus, they constitute intrinsic motivation. Reward and punishment usually are controlled by one's parents or teacher; thus they constitute extrinsic motivation. Hence, "the use of reward and punishment seriously affects the informative utility of successful and unsuccessful attempts at problem-solving."[42] One reason for this is that success followed by strong external reward will tend to increase the likelihood of the same kind of behavior, and this result may or may not be desirable. If the learning is an achievement of a transitional state en route to more powerful learning, repetition of the behavior is not desirable. A second reason is that a behavioral error followed by an external punishment is more likely to disrupt a behavior than to provide a basis for its correction.

5. Procedures for Stimulating Thought in a School Setting. Instruction, according to Bruner, should make learners self-sufficient problem solvers or discoverers. But, Bruner does not restrict discovery to the act of finding out something that before was unknown to humankind. Rather, discovery includes "all forms of obtaining knowledge for ownself by the use of one's own mind."[43] Discovery

> whether by a schoolboy going it on his own or by a scientist cultivating the growing edge of his field, is in its essence a matter of rearranging or transforming evidence in such a way that one is enabled to go beyond the evidence so reassembled to additional new insights.[44]

Teachers should aim to give students a firm grasp of their subjects in such way as to promote students' being self-propelled thinkers who will proceed to learn on their own when their formal schooling is ended.

NOTES

[1] Robert M. Gagné, *The Conditions of Learning*, 2d ed., New York: Holt, Rinehart and Winston, 1970, p. 3.

[2] Ibid., p. 326.

[3] Ibid., p. 3.

[4] Robert M. Gagné, *Essentials of Learning for Instruction*, Hinsdale, Ill.: Dryden Press, 1975, pp. 4–5.

[5] Gagné, *The Conditions of Learning*, p. 237.

[6] Ibid., p. 4.

[7] Ibid., p. 34.

[8] Ibid., p. 78.

[9] Ibid., p. 62.

[10] Ibid., p. 65.

[11] Ibid., p. 106.

[12] Ibid., p. 123.

[13] Ibid., p. 125.

[14] Ibid., p. 67.

[15] Ibid., p. 191.

[16] Ibid., p. 191.

[17] Ibid., p. 197.

[18] Ibid., p. 214.

[19] Ibid., p. 216.

[20] Gagné, *Essentials of Learning for Instruction*, pp. 64–68.

[21] Ibid., p. 55.

[22] Robert M. Gagné, "Learning Hierarchies," in Harvey F. Clarizio, Robert C. Craig, and William A. Mehrens (eds.), *Contemporary Issues in Educational Psychology*, Boston: Allyn & Bacon, 1974, p. 230.

[23] Ibid., p. 234.

[24] Gagné, *Essentials of Learning for Instruction*, pp. 28–46.

[25] Jerome S. Bruner, Jacqueline J. Goodnow, and George A. Austin, *A Study of Thinking*, New York: Wiley, 1956, pp. 245–246.

[26] Ibid., p. 14.

[27] Jerome S. Bruner, R. R. Olver, P. M. Greenfield, et al., *Studies in Cognitive Growth*, New York: Wiley, 1966, p. 319.

[28] Jerome S. Bruner, *The Relevance of Education*, New York: Norton, 1971, p. xi.

[29] Ibid., p. 5.
[30] Jerome S. Bruner, *Toward a Theory of Instruction,* Cambridge: Harvard University Press, 1966, p. 27.
[31] Ibid., p. 28.
[32] Ibid., p. 45.
[33] Bruner, Goodnow, and Austin, *A Study of Thinking,* p. viii.
[34] Bruner, *Learning About Learning,* p. 121.
[35] Bruner, *The Relevance of Education,* p. 111.
[36] Ibid., p. 131.
[37] Ibid., p. 70.
[38] Bruner, *The Process of Education,* p. 6.
[39] Bruner and Anglin, *Beyond the Information Given,* p. 222.
[40] Bruner, *Toward a Theory of Instruction,* p. 44.
[41] Bruner, *Learning About Learning,* p. 202.
[42] Ibid., p. 207.
[43] Bruner and Anglin, *Beyond the Information Given,* p. 402.
[44] Ibid., p. 402.

BIBLIOGRAPHY

BRUNER, JEROME S. *On Knowing; Essays for the Left Hand.* Cambridge: Harvard University Press, 1962. A series of essays derived from papers, articles, and addresses, revised to provide continuity. Part 1 is on how one comes to know; Part 2 on how to teach and learn; and Part 3 on how one's conception of reality influences action. Provocative and stylistically excellent.

BRUNER, JEROME S. *The Process of Education.* Cambridge: Harvard University Press, 1960. The chairman's report of the major themes, principal conjectures, and most striking tentative conclusions of a 1959 conference of 35 natural scientists, psychologists, and educators on teaching science and mathematics in elementary and secondary schools. The report emphasizes teaching for understanding the structure—pertinent relationships—of a subject matter rather than for mastery of facts and techniques.

BRUNER, JEROME S. *Toward a Theory of Instruction.* Cambridge: Belknap Press of Harvard University, 1966. Presents Bruner's conclusions concerning what should go into a theoretical basis for teaching procedure. Bruner writes on a theoretical level but his ideas are highly thought-provoking.

BRUNER, JEROME S. *The Relevance of Education.* New York: Norton, 1973. Bruner emphasizes that educational reform must begin with an understanding of how children acquire information and convert information into action. Educational strategies must expand, not constrict, the learning skills of children and youth.

BRUNER, JEROME S. (ed.). *Learning About Learning: A Conference Report.* U. S. Department of Health, Education, and Welfare, Cooperative Research Monograph No. 15, 1966. Report of the working conference on research on children's learning. A major attempt to answer some important questions about the nature of the learning process. Major problems studied are (1) inducing a child to learn and sustaining his or her attention, (2) learning ideas and skills in one subject in such a way that they will assist progress in others, and (3) promoting optimum sequences of learning materials.

BRUNER, JEROME S., and JEREMY M. ANGLIN. *Beyond the Information Given: Studies in the Psychology of Knowing*. New York: Norton, 1973. Brings together Bruner's major contributions in his study of knowing as it relates to perception, thought, infancy, childhood, and education. Centers on the human process of knowing, experience, and achievement of insight, understanding, and competence.

BRUNER, JEROME S., JACQUELINE J. GOODNOW, and GEORGE A. AUSTIN. *A Study of Thinking*. New York: Wiley, 1956. A study based on research conducted at the Institute for Advanced Study (Princeton) and at Harvard University. Focuses on the formation and use of concepts. Technical, but an average student can read the introduction with profit.

BRUNER, JEROME S., R. R. OLVER, P. M. GREENFIELD, et al. *Studies in Cognitive Growth*. New York: Wiley, 1966. A study of intellectual development in children, based on the work of the Center for Cognitive Studies at Harvard. Has important implications for an understanding of child development as well as discussing how to teach meaningfully.

GAGNÉ, ROBERT M. *The Conditions of Learning*, 2d ed. New York: Holt, Rinehart and Winston, 1970. The conditions of learning set forth are eight distinguishable classes of performance change and the conditions associated with each. Emphasis is placed upon the hierarchical nature of the eight conditions and the use of reinforcement to implement them all. Sets the stage for the teacher's pursuing an educational technology.

GAGNÉ, ROBERT M. *Essentials of Learning for Instruction*. Hinsdale, Ill.: Dryden Press, 1974. Describes learning in terms of an information processing model. Describes instruction as an arrangement of external events to activate and support the internal processes of learning.

GAGNÉ, ROBERT M. "Learning Hierarchies," in Harvey F. Clarizio, Robert C. Craig, and William A. Mehrens (eds.), *Contemporary Issues in Educational Psychology*, pp. 224–239. Boston: Allyn and Bacon, 1974. Describes the sequential nature of learning and its transfer from simpler to more complex capabilities. Emphasizes skill entities in place of "knowledge" entities.

GAGNÉ, ROBERT M. "Some New Views of Learning and Instruction," *Phi Delta Kappan* (May 1970), pp. 468–472. Treats learning as information processing. Emphasizes importance of prerequisite intellectual skills necessary for each of the eight conditions of learning. Learning is described as being mechanistically cumulative.

GAGNÉ, ROBERT M., and LESLIE J. BRIGGS. *Principles of Instructional Design*. New York: Holt, Rinehart and Winston, 1974. Describes principles of design and development of plans and procedures for behavioristic instruction. Applies Gagné's eight conditions of learning to five categories of learning outcomes through the use of performance objectives. The five categories are intellectual skills, cognitive strategies, verbal information, motor skills, and attitudes.

SAHAKIAN, WILLIAM S. *Psychology of Learning: Systems, Models, and Theories.*

Chicago: Markham, 1970. Chapter 21 (pages 380–383) contains a biography of Gagné along with a summary of his eight types of the cumulative learning model.

SHULMAN, LEE S. "Psychological Controversies in the Teaching of Science and Mathematics," Harvey F. Clarizio, Robert C. Craig, and William M. Mehrens (eds.). *Contemporary Issues in Educational Psychology*, pp. 190–205. Boston: Allyn and Bacon, 1974. Contrasts views of Robert M. Gagné and Jerome S. Bruner in regard to the meaning of discovery. Whereas Gagné's discovery takes place within guided programmed learning, Bruner sees discovery as an actual creative process.

SHULMAN, LEE S., and EVAN R. KEISLAR (eds.). *Learning by Discovery, A Critical Appraisal,* Chapter 7, "Some Elements of Discovery" by Jerome S. Bruner. Chicago: Rand McNally, 1966. Treats discovery as it relates to a given culture. Bruner perfers the term problem solving rather than discovery in discussing creative learning.

Part IV
HOW MAY PSYCHOLOGY BE APPLIED TO CLASSROOM SITUATIONS?

A textbook on the psychological foundations of education would be incomplete without sections on the nature of intelligence and the classroom application of psychological principles. In Part IV, Chapters 17 and 18 discuss the nature of intelligence and its measurement as they are related to the teaching-learning process. Then, Chapters 19 to 21 concentrate on the teaching-learning process as such.

In these last three chapters we avoid merely providing students with an assortment of techniques. Instead, we restate, in summary form, theories that are developed earlier in the book and discuss the implications of respective theories for classroom practice. In no instance are theory and practice divorced, but Part IV does give teaching practices serious attention; Chapters 19–21 essentially are "how-to-teach" chapters.

Chapter 17
HOW IS INTELLIGENCE RELATED TO TEACHING AND LEARNING?

Due to the historical sequence of emerging psychologies of learning, the psychological underpinnings of modern education have become extremely diverse and mutually contradictory. Once a psychological position has been developed and popularized, centuries have been required for its influence to wane. As new positions are developed, they do not replace the old ones; they are merely grafted on to them. The result is an ideological hodgepodge of bewildering complexity. In the resultant educational atmosphere, one of the most perplexing problems involves the relationship of intelligence to learning. Consequently, a key to the significant differences in the outlooks and practices of teachers is their thinking in regard to the nature of intelligence and its development.

Although human beings of a given culture are more alike than they are different, they do differ tremendously. Furthermore, even though forces appear to be at work in the American culture that tend to induce even greater similarities of individuals, differences continue to be of great importance. So, we should always take them into account in planning teacher-student relationships.

Not only should teachers have a general knowledge of the nature and significance of individual differences, but they also should have some understanding of the technical aspects of how and in what ways people differ from one another and how significant this difference is to the operation of educational programs.

In the United States we attempt to educate all the children of all the people through the twelfth grade. Furthermore, for social reasons, we tend to keep children moving along through school so that most of those of a given age are concentrated at a single grade level, for example, most 8-year-olds are in the third grade. Whether this is the best possible practice is debatable, and there are notable exceptions to it. Nevertheless, it is the prevalent procedure and teachers must prepare themselves as best they can to cope with the situation.

Because of our general practice of promoting pupils according to age rather than achievement or ability, a teacher can expect to find a wide range of difference in intellectual ability among students in his or her classroom. A typical four-year comprehensive high school will enroll freshmen with measured IQs from 60 to 125 or higher, reading levels from the third to beyond the twelfth grade, and arithmetic levels from the fourth to fourteenth grade.

Today, in much of the literature of education, development of the capacity to think, that is, to make intelligent decisions, is a paramount goal. This is not to say that moral education is disregarded but rather that the method of intelligence is recommended in this area as well as in others. Why do many educators of today stress development of intelligence as a primary goal of education? One reason is the relation between the level of general intelligence of a citizenry and the successful functioning of democracy. This relationship has been noted for many centuries, often for the purpose of proving that, since the masses were so lacking in intelligence, democracy was an impractical ideal. But, by the late eighteenth or early nineteenth century, democracy had come to be widely accepted in a few countries not only as an ideal social arrangement but also as a practical system of conducting human relations. Those who thought democracy practicable, like Thomas Jefferson, felt that its potential for good could be realized only as the masses were educated. Jefferson recommended free public education—not much, but a little— for everyone. His assumption was that a system of free, compulsory public education would raise the general level of intelligence of a people.

Most people will say that intelligent behavior among the masses is prerequisite to successful functioning of democracy and that education is essential to mass intelligence. Yet, many of these same people do not have a very clear conception of what it means to be intelligent. Furthermore, they often are for intelligence only up to a point; when its application has reached a certain intensity and comprehensiveness, they become frightened of it. Consequently, they may regard a limited amount of intelligence as a necessity, but any excessive amount as subversive.

Although there may be disagreement as to the seriousness of the problems now confronting mankind, there probably would be little objection to the statement that numerous social difficulties exist that people have so far failed to alleviate to any significant degree. In addition to population growth and war, we might include in our list of problems extreme poverty and outright hunger in large parts of the world, political and economic centralization, bureaucratization, growing mechanization of life in industrial countries, and increasing pressures toward conformity.

To what extent can gains in the general level of intelligence help us achieve solutions, or even partial ones, to problems like these? No one can answer with certainty. In some areas of life we allow intelligence to operate comparatively unhampered. Especially in science and technology the method of intelligence seems firmly established and highly rewarded. A scientist or technician is rewarded for discovering flaws in old scientific or technical ideas, particularly ideas relating to design and manufacture of material goods. An inventor who devises a new military weapon or a new design for an automobile motor may become a national hero. It does not matter seriously that his or her invention makes obsolete all that has come before it.

But as James Harvey Robinson has pointed out,

> Our most important opinions—those, for example, having to do with traditional religious and moral conviction, property rights, patriotism, national honor, the state, and indeed all the assumed foundations of society—are . . . rarely the result of reasoned consideration, but of unthinking absorption from the social environment in which we live. Consequently, they have about them a quality of "elemental certitude," and we especially resent doubt or criticism cast upon them.[1]

Thus, we live in a paradoxical world. We tend to use the method of intelligence with boldness and zest in certain areas of living, and we reject it with great determination in others.

Children and youth vary in intelligence, physique, personality, aptitude, interests, motivation, and achievement. But, because of the importance that both parents and schools attach to the term intelligence, we devote the major part of this chapter to a discussion of its meaning and its significance to the teaching-learning process. Considerable controversy and confusion have surrounded the use of the term. Hence, the purpose of this chapter is to cut through some of the uncertainty by describing, in comparative fashion, the major positions that have been taken with respect to the nature and sources of intelligence and to give the reader some help in evaluating the positions against one another.

Each basic psychology of learning—mental discipline, natural unfoldment, apperception, S-R conditioning, and cognitive-field psychology—has its unique meaning for the concepts *intelligence* and *intelligent*. During the development of modern education, each psychology has had, or is having, its turn at the center of the stage. With every change in dominant psychology, schools have shown the consequences of application of the meaning of intelligence then in vogue. Consequently, confusion in regard to the nature of learning has carried with it a parallel perplexity concerning the nature and meaning of intelligence.

Representatives of all schools of thought take at least some interest in the intellectual development of individuals. However, they do not define intelligence in the same way, and they differ sharply in regard to whether intelligence should be the immediate end of education or merely a subsidiary goal or byproduct. Each psychological position has its own characteristic way of defining intelligence and of evaluating the proposal that promotion of intelligence be the central goal of education.

Prior to the 1600s it was thought that little, if anything, could be done to improve the intelligence of an average human being. Until the coming of the "Age of Enlightenment" in the seventeenth and eighteenth centuries, it was generally assumed that attempts to improve the quality of the intellect of an ordinary person were doomed to defeat. This pessimistic and fatalistic view of the human race dated from ancient times. However, a much more optimistic view developed in the eighteenth century. Liberal thinkers of France, England, the American colonies, and elsewhere, influenced by Locke's *tabula rasa* theory of sense empiricism, concluded that the intelligence of any normal person could be improved indefinitely through education. Faculty psychology, too, contributed to this line of thinking; intelligent behavior was assumed to be a product of the use of certain faculties (such as reason, memory, and imagination), which were strengthened by exercise.

Those who were optimistic about the improvement of intelligence tended to favor extension of formal education to the lower classes and improvement of education for everybody. However, during the time that the mental discipline approach to learning was the prevalent one, those who felt that education could improve the intelligence of students assumed that benefit could come only from either disciplinary drill or reading the classics.

HOW HAVE MENTAL DISCIPLINARIANS VIEWED INTELLIGENCE?

According to the doctrine of mental discipline, the chief purpose of education is to strengthen the mental faculties, especially will and reason, through appropriate kinds of drill. Although mental disciplinarians often fail to define their terms carefully, it is evident that their view of the meaning of intelligence is different from that of persons who reject this approach to teaching and learning. To mental disciplinarians, intelligence is a condition characterized by relatively high development of the faculty of reason. An intelligent person is a highly rational person. The faculty of reason, when well exercised and developed, qualifies its owner to reason intelligently in regard to most any matter.

Persons whose theory of mental discipline is tied to a theology are likely to stress strengthening of faculties such as will, moral discernment, and religiosity. In contrast, those whose theory of mental discipline is related to a nonreligious classical humanism are more likely to stress such faculties as reason, memory, and imagination, all of which might work together to produce "intellectual capacity."

Mental disciplinary attitudes in regard to individual differences date back to and before the time of the ancient Greek philosophers. Aristotle tended to divide people into two kinds: those with and those without a "deliberative faculty." He taught that human beings who lack the deliberative faculty are by nature slaves. He thought that inferior persons have enough ability to follow directions given by others but not enough to direct their own lives. Accordingly, they differ from lower animals in that, rather than being driven by instinct, they do engage in reason, but only passively. Thus, Aristotle believed that, although natural slaves are men and not brutes, they differ in kind, not merely degree, from those men who are naturally free. Consequently, he considered the use of slaves similar to the use of domesticated animals.

Ancient aristocrats, represented by Aristotle, denied anything like natural equality of persons and justified the institution of slavery in terms of natural inequality. As free people were distinguished from slaves, so education was distinguished from training. It apparently never occurred to an ancient aristocratic thinker that a manual worker of any kind should, for any reason, study cultural subjects such as poetry and music. Workers were trained to master specific jobs and there their education stopped. Adler and Mayer state the role of education in the ancient world, as conceived by the aristocratic class thus:

> Education, liberal in purpose and character, is for free men, for citizenship, leisure, and lofty pursuits. Slaves, serfs, manual workers, and even skilled artisans are trained, much as animals are trained.[2]

The idea of there being a natural aristocracy, that is, a group superior to most people because of its inheritance, continued to be accepted without much question down to the eighteenth century. In fact, in colonial America the sharp class structure reflected the wide-spread belief that people differ naturally, ranging from those who are fit only to rule to those who are fit only to serve. Such colonial leaders as Alexander Hamilton and the Adamses certainly believed in a natural aristocracy. Although Thomas Jefferson personally may have believed that all human beings are born potentially equal, as his statement in the Declaration of Independence seems to imply, he was clearly aware of the social fact of inequality. In a letter written in 1814 he stated,

> The mass of our citizens may be divided into two classes—the laboring and the learned. . . . At the discharging of the pupils from the elementary schools the two classes separate—those destined for labor will engage in the business of agriculture, or enter into apprenticeship to such handicraft art as may be their choice; their companions, destined to the pursuits of science, will proceed to the College.[3]

Faculty psychology emphasized that people are born virtually equal and that individual differences are developed thereafter. The central thesis of faculty psychology is that each person has a single unitary mind; this mind has several specific faculties, such as memory, will, and reason; and the strengths of these faculties depend upon the degree to which they are exercised. Within this pattern of thinking, individual differences might be construed as the result of different amounts of exercise of the various faculties of the mind (see Chapter 10, pp. 240–251 for a detailed treatment of mental discipline).

A curious pseudo science, designed for the purpose of measuring individual differences, arose in connection with faculty psychology. This was phrenology. Phrenologists felt it reasonable to assume a direct relationship between the development of one's faculties and the contour of one's skull. Early in the nineteenth century, E. G. Gall, a prominent phrenologist, listed 27 powers of the mind. He then attempted to link them with 27 regions of the brain. He assumed that development of a specific mental function depends on development of the corresponding brain area. Furthermore, he thought that such cerebral development exerted pressure on the skull, pressing it outward in the form of bumps.

Phrenologists such as Gall thought that they could measure the relative development of a person's faculties by feeling his or her skull. Consequently "bump feeling" was taken very seriously by some of our most prominent early American educators. For instance, Horace Mann (1796–1859), who was secretary of the Massachusetts State Board of Education from 1837 to 1848 and a leading figure in American education, was enthusiastic over the "science" of phrenology.

HOW DO PSYCHEDELIC HUMANISTS VIEW INTELLIGENCE?

Any drastic departure from a mental disciplinary approach to education is possible only through the adoption of some fundamentally different assumptions about the moral nature of human beings and their relationship to their environments. The psychedelic humanistic approach is based upon the assumption that people are innately good and active. Let us follow the train of thought that emerged as the result of Rousellian romantic-naturalistic influences.

If the human being is a part of nature, and if all of nature is intrinsically good, then the human being is naturally good. (This line of reasoning is developed in considerable detail in Chapter 10, pp. 251–254). If a child is born good, and his (or her) natural tendencies lead him to remain so, then it follows logically that children should be reared permissively; there is no need for their being disciplined at any time. A permissive classroom is one in which there is virtually unlimited freedom. A permissive situation, then, is an extreme laissez-faire one. Permissive, as used here, may be considered the opposite of such terms as teacher-centered, centralized, directed, and autocratic.

The term permissive should not be confused with democratic. A democratic group is led, and in the process it may be subject to a variety of restraints. Accordingly, in a democratic classroom there is not *unlimited freedom* but rather *equally limited freedom.* Consequently, we may think of democracy as an emergent synthesis arising from the inadequacies of both anarchic laissez-faire and autocratic forms of organization.

How exponents of natural unfoldment or psychedelic humanism define intelligence is not entirely clear. Conceivably, they might employ any of the extant definitions. However, it is clear that they regard the development of intelligence as something that "just naturally happens." Thus, there is no need for formal teaching to enhance the intelligence of children; it just grows on its own. One's intelligence is closely identified with one's knowledge, and

> in the last analysis, knowledge rests on the subjective: I *experience;* in this experiencing, I *exist;* in this existing, I in some sense *know,* I have a felt assurance. All knowledge, including all scientific knowledge, is a vast inverted pyramid resting on this tiny, personal, subjective base.[4]

This tiny, personal, subjective base is the experienced "I."

HOW HAVE HERBARTIAN APPERCEPTIONISTS VIEWED INTELLIGENCE?

Apperceptionists, in the tradition of early mentalistic associationism, have had a characteristic manner of defining intelligence as an acquired ability. Remember that they have regarded learning as a process of storing away ideas. Hence, they have equated intelligence with capacity to associate and retain ideas and call them forth when needed in proper association with one another. Intelligence refers to a person's acquired general effectiveness at storing "mental marbles" in an organized fashion and selecting efficiently those that are appropriate as the need arises. The active nature of intelligence, however, resides in the store of "marbles," not in the "container." (See Chapter 10, pp. 254–265 for an explanation of apperception.)

Intelligence, then, is a product of learning. All people, except those who obviously are defective, have the same potential at birth, which is a unique kind of emptiness and receptivity. The intelligence that they achieve stems from the opportunities for learning that they have. This means that the intelligence of any normal person can be improved indefinitely through imposed education; one's apperceptive mass can be expanded continuously and it has an unlimited capacity.

HOW HAVE SCIENTIFIC PSYCHOLOGISTS APPROACHED THE STUDY OF INTELLIGENCE?

Early twentieth-century scientific psychologists usually thought of intelligence as a general capacity or potential for learning that could be directed along most any line of endeavor. However, they advanced several competing ideas concerning its exact nature and its source.

What Is the Nature of Intelligence?

Alfred Binet (1857–1911), a French psychologist, in 1905 designed the first widely used test of mental ability as a means of identifying academically promising students in the schools of Paris. He gave little attention to a theoretical definition of intelligence. But, for him, intelligence was unitary in the sense that each person had a certain amount that could be used for most any purpose; it was a general ability to learn. Accordingly, if a person did better in one field of activity than in another, it was due, not to any fundamental variation in intelligence relative to the two fields, but to factors such as learning, interest, and motivation. To illustrate: a person who learns to play a musical instrument brilliantly does not have a different kind of intelligence from that of a brilliant engineer, chef, actor, or seamstress. Rather, he (or she) chooses to direct his talents toward music because a combination of environmental factors impels him in this direction.

Lewis Terman (1877–1956), an American psychologist, saw intelligence as ability to do abstract thinking, an ability which can be directed toward repairing an automobile motor just as well as toward solving a problem in quantum mechanics. William Stern (1871–1938), a German professor, regarded intelligence as adaptability to new problems and conditions of life. To him, solving a problem involving marital discord was as good an example of the functioning of intelligence as devising an original algebraic formulation.

The concept of intelligence as an unitary or general capacity eventually came under considerable criticism. Charles E. Spearman (1863–1945), an English psychologist, thought that two factors contributed to every intelligent act: g, a general factor operative in all situations, and s, a specific factor operative only in situations where that specific factor is involved. Thus, he thought that a person's capacity to act in any situation depends both upon his (or her) general capacity and upon the special capacity involved in that particular act. To illustrate: a person might have a fairly mediocre general intelligence but a very high order of special capacity in, say, music.

To split intelligence still further, the American psychologist Edward L. Thorndike divided it into three kinds—mechanical, social, and abstract. He thought that each kind of intelligence is manifested by the quality of responses that a person can make to stimuli in whichever of the three areas that is involved. A person might have a high degree of mechanical intelligence without a corresponding level of social or abstract intelligence. In this case he might be highly competent in working with motors, but be ineffective in working with other persons or solving problems in higher mathematics. Similarly, a person might be extremely adept in persuading others, in which case he (or she) might perform brilliantly as a salesperson, but be incapable of changing a tire or passing an introductory course in philosophy. Or, a person might be extraordinarily able in dealing with abstract ideological matters and yet highly inept socially and mechanically.

For Thorndike, a person's intelligence was his (or her) capacity to form links or bonds between sensory stimuli and motor responses to retain these links, and to repeat the proper sequence of motions when confronted with an appropriate stimulus at some time in the future. So, Thorndike maintained that a person's intelligence is represented by the sum total of the stimulus-response bonds that have been formed. He made clear, however, that the person's intelligence actually is not the bonds themselves but the capacity to form them; it is a function of the way an organism is put together.

All of these early twentieth-century definitions of the nature of intelligence assumed that, whether intelligence is unitary or composed of two, three, or more somewhat independent factors, it is basically a capacity—a learning potential. This capacity, whatever its origin, was assumed by early twentieth-century psychologists to be relatively fixed once a person reached adulthood.

The early workers in the area of intelligence who were adherents of a mechanistic stimulus-response psychology construed the nature of intelligence as capacity to form new responses to stimuli in a rapid and accurate manner in situations that so permit. However, today the idea that one's intelligence is a fixed characteristic is being challenged by much more flexible conceptions: Functionally defined, one's intelligence consists of the effectiveness of one's approaches to situations in which competence is valued in a given culture. David Wechsler, an authority on adult intelligence, defines intelligence as "the aggregate or global capacity of the individual to act purposefully, to think rationally and to deal effectively with his environment."[5]

What Is the Source of Intelligence?

Traditionally, the two basic sources of individual differences of any kind have been considered to be heredity and environment. Although it is true that heredity and environment do influence human traits, they also influence each other, and human traits cannot be separated into those which depend entirely upon heredity and those which depend completely upon environment. (See Chapter 8, pp. 429–430 for a discussion of the futility of the nature-nurture controversy.) For any individual, the presence or absence of a certain type of heredity structure can provide or limit opportunity for development, but it cannot insure that a certain kind of behavior will or will not be manifested. A person's genes help provide and limit opportunity but do not determine what will be made of that opportunity.

The crucial question in regard to the source of intelligence is to what degree is it (1) genetic endowment, (2) a product of learning, or (3) a combination of the two? If intelligence is genetic endowment as was thought by Thorndikean connectionists, then it bears a one-to-one relation to the quality of genes that determine the structure and functioning of the organic-neural-endocrine system. Intelligence is a function of the way an organism is put together; it hinges upon physical structure. From this point of view, it is relatively fixed in each individual; a person can function only to a certain point of efficiency—he (or she) can do no more. To expect additional achievement would be like expecting the runner of a 4-minute mile to increase his speed so that he was running the mile in, respectively, 3½ minutes, 3 minutes, then 2½ minutes.

Connectionistic psychologists have thought that the two traits deemed crucial to intelligence—complexity and modifiability of the nervous system—are transmitted from parents to offspring. Thus, intelligence, like other physical traits, is determined by physical inheritance, and its level, once maturity is reached, is constant for each individual, just as are the colors of his (or her) eyes and skin. Since intelligence was given a physiological basis and a given person's neural structure was not likely to change, it was only logical to suppose that an organisms potential for intelligent behavior also would not change.

If intelligence is solely the product of learning, then all people, except those who are obviously defective, have the same potential at birth. So, the intelligence level that they achieve stems from the opportunities for learning that they have had. Since the potential of each person is very high, few persons ever come close to reaching their maximum biological potential. It should be obvious to readers that this outlook is consistent with Locke's *tabula rasa* idea and the Watsonian version of early twentieth-century behaviorism.

At about the same time that Thorndike was emphasizing innate differences in intelligence, John B. Watson was writing about human behavior and learning in such a way as to imply that all healthy normal people are essentially equal at birth. However, like Thorndike, he was aware of great differences among them, but he credited these to differences in environment. Watson was convinced that in any normal person the capacity for forming neural bonds was so great that he or she would never make full use of it. He therefore assumed that an average person does not learn up to capacity, and the amount he does learn is purely a function of the environment. So, Watson believed that almost any normal person could acquire the same complicated conditioning that, say, a skilled surgeon could achieve. Thus, on the matter of intelligence, Watson was an environmentalist.

Every environmental determinist, if consistent, necessarily accepts the notion that intelligence, at least in large measure, is learned. This is a comforting belief for persons who are required to work with seemingly retarded people. It provides a source of never-ending optimism. To a considerable extent welfare workers, sociologists, and some public school teachers find the extreme environmental determinist point of view satisfying.

Some of the studies of changes of IQ in individuals give support to the hypothesis that intelligence is learned rather than inborn. However, other research rather strongly supports the notion that one's potential intelligence is a matter of genetic endowment and is therefore relatively fixed. Actually, research provides us with no conclusive data to support either of the extreme positions that we have just described.

If intelligence is the product of both genetic endowment and learning, then there are two possible positions in regard to the nature of this product. Behavioristic oriented psychologists such as Arthur E. Jensen speculate in regard to the actual existent relative strength of the two factors and draw conclusions in this regard. For example Jensen states that, "on the average, genetic factors [in intelligence] appear to be about twice as important as environmental factors, including prenatal influences."[6]

Cognitive-field psychologists, in contrast to most behaviorists, view intelligence as the product of a person's purposive interaction. So, in this view, intelligence is a product of the interaction of a human self and its perceived environment. That is, in asserting the basis of one's intelligence, it is assumed that both poles—one's person or self and one's psychological environment—are important but that it is impossible to assess the relative importance of either pole.

In the interactive process the quality of perception is of crucial importance. A person may have a physical organism, including sensory organs, of excellent quality, but his (or her) perceptions of himself and his environment may, because of previous learnings, be extremely faulty. Conversely, a person may have a mediocre physical organism, including sensory organs, but, because of previous learnings, his perceptions may be first rate. Since, to date, there is no known scientific way of determining the relative importance of genetic physical structure and learning as a source of intelligence, we may relegate this argument to the same limbo as that over how many angels can dance on the point of a needle.

HOW DO CONTEMPORARY BEHAVIORISTS VIEW INTELLIGENCE?

In the first quarter of the twentieth century the two dominant S-R conditioning psychologies were Thorndikean connectionism and Watsonian behaviorism. Today's S-R conditioning theories or behaviorisms are modifications and refinements of these two earlier psychologies.

The characteristic contemporary behavioristic position in regard to the source of intelligence is that it, like all behavior, is the result of a given genetic inheritance plus the influence of an impinging environment. Each child at birth has a certain organic capacity for intellectual development. The degree of stimulation of the organism by the environment then determines the intellectual level of the functioning organism.

D. O. Hebb distinguishes two intelligences. Intelligence A is one's innate potential for the development of intellectual capacities; intelligence B is one's level of development at sometime after birth when one's intellectual functions may be observed. One's IQ is a measurement of one's intelligence B; from this measurement one's intelligence A might be inferred. But, Hebb warns,

> The extent to which intelligence can be developed may be low, in which case no environment can produce a high IQ; then heredity sets a limit on the development. But the child may have inherited a better brain, capable of developing a high IQ, and yet in a poor environment his IQ remains low—just as with a child that inherited a poorer brain.[7]

Arthur R. Jensen, who sees a strong correlation between intelligence and educability, writes, "it is the general intelligence factor— the g which all tests of mental ability share in common—that correlates most highly with achievement."[8] ". . . something over 60 percent of the true variance in individual differences in scholastic achievement is accounted for by individual differences in intelligence."[9]

WHAT DO COGNITIVE-FIELD PSYCHOLOGISTS MEAN BY INTELLIGENCE?

Cognitive-field psychologists define intelligence as the ability to respond in present situations on the basis of a discerning anticipation of the possible consequences and with a view to controlling the consequences that ensue. One's intelligence so defined consists of the number and quality of one's insights, that is, the differentiations, generalizations, and structurizations of one's life space. Within this frame of reference, successful behavior rightfully may be called intelligent only when a person might have done otherwise and his (or her) actions were premised upon an envisioning of what he was doing and why. Learning is enhancement of one's intelligence. This means that all of its forms— development of logical organization, social insight, appreciation, information, and skills—have a common element. They all involve a change in the experiential situation of a person that gives him a basis for greater predictability and control in relation to his behavior; they enhance the person's intelligence.

When one is behaving intelligently, one is pursuing some purpose and one has some degree of foresight as to how the purpose is to be achieved. So, intelligence is that capacity to act with dependable *foresight,* which is the product of the *interaction* of a person and his perceived psychological environment.

How Is Intelligence the Ability to Act with Foresight?

When we think of intelligence as the ability to act with foresight, we are not contradicting the notion that it is a capacity; rather, we are making different assumptions about the nature of this capacity. When a person acts with foresight, he (or she) looks ahead; he tries to anticipate the consequences of acting in a particular way; and he makes forecasts regarding the outcome of alternative lines of action. These forecasts are based upon experience. They are made possible by the fact that experience has equipped the person with a number of functional generalizations, rules, or principles that are invoked as needed to predict the consequences of present action. For example, having learned by experience that although rattlesnake bites are not usually fatal they do make one very ill, a person will behave very cautiously in rattlesnake country so as to avoid getting bitten.

When intelligence is defined in such manner, the quality or level of a person's intelligence hinges upon the number and accuracy of generalizations or rules learned plus the person's ability and willingness to invoke these rules, flexibly and imaginatively, in situations that call for them. Seldom does a rule learned from past experience fit a new situation precisely. Consequently, ability to recognize what is appropriate to a situation and to take proper action is, from this point of view, an indication of intelligence. Thus, we cannot separate intelligence from what we usually call originality or creativity. Brilliant children or adults differ from their less brilliant fellows in both what they are able to think about and what they are able to do with their thoughts.

When two situations seem superficially alike, more intelligent persons characteristically discern significant differences that would escape less intelligent persons. They do not slur over fine distinctions whenever such distinctions are relevant to solving a problem at hand. Thus, in difficult situations, they are able to test their hunches or hypotheses intellectually so that in their overt behavior they appear to do a minimum of fumbling and they choose the correct act sometimes almost instantly. But not in every kind of situation is an intelligent choice instantaneous; Einstein required several years to develop and perfect the theory of relativity.

What Are the Limits of Human Intelligence?

The cognitive-field conception of intelligence assumes that, although influenced by hereditary factors, problem-solving ability is susceptible to change in a normal person and can improve through education. If one's education includes not only opportunity for problem solving but also opportunity to study the problem-solving process as such and to achieve generalized insights about it, most new problems will be approached more intelligently than they would have been before. Thus, as a person acquires more, and more adequate, generalized insights he (or she) becomes more intelligent.

Experiments with twins, siblings, and children in foster homes indicate that children living in privileged environments test higher in intelligence than do children in less privileged environments. Children moved from unfavorable to more favorable environments tend to measure higher in intelligence than their twins who remain in the more unfavorable environments (see Chapter 18, pp. 441–443 for a description of some of these experiments). G. D. Stoddard in 1943 wrote: "It can be predicted with some confidence that when homes and schools give the child what he truly needs, at all ages from the first year upward, there will be a radical revision in the norms and standards of mental tests."[10]

A 1961 article by Martin Mayer reported data on intelligence score variability as dramatic as any the authors have seen.[11] Mayer reported how New York City, among others, was making a determined effort to "build a fire" under slum youngsters in order to improve academic performance and increase the proportion who graduate and go on to college.

In Manhattanville Junior High School 43, a few spectacular results had been observed. One boy leaped from a measured IQ of 97 on entrance to 139 before high school graduation. Another who started with an IQ of 74 ended with a scholarship to New York University. Another started with an IQ of 99 and finished in the top 15 percent on the College Entrance Board's examination and with a full scholarship to Amherst.

Human beings and lower animals develop insights not only in learning but also in learning how to learn. Harry F. Harlow, a psychologist who has experimented extensively with animals writes as follows:

> The learning of primary importance to the primates, at least, is the formation of learning sets; it is the *learning how to learn efficiently* in the situations the animal frequently encounters. This learning to learn transforms the organism from a creature that adapts to a changing environment by trial and error to one that adapts by seeming hypothesis and insight.[12]

Exponents of cognitive-field theory, more than representatives of any other system of modern psychology, have emphasized that capacity for intelligent behavior can be modified by learning almost infinitely. Given a healthy physical organism to provide the vehicle for perception, a stimulating environment, challenging and fruitful problems, and a non-restrictive self-concept, there seems to be no limit to a person's possible perceptions. So, with the proper conditions there is no reason why a person's intelligence should not increase throughout life. Of course, old age may produce a physiological deterioration that reduces the capacity for differentiating new perceptions. On the other hand, it is possible to cite numerous cases of persons who have retained a remarkable capacity for intellectual growth and creativity until the age of 90 or beyond.

To a large degree a person's intelligence is dependent upon the degree of his (or her) change in motivation, bodily coordination, and time perspective, his differentiation of aspects of his person from those of his environment, and his discernment of levels of concrete and imaginative reality. As a child develops by means of these processes, he learns increasingly to understand and control his environment. However, teachers have no reason to fear that a student will soon acquire complete understanding and will see no further need to learn. The only persons who may think they know everything are the ones who know practically nothing. Once a student launches a serious study of his environment, his life space accelerates its rate of expansion. As his understanding expands to encompass newly gained regions of his life space, his life space also grows to such a degree that his motivation for study actually multiplies. This is illustrated graphically in Figure 17.1.

By the time Helen is four years old she has some insights and understandings. However, there still are many things around her that she does not understand but which are part of her life space in the sense that she realizes that they have something to do with her. When Helen reaches her eighth birthday, she has expanded her world of understanding to encompass more and more of her psychological environment. But, interestingly, because of the dynamic nature of human beings, Helen's psychological environment also expands. A teacher's job, then, is one of enhancement, enrichment, and acceleration of this psychological growth process. Teaching, in its best sense, consists of promotion and enrichment of the interactive learning process, both qualitatively and quantitatively.

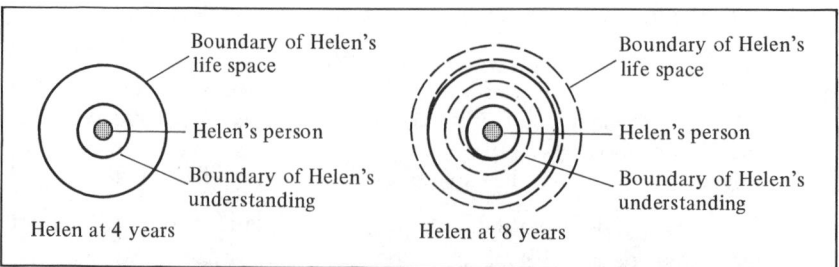

Figure 17.1   Helen's understanding of her life space at ages 4 and 8.

Such teaching is a process of helping students both broaden and put greater quality into their psychological worlds.

The view of intelligence herein described rejects the notion that the intelligence of anyone, including adults, is fixed. With an increase in age and experience, a person may show increased flexibility of behavior and imagination. Furthermore, a person's gain in intelligence may not be equated with a gain in age: it may be much faster in rate, or much slower. Adults may continue to gain in intelligence as long as they live. On the other hand, for certain individuals intelligence may appear to be relatively fixed; for various reasons they have ceased growing intellectually. The point is, we cannot say that it is because of innate limitations that such persons cease growing. Some qualifications of this position, however, are necessary.

Perception hinges in part on the purpose and efficiency of sensory organs and other physical structures. If the goal is to pounce on a field mouse, then a high-flying eagle can behave more intelligently than a human being, not only does its position vis-à-vis the mouse confer an advantage, but it can see more acutely. Obviously, poor eyesight, deafness, "taste blindness," and other sensory defects reduce the capacity for dependable perception. On the other hand, human beings as well as other creatures can often go far in compensating for impaired sensory capacity, for example, consider Helen Keller.

Some nonphysiological factors also are central to the development of a person's intelligence. Thy include the opportunity a person has for exposure to a rich environment, the length of time he (or she) has had to improve his perceptions, goals, and values, the cultural milieu in which he is placed, his concept of self, and his feeling of threat.

The two latter points need to be expanded. A person is unlikely to behave any more intelligently than he (or she) thinks he can. If a person is convinced that he is stupid with respect to certain tasks, his conviction will limit his capacity for perception in connection with these tasks. All teachers have known students who had persuaded themselves that they could not learn arithmetic, the parts of speech, or spelling. Once convinced, they found it quite impossible to learn these things. On the other hand, over-confidence as to what one can learn can lead to equally serious inaccuracies of perception.

A sense of threat also limits capacity for accurate perception. When people feel a threat, they are inclined to restrict their perception to the source of threat; they become aware of little else. In addition to a "tunnel vision" effect, threat tends to make persons defensive and rigid concerning their present pattern of attitudes, values, and beliefs. That is, threat produces "closed-mindedness," within which capacity for intelligent action is reduced.

In consideration of the foregoing point of view concerning the flexibility of intelligence, a further word of caution is necessary. It is by no means easy for a person continuously to improve the number and quality of his or her perceptions. Although one's perceptual field, or life space, undergoes continuous modification, these changes more often involve minor attitudes, values, and beliefs that are not central to one's personality structure. Religious convictions, for example, are not so likely to change readily—not like one's taste in clothing or automobiles.

The essential ingredients for continued growth in intelligence are open-mindedness to new ideas and willingness to criticize one's most cherished convictions. Since for most persons attainment of these ingredients is very difficult, their intelligence quotients (IQs), as revealed by any known measuring device, do not change markedly over the course of time, and in the case of some persons the IQ may even regress. There is reason to suppose, however, that one's degree of open-mindedness and one's ability for self-criticism are largely a function of one's education. (See Chapter 18 pp. 429–433 for a definition of IQ.)

In discussing intelligence we should consider another dimension of experience—emotion. Faculty psychologists, apperceptionists, and behaviorists have tended to separate emotion and thought. But, for cognitive-field psychologists, thinking never occurs apart from feeling. A person who habitually displays a given level of intelligence also experiences emotion as he or she thinks. So emotion is one aspect of the process we call thinking. Of course, some types of feeling, if experienced with intensity, may hinder rational decision. One of the most common is the fear a person feels when he thinks some aspect of his self is under threat. However, the most careful thought may be accompanied by considerable amounts of fear, discouragement, elation, or other feeling states.

NOTES

[1] James Harvey Robinson, *The Mind in the Making*, New York: Harper & Row, 1921, p. 61.

[2] Mortimer J. Adler and Milton Mayer, *The Revolution in Education*, Chicago: University of Chicago Press, 1958, p. 72.

[3] Ibid., p. 3.

[4] Carl R. Rogers, "Some Thoughts Regarding the Current Presuppositions of the Behavioral Sciences," in William R. Coulson and Carl R. Rogers, (eds.), *Man and the Science of Man*, Columbus, Ohio: Merrill, 1968, p. 60.

[5] David Wechsler, *The Measurement and Appraisal of Adult Intelligence*, 4th ed., Baltimore: Williams & Wilkins, 1958, p. 7.

[6] Arthur R. Jensen, *Educability and Group Differences*, New York: Harper & Row, 1973, p. 355.

[7] D. O. Hebb, *Textbook of Psychology*, 3d ed., Philadelphia: Saunders, 1972, p. 163.

[8] Jensen, p. 73.

[9] Ibid., p. 72.

[10] George D. Stoddard, *The Meaning of Intelligence*, New York: Macmillan, 1943, p. 392.

[11] Martin Mayer, "The Good Slum Schools," *Harper's Magazine* (April 1961): 47ff.

[12] Harry F. Harlow, "The Formation of Learning Sets," *Psychological Review* 56 (January 1949):51.

BIBLIOGRAPHY

References pertaining to Chapters 17 and 18 are at the end of Chapter 18. These two chapters should be studied as a unit.

Chapter 18
HOW IS INTELLIGENCE MEASURED?

Many psychologists and educators, especially those sympathetic to cognitive-field psychology, take the position that the most advantageous way for today's teachers to deal with the concept of intelligence is to consider it *learning acumen* defined in terms of keenness of perception, discernment, and discrimination. Learning acumen, so defined, is a person's capacity to act with dependable foresight, which is the product of the person's interaction with his (or her) psychological environment. So construed, a person's functional intelligence is capable of constant improvement through further education. To a great extent, it is the effective utilization of tools provided by one's culture. So, the intelligence, or mind, of a person depends greatly upon the language of his culture.

Teachers should distinguish between the concepts *intelligence* and *IQ*. One's intelligence is simply the level of clear-headed efficiency at which one operates. One's IQ is a measure of how far a person's mentality has progressed in comparison with that of other individuals of the person's age; it is a measure of how mentally big or small one is for his age.

Prior to the twentieth century the prevalent trend was to place individuals into one of several distinct intellectual classes such as brilliant, bright, or dull. It was assumed that the class into which an individual fell was largely a hereditary matter. Early in the twentieth century, attempts were launched to devise graduated scales of intelligence. In recent years, many such scales have been devised, but the legitimacy and usefulness of such quantitative measures of intelligence are now being seriously challenged. (Some states are even passing laws that either limit or prohibit their use.)

HOW HAVE INTELLIGENCE TESTS BEEN DEVELOPED?

In 1905, Binet introduced the first scale of intelligence; it was graduated in terms of *mental age*. Regardless of their chronological age, when children can pass the items that are passed by the average 10-year-old, their mental age (MA) measures 10. A shortcoming of this scale was that it often was erroneously assumed that, if a 12-year-old child measured a mental age of 10, when he (or she) became 15 years old he still would be only two years behind the average of his group. Actually, provided his motivation and stimulation proceeded on about the same level as before, at age 15, he was likely to be two and a half years behind the average of his group.

To remedy this deficiency, in 1911 William Stern introduced the concept *mental quotient* to be measured by dividing a person's mental age by his chronological age. This quotient would remain relatively constant; if it was .80 at age 12, it probably would be approximately .80 at age 15. When Terman issued the Stanford Revision of the Binet Scale in 1916, he renamed Stern's quotient the *intelligence quotient*. In the process he multiplied the quotient by one hundred to eliminate decimals. The result was the IQ as we know it today.

Terman and his associates thought that one's IQ remained fairly constant; the relative level of intelligence of an adult was predictable in early childhood. The two traits crucial to intelligence—complexity and modifiability of one's nervous system—were transmitted to one through one's genetic familial inheritance. Intelligence, like other physical traits, was determined by physical inheritance, and its level is relatively constant for each person just as are the colors of one's eyes and skin.

Intelligence, so defined, was measured by tests that attempted to sample what a person had learned and how effectively he could solve problems of increasing degrees of difficulty. Once a person's mental age was derived by means of such a test, an IQ was obtained by dividing the person's mental age by his chronological age and multiplying the quotient by one hundred. Intelligence, so measured, supposedly was innate and one's IQ remained reasonably constant throughout one's life. Although most psychologists have abandoned this rather simplistic point of view, it persists in the thinking of many parents, teachers, and school administrators.

Psychologists have recognized that no one, as yet, has devised a test to measure intelligence directly. Instead, intelligence tests measure achievement. Then a person's intelligence is inferred from the level of his (or her) achievement. When IQs are assumed to be constant relative mental abilities based on people's genetic patterns, intelligence tests are based upon the assumption that all people who take a given test have had approximately equal opportunity to learn the things that the test measures.

Today, psychologists and educators more often think of each person's intelligence as depending upon a combination of genetic structure and environmental experiences. They recognize that the hereditary basis of each person's intelligence can give rise to a wide range of actual tested intelligence. The height of a person's score depends partly upon how favorable the person's environmental experiences have been for mental development.[1]

The historical development of the meaning of measured intelligence has been unfortunate. Since instruments that traditionally have been called intelligence tests do predict students' academic success reasonably well, they might very well continue to be used for this purpose. But, "intelligence" tests should be identified by a more appropriate title, perhaps as tests of "educability" or tests of "academic power and readiness."

Although not all psychologists have intended such, people in general tend to assume that a person's relative intelligence is innate. So, parents would prefer their children to have most any other deficiency rather than to be identified as "mentally retarded." They often do not realize that there is no way of establishing just how much of a person's mentality is hereditary or genetic and how much of it is environmental.

It is unfair both to students, and the society of which they are a part, to evaluate and predict their overall ability and potential in terms of typical tests of scholastic aptitude alone. One's measured intelligence should be considered only a significant part of a total personality structure. For example, not all highly intelligent people are highly creative, but many highly intelligent people are highly creative and, "Creative people come from the upper half of the intelligence distribution."[2] Creative people also differ from the noncreative in personality orientation, valuing complexity, and richness of experience, as well as in their degrees of intelligence.

It can be argued that some other selection procedures that are in common use are often even more unfair to some individuals than are intelligence tests. So, many testing experts think that, "Rather than to 'stamp out' mental testing, we need to remodel and update it."[3] Two changes that are contributing to this remodeling process are the interpretation of intelligence as only a part of a larger pattern of measurement and a shifting of emphasis in testing from selection to classification procedures. There is a growing feeling that it is more defensible positively to measure and use (classify) people's respective talents in the best way possible rather than negatively, outrightly either to select or reject persons for given roles based on the results of tests.

WHAT IS THE MEANING OF IQ?

The average person thinking about mental testing probably thinks in terms of IQs. Although many people have definite opinions concerning the fairness or unfairness of intelligence tests, they continue to think that individuals do differ in intelligence and that a person's relative intelligence or IQ is, to some degree, important. For us to evaluate the use of intelligence tests as predictors of success in various pursuits we need a working knowledge of the meaning of the concept *coefficient of correlation* and of the nature and value of *standardized tests*.

What Is a Coefficient of Correlation?

A coefficient of correlation is a stated numerical relationship between two sets of scores or measures. Numerical description of a correlation enables us to realize the degree of relationship that exists. The degree or size of a correlation refers not to positiveness as opposed to negativeness but to the distance from zero (whether positive or negative). Coefficients of correlation vary from a perfect positive (+1.00) through (0.00) to a perfect negative (−1.00). A positive correlation between verbal aptitude and intelligence means that persons who tend to score high in verbal aptitude also tend to score high in intelligence. A negative correlation would exist if persons who scored high on one test scored low on the other.

A zero correlation signifies that there is no relationship between the scores different persons get on the two tests that are being evaluated against each other. A correlation of 0.50, then, means that there is a fairly strong, but only a fairly strong, positive relationship between respective persons' scores on vocabulary and intelligence tests. Actually it means that scores on one test can be predicted from scores on the other tests 13 percent better than they could if there were no correlation at all, that is, if prediction had to be based upon pure chance.[4]

How Do IQ Scores Correlate with School Grades?

"The [coefficient of] correlation between IQ or its equivalent and school grades at all levels from kindergarten to college usually turns out to be between .40 and .60"[5] So, tested intelligence shows a definite relationship to school learning, but it is difficult to establish which one is the cause and which is the effect. The correlation that exists between IQs and school grades means that, under ordinary circumstances, it is unlikely that a student measuring a quite low IQ will perform above average in his (or her) schoolwork; and it is unlikely that a student measuring a high IQ will fail. So, in general, we can use IQ tests to predict students' degree of success. But, there are students with only average IQ scores who do excellent school work, and there are high-scoring students who fail. Correlations mean probabilities, never certainties. Hence, all evaluations of potential school performance, using any means including intelligence tests, should be only tentative.

A valid measurement of intelligence can be achieved only through the use of one or more standardized intelligence tests. There also are standardized tests of interests, aptitudes, and personality structures.

What Is a Standardized Test?

A standardized psychological test is an instrument so constructed as to achieve an objective measure of a sample of a person's behavior. For example, when a psychologist or psychometrist sets out to measure the vocabulary of a child or youth, he (or she) observes that person's performance with only a limited number of words. However, he carefully selects these words with the goal of having them typify the child's total vocabulary. Thus, testing discovers in short order what less systematic observation of a child's daily life could unearth only in a much longer period of time. Tests are a quick and relatively objective method of systematically observing a child in a variety of situations. Since standardized tests judge all children by the same standards and hence minimize the influence of personal biases, these tests appear to be more "scientific" than are personal observations and interviews.

Teachers use systematic testing to the best advantage when they are acquainted with tests to the point of knowing what to, and what not to, expect of them. Thus, it is essential that the purposes and limitations of each test be known. Teachers who realize that the use of standardized tests possibly—but not necessarily—is the most accurate method yet devised of estimating the nature of certain human characteristics will be able to benefit both the students and themselves through the use of standardized test scores. On the other hand, those who blindly become test enthusiasts probably will do more harm than good through their use of tests. Thus, it is essential that we know what tests can, and what they cannot, do. We now list some of the capacities and limitations of standardized tests.

What Can Standardized Tests Do?

1. Within limits, tests can provide comprehensive pictures of the intelligence, aptitudes, interests, and personalities of individuals.
2. Tests, to a large degree, can minimize many of the biases that often creep into the evaluation of people.
3. Tests can provide a rapid means of evaluating students.
4. Each test has a unique function that it can serve best; however, some tests are valuable for more than one purpose.

What Are Some Limitations in the Use of Standardized Tests?

1. Test scores cannot be pure measures of people's innate abilities.
2. Tests do not reveal some kind of universal human abilities, the natures of which are sharply defined and well understood.
3. Tests cannot exactly measure any general ability, capacity, aptitude, or other trait with absolute certainty.
4. A test that is very good for one purpose may provide useless or even misleading information when used for a purpose for which it was not devised.
5. Results of one standardized test, regardless of its excellence, do not alone provide a sound basis for student evaluation, counseling, and guidance.
6. Intelligence tests do not measure some faculty which, although differing in degree, is essentially the same in all human beings.
7. Intelligence tests that measure academic aptitude do not necessarily measure capacity for intelligent behavior in life.
8. Although bright students usually become bright adults and dull students usually remain dull, a person will not necessarily continue to score at a certain level merely because he or she did so on one occasion.

HOW ARE INTELLIGENCE TESTS ADMINISTERED AND EVALUATED?

Intelligence is measured by finding out how much a person knows and can do. Thus, intelligence tests are designed to find how much a person knows about certain matters and how well he (or she) can solve certain types of problems. On the basis of the person's relative performance, examiners infer an IQ score.

Should we give almost any standardized intelligence test to a given number of people of each age from, say, 4 to 40, take the mean or average score of each age, and plot those means on a curve, they would approximate the curve shown in Figure 18.1; this is the intelligence growth curve upon which all standardized intelligence tests are based.[6] From birth to age 15 or 16 intellectual growth is rather constant. Measured intelligence then levels off through the twenties up to the thirties. Then, there is a very slow decline of measured intelligence as people grow through adulthood. This is what actually occurs in curves of measured intelligence; functional intelligence may not conform to such curves. In computing adult IQs some tests allow for this decline.

Intelligence is measured by either individual or group tests of mental ability. An individual test is administered to one person at a time by a trained practitioner who usually is a psychologist or psychometrist. A group test is designed to be administered to an entire classroom of youngsters at one time. It can be scored quite easily either by a teacher or a machine; there is only one right answer to each question.

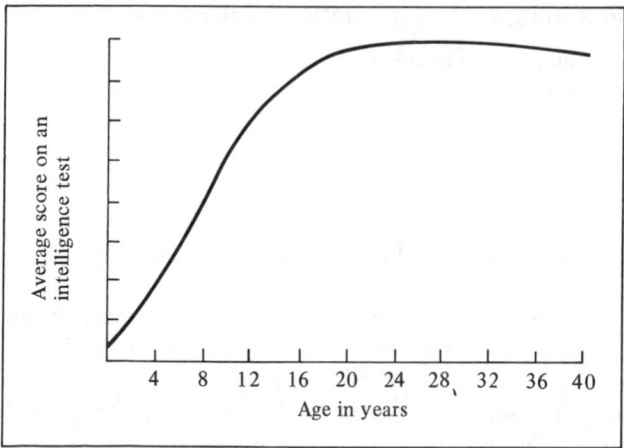

Figure 18.1   Representative curve of the growth of measured intelligence.
(An adaptation from Joseph M. Matarazzo, *Wechsler's Measurement and
Appraisal of Adult Intelligence*, 5th ed., Baltimore: Williams & Wilkins,
1972, p. 110.)

The two best-known and most widely used individual tests are the
Wechsler Intelligence Scale for Children (WISC) and the Stanford-Binet
Intelligence Test (SBIT). The latter is a revision, performed at Stanford
University, of the earlier Binet scales. The Stanford-Binet seeks to find the
general intelligence of a child by means of a many-sided survey of his (or
her) mentality. The WISC is treated in some detail later in this section.

Although group tests rank far ahead of individual tests in frequency
of use, individual tests have some definite advantages. Some of the sub-
tests of individual tests are nonverbal, which makes it possible to administer them to any person who can understand spoken directions. Also,
the examiner can make sure that the individual testee is exerting his
maximum effort. Furthermore, the examiner has ample opportunity to
study the performance of students qualitatively. Thus he (or she) can
learn a great deal about them. Finally, each particular group test is more
limited in function than is an individual test. A group test often is geared
to serve a particular function and do it well, but it is appropriate only
for a given age, grade, or occupational group. For example, the Henmon-
Nelson Tests consist of a series—one for grades 3–6, one for grades 6–9,
and one for grades 9–12. Likewise a scholastic aptitude test such as that
of the College Entrance Examination Board differs in form and purpose
from the Army General Classification Test.

To make the best use of intelligence or mental ability tests, teachers
should understand some key concepts that are related to testing procedures. These are *scoring formula, arithmetic mean, variability, average
deviation, standard deviation, normal distribution curve, mental age,
intelligence quotient,* a *percentile,* and *stanine scores.*

What Is a Scoring Formula?

Although some standardized tests are scored merely by counting the number of correct answers, usually a test is accompanied by a special formula for deriving its score. To score a multiple-choice test accurately the formula most often specifies that the grader count the number of items right and subtract some fraction of the number wrong. The fraction of the number wrong to be subtracted is the reciprocal of a number one less than the number of choices on each question. (The reciprocal of 3 is $\frac{1}{3}$.) A true-false test with two possible answers for each question should be scored by taking the number right less the number wrong. A selection test with four possible answers for each question should be scored by taking the number right less one-third the number wrong. Statistically, when this procedure is followed those students who know no correct answers probably will score zero. A student will receive a positive score to the degree that he (or she) has accurate hunches or insights concerning the correct answers for the questions.

What Is the Arithmetic Mean?

The two principal descriptive characteristics of a distribution of the intelligence of a group of individuals are its *central tendency* and its *variability*. These same characteristics also are used in describing distributions of other traits. Although the arithmetic mean is the measure of central tendency most often used, there are two others—the median and the mode. The median simply is the middle score in a distribution; the mode is the most common score.

The arithmetic mean is the average of a group of scores. To find it, one merely adds all the scores together and divides the sum by the number of scores. If four students measure IQs of 70, 90, 95, and 113, the mean is 92. This is found by adding the scores and dividing their sum by 4. For some purposes, the median and the mode are more useful than the mean. However, the mean is the central point of reference for key concepts related to testing procedures. Furthermore, it is the score most representative of an entire group tested. Thus, a mean or average score provides a means of comparing an individual child's score with that of members of his (or her) group. It also may be used in comparing scores of various groups.

What Does Variability Mean?

Some measure other than the mean must be used to determine just how far above or below the average the score of a child or youth falls. Two groups may show the same averages on the same test and yet have a great difference in variability. Variability means the extent to which scores are spread or scattered. The measures of variability most commonly used and encountered are the range, the average deviation, and the standard deviation of a group.

To find the range, one simply subtracts the lowest score from the highest. The disadvantage of using the range in speaking of variability is that only two pieces of information—the single highest and lowest scores—are considered. Thus, there is no indication of the pattern of the distribution in relation to the mean. In contrast, the average deviation and the standard deviation are based upon the total dispersion of all the scores.

What Does Average Deviation Mean?

An average deviation is found by finding the numerical degree of deviation of each score from the mean, then finding the average of those deviations. So, average deviation is the sum of the deviations divided by the number of deviations. The average deviation is less influenced by extreme scores than is either the range or the standard deviation.

What Does Standard Deviation Mean?

Since a standard deviation involves the degrees of the quality being measured, it is the most commonly used measure of variability or dispersion of a group of test scores. A standard deviation is a numerical index of how much a dispersion of scores deviates from the mean. Thus, it denotes the pattern of distribution in relation to the mean. A standard deviation, indicated by the symbol SD or σ (sigma) is obtained by taking the square root of the average of the squared deviations. Steps in this process are:

1. Find the deviation of each person's score from the mean.
2. Square each of these deviations.
3. Find the sum of these squared deviations.
4. Divide this sum by the number of scores in the group.
5. Find the square root of this average. This is σ or SD.

In contrast to the range of a group of scores, each score in a distribution, not merely the top and bottom one, makes its contribution to a standard deviation. When scores cluster near the mean, the standard deviation is relatively small; when they spread away from the mean, it is relatively large.

The use of standard deviation is valuable in that it enables the qualitative measure of a particular trait to be divided into approximately six equal parts. The spread in the trait being measured is about the same from the mean to one SD above or below the mean as it is from 2 SD to 3 SD above or below the mean. Note that standard deviations equate the degrees of the trait being measured, not the number of people scoring any particular score. On a normal curve, as we move farther away from the average or mean, the amount of change in each succeeding given numerical fraction of the group becomes greater.

What Is a Normal Distribution Curve?

When an intelligence test is given to a large number of children representing a cross section of a population, the scores will tend to fall into a normal distribution or bell curve. It is called "normal" because of its repeated recurrence in the frequency distributions of sets of measures such as those of human characteristics studied in psychology and education. In a normal distribution curve, scores are distributed symmetrically on both sides of the mean. Also, the cases concentrate near the mean and gradually become less frequent away from the mean. Furthermore, there are equal numbers of cases at various equal distances above and below the mean.

If the scores on a test constitute a normal distribution, about two-thirds (68 percent) of the scores will fall within one SD above and below the mean, 95 percent of the scores will fall within two SDs above and below the mean, and three SDs above and below the mean will include almost all of the scores. Figure 18.2 shows a normal distribution curve.

A normal distribution curve indicates that, although there are some extremes in measured intelligence, most children tend to be much alike. However, our growing tendency to have an increased number of children in school for an increased number of years has caused a greater spread in intelligence of students in most classes. Schools now contain virtually

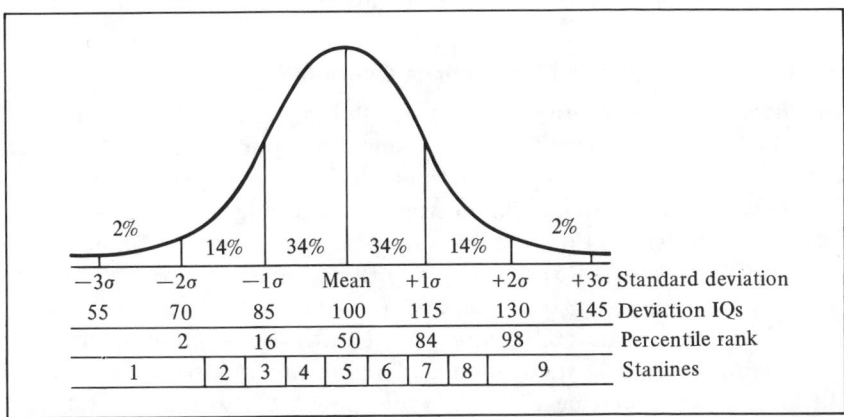

Figure 18.2 Normal distribution curve with standard deviations, WISC IQs, percentile ranks and corresponding stanine scores.

the whole child and youth population representing the entire range of human differences as measured by intelligence tests. In a typical school class, the mental ages of students cover a range of about six years. Consequently, the upper 50 percent of students in a grade are capable of about the same quality of learning as are the lower 50 percent of those in the next higher grade.

The normal distribution curve in Figure 18.2 is a typical bell curve. It is used here to show the interrelationships of standard deviations, IQ scores, percentile ranks, and stanine scores. We now turn to discussions of the latter three concepts. But first we must define *mental age*.

What Do We Mean by One's Mental Age?

Intelligence is measured in terms of either mental age (MA), intelligence quotient (IQ), percentile rank, or stanines. Mental age, introduced by Binet in 1905, is a year-month notation, which represents an absolute level of capacity. Absolute, as used here, is an antonym of relative. It means that a mental age is not determined by a relationship of other units. Rather than stating a relationship—as the IQ and percentile do— MA states a maximum level of achievement. A scored MA of 9 years, 6 months, means that the person being measured can perform a group of tasks which can be performed by an average 9½-year-old. However, since people's scoring abilities on intelligence tests hold about constant from the age of 15 or 16 to 30 and beyond, the MA of an average mature person is taken to be about 15 or 16.

Mental age is determined entirely by a subject's performance on a test and by a table of norms found by testing a large number of children of each age. An MA of 10 means the same regardless of the chronological age of a subject. Even though a 4-year-old with an MA of 6 probably does not act the same way in a given situation as a 6-year-old with an MA of 6, test scores would not indicate any difference between them.

What Do We Mean by an Intelligence Quotient?

Intelligence quotient originally represented the relationship of mental age to chronological age. The use of mental age implemented placement of pupils in grade levels adapted to them, but it gave no help in anticipating the level upon which children would be learning three or four years later. Four students, at present measuring the same mental age, might be far apart in their schoolwork four years from now. Suppose that student A is 6 years old, B is 8, C is 10, and D is 12, and all four measure a mental age of 8 years and so are placed in the same class. Four years hence, provided their motivation and opportunity remained constant, A's mental age would be 13.3, B's would be 12, C's would be 11.2, and D's would be 10.7.

For the testing process to be serviceable, something new was necessary. This was the intelligence quotient—IQ. By definition, IQ equalled mental age divided by chronological age and multiplied by 100; $IQ = MA/CA \times 100$. Then, through transposing, one could derive the formula $MA = CA \times IQ/100$. Teachers have had greater use for the latter formula. Its application indicates that a 12-year-old with an IQ of 80 is capable of working at approximately a 9½-year level; his MA is 9.6.

The principal advantage of the use of IQ as contrasted with a statement of a retardation or acceleration of so many months in mental age is that it makes it possible to compare relative degrees of measured intelligence of children and youth of different ages. An IQ of 100 means normal or average capacity for performance regardless of a child's age. IQs of 90 or 110, for children of any age, indicate comparable degrees of retardation or acceleration.

The concept IQ continues to be employed, but the tendency is away from computing it in the original way, that is, by dividing a person's mental age by his or her chronological age and multiplying the quotient by 100. For example: David Wechsler has formulated the concept *deviation IQ*, which is somewhat different, but more functional, than the earlier meaning of IQ.[7] Within Wechsler's system, each person tested is assigned an IQ that, at his age, represents his intelligence rating as related to the mental abilities of other people of his chronological age.

Deviation IQ is the amount by which a subject's performance deviates above or below the average performance of individual's of his own age group. Wechsler's verbal tests test people's information, their comprehension, their ability to repeat a span of digits, their identification of similarities, and their competency in arithmetic and vocabulary. His performance tests test persons' competency to arrange pictures, to complete pictures, to make block designs, to assemble objects, and to relate digits and symbols.

An IQ of 100 on the WISC is set as the mean score for each age, and the standard deviation is set equal to 15 IQ points. When any standardized IQ test is given to a cross section of a large number of children, it can be assumed that the mean IQ will be approximately 100 and the standard deviation of the IQ will be approximately 15 or 16. Wechsler, however, has developed his tests and norms in such a way that the SD is definitely 15. So, the deviation IQ is really a position on a scale of standard deviation indicated in standard deviation units.

When the intelligence of a large number of children representing a cross section of Americans is measured by means of the WISC, certain general results may be anticipated. The middle 68 percent (one σ each side of the mean) will measure IQs between 85 and 115; 95 percent (between -2σ and $+2\sigma$) will score IQs between 70 and 130. Practically all children (between -3σ and $+3\sigma$) will score IQs between 55 and 145 (see Figure 18.2).

What Is a Percentile?

A *percentile* is the percentage of people whose scores fall below that numerical point on a curve. Thus, when we divide the scores made by a large group of children on a given test into 100 equal parts, each part is a percentile. When a person scores in the ninetieth percentile on a test, it means that 90 percent of the people being tested have scores below that score. Hence percentile scores are in terms of people, not test items. Table 18.1 means that 90 percent of people measure an IQ of below 119 on the WISC.

The amounts of ability represented by each percentile are not equal. In fact, when the distribution of scores is normal there is about the same amount of difference in the measured trait between the ninety-eighth and ninety-ninth percentile as between the fiftieth and sixtieth. This is shown in Figure 18.2, page 437.

What Are Stanine Scores?

A more recent development in the interpretation of tests is the use of stanine scores (*stanine* is derived from *standard nine*). Stanines are normally distributed scores that range from a low of 1 to a high of 9; the mean is 5 (see Figure 18.2).

Each unit on a stanine scale, except units 1 and 9, is one-half a standard deviation in extent. The middle score, stanine 5, extends from one-fourth of a SD below the mean to one-fourth of a SD above it. Then stanines 2, 3, and 4 and 6, 7, and 8 extend one and one-half SDs each way beyond stanine 5. Each of stanines 1 and 9 extend more than a full

Table 18.1 RELATIONS OF IQ ON WISC TO PERCENTILE RANK

PERCENTILE RANK	EQUIVALENT IQ
99	135+
97	128
95	125
90	119
80	113
75	110
70	108
60	104
50	100
40	96
30	92
20	87
10	81
5	75
3	72
1	65

Table 18.2 PERCENTAGE OF NORMALLY DISTRIBUTED SCORES
IN EACH STANINE

STANINE	PERCENTAGE OF GROUP
1	4
2	7
3	12
4	17
5	20
6	17
7	12
8	7
9	4

SD at the outer limits of the curve. The approximate percentage of the scores that are in each stanine is shown in Table 18.2.

HOW ARE INTELLIGENCE TEST SCORES RELATED TO THE HEREDITY-ENVIRONMENT ISSUE?

In the last fifty years more than 50 studies have been made that have involved the heritability of human intelligence as it appears to be manifested by the correlation of children's and youths' IQs with the different degrees of similarity between their heredities and their environments. Theodosius Dobzhansky has developed a comprehensive statement of the results of these studies.[8] To accomplish this, he has drawn from earlier studies by L. Erlenmeyer-Kimling and L. F. Jarvik,[9] J. N. Spuhler and G. Lindzey,[10] and A. R. Jensen [11] (see Table 18.3).

The results of Dobzhansky's study seems to show that the closer the genetic relationship is among people, the more they are alike in measured intelligence. But, some psychologists and many sociologists challenge this study's giving complete support to the heritability of intelligence. They point out that in situations where children's heredities are much alike, so are their environments. There are ranges of environmental influences as well as ranges of biological heredity. Furthermore, there is a tendency for positive hereditary factors to be paralleled by positive environmental ones. As stated by Vernon, "the only reasonable conclusion seems to be that we cannot prove nor disprove genetic differences"[12] between races or ethnic groups.

A study of Table 18.3 gives us some general idea of how the heredity-environment issue is related to intelligence test scores. With this in mind, let us examine a few specific studies that are related to this question.

In 1935 a study was conducted to see how a group of children would perform on various intelligence tests.[13] During a period of one month, 14 different intelligence tests were administered to 149 children in the high sixth and low seventh grades. There was found to be no correlation be-

Table 18.3 MEDIAN CORRELATION COEFFICIENTS BETWEEN IQs OF PERSONS OF DIFFERENT DEGREES OF GENETIC AND ENVIRONMENTAL RELATIONSHIPS (A RESTATEMENT OF DOBZHANSKY'S TABLE)

RELATIONSHIP OF PERSONS	MEDIAN CORRELATION COEFFICIENT
Identical twins reared together	+0.87
Identical twins reared apart	+0.75
Fraternal twins of same sex	+0.56
Biological siblings reared together	+0.55
Biological parent and child	+0.50
Fraternal twins of opposite sex	+0.49
Biological siblings reared apart	+0.47
Grandparent and grandchild	+0.27
First cousins	+0.26
Unrelated children reared together	+0.24
Foster parent and child	+0.20
Unrelated children living apart	−0.01

tween the order of taking the tests and the results obtained. No child showed an IQ variation of fewer than 21 points. The average variation was about 42 points; that is, the average child scored 42 points lower in IQ on one test than he (or she) did on some other tests in the 14. One child showed a spread of 84 points between his lowest and his highest IQ scores.

Other studies have been made to determine how specific children would score on the same or similar IQ tests over a period of time within which their psychological environments were significantly changed. These studies seem to indicate that, whatever it is that an IQ test measures, it can be raised, or lowered, through a marked change in environment. We give examples of three different kinds of studies that have contributed to a knowledge of the effects of changes in environment upon IQ scores.

1. *A study of identical twins reared in different kinds of environments.* Newman, Freeman, and Holzinger in 1937 reported a complete case study of 19 pairs of identical twins reared apart.[14] They found that, whereas the average IQ difference of the identical twins reared together was 5.9 points, it was 8.2 for the twins reared apart.

2. *A study of two groups that, on the average, had different hereditary potentialities but similar environmental influences.* B. S. Burks in California studied a group of adopted children placed in foster homes during the first year of their lives and a control group of "own children" matched with the adopted children in regard to age and sex of children and locality and occupational level of homes. She estimated the average IQ of the adopted children at the time of adoption to be approximately 100. When tested from ages 5 to 14 they average IQs of 107.4. However, the mean IQ of the control group of "own children" was 115.1. This seems to be evidence "that a superior home can produce a moderate increase

in a child's tested intelligence, but cannot bring him to the level of individuals who have both superior heredity and superior environment on their side."[15]

3. *Studies of groups of children measured before and after experiencing a decidedly changed environment.* Several studies were pursued in the child study laboratory of the University of Iowa during the late 1930s which are pertinent to the problem of constancy of IQs. B. L. Wellman has reported these studies.[16] One was an investigation of the effect on IQ of a child's attending the University of Iowa Nursery School; 228 children with an average age of 40 months and a mean IQ of 117.3 in the fall measured a mean IQ of 124.3 in the spring. The following fall they measured a mean IQ of 123.9; this grew to a mean of 127.7 in the spring. Thus, in a 20-month period, average measured IQs were raised 10.4 points.

In 1968, Heber experimented with ghetto children whose mothers measured IQs below 70 (the IQs of their fathers were unknown).[17] Part of the children, his control group, continued their usual routines. The other part, the experimental group, were given special care and training. Four years after the training period, whereas the IQs of the control group averaged 90, the IQs of the experimental group averaged 127.

HOW CAN WE MAKE THE BEST USE OF INTELLIGENCE TESTS?

Intelligence tests can serve as a useful adjunct to other kinds of information about students, provided both teachers and parents come to understand what can and what cannot be accomplished through the use of intelligence test scores. We explain in Chapter 17 how intelligence testing gained its impetus through the application of connectionistic-behavioristic psychology. Within the early behavioristic position, intelligence was defined as organic capacity to make quick, appropriate responses. This capacity was regarded as being rooted in the physiological make-up of each organism, hence largely hereditary.

Sufficient studies of the marked variability of specific individuals' IQs have been made that psychologists have come to see the nature and origin of intelligence in a different light. Perhaps we are on the safest ground when we begin with the assumption that no available "intelligence" tests measure completely satisfactorily what a cognitive-field psychologist means by intelligence. Opinions vary as to what present IQ tests do measure, but most commonly they are thought to measure a certain kind of academic capacity—that which we commonly associate with success in college preparatory curriculums in elementary and high schools and with later success in college. The scholastic potential that these tests measure in some cases will vary over a wide range. By instituting the right sort of learning environment, it seems fairly well established that IQ scores for given individuals can be raised markedly. Since a capacity is itself regarded as a function of person-environment interaction, we should cease thinking of anyone as having a fixed capacity or potential, along academic or any other lines.

NOTES

[1] See Ira J. Gordon, *Human Development: A Transactional Perspective*, New York: Harper & Row, 1975, pp. 244–246.

[2] Leona E. Tyler, *Individual Differences*, New York: Appleton-Century-Crofts, 1974, p. 101.

[3] Leona E. Tyler, Ibid., p. 28.

[4] The formula for finding *efficiency of prediction* in percentage is $100 \ (1 - \sqrt{1 - r^2})$ where r represents the coefficient of correlation.

[5] Leona E. Tyler, p. 44.

[6] See Joseph D. Matarazzo, *Wechsler's Measurement and Appraisal of Adult Intelligence*, 5th ed., Baltimore: Williams & Wilkins, 1972, pp. 107–114.

[7] David Wechsler, *Wechsler Intelligence Scale for Children*, Psychological Corporation, 1949, pp. 3–4. (The WISC sets the deviation IQ at 15, the SBIT sets it at 16.)

[8] Theodosius Dobzhansky, *Genetic Diversity and Human Equality*, New York: Basic Books, 1973, p. 13.

[9] L. Erlenmeyer-Kimling and L. F. Jarvik, "Genetics and Intelligence: A Review," *Science* 142 (December 1963): 1477–1479.

[10] J. M. Spuhler and G. Lindzey, "Racial Differences in Behavior," in J. Hirsch (ed.), *Behavior—Genetic Analysis*, New York: McGraw-Hill, 1967.

[11] A. R. Jensen, "How Much Can We Boost IQ and Scholastic Achievement?" *Harvard Educational Review* 39 (Winter 1969): 1–123.

[12] Philip E. Vernon, "Genes, 'G' and Jensen," *Contemporary Psychology* 15 (March 1970): 162.

[13] P. L. Boynton and Rosa F. Parsons, *Pupil Analyses in the Peabody Demonstration School*, Bulletin 24, no. 9, George Peabody College for Teachers, 1935.

[14] Leona E. Tyler, *The Psychology of Human Differences*, 3d ed., New York: Appleton-Century-Crofts, 1965, p. 451.

[15] Ibid., pp. 457–458.

[16] Beth L. Wellman, "Iowa Studies on the Effect of Schooling," in Guy M. Whipple (ed.), *Intelligence: Its Nature and Nurture*, Part II, Chapter 26, The Thirty-Ninth Yearbook of the National Society for the Study of Education, Public School Publishing Co., 1940, p. 383.

[17] See R. Heber, *Rehabilitation of Families at Risk for Mental Retardation*, Madison: University of Wisconsin Regional Rehabilitation Center, 1968.

BIBLIOGRAPHY

ANASTASI, ANNE. *Differential Psychology*, 3d ed. New York: Macmillan, 1958.
  An excellent introduction to major concepts which pertain to individual and group differences. Sources and nature of differences and their

measurement are treated in detail. Chapters 13 and 14 on genius and sex differences are particularly interesting.

CASPARI, E. "Genetic Endowment and Environment in the Determination of Human Behavior: Biological Viewpoint," in R. E. Ripple (ed.), *Readings in Learning and Human Abilities*, 2d ed. New York: Harper & Row 1971. A discussion of the biological and environmental determinants of behavior. Stresses individuality of persons.

COLEMAN, J. S., et al. *Equality of Educational Opportunity*. Washington, D.C.: U.S. Office of Education, 1966. Found a lack of difference of educational opportunities for individuals of different races or colors. Families, not schools, make the greatest difference in achievement of success.

CRONBACH, LEE J. *Essentials of Psychological Testing*, 3d ed. New York: Harper & Row, 1970. A standard text on psychological and educational testing of ability and personality. Emphasizes general principles of psychological testing. Provides lists of tests. One of the best surveys of the field of psychological testing.

DOBZHANSKY, THEODOSIUS. *Genetic Diversity and Human Equality*. New York: Basic Books, 1973. An eminent geneticist discusses differences in human intelligence. The broad overlap of various curves for IQs and the universal educability of human beings refute the position of their being a genetically superior race. Human's adaptedness depends primarily on cultural, not genetic, inheritance.

EELLS, KENNETH, et al. *Intelligence and Cultural Differences*. Chicago: University of Chicago Press, 1951. "A study of cultural learning and problem solving." The validity of standardized intelligence tests as a measure of intelligence of children from widely varying cultural backgrounds is examined.

ERLENMEYER-KIMLING, L., and L. F. JARVIK. "Genetics and Intelligence: A Review." *Science* 142 (December 1963): 1477–1479. One of the most recent reviews of research on the relation of genetics to intelligence.

EYSENCK, H. J. *Race, Intelligence and Education*. New York: Library Press, 1971. A British psychologist's approach to the nature-nurture problem.

FULLER, JOHN L., and W. ROBERT THOMPSON. *Behavior Genetics*. New York: Wiley, 1960. Consideration of the nature of intelligence, personality, temperament, and the evidence relating to their inheritance (Chapters 7 and 8). Treatments of the relation of heredity to individual differences (Chapter 10).

GAGE, N. L. "I.Q. Heritability, Race Differences, and Educational Research." *Phi Delta Kappan* 53 (January 1972): 308–312. Summarizes the development of the meaning and role of intelligence tests, and discusses the relevance of tested intelligence to racial differences, notes that available evidence gives inconclusive results.

GUILFORD, J. P. *Intelligence, Creativity and Their Educational Implications*. San Diego, Cal.: Knapp, 1968. The author is a recognized leader in measurement of abilities and aptitudes. This book introduces the reader to Guilford's concepts and ideas.

HERSCH, JERRY. "Jensenism: The Bankruptcy of 'Science' without Scholarship." *Educational Theory* 25, no. 1 (Winter 1975): 3–27. A vitriolic response to Jensen's article in the *Harvard Educational Review* by a professor of psychology and zoology. Genetic formulas are employed to disprove Jensen's thesis in regard to innate racial differences in intelligence.

JENCKS, CHRISTOPHER, et al. *Inequality: A Reassessment of the Effect of Family and Schooling in America.* New York: Basic Books, 1972. Distinguishes between equality of opportunity and equality of condition. There is no direct correlation between expenditures in schools and effects on society. Family status is the greatest factor in economic success.

JENSEN, ARTHUR R. "How Much Can We Boost IQ and Scholastic Achievement?" *Harvard Educational Review* 39 (Winter 1969): 1–123. Develops a definition of intelligence and weighs the contribution of heredity much greater than that of environment. Implies that different racial pools differ in intelligence.

JENSEN, ARTHUR R. "Discussion: How Much Can We Boost IQ and Scholastic Achievements?" *Harvard Educational Review* 39 (Spring 1969): 273–356. Six psychologists and a geneticist react to Jensen's article on the relative influence of hereditary and environmental factors on human intelligence and the value of compensatory education programs.

JENSEN, ARTHUR R. *Educability and Group Differences.* New York: Harper & Row, 1973. Reviews genetic nature of human heredity. Distinguishes between intelligence and educability. Heredity vs. environment is a pseudo-question. Heredity and environment is the real problem. Compares intelligence test scores of different ethnic groups.

LINDVALL, C. MAURITZ, and ANTHONY J. NITKO. *Measuring Pupil Achievement and Aptitude*, 2d ed. New York: Harcourt Brace Javonovich, 1975. Presents basic principles of testing and evaluation. Chapter 8, "Tests of Scholastic Aptitude," is particularly pertinent to these chapters.

MCCLELLAND, DAVID C. "Testing for Competence Rather Than for 'Intelligence,'" *American Psychologist* (January 1973): 1–14. Questions the overwhelming validity of intelligence tests. Skeptically reviews the evidence for validity of intelligence and aptitude tests.

National Society for the Study of Education. *Intelligence: Its Nature and Nurture*, Thirty-Ninth Yearbook Part I, *Comparative and Critical Exposition.* Chicago: National Society for the Study of Education, 1940. A rather technical symposium by psychologists on the nature and development of intelligence. It considers the meaning, deviations, physiology, and significant factors of intelligence.

NOLL, VICTOR H., and DALE P. SCANNEL. *Introduction to Educational Measurement*, 3d ed. Boston: Houghton Mifflin, 1972. A general orientation to measurement and evaluation. Introduces measurement theory and elementary statistical methods. See especially Chapter 11 on the measurement of general intelligence.

TYLER, LEONA E. *Tests and Measurements*, 2d. ed. Prentice-Hall, 1963. A concise treatment of "consumer knowledge" of individual differences, tests, and measurement. Unusually clear and readable.

TYLER, LEONA E. *The Psychology of Human Differences*, 3d ed. Appleton-Century-Crofts, 1965. An analysis of quantitative studies of individual differences. The author appraises sex, race, nationality, and class, as well as individual differences in intelligence, school achievement, vocational aptitude, personality, interest and attitudes, and perception.

TYLER, LEONA E. *Individual Differences*. New York: Appleton-Century-Crofts, 1974. One of the most readable books on individual differences. Recommended reading to accompany a first course in educational psychology.

VERNON, PHILIP E. "GENES, 'G.' and JENSEN." *Contemporary Psychology* XV (March 1970): 161–163. A critical review of Professor Jensen's *Environment, Heredity, and Intelligence*.

WELLMAN, BETH L., and EDNA L. PEGRAM. "Binet IQ Changes of Orphanage Preschool Children: A Reanalysis." *Journal of Genetic Psychology* 65 (December 1944): 239–263. A reanalysis of the data collected in 1938 by Miss Wellman and three others on their experiment in raising IQs of orphans through environmental stimulation. This article substantiates the earlier conclusions.

Chapter 19
HOW IS TEACHING RELATED TO LEARNING?

In Part III of the book we consider various learning theories that teachers might adopt. We now are ready to examine how the respective theories are related to teaching principles and procedures. But first, as a necessary preface to our inquiry into the relationship of learning theory to teaching practice let us examine the unique role of teachers in our culture.

WHAT IS THE ROLE OF TEACHERS IN MODERN AMERICA?

When we consider the role of teachers in modern America we should study both of its aspects, namely, teachers' relationship to preservation and improvement of the culture and their relationship to their students. A *culture* is the established way of life or social heritage of a people. It is constituted of all those socially transmitted results of human experience through which a group of people carries on its way of life. It includes language, customs, morals, tools, institutions, knowledge, ideals, and standards.

What Are the Possible Relationships of Teachers to the Preservation and Improvement of the Culture?

Most people would probably agree that one of the principal functions of teaching is to preserve, by transmitting to the young, that part of the culture that is regarded by most people as good. However, performance of this task alone makes education a highly conservative force. Teaching that does no more than merely conserve a culture is appropriate to a static culture but not to a dynamic, rapidly changing culture such as ours. Hence teaching in a fast-moving culture, must operate in relationship to change with the goal of keeping cultural innovations socially beneficial. Although there is general support for this two-fold function of teaching, that is, cultural conservation and cultural improvement, it is difficult to get agreement on just how the two tasks are to be performed simultaneously.

Teachers may hold any one of four basically different attitudes in regard to their proper function in preserving and improving the culture. They may envision themselves as (1) ignorers of the culture, (2) cultural architects, (3) conservators of the culture, or (4) democratic leaders in developing insights pertinent to amending the culture (to amend a culture is to modify it in some way for the better). Let us explore each of these attitudes briefly.

TEACHERS AS IGNORERS OF THE CULTURE

Teachers who adhere to this view consider the prevailing culture to be a necessary evil, outside nature, that should be either ignored or neutralized as far as possible. Hence, they align themselves with psychedelic humanism. Within this extreme laissez-faire position, they encourage each student to disregard the prevailing folkways and mores of his (or her) culture and to "do his own thing."[1] They are interested in encouraging each student's autonomous self-development and self-actualization to the point that they have little interest in either cultural conservation or improvement.

TEACHERS AS CULTURAL ARCHITECTS

Teachers who adopt this view see themselves as radical innovators. So, in their thinking they design the specifications of an ideal culture. They then teach the attitudes, values, and knowledge that will cause new generations to move in the direction of this ideal. They are likely to promote ideas toward which resistance will develop, and they are not reluctant to indoctrinate and propagandize students in order to achieve their purpose. Since teachers who see themselves as cultural architects are discontented with affairs as they are and want to introduce a new cultural design, their point of view has been called "social reconstructionism."

TEACHERS AS CONSERVATORS OF THE CULTURE

Teachers who accept this role see themselves as preservers of traditional attitudes, values, beliefs, and knowledge. To the best of their ability they analyze the present culture and attempt to transmit this, intact, to new generations. They recognize that accidents of history will induce cultural changes, and they may think that if these changes contribute to the welfare of people they will be perpetuated. However, they never see themselves as active agents of cultural change. Teachers who operate within this framework are called "conservatives." Since unorthodoxy bothers conservatives, they are likely to try to suppress any unconventional thinking on the part of the students. In a manner very much like that of social reconstructionists, who also have specific objectives in mind, conservative teachers often indoctrinate their students and propagandize their objectives into their thinking and behavior.

But, regardless of the degree to which teachers may be dedicated to conservation of their culture, their task is becoming impossible to perform. With the loss of the old sense of community and the accompanying decay of the cohesive and relatively consistent value pattern that accompanied it, there is no longer a harmonious structure of attitudes, values, and beliefs for teachers to promote. Confronted with a culture filled with confusion and contradictions, which elements are a conservative teacher to select and teach? Is it not reasonable that teaching today should help students examine as objectively as possible their disjointed culture in the hope that as they live their lives they will be able to work some integration into it? But this is a job for neither a laissez-faire "teacher," an impetuous seeker of change, nor a conservative who is frightened of change.

TEACHERS AS DEMOCRATIC LEADERS IN DEVELOPING INSIGHTS PERTINENT TO AMENDING THE CULTURE

In contrast with either an ignorer, an architect, or a conservator position, a teacher may develop an emergent synthesis from the three positions and visualize himself as functioning much as a head scientist in a laboratory. When the subject matter under investigation is the culture, the primary purpose of investigation is neither solely to ignore, to change, nor to preserve it, but to appraise it and strengthen its tenability. Accordingly, an attempt is made to uncover contradictions and conflicts in a culture and to determine possible ways of resolving them, or at least preventing them from causing serious trouble. The ultimate hope of democratic teachers is that the culture will be progressively refined by a citizenry that has learned the habit of studying problems in a reflective and democratic manner. So, teachers with this view should foster social change, but strive to keep it orderly and constructive.

Teachers, as democratic leaders, do not discard their personal preferences. Like either social reconstructionists or conservators of culture, they too hold certain cultural goals in preference to others. However, their method of teaching, unlike that of either ignorers of culture, social reconstructionists, or conservators of culture, is the method of democracy. In a very real sense, each teacher and his or her students, together, are gaining more adequate insights for building their culture.

Teachers who function as democratic leaders believe that, since people are cultural beings, there need not be assumed any ceiling or limit to the possibilities of human nature. When human nature is assumed neither to be tied to an autonomous natural unfoldment process nor to be static or inert, it encompasses all the institutional achievements of dynamic society. Accordingly, with sufficient application of human intelligence, a society can continue growth in the direction of more adequate and harmonious living for all individuals involved. So, if teachers are to aid substantially in cultural progress, they must encourage students to study the existing cultures of their own and other societies, but always with a view toward progressive refinement of those cultures.

What Are the Possible Relationships of Teachers to Their Students?

We may visualize three broad types of relationships between respective teachers and their students: (1) authoritarian, (2) laissez faire, and (3) democratic. Each form of relationship produces a distinctive type of situation within a classroom, characterized by more or less predictable results and carrying with it definite implications concerning the teacher's commitment in regard to how students learn. Furthermore, a particular type of relation of a teacher to his (or her) students presupposes a correlative relationship of the teacher to the culture. Whereas an authoritarian teacher considers himself either a cultural architect or conservator, a laissez-faire teacher deliberately adheres to a policy of noninterference with students' individual freedom of choice and action, and a democratic teacher sees his cultural role as that of a leader in developing insights that may contribute to the culture's amendments.

AUTHORITARIAN TEACHERS

Authoritarian teachers exercise firm, centralized control. They closely direct the actions of their students. They do all the planning for their classes and issue all the directions. Furthermore, they tell students what to think as well as what to do. In an authoritarian classroom, a teacher regards himself as the sole active agent and considers students passive receivers of instructions and information.

In the experiments with group climates conducted by White and Lippitt,[2] it was found that boys in authoritarian groups tended to be apathetic and dependent and to demonstrate little capacity for initiating group action. When the leader left the room, they accomplished very little. Although they did not seem to resent authoritarian leadership strongly, they occasionally showed evidences of hostility, as expressed in aggressive acts toward fellow group members.

LAISSEZ-FAIRE TEACHERS

Laissez-faire teachers go to the opposite extreme. Since they are committed to noninterference with students' choices and actions, they deliberately abstain from student direction or lesson planning, so they do not really lead at all. They are present, they may answer questions, but essentially they let students follow their own initiative. Students decide what they want to do and how they will do it.

In the White-Lippitt experiments, boys in the laissez-faire group got along together much better than those in the authoritarian group; they showed less tendency to direct resentments at fellow students. They did get some work done. However, they acted insecure; for example, they repeatedly asked for help and, after the experiment was completed, expressed dissatisfaction with its leadership.[3]

DEMOCRATIC TEACHERS

In a democratic teaching-learning situation the teachers fulfill the role of democratic group leaders. Their function is analogous to that of a head scientist in a laboratory. Their chief purpose is to lead their students in the study of significant problems in the area in which they are teaching. Such study presupposes interchange of evidence and insights, give-and-take, and respect for one another's ideas. In a democratic classroom the teacher's ideas are subject to both student and teacher criticism just as are those of students. In this way both the students and the teacher learn together. Although the teacher may be an authority on his (or her) subject, and to teach it best he should be, the situation is arranged so that students are encouraged to think for themselves. Accordingly, a democratic teacher is most likely to hold an outlook toward learning that emphasizes purposiveness in human experience and behavior.

In the White-Lippitt experiments, democratic groups evidenced a more friendly and confiding atmosphere than did authoritarian groups. Members seemed as able to extend mutual recognition to each other as did members of the laissez-faire groups. However, they worked on a higher level of efficiency and were much less dependent on the leader than were the laissez-faire groups. Furthermore, they showed more initiative and worked more effectively in the absence of a leader than did the authoritarian groups.[4]

The traditional relationship between teachers and their students has been authoritarian. Until the twentieth century, teachers tended to be despots—often benevolent, but despots nevertheless. During this century, despotism in the classroom has begun to disappear, but when this has happened, a laissez-faire attitude frequently has taken its place. Or, perhaps more often, teachers have come to alternate between a friendly despotism and situations close to laissez faire. There are some good reasons why consistently democratic relations could well be substituted for both autocratic and laissez-faire modes of operation. It ill behooves a nation that is straining itself in democratic directions to maintain in its schoolrooms nondemocratic relationships between teachers and students. Furthermore, evidence now available indicates that students probably learn more effectively in a democratic than in either an authoritarian or a highly permissive classroom.[5] Democratic learning situations seem to produce more retention and more transfer. Thus, even if there were no other reason for democratic relations between teacher and students, the general adoption of such relations would at least permit taxpayers who support education to receive more for their money.

In recent years and in many places, the idea of democratic schools and classrooms has fallen into ill repute. There are two basic, but unfortunate, reasons for this. (1) Laissez-faire situations often have been erroneously mistaken for democratic situations. Truly democratic teachers, however, have no enthusiasm whatsoever for laissez-faire classrooms, and they feel that it is tragic for an educator to call an uncontrolled and undirected classroom "democratic." (2) The meanings of the terms democracy and democratic have become perverted. As applied to teaching, they often have come to mean "easy," "soft," or "undisciplined." Yet, in fact, making allowances for the maturity and capabilities of students, a democratic group may work at the maximum level that health permits, and its manner of operations may be fully as rigorous as that of any scientific investigation.

There is a close connection between the respective types of relationships of teachers to students and the relative amount of usage of each of four different levels of teaching and learning. These levels are the subject of the remaining part of the chapter.

WHAT ARE THE LEVELS OF TEACHING AND LEARNING?

Teaching-learning situations may be characterized according to where they fall on a continuum that ranges from thoughtless to thoughtful modes of operation. But, it is helpful to divide their total range into four classifications: (1) autonomous development level, (2) memory level, (3) explanatory understanding level, and (4) explanatory understanding or reflection level. Notice that, in describing levels of teaching and learning, the expressions *exploratory understanding and reflection* may be used interchangeably. The autonomous development level emphasizes the importance of students' feelings and minimizes the value of hard thinking based upon empirical data. The memory level is relatively thoughtless, the explanatory understanding level is more thoughtful, and the exploratory understanding or reflection level is the most thoughtful of all.

In this chapter we summarize the differences between the various levels of teaching and learning and treat, in some detail, the nature of the autonomous development level and the memory level. We then devote Chapter 20 to the explanatory understanding level and Chapter 21 to the exploratory understanding level of teaching and learning.

What Is the Meaning of Understanding?

The term *understanding* has been used so ambiguously by psychologists and educators that teachers are likely to use it rather glibly without being able to define it clearly. For example, a teacher may ask students, "Are you sure you understand this?" when not really knowing the meaning of the question. One may be fairly sure that the students do not know either.

The *American College Dictionary* gives the following definition of the verb *understand:* "1. to perceive the meaning of; grasp the idea of; comprehend. 2. to be thoroughly familiar with; apprehend clearly the character or nature of. 3. to comprehend by knowing the meaning of the words employed, as a language. 4. to grasp clearly as a fact, or realize."[6]

A serious student of educational psychology will be dissatisfied with definitions of this kind. Although helpful to a degree, they are not sufficiently operational. That is, they do not show what psychological action a person takes when he or she comes to understand something. In the sections to follow, we present two key definitions of understanding, then show how they may be combined into one.

UNDERSTANDING AS SEEING RELATIONSHIPS

This definition of understanding is implied in the first category of dictionary definitions. One meaning for comprehend is "to take in or embrace"; the Latin root is *comprehendere,* meaning "to seize." In other words, we have here the idea of reaching out and gathering in individual items. As they are pulled together, they are understood. However, the definition implies still more; it involves inclusion or embracement of a group of particulars under a single overarching idea.

Seeing solitary facts in relation to a general principle is the essence of understanding implied by our first definition of the term. Although we are about to suggest that there is significantly more to understanding than this, teaching probably would be more effective than it is now if all teachers grasped even this limited definition. Too few teachers realize that any item of factual knowledge is quite meaningless unless students see how it is embraced by a general principle. A fact must be seen as either supporting or casting doubt upon some principle or it means very little. Yet entire textbooks have been written that contain little more than "descriptive facts." Teachers often labor away a professional lifetime without trying to teach students the generalizations that would be necessary for them to "pull together" the facts that they are required to memorize.

UNDERSTANDING AS SEEING THE TOOL-USE OF A FACT

This brings us to a second definition of understanding. We may say that a person understands any object, process, idea, or fact if he (or she) sees how it can be used to fulfill some purpose or goal. As soon as one sees what something is for, one, to some degree, understands it. Of course, the degree of one's understanding is always relative. If a person knows that a camera takes pictures, he (or she) has begun to understand a camera. But if he is going to use a camera successfully, he also needs to know the details of its operation and the consequences of his using different types of lenses, film emulsions, lighting, and picture compositions.

It is from one's experience that one's understanding grows. Within experimental experience, one tries first one course of action and then another, preserving only those that work best. Thus, through experience, the features of each person's environment progressively develop a "pointing quality"—dark clouds "point" to rain, Johnny's out-thrust jaw and angry squint "point" to a poke in the jaw for Freddy. This pointing quality which we give to features of our environment permits us to behave intelligently—to act with foresight because these are signposts along the way. The pointing quality of things tells us the probable consequences of using them, which is to say, how to use them with maximum effectiveness.

UNDERSTANDING AS SEEING BOTH RELATIONSHIPS AND TOOL-USE

It is important to realize that understanding as seeing the relation between particulars and generalizations and understanding as seeing the tool-use of things are complementary processes. Hence, in order to have a fully adequate definition of understanding, we need to consolidate the two definitions.

Because it ignores the role of purpose, understanding as merely seeing relationships is not an adequate concept. Suppose one sees the relationship of certain specific facts to the principle of flotation, as we portray in the example of a Herbartian lesson plan in Chapter 10 (p. 260). A student reaction to a forced acquaintance with such relationships might simply be "So what?" and no attempt would be made to delve deeply into the implications of the principle, to remember it for future use, or to transfer it to new situations. In other words, an understanding that is confined to seeing relationships between particulars and a concept is a fragile and superficial achievement. But suppose a student is a boat hobbyist. He builds boat models and operates them upon a local lake. He is involved in developing a design and needs to know how much of the boat will be submerged when it is carrying four persons whose average weight is 130 pounds. To this student the principle of flotation, and the concrete facts subsumed under it, will seem of vital importance.

Thus, what we may label "functional understanding" is much more likely to occur if a learner, in learning generalizations and the specific facts pertinent to them, sees how some purpose is served thereby. So, we should not divorce the problem of teaching for understanding from that of promoting student motivation.

If understanding is best achieved when we want to use that which is to be understood, it is equally true that, when motivation toward understanding is present, what is understood will inevitably consist primarily of principles derived from a pattern of specific facts. At this point, we must restate an assertion made in Chapter 12 to the effect that specific insights tend to be generalized. As soon as one achieves an insight, the thought occurs, "Possibly this idea will work in other—or all—similar situations." Accordingly, the insight's general value is tested through its repeated use in similar situations. If it fails to work, it will be discarded as having extremely limited worth. If it seems always to work, it will become a valued possession that will be added to the person's intelligence. Of course, most insights are valid in varying degrees of predictability; they fall somewhere between the two extremes just suggested.

We now have pushed our analysis to the point where we can offer a third definition of understanding. Understanding occurs when we come to see how to use productively, in ways that we care about, a pattern of general ideas and supporting facts.

UNDERSTANDING AS A NOUN

So far we have been discussing what the verb understand means. In the literature of education, we also regularly encounter the noun understanding or understandings. The noun form refers to the product of acts of understanding. We go through an experimental process of trying to see how certain relationships may be put to use. We find a relationship between something done and the consequences of doing it. This is our understanding.

An *understanding*, then, is a generalized meaning or insight. Often it may be put into words, but not always. The understandings a person achieves in regard to driving a golf ball, running the high hurdles, casting a fly, timing a motor, or writing a sentence may lie, in part, in a "feel for the act" that would be difficult to verbalize. But, most persons who have thought about such achievements are able to make statements about the probable consequences of attempting them in alternative ways. Other names for understandings are *generalizations, theories, generalized insights, general ideas, concepts, principles, rules, and laws.*

How Does Explanatory Understanding Differ from Memory Level Teaching and Learning?

Both memory level teaching and explanatory understanding level teaching are teaching centered. However, in the memory level teachers concentrate on factual, short answers, whereas in the explanatory understanding level teachers explain answers to students in the form of rules, relationships, or generalizations. When an explanatory understanding level of teaching is successful, students will know, in addition to facts, some principles by which the facts are related. In contrast, memory level teaching tends either to ignore principles, or at best to treat them on such a superficial level that they have little meaning for students.

It is well to recognize that most behavioristic psychologists of learning, in actual practice, represent a combination of memory and explanatory understanding levels of learning. Since these psychologists center upon behavior that is the result of forces exerted upon individuals, explanation for what persons do is sought in the circumstances that surround them, the stimuli that impinge upon them, and the facts and principles that they have learned. Consequently, a child or youth is something to be molded in the proper fashion. For behaviorists, a verbalized understanding is a concept characterized as a learned common, generalized response to a number of stimuli of a given class. Teaching, then, is a matter of setting objectives for students and creating the proper environment to ensure their reaching these behavioral or performance objectives. With these purposes or goals in mind, teachers strive to transmit facts and principles in the form of memories and understandings to students through telling, showing, guiding, rewarding, punishing, and, at times, forcing and coercing them.

How Does Exploratory Understanding or Reflection Level Differ From Explanatory Understanding Level Teaching and Learning?

Explanatory understanding level teaching is teaching that seeks to acquaint students with the relationships between a generalization and the particulars, that is, between principles and solitary facts, and that develops the uses to which the principles may be applied. When teachers teach students rules governing the use of, say, subjunctives, they are instructing on an explanatory understanding level. To the degree that they succeed, their students will be able to identify cases in which a given rule applies and then use the rules as a guide. Teachers are seeking the same kind of result when they teach rules of spelling, rules for dividing fractions, or rules for repairing a motor. They are likewise operating on the same level when they teach theories in physics, chemistry, or football. (A rule or principle, by definition, is a theoretical statement.)

Explanatory understanding or reflection level teaching and learning leads to understandings just as do explanatory teaching and learning, but with reflection the search for understandings is pursued in a different fashion. Instead of students' being given a collection of facts and generalizations by a teacher, they are confronted with something that is problematic—either unclear or puzzling. Students' reflective learning may be based upon the inadequacies or disharmonies of the mental furniture that they bring with them to school, that is, their own attitudes, values, and knowledge. Or it may begin with some observed inadequacy, inconsistency, incompleteness, or irrelevance in the subject matter. In any case, if reflective learning occurs, problematic situation appears about which students center their thinking and research. In the reflective process, students examine existing facts and generalizations and seek out new ones.

There are crucial differences between explanatory understanding and reflection level teaching. The latter requires more active student participation, more criticism of conventional thinking, and more imagination and creativeness. The classroom atmospheres associated with the two approaches differ markedly. Reflective teaching leads to the development of a classroom atmosphere that is more alive and exciting, more critical and penetrating, and more open to fresh and original thinking. Furthermore, the type of inquiry pursued by a reflective class tends to be more rigorous and "work producing" than that pursued in an explanatory understanding level learning situation.

Since reflective teaching is problem-centered teaching, that which distinguishes reflective from nonreflective teaching and learning is the presence of genuine problems that students feel a need to solve. At the outset of a study, a real question develops for which students have no answer, or at least no adequate one. Through the study, the students and teacher, working cooperatively, develop what is for them a new or more adequate solution. Although the teacher is conscious of performing a unique function in a classroom in relation to a group of students, he (or she) still deems himself a part of the group as its members participate in the learning process.

Testing, like teaching, may be conducted on any one of three levels —memory, explanatory understanding, or reflection. Although there are many kinds of techniques and instruments that may be used for evaluating student progress, formalized testing continues to hold a very prominent position among them, especially in the minds of students. When students consider their teachers' evaluation of their achievements they usually think first of all of tests. Thus, they tend to gauge their levels of learning to the level of testing that their teachers employ; this is where the pay-off occurs. Hence, the nature of teachers' systems for evaluation of student learning has very great influence upon the quality of learning that actually develops.

Teachers' programs of evaluation not only govern their students' study habits, their manner of interaction in class, and the number and quality of their learnings, but they also greatly influence the teaching-learning level upon which their learning efforts proceed. For example, even though teachers strive to teach on either an explanatory understanding or a reflection level, so long as they continue to give memory level tests, most of the learning that ensues will be accomplished on a memory level. So, they should give careful consideration to the nature of their testing programs and other evaluational procedures. To quote Benjamin S. Bloom, "The point to be emphasized is that the type of mental process the student *expects* to be tested will determine his method of study and preparation."[7] (See Table 19.1 for a summary of the levels of teaching and learning and the evaluation procedures that are appropriate to each level.)

WHAT IS THE AUTONOMOUS DEVELOPMENT LEVEL OF TEACHING AND LEARNING?

The autonomous development level of teaching and learning is based upon *psychedelic humanistic* educational psychology and a *radical* (as contrasted with a *moderate*) *existentialist* educational philosophy within which people basically are considered forwardly active selves. Hence, education should be completely student-centered. Each student's feelings constitute the final authority for his (or her) test of truth. Accordingly, teaching is a laissez-faire process within which the teacher promotes each student's heightened intuitive awareness of himself and the artistic expression of his self-actualization.

A *radical existentialist* stresses three basic human awarenesses; "the teacher's imperative is to arrange the learning situation in such a way as to bring home the truth of these three propositions to every individual."[8] These awarenesses are: I am a choosing agent; I am a free agent; and I am a responsible agent. My responsibility, however, is only for how I live my own life. Thus, a radical existentialist teacher, or student, is always searching for personal truth. In teaching, the teacher awakens awareness, freedom, and responsibility in each student. But, since each person's own feelings are the final authority for the truth that is gained through this process, there is to be no analysis, prescription, or imposition of the activities of anyone by any other person, including the teacher.

Since, within autonomous development, the students as well as the teacher are considered to be autonomously proactive—forwardly active —selves, as opposed to their being either passive or interactive beings, teaching proceeds in a highly permissive atmosphere within which each individual develops largely on his (or her) own through the exercise of

Table 19.1 LEVELS OF THE TEACHING-LEARNING PROCESS AND THE TESTING PROCEDURES APPROPRIATE TO EACH LEVEL

LEVEL OF TEACHING LEARNING	UNDERLYING LEARNING THEORY	ATTRIBUTES OF THE TEACHING AND LEARNING PROCESS
1. Autonomous development (Neoprogressive education)	Natural unfoldment theory of psychedelic humanism or romantic naturalism; learners are autonomously proactive —forwardly active	Promotion of intuitive awareness of each self; artistic expression of self-actualization; negative education—no coercion, prescription, or imposition, one's feelings are the final authority for truth; student-centered
2. Memory a. Verbal-factual; mentalistic	Mental discipline theories of mind substance family; learners are active	Rote memory; training faculties of rational minds; repetitive drill, catechetical; teacher-centered
b. Behavioral; physicalistic or mechanomorphic	S-R conditioning theories of behavioristic family; learners are passive or reactive	Conditioning or behavior modification; formation of either S-R linkages or R-S reinforcements; reductionistic; teacher-centered
3. Explanatory understanding	Apperception; learners are passive	Teacher explanation and student grasp of generalizations, relationships, rules, or principles; teaching facts in relation to principles and the tool-use of generalizations and their supporting facts; teacher-centered
4. Reflection or exploratory understanding; problem-centered (not progressive education)	Cognitive-field theory; learners are situationally, perceptually interactive (SMI)	Purposive involvement and perplexity, problem raising and solving, and getting an intelligent "feel" for a principle, idea, or act; requires personal involvement, not merely interest; teacher-student-centered cooperative inquiry and evaluation; goal is student perplexity just short of frustration and resultant learning

his feelings, and each "does his own thing." Such teaching is student-centered as contrasted with both memory and explanatory understanding levels, which are teacher-centered, and exploratory understanding or reflection level, which is teacher-student-centered.

So, within the autonomous developments of psychedelic humanism, the teacher's function in education is more negative than positive in the

NATURE OF LEARNINGS	BASIS FOR APPROPRIATENESS OF TEST ITEMS	NATURE OF APPROPRIATE TESTS	METHOD OF TEST EVALUATION
Self-directed active unfoldments; expressed intuitive awareness; unfolded or developed natural needs or instincts and accompanying feelings		No testing; students alone evaluate their achievements according to their respective feelings	
Disciplined minds or mental faculties and retained factual materials	Recall of retained memories	Factual essay or short-answer true-false or completion	Check students' answers against list prepared at time the test is made up; teacher-centered
Either proper responses or increased probability of desired responses	Manifestation of previous conditioning or reinforcement	Sampling of desired responses	Check students' responses against a prepared list; teacher-centered
Teacher imposed understandings, insights, principles, relationships, concepts, generalizations, rules, theories, or laws	Recognition, explanation, or use of understandings, insights, principles, generalizations, rules, laws, or theories	Factual and explanatory essay or short-answer, true-false, selection, or completion	Check students' answers against prepared list, but, on essay tests, credit a student for "right" answers even though he or she uses words other than the instructor's; teacher-centered
Purposely acquired exploratory understandings, insights, principles, relationships, concepts, generalizations, rules, theories, or laws plus enhanced scientific outlook and instrumental thinking	Essay questions that are real, unanswered problems for the students and pertinent to the study having been pursued; real problems involve both generalization and tool-use of ideas as well as some degree of creativity	Reflective or problem-centered essay	Check students' answers on basis of criteria agreed upon prior to the test— probably pertinence and adequacy of data applied to the solution and harmony of the data, problem, and answer; teacher-student-centered

sense that there is little or no leadership, direction, coercion, prescription, or imposition of student thoughts or behaviors. Intellectual development is something that "just naturally happens." Hence, there is no need for any kind of formal teaching. Instead, student-planned, permissive types of projects are promoted for the purpose of releasing the students' latent talents. Students, as much as possible, are permitted, even encouraged, to live close to nature so that they may indulge freely their natural impulses and feelings. Inasmuch as creativity is an inherent characteristic of children and youths, it should be left to unfold in the highly permissive atmosphere of a child-centered school. Either Nature or the Creator has *enfolded* certain ideas, talents, and purposes into each child, and these should be permitted to *unfold* as he or she proceeds in school. Accordingly, each student should be permitted to choose his activities throughout the school day.

CAN AUTONOMOUS DEVELOPMENT BE TESTED?

Autonomous development, as an approach to teaching and learning, implies not only that students are active, but that they are forwardly so or proactive. Since the desired end product of education is a completely autonomous person, teachers have little interest in imparting measurable objective knowledge about reality, truth, and goodness.

An autonomous development approach to learning betokens a negative education within which there not only is no coercion, prescription, or imposition, but also there is neither teacher leadership nor student-teacher cooperative learning and evaluation. Each student's feelings are the final authority for truth. The educative function of teachers is to promote intuitive awareness of each student's self and artistic expression of his or her self-actualization.

School learnings are in the form of naturally unfolded or developed needs and accompanying feelings being actively expressed by self-directed active persons. Hence, there can be no valid systematic, teacher-developed testing program. Students alone can evaluate their respective achievements in accordance with their individual feelings.

WHAT IS THE MEMORY LEVEL OF TEACHING AND LEARNING?

Memory level learning may be either a mentalistic, verbal-factual process or a physicalistic behavioral process. Mentalistic-memory level learning is that kind of learning that embraces committing factual materials to memory and nothing else. It is possible for a person to memorize virtually any type of material, including that which seems quite nonsensical. But the more meaningful is the material to be learned, the easier it is to memorize it. Furthermore, the more meaningful the learned material, the longer it tends to be retained. A collection of "nonsense" syllables might conceivably be remembered for a lifetime if a person had sufficient reason for retaining it. However, when one develops a reason for retaining something, it is no longer nonsensical.

Physicalistic-behavioral memory level of teaching and learning consists of the formation in students of either S-R linkages (classical conditioning) or R-S reinforcements (instrumental conditioning). A student's learning consists of his or her developing the proper sequence of responses and an increased probability of the proper responses. The learning process is comparable to other organic processes such as digestion and respiration.

Since behaviorists view education as a matter of behavioral engineering or technology, they think of a teacher as a designer and manager of instruction and an evaluator of specific student learnings. Hence, they view educational goals as specified behaviors that students will manifest when they have been properly processed; these are physically memorized behavioral or performance objectives. After the general performance objectives are established, they are translated into increasingly specific, lesser ones and arranged in appropriate sequences for instruction. Instruction consists of shaping, and increasing the incidence, of desired behavior through presentation of appropriate stimuli at the proper time.

Behavior modification and performance-based instruction are anchored on three basic assumptions: (1) Learning of any degree of complexity, even critical thinking, can be achieved by one's progressively mastering or memorizing a large number of small sequential components. (2) All attainable educational goals can be explicitly stated in terms of physicalistic behavior. (3) Any educational objectives that are not definable in behavioral terms are either irrelevant or unattainable.

At first glance, memory level learning seems to exemplify either a mental discipline or an S-R conditioning theory of learning; either a bad-active or neutral-active substantive mind is trained, or simple relations are formed between the stimuli and responses of a neutral-passive biological organism with no particular thought or purpose being involved. But cognitive-field psychologists deny that either is the case. Instead they insist that, if anything is learned at all, insight of a sort is always present. What characterizes memory level learning, to a cognitive-field theorist, is the fact that the insights so acquired usually have no significant relationship to the material being studied. However, the learned material still is patterned by the learner during the process of learning it. Even "nonsense" syllables, when learned, are not completely unpatterned.[9]

One's capacity to memorize and retain material probably bears no positive relationship to one's capacity for intelligent behavior. Geniuses are notoriously forgetful, although not usually in their areas of major interest. Conversely, a mentally defective person may be highly proficient in memorization. For instance, Polly was a 13-year-old girl with a somewhat limited mental capacity. She had a quite brilliant memory of the "shotgun" variety. That is, she memorized indiscriminately anything she heard, and often could repeat verbatim an overheard conversation or a radio newscast. After hearing it once, she could recite faultlessly the words of every popular song being broadcast at the time. Nevertheless,

Polly's "thought power" was so impaired that, if asked to close an outside door of the house, she could not decide on which side of the door to stand to avoid shutting herself out.

Every experienced teacher can recall numerous students who developed a considerable capacity to memorize standard curricular materials in most or all school subjects. Such students usually make high grades. However, when placed in situations requiring reflection, they may be at a loss. If, occasionally, they take a course with a teacher who employs problem-centered teaching, they may become extremely frustrated and do very poor work. Conversely, an experienced teacher also can recall students whose grades were spotty but who achieved magnificently once they got out of school. There is a fairly good chance that in such cases poor achievement in school is a result of rebellion against required rote memorization.

Memory level teaching may, of course, contribute indirectly to intelligent behavior. If memorized facts become pertinent on an occasion when a problem requires solution, they contribute to usable background and hence to the effectiveness of problem solving. However, memorized facts usually contribute little to effective student growth. One reason is that, as already suggested, they tend to be forgotten quickly. Another is that a large proportion of the facts memorized in school are irrelevant to future thought needs. In summarizing the value of rote-memory teaching we might even say that the best way to make sure that a student will not remember many facts is to place the major emphasis upon teaching facts.

Despite all the legitimate criticisms we may make of rote memorization, it would be unrealistic to suppose that a teacher can always avoid it. In any ordinary school situation, on occasions even the most imaginative teacher will have no better approach than memory level teaching. This may occur on days when lack of time has prevented planning anything else. Or it may happen when the teacher does not know how else to handle the material to be covered.

One might ask, Can the fundamental skills, such as spelling, be taught otherwise than through a process of straight memorization, using drill procedures. Generally speaking, they can be taught more efficiently through other procedures. However, much more study will be required to develop procedures for teaching all the fundamental skill subjects in ways that will free us entirely from rote memorization.

WHAT TESTING PROCEDURES ARE APPROPRIATE TO MEMORY LEVEL TEACHING AND LEARNING?

In the process of appropriate mentalistic memory level testing, either factual essay or short-answer "objective" tests are employed to check for recall of memories that have been retained in the students' minds.

Questions on factual essay tests are in the form of "What are the four levels of teaching and learning?" Objective tests geared to this level take the form of "The four levels of teaching and learning are (1)————, (2)————, (3)————, and (4)————."

Within behaviorism, testing, like teaching, centers upon behavioral modification or change. The desired behaviors of students are sampled in such a way as to measure the manifestations of previous conditioning. In testing for learned physicalistic behaviors, teachers take a sampling of the behavioral modifications that had been included in a statement of behavioral objectives that was developed prior to the beginning of the course. These modifications all are in the form of observable responses. Hence, teachers who are teaching on this level would expect their students to be able to list or name the four levels of teaching and learning. Consequently, they would use test items much like those used in mentalistic memory level testing.

NOTES

[1] See "laissez-faire," *Webster's Third New International Dictionary*, Springfield, Mass.: Merriam, 1966, p. 1265.

[2] See Ralph K. White and Ronald Lippitt, *Autocracy and Democracy: An Experimental Inquiry*, New York: Harper & Row, 1960, pp. 51–55, 66–80.

[3] Ibid., pp. 55–58, 61–64.

[4] Ibid., pp. 58–65.

[5] See Ernest E. Bayles, *Democratic Educational Theory*, Chapter 1, "Experiments with Reflective Teachings," New York: Harper & Row, 1960.

[6] See "understand," *The American College Dictionary*, New York: Random House, 1964, p. 1321.

[7] Benjamin S. Bloom, "Testing Cognitive Ability and Achievement," in N. L. Gage (ed.), *Handbook of Research on Teaching*, Chicago: Rand McNally, 1963, p. 392.

[8] See Van Cleve Morris, *Existentialism in Education*, New York: Harper & Row, 1966, p. 135.

[9] See George Katona, *Organizing and Memorizing*, New York: Columbia University Press, 1940.

BIBLIOGRAPHY

The bibliography for Chapters 19, 20, and 21 is at the end of Chapter 21.

Chapter 20
HOW MAY TEACHERS TEACH FOR EXPLANATORY UNDERSTANDING?

At the close of the preceding chapter a distinction was made between memory level, explanatory understanding level, and exploratory understanding level teaching and learning. However, no attempt should be made to draw extremely fine lines between these levels. Memory level learning, at times, can contribute to understanding or help provide a background for reflection. Likewise, explanatory understanding level learning can foster learning of individual facts—though seen in a related fashion—and may progress into reflection level learning. Furthermore, students will learn large numbers of facts and understandings whenever they become involved in reflection level learning.

However, it would be a mistake not to make a reasonably clear distinction between the three levels; each is quite distinctive. Many educational psychologists consider a memory level learning that seeks nothing else—neither understanding nor reflection—a waste of time on the part of both students and teachers. Nevertheless, teachers sometimes get caught in a bind of pressures and distractions which make it temporarily impossible for them to do much else than resort to memory work of some kind. Since many educational psychologists think that memory level learning per se is not worth striving for, we do not devote a chapter to it as we do for each of the other levels.

To the extent that memory level learning ever can be justified, the problem of teaching on this level takes care of itself; teachers need only teach as they usually have been taught. However, there are a few general considerations worth noting about memory level. Some persons, for reasons not yet understood, have better memories for unrelated facts than do others. A few individuals have what is known as a "photographic memory"; that is to say, they seem able to retain almost indefinitely even the most meaningless of the mass of potpourri which they encounter. Other individuals are notably forgetful concerning all matters with which they are not deeply involved.

There is little or no evidence that either of these traits bears any significant relationships to a person's ability effectively to solve the problems which arise in his (or her) life. In short, a person with a "photographic" memory is not necessarily either more or less "intelligent," as we have defined the term on page 421, than is a forgetful person. We have described the real-life case of Polly, the idiot savant who could remember virtually everything with remarkable precision (see p. 463). Another case in point is that of the late John von Neumann, one of the greatest creative mathematicians ever to live in the United States. He had great difficulty remembering not only all the commonplace small routines of life but even some of the larger ones. The story is told that when he was required to travel away from home—even to some important conference where he was scheduled to deliver a paper—someone (his wife, we assume) pinned a sheet of paper to the outside of his coat explaining which airplane flight he was supposed to take, at which hotel he was to stay, and other necessary information so that people along the way could help him arrive at his destination and meet his commitments.

Teachers would be well advised to remember that students who seem unable to remember lists of facts, even until the next day's quiz, may have a much higher functional intelligence and a much greater potential contribution to human culture than do some other students who make a perfect score on every quiz. Accordingly, when testing is pitched on a strictly rote-memory level, test results should be given very little weight in one's trying to estimate a student's potential.

We now turn to the major theme of the chapter—explanatory understanding level teaching. Explanatory understanding level teaching seeks to give students patterns of general ideas and supporting facts in such a way that they will see the relationships between the generalizations and the particulars or facts that support them; it is giving students rules. (At this point readers should review the meaning of understanding developed in Chapter 19, pages 454–456.)

To repeat, an understanding may be gained in either of two quite distinctive manners. We may identify the two processes as learning on an explanatory understanding level and learning on a reflection or exploratory understanding level. When teachers give understandings to students, the class is operating on an explanatory understanding level. When students and the teacher cooperatively and exploratively develop understandings, the class is operating on a reflection or exploratory understanding level.

Johann F. Herbart, Charles H. Judd, Henry C. Morrison, and the contemporary educators Robert M. Gagné and Jerome S. Bruner have provided perhaps the most significant leadership in the development of explanatory understanding level teaching, based upon their respective conceptions of the nature of understanding level learning. Many others, too, have made important contributions, but these five stand out as perhaps the most prominent innovators in explanatory understanding level teaching and learning.

Since Herbart's, Gagné's, and Bruner's positions are treated in some detail in Chapters 10 and 16, we, in this chapter, only summarize the aspects of their theories that pertain to the exploratory understanding level of teaching and learning. But the respective positions of Judd and Morrison are treated in some detail.

HOW DID HERBART'S APPERCEPTION THEORY INVOLVE UNDERSTANDINGS?

Johann Friedrich Herbart wrote no treatise on the meaning of understanding, yet his approach to the teaching-learning process indicated that he was aware of one aspect of understanding—that is, relating the isolated fact to the general principle or rule which gives it meaning.

In Steps 3 and 4 of a Herbartian lesson plan as developed by American Herbartians (see p. 261), students are asked to identify common elements in a body of factual material and to make a general statement that will link them together, that is, they are asked to take an assortment of related facts and formulate the relationship into a rule, principle, or law. Then in Step 5 students are expected to demonstrate that they see clearly the nature of the principle by applying it in novel situations. A number of school subjects today are taught with essentially the same aims. These are the subjects in which the crux of the subject matter is the learning and application of principles. English grammar and mathematics are usually taught this way. In contrast, foreign language, history, geography, and many other subjects often are taught on a memory level basis.

HOW WERE JUDD'S GENERALIZATIONS EXPLANATORY UNDERSTANDINGS?

Between 1915 and 1920, two of the most eminent educational psychologists of the time, Edward L. Thorndike and Charles H. Judd (1873–1946), carried on a running debate in regard to the nature of learning and its transfer. Whereas Professor Thorndike continued to champion his identical elements theory, Professor Judd insisted that generalizations, not identical elements, were transferred to new situations. A generalization is a statement or understanding of relationships. It may also be called a principle, rule, or law. "Generalization is another name for the relating of experiences in such a way that what is gained at one point will redound to the advantage of the individual in many spheres of thought and action."[1]

The basic educational issue of identical elements versus generalization of experience has persisted through the years. In its current form, the issue is whether teachers should condition students with lists of specific essential serial *performances* or whether they should facilitate students' development of significant *understandings* that are instrumental to students' development of effectual activities or behaviors.

How Are Generalizations Learned?

Judd recognized two possible kinds or levels of learning: rote memorization with little, if any, meaning and generalized knowledge with many intellectual associations. He placed very little value on the first level and a high premium upon the second. He was convinced that knowledge always should be in the form that makes generalizations possible; that is, it should have many intellectual associations and many possibilities of new associations. He even emphasized his generalizations theory when discussing the teaching of basic skills. Thus, he stated, "when new skills are cultivated by an individual, the muscles are brought into coordinated action through elaborately organized patterns developed in the nervous system."[2] Furthermore, "generalizations which epitomize great numbers of experiences are the highest products of racial and individual intellectual effort."[3]

Judd's dart throwing experiment to test the value of generalizations has become something of a classic. Success in hitting a target under water requires readjustment of one's ordinary habit of throwing a dart. Since the light coming from the target is refracted as it leaves the water, there is an apparent displacement of the target. Judd selected two groups of boys comparable in those variables that seemed relevant. One group, the experimental one, was instructed in the principle of—generalization in regard to—the refraction of light; the other, the control group, was not. Both groups of boys were then asked to throw darts in such a way as to hit underwater objects with them. At the beginning of the experiment, none of the boys had any skill in throwing darts.

Both groups of boys were instructed to hit targets placed 12 inches under water. The boys who had had theoretical training in the principles of refraction did as poorly at this first task as did the control group; they had to learn to throw darts before their theoretical training could help. Once this was accomplished the target was moved to a position four inches under water. Immediately the experimental group showed a conspicuous superiority over the control group. Their understanding of the nature of refraction had given them cues as to where to aim the darts in order to hit underwater objects which are not where they appear to be. Judd's experiment and his interpretation of it is related in detail in his various books.[4]

More recent research supports Judd's position. In 1957, Kittell measured the relative effects of three amounts of direction on sixth graders' discovery of established principles on transfer to differing situations and on their retention of learned principles.[5] He concluded that

> Evidence from this experiment in conjunction with that of similar experiments indicates that furnishing learners with information in the form of underlying principles promotes transfer and retention of learning principles and may provide the background enabling future discovery of new principles.[6]

HOW HAVE MORRISON'S IDEAS PROMOTED EXPLANATORY UNDERSTANDING LEVEL TEACHING?

Henry C. Morrison (1871–1945) was an influential figure in American education during the 1930s and devised a unit plan which at one time was in rather wide-spread use. Like Herbart and Judd, Morrison is now considered outdated and his books no longer are required reading except in a few schools of education. Nevertheless, some of his ideas still are too avant-garde for many educators of the 1970s to accept.

Within an idea-centered frame of reference, Morrison describes various types of learning, including conditioning, "bonding," and trial and error.[7] However, the kind of learning he felt schools should promote is none of these as such, but a special form which he referred to as *personality adaptation*. In developing his position, he borrowed freely from various schools of thought, yet to call him an eclectic would be an oversimplification. Because of his emphasis upon personality adaptation, to some degree he developed a synthesis of the prevailing outlooks on learning.

Personality adaptation is somewhat different from biological adaptation. Biological adaptation, in its most general sense, is the structural and functional process and product that occurs whenever an organism achieves a better adjustment to the conditions of life. Personality adaptation is a psychological process of permanent personality change; it is a change in insight. It consists of revised attitudes, values, beliefs, knowledge, and whatever else constitutes a psychological person.

Morrison distinguished *adaptive responses* from *true adaptation*. An adaptive response is a habit learned more or less by rote that its bearer does not understand and therefore uses blindly. Morrison thought that much human behavior is on this level. But he deplored any kind of teaching that leaves students only with adaptive responses instead of true personality adaptations.

The proper task for education, said Morrison, is the creation of true adaptation, which is a permanent change in outlook as indicated above. Or, put in language which Morrison frequently used, it is personality change. To him, the term personality meant a total person in its psychological and sociological sense, not those superficial aspects of a person's make-up that we sometimes signify when we say, "Jane has a nice personality." Specifically, Morrison said personality is the "sum total of what an individual has come to be by learning the cultural products of social evolution."[8]

What Was Morrison's Recommended Teaching Procedure?

Fundamental to comprehension of Morrison's teaching procedure is an understanding of his concept *mastery*. The outcome of all teaching is mastery—not mere memorization of facts, but mastery. Mastery is reached only when planned understandings have been grasped thoroughly. An understanding, as we have seen, is a generalization seen in relation to the pertinent facts and to the uses to which it might be put.

Each subject field, according to Morrison, was to be divided into units. Each unit should present a specific understanding with such thoroughness that mastery is achieved by most students. Note that Morrison did not mean by a "unit" what is commonly meant today. In contemporary parlance, a unit usually is a block of work that, to a teacher or textbook writer, comprises a logical work-task. A unit, therefore, is typically conceived as simply a piece of work, based upon a certain quantity of related facts in a textbook or other source. Morrison's conception of a unit of work was psychological. To him, a unit was a generalization and its related facts, as a student should come to see them. A unit was never "covered" until all or almost all students thoroughly understood the generalization—its factual origins, its probable reliability, and the kinds of situations in which it could be used in the future.

Some subjects, for instance algebra, contain many units, each of which may be grasped by most students in a fairly short time. Other subjects, for instance a foreign language, contain only one unit; the whole subject must be mastered before a student has anything worthwhile. The point is, a unit represents an insight that is relatively complete in itself. This insight may be relatively simple and readily grasped, or it may require years of study. Hence, a unit, as Morrison conceived it, may require anywhere from a class period to many years to be mastered. Each unit is developed according to a sequence of steps, which, although Morrison disclaimed their relationship to the famous five steps of the Herbartian method, are nevertheless reminiscent of the Herbartian steps.

Morrison's contribution was a major one and most current teaching would undoubtedly be greatly improved if Morrison's thinking were more widely understood. His notion that mere collections of descriptive facts have no meaning, provide no basis for understanding, and therefore constitute unteachable subject matter is of especial importance.

What Is Mastery Teaching of the 1970s?

The ideas, research, and operational procedures of Benjamin S. Bloom, James H. Block, and others have developed a contemporary version of mastery teaching and learning that harks back to Morrison's position. However, this contemporary version is anchored to a behaviorism that emphasizes discrete psychomotor, cognitive, and affective objectives. So, it has a much lesser place for true understanding level learning than did Morrison.

Contemporary adherents think that, "Mastery learning offers a powerful new approach to student learning which can provide almost all students with the successful and rewarding learning experiences now allowed to only a few."[9] So, modern educational technology now provides the means for achievement of Morrison's ambitions.

Modern mastery learning has emerged as a corollary of programmed instruction. By setting the level formerly required for a grade of A in a nonmastery class as the definition of mastery for mastery classes, Professor Bloom and his associates have brought four-fifths of their students to reach a level of achievement that less than one-fifth had attained under nonmastery conditions.[10]

Teaching for mastery, then, entails the formulation of a set of instructional objectives or tasks that all students will be expected to achieve to a particular mastery performance standard, then breaking the course into a sequence of smaller learning units. The teacher follows a "cycle of group-based instruction formative testing, and certification or prescription/correction for each student on each unit until all the learning units have been completed."[11] Each student's grade is determined solely on the basis of his or her absolute, as opposed to relative, performance over the learning material.

HOW ARE GAGNÉ'S HIGH-ORDER RULES RELATED TO EXPLANATORY UNDERSTANDING?

Gagné's intellectual skills involve organisms' knowing how to perform acts. His cognitive strategies are a special kind of intellectual skills, in the form of internally organized capabilities, that learners use to guide their processes of attending, learning, remembering, and thinking. Thus, learning strategies, in a sense, are understandings developed internally as concomitants of behavior.

Gagné's sixth, seventh, and eighth learning types are concept learning, rule learning, and problem solving. Concept learning is making a common response to a class of stimuli. Rule learning is forming a chain of two or more concepts so as to enable one to respond to a class of stimulus situations with a class of performances. In problem solving one applies previously learned rules to achieve a solution of a novel situation. So, all three involve gaining explanatory understandings through a behavioristally characterized learning process. But, in no sense is the process of gaining understandings in an exploratory fashion brought into the picture.

HOW DOES BRUNER EMPHASIZE TEACHING FOR UNDERSTANDING THROUGH CONCEPTUALIZATION?

Jerome S. Bruner is a cognitive psychologist who strongly advocates a combination of explanatory and exploratory understanding levels of teaching and learning. However, he uses a somewhat different vocabulary and manner of describing his views than do others within the same frame of reference.

Bruner's principal concern is with how people actively select, structure, retain, and transform information and how they go beyond discrete information to achieve generalized insights or understandings. He has great interest in how people adopt models of reality from their culture and adapt them to their individual uses. His "models" are expectancies, and expectancies are insights.

All three modes of representation—the enactive, iconic, and symbolic—involve, to some degree, people's striving for understanding. But, it is within the process of symbolic representation, centered on language, that people achieve genuine reflective thinking or exploratory understanding. Symbolic representation is an instrument for conceptualization or categorization, which is the principal product of reflective thinking and learning. It is through goal-oriented strategies that conceptualization occurs.

Bruner thinks that teachers should encourage students to discover the value and the amendability of their considered guesses and should promote students' confidence in their ability to solve problems by thinking. Education should concentrate more on the unknown and speculative, and gained knowledge should be placed in the context of action and commitment.

HOW MAY THE EXPLANATORY UNDERSTANDING LEVEL OF TEACHING BE IMPROVED?

As now organized, many courses are built around concepts and generalizations. This is true of languages, provided the "rules" are taught. It also is true of mathematics, which is one of the courses par excellence so far as generic learning is concerned; it is practically all rules, once the fundamentals of arithmetic are taught (by rote, all too often). Home economics, too, rises to the level of coding when a student learns generalizations about nutrition, cooking, baby care, housekeeping, and so forth. Readers can name the remaining school subjects which commonly are focused on concepts and generalizations, rather than on the memorization of discrete facts.

Unfortunately, there are certain regularly required courses which are nothing but arrays of facts arranged chronologically or topically; there is no apparent rationale either to the selection or arrangement of factual materials included. Among the worst offenders on this score have been the social studies. However, readers will be able to think of several other culprits, including the natural sciences. Biology, for example, may emphasize taxonomy—classification—to the point where everything else is omitted or treated only incidentally; albeit, in certain areas of biology, it is difficult to escape if-then generalizations and the building of at least partial structures. Ecology, genetics, and speciation are examples of such areas.

The following suggestions may be of value to teachers who wish to implement classroom explanatory understanding level learning. Some of the points are suggested in Bruner's works, others come from several different sources, and some are our own. They center upon teachers, the teaching process, and appropriate evaluation.

What Are Some Necessary Characteristics of Teachers Who Teach on an Explanatory Understanding Level?

It appears evident that a teacher must manifest a certain kind of attitude, values, and knowledge to be able to teach effectively on an explanatory understanding level. Let us examine some of the factors that are involved in a teacher's acquisition of these traits. They are as follows: (1) the way in which a teacher has learned the subject, (2) the degree to which the teacher has learned the subject, and (3) the personality characteristics of a teacher.

THE WAY IN WHICH A TEACHER HAS LEARNED THE SUBJECT

If prospective teachers have been taught on an understanding level the subjects which they in turn plan to teach, then it is unlikely that they will need much further instruction. It is a truism that the way in which teachers have learned will reflect itself in the way they teach. If a teacher has not himself learned his (or her) subjects by moving from instances (facts) to categories (concepts) to codes (generalizations), then it would appear that he needs to relearn his subjects over again, following those steps. The practical problems involved in doing this might in many cases seem insurmountable. It certainly suggests the need for changed methods of instruction in many college classes, for more discriminating selection of the "master teachers" with whom student teachers or interns work, and for changed in-service teacher education programs.

THE DEGREE TO WHICH A TEACHER HAS LEARNED THE SUBJECT

Bruner has written

> It takes no elaborate research to know that communicating knowledge depends in enormous measure upon one's mastery of the knowledge to be communicated. . . . It is also quite plain from recent surveys that many primary and secondary school teachers are not, in the view of various official bodies, sufficiently well trained initially to teach their subject.[12]

Our only advice to prospective or in-service teachers is, "If you are not a master of your subject, then take whatever steps are necessary to insure mastery." For the undergraduate, this may mean studying far beyond the minimal graduation requirements. For those already teaching it may mean returning to college for study in depth of the subjects they now teach or it may mean a carefully planned program of self-study.

THE PERSONALITY CHARACTERISTICS OF A TEACHER

It is fairly simple to deduce what kind of person is most likely to be successful at explanatory understanding level teaching. He (or she) must be fairly bright—by which we mean capable of exercising intelligence on a fairly high level. He must have the kind of mind-set that finds it easy to see particulars in relation to one another—the kind that leans toward conceptualization, generalization, and abstraction. Another way of putting it is to say an effective teacher is a person with a penchant for theorizing and who understands that "nothing is so practical as a good theory."

Another capacity of crucial importance is patience. Teaching for understanding is not something that can be hurried. The "frantic ground-covering" type of teacher is suited only for memory level or rote teaching. To discuss other personality characteristics would run us into a series of clichés that potential or practicing teachers already have heard entirely too many times. Of course, a teacher should be dedicated, conscientious, honest, tactful . . . etc., etc. Readers can make up their own list of what is required.

What Is the Explanatory Understanding Teaching Process?

Most advocates of explanatory understanding level teaching have taken for granted that a teacher begins with truths that he (or she) knows but which students do not. Students struggle to find these truths, with the teacher providing what cues are necessary along the way. Students have successfully completed their learning task when they emerge with an understanding of the preordained truths that the teacher already knew. This approach permits inquiry, investigation, and exploration on the part of the students—all of which undoubtedly does not help them greatly in understanding the foregone conclusions that they eventually will reach. But there is an issue here that is of notable importance and Richard Brown states it brilliantly as follows.

> Are the proponents of the revolution willing to follow through where they argue that they want to make the student a fledgling scholar, a free inquirer after truth? Or do they want him merely to find on his own the truths they already know? In dealing with the original sources . . . should the student do any more than play a game with the compiler of the materials, looking for clues so that he may come to a preordained answer? Dare he find things the compiler did not know were there, or ask questions which will carry him outside the materials altogether?[13]

Professor Brown obviously sees the issue between teaching that remains on an explanatory understanding level and teaching that moves to the level of reflection. If students dare to find things that the compiler did not know and if they dare ask questions that lead outside the previously prepared materials, then clearly reflective teaching and learning are operating. This will be explained in the ensuing chapter. But now let us examine the attributes of an effective explanatory understanding level teaching process.

To teach effectually on an explanatory understanding level, a teacher must (1) keep his or her objectives clear, (2) understand the proper role of practice, (3) practice productive motivational techniques, (4) pace students and lessons advantageously, and (5) use lesson plans properly.

KEEPING OBJECTIVES CLEAR

In several of his writings Bruner stresses that most students will make an effort to achieve the learning goals that a teacher announces to them. However, this does not mean that prior announcements of conclusions are desirable; such action would destroy the "discovery aspect" of learning. What should be explained to students before the learning act is the kind of learning that they are expected to achieve. Teachers are either misled or shoddy if, in making assignments, they request their students to memorize something, to spend so much time at drill, or just to "learn this by tomorrow" (which students almost always construe to mean "memorize"). Students must be taught, but not through mere memorization, the nature of a concept, a generalization, and a structured subject. This can be done by an inductive type of questioning coupled with the study of examples showing people in the process of achieving these goals. When students not only can explain in their own words but also can invent their own examples of these processes, then they are ready for effective statements of objectives.

Obviously students should be taught as soon as possible the road to abstract thought. Once this is done, it is possible to proceed with the content of the subject. Assignments will carry instructions such as this: "Here we have some facts that seem unconnected. See to what extent you can categorize them," or "We have reached three generalizations concerning this topic. Try to see if you can combine them into a single, more inclusive generalization," or "After conceptualizing the known facts, we have invented a generalization. See how many presently unknown but possible facts you can deduce from the generalization." If students are always reminded that the object of learning is some level of conceptualization, and if no other approach works, then this is the way they will learn.

THE ROLE OF PRACTICE

Practice—sometimes extending over a long period of time—often is necessary to achieve a learning task. This is perhaps more true of gaining voluntary control of motor skills than of cognition of an academic sort, but practice is an important factor in both. In the past, practice has all too often been construed as repetitive drill—the repeating of a static item in identical form. As observed earlier in the book, one of the early proponents of repetition as a means of learning, Thorndike, as a result of further experimentation, later retracted his original assertions in regard to the value of repetition (see p. 273). Only the most naive teachers now know so little about learning that they think they can teach anything of significance by mere repetition.

Practice, on the other hand, has a special connotation. Practice can be construed as the experimental trying out of an act or idea in what may appear to be a repetitive process. However, a crucial difference between mechanical repetition and experimental practice is that with practice the subject performs the act a little differently each time and observes or experiences the consequences. Bruner maintains that generic learning cannot occur in the absence of a changing situation. Accordingly, he comments on a statement of Kurt Lewin as follows: "Kurt Lewin had a subtle point when he urged that the best way to understand the nature of a social process was to try to change it, for only in the face of changes in events does one begin to have the information necessary to abstract generic properties."[14]

PRODUCTIVE MOTIVATION

Educators who operate within an explanatory understanding level frame of reference assume that once a student is acquainted with a subject, told of the expected goals in learning it, and begins to experience some success, motivation generates rather spontaneously. This is not a false theory of motivation, but it may be an inadequate one. It is true that some students become very much interested in a subject merely through exposure to it. But this is the exception rather than the rule.

Like others before him whose chief focus was on teaching for explanatory understanding, Bruner does not come to grips with the problem of inducing students to want to involve themselves in study. It appears that teaching that does not go beyond the objectives of helping students see the relatedness of things seeks motivation from wherever it can be found. Bruner stresses the importance of students having a purpose for learning. However, he is not clear—and sometimes is contradictory—with respect to how such purpose can be instilled. Much of his discussion seems to center on extrinsic purposes—those arising from something other than the fascination of the subject matter itself.[15] But he also refers to a natural tendency toward curiosity and drops it at that. Then, in one book he devotes a chapter to motivation and attributes it to cultural pressures on the learner deriving from the general social milieu.

In any case, student motivation is one area in which Bruner and his like-minded forerunners do not have much to say. The reason is not concealed: Professor Bruner is wary enough to try to steer some middle path between vitalism and the unadulterated environmentalism of most advocates of behaviorism. What seems to be lacking is an emergent synthesis that will suggest fresh lines of inquiry. Cognitive-field psychologists have worked on this problem and further treatment of it appears in Chapter 21.

PACING ADVANTAGEOUSLY

We come now to one of the major points concerning classroom procedure. By "pace" we refer to speed of movement from one topic to another; it logically follows that the number of topics studied in a year is of great significance. The pace of learning on both levels of understanding is usually slow. It is much more analogous to the steady thrust of a glacier than to the speed of a greyhound. As we pointed out earlier in the chapter, categorizing, generalizing, and structuring cannot be rushed. This is the case even in spite of "intuitive leaps" (see p. 475)—after all, the leaps produce only hypotheses and not firm knowledge. If a learner is to emerge with something solid, each leap must be followed by a careful series of verifying tests.

Any subject matter worth confronting students with is worth careful, penetrating, thorough study. If it is not worth this kind of study, it is not worth inclusion in the curriculum. Typically, we try to teach too many items—and they remain nothing more than items—quickly to be forgotten. To achieve genuine understanding, and consequent retention and transfer, it may be necessary to eliminate half or more of the present curriculum. The problem of the relationship of teaching methodology to curriculum needs a great deal more study than it has received to date.

PROPER USE OF LESSON PLANS

Historically, carefully drawn day-by-day lesson plans have been considered essential to explanatory understanding level teaching and learning. It appears likely that, until a teacher has structured his (or her) subject matter in his own thinking, he not only should read and think copiously, but also should take notes which can be translated into lesson plans as necessary. But, Herbartian lesson planning is overly rigid and leads to indoctrination. Morrison's mastery units represent an advance over Herbartian lesson plans. However, they, too, set the stage for a teacher's indoctrinating students in a rather mechanistic fashion. Bruner appears to have nothing to say on the subject of lesson plans. Possibly he assumes that a competent teacher will have his lesson plans in his head.

Our own feeling is that a beginning teacher, striving for explanatory understanding level teaching, should have a tentative plan for each class session. For safety, he should probably have an alternate plan in case the first does not work. We do not recommend a rigid plan with 1-2-3 steps. Thought does not take this pattern. Plans should be informal and flexible. They should include reminders of factual material to be presented when needed, key questions to ask, and tentative conclusions. One manner of distinguishing explanatory understanding from reflection level teaching is the tendency of the former to adhere quite closely to lesson plans as drawn and to wrap up each unit in a complete package with no loose ends. This tendency has significant implications for motivation, as we shall see in the next chapter on reflection level teaching.

The proper use of lesson plans in reflective teaching was summated, and not facetiously, by Boyd H. Bode when he wrote, "the lesson plan has its merits, provided we do not use it, i.e., provided we do not follow it as a plan of campaign in the classroom. . . . It is as preposterous to concoct a recipe for learning as for invention."[16]

How Is Explanatory Understanding Level Learning Evaluated?

Either factual explanatory essay tests or short-answer, true-false, selection, or completion tests are most appropriate for testing students' understandings that are learned on an explanatory understanding level. Through the use of these, students demonstrate how well they can either recognize, explain, or use the understandings or generalized insights that the teacher has expected them to acquire.

In testing on an explanatory understanding level, just as on both aspects of the memory level, the teacher checks students' answers against a prepared list of answers. However, the process differs somewhat from that of memory level testing in that so long as the answers are correct the teacher credits students for "right" answers even though they may use wording somewhat different from that of the instructor. An appropriate explanatory understanding level essay test question would be "Describe how the four levels of teaching and learning differ from one another." An appropriate objective test item might be as follows: "Select the word that completes the sentence best: When a teacher teaches on an explanatory understanding level, he gives his students (1) advice, (2) generalizations, (3) thoughts, (4) memories."

NOTES

[1] Charles H. Judd, *Educational Psychology*, Boston: Houghton Mifflin, 1939, p. 514.

[2] Ibid., p. 496.

[3] Ibid., p. 514.

[4] Ibid., pp. 507ff.

[5] Jack E. Kittell, "An Experimental Study of the Effect of External Direction During Learning on Transfer of Retention of Principles," *Journal of Educational Psychology* 48 (November 1957): 391–405.

[6] Ibid., p. 404.

[7] Henry C. Morrison, *Basic Principles in Education*, Houghton Mifflin, 1934, Chapter 4.

[8] Ibid., p. 39.

[9] James H. Block (ed.), *Mastery Learning Theory and Practice*, New York: Holt, Rinehart and Winston, 1971, p. 3.

[10] Benjamin S. Bloom, "An Introduction to Mastery Learning Theory," in James H. Block (ed.), *School, Society, and Mastery Learning*, New York: Holt, Rinehart and Winston, 1974, p. 6.

[11] James H. Block, "A Description and Comparison of Bloom's Learning for Mastery Strategy and Keller's Personalized System of Instruction," in James H. Block (ed.), *School, Society, and Mastery Learning*, New York: Holt, Rinehart and Winston, 1974, p. 18.

[12] Jerome S. Bruner, *The Process of Education*, Cambridge: Harvard University Press, 1960, p. 88.

[13] Richard H. Brown, "History and the New Social Studies," *Saturday Review* (October 15, 1966): 80–81.

[14] G. S. Bruner, "Going Beyond the Information Given," in H. Gruber (ed.), *Contemporary Approaches to Cognition*, Cambridge: Harvard University Press, 1957, p. 61.

[15] G. S. Bruner, *The Process of Education*, Cambridge: Harvard University Press, 1960, Chapter 5.

[16] Boyd H. Bode, *How We Learn*, Boston: Heath, 1940, p. 156.

Chapter 21
HOW DO REFLECTIVE TEACHING AND LEARNING PROCEED?

Much of the inefficiency in education that research has exposed stems from the way most school subjects are organized and presented. Subjects often remain meaningless to students, not because of students' intellectual deficiencies, but because human mentalities work in such a way that the subjects, as organized and taught, may have little meaning for them. Explanatory understanding level teaching gives students a tool for more intelligent behavior. It equips them with generalized insights that can be applied in problematic situations both in and outside school. But, explanatory understanding level teaching, if it remains merely that, casts the students as a passive agent and the teacher as an active agent. The teacher tells and the student listens or the teacher stimulates and the student responds. Thus, this level of teaching is basically uncritical and authoritarian.

Teachers who are committed to the reflection level of teaching and learning think that the quality and quantity of what students come to know, think, and do are inseparable from the way in which their learning is acquired. What children and youth learn along with their learning subject matter is as significant as the subject matter itself. Students may passively absorb content as it is presented by an authority or they may actively follow directions and move around according to instructions. But, in either case, they are learning to follow directions passively, to appear to accept what they are told, and to believe that education consists of those who know telling those who do not.

In contrast with the results of authoritarian education, students may democratically and reflectively learn both how knowledge changes, grows, and is subject to interpretation and what "good" thinking is and how difficult it is to accomplish. Within this process they may develop intellectual habits of curiosity, inquiry, persistence, and carefulness. Thus, they may learn both to discern the difference between relevant and irrelevant information and reliable and unreliable sources.

When reflective teaching and learning are successful, students emerge with (1) an enlarged store of tested insights of a generalized character, and (2) an enhanced ability to develop and solve problems on their own. The latter product is as important as the former. If only the first were accomplished, no claims could be made for reflection level which could not also be made for explanatory understanding level teaching. However, within genuine problem-centered teaching, students learn the very nature and techniques of problem-solving processes. And, if well taught, problem-solving approaches and procedures that are learned in school carry over to be applied to a wide range of problems both in and outside school.

An understanding of how to solve problems according to principles of scientific reflection is perhaps the most useful intellectual tool a person can possess. If the central goal of education is to foster intelligence, reflective teaching should be the basic approach used by teachers everywhere. Let us visit a fifth grade social studies class being taught reflectively and see whether we can discern what is unique to reflection level teaching procedures.

HOW MAY A CLASS REFLECTIVELY STUDY THE PONY EXPRESS?

Let us now follow the teaching-learning procedure of a fifth grade class's reflectively studying the Pony Express.[1] The key provocative question that was developed was as follows: "If the Pony Express was such an exciting and successful venture, why was it suddenly discontinued after less than two years' service?"

One day a class was listening to a member giving a report on the Pony Express. The student reporter related the following to the class.

A newspaper advertisement in 1860 read:

WANTED

Young men not over eighteen.
Must be expert riders,
willing to risk death daily.
Orphans preferred.
Wages, $25 a week.

This notice brought a group of young men together who would carry a parcel from St. Joseph, Missouri, to Sacramento, California, in ten days' time. The stagecoach took 25 days to complete this trip, and many business-men and government workers in the East and West wanted important long-distance mail to travel much faster. The newspaper advertisement helped create an organization that cut fifteen days off the time needed for mail to go from coast to coast.

Pony Express stations along the way provided food and care for both riders and horses. Fresh horses were available at each station, and about every 70 or 80 miles a different rider would take over. Sometimes a rider would reach a station and find it either burned down by Indians or deserted, and he would have to go on to the next station. No matter whether it snowed or rained or whether Indians or thieves attacked, the mail was to go through. Every Pony Express rider was given a revolver to protect himself. However, his main job was not to fight, but to avoid trouble if possible and reach his next station. Obviously, the job of Pony Express riders was most exciting, and the Pony Express was highly efficient for its time. People generally were enthusiastic about the new venture and, in a way, it made heroes of the riders.

The student reporter talked at some length about the excitement and glamour of the entire affair, mentioning a particular rider, Buffalo Bill, and recounting a ride that he had made on a certain day. After telling about the enthusiasm that developed for this thrilling and efficient operation, the reporter said, "Having been begun in 1860, the Pony Express was discontinued in 1861 after less than two years of operation." He then sat down.

The class was somewhat surprised. After finding out what a grand and successful operation the Pony Express was, they learned that it was suddenly disbanded. Why? They started asking questions. In the follow-ing report of the discussion that ensued, "Reporter" indicates the student reporter who related the history of the Pony Express. "Student" indicates anyone who responded to the reporter's particular statement. A number of students participated in the discussion.

STUDENT: Why was the Pony Express stopped?
REPORTER: Why do you think it was stopped?
STUDENT: Were all the riders killed?
REPORTER: No.
STUDENT: Did they all quit?
REPORTER: No.
STUDENT: Did people stop writing letters?
REPORTER: No.
STUDENT: Did they get faster stage coaches?
REPORTER: No.
STUDENT: Was a railroad built?
REPORTER: No. The railroad wasn't completed until 1869.
TEACHER: Perhaps you should tell the class how they can find the answer.

REPORTER: O.K. If you read the middle part of Chapter Ten in your book, it tells why the Pony Express stopped.

STUDENT: Wait a minute. Did they start using the telegraph?

REPORTER: Why would people send mail by telegraph? We don't send telegrams when we want to write to someone, do we? We use telegrams for emergencies, don't we?

STUDENT: I've found it! I looked in my book and it says the telegraph was just invented by Morse and so they didn't need the Pony Express to carry mail. That's why they stopped it.

REPORTER: But we don't send letters by telegraph. Telegrams are for emergencies and special occasions.

TEACHER: Boys and girls, perhaps you should all read your text and see whether you can find why the telegraph would eliminate the Pony Express, even though today we don't use the telegraph to send letters.

(Here about ten minutes of silent reading and thinking elapses.)

STUDENT: Oh. I've got it. Way back at the first you said that business-men wanted faster time for their mail orders for shipments and things like that. Regular mail was carried on stage coaches all the time and only very important things went by Pony Express—things like you would put in a telegram. So, with the telegraph, the important special messages could go that way.

TEACHER: Well, class, shall we see whether our reporter can verify that explanation?

CLASS: Yes.

The reporter than verified his explanation by rephrasing the students' questions so as to make them hypotheses and then testing the hypotheses with all available evidence. For example, the first student's question, "Were all the riders killed?" implied the hypothesis, "The riders were all killed." The reporter tested the hypothesis with information that he had gained from his reading and rejected it. The exchange of questions and answers in this simple example illustrates the process of hypothesis formation and testing. The hypothesis concerning the telegraph almost stood the test, except for the fact that it did not make sense to send all letters by telegraph. It was only after the fact was established that most ordinary mail was carried by stagecoach and that the Pony Express was used only for messages of special business and governmental importance, that it made sense for the telegraph to have replaced the Pony Express.

The example, though simple, does show that a correct answer—the telegraph replaced the Pony Express—must still be tested and may be found less than wholly correct or convincing until other information is added to complete the picture. Notice how the notion of the telegraph sent pupils looking for what special way it served. The special way was the need by business and government for fast service for important messages.

Because of space limitation the preceding discussion between students and between students and teacher is to some degree in outline form. In actual practice there would be more digressions, and many statements would be made that were not pertinent to the problem at hand. The latter part of the discussion particularly would be more involved and much longer than is reported.

Now, just what is there about this teacher-student and student-student reflective classroom procedure that makes it different from either memory or explanatory understanding level teaching? Perhaps it could be summarized by describing the classroom atmosphere as one of teacher-student mutual inquiry within which genuine problems are developed and solved.

Reflective teaching, then, involves *problem raising* and *problem solving*. In problem-centered or reflective classes, instruction begins with introduction of an "I don't know" or problematic situation—one in which students are faced with a question they cannot answer. The problem should be so compelling that students really want to study it, but not so overwhelming that they are prone to give up. Accordingly, it should generate an urge to analyze the possible obstacles and dilemmas in the situation, to understand them, and to devise means for resolving the difficulties. After aiding students in raising a problem, the teacher then helps them investigate it until the best possible answer is found. Problem solving consists of formulating hypotheses and testing them with all available pertinent evidence. Facts are gathered in profusion, but teachers make no attempt to encourage fact learning or fact recall as such. Problems that make for ideal classroom study involve situations that are difficult enough to be challenging, yet simple enough that most students in a class will be able to cast and test hypotheses leading to a solution.

When students acquire exploratory understandings, they make genuine discoveries. But, for students to discover something, they need not necessarily invent it. They need only to explore a matter in such a way as to make sense of it. Within reflective learning students continue to acquire traditional learnings, but they acquire them as verifying or substantiating data. Hence, teachers who adhere to exploratory teaching and learning in no way disparage the importance of subject matter.

HOW DOES REFLECTIVE THINKING AND LEARNING DIFFER FROM CLASSICAL-HUMANISTIC REASONING?

For us to understand the nature of reflective learning and thinking, we should distinguish it from the mental disciplinary pure reasoning process that became characteristic of the classical humanism that emerged at the close of the Middle Ages and still is very much with us (see p. 245 for further explanation of this position). Whereas contemporary reflective thinking is a process that has much in common with modern experimental science, the reasoning of classical humanism is a purely mentalistic intellectual process whose use extends back into ancient times. Although some aspects of classical humanism have contributed much to the development of reflective thinking, the current conception of the reflective thinking process, as it is implemented by cognitive-field psychology, is quite different from the classical concept of rational thinking or reasoning as it has been implemented by mental discipline.

When a person reflects, he (or she) turns his thoughts back upon an existing idea or article of knowledge that has been taken, to some degree, to be dependable. Thus, reflection level teaching-learning is careful, critical examination of an idea or supposed article of knowledge in light of the *empirical* or *testable* evidence that supports it and the further conclusion toward which it points. In other words, teacher and students are cooperatively involved in both problem development and problem solution. So, such learning is based upon, and has much in common with, a modern scientific outlook and approach. It reflects the conviction that students study and learn best when they are seeking both the intellectual and emotional relevance of their learning to significant aspects of their lives.

For classical humanists, people are *rational animals*. This means that they are biological organisms in the same way that the lower animals are. But, in addition, they are endowed with a unique rational or reasoning faculty, which is the principal characteristic of their substantive minds; no other animals have this faculty or trait. Within classical humanism, knowledge consists of a body of principles that have been reasoned out by scholars throughout time and set down in the great books. Hence, scholarship consists of an armchair rational investigation of the nature of absolute Truth, Beauty, and Goodness. So, the appropriate method of acquiring true knowledge is purely rational, as contrasted with experimental, thinking.

Education, for classical humanists, consists of training students' predominant faculty, reason, along with developing their subordinate faculties such as memory, perception, and imagination. An intelligent person is a highly rational individual; his (or her) faculty of reason has been well developed. An individual's reasoning faculty, when well exercised and thereby developed, qualifies its owner to reason logically and accurately in regard to any matter in most any situation. So, learning consists of one's emulating the great intellectuals of history in exercising, and thereby developing, the faculties of one's mind, particularly the one of reason.

In contrast, education that centers on reflection level teaching and learning consists of both students' and teachers' experimentally reconstructing their respective life spaces in such way as to add to their meaning and thereby to increase the involved persons' abilities, both individually and collectively, to direct the course and contents of their future life spaces.

HOW IS REFLECTION LEVEL LEARNING PROMOTED?

Reflective level learning is promoted best through the application of cognitive-field psychology wherein learning consists of one's either gaining new insights or understandings or changing old ones in an exploratory, experimental method. According to the outlook of cognitive-field psychology, each individual, when behaving intelligently, is trying cognitively to reconstruct his (or her) life space in terms of the way in which its various functional regions—objects and activities—can be made to serve his purposes more effectively. The predominant, overarching purpose is the maintenance and enhancement of one's self. This entails the progressive improvement of one's ability to structure one's psychological person and environment to serve one's own purposes. Within such experimental experience, one tries first one course of action and then another, preserving only that which works best. It is from such experimentation that one's understandings grow.

As soon as one achieves an insight, the thought occurs that possibly this idea will work in other, or even all, similar situations. Accordingly, the general value of the insight is tested through its repeated use in similar situations. If it fails to work, it will be discarded because of its extremely limited worth. If it seems always to work, it will become a valued possession that will be added to the person's intellectual make-up —the cognitive structure of his or her life space. Of course, insights are valid in differing degrees of predictability.

A person's *immanent purposes* are always involved in his (or her) exploratorily gaining understanding. The understander must have a goal, and he must see that which he seeks to understand in relation to that goal. Moreover, he must see how what he is trying to understand can be made to assist in the attainment of the goal, or how it can be kept from hindering such achievement. It is as important to understand things that get in our way as it is to understand those that help us along. A rattlesnake may well be understood as something to be avoided just as a good book may be understood as something to add savor to life.

Understanding occurs in its best form when students come to see how to use productively, in ways they care about, a pattern of verified general ideas and the facts that support them. If a person really understands a principle, he (or she) can probably (1) state it in his own words, (2) give an example of it, (3) recognize it in various guises and circumstances, (4) discern the behaviors or lack of behaviors that may represent it, (5) see the relationships between it and other principles or generalizations, (6) see the uses to which it may be put, (7) use it in diverse situations, (8) anticipate the consequences of its application, and (9) state a principle that is opposite to it.

A cognitive-field–oriented teacher will be drawn toward teaching on the reflective or exploratory understanding level to the degree that he or she can develop means to promote it in his classes. But at times most any teacher, so oriented, will find it necessary to fall back to an explanatory understanding level of teaching. In so doing, the teacher will recognize that, although explanatory level teaching is based on the idea that people are neutral and passive, it can be employed by one who thinks that people are neutral and interactive. It can lead to more intelligent behavior on the part of students, but it does not carry the quality of experience with it that is needed to enhance the development and use of student intelligence to its fullest potential.

We now proceed to a study of the basic procedures that are involved in reflective teaching and learning. These include both problem-raising and problem-solving techniques. Problem raising is a process of persons' discovering and identifying inadequacies and disharmonies in their outlooks or the cognitive structures of their life spaces. Problem solving, in turn, is a process of individuals' reconstructing their outlooks or cognitive structures so as to make them more adequate and harmonious. Problem raising is the first of the five aspects of reflective thinking or learning; problem solving encompasses the other four.

WHEN IS A PROBLEM A PROBLEM?

Too many teachers who have attempted a problems approach to teaching have not adequately understood the psychology of learning as it relates to problem-centered study. Older psychologies—mental discipline, apperception, and behaviorism—had little to say about problem-centered study. Nor have neobehaviorists, with their more sophisticated S-R conditioning theories, contributed much understanding of reflective teaching.

Often problem-centered teaching has failed because what teachers have chosen as "problems" have not actually been problems in a psychological sense. Contributions of cognitive-field psychologists enable us to understand better what happens to a person psychologically when he (or she) has a problem. A learning problem is not just an objective issue to be resolved; it must involve psychological tension in a learner.

The analysis of a problem in psychological terms should help resolve a common dilemma that arises in connection with a problems approach to teaching. The dilemma is this: students have a great variety of real problems, but often the "problems" that a teacher thinks students should study arouse little tension in students. If students do feel personally some of the problems posed by a teacher, they feel some much less intensely than others. Consequently, the motivation that should accompany problem-centered study often does not develop.

Problems are either personal or societal in nature. *Personal* problems hold a dominant place in the life spaces of students. *Societal* problems represent the social needs that some adults believe exist in a community, region, or nation. They constitute part of the social matrix and, as such, are at least in the foreign hulls of the life spaces of students, but often they constitute no part of their actual life spaces.

Societal problems are felt personally by someone or they never would have been identified as problems in the first place; but commonly they are perceived only by some adults, and sometimes only by experts in fields of knowledge relevant to specific questions. To students, societal problems often seem quite remote; the students' function of living does not bring them into play. Posed by a teacher, societal problems, unless students feel themselves personally involved with them, are not real problems at all.

Are Students Motivated by "Other Persons' " Problems?

Reactions of students to the two types of problems—personal and societal—are likely to be quite different. Students can see the point of studying problems in which they are personally involved. The necessary emotional steam already exists; often all a teacher needs to do is to direct study so that it will be as mature as possible. But when students are asked to study problems that they do not accept as their own, they are likely to remain unresponsive. Since no personally felt psychological goals are involved, a personally motivated search for solutions is unlikely. Because of this detachment, relevant facts are seen not as data contributing toward a solution but only as lessons to be learned. Consequently, the quality of learning that results when students study someone else's problems is likely to be little different from that produced by conventional textbook-recitation teaching.

Textbook writers often include "problems" at the ends of chapters. But, these more often are tasks than problems. There is little reason to suppose that, without skillful preliminary discussion led by a teacher, these "problems" as stated will induce any significant kind of psychological tensions in students. All too often textbook writers, authors of syllabi and courses of study, and classroom teachers themselves label as problems exercises that do not function as true student psychological problems at all. The following are examples of "problems" that really are tasks, not problems.

To learn about the public utility companies of your community.

To see how many articles devoted to farming and rural life appear in the local newspaper.

To find out how many ways there are to send money from one city to another.

To find out what instructions are given to Boy Scouts for the protection of forests.

To learn more facts about life insurance.

To determine the advantages and disadvantages of good roads.

Since study of other people's problems results in learning that qualitatively is little different from traditional fact memorization, some writers have suggested that teachers exclude from study any problem in which students do not already feel involved, and confine instruction to problems that students feel spontaneously because of their life situations. Thus, they argue that the role of a teacher is to help students define carefully problems that already exist for them, and then to help them conduct whatever research and discussion seem to be appropriate in solving these problems. Although it should not be denied that in any school there is an important place for this kind of problem study, exclusive emphasis on it is highly reminiscent of the Roussellian natural unfoldment outlook. There is a strong flavor of "letting students do as they please." Of course, in the hands of a capable teacher, considerable freedom may be permitted students in selection of their problems and at the same time considerable rigor may be demanded in their study.

Why Classroom Study of Serious Societal Problems?

One might defend the confinement of problem-centered study to problems that students already feel on the ground that it teaches them methods of problem solving that will be useful all through life. However, there are a number of significant, persistent societal problems that, for the good of the community, state, and nation, students should come to understand and appreciate. The study of those problems, about which normally only specialists or other adults are concerned, may be of great importance in preparing students for intelligent citizenship. But how can we motivate students to study, in a serious and sustained way, problems that do not seem real to them? In this question is the crux of problem-centered teaching. Failure to give serious consideration to it is the reason why a problems approach so often bogs down, why students are uninterested, and why, after having tried "problem-centered teaching," teachers frequently return to "teaching the facts straight."

In recent years, teachers have tried to devise ways of involving students in problems that are not intrinsically challenging to them. "Solutions" to the enigma in which teachers find themselves have included suggestions that they explain to students just how the problems are bound to affect them eventually, that students be confronted face to face with the problems (as when we take a middle-class group to visit a slum), and that teachers use more eye-catching teaching materials (such as pictures).

But, as every practicing teacher knows, these "solutions" often fail to produce real intellectual involvement. Students still do not feel the problems as their own. Of course, some students always will do whatever work a teacher assigns, and seemingly do it with enthusiasm. But what seems to be intellectual involvement and a desire to study a genuine problem often is a desire to achieve other goals such as high marks, praise, and social status.

Instead of striking out blindly and trying everything they can think of, willy-nilly, to motivate students to study seriously what does not seem to them any of their own concern, teachers may try a drastically different approach; they may view their teaching problems in the light of a clear and adequate understanding of the learning process. Basic to such understanding is knowledge of what it means for a person to experience a problem as a felt tension, and formulation, based on this knowledge, of an approach to teaching that holds promise in many cases of effectively translating the "problems of others" into the problems of students.

How Is a Problem a Felt Tension?

To have a problem, a person must have a goal or goals that he (or she) accepts as his own. A problem arises when the person finds it impossible to proceed quickly and directly to the goal. When a student cannot achieve his goal readily, it is either because he sees no open path to it or because he sees two or more competing paths, or two or more competing goals, and cannot decide which to pursue. These are the familiar "no-path" or "forked-path" situations described by John Dewey. (See Figure 4.1, p. 93.)

Cognitive-field psychology provides a psychological basis for a problem-centered, exploratory understanding level of teaching and learning. Whereas behavioristic teaching required only enough tension in students to cause them to behave in ways that might be conditioned, problem-centered teaching requires the promotion of tension in students to the point that they are involved and perplexed, but not frustrated.

Since teachers, in teaching reflectively, should strive to keep their students involved and perplexed to a point just short of frustration, they should be able to recognize when people are approaching the frustration point. When a student stays right in there and battles with conflicting or problematic ideas, we know that he or she is perplexed but not frustrated. However, when a student becomes unduly aggressive, perhaps impudent, in his relations with others, he or she is displaying "fight." Or, if a student passively submits to a situation and appears to be doing nothing at all about it, this is psychological "flight." Both psychological *fight* and *flight* are symptoms of frustration.

Within a cognitive-field frame of reference, a person has a problem when he (or she) finds himself in either a goal-barrier situation or one of three kinds of conflicting goal situations. These situations are shown in Figure 21.1. The form that a situation takes depends largely upon what the person involved *makes of* that situation. In a goal-barrier situation, there is a goal region in a person's life space that has a positive valence, and there is a barrier between the person and the region of positive valence. Learning here consists of the person's finding a way either to change his or her life space so that the barrier disappears or to surmount or detour the barrier.

In a conflicting goal situation, there are two or more conflicting goal regions toward which or away from which a person wants to make psychological movement. Conflicting-goal situations lend themselves best to reflective or problem-centered teaching. In a Type I situation, a person has two conflicting goals or two psychologically opposite regions of his (or her) life space, both with positive valences. (Positive goal regions being psychologically opposite means that both cannot be achieved at the same time.) In the illustration of Type I, vector *vb* represents a psychological force equal to the valence of region *b*, and vector *va* represents a force equal to the valence of region *a*. In a Type II situation, the person is faced with two psychologically opposite significant regions of his life space, each having a negative valence; he (or she) wants to escape both, and they are of such nature that this is impossible. In a Type III situation, a region of positive valence and a region of negative valence are in the same psychological direction from the person; they are functionally similar or perhaps identical. Movement toward or away

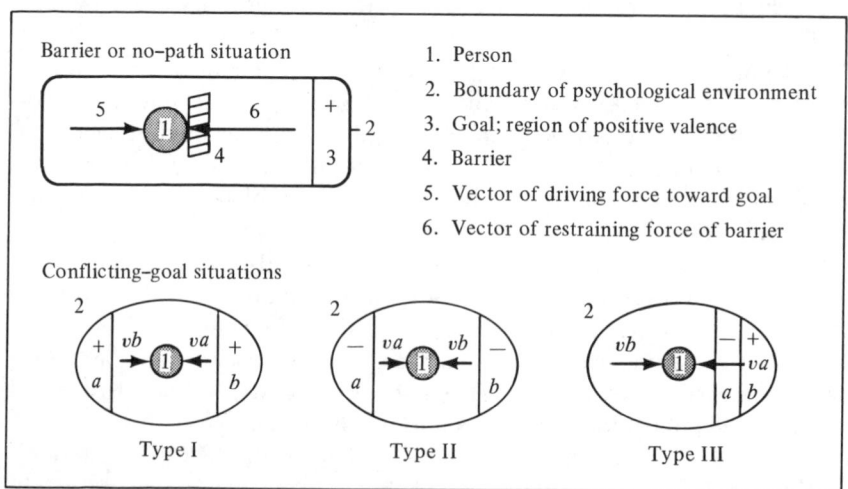

Figure 21.1   Field-conflict situations.

from regions is determined by the relative strength of the pertinent psychological forces at the time of movement.

Superficially, Type I and Type II situations appear much alike; however, they are crucially different. Quite often, whether a conflict situation is Type I or Type II depends largely upon what the individual *makes of* the situation in which he finds himself. A person in a Type II situation is like a ball being pushed from opposite directions by two sticks; once it gives a little, it flies off to the side, out of the picture. A person in such a situation is trying to escape two opposite negative driving forces and is likely to become completely frustrated and, like the ball, leave the field—psychologically to flee from the scene or become irrationally aggressive, that is, to engage in either flight or fight. This means that the person suddenly moves from a relatively concrete level of his life space to an extremely imaginative level (see pp. 376–378). In contrast, a person in a Type I situation, like a ball being pulled in opposite directions, usually will stay in the field, that is, remain engaged with the problem and try to resolve his conflict at the level of reality at which he meets it. He is attracted to two goals, both with positive valences. The goal toward which he moves is the one with the higher value or valence. (Should his two opposing goals be exactly equal, would he be like the donkey who starved to death while standing exactly half-way between two stacks of hay?)

Since Type II situations (two opposite negative goals) give rise to frustrations, they should be avoided in teaching procedures. Contrastedly, since Type I situations (two opposite positive goals) involve and perplex but do not frustrate students, they should be sought.

A Type III conflict situation develops when a person contemplates violating one of the basic mores of her society, especially if it is for the first time. The person wants to perform the tabooed act and simultaneously she (or he) wants not to do it; thus it has both positive and negative valence. The person involved might perceive the taboo not as a negative goal region but as a barrier between her and the positive goal region. In this event, the barrier would have a negative valence which would need to be counteracted by the stronger positive valence of the act, if it is to be performed.

What Level of Tension Is Best?

A characteristic of a goal-centered problematic situation is the presence of a certain amount of felt tension or discomfort. A person confronted with either a no-path or a conflicting-goal situation feels to some degree doubtful, puzzled, bewildered, and uncertain. How strongly he (or she) feels this way depends upon at least three factors: (1) the desirability of the goal or respective goals; (2) the apparent difficulty of the obstacle;

and (3) his own personality make-up. Whether a person finds himself between opposite positive goals that he is trying to achieve or opposite negative aversions that he is trying to escape often depends largely upon *how the person construes himself and his psychological environment.*

In a sense teachers must be tightrope walkers. They get the best results when they keep their students in a state of full enthusiasm. When they have students involved to the point that, during discussions, they sit on the edges of their seats, arms waving and eyes glistening and all wanting to talk at once, teachers have a potentially fine teaching situation. However, there is a rather fine line between this type of situation and situations in which students either become so excited that their emotions are chaotic, feel despair because the problem is too difficult, become frustrated because of too great a personal involvement, or are bored because a supposed problem is too easy.

The necessity for teachers' maintaining control of learning situations cannot be over-emphasized. One of the difficulties that commonly arises when a teacher attempts reflective teaching is his or her loss of control. When youngsters are highly excited, as well as when they are bored, they are difficult to manage. A teacher following the reflective approach usually learns from experience when it is time to sidetrack a discussion that is producing too much heat.

HOW DOES PROBLEM RAISING PROCEED?

Problem raising consists of both recognition and definition of a problem. For a problem to be a problem a person needs not only to feel a tension in a situation but also to have some idea of the nature and cause of the tension. A problem arises in the thinking of a student whenever, by some means, he (or she) is induced to be either dissatisfied with, or doubtful concerning, some aspect of his present knowledge, attitudes, or values. The dissatisfaction or doubt represents either a forked-path or a no-path situation within the student's life space that is characterized by conflicting goal regions. When a student has a real problem, he should be asking himself questions such as "Is an existing insight, attitude, or value adequate? Is it valid? Is an alternative to it more promising? In adherence to a given pattern of thought, is there a basic contradiction? What are the real issues in regard to the ideas that I hold? What are the available alternatives in thought and action?"

Whenever two or more competing alternative ideas, attitudes, or values are at stake, there is an issue. And since, by definition, all issues are controversial, controversy is a fundamental aspect of any truly problem-centered teaching. Controversy involves either interpersonal or intrapersonal conflict. *Interpersonal conflict* arises when individuals or groups hold ideas that are sharply opposed to those of other individuals or groups. We often refer to conflicts of this type as "controversial issues."

Persons on each side of an interpersonal conflict or dispute may be quite consistent, each in his or her own outlook, even though the outlook is in sharp disagreement with that of the opposing party. In our culture such conflict may arise between social classes, between racial, religious, ethnic, or age groups, between representatives of capital and labor, and between the sexes.

When a student becomes aware of his own incompatibilities of outlook, the resulting internal struggle may be referred to as an *intrapersonal conflict*. The content of an intrapersonal conflict may be little different from that of an interpersonal one. Yet it tends to foment greater tension in the individual. Since extreme intrapersonal tension is hazardous to an individual's personality structure, this level of intrapersonal conflict should not be deliberately promoted. Nevertheless, for a reflective learning situation to exist at all, issues must come to be felt by students in such a way that each finds himself to a significant degree in controversy with himself. Hence, each individual must be attracted to some extent by two or more competing hypotheses and feel temporarily unable to make a choice between them; otherwise, for him, no problem exists. Accordingly, if teachers are to teach reflectively, they must help students expose contradictions and inadequacies in their own thinking and action to their own critical examination.

How May Teachers Bring Students to Recognize Contradictions and Inadequacies in Their Thinking?

For teachers to accomplish much in helping students see their inconsistencies, they need a good idea of what kind of contradiction students are likely to hold. This knowledge will enable reasonably skillful teachers to pursue a line of discourse and questioning that will expose students' ideological inconsistencies and inadequacies to themselves. Some techniques for exposing contradictions and inadequacies and thereby raising problems in the thinking of students are teachers' use of a subject matter switch, their introduction of disturbing data, their permitting students to make mistakes, and their helping students convert some societal problems into personal ones. The examples of these techniques that we give are hypothetical ones and, of course, are very much simplified. To make the contradictions and inadequacies explicit to most students in a class, much more discussion than is herein described would be necessary.

A SUBJECT MATTER SWITCH
A subject matter switch is accomplished when a teacher helps a class generalize—reduce to a principle—a particular idea that is expressed by a student, then demonstrates how a further thought that is held by the same student is incompatible with the generalized principle and, consequently, with the first idea. For example, a student expresses the opinion

that "Government price supports for cotton are ridiculous." The teacher then seeks agreement with the principle that "The federal government should not interfere with the economy." The teacher than places the principle in a different context, that is, gives it a different subject matter with a question like "Do you favor a protective tariff on cotton?" The student, who also adheres firmly to the principle that "A high protective tariff brings prosperity to a nation," is placed in a position that forces him (or her) to make some kind of revision of either one or both of his contradictory opinions, should he attempt to extricate himself from the contradiction. To achieve the desired result, the teacher must hold the student closely to the issue. If students are permitted to qualify their opinions by introducing exceptions, they may extricate themselves readily without having to do any serious thinking.

Teachers should realize that often, even when a subject matter switch does not provoke thinking in the particular student who is trapped by it, it does motivate constructive thought in several other members of the class. The word trapped is used here advisedly; yet some rationale for its use is needed. A teacher who wishes to teach reflectively is probably justified in using almost any device that helps get reflection going. Some such devices may seem so teacher centered that the whole procedure may appear to be rigged in favor of the teacher's biases. But, this is only the beginning aspect of an inquiry. When it comes to casting and scrutinizing hypotheses and drawing conclusions there should be no rigging. Although the teacher performs key functions throughout the reflective process, the relationship between the students and the teacher must be continuously centered in mutual inquiry.

INTRODUCTION OF DISTURBING DATA

Another means of inducing students to feel problems is to introduce them to data from outside their life spaces that lead them to doubt some currently held item of knowledge, attitude, or value. The teacher may ask students to read a book, to watch a television program or motion picture, to go on a field trip, or to engage in some other activity that confronts them with facts contrary to those that they have taken for granted. Of course, this approach, like any other, may not work. Students may refuse to admit the new facts into their life spaces. Unless they recognize the significance of the facts and truly come to doubt their existing ideas, no problem is created.

PERMITTING STUDENTS TO MAKE MISTAKES

Teachers usually do not let students make enough mistakes. Their making mistakes often encourages students to reexamine things that they had previously regarded as true. It is much more educative to let students do something their own way, experience the consequences, and see their mistakes than to tell them the "right way," which they then follow more or less blindly. Of course, some situations preclude this. A shop teacher might achieve maximum student motivation for study of safety practices by allowing a student to cut off a finger with a power saw, but a teacher would not be morally justified in using such means to establish an efficient learning situation. However, a teacher has many opportunities to permit students to make problem-raising mistakes without unduly endangering anyone.

CONVERTING SOCIETAL PROBLEMS INTO PERSONAL PROBLEMS

There are numerous areas of adult and societal concern about which students normally have some more or less superficial attitudes, evaluations, and knowledge. These include politics and government, international affairs, economics, business, labor and employment, pure and applied science, morality, various arts, and personal relations. The ideas that students have acquired are often sketchy, disorganized, and poorly understood. Nevertheless children, and especially adolescents, do have attitudes, opinions, and some knowledge about most operations with which adults are concerned. This can be demonstrated by a reasonably free classroom discussion of any one of these subjects. Our question now is, "How may a reflective approach to learning serve to build a psychological bridge between adult-societal problems and student-personal concerns"?

When students appear in public school classrooms, the total knowledge, both true and untrue, that they have is usually more than teachers realize. With modern media of communication, frequent opportunities for travel, and continuously rising educational levels of parents, it seems likely that a great many youngsters have more factual knowledge than they can make much sense of. So, one of the major jobs of a modern school is to help students both verify and make sense of the welter of information that they acquire outside their schools.

Although students willingly make statements about matters in such areas as government, economics, international affairs, and the relationship of science and religion, the commitment that they feel toward such statements varies greatly. In some instances, students' commitments are so slight that they will abandon their pet ideas with little hesitation. At the other extreme, statements may represent convictions so highly cherished and strongly held that students resist bringing them under any kind of critical scrutiny.

Ideas and attitudes that students hold concerning matters that are also of concern to adults constitute the psychological bridges between youth and adult interests. If a student feels enough personal attachment to a view to care, the moment the position becomes a subject of doubt the student is likely to want to start thinking about it. At that point, if teaching is skillful, he can be led to want to study a subject about which he or she previously felt little or no curiosity.

By using the challenge of students' attitudes, goals, and knowledge as a lure, teachers may arouse real interest in situations that otherwise would never have been felt by students to be in any way problematic. Consequently, in relation to areas in which students at first feel no personal goal or involvement, a learning problem can be created and thereby genuine student involvement can be achieved. Accordingly, students can be led to see that their problems involve the various subject matters of the social sciences, the natural sciences, and the humanities.

What Kinds of Questions Induce Problems?

The essence of a problematic situation is that there is something in it that is unknown. The unknown can be uncovered only when right questions are asked. One of the best questions is also the simplest: "Why?" "Why did you say that?" "Why do you have the opinion you have stated?" Because of the demise of several fish in the classroom aquarium, a class of fourth graders embarked upon an enthusiastic study of the biology and ecology of fish life. The students had been caring for the fish according to what they thought were "right principles." These included the assumption that fish need to eat as much in proportion to their size as do fourth graders, whether or not by design, allowed the children to make a mistake—to overfeed the fish. He then posed the question, "Why did the fish die?" and thereby launched a reflective study.

So the heart of a reflective-learning situation is a good thought-provoking question. Such a question is not one that points to a highly structured answer that can be given in a neat, pat word or two. The following questions are the kind that do *not* promote reflective thinking.[2]

1. Who were the first settlers in this land?
2. Where did they go before coming to America?
3. What was the name of the boat on which they came to America?

In contrast to these nonprovocative questions, the "springboard" questions in the following list are much more likely to activate the degree of psychological dissonance or uncomfortableness that is necessary to motivate students toward their thinking reflectively. Note that we include only the "bare bones" of the questions. In actual classroom practice, each question would need to be prefaced by a certain artful "buildup."

1. If the writers of our Constitution believed in equality, why did they agree to count each Negro as only ⅗ of a person when determining how many representatives each state could send to Congress?
2. If warm air rises, why is it cold high in the mountains?
3. If heat cannot travel through a vacuum, how can we get heat from the sun through the vacuum of deep space?
4. Our text states that big freight trains travel 100 miles an hour. We

know that trucks are limited to 55 to 60 miles an hour by law. Why do authors of our book say that trucks can deliver freight faster?
5. If Columbus discovered America, how did it happen that people were here to greet him?

What Is the Lullaby Effect?

We suggest the use of the expression *lullaby effect* as a reminder to teachers that they should help students avoid careless and incomplete thinking as it may be evidenced by students' jumping to unwarranted conclusions, making hastly generalizations, or achieving premature closures. Generally speaking, people—adults and children alike—are so eager to reach a solution that they tend to accept a hypothesis that "sounds good" without testing it sufficiently. Better thinkers, however, avoid being lulled into false security by the first answer that seems to let their "minds go back to sleep." The soothing and lulling effect of persons' accepting easy answers that only appear to be correct may be identified by calling it the "lullaby effect." The lullaby effect with its tendency to release people from further thinking should be remembered and counteracted by our continuing to test all hypotheses, especially those that quickly appear to be correct.

A few questions and quick, apparent answers to them will illustrate the lullaby effect.

1. Question: Why is Eskimo life so difficult? Answer: Because the farther north one goes, the colder it is.
2. Question: Why is winter colder than summer? Answer: Because the sun is farther away.
3. Question: Why are some countries still "underdeveloped"? Answer: Because they do not have sufficient natural resources.

The answers given to these three questions all have two features in common; they "sound good" and they are incorrect. Yet they are answers that will likely be accepted, if great care is not taken to avoid the lullaby effect.

The use of springboard questions does not permit a teacher to have the security of giving fixed answers of such nature that one is right and all others are wrong. So, in some instances, a teacher may be pressed by the class to admit some limitations to his or her knowledge. Consequently, even if intellectual authoritarianism should be desired, it cannot be maintained. But, at the same time, teachers should be highly knowledgeable in their subject areas, and they should encourage students also to become the same. Psychologically, an accepting, open atmosphere is necessary to stimulate students to volunteer. But, a teacher's accepting the basic worth of the thinking of each and all students is not the same as his or her accepting the intellectual correctness of each and every idea offered. Therein lies the need for a teaching art that enables a teacher to cast doubt on a proposition that is offered in class without seeming to cast doubt upon the integrity of the persons who presented the proposition.

How Does the Problem-Raising Aspect of a Unit on Race Proceed?

We now develop the problem-raising aspect of a reflective unit on the meaning of *race*. The problem herein described was selected through the authors' conversations with a number of high school students. The students had various definitions of the term race, they recognized that their definitions were cloudy, and they wanted to bring them into sharper focus. So, it was assumed that for most high school students of today the meaning of race probably constitutes a real problem. It also was assumed that this problem could emerge in a senior problems, social studies, history, psychology, sociology, or biology class on any one of the senior high school grade levels.

The problem and the aspects of its solution were developed by means of members of a college undergraduate class in educational psychology playing the roles of high school students. Throughout the unit the teacher is designated by "Teacher" and each of the participating students by "Student." All members of the class participated to some degree, but individual students are not identified. Only the more incisive and significant statements are recorded; limited space precludes our including every detail of the class discussion. To repeat, problem raising consists of both *recognition* and *definition* of a problem. The class discussion proceeded as follows.

> TEACHER: I noticed in our reading assignment for today that the term race appears several times. What does that word mean to most of you?
>
> STUDENT: Why, there are three races—white, black, and yellow.
>
> STUDENT: I don't think it is that easy. I know some white people who are called Negroes.
>
> STUDENT: To me, race is a cultural word, the color of people's skin is not the real difference.
>
> TEACHER: When you say there are three major races, are you stating the way things really are or are you merely classifying people for convenience? In other words, what is the basis for your distinction?
>
> STUDENT: Biologists say that there are three races, maybe four.
>
> STUDENT: That may be so, but cultural differences are also called racial features. For instance, people in the United States think of Jews as a race and in Germany Hitler talked about the Nordic race.
>
> TEACHER: When people refer to the Jewish race, are they thinking of biological traits, social traits, or what?
>
> STUDENT: They are thinking about the fact that Jews have been different down through history.

TEACHER: Oh! Then we identify them as a race because of their ancestors?

STUDENT: Partly because of their ancestors, but also because of things they do, such as make money.

STUDENT: We are getting clear away from our discussion; one's race depends upon his genes.

TEACHER: So, you think race is purely biological. How many of you think race is purely biological? (A show of hands indicated that about one-half of the class would answer this question in the affirmative, but the other half definitely would not.)

TEACHER: So, according to biologists, there are three definite races plus a fourth that even the experts can't agree upon. Then this fourth could be almost any group, so the problem of race is wide open.

STUDENT: It is not quite that way. We can limit our definition of race to inherited physical characteristics that one group, and not others, has. It is the physical characteristics of a person and his ancestors.

TEACHER: For instance?

STUDENT: Color of skin and type of hair.

STUDENT: But, as I see it, everyone to some degree has a mixed blood.

TEACHER: Do you mean that everyone is some sort of a hybrid?

STUDENT: I think we're making too much of this. Race is simply a biological variation of *Homo sapiens*—a subdivision of the species.

STUDENT: Then, according to you, it is very easy to place each of us in a certain race.

STUDENT: I'm beginning to think that we should just quit talking about races; we should do away with the idea.

STUDENT: We can't do that. Race means something to everybody; if they didn't have the word race, they would use some other word.

STUDENT: The trouble is that race started as a biological word, then people have added a lot of other meanings to it.

TEACHER: Let us be more specific in regard to our problem and the issues involved. Just what are we trying to decide?

STUDENT: What a race is.

TEACHER: O.K. How many of you want to pursue this question further and attempt to arrive at an answer? (Most of the class members favored this procedure.)

TEACHER: All right, now we may look at the meaning of the word race in at least two different ways. Do specific races, each spelled with a capital letter, exist in the very nature of things, the way gravity and the planets supposedly do, or is a race merely what people call it?

STUDENT: I'm not sure I understand the first meaning, but I am more concerned with the second.

TEACHER: You may recall that a few weeks ago we developed the difference between realism and nominalism in regard to the source of large concepts. The question that I am raising is, Do we want to find the real meaning of a concept *race*, which transcends or extends beyond any and all existing races, or do we want to conceive of race as a name for an idea that men have developed?

STUDENT: I, too, am more concerned with the second type of meaning.

TEACHER: How many prefer to concentrate upon the meaning of the named idea race and leave any transcendental or absolutistic definition out of our discussion? (Most students agreed with the two who had expressed more interest in the nominalistic meaning.)

TEACHER: O.K. We shall assume that a word means what it means because of the meanings people give it, not because of its being derived from some basic transcendental source. Now, we must decide one more question. Are we concerned with what the word race does mean, what it should mean, or both?

STUDENT: When we discussed democratic and reflective procedures, we decided that we should study both how things are and how they should be.

TEACHER: Any other reaction or ideas?

STUDENT: Just how much are we going to change things by thinking how race should be defined?

STUDENT: I get your point. But how much are we going to change things by merely studying how things are? I think we should figure out both what race means and what it should mean.

TEACHER: How many concur with this position? (About two-thirds concurred; the other third expressed the idea that their treatment would be too superficial to attempt any "oughts" in regard to the meaning of the word.)

The next step was to make a precise statement of the problem at hand through using the contributions of the students. The statement of the problem was then reworded until it was acceptable to all members of the class. The problem was "What does the term race mean to all kinds of people, including experts, and what should it mean to us?"

At this point, we should remind ourselves of the fact that in any fertile group inquiry, two types of discussion are always in progress—one the public discussion that an observer can hear, the other a series of private discussions within which each interested student debates the issue with himself. Most of the questions and assertions that are uttered aloud emerge from, or are influenced by, the concurrent private, silent debates. The primary aim of vocal discussion is to help each individual in the classroom, including the teacher, push forward his or her private thinking. Hence, during the course of a single discussion, Mary may reach a conclusion that seems quite satisfactory to her, John may have his faith in a conclusion that he once held badly shaken, and Fred may merely formulate a hypothesis. In each case, the student may have thought the problem through to a further degree than at any previous time. Hence, in a discussion that appears rather chaotic to an observer, members of the group involved may actually achieve a considerable amount of pointed thinking.

HOW DOES PROBLEM SOLVING PROCEED?

Helping students see problems is only the first of five aspects of reflective teaching-learning. However, this aspect is very important in that it provides the motivation and direction for the problem-solving aspects of reflective inquiry. Once doubt or uncertainty has been induced, reflective teaching and learning enter the problem-solving phase.

Problem solving consists of formulating and testing hypotheses; it envelops the last four aspects of the reflective teaching-learning process. We should emphasize here that the parts of reflective thinking, teaching, and learning are *aspects*, not *steps*. They seldom are followed in a consecutive orderly fashion. They may develop in any order or any or all of the aspects may develop concurrently. Reflective processes commonly are characterized by confusion, hesitation, and irregularity.

Formulation and testing of hypotheses should be conducted in an atmosphere that resembles as far as possible that of a scientific laboratory. The same open-minded and objective attitudes that characterize any scientific investigation should prevail. Hence, the teacher's role should be analogous to that of a head scientist in a laboratory; the teacher should help students construct hypotheses, then assist them in testing them out.

How Are Hypotheses Formulated and Their Logical Implications Deduced?

Formulation of hypotheses—considered guesses or hunches—constitutes the second aspect of reflective learning. Deducing the logical implications of the hypotheses constitutes the third. Often, the two aspects are so intermingled that it is difficult to distinguish one from the other. In reflective teaching, students are encouraged to formulate as many hypotheses as possible in regard to what might resolve the discrepancies or inadequacies in thought that have been exposed. Simultaneously, a class is urged to deduce as many of the logical implications of each hypothesis as its members can muster. Within this aspect students think "If this hypothesis holds, what checkable consequences should result from its operation?"

In the unit on the meaning of race, hypotheses are the various alternative definitions of the concept that gave rise to the problem in the preceding dialogue. We now proceed with the second and third aspects of the unit.

TEACHER: Let us restate our problem. It is "What does race mean to all kinds of people, including experts, and what should it mean to us?" Now, let's see how many possible answers there are to this question.

STUDENT: The use of the word race does a lot of harm, and no good; let's drop it.

STUDENT: But, there are some racial characteristics.

TEACHER: For example?

STUDENT: Sickle cell anemia is characteristic of Negroes.

TEACHER: Is this a disease?

STUDENT: Yes, and its incidence is much higher in Negroes.

TEACHER: Could you say that a person who has sickle cell anemia is a Negro?

STUDENT: No, I couldn't do that.

TEACHER: If a person has three white grandparents and one black one, which race is he a member of? (This question opened up a great deal of discussion and disagreement.)

TEACHER: Can we say that, even though a person is much more "white" than "black," in the U.S.A. he is a "black"?

STUDENT: Are we concerned with the definition of the word in this country?

STUDENT: This should be our first concern.

STUDENT: If we even do this, we will be doing quite a lot.

STUDENT: Some minority groups think they can help their position by emphasizing their race.

STUDENT: But other racial groups have made themselves a part of the American culture. Chinatown has been pretty American.

STUDENT: A member of any minority group has things stacked against him.

TEACHER: This morning on the "Today Show" a Negro professor at a New York university appeared. New York public universities pay top salaries. Do you think this man still finds the cards stacked against him?

STUDENT: Yes, I do.

TEACHER: How many agree that he does? (About one-half of the class agreed.)

TEACHER: It now seems to be the time for us to "handicap" ourselves with some information. Let's all go to the library and find at least one article on the subject of race. Each of you be prepared to give us the high points of what you find out.

At the next class, students contributed the ideas that they had gained through their reading. The teacher then asked each student to write out, in one short paragraph, the very best statement on, or definition of, race that he (or she) could devise.

Between classes the teacher and several class members summarized the contents of the statements. The summary in terms of the ideas stated and their frequency was as follows (ideas stated only once are not included).

1. Race primarily is a biological concept. (15 times)
2. In light of the improbability of there ever having been any pure races, the increasing miscegenation—cross-breeding—that is occurring, and the emotionality surrounding the term race, the concept of race has always been ambiguous and is now becoming archaic. (13 times)
3. The term should be either discarded or disregarded. (11 times)
4. The only term with which people should be concerned is the human race. (4 times)
5. A biological definition is inadequate. (3 times)
6. We can't ignore the term, so we should understand it. (3 times)
7. Race should be replaced with ethnic groups. (2 times)

This summary was dittoed and distributed in the next class. The various ideas were taken as hypotheses whose implications were to be tested through further reading and thought.

How Are Hypotheses Tested?

In the fourth aspect of reflective thinking, teaching, and learning, students are encouraged to examine the hypotheses in the light of all obtainable, pertinent evidence. Provided the teacher promotes an atmosphere of mutual inquiry, problem-centered study in school may encompass a variety of evidence-seeking activities. It is likely to include the use of individual and group research, home study, field trips, and guest speakers. It may also include considerable explanation and illustration on the part of the teacher. An informal lecture can be a highly useful tool both for providing data for students' consideration and for instigating and promoting further reflection.

In the process of testing hypotheses, teachers do not play the role of softhearted baby-sitters. At times they must be quite tough-minded in their insistence that students examine and consider all pertinent available evidence. Teachers also must guard against students' making hasty generalizations, arriving at snap conclusions, achieving premature closure, or taking other liberties that either impede or pervert the reflective process.

At this point in the study of the meaning of race the class reviewed the summary of hypothetical statements. The instructor next divided the areas and sources of inquiry among the students so that the investigation would be reasonably comprehensive. The entire class moved to the library during several class meetings to gather as much more pertinent information as possible in the time available. Then, the students returned to their classroom and continued their inquiry.

First, several students presented definitions that they had taken from dictionaries, encyclopedias, and other books. Next, other students presented some new ideas that they had gained from their reading. At this stage of the study several sharp disagreements arose. Samples of student expressions are as follows:

STUDENT: Why are we talking about race at all? We are just building up more prejudice and racism.

STUDENT: Each individual has his own definition, so let's let it go at that.

STUDENT: Cultural distinctions are not racial ones.

STUDENTS: William A. Boyd and Isaac Reisman, in *Races and People,* say that physical features are useless criteria of race.

STUDENT: Although a biological definition is the most ideal, it is not the most practical. A word can mean many things to people.

STUDENT: The best we can do with the word is to try to understand what it really means in relation to the evolution of human beings, to separate fact from fiction, and to pass on our knowledge to others. Then, hopefully, as people learn to live together, the word will disappear from their vocabularies.

STUDENT: Ashley Montagu, in *The Concept of Race,* says that the term race has had a long and tortuous history. Biologists see it as the subdivision of a species, and laymen have an emotionally muddled interpretation of the word. But anthropologists see the term as facts forced into predetermined categories. The major idea Montagu brings out is that the meaning of the term race is far from being a solved problem, and that people generally refuse to see this. The ethnic groups formed by virtue of community, language, religion, and social beliefs just add to the confusion. If race is to be a scientific term, it must have a genetic meaning; geographical, linguistic, and ethnic grouping then would be unnecessary. However, race is a trigger word because it is loaded with prejudice and misunderstanding.

STUDENT: If we are to form an operative definition of race, we should limit it to the inherited physical characteristics that are predominant in one group of people as opposed to another group. The prejudice implied in the word race should be limited to noticeable anatomical features so as not to confuse Jewish "race" and Negro race and consider both to be races.

STUDENT: Basically, there are physical differences in people. Therefore, people need some way of explaining or understanding this. The word race is an attempt to do this. It describes three (or possibly more) sets of physical characteristics, each set belonging to one of the races. It should be based only on these biological aspects, because within each race there are many cultures.

STUDENT: Race started out as a biological term, but society has taken the term and added other meanings to it. The easiest answer would be to do away with the word, but I think that it is here to stay for a long time yet, and if we're going to find answers to our problems today the change is going to have to come from within the people themselves. The older generations won't or can't change their feelings and ways of thinking, so it is up to the younger generations to accept changes in their society, and this takes time.

STUDENT: I think that defining race biologically is a complete waste of time and meaningless. Race does, however, imply or refer to characteristics that exist in some way or another, and quite obviously it causes much strife within our society. So, I think that we can't ignore the term.

How Are Conclusions Reached?

The fifth aspect of reflective teaching-learning is drawing conclusions. This is perhaps the most difficult aspect of a teacher's endeavor to promote reflective learning through reflective teaching. However, the basic, guiding principle of reflective teaching and learning is that the teacher and students should strive to achieve at least a consensus on the conclusion, unanimity being the ideal. But even though a student may represent a minority of only one person, he (or she) should not be coerced in any way to swing his position to the conclusion of either the group consensus or the majority.

So, ideally, problem-centered study should culminate in at least a tentative conclusion about how the problem might be alleviated or solved. However, in many instances a definite conclusion will not be achieved. Furthermore, when a conclusion is reached, the teacher should emphasize its tentativeness and relativity. An irrevocable conclusion is like a locked door whose only key has been thrown in the sea. Students should be taught that the door to knowledge must always be left unlocked, even ajar. Nevertheless, at the termination of an inquiry, a conclusion should be considered to be a warranted assertion; it should provide greater predictive accuracy than any alternative hypotheses that have been entertained and examined.

A conclusion may involve either reacceptance of the idea that was originally brought under question, modification of the idea, or formulation of a substitute one. The important concern is that students push their thinking further than it had gone before. They need not necessarily arrive at an answer that has been preconceived by the teacher. Teaching for reflection is *provocative* rather than *evocative*. Reaffirmation of the same idea that the teacher had earlier induced students to doubt is quite acceptable, provided that in the course of their study the students come to understand the idea better and to have a better grasp of the evidence pertinent to it.

The high school class discussed above had completed the first four aspects of reflective inquiry. It had stated the problem in definite terms; it had formulated some hypotheses and deduced their implications; and it had gathered much pertinent data and tested the various hypotheses. The culminating task was to formulate a tentative concluding statement in regard to the hypothesis or hypotheses that seemed most tenable.

In drawing the class's conclusions, the first step was for a committee to construct a carefully formulated summary that incorporated the statements earlier listed as hypotheses. The class then discussed each clause of the summary, and either made changes in it until a consensus would support it, or deleted it. The teacher reminded the students that their decision should rest upon what the data—pertinent information— supported, not upon personal whims. Out of a class of 30, there were from none to three dissenting votes in regard to the final form of each clause. The class's concluding statement in regard to the meaning of the term race was as follows:

CLASS: Since we cannot ignore the concept race in our American culture, we need an understanding of its meaning. Race is primarily a biological concept. But a biological definition, in itself, is inadequate; cultural aspects also enter into its meaning. Because (1) there is an improbability of there ever having been any pure races; because (2) miscegenation is increasing; because (3) the concept race serves little long-range beneficial personal-social purpose; because (4) it has been and continues to be ambiguous; and because (5) it is emotionally loaded, the term race now should either be discarded or considered archaic. So, we should move toward elimination of the concept race as such. The only race with which enlightened people should be concerned is the human race.

TEACHER: Does our conclusion imply that we should strive to build one unified culture to replace various cultures? If so, should the one culture be a pluralistic one, that is, should it be one that reflects a unity of people but recognizes and accepts diversity within the unity? Or should people attempt to blend themselves into one generalized race? Perhaps these questions involve problems for our further study.

The teacher then urged dissenting students to develop cooperatively an alternative statement that they would support and report it to the class. These students were allotted some class time to do this as a group. The teacher also reminded the class of the many insights or understandings that they had gained during their study. These ranged from simply learning some new words—for example, miscegenation—to gaining a more meaningful and effective grasp of the race problem. The class then moved ahead to a new problem or area of inquiry.

Throughout the study, the teacher had made it clear that he preferred and expected serious thinking on the part of his students. His role had been to elicit compelling questions pertinent to the area of study and to lead the ensuing inquiry along lines of gathering pertinent evidence and doing logical thinking.

HOW CAN CLASSROOM ATMOSPHERE PROMOTE REFLECTIVE LEARNING?

A teacher's success in inducing reflective learning hinges upon his or her ability to bring students to involve themselves in issues to the point of perplexity and yet to remain curious and open-minded in regard to their solution. The aim of this section is to consider means of keeping students so involved without frustrating them, and to explore ways in which they can be made more receptive to knowledge and points of view based on empirical—scientific—evidence.

The type of atmosphere in which a person feels so secure that he (or she) dares entertain evidence contrary to his present knowledge and values seems best achieved in a small, face-to-face group in which warmth and considerable permissiveness have been deliberately cultivated. Some techniques which a teacher may use in creating such an atmosphere, and in leading a class to change its views and thereby its behavior, are (1) encouraging group membership, (2) reducing threat and promoting open-mindedness, (3) practicing democratic group leadership, and (4) fostering group decisions.

How May Teachers Encourage Group Membership?

A student is more likely to drop prejudices, revise his (or her) moral values, or make almost any other type of significant ideological change, if he is a member of a group of individuals who are making the same change together. Although significant learning may occur in discussion groups formed of strangers, learning in areas of strong prejudice such as in the areas either partially or largely closed to reflective thought seems more likely to occur in groups characterized by friendships and some degree of mutual intimacy. Thus, there may be sound pedagogical advantages in helping students become well acquainted with each other, whether simply through classroom informality or by deliberately fostering out-of-school contacts.

In establishing group feeling, there are possible advantages to be gained from group study and group projects. However, when this sort of thing is attempted, it is best to divide a class into small groups and to see that the same students do not always work together. A committee system can ordinarily be made to work fairly well for gathering information. Whether it can be made to function in reflective evaluation of data and the productive solution of problems depends on the maturity of students and their familiarity with the rules of reflection. Generally, a teacher must be central to reflective deliberation if it is to be productive.

Encouragement of full and free communication among its members will heighten the cohesiveness of a group. If students understand each other, they will almost inevitably work together better as a group. Teachers should urge and help students to state opinions and propositions meaningfully. Also, they should discourage use of emotive language, particularly when students are inclined to direct personal jibes at each other. Furthermore, they should make certain that every member has a chance to be heard and is correctly interpreted.

A deep-seated desire of human beings is for security, and a common means of achieving security is through membership in a group. When a person feels that he (or she) has a place in a group, that he "fits in," that he is wanted, he feels secure. As Lewin points out, "The social climate in which a child lives is for the child as important as the air it breathes. The group to which a child belongs is the ground on which he stands. His relation to the group and his status in it are the most important factors for his feeling of security or insecurity."[4] One achieves membership in a group by conforming, at least to a degree, to the mores of the group.

Individuals are, however, not completely subject to group control. They may develop beliefs and values that are novel to a group and get them accepted by others in the group. With widening acceptance, the new beliefs and values may become effective in controlling group behavior. However, there is little chance that large changes will occur in individuals outside their relationship to their primary group associations.

How May Teachers Reduce Threat and Promote Open-Mindedness?

When students regard their convictions to be under fire, they feel threat to their egos. The intensity of the threat depends on its source, its power, and the valuation placed on the ideas that are in jeopardy. Unless threat can be largely eliminated, students are not likely to entertain evidence contrary to present convictions or, when facts warrant, to change their minds. Several techniques are available for keeping a sense of threat to a minimum.

A teacher should always treat student opinions with respect. This does not necessarily mean that a teacher expresses approval; but he (or she) avoids ridicule, sarcasm, or any expressions that might be so interpreted by students. Furthermore, he does not cast aspersions on the intelligence or motives of students who render serious opinions. Opinions offered in good faith are taken for what they are—the best insights which students have been able to achieve up to then. Students need to feel complete freedom to express their opinions without danger of censure, no matter how ill-formed or unorthodox they may be.

On occasion, as during relatively undirected discussion preceding serious study of an issue, it may be advisable for a teacher to give students plenty of opportunity to express the very views that he hopes later to bring under question. It may even help for him to express considerable sympathy with these ideas for the time being. Lewin has written, "a feeling of complete freedom and a heightened group identification are frequently more important at a particular stage of re-education than learning not to break specific rules."[5]

When a teacher wishes to challenge an opinion expressed by a student, he (or she) should do it in such a way that conflict is internalized. That is, the student is made to feel the conflict within his (or her) own personality. If he sees the conflict merely as a contest between him and someone else, he may not feel a problem, or at least not the problem which the learning situation demands. Accordingly, when a teacher wishes to contest the opinion of a student, he may best handle it something like this: "You have an opinion, and I think I understand and appreciate your reasons. But there are contrary opinions which are widely held in this country. I wonder if there is any merit in a point of view such as . . . ?" Thus, the student is asked to entertain, not an opinion of the teacher or a classmate, but simply an opinion which "some persons" hold.[6]

It is well to arrange the learning situation so that facts "speak for themselves." Other things being equal, facts—especially if impersonal, sharply relevant, and simple enough to be easily grasped—are more likely than expressions of opinion to break through an emotional barrier, particularly if the facts come to students in life situations. It may then only be necessary to remind a student of their relevance and their bearing on a problem. For example, a trip to a slum may speak eloquently against the notion that everyone is adequately housed, or the witnessing of a congressional investigation over television may show quite convincingly that traditional American principles of fair play are not always employed. Lewin has suggested that "An individual will believe facts he himself has discovered in the same way he believes in himself or in his group."[7]

In most instances it probably pays to minimize, or at least not encourage, emphasis on personal opinion in discussion. Issues may be handled as issues and propositions discussed on their merits. The learning enterprise should focus on raising questions about what will come of acting in accordance with a given proposition by saying, "Here is an opinion which is before the class. Let us take it as a proposition to be tested. If it is true, what consequences may we deduce from it?" If propositions are relevant to beliefs of students, then students often make their own connections. Even though beliefs are not studied directly, significant revisions may come.

How May Teachers Practice Democratic Group Leadership?

The aim of democratic group leadership is to translate a democratic philosophy into group action. Thus, democratic group leadership combines traditional democratic philosophy with a relatively recent personal-social psychology such as cognitive-field psychology described in Chapters 14 and 15.

DEMOCRATIC PHILOSOPHY

We define democracy as a social arrangement in which all members of a group share equally in determining which freedoms and restraints shall apply. It is presumed that, in general, freedoms and restraints shall apply with the same force to all. But democracy must allow for the granting of special powers for special purposes (as in the case of its executive officers). If we think of democracy as a system of *equally limited* freedom, characterized by shared decisions regarding which specific rules are to prevail, then we have a simple criterion for distinguishing democracy from other social arrangements. A social system may provide *unlimited freedoms*, in which case it is called anarchy. Or it may provide *unequally limited freedoms*, in which case it is called autocracy. Or it may provide for *equally limited freedom*, in which case it is called democracy.

THE NATURE OF A DEMOCRATIC GROUP

A democratic group is self-governing. But it must provide for situations where disagreement occurs. Ideally, democratic decisions are by consensus, that is, mutually agreeable decisions reached through discussion and compromise. Then, by common consent, action is taken. However, if it is time for action and consensus is not yet possible, a democratic group votes. Each person has an equal vote, and a majority vote wins. So, votes are taken to facilitate action, not to enforce views or opinions.

Successful and permanent operation of democracy seems to require that a group maintain certain conditions that although not a part of the central idea of democracy, contribute to its functioning. For example, if participation is to be full and free, a group must establish an accepting atmosphere—an atmosphere in which every member is considered important and his or her opinions are guaranteed a hearing. Participation implies reasonable freedom of communication, and freedom of speech and thought. If any single individual or minority group gains disproportionate control over agencies of communication and opinion, the society has lost equality of participation in decision making.

If a democratic society is to survive over time, a majority of its members must learn to make reflective decisions where socially important questions are involved. A democratic society assumes competence on the part of its members; any different assumption would lead to distrust and rejection of the principle of equal participation. If democracy is to survive, its members must take steps to insure that the principle of reflection is employed as widely as possible in making choices of group concern.

THE ROLE OF DEMOCRATIC LEADERSHIP

The role of democratic leadership is to help a group realize its own potentialities for growth. Such a statement becomes meaningful only when growth is defined in operational terms. One attempt at an operational definition specifies a number of "dimensions" of group growth, including the following.[8]

1. Progress toward closer intercommunication among members. This includes increasing understanding and acceptance by members of standards of language usage, with especial reference to problems of semantics.
2. Progress toward seeing the functioning of the group objectively. This includes both capacity of all participants to make, and agree with, interpretations about the proper functioning of the group and its individual members, and ability to accumulate, and make use of, relevant information about itself.
3. Progress toward achieving shared responsibilities. This includes personal movement toward sharing functions of leadership, as well as participation in the determination of goals and cooperation in their achievement.
4. Progress toward achieving group cohesion. Cohesion should be sufficient to make possible absorption of new ideas without group disintegration, assimilation of new participants in a way which will strengthen rather than weaken group feeling, maintenance of long-range goals when a situation so demands, and putting to constructive ends whatever internal conflict may arise.
5. Progress toward acquiring the capacity to inform itself, to think clearly, and to make creative choices when problems must be resolved. This embraces learning to make maximum use of whatever contributions members are potentially capable of supplying and uncovering and rectifying falacious conclusions.

If a group is to move in these directions, what functions does a democratic leader perform? He (or she) may execute or administer, serve as judge or arbiter, be an advocate (or shaper of opinion), render expert advice, and serve as discussion leader. Although a discussion leader may on occasion assume any of the above roles, his function as discussion leader is distinctively different from and more inclusive than that of any of the others; he helps the group members, including himself, achieve self-growth. Or, as one writer puts it, he tries to "release the creative talents of the members of a group, help them solve their own problems, and reach their own decisions."[9]

How May Teachers Foster Group Decisions?

No matter how great their internal rapport, groups do not change ideas and beliefs automatically. As we have observed, the most effectual situation for producing group change appears to be a democratically led discussion. For purposes of this analysis, probably the most important requirement of discussion (or other modes of study) designed to change basic attitudes is that it have the quality of freely permitting self-learning. (This should not be taken to mean absence of directedness.) We have already noted that students resist outside pressure to change opinions. As Lewin has indicated, the object in achieving change is not to apply pressure from outside but to remove counterforces within the individual.[10]

Although a teacher can and usually must help in eliminating these counterforces, students must perform the actual removal. If they can explore a problem independently, feeling no authoritarian pressure from above to explore it in a particular way or emerge with particular conclusions, they are much more likely than otherwise to undergo real and permanent changes in conceptual patterns. They need to be encouraged to use investigatory techniques of their own, to explore by themselves provocative readings, trips, interviews, and radio and television programs. A teacher's role here is to suggest possible directions of exploration and to help students evaluate facts which are exposed.

For maximum change, reflective discussion of problems should culminate in group decisions. That is, in addition to discussing and studying a problem, students as a group should consider what conclusions are warranted, what the conclusions mean to them, and what if anything they intend to do about them. Students need to communicate their views to each other, so that intentions of each are known to all. If it is evident to individuals that most members of a group have revised their outlooks and expect to change their behavior in stated ways, then members who are reluctant to change because of long-standing attachment to certain views may find change easier. This should not be interpreted to mean that a group or its leader should pressure individual members to accept conformity. We are referring to changes which individuals see the logic of making but find difficult because of opposing forces. The opposing forces are often social pressures exerted by peer culture, community mores, or parental dictates. These may be combated more successfully if a student feels that others intend to combat them with him or her.

IN WHAT SUBJECT AREAS IS REFLECTIVE TEACHING APPLICABLE?

Many teachers see reflective or problem-centered teaching as a possible approach to instruction in a very limited number of courses, such as social studies, literature, industrial arts, or home economics. These teachers are unable to imagine the use of problem-centered teaching in such subjects as mathematics, physics, music, physical education, and foreign language. However, such teachers have an inadequate conception of reflective teaching procedures.

With respect to subjective areas, it appears that the essential characteristics of reflective teaching have enough flexibility to be employed in all school subjects, including those which seem on the surface to be rather cut and dried. Problem-centered teaching does not require development of elaborate unit plans. It emerges whenever a teacher, through adroit questioning and use of negative evidence, induces students to doubt that which they now accept, and then helps them analyze critically the issue that has arisen. In most conventional subjects, opportunities regularly appear for a teacher to operate in this manner. Passages in a textbook, assertions made by students, a news story, a motion picture or TV show—any of these may serve at times as a springboard for creation of problems. Problem-centered teaching seems to spring into existence in those situations where minds of teacher and students engage. It grows more from a unique relationship between teacher and students than from any different nature of formal course materials.

Of course, some courses and some types of course organization lend themselves more readily to reflective teaching than do others. A course construed broadly—that is, whose subject matter is not narrowly prescribed—is probably a better tool than is a more narrow course. Thus, as usually defined, general business is a better course for reflection-level teaching than is shorthand; problems of democracy better than economic geography; history and philosophy of mathematics better than algebra; world literature better than freshman composition. This difference, however, is not inherent in the nature of the subject matter as such but lies in the frame of reference within which it customarily is treated.

A course in which problem-centered teaching is used cannot be bound rigidly to a textbook. Real problems are psychological; data used in solving them are rarely organized in the same pattern as textbooks and courses of study. The "logical" organization of a book simply does not usually coincide with the logic of live thought. Hence, courses should be allowed to cut across subject matter lines whenever such deviation makes sense in terms of the particular problem being studied.

Determination of which subjects, or which topics within a subject, should be handled as problems cannot be made without reference to a specific classroom situation. In each case, a teacher should reckon with the maturity and experiential background of students, community attitudes, his or her own preparation and skill, and anticipated consequences of having a class delve deeply into the subject.

HOW ARE PROJECTS AND UNITS RELATED TO TEACHING FOR UNDERSTANDING?

Some teachers, as well as some writers, erroneously assume that all projects and units are aimed toward engendering student understanding of either an explanatory or an exploratory nature. Project and unit teaching is not necessarily reflection level teaching, nor is it always even teaching for understanding on either an explanatory or an exploratory level. The outcome of project and unit teaching depends upon the wisdom and techniques of each particular teacher.

A project is an individualized work assignment. Although all members of a class may be given the same general kind of task, each student is free to arrange variations. Furthermore, although there may be a deadline for completion of a project, students work on an individualized time schedule. Projects involve physical activity and almost always result in some kind of physical product. Examples of projects are making a table in a shop class; raising a calf in an agriculture class; making an insect collection in a biology class; or making a clippings scrapbook in a social studies class.

A unit, in its most general sense, is a collection of subject matter which is unified by a single theme. The unit concept has been applied extensively in academic or semiacademic courses, such as English and social studies. In a given course, units constitute the organizational foci. A succession of units, arranged sequentially in some presumably logical fashion, gives a course its form. Obviously, unit organization is designed, among other things, to make a course independent, or relatively independent, of a textbook. Since teachers themselves usually are responsible for developing each unit and collecting teaching materials to go with it, a unit organization offers considerable flexibility. Units may be selected and designed to fit a particular situation. Educators have devised a great variety of unit plans, the nature of which depends largely on how the educator defines the learning process and what he or she sees as the goals of education.

So far as contemporary practice is concerned, most teachers view a unit as very much like a textbook chapter except that, to a large degree, it is their own creation. They see a unit of work as simply a block of subject matter dealing with a common subject. For example, a geography course may contain a unit on France. This simply includes all the factual data on France which the course provides, pulled together in a bundle so that they can be studied together.

Popularization of project teaching and unit teaching may have done more harm than good in the sense that, to many teachers, these approaches have been seized upon as the heart of the educational process. Teachers may develop collections of projects and units that look good to them and consider their major teaching problem solved. Consequently, project and unit teaching may misdirect teachers' efforts. Instead of regarding as all-important the development of the kind of unique interaction among teacher and students that leads to reflection and understanding, they are likely to focus on the more or less mechanical arrangement of predetermined subject matter so it will look neat on paper. Teachers so occupied lose sight of what is central in all learning: the intelligent interplay of a person's ideas with those of others.

Because there is so much confusion over the meaning of a unit and particularly because units often are handled in a kind of pseudo problem-solving manner, it is well to sharpen the distinction between the "problem-like" unit and true reflective problem solving. Fortunately, Elizabeth Berry has provided us with a very apt illustration which could fit any of the subjects of English, social studies, or journalism—and, by implication, probably almost any other. Berry uses the term process unit as equivalent to what we mean by a true problem-centered, or reflective, unit. In her own words, the story is as follows:

A few years ago I visited and observed in the classroom of an English teacher who was conducting a unit on "The Role of the Newspaper in the World Today." This teacher began the unit by announcing that the students were going to undertake a unit on the aforementioned title. The teacher spent considerable time telling the students why it was important for them to make a study of the newspaper, then she told them that the next day the class would set up objectives for the unit study.

In the meantime, class members were to give some attention to the objectives. The next day in class, the students agreed upon a list of objectives for the unit, questions they wished to answer. It was interesting to note that their questions were primarily material that the teacher had given them in the lecture the day before. The teacher then announced a series of activities that the class would undertake in the study of the unit. These activities proceeded in a systematic way. As each activity was undertaken, the teacher brought to the class any materials needed, gave specific instructions on how each piece of work was to be done, and saw that these activities were carried out. Some of the activities undertaken included the daily reading of the local newspaper and a discussion of local news items. No attention was given to the accuracy of reporting. There seemed to be a feeling that if an article appears in the press it is valid. A local newsman spoke to the class and built up a strong argument for his paper and the press in general. He was a delightful speaker and won the support of the group. The students then wrote letters to the editor on a rather non-controversial subject. The letters were graded, returned to the students, and presumably mailed. Students were encouraged to write articles of school interest for the school newspaper. Several did. Some vocabulary words relating to the press were studied. During the month that the unit was in progress, the daily work laboriously dragged on. By the end of the unit, the students were restless and ready for a change. The teacher, realizing that the students had lost interest, decided to bring the unit to an end with a class evaluation. In the evaluation, the students agreed that they had learned how to read the newspaper, recognized the importance of reading, and expected to confirm their interest by making a daily reading of the newspaper a part of their lives. The teacher then announced that it was time to move on to another unit, which would be a study of *Macbeth*.

After I had observed the teaching of the newspaper unit, I determined to try this unit using a different approach, method, and plan. I decided to use the unit process. My own personal goals were not only to help students improve their use of specific language skills, but also to make them critical readers of newspapers. From past experiences, I knew that many of the students believed that anything in print was truth. They had probably developed such a belief because most of their educational experience had been rooted in a firm belief in the word of the press. Many had gone through school proving their points with such remarks as this, "I can prove it because I read it in . . . ." Also I had observed that many of my students equated being arrested with being guilty, considered all advertising as an honest presentation of fact, thought almost any sale a good buy, and generally felt that the highest honor that a girl could achieve would be a photograph in the society section.

Now I could have told the students the strengths and weaknesses of a newspaper, of its worth and limitations. But I knew that learning comes from within, not from without, and that students are more apt to use fruitfully knowledge gained through self-discovery. For this reason, I presented the unit in a problem solving context. I did this by making reprints of articles on the same subject but from different newspapers. I used three different newspapers for this and selected an article from each on the same topic but with varying interpretations. I passed out reprints of the first article for the class to read. Class discussion followed, but there were few comments. In general, the class members agreed with the reporter. I then gave them a second article to read. There were some comments that this article was not in complete agreement with the first, but not much excitement about it. Then I gave them the third article. But this time students were puzzled at discrepancies and differences of opinion in reporting the news. I let them wrangle over these differences in class discussion before I took action. In other words, I allowed them to come face to face with a felt difficulty and problem. Finally I halted the discussion and said, "What is the issue in this discussion? What is it that you want to know? Let's define the problem."

Now the students entered the second phase of the unit process, when they defined the problem as they saw it in view of their recent experiences. I did not define the problem for the students. Through the use of the chalkboard to examine carefully selected answers, I patiently took time for the students to agree upon a statement of the problem and a series of questions that they should answer if they were to become intelligent readers of the news. Now I asked how the class could proceed to make a study of this problem so as to gain the needed insight. The students suggested numerous ways: (1) Daily reading of different papers to see differences or similarities in reporting, (2) Reading news magazines for a similar purpose, (3) Searching for books in the library that discuss the magazine and newspaper field, (4) Calling in local reporters for class interviews, (5) Getting personal accounts of news reporting from biographies of famous newsmen, (6) Interviewing people in the community who had complained about being misrepresented in the news, (7) Practicing news reporting themselves to see what difficulties arise. I shared in the suggestions for this co-operative research, but I did not dictate them. For I did not wish to kill initiative and creativity.

Next the class co-operatively agreed upon a plan of action. They then proceeded to carry out their plans, and I acted as a catalyst and guide. As the students began the study and exploration, they found a need to go to the library for resource materials pertaining to the problem at hand. The librarian helped the students find books and materials relating to their study. Perhaps it was necessary for both librarian and students to consult the card catalogue, the *Reader's Guide*, encyclopaedias, and bibliographies. In addition, students used the library to investigate current magazines and newspapers. It was through the resources of the library, for example, that they were able to compare original articles with *Reader's Digest* condensations of them. It was from the *Reader's Guide* that students discovered articles on "How to Read the Chicago Tribune" and "All the News that Fits the Pattern." (April and May issues of Harpers, 1949.) The students found especially helpful William H. Burton's *Education for Effective Thinking* and S. I. Hayakawa's *Language in Thought and Action*. Copies of Liebling's *The Press* and Edgar Dale's *How to Read a Newspaper* were also found on the library shelves. In addition there were the autobiographies of newsmen and journalists telling their own personal experiences in the newspaper field. The unit took the students to the school library, to the public library, and into the community. It made them active researchers and problem solvers.[11]

WHAT IS UNIQUE ABOUT THE REFLECTION OR EXPLORATORY UNDERSTANDING LEVEL OF EVALUATION?

Although the mentalistic-memory, the physicalistic-memory, and the explanatory understanding level of teaching and learning each has its unique characteristics, the three also have a common significant trait, namely, all three are teacher-centered processes. The teacher sets the objectives for the students and the teacher measures the relative achievement of those objectives. In some cases learners are considered to be active, but in more cases they are assumed to be either passive or intermittently active and passive. Seldom, if ever, are they considered to be perceptually interactive, as is the case in reflective teaching and learning.

If teachers assume that their students are active and if they pursue either memory or explanatory understanding level teaching, they do so for the purpose of making sure that the students' active natures either are exercised or unfold in the proper manner. If teachers assume that their students are basically passive, and this is most often the case, they bring the proper stimuli or ideas to impinge upon the students and thereby inculcate the designed behaviors or understandings.

The seminal concept that has provided the originative power for the reflection or exploratory understanding level of teaching and learning has been *perceptual interaction*. To repeat, perceptual interaction, that is, simultaneous mutual interaction (SMI) is a cognitive experiential process within which a person, psychologically, simultaneously reaches out to his (or her) psychological environment, encounters some aspects of it, brings those aspects into relationship with himself, makes something of those aspects, acts in relations to *what he (she) makes of* them, and realizes the consequences of the entire process. Perceptual interaction, so defined, is supported and amplified best by a cognitive-field psychology of learning.

The results of reflection level teaching and learning, as is the case with the explanatory understanding level, include understandings, principles, rules, or laws, but not these alone. The reflective level implies that these results are *purposively acquired.* Consequently, reflection level learning enhances students' scientific outlook and experiential-instrumental thinking and thereby points them toward doing further creative thinking on their own.

Since reflective teaching entails problem-centered, exploratory personal involvement, testing that is compatible with it will likewise be centered on genuine problems. When one is teaching on a reflective level one should be trying, in testing as well as in all other evaluational procedures, to ascertain whether each student is able to apply adequate information to the solution of a problem in such a way as to harmonize the problem, all available pertinent data or facts, and the answer. The most practicable instruments for the accomplishment of this purpose are problem-centered essay tests. A reflection level essay test usually consists of four, three, or even fewer carefully constructed questions. Each question should be pertinent to the study that the students have been pursuing and should constitute a real problem for them. A sample reflection level test question is as follows: "How is the listing of the behavioral objectives of a course related to the course's being taught reflectively?"

The best type of reflection level question is one to which there is possibly more than one true answer. So, answers cannot be written out at the time the test is constructed. Each answer must be evaluated on its own merits. In an adequate answer many facts will be used, but the number of facts listed as such will not be the basis for evaluation. Instead, answers will be evaluated on the basis of some criteria or measuring sticks that the teacher and students have agreed upon prior to the time of the test. These criteria probably will be *pertinence* and, *adequacy* of the data that are applied to the solution of the problem, *harmony* of the problem, data, and answer, and perhaps one or two others.

Teachers who are committed to reflective teaching would neither test their students on a memory level nor use so-called true-false tests. Instead, they would prefer to use essay tests, and they would strive to make their questions truly reflective. At times the teachers might use selection tests, but they would realize that in so doing they would be drawing their students away from reflective thinking.

HOW EFFECTIVE IS REFLECTIVE TEACHING?

A person who experiences reflective learning should thereby gain an increased store of generalized insights related to the subject studied; and these should be incorporated at the personality level so that a permanent change in him (or her) occurs. Furthermore, the person should show a greater disposition and ability than before to apply the method of scientific reflection to problems outside the school subject in which reflective learning occurs.

It is difficult to measure insightful changes which occur in people as a result of school experiences. The most significant changes may not be evident in a person's outward behavior while he or she is still in school. Nevertheless, the results of objective studies of the accomplishments of reflective teaching as compared with those of the other two levels are markedly favorable to reflective teaching.

It might seem valid that, on a test designed to measure recall of facts, students taught on a memory or an explanatory understanding level would fare better than those taught reflectively. However, if we are to take at face value a group of studies extending from 1940 into the 1950s, this apparently is not the case. These studies, all designed to test the results of reflective teaching, have been reported by Bayles.[12]

The studies were conducted by public school teachers in Kansas and Missouri and culminated in the form of master's theses. Four of the six studies reported were conducted in high school social studies and the other two in fifth- and sixth-grade classes.

The general procedure was as follows: students were given IQ tests to determine the average IQ of a class. Only those classes were used which were approximately "average." Then, insofar as the teachers were able to do so, the classes were taught reflectively. The teachers measured the effects of reflective instruction by giving various standardized achievement tests and by observing such changes of students' overt behavior as made it possible to infer the quality of their learning.

The control group used in evaluation of test results was in each case the group upon which the test had been standardized. All tests used had been standardized on groups of students of average or better IQ. The control against which teachers judged student behavior was much more subjective—the behavior of students of other classes which the teachers had taught in conventional fashion. However, since each of the teachers was experienced and able, subjective impressions reported by them were considered worthy of respect.

The results of each study were very clear cut. Irrespective of whether the achievement tests emphasized fact recall or the application of principles, students who had been taught reflectively scored conspicuously higher in almost all cases than the national or regional norms. Those who did not actually score higher than the norms made exceptionally large gains during the school term. With respect to informally gathered data, teachers reported the following results: (1) apparent heightened interest among students; (2) more work done; (3) more voluntary reporting of data which had been encountered out of school—data gathered from radio, newspapers, magazines, and so forth; (4) increased tendency to be critical—to demand evidence; (5) increased participation in discussions, particularly among students formerly reticent; and (6) much more reading. Some of the teachers obtained librarians' records of magazines and books checked out by students; they found that those in their reflectively taught classes were reading more than any other students in school.

To measure the amount of gain during a term, one of the investigators continued for a period of six years to give achievement tests to respective classes at the beginning and end of each school term. She found that the net gain in learning increased from year to year. This indicated that with continued experience with reflective teaching a teacher becomes more effective. If the six teachers participating in these studies had had several years of reflective teaching experience behind them (most were trying it for the first time), it seems likely that the studies would have revealed even more spectacular results.

Many teachers, when discussing the merits of reflective teaching, argue that it works only with the best students. One of the studies reported by Bayles suggests that this is not true; in the instance reported, reflective teaching was used in a class containing a wide range of ability. Students of low ability made greater percentage gains than did those of high ability. However, the investigator concluded that her teaching had not been pitched on a challenging enough level for the high group. Probably a safe conclusion is that reflective teaching, when effective, tends to bring students of all levels of ability up to maximum or near maximum performance.

There is one more significant conclusion. The teachers who participated in the studies which Bayles reports adapted reflective teaching to school situations which were quite conventional. The fact that they achieved good results suggests that effectiveness of teaching in our public schools could be greatly increased without drastically upsetting the conventional framework of subject matter and school organization. It is reasonable to assume that, in a school administratively committed to reflective teaching, results would be even more impressive.

In concluding, we should remind ourselves that, regardless of the level of learning pursued, students need facts in order to understand anything. Furthermore, they need both facts and understandings in order to learn reflectively. However, teachers need not be reluctant to experiment with both explanatory understanding level and reflection level teaching and testing for fear that their students will not learn a sufficient number of facts. When students are taught and tested on the reflection level, they acquire many facts as well as understandings, and likewise when they are taught and tested on the explanatory understanding level they acquire much factual information. However, this process does not work in reverse; there is little about factual learning as such that contributes to understanding, and little about teaching for understanding in a nonreflective way that contributes to a student's reflective powers and habits.

NOTES

[1] This teaching-learning unit was developed, implemented, and recorded by Dr. William B. Lieurance, using an actual class in a school situation, as a part of the Tri-University Project in Elementary Education at New York University in 1968.

[2] See Grant Bateman, William B. Lieurance, Agnes Manney, and Curtis Osburn, *Helping Children Think*, Tri-University Project in Elementary Education, New York: New York University Press, 1968, pp. 2–8.

[3] One of the most useful references on means of analyzing the social structure of groups and techniques to use in establishing greater cohesiveness is Helen Hall Jennings, *Sociometry in Group Relations: A Work Guide for Teachers*, American Council on Education, 1949.

[4] Kurt Lewin, *Resolving Social Conflicts*, New York: Harper & Row, 1948 p. 82.

[5] Lewin, *Resolving Social Conflicts*, p. 68.

[6] See Kurt Lewin, "Group Decision and Social Change," in Theodore Newcomb and Eugene Hartley (eds.), *Readings in Social Psychology*, New York: Holt, Rinehart and Winston, 1947, pp. 330–344.

[7] Lewin, *Resolving Social Conflicts*, p. 68.

[8] National Training Laboratory in Group Development, *Report of the Second Summer Laboratory*, Washington, D.C.: Department of Adult Education, 1948, pp. 113–114.

[9] Franklin S. Haiman, *Group Leadership and Democratic Action*, Boston: Houghton Mifflin, 1951, p. 71.

[10] Lewin, "Group Decision and Social Change," in *Readings in Social Psychology*, p. 342.

[11] Elizabeth Berry, "The Unit Process," *The Educational Forum* 27 (March 1963,): 364–366. Recommended is her textbook, *Guiding Students in the English Class*, Appleton, 1957. This material is used by permission of Kappa Delta Pi, an honorary society in education, owners of the copyright.

[12] "Experiments with Reflective Teaching," *Kansas Studies in Education* 6, no. 3 (April 1956): This monograph is reproduced in essentially its original form in Chapter 1 of Bayles book *Democratic Educational Theory*, New York: Harper & Row, 1960.

BIBLIOGRAPHY

ANDERSON, HAROLD H. (ed.). *Creativity and Its Cultivation*. New York: Harper & Row, 1959. Addresses presented at the Interdisciplinary Symposia on Creativity, Michigan State University. Top authorities cover numerous facets of the subject. Excellent.

ASCHNER, MARY JANE, and CHARLES E. BISH (eds.). *Productive Thinking in Education*. Washington, D.C.: The National Education Association and the Carnegie Corporation of New York, 1968. A report on two conferences on productive thinking. Part 4, "Education for Productive Thinking," and Chapter 12, "Summary and Interpretation," are especially pertinent to these three chapters.

BASSLER, OTTO C., and JOHN R. KOLB. *Learning to Teach Secondary School Mathematics*. Scranton, PA: Intext Educational Publishers, 1971. A systematic behavioristic approach to teaching secondary school mathematics. Adheres to the tenets of scientific realism as well as behaviorism.

BATEMAN, GRANT, WILLIAM B. LIEURANCE, AGNES MANNEY, and CURTIS OSBURN. *Helping Children Think*. Tri-University Project in Elementary Education. New York: New York University Press, 1968. Pages 6–8, 19–21, 26–31, and 49–79 describe approaches to, and units in, teaching reflectively in the various elementary grades. Pages 81–97 contain "springboard" questions that may be used to initiate reflective learning. This book is probably the best source for elementary school teachers.

BAYLES, ERNEST E. *Pragmatism in Education*. New York: Harper & Row, 1966. Pages 109–127 depict elementary school units for teaching spelling, arithmetic, art, nature study, and grammar reflectively. Pages 127–140 describe secondary units in literature, American history, and natural science.

BEVANS, WILLIAM. "Perceptual Learning: An Overview." *Journal of General Psychology* 64 (January 1961): 69–99. Characterizes perceptual development as a process of progressive refinement, definition, and specificity rather than of building associate linkage.

BLOOM, BENJAMIN S., et al. *Taxonomy of Educational Objectives: Handbook 1: Cognitive Domain*. London: Longmans, Green, 1956. Develops six general areas of educational objectives and test exercises, namely, knowledge, comprehension, application, analysis, synthesis, and evaluation.

BONNER, HUBERT. *Group Dynamics*. New York: Ronald Press, 1959. One of the best general texts in the field. Covers history of research on groups and present status of group work.

BRETHOWER, DALE M. *Programed Instruction: A Manual of Programing Techniques*. Chicago: Educational Methods, 1963. A book on linear programming making use of a linear programmed format. Interesting to peruse for illustrative purposes.

BROPHY, JERE E., and THOMAS L. GOOD. *Teacher-Student Relationships: Causes and Consequences*. New York: Holt, Rinehart and Winston, 1974. Behavioristic-oriented summaries of research on student differences that affect teacher expectations and attitudes. The effect of the latter on teacher-student alternating interaction patterns and student performance.

BRUNER, JEROME S. *The Process of Education*. Cambridge: Harvard University Press, 1960. The chairman's report of the major themes, principal conjectures, and most striking tentative conclusions of a 1959 conference of 35 natural scientists, psychologists, and educators on teaching science and mathematics in elementary and secondary schools. The report emphasizes teaching for understanding the structure—pertinent relationships —of a subject matter rather than for mastery of facts and techniques.

BRUNER, JEROME S. *Toward a Theory of Instruction*. Cambridge: Harvard University Press, 1966. Presents Bruner's conclusions concerning what should go into a theoretical basis for teaching procedure. Highly recommended to be read in connection with the section of Chapter 21 entitled "How Is Reflection-level Learning Promoted?" Bruner writes on a theoretical level but his ideas are highly thought-provoking.

CARTWRIGHT, DORWIN, and ALVIN ZANDER (eds.). *Group Dynamics*, 3d ed. New York: Harper & Row, 1968. A collection of readings, all of which are relevant to classroom procedures. Readers will detect a strong Lewinian influence. A very useful reference.

Combs, Arthur W., Robert A. Blume, Arthur J. Newman, and Hannelore L. Wass. *The Professional Education of Teachers: A Humanistic Approach to Teacher Preparation*, 2d ed. Boston: Allyn & Bacon, 1974. An application of modern "perceptual-humanistic" psychology to problems of teacher education. Teaching is described as a "helping" relationship.

Coulson, John E. (ed.). *Programmed Learning and Computer-Based Instruction*, New York: Wiley, 1962. Proceedings of the Conference on Application of Digital to Automated Instruction. The last half of the book, on linking computers to teaching devices to provide a more sophisticated kind of feedback, is interesting.

Ebel, Robert L., (ed.). *Encyclopedia of Educational Research*, 4th ed. New York: Macmillan, 1969. Benjamin S. Bloom, "Higher Mental Processes," pages 594–601, treats theories of learning, schools of psychology as related to teaching and learning, analysis of problem-solving processes, and education for improvement of thinking abilities. Margaret Ammons, "Objectives and Outcomes," pages 908–912, summarizes historical approaches to educational objectives and their evaluation and discusses meaning of "behavioral objectives."

Eisner, Elliot W. "Educational Objectives: Help or Hindrance." *School Review* 75 (1967): 250–282. Reviews history of specific objective movement back through 1918. Develops case for and against the use of specific educational objectives.

Engelmann, Siegfried. *Preventing Failure in the Primary Grades*. Chicago: Science Research Associates, 1969. Chapter 4, "Reading for the Non-reader," explains how to teach reading in order to help children get the ideas surrounding the use of words. Hence, it opens the way for a teacher to teach beginners how to read using reflective processes.

Fenton, Edwin. *The New Social Studies*. New York: Holt, Rinehart and Winston, 1967. Emphasizes an inductive approach to teaching to teach the concepts that make up the structure of social science. Makes much of teaching strategies.

Fraenkel, Jack R. *Helping Students Think and Value*. Englewood Cliffs, N.J.: Prentice-Hall, 1973. A well-organized presentation of strategies for teaching social studies on an explanatory understanding level. Presents strategies for developing thinking with little place for reflective thinking.

Gage, N. L. (ed.). *Handbook of Research on Teaching*. Chicago: Rand McNally, 1963. See Chapter 17, "Research on Teaching the Social Studies," by Laurence E. Metcalf. Pages 941–943 present two reflective units, one on who discovered America by Ernest E. Bayles and one on the election of 1800 by Alan F. Griffin.

Galanter, Eugene (ed.). *Automatic Teaching: The State of the Art*. New York: Wiley, 1959. A concise book of very well-selected readings. See especially the articles by Crowder and Lumsdaine. The latter is one of the best writers in the field—he is able to include both wit and satire in his prose.

Goldmark, Bernice. *Social Studies: A Method of Inquiry*. Belmont, CA: Wadsworth, 1968. An excellent book to lead students to think about thinking.

Green, Edward J. *The Learning Process and Programmed Instruction*. New

York: Holt, Rinehart and Winston, 1962. Green vacillates between an extreme Watsonian behaviorism and an advocacy of Skinner's operant conditioning. His arguments are polemical and dogmatic; nevertheless the book is very well organized and written. Green seems convinced that there is nothing about human beings which cannot be learned by studying rats; also that anything which can be taught at all can be taught better by a machine.

HAUBRICK, VERNON F. (ed.). *Freedom, Bureaucracy, and Schooling.* Washington, D.C.: Association for Supervision and Curriculum Development, 1971. An examination of current bureaucratic school practices and the teacher-student relationships they entail. See especially Chapter 1, "Freedom and Bureaucracy in the School," by Donald Arnstine who writes, "Stronger leadership, tighter controls, and human relations programs very seldom change the attitudes of workers and students, unless the change is for the worse."

HULLFISH, H. GORDON, and PHILIP G. SMITH. *Reflective Thinking: The Method of Education.* New York: Dodd, Mead, 1961. A noneclectic argument to the effect that unless education dedicates itself to teaching students to think, it dedicates itself to nothing at all. Highly recommended reading.

HUNT, MAURICE P., and LAWRENCE E. METCALF. *Teaching High School Social Studies,* 2d ed. New York: Harper & Row, 1968. Part 1 contains a general treatment of reflective teaching that applies equally to all subjects and grade levels.

JOURARD, SIDNEY M. *Healthy Personality: An Approach from the Viewpoint of Humanistic Psychology.* New York: Macmillan, 1974. One of the best presentations of psychedelic humanism. Human beings are taken to be free, good, and active.

JUDD, CHARLES H. *Educational Psychology.* Boston: Houghton Mifflin, 1939. A comprehensive educational psychology text that emphasizes the learning of generalizations as opposed to atomistic learning. Readers will be impressed by the richness of content.

KLAUSMEIER, HERBERT J., ELIZABETH SCHWENN GHATALA, and DOROTHY A. FRAYER. *Conceptual Learning and Development.* New York: Academic Press, 1974. A cognitive view of concepts within a behavioristic orientation. Model of conceptual learning and development to serve as a guide to research. Attributes of public concepts are various degrees of learnability, usability, validity, generality, power, structure, instance perceptibility, and instance numerousness.

KOLESNIK, WALTER B. *Humanism and/or Behaviorism in Education.* Boston: Allyn & Bacon, 1975. Treats humanism and behaviorism as the two dominant psychological theories in contemporary education. An attempted synthesization of the two conflicting positions.

LEWIN, KURT. *Resolving Social Conflicts.* New York: Harper & Row, 1948. A fundamental reference. Lewin's experimental work paved the way for much that is now known about the dynamics of groups.

LUMSDAINE, ARTHUR A., and ROBERT GLASER (eds.). *Teaching Machines and Programmed Learning; A Source Book.* Washington, D.C.: The National Education Association, 1960. A collection of 48 readings—the most comprehensive collection of the subject. Articles by most of the big names in the field. A very useful reference.

LYSAUGHT, JEROME P., and CLARENCE M. WILLIAMS. *A Guide to Programmed Instruction.* New York: Wiley, 1963. Perhaps the best introductory book in the field. Short and readable, it offers a balanced treatment and is one of the best sources of references, including journals and journal articles.

McBURNEY, JAMES H., and KENNETH HANCE. *The Principles and Methods of Discussion.* New York: Harper & Row, 1939. One of the best treatments of "reflective discussion." The authors reject any discussion that is a mere pooling of ignorance.

MAGER, ROBERT F. *Preparing Instructional Objectives.* Belmont, CA: Fearon, 1962. Instructional objectives are to be stated and measured in terms of observable terminal behaviors. Divides objectives into content and non-content ones. By implication, rules out reflective teaching.

MEYER, AGNES E. *Education for a New Morality.* New York: Macmillan, 1957. A provocative little book with profound implications for what and how we teach. It suggests a philosophy of education that might close the gap in our thinking between science and humanism.

MILES, MATTHEW B. *Learning to Work in Groups.* New York: Teachers College Press, 1959. The contributions of many experimental and research studies of the nature of group dynamics brought together and focused on the process of helping people to learn to work in groups.

MILLER, GEORGE A., EUGENE GALANTER, and KARL H. PRIBRAM. *Plans and the Structure of Behavior.* New York: Holt, Rinehart and Winston, 1960. A creative treatment of the psychology of the cognitive processes. Ideas developed in communication and computer theory are applied to psychology. A TOTE—Test-Operate-Test-Exit—unit based on "feedback" is conceived as an alternative to reflex arc theory.

MORRIS, VAN CLEVE, and YOUNG PAI. *Philosophy and the American School,* 2d ed. Boston: Houghton Mifflin, 1976. Introduces students to the problems of teaching and learning through the medium of philosophy. Develops philosophical models of teaching and learning.

MORRISON, HENRY C. *Basic Principles in Education.* Boston: Houghton Mifflin, 1934. The bases of Morrison's theory of teaching and learning. See Chapter 4 for his concept of adaptation—learning with understanding but not reflection.

MORRISON, HENRY C. *The Practice of Teaching in the Secondary School.* University of Chicago Press, 1932. Morrison's theory of education, with a detailed statement of his idea of the "mastery unit."

OSGOOD, CHARLES E., et al. *The Measurement of Meaning.* Urbana, Ill.: University of Illinois Press, 1957. Technical, but provocative. Chapter 1 contains a section entitled "Meanings of 'Meaning.' "

PATTERSON, C. H. *Foundations for a Theory of Instruction and Educational Psychology.* New York: Harper & Row, 1977. Presents basic ideas of Montessori, Piaget, Skinner, Bruner, Rogers, and others as they relate to instructional processes. Develops the psychological foundations for a generalized theory of instruction.

POSTMAN, NEIL, and CHARLES WEINGARTNER. *Teaching as a Subversive Activity.* New York: Delacorte Press, 1969. Sharply critical of today's schools.

Develops "inquiry method" as the solution. Students generate their own stories by becoming involved in their learning. A mixture of laissez-faire and social architect views.

RATHS, LOUIS E., ARTHUR JONAS, ARNOLD ROTHSTEIN, and SELMA WASSERMANN. *Teaching for Thinking.* Columbus, Ohio: Merrill, 1967. Perhaps one of the best methods books on teaching reflectively. See especially the introduction and Chapter 1.

ROGERS, CARL R. *Freedom to Learn.* Columbus, Ohio: Merrill, 1969. A plan for self-directed procedures in education. Emphasizes openness, spontaneity, and learning how to learn. A contemporary presentation of autonomous development and psychedelic humanism.

SAETTLER, L. PAUL. *A History of Instructional Technology.* New York: McGraw-Hill, 1968. Treats theories of learning in relation to technology of instruction, including programmed instruction. See especially Chapter 4.

SAUCIER, WEEMS A., ROBERT L. WENDEL, and RICHARD G. MUELLER. *Toward Humanistic Teaching in High School.* Lexington, Mass.: D. C. Heath, 1975. Psychological and sociological basis for moderate humanistic teaching of various high school subject areas. Humanistic teaching of specific high school subjects. Gestalt-field oriented.

SEVERIN, FRANK T. *Discovering Man in Psychology: A Humanistic Approach.* New York: McGraw-Hill, 1973. A symposium of articles by authors of both psychedelic and scientific humanistic bents.

TABER, JULIAN I., ROBERT GLASER, and HALMUTH M. SCHAEFFER. *Learning and Programmed Instruction.* Reading, Mass.: Addison-Wesley, 1965. Probably one of the best-written and scholarly expositions of Skinner's linear programming. Includes a concise theoretical treatment of Skinner's concept of operant conditioning.

TRAVERS, ROBERT M. W. (ed.). *Second Handbook of Research on Teaching.* Chicago: Rand McNally, 1973. Perhaps the best comprehensive source of information concerning contemporary research on teaching.

USHENKO, ANDREW. *The Field Theory of Meaning.* Ann Arbor: University of Michigan Press, 1958. A highly technical discussion that attempts to harmonize the theory of meaning with field psychology. For advanced students.

WALKER, MARSHALL. *The Nature of Scientific Thought.* Englewood Cliffs, N.J.: Prentice-Hall, 1963. Written by a physical scientist for general readers. Basic purpose of science is prediction; basic procedures are use of conceptual models.

WILLOUGHBY, STEPHEN S. *Contemporary Teaching of Secondary School Mathematics.* New York: Wiley, 1967. Presents an approach to teaching high school mathematics that harmonizes with cognitive-field psychology and reflective teaching. Does not use all of the language of reflective teaching, but emphasizes teaching for genuine discovery.

WYNNE, JOHN P. *Theories of Education.* New York: Harper & Row, 1963. A philosophical-historical treatment of educational theories. Decribes principles, psychological approaches, methods, and practices implicit in each theory. Excellent background material for this book.

Epilogue
HOW MIGHT COGNITIVE-FIELD PSYCHOLOGY PROVIDE AN EMERGENT TEACHING THEORY AND PRACTICE?

The primary purpose of a course in psychological foundations of education is to aid students in critically evaluating psychological theories and principles from the point of view of their applicability to classroom practices. However, when we do this we see that, whereas certain aspects of respective theories of learning and teaching support or supplement one another, some others openly conflict or disagree. Furthermore, when we study the major outlooks in regard to learning and teaching that have arisen in Western civilization and are still with us, it becomes quite evident that actual educational procedures often reflect inconsistent hodge-podges of bits of several systematic theories developed from time to time. Thus, educators often are not able to provide effective educational leadership because they themselves are not certain of where they think they are headed.

In teaching, an educator has at least three possible choices of action. He (or she) may conform rigidly to one recognized, systematic theory of teaching and learning—mental discipline, natural unfoldment, appercep-tion, S-R conditioning, or classical Gestalt theory; he may eclectically—selectively—borrow freely from the various outlooks and arrange his ideas into a mosaic or patchwork that is available for him to draw upon as need arises; or he may develop an *emergent synthesis*—a genuinely new outlook that benefits from knowledge of previously developed psychological theories but is not an eclectic compromise among them.

HOW SATISFACTORY ARE THE THEORIES OF LEARNING THAT HAVE PRECEDED COGNITIVE-FIELD THEORY?

Adherents of a positive-relativistic cognitive-field psychology think that this approach may come to function as an emergent synthesis capable of transcending many of the difficulties underlying other positions and at the same time providing a psychological base for a set of school practices that will reflect a knowledge of pertinent scientific evidence and will be both adequate and internally consistent. The first step in development of such an emergent synthesis is an evaluation of other existing major learning theories.

How Defensible Are the Premises of Mental Disciplinarians?

People who make absolutistic judgments about the moral and actional nature of human beings encounter great difficulty in attempting to prove, or disprove, their theses scientifically. However, whether a person's study of a "mind training" subject such as geometry strengthens his (or her) thinking faculty is susceptible to scientific test. And, attempts to support mental disciplinary propositions experimentally appear to have been un-successful (see p. 249). Within a prescientific frame of reference of faculty psychology or classical humanism, mental discipline seems quite harmonious; however, we may seriously question its adequacy for schools in a modern scientific age. (An outlook or thought pattern that is scientifically most satisfactory is one that is both *adequate*—consistent with known facts or pertinent data—and *harmonious* in the light of all obtainable pertinent data.)

What Are the Strengths and Weaknesses of Apperception?

Apperceptionists have recognized that students acquire new learning in relation to what they already know, but they have failed to define the learning process in other than mechanistic terms. Thus, in considering children as passive minds, they opened the way for behaviorists' treating them as passive masses of protoplasm. They have recognized a principle of activity, but they attributed the activity to ideas, not persons. Consequently, apperception has implied a policy of student indoctrination; teachers, who are specialists in mental chemistry, fill the apperceptive masses of their students with proper ideas. Apperception indeed is internally harmonious, but we can question its adequacy, particularly for schools in a democratic society.

How Adequate Is Neobehaviorism?

The psychology of behaviorists and neobehaviorists, likewise is internally harmonious but, to cognitive-field theorists and other critics, it lacks adequacy.[1] Behavioristic psychologies are "scientific" in the sense that, in the main, propositions that emerge from them are quite susceptible to scientific test. Furthermore, the results of an education based upon them can be rather objectively measured. However, criticisms of behavioristic psychologies, when such psychologies are used as guides in teaching, lie in the apparently poor results that follow. This does not mean that, when teaching takes the form of more or less mechanical drill, students do not learn anything. Actually, the amount they learn seems to depend largely on how highly motivated they are; students do not necessarily learn in the way teachers think they do.

WHAT IS THE COGNITIVE-FIELD EMPHASIS IN TEACHING?

Cognitive-field psychologists certainly do not object to having students learn facts and remember them for future use. However, their emphasis is upon the students' growing to see the world and themselves differently, and it is within this process that facts are acquired and used. Accordingly, adherents of cognitive-field psychology emphasize that facts are learned best when they are regarded by learners as instruments for serving purposes that they feel are important. A growing number of teachers, including those educated in the behaviorist tradition, also would accept the legitimacy of this statement; almost everyone wants students to be able to use what they learn. However, in contrast to neobehaviorists, cognitive-field psychologists are interested mainly in reflective learning and the ways in which its quality can be improved. Consequently, an educational program consistent with a cognitive-field psychology focuses on teaching students to think more effectively in a wide variety of situations; it entails problem-centered teaching. Adherents of cognitive-field psychology and its cognate—reflective teaching—recognize that there are few, if any, teachers who can hold teaching and learning on a reflective level all the time. Thus, teaching that is focused on reflection will slip into an explanatory understanding level part of the time. But, it seldom, if ever, will be based on a memory level per se.

A sizable amount of psychological research has been conducted within a cognitive-field frame of reference. However, cognitive-field theorists base their psychological principles upon research that has been conducted by behaviorists as well as upon their own. They note that, provided lower animals or persons are credited with being genuinely purposive, the results of most psychological research supports cognitive-field psychology. For example, the results of experiments, such as those developed by B. F. Skinner to test operant conditioning, also support cognitive-field theory; it is only necessary to assume that the person or animal being studied is attempting to take care of its welfare the best way it knows how.

HOW DOES COGNITIVE-FIELD PSYCHOLOGY ELIMINATE WEAKNESSES OF BOTH TRADITIONALISM AND PERMISSIVISM?

Although not without some distinctive weaknesses of its own, teaching based on cognitive-field psychology appears to be an emergent position that, if widely adopted in our schools, might eliminate some of the inadequacies of earlier psychologies. The approach to teaching implied by this psychology, although in many respects distinctively different from other approaches, should at the same time have some appeal for both traditionalists and progressives.

Cognitive-field psychology may come to command the support of both traditionalists, who have thought that teachers should be centers of authority and progressives, who have felt that classrooms should be child-centered. Traditionalism is criticized on the ground that it does not permit children enough freedom for intellectual exploration, and progressivism on the ground that it assumes that adequately worthwhile learning will necessarily result if children are given free rein and allowed to plan their own activities.

The adoption of cognitive-field psychology as a basis for teaching would lead to greater student participation than is permitted by traditional teachers, but participation would be of a different kind from that advocated by Roussellian psychedelic humanists. In contrast with either authoritarian or laissez-faire classrooms, the ideal classroom, consistent with cognitive-field psychology, would be democratic. Although cognitive-field psychology is not a compromise between the psychologies underlying traditionalism and permissivism, it does lead to a kind of middle position: a position that permits students a considerable amount of freedom, but only within certain confines, as they think their way into restructuring their life spaces.

A large group of present liberal arts scholars also want to teach students to think more effectively. Most of these persons, however, are inheritors of the classical tradition in education, and to the extent that they think in psychological terms they still cling to a mental discipline psychology. But if they were to make a careful study of systematic psychologies in relation to contrasting educational philosophies, it seems likely that the only modern school of thought in psychology that they could accept would be a cognitive-field psychology. This is because cognitive-field is the contemporary scientific psychology that perhaps harmonizes best with the professed aim of scholars in the arts and sciences of giving education an intellectual emphasis. Joseph Wood Krutch, a prominent liberal arts scholar, literary critic, and author, has written a book pleading for rejection of mechanistic psychologies (such as connectionism and behaviorism) and for adoption of a nonmechanistic psychology whose main interest would be a study of reflective and creative mental processes.[2] Wide-spread acceptance of cognitive-field psychology possibly would restore an intellectual emphasis in education and at the same time provide a psychological basis for education free of the criticisms validly made of the old "mind training" approach. A common, constant purpose of cognitive-field psychology is the enhancement of intelligence as teachers aid students in changing or reconstructuring the cognitive structures of their life spaces. In accomplishment of this purpose there is teacher-student, purposing, planning, fulfillment, and evaluation of the learning tasks at hand.

NOTES

[1] See Sigmund Koch, "Psychology and Emerging Conceptions of Knowledge as Unitary," in T. W. Wann (ed.), *Behaviorism and Phenomenology*, Chap. 1, University of Chicago Press, 1964, pp. 1–41.
[2] Joseph Wood Krutch, *The Measure of Man*, Indianapolis: Bobbs-Merrill, 1954.

NAME INDEX

SUBJECT INDEX